SEMIOTEXT(E) FOREIGN AGENTS SERIES

Originally published as *Sphären II. Globen* by Editions Suhrkamp, Frankfurt.
© Suhrkamp Verlag Frankfurt am Main 1999. All rights reserved

This edition Semiotext(e) © 2014

Published by Semiotext(e)
PO BOX 629, South Pasadena, CA 91031
www.semiotexte.com

Chapter 8 originally appeared in Peter Sloterdijk, *In the World Interior of Capital* (Cambridge: Polity, 2013) and is printed in *Spheres 2* with the permission of Polity Press.

Special thanks to Ellen Davis and John Ebert.

Cover art by Channa Horwitz. *Circle and Square or Square and Circle*, 1968.
© the Artist and François Ghebaly Gallery, Los Angeles.

Design: Hedi El Kholti

ISBN: 978-1-58435-160-3
Distributed by The MIT Press, Cambridge, Mass. and London, England
Printed in the United States of America

SPHERES

VOLUME 2: GLOBES

MACROSPHEROLOGY

Peter Sloterdijk

Translated by Wieland Hoban

For
Heinrich Klotz
teacher, founder, mover
in friendship and gratitude

Contents

Prologue: Intense Idyll   13

Introduction: Geometry in the Monstrous   45
The Project of Metaphysical Globalization

     1. The Atlas   45
     2. The Parmenidean Moment   70
     3. Carrying God   91
     4. The Morphological Gospel and Its Fate   112

Access: Anthropic Climate   135

1. Dawn of Long-Distance Closeness   151
     The Thanatological Space, Paranoia and the Peace of the Realm

2. Vascular Memories   187
     On the Reason for Solidarity in Its Inclusive Form

3. Arks, City Walls, World Boundaries, Immune Systems   237
     The Ontology of the Walled Space

     Excursus 1: Dying Later in the Amphitheater   307
     On Postponement, the Roman Way

     Excursus 2: Merdocracy   321
     The Immune Paradox of Settled Cultures

4. The Ontological Proof of the Orb   335

     Excursus 3: Autocoprophagia   405
     On Platonic Recycling

     Excursus 4: Pantheon   411
     The Theory of the Dome

5. *Deus sive sphaera*, Or: 441
The Exploding Universal One

Excursus 5: On the Meaning of the Unspoken Statement   553
"The Orb Is Dead"

6. Anti-Spheres   565
Explorations in the Infernal Space

Parenthesis: On Depression As a Crisis of Extension   583

7. How the Spheric Center Has Long-Distance Effects through   637
the Pure Medium
On the Metaphysics of Telecommunication

Excursus 6: The De-crowning of Europe   753
An Anecdote about the Tiara

8. The Last Orb   765
On a Philosophical History of Terrestrial Globalization

Transition: Air Conditioning   961

Notes   969

Photographic Credits   1021

SPHERES

VOLUME 2: GLOBES

MACROSPHEROLOGY

Verily, Zarathustra had a goal, he threw his ball: now you friends are heirs of my goal, to you I throw the golden ball.

More than anything I like to see you, my friends, throwing the golden ball!

— Friedrich Nietzsche, *Thus Spoke Zarathustra*

Mosaic showing a group of philosophers from Torre Annunziata, probably 1st century BC

Intense Idyll

When someone asked him what was the object of being born,
he replied: "to investigate the Sun, Moon, and heavens."
— Diogenes Laertius, *Life of Anaxagoras*[1]

But soul is also longing, and the eternal longing of the soul
always goes towards space.
— Max Bense, *Raum und Ich*[2]

Seven elderly men in an idealized landscape, not far from a
Greek city—perhaps Acrocorinth, perhaps Athens, certainly
not Sparta.

These gentlemen, every one of them bearded, are gathered
in conversation under a tree, near a sacred grove whose entrance
is marked by pillars; placed on the crossbeams are offerings in
bulbous vessels.

Everything in this scene points to a state of exception: the
place is not a place like any other, and whatever is being discussed there is no ordinary matter. Clearly the participants are
animated by an acute argument. The man standing on the left

has just ended his speech, the chairman gives a concise answer by pointing his staff at the orb, and a kind of amazement spreads among those gathered. It seems as if an idea were spreading through the round, coming upon them like a seizure. There is a touch of indignation in the air; one cannot shake off the feeling that just now, the fascination of the argument has given way to a general dismay. Probably a startlingly bold thought has entered the discussion, the kind that imposes itself on the group with the force of the unprecedented. There is no reason not to imagine this as the moment in which something never before dared and never before thought, something none had ever believed possible, seizes hold of the discussants in an almost pathological fashion. The fruitful moment in this *dotta conversazione* has arrived. The making of words has transformed into thinking; rising up from futile chatter, world-moving ideas begin their flight. An evidence like none before it captivates the intelligence of those present.

How is it possible to read such things into this picture? That the scene is a scholars' discussion is indicated by the typical philosophers' beards of the participants and the scrolls in the hands of some members; and that the situation is an emergency of thought is demonstrated by the presence of an object that one must surely assume is the reason for this gathering and this shared enthusiasm.

One of the men, the one sitting in front of the tree—he appears to be the senior member of the round—is pointing with a rod, the teacher's *radius*, to the structure sitting in a small box on the floor in front of the semicircular learned *schola*, three quarters of it protruding from its container: a light blue orb, covered with a web of crossed reddish lines. A glance at the object is enough to explain the dismayed enthusiasm that, if our interpretation is correct, has overcome the seven scholars. The thing protruding from the little box, like a saintly image from its shrine, is nothing other than a *sphaira*, an orb of the earth and the heavens, that symbol of totality which has been both revered and investigated by geometricians and metaphysicians alike since the days of Empedocles and Parmenides.

Reverent investigation: the contradiction in this phrase is resolved as soon as one calls to mind that for the ancients, especially after the Platonic reform of declamatory wisdom into a philosophy of arguments, the orb had been an emblem of the divine existent as a whole[3]—the symbol of the encompassing or being-around, *periéchon*, which includes all physical and intellectual categories of the existent and thus also pervades the intelligences bending over the almighty orb at this moment. What passes through the round of bearded discussants like a shudder is the simultaneously arousing and calming certainty, realized anew and regained in free contemplation, yet created as if for the first time, that they, these reflective mortals, can never remove themselves from this space-orb—even if, at this moment, they stand facing the image of the whole as if it were a soulless object or an arbitrary sign.

The gathering around the *sphaira* marks one of the rare moments in the history of thought in which cult and discourse merge without obstructing each other. Just as the officiants of religious cults erect statues in honor of their preferred deities, the scholars have set up this image of the orb of being and the cosmos to honor it with appropriate debate. The orb is the divine image of the thinkers, the box or the podium is its portable altar, the grove before the city gates is its temple district, and the men in the colored cloaks evidently embody the holy office and the congregation at once.

But the *sphaira*, the One as a form, is the God who makes humans think. It is not through prayers and invocations that this One can be reached, but rather through analyses, measurements and proofs. Its cult consists in the precise consideration of its qualities; this time, the piety of thought proves itself in the ability to see to the heart of the form's construction. The orb wants to be viewed and honored as much as calculated and assessed. Its interior demands a congenial spirit to enliven it—and enlivening here means producing and gauging. Intelligence is spheric tension; insight becomes circumspection in the monstrous. In the experiences of evidence ignited in the noetic soul when correct thinking occurs, God, the One, the unanimous, shows himself to the thinker-looker. Through logical enthusiasm, he[4] confirms to his admirers that he is present in them: his presence is the unity of circumspection and encompassment. At the time of this scene, we are still living in an age where being seized by evidence can be viewed as a point of intersection between statements and ecstasies; even in conceptual work, the blessing comes from above. Because these are mortal humans reaching for the One with fallible concepts, only the divine itself can grant success to the attempt through current evidence and fill the concepts with clear content. Wherever the orb is thought in the correct manner, however, it is present in the midst of its analysts. In the concept with the power to prove itself and the image that is capable of being, the divine spirit—whose existence can here still be posited with untainted naïveté—approaches the human.

When the Athenian or Acrocorinthian seven look at the orb, trembling with a shared breath of spirit, it is because, at this moment, they are part of the pentecostal event in the history of thought: what takes hold of them is the outpouring of evidence in tongues of logical fire. This evidence is at once intimately moving and public; it enables both silent meditation and heated debate. One therefore notes that there is no hypnotic or religioid spell cast over the group; each of these wise men enters into his own relationship with the encompassing in a state of emancipated thoughtfulness and free motivation. Each of them experiences in his own particular way what the orb gives him to think about. Indeed, one could even say that what would later be called individuality only became possible through logically matured thought about this one orb—for one can only be an individual in the substantial sense of the word through reference as a singular, knowing life to the One (just as the drop testifies to the cloud from which it falls), and by allowing the encompassing to speak through the self, the discreet vessel of the monstrous.

Because this is the first time that individuals are appearing under a new motif of individualization, a new dimension of socialization also comes into view at this moment: the shared experience of the idea of unity and totality has resulted in a commonality with no precedents in tribal or familial relations. From this moment on, the learned *schola* is sworn to a communitary enthusiasm; it will in future be held together by, to use an anachronistic turn of phrase, a "problem awareness" that removes them from all other human groups. It seems as if an incomparably novel reason to be together with intelligent beings had come into the world, and as if this pentecostal discourse on the sphere had given rise to something of which we still do not fully understand, even after two and a half millennia of the most powerful effects, what it means and how far it will extend. For it is clear that a form of affiliation has taken shape here whose motive is neither political self-preservation nor procreation and child-rearing, but rather ascetic and solidary research into the truth about the round whole, the complete, the unanimous, the One. Whoever participates in this research is now clearly more than a mere member of their tribe or people; they have crossed over, assuming they are serious in wanting to know— though what does "serious" mean in such matters?—to a logical counter-society that bases itself on the natural commune without allowing itself to be defined by it. Precisely this unfathomably counter-natural idea of commune, an anticipation of religious orders, was laid out by the founder of the *mundus academicus*, Plato, in his school project, and there is also a hint of retrojective academicism surrounding the *schola* of Torre Annunziata: these ancient seven were already learning for the school, not for life. The first proponents of the *bios theoretikós* knew that freedom to theorize could only be attained by breaking with the city, and with what would later be called the people's community.

Through the invention of the theoretical game of philosophy, subsequent societies—whether cities, kingdoms or empires in their constitution—were endogenously split. A form of thought irrupted into the world that declared itself the emergency in what applies and what is, yet is only seen from the outside by most people, even the politically, economically or journalistically powerful. Unless it decided to prevent thought outright, every real-life society would have to deal with this snub—whether by evading it through admiration, as the ancient world did, or hiding behind a skepticism towards higher knowledge and its embodiments, which helped the vitalistic moderns to lead a life of ignorance without feeling any lack of autonomy.

The picture from Torre Annunziata already points unmistakably to the rupture between knowledge and society: the scene, wholly infused with the post-Socratic, free-school, secessionist spirit, is no longer set in the city, but rather before the gates—not so far that the participants in the sphere conversation had to become hermits, but far enough that the smoke and noise from the markets could not infiltrate the grove of ontology. The party grimaces have left the faces, leaving only the beautiful effort of the concept. Fragrance and quiet; convivial precision. The cicadas fill the argument-enriched air with a second chirping.

No intellectual should ever forget this situation: seven scholars facing a striped orb, bearded gentlemen in a cheer whose cause is inscrutable to all outsiders, removed from the city, devoted to a subtle dissidence, sworn to an eternal *question* through shared logical intuitions—that is the primal scene of academic pacifism. In that small picture, happiness and the monstrous lie calmly in each other. Henceforth, there would be no more theory without the will to this idyll, no school without leisure, and none of what was known in Old Europe as freedom of research without being uprooted from vulgarity. Such theory claims the privileges of the highest life for itself. The attraction of the divine orb even overtook interest in the productions of the Dionysian theater; for burgeoning philosophy, the monstrous within order went further than the monstrous in tragedy.

How should we go about reconstructing the wording and development of the arguments? Is it possible to translate the pictorial outer view of the philosophers' pentecost into a view from within and a hearing at close quarters? Tradition is silent on the legends that belong to the picture and reveals nothing of its immanent text, leaving the picture-reader of later times with the task of letting the scene speak purely through its iconic elements. The dating of the philosopher mosaic from Torre Annunziata—which can today be viewed at the Museo Nazionale in Naples—to the first century BC does little to help understand it; in addition, the existence of a counterpart from the Villa Albani in Rome makes it all but certain that both mosaics are based on a lost original painting whose origin, age, context and program are all the more obscure.[5] No great deduction is required to assume that, going by the formal language and pictorial rhetoric, its origin lies in Hellenism, the age of academic idylls and the scenario of *otium*. These clues do not open up the picture, however, for what speaks through the significant picture is not the sluggish epoch, but rather the event which the picture uses for its own ends.

The pictures offers a first entrance to the inner language space of the scene via the number of wise men, namely seven—a number that is self-explanatory in many respects: older Greek culture, and even more so the Hellenistic era, had invented their early days in myths of heroic founders and numerological symbolism, especially in the legend of the Seven Sages, who supposedly brought wisdom and science to Greek men in the days of the great ancients.[6] That all seven populate the scene in fictitious synchronicity can be accepted as a legitimate artistic sleight of hand. Among the educated, it would also have gone without saying that the participants and speakers from Plato's symposium—likewise seven—were present on the connotative horizon. What makes the mosaic from Torre Annunziata unique, however, is that the convention is not depicted as an allegorical philosophy faculty, with each figure representing a scholastic type or intellectual temperament. We are not dealing with a Hellenistic sketch for *The School of Athens*; the singularity of the philosophers' scene lies in the fact that it shows some of the greats of early thought at the moment of a shared commitment to a single topic, as if the viewer were meant to become a witness to a debate that was constitutive for philosophy. One could say that what comes into the picture here is the outpouring of the primal question itself. For a moment, as it were, the very meaning of thought lies at the assembly's feet. There is an orb here, summoning the observer with two unconditional imperatives: "Come, think me!" and "Be subsumed in me!"

Future generations are given the task of understanding that there was a pentecost which was a discussion. Its subject made it impossible to end, and hence that pentecostal clarity, the evidence of the philosopher, subsequently had to spread across an entire age—the time of the movedness of thinkers through the intellectual light emanating from the highest spatial idea. One can only entertain doubts as to the subject of the conversation depicted to the extent that it is possible to consider whether scholars, monomaniacs and monothematicists have always thought only of the One that lies before them as the sphere, rounded into beauty, or whether they are also thinking of the sundial guarding the scene from atop a pillar at the back. In truth, the clock and the orb are grouped as if to emphasize their shared bond and their conflict, positioned almost exactly on a vertical line slightly to the right of the picture's center. With its hour lines, the sundial refers—almost banally, in retrospect—to the time that is henceforth measured and elapses, while the sphere, covered in mathematical lines, represents the quantified and conceptualized world-whole in its event-free resting form. We are now transported, by the one instrument as much as the other, to the incipient era of measuring, ascertaining, objectified reason.

The answer to the question of the conversation's subject can be found in the attitude of the men: their intentions gather undivided in the object lying before them, which passes the central idea of their verbal exchange on to them through the mere fact of its presence. The mosaic artist who captures the philosophers at the moment of their illumination through the One Orb, encompasses the scene with a visual idea that can claim the status of a theorem. With the eloquence of the obvious, the *image* of the discussing figures embodies the thesis that a philosopher is someone who has a clock behind them and an orb in front. The thinkers of Hellenism and their heirs exist under the law of time as intelligences that contemplate what is other-than-temporal. With the two scholarly emblems, the clock and the sphere, the philosopher mosaic communicates that in the third, second or first century before the turn of the eras, there was no need to hesitate when it came to naming the essence and theme of first philosophy. Understanding being and time and illuminating the constellation they form together: this and nothing else is the concern of this verbosely opaque profession.

What information on the constellation of being and time is transmitted in the present case is made unmistakably clear in the

Neapolitan mosaic: through their stance, the seven who are present reveal themselves as staunch partisans of being—and thus of the glorified space. They turn their backs on the sundial and the realm of things that blossom and wither in time. It is in this position, this decision that the good news of the summer seminar lies. By turning away from the clock and towards the orb, the sages embrace the possibility of separating themselves in time from time and entering absolute space, divine immanence, spheric abundance. That is the magic of the pictorial program, and its sublime wager: one must look at the orb if one wishes to become part of its carefree realm. It is under its auspices, and only thus, that the ontologists' paradise opens up. The most powerful eidos deserves the longest viewing and the most subtle asceticism. All those who want to enter the orb must therefore view it patiently; whoever wants to view it must sit before it. And whoever is sitting before it will finally grasp what an intelligence resolved to examine is capable of. Here the world has become concept—from now on, its *being* consists in making space for the space, imaging the image, and measuring the measure. The image of the orb assists this process of becoming understood being. An image, *this* image, an orb, *this* orb, contains everything that later understanding and image forming would strive for to this day, and perhaps for all time. Even Hegel, undoubtedly without knowing it, was only a commentator on the mosaic of Torre Annunziata. And even Heidegger, in his late lectures, returns home to this sublime orb with the air of one who regrets speaking too much of time. Needless to say, the post- and anti-Hegelians battle vigorously for the legacy of the orb, which reportedly burst apart, meaning that the humans plummeting from it can only exist as if in free fall.

The *sphaira* in the web of uranometric lines

One thing, at least, must be conceded: never again would it be possible to view the true metaphysical activity of Western philosophers and scientists in a manner so devoid of coding or pretext: what they do is *imagining*, in every possible sense of the word.[7] They envisage the orb by making it an actually present model; and, by attempting to see in the envisaged orb the existent as a whole, and ultimately the manifesting God, the over-good reason, the supra-essential essence itself, they provide the way of thinking that reaches for the One, whole and universal with an instrument both massive and subtle to objectify the totality of the existent.

With the introduction of the sphere motif into the debate on the "world ground" [*Weltgrund*], the god of the philosophers ceased to be merely an invisible, magically enlivened all-around, a nebulous close-distant other somewhere yonder up there to which the eye that dreams of ancestors looks up, and which acute misery implores. Rather, God becomes a precise absolute, an encompassing entity that rouses mathematicians and provokes cosmographers. For through the orb's imagining, the circumspective navigation in an expansive space that attracts both incisiveness and the melting soul, the intellect itself becomes philosophical; it is granted an exact joviality normally reserved for the panoptic God in his world-positing self-referentiality.

It was with this triumph of imagining that philosophical, rational and collegial theology began a career spanning multiple eras. It speaks of orbs in order to establish, by means of an inter-intelligent complicity with its object—the greatest and realest orb—a sympathetic connection between itself and the One currently encompassing this life here and everything else. Thinking the orb means surrendering oneself to the monstrous as a local function thereof.

Whoever considers doing so will have less difficulty calling to mind the spoken words that echo through the idyllic pictorial space. What can speakers articulate but the things they have before them in sensual-symbolic concretion and noetic current-ness? And what do they have before their eyes, under the aforementioned premises, but the strongest reason for optimism? The assembled philosophers had to convert to a radical optimism because they had placed the image of the best before them, and gradually reached the conviction that they could not be excluded from this image and its original if the sphere were truly meant to be the pictorial and conceptual embodiment of the whole. The all-holding orb encompasses and also carries its exegetes; it contributes to every true statement made about it. Whoever begins to understand this will recognize themselves as a local function of the global optimum.

"In a sense, you are gods and sons of the best"—this is what the speaker with the *radius*, the teacher's staff in which the master's speaking rights are condensed, currently seems to be explaining in response to an argument from the man on the left. "Understand, friends, transformed spheric comrades, what the form over there means for each one of us! We are those contained by the orb, we are held in the ring of being, we are not missing from the whole, even if we are initially under the illusion that we face the *sphaira* as separated. Yet every semblance of distance is deceptive: we are intimately involved in the best, though earthly impoverishments afflict us; we are accomplices of the round, the One, even if the dominion of time makes it seem as if we were only running in cheerless straight lines and muddled curves. We are encompassed and saved, even though we feel at the mercy of need through current or chronic misery."

The thetical spark ignites in the moment: everything is mercy, everything is circular. *Eíso pánta.*[8] For now and for the future, those present are infused with an evidence that transforms and transfigures them. Were the scholars prepared for such an illumination when they began their conversation? Naturally, as citizens of their towns and students of wise men and women before their time, they would have sensed that matters of consanguinity and urban chitchat are not the only things that should define the horizon of human life. But did this alone prepare them for the uprooting, transforming, dispossessing evidence? Could they foresee that they would be transferred from their tribal and political ties into the kinship system of a deadly perfection? That they would encounter an orb which did more for them than their mother or father? That they would be taken up into a spatial figure which would stay firmly around them under any circumstances, in every agony and every excessive strain, like a geometric guardian angel, an invulnerably exact ally? No ordinary human intellect, even one opened a crack through scientific practice, could have suspected and expected so much, something so great, in advance. The intellect seized by the sphere idea was henceforth incurably ill, struck with a pathos of which one cannot say whether it is light or dark: amazement.

Under this stimulating shock, a conversation unfolds between the orb thinkers in which analysis and praise compete. Analytical praise: this sets the tone of rational theology or cosmotheology that celebrates its European inception here—a tone that imposes itself, for one consequence of the spheric pentecost is that any non-rejoicing theoretical language is merely an indication that the flash of evidence has not struck that candidate. The unenthusiastic person is one who has simply failed to understand where they are in relation to themselves and the whole. Whoever does not declare themselves an optimist stands insensate before the round symbol as if before an impenetrable externality, a mathematician's toy that has not yet been recognized as the generative cell of thought and being. The non-optimist has not succeeded in the leap to unanimity, having still not been seized by the new ordered truth of the orb. For being an optimist is no longer a matter of character or mood; it now means nothing other than exposing oneself as a thinker to the best reasons, in order to be dispossessed, heartened and heightened. In the face of the orb, the thinker is damned to optimism. From now on, habitual critical philosophizing suggests an impaired intelligence that does not have its second-rate impulses under control.

But how is one to speak of the orb once the thinkers have been taken over by critical euphoria? The style of metaphysical optimism can only be one of superlatives in its first phase because it corresponds to the orb's nature that its thinkers honor it with the highest accolades and decorate it as if with ontological medals. In reality, understanding the orb means attributing the best qualities to it. One could even claim that rational theology, which would remain affiliated with cosmology until Epicurus' turn towards concern for the withdrawn soul, was born from the invention of its own unique part of speech: the exact superlative, which is only meaningful and necessary in conjunction with exact optimism.

Exact optimism: this is the substance of the later ontotheology, which later became known by the more straightforward name "ontology." Its underlying principles are easily expounded, though it is difficult to absorb them to their fullest extent: the One Being is the epitome of wealth. Wealth, however, is always a wealth of differences; the intelligence that knows it belongs to the One comes into itself as the overabundance of coercions to think—that is to say, to find one's bearings in the confusing multiplicity of differences, oppositions and contradictions. Thus the doctrine of the existent as a whole can only be a hermeneutics of abundance. Its language will unfold as a cascade of distinctions that tumbles into the endless. To find the right bearings in thought, one must always begin with the One that lacks absolutely nothing, even if *we*, in practice, do not begin to think until subjected to deprivations and castrations. These premises create a theoretical climate that has become deeply alien to the complaint-addicted moderns, who motivate all that is through deficiencies to the last—so alien that at the slightest contact with any mode of thought coming from wealth, they raise the alarm: unmask the one who insults deficiency! What is commonly termed the end of metaphysics is usually also the start of the effort to give *ressentiment* a theoretical license—most openly in those philosophically lecherous versions of psycho-analysis that claim the truth of the subject lies in castration and the admission of deficiency.

By contrast: placing abundance at the start casts an aristocratic light on everything that is the case. The real has infinitely more of everything than can be motivated by using and compensating. It is not the too-little that explains the existent as a whole, but the too-much. Being and abundance are merely different words for the same thing: in the horizon of traditional ontology, the real is always the undeprived, the complete, the encompassing and the overflowing. It is the untorn, the uncastrated. It presents itself as cornucopian wealth, divine inclusivity, heavenly length, breadth, depth—and as a multitude of further dimensions for which we, who initially remain caught up in everyday physics, have neither names nor concepts for the time being.

This principle of abundance is also mirrored in philosophical references to the whole: when it speaks of the optimum, language can only celebrate—or rather, join in the celebration, as the festivities and the words unfold in parallel. It was in this spirit that Plato let Timaeus conclude his speech on the cosmos as the perceptible God (*theós aesthetós*) on the highest note, by declaring through his speaker that this world, which encompasses every-thing visible, is "the greatest, best, most beautiful and most perfect." In these contexts, the tone is the message; the superlative is the matter itself. That the great critics from the unrelenting feuilleton would later be reluctant to follow such elevations is of little consequence; indeed, it forms part of the jovial picture of the whole, for at successful celebrations one laughs not least about those morose guests who want to spoil the fun with their refusals. One should know, however, that optimism too is subject to entropy, and that the positings of enthusiastic ontology are crushed by an inevitable de"con"structive decadence in the course of thinking time. But before the entropic discourses were able to academicize themselves and erudite chagrin was going about its globalization, the friends of space held the floor at Plato's school. For almost an epoch, they had the attitudes and the arguments to teach with authority and logical success what the belated topophile Gaston Bachelard would repeat retrospectively, and as if for the last time: "In its germinal form, therefore, all of life is well-being. [...] Space, vast space, is the friend of being."[9]

How should one celebrate the divine orb analytically? What must be uttered about it for it to be simultaneously praised and understood? In an ingenious interpretation of the mosaic from Torre Annunziata, Otto Brendel developed the suggestion of reading the scene as a *schola* that gathered around the proto-philosopher Thales to expound his teachings—albeit a very Platonically tinted Thales transformed by later tradition, who, in this conversation of the sages, already delivers insights that would only become available to subsequent centuries.[10] Thales, the man holding the *radius*, is described in a later tradition as the cosmotheologian *par excellence*, in whose thought the philosophy of origin—everything comes from water—and the philosophy of shape—the whole is a perfect orb—supposedly merged to form a notable, very Platonic synthesis.[11] Brendel now compiles in what could be called a very suggestive manner, if one accepts the shape-philosophical anachronisms as interpolations from a later perspective, excerpts from Plutarch's *Banquet of the Seven Sages* and the anecdotes about Thales from the first book of Diogenes Laertius in order to reconstruct the possible course of the philosophers' conversation.[12] What results from this is a theological-cosmological litany in which the eminent spheric attributes are studied *ad maiorem gloriam globi*.

If it is true that this object can only be examined in the tone of a laudatory analysis, the references of Laertius and Plutarch to the pronouncements of Thales would provide us with an excellent model to illustrate how a thinker from ancient times might have dealt with the task of grasping the orb of being in praise—although the historical Thales would have been out of his depth with this assignment. Philosophy becomes exact boasting, as well as the feat of speaking of overwhelming things with a dry soul.

Seven qualities are ascribed to the super-object termed the "orb of the existent as a whole," seven answers to ontological riddles, seven attributes in the most exalted tone—a tone that nonetheless retains its argumentative fiber, for the logical aspect changes with each statement, as if a litany could be followed by a table of categories. The fact that the aphorisms honoring the orb contain one superlative after another confirms the character of Thales' words: their type is that of exact hyperbole, whose theology-enabling function cannot be emphasized enough—because theology, including the philosophical variety, is never more than a competition of proclamation and boasting in favor of the gods allied with its eulogists.[13]

Measured time

The first words of honor are the statement that the orb is none other than god, and as such constitutes the oldest, *presbýtaton*. Just as it would be logically unproductive and morally inadmissible to ask about things preceding God, it would be unwise if one attempted to go back to causes older and deeper than the orb. God and the orb are equally immemorial. As the oldest thing, it is the unbecome, the parentless, the unbegotten, and is its own being and continuance. As the origin and archetype of all things it contains, it is the necessary, sufficient and excessive reason for itself and its contents. It does not yet harbor the modern enigma of infinite regression, as even a potentially interminable reflection would be forced to succumb to its edifying orbit.

Its second quality depends immediately on this: it must simultaneously be the most beautiful, *kálliston*, because everything that belongs to the orb bespeaks the radiance of the first reason, both for the seeing eyes and those of the spirit. As a perfect beauty, the oldest orb must be called the *kósmos*, or all-encompassing heavens; it shows the glittering of a manifestation that could not be seen or imagined more beautifully. From the ancient perspective, beauty is possessed above all by that which refers to itself and equals itself in a perfect fashion, a condition that no object meets better than the orb, which is animated *everywhere* from its center, and which, infused with magical symmetries, is capable of revolving around itself by its own agency.

After age and beauty, the third attribute is size. Hence the next voice in the chorus of orb thinkers, in keeping with its predecessors, says it is the greatest, *mégiston*, because it forms the utmost coherent space (*tópos*), which encloses everything so completely that not even a speck of dust could be outside of it. It is the maximum for which one cannot conceive of any opposite, anything foreign or other. The orb is the universal container, the *continens*, the only continent of the One Existent of which one could rightfully say that it contains everything, yet is contained by nothing. If it is capable of this, then only because the record set by the maximum integrates all that is into its everlasting victory. The greatest takes up the complete existent into its grandiose procession. Though this would initially, and for a long time, only be said of the three-dimensional orb, one should not forget that the twentieth century began to grasp space as a matrix in which all geometries and all multiplicities are possible.

These honors could not be taken even further if it were not possible and necessary to spiritualize them: this occurs through

Spherical clock at the German Embassy in Athens; conception
by Karl Schlamminger, architecture by Eberhard Schultz

the statement that the orb of being is at once the wisest, *sophóta-ton*. Indeed: only inwardly directed enlivenment, wisdom, knowledge—the form of reflection, in modern parlance—can help the oldest-most beautiful-greatest to attain even more heightened accolades. The knowledge of the circular optimum evidently wants to move in circles itself: it can only do so because time (*chrónos*) is orb-shaped in this interpretation. Does time not likewise have the shape of something that returns into itself while moving forward into the endless? Is not every future tied by a great loop to origin? Consequently, we can say that time, like space, contains everything, and ideal containers are only imaginable as round. As the wisest, the orb is memory, foresight and presence of mind at once—praise that foreshadows the idea of a world spirit. As curved time, the sphere invents and designs things, holds them in existence and preserves them in the memory.

This becomes more specific in the fifth declaration in praise of the orb, namely that it is infused with the fastest, *táchiston*—the mind (*noús*), which covers every distance in an instant and connects all points on the inside of the vault of being with a moment's delay. The mind is capable of this primarily because it endogenously enlivens the sphere through its even distribution and lends it the divine attribute "omnipresence of the middle." Infinitely wise and swift of thought, the eternal sphere is the house of the world spirit.

If the orb is credited with the utmost age, beauty, size, wisdom and speed, it cannot fail to be given the majestic attribute of strength as its crowning quality; thus it is also the strongest, *ischyrótaton*, in so far as it is driven by the world force of necessity (*ananké*). That force's most important deed was the integration of outer space into the borders of the spheric vault, which embody

Urania pointing her rod at a heavenly sphere; Pompeii, House of the Vettii

not only beauty and splendor, but also determination and the seriousness of laws. The orb is a held-holding body of order, a dome of force upon which its explorers, the mathematicians and philosophers, have drawn a network of lines—the so-called *aráchne*, denoting spider and web at once, the symbol of divine overview and ruling necessity, which even weaves together that which seems most distant and unrelated according to strict, albeit largely unidentifiable laws. To hold the greatest together with the power of a boundary, then, the strongest is just strong enough; this is why the orb must be viewed less as a static geometric figure than an energetic, not to say imperial revelation of power. In it, thought about being attains its most majestic form. It is not least for this reason that the *sphaira* demands to be seized by the powerful of the world; as the symbol of the strong-good boundary of the world, it became indispensable for the later imperio-theologians and interconnectors.

Now only the seventh of the analytical praises remains to be formulated—and one would think that this too can be uttered only in the mode of the exact superlative. The last attribute, however, is something of a special case. If we can imagine that the previous six statements are distributed between the anonymous sages in the scene, what remains is a summing-up that can only be delivered by the speaker in the middle, the idealized Thales, the man with the teacher's pointer. With the aid of his rod (which he borrowed from Urania, the astral muse), and perhaps already unduly similar to the Academy founder Plato, Thales can conclude the optimistic litany by using the highest boasting tool of the teacher, called *radius* by the ancients, creating the most direct intention towards the opulent body of being. The seventh accolade, however, appears in a plainer language form; on the grammatical surface, it dispenses with the superlative form and simply calls its object the divine, *theion*—though not without adding: "that which has neither beginning nor end." If we look more closely, it transpires that these formulations do not simply conceal a semantic superlative because it would be rhetorically nonsensical to attempt a formal superlative of the divine, the very essence of the *summum* and *super*; it is rather because it completes the transition from laudatory, affirmative and extraverted theology to the negative, austere, in a sense homecoming and increasingly silent word of God. The two negations—"neither beginning nor end"—form, together with synonymous descriptions such as "unbegotten" or "unborn," the bridgehead for the second form of theology, namely the apophatic, disputing, negating form that surrounds the mystical object known as God in a wreath of overturned definitions until, surrounded by negated epithets, it slips from the network of imagining thought and ascends to a supra-conceptual glory. It is precisely this ascent that is triggered by the last word in the litany in honor of the orb. With it, we depart from the space of positive assertions of abundance and affirmative boasting. But would not everything suggest that the boasting which goes undone is the greatest of all?

If the seven sages in the theory garden outside Acrocorinth or Athens are fundamentally optimists, the reasons for this surely include one that motivated their entrance into the picture in question. Together with their portraitist, they are confident that later times will carry on the memory of their conversation and the impulse emanating from the pentecostal discussion event. There are good reasons for this assumption, at least in the stretch of the history of ideas where the equation of ontology and optimism defended its validity. Where else could the basic doctrine underlying the philosophy of the bestness and completeness of being have been presented so comprehensively and so simply? Where else would the ontology of the finished world have introduced itself so cheerfully and engagingly? Where else would mortals have been given such a convincing demonstration that their lives were superfluous, in the strict sense of the word, because the addition of the human to the perfect cannot enrich the latter—which is simply another way of saying that space is deeper than time and the old deeper than the new? And where else in the field of Old European thought was it expressed in such an appealing fashion that the highest achievement of human wisdom can only be to integrate oneself into the primal abundance of being in contemplative gratitude?

Indeed, orb ontology assigns mortals a place in a perfect world where new things can only exist as a result of deterioration. This already shows us, the children of a chronolatrous culture of innovation and event overwhelmed by becoming, the limits of thought and existence in the old orb of essence. Where being seeks to be everything, curiosity—like all cognitive pathos—should finally come to rest in the first, oldest and best; we moderns, however, are challenged to pursue a projective mode of thought that flees from origin and runs ever further forwards—a thought that opposes homesickness for the unchanging and harboring and follows the pull towards what is unattached, has never before existed, and was promised from afar. This much is certain: the relationship between being and time did not allow itself to be captured, for our sake, within the boundaries the picture from Torre Annunziata sought to lay down. With time, time itself penetrated the orb, whether in the Hegelian form—

Byzantine imperial statue, bronze, dated between the 4th and 7th centuries

time is the existent concept—or the Heideggerian form—being is time. Both are statements which we stumble upon like giant toys, and which call out mockingly to us, their dwarfish finders: "Keep playing!"[14]

The history of ideas and symbols in Old Europe overwhelmingly confirmed the cosmological demands of ancient orb piety. An entire epoch stands in the shadow of the wondrous conversation to which the philosopher mosaic bears witness. At the founding celebrations for his newly established imperial capital Constantinople, previously called Byzantium, on May 11, 330, the Emperor Constantine strode through the streets in a procession with an orb in his hand—a symbol that had become a stereotypical feature of the Caesars for centuries. For a millennium, his statue on the Column of Constantine showed him in the pose the emperor had assumed for the consecration of his city.

In the subsequent millennia, the orb would be adorned with a cross and placed in the hands of baptized kings and emperors at coronation ceremonies. Through the passing on of the *globus cruciger* from priestly to princely hands, the orb game would survive for centuries and keep itself in the heart of European world history. The human being—this much was at least understood by some thinkers of the Christian age—is the creature that has a world orb placed in its hand. It is the ecstatic animal that must, at some point, answer these questions: did you perceive your kingship? Did you become what those who catch the world orb become? Were you there when they wanted to give you the orb? If not, why not? Name the reasons you consider stronger than your vocation to play the orb game! Why did you not catch the golden ball?

We should not fool ourselves: all newer philosophy—with the exceptions of Nietzsche, Kojève, Bense, Foucault, Deleuze, the incomparable ones and their friends—is the list of excuses from theorists for their inability to catch the orb of being. The moderns were never short of arguments when it came to painting an impoverished picture of humans. How would a deficient creature be capable of encountering being? How might the alienated withstand abundance, especially as there is no correct life in the wrong life? How could the exploited, dispossessed and fragmented conduct direct conversations with the whole? How should people who have devoted themselves to utility indulge in the nonsensical luxury of existing? Why should they spare any thought for being, if the precedence of democracy over ontology has already been asserted? What is a bulging orb about anyway, if presence is impossible? And why should one court a whole that analytical minds assure us is either a mere formal concept or a narcissistic phantasm?

Johann Wolfgang Goethe's *Altar of Good Fortune* (Weimar, 1777)

In the twilight of the orb epoch, a German poet would place a large orb of stone on a cubic pedestal on the property surrounding his summer house by the River Ilm, outside the gates of Weimar—as if it gave him satisfaction to declare his allegiance once more to the saturated world symbol of the Greeks against the dominant mentalities of the unfulfilled present with this provocatively pantheistic gesture, a tribute to fortune. In the shapes of cube and orb, the artist even resorted twice to geometric symbols of totality, each effecting a mediation between calm and movement in its own way. As if for the last time, the orb placer invoked the bright demonism of an unfragmented life in a complete world. When the young Goethe had his *Altar of Good Fortune* erected in April 1777, he addressed future generations with a hidden riddle whose answer was to be found in the times to come. In the light of the sphere tradition, the Weimar question to posterity can perhaps be formulated thus: what is to become of the orb in a time without kings—or: what is to become of the kings in a time without orbs?

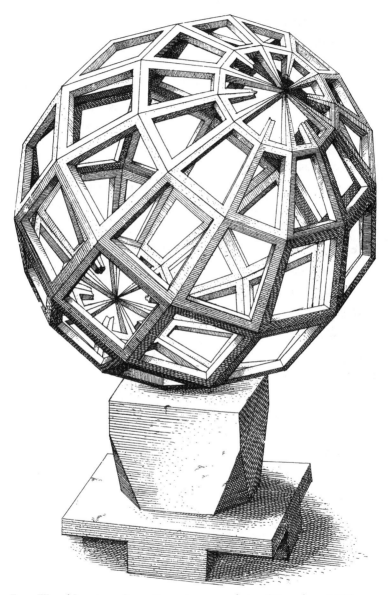

From Wenzel Jamnitzer, *Perspectiva corporum regularium* (Nuremberg, 1568)

Geometry in the Monstrous

The Project of Metaphysical Globalization

> The fundamental event of the Modern Age is the conquest
> of the world as picture.
> — Martin Heidegger, *The Age of the World Picture*[15]

I. The Atlas

If one had to pinpoint the dominant motif in the metaphysical
era of European thought in a single word, it could only be
"globalization." The affair between occidental reason and the
world-whole unfolded and exhausted itself in the sign of the
geometrically perfect round form, which we still label with the
Greek "sphere," and even more widely the Roman "globe." It was
the early European metaphysicians, mathematicians and cosmologists who forced onto mortals their fateful new definition:
orb-creating and orb-inhabiting animals. Globalization began as
the geometrization of the immeasurable.

Through this process, which forms the centerpiece of Greek
theoría, the question of what position humans occupy in nature
takes on a radically technical meaning. For humans, and they

alone, in so far as they conceive the shape of the orb, place themselves within an intelligible, formal and constructive relationship with the world-whole.

Now, after the encounter between being and the circle, having a place in nature means occupying a point in a large orb, whether central or peripheral. With the imagining of the orb, its production immediately begins; it opens the graphic and technical game with totality and its image, as the geometrically illuminated Europeans have done since high antiquity. "For no beast," as Nicolas of Cusa would say in his hyper-lucid treatise on the metaphysics of the round, *De ludo globi*, "produces a ball,"[16] and certainly no animal can play with or aim one. Globalization or spheropoiesis on the grandest scale is the fundamental event of European thought, which, for two and a half thousand years, has not ceased to provoke radical changes in human thinking and living conditions. Something that is entering a phase of greater compaction (and more nervous interpretation) today as a mere geopolitical fact was initially a binding thought figure for philosophers and cosmologists. Mathematical globalization preceded its terrestrial variety by over two thousand years.

> We recognize… we truly recognize! This must be realized and felt again. And the spirit that carries and develops this recognition must be defended against aberrations of the spirit and life.[17]

Today, we can read this exclamation by the young Max Bense— in a text from 1935 bearing the idea-politically suggestive title *Aufstand des Geistes. Eine Verteidigung der Erkenntnis*—as if he

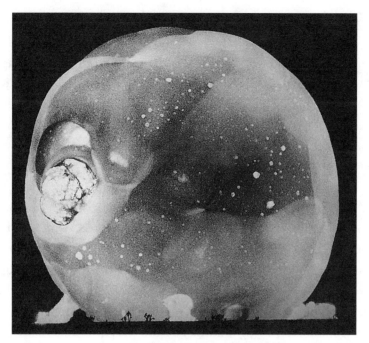

Hydrogen bomb test in Nevada, early 1950s, picture taken from c. 20 miles away

had wanted to postulate the axiom for an intellectual ethics of globalization. Globalization can only be understood by opening up to the realization that the thought figure of the orb is an ontologically, and thus technologically and politically serious matter. Thinking means playing a part in the history of this seriousness. This serious history is the history of being. Hence being is not simply some time or other, but rather the time it takes to understand what space is: the realest of all orbs.

The breakthrough to the concept of the actually existing orb brought the muddle of human history to its conclusion—as the epoch in which the real, lost in unclear fibers of time, still had to be recounted—and ushered in post-history: the state in which space has absorbed time. After the stories, the simultaneous world. For those who recognized it, the orb triumphed over the line, and the calm of essence over the twitchiness of becoming. Post-history, therefore, is as old as the philosophical theory of the orb; what this refers to today is the attempt to imitate on the terrestrial orb what Plato had already demonstrated in the cosmic orb: relaxation in the apocalypse of space.

The starting date of the original globalization can thus, as an era at least, be determined with reasonable accuracy: it is the cosmo-logical enlightenment among the Greek thinkers, who set the great orb rolling through their combination of ontology and geometry. Perhaps Heidegger was right to equate the Modern Age with the golden age of the pictorialization of the world and the existent, but the beginnings of events nonetheless extend back to the culminating thought of the Greeks. The representation of the world-whole through the orb was the decisive act of the early European Enlightenment. One could, by way of definition, say that original philosophy was the shift to monospheric thought— the imposition of interpreting the existent as a whole through the morphological idea of the orb. This formalizing act of force involved thinking individuals in a strong connection to the middle of being, and swore them to the unity, totality, and roundness of the existent. That is why geometry preceded ethics and aesthetics in this case: first comes the sphere, then morality. By making the rule of orb construction explicit and conceiving the ideal periphery, where every point is equidistant from the center, the early mathematicians provided a tool of unprecedented rationality for the world picture-producing energies of Western man. From that point on, humans could, and had to, localize themselves in an encompassing—the *periéchon*—that was no longer only a womb or vegetative grotto, a herd or a cultic commune animated in dance, but a logical and cosmological construction form of timeless validity. Every intelligence was now forced to verify its position in relation to the middle: are we close to the center of being, and are we enjoying jovial circumspections from its vantage point? Or is it, on the contrary, our distance from the middle that allows us to clarify where and who we are? Are we contained in the circle or placed outside of it? Are we related to the middle or alienated from it? As soon as the unconditional orb has subjected the scope of everything existent to representation, philosophers can tell ordinary mortals to their faces that they are blind, and do not see the orb for all the things around it. And as they are incapable of counting to one, they are also powerless to think truly.

It was not the malicious pedantry of the eternal schoolmaster that led the first European thinker of all-encompassing unity, Parmenides, to separate off the path of truth from that of opinion; it was his sharpened insight into the unanimous "structure" of the universally round that forced him to acknowledge the difference between those who lift their gaze and look out at the beautifully rounded, the one-shaped, and those who always remain lost in the diverse muddle around them. The simplest geometric form ascends to the rank of the absolutely valid ideal, which would be the measure of all things for the uneven life and the rugged world over an entire epoch. The pure sphere created in thinking-as-circumspection-in-the-unanimous becomes a critique of empirical, imperfect, un-round reality. Where there were mere surroundings, there will now be the orb—with this imperative, geometry crosses over to the ethical field. It inspires the leap of the soul into the whole; it gives transference its full ontological gravity.

The whole of the existent is now interpreted in terms of spatiality, sense and soul: the project of the world soul has entered its phase of precision. Mortals are invited to exit their unpromising temporal segments, where they while away their lives hanging from threads of worry; they suddenly have a chance to look up from the trough of concern and emerge into the large, friendly space, where everything is simultaneous, illuminated and open. Once early philosophical-cosmological thought had chosen the sensible-supersensible figure of the orb as the archetype of perfect beauty, it lent the human condition the form of a game that entertains, empowers and exceeds its players. Whoever plays with balls will, when the seriousness of the idea overtakes the game, find themselves face to face with an oversized, over-beautiful and over-round orb that inevitably rolls over its players. Would it be geometry, then, that is nothing but the beginning of terror?

In the surviving images from everyday culture in antiquity, there initially seems to be little evidence of this great turn towards the timelessly round. From the Greek spheric dawn, alongside discursive expositions in philosophical texts from Anaximander to Plato, only two-dimensional pictorial documents of the *sphaira* have reached us, all of them flat and conventional. Next to works of a type similar to the philosopher mosaic from Torre Annunziata, the majority are depictions on coins, in whose visual programs the *sphaira*, together with portraits of rulers and imperial insignias, plays a central part. One of the faces one recognizes on old coins is that of the goddess Nike, who is writing news of victory on a round shield floating before her, her foot placed on a ball lying on the ground. This habitus was adopted by the later Caesars—the *sphaira* under the ruler's sandal became a set phrase in the language of

Sphaira under the emperor's foot

power images. On an earlier coin, the philosopher Anaxagoras is depicted sitting on an orb, and the figure of Italia likewise; a small Hellenistic gem even shows an Eros sitting atop the sphere. In Roman relics it is the goddess Fortuna who rests her light foot on the orb. The image of the orb descends into the purely formulaic when presented laconically together with a helm—enough to convey to the educated the connection between state cybernetics and cosmic piety. On Caesar's coins, the sphere, the staff of Mercury and the *fasces* are combined to form a complex of insignias, as if postulating the unity of absolute power and world happiness. From the Hellenistic period onwards, as one scholar aptly remarked, the *sphaira* had become the standard "hieroglyph for the entire universe, especially the heavens";[18] under the Roman emperors, the association between the sphere and the ruler's portrait developed into a mandatory motif for anyone who wanted to seize or proclaim power. When the *sphaira* changed into the *globus cruciger* among

Beneath the feet of Fortuna: Albrecht Dürer, *Nemesis (The Great Fortune)* (1502), detail

The globe under the foot of Saint Francis of Assisi: Bartoleme Estéban Perez
Murillo, *Saint Francis Embracing the Crucified Christ* (Seville, c. 1668), detail

the Christianized lords of late antiquity and the Middle Ages, the
old equation of the orb symbol and kingship was continued with
an additional sacramental elevation. And even when the image of
the globe outstripped the cosmic orb from the nineteenth century
onwards, the earth, emancipated from heaven and standing on its
own, still profited from the classical sphere's connotation of totality.

Contemporary media theorists may notice that the image of
the sphere on the old coins testifies to a twofold circularity: it is
imprinted on objects that were themselves already agents and
media of a relative globalization in the economic sense, for in their
time, Roman coins were in circulation in the entire *inhabited
world*. The imago of the cosmos on the coin is part of a pictorial
history that leads not to art, but to the political and technological
seizure of power. For even if ancient Hellenistic coins only

Roman coins from the time of Caesar

circulated in the Roman ecumene, their movement displayed the same dynamics that would incorporate the entire earth from the start of the Modern Age onwards. Money and the globe belong together, as the typical movement of money—return of investment—is the central principle of the circumnavigation of the world.[19] Images of spheres on coins: viewed from the outcome, the program of European world history and media history reveals itself in these unspectacular relics of ancient culture. In modernity, money, as both real and speculative capital, placed humans under the dominion of absolutely posited traffic. Whatever controls the circulation gains possession of the whole. At the end of this exposition, I will show why the principal idea of the Modern Age was proved *not* by Copernicus, but by Magellan. For the basic fact of the Modern Age is not that the earth travels around the sun; it is that money goes around the earth. The theory of the orb is simultaneously the first analysis of power.

That is why in antiquity, as soon as the spherical shape could be constructed in geometric abstraction and viewed in cosmological contemplation, the question immediately arose who should be the master of the imagined and produced orb. In the older pictures the goddesses of victory, the Fortunas, the emperors, and later the missionaries of Christ placed their feet on the sphere; scientists grouped their instruments around them, marked tropics

The orb as a base for a bust; detail from G. B. Piranesi, *The Roman Circus* (1756)

and meridians on it and drew the equator; early on, the Catholic Church planted the cross on top of the orb and proclaimed Christ cosmocrator and lord over all spheres; in the twentieth century, finally, the globe was integrated into the logos and advertisements of countless firms operating worldwide. It is the shared sign of power and intellect—even if, in the age of regional advanced civilizations, these two factors confronted each other as irreconcilable opposites, united by mutual suspicion and depending on each other only in antagonistic cooperation.

When the Romans stormed Syracuse and captured the splendid globe of Archimedes from his house, the commander Marcellus had it taken to Rome and exhibited in the temple of Virtus, best translated as the goddess of military motivation. The

Globus cruciger of Hohenstaufen

words of Archimedes to the Roman soldier who killed him—
"Do not disturb my circles!"—were soon understood also by the
generals of the republic, and later the Caesars, in their own way.
For how were these lords to make sense of their contributions to
the formation of the Roman Empire, if not as an attempt to draw
increasingly wide and well-defended circles with a compass of
legions around the capital chosen by the gods and ensure it
remained undisturbed?

Hand of Elizabeth I of England on the earth globe

The image of the largest orb thus raises the question of the location of the middle, and consequently the identity and residence of the overlord; at the same time, it forces pictorially-imagining thought to offer a solution to the problem of whether the all-encompassing orb can be *placed* on a support or a ground. On what foundation could the cosmos—as an image, as a concept and as a reality—be made to stand? In what shell or enclosure could—in the imagination and in actuality—the orb of orbs be embedded? Who or what should carry that which carries everything? Or should we already permit the bold thought that the encompassing contains itself and *floats* in the void on its own unconditional authority, unsupported by anything external?[20]

When ancient thinkers and artists faced the difficulty conveyed by these questions, what came to their aid was the mythological tradition that suggested a Titanic candidate for the role of the cosmos-carrier. It was this myth that informed the most powerful visual globe work of the Old World, for with its help, in one of the most fruitful moments of ancient pictorial

Celestial globe on the shoulders of the Farnese Atlas, 1st or 2nd century AD,
Museo Nazionale, Naples

creation, the question of the stand and carrier of the whole found
an answer as clear as it was enigmatic.

In 1575, under the pontificate of Gregory XIII, excavators in
Rome uncovered fragments of a monumental statue that could
easily be identified as Atlas carrying the celestial globe. After

extensive restoration, this sensational find was incorporated into the antiques collection of the House of Farnese; in the eighteenth century, together with the family's other art treasures, it entered into the possession of Charles IV of Naples, the son of Philip V of Spain and Elisabeth Farnese. For this reason the figure stands today in the Museo Nazionale in Naples, even though, in its spirit and styling, it cannot be at home anywhere but the Rome of the Caesars, and indirectly also that of the popes.[21]

In its stout pathos and immanent monumentality—the sculpture is seven feet tall—the *Atlante Farnese* could strike the inexperienced observer as beckoning from the hallowed early days of thought and art. If, furthermore, one considers that this work features the oldest globe in the world, and almost the only one to survive from antiquity—the documented celestial globe of Archimedes from the third century BC was lost, as was the great earth globe of Crates of Mallus from the second century BC[22]—this unique art object could arouse almost numinous feelings. This Atlas, with his bearded, long-suffering Titan's head, tilted painfully to one side, burdened with the weight of the world, athlete and thinker in one, could, in the viewer's initial dismay, be regarded as the petrified form of a Presocratic saying: a reminder of a time in which humans and Titans were able to empathize with one another. In its subdued torment and formalized endurance, this humanely powerful figure of Atlas seems to be whispering to its observer the theorem that existence means carrying the weight of the heavens.

At second glance, the work's archaic aura vanishes entirely, and the more intensely one examines it, the more clearly it reveals itself as a construct already marked by late imperial ideas of function and scientific concepts. In truth, this sphere-bearing

Atlas is by no means the document of a mythical early period—in two different ways.

Firstly, the orb on his shoulders and between his hands is no longer the old Homeric or Hesiodic heaven which, according to mythology, Zeus commanded the Titan to carry as a punishment for participating in the uprising of the old telluric gods against the Olympians. In reality, the old Homeric *uranós* could not be depicted as a *sphaira*, only as a hemisphere above the flat earth—a view that corresponds most clearly to the intuitive, pre-theoretical conception of the world. For the ancient imagination, it was undoubtedly natural to prevent a notional hemispheric sky from falling down on the earth through a real counterforce; hence, in some ancient depictions, the sky was held up by pillars, just as temple beams were supported by a row of columns. In old Peloponnesian legends, the sky rests on mountaintops as if they were pillars, lending expression to the understandable mythological explanation for the distance between the earth and the sky.

It testifies to the triumph of the Greek enlightenment, on the other hand, that the archaic figure of the Titan was burdened with the modern mathematical object of the complete sphere. For what Atlas is carrying on his shoulders is already the sky of the philosophers, which, with Plato and Aristotle, became synonymous with the world as such or the cosmos. The geometric modernity of the ideal spherical form—reinforced by the line system comprising the equator, the tropics and the colures—nonetheless continues to be connected with the pre-scientific celestial poetry of antiquity, which had painted the complete catalogue of constellations on the curvature of the nocturnal world vase. The images are fashioned in high relief, as if one were seeing the stars in the night sky not from the earth, but from some location beyond earthly nights. Of the forty-eight canonical constellations of antiquity, forty-two can be made out clearly on the Farnese globe.

What the Titan is bearing on his shoulders thus constitutes a poetic-scientific bastard of a sky, a product of mythology as much as geometry, a sky for story-readers and prognosticators of natural events, crafted in an age when a warm agreement between science and imperial world-imagining had begun to establish itself. It addresses a mathematically or philosophically literate audience that is, however, still sufficiently educated in mythology and literature to read the symbols of constellations as if they were accessible episodes from Ovid's *Metamorphoses*.

In this sense one can say that as well as the philosophical sky, the Farnese Atlas also carries a literary one by setting up, together with the new, bafflingly clear mathematical lines, a long-familiar library of astral legends before the observer. In the center of our picture one recognizes the primeval Greek ship, the Argo, emblem of the Hellenic entrepreneurial spirit and central symbol of a thalassophilic culture pervaded by a consciousness that humans, or at least those who can feel what Greeks feel, are creatures that always have something to search for on other shores. Here the Argo is depicted as half a ship, because only half of it appears above the horizon in the southern winter sky, and it dives under once more come spring. The ship is flanked on the right by centaurs, above which one recognizes the Hydra and the crater, and on the left by the figure of the Great Dog. Each of these images is connected to a micro-universe of stories that enable the world's event character to develop among images of scenic animation. Though the *sphaira*, as a total figure, already advanced the philosophical calming of the existent in a single sublime outline, labeling it with the constellations kept the memory of life's primal dramas alive in prototypical sequences of events. Aby Warburg celebrated the constellation-covered celestial globe in emotional words as the true manifesto of Greek genius—the humane synthesis of mathematics and poetry.[23]

In a second sense too, however, this sculpture reveals itself upon calmer inspection as a late, almost modern work. For this Atlas has been transferred from the age of Titans to that of athletes; its inner date is not the era of Titanomachy, in which ancient gods of power and the elements fought for cosmic dominance with younger gods of form and virtue; nor is it situated on the edge of the ecumene, by the pillars of Hercules behind which the early Greeks believed the Mediterranean world ended. Its place is at the center of a stadium, or even more a Roman arena, where professional fighters and athletes of violence, like second-order barbarians, were wont to exhibit their impressive bodies in spectacular, bloody feats of strength. This is supported by the cited dating suggestions from historians of art and ideas, who consider the work a Roman creation from the Augustan period. If one were to take the location of the vernal equinox on the globe as indicative of its time of production, it would point to an original sculpture from around 300 BC; the Roman find would then be a replica that had retained an obsolete notion of the stars from a Greek model. This would in turn suggest that for its Roman users, the globe had lost its possible scientific function and become no more than an educational piece of plunder and an imperial showpiece.

And indeed, everything suggests that the *Atlante Farnese* was not used as an instrument of astronomical enlightenment by its Roman owners. Rather, its installation shows that it was perceived as symbolizing a new existentialism of power. The muscular Titan bends beneath his burden as if he had not only to carry the vault of heaven, but also a world of new rulers above.[24] For an Atlas who must carry the sky of the mathematicians belongs, in worldview-historical terms, at the side of an emperor who had to make the earth his own personal concern. It is no coincidence that such figures started appearing in Rome at the very time when the Romans were rehearsing their new imperial role. The moral meaning of physically carrying the sky was quite simply that of governing the world edifice—an idea that Augustus would already have found plausible. We must take into account that from the Hellenistic period on, the "cosmos" was not only the celestial space as a beautifully arranged whole; the term applied equally to the human space or the ecumene—the cosmopolis, in so far as this became a target of imperial interest and anthropological curiosity. Thus the meaning of Atlas' role shifted from a mythical forced service to a sacred political office. Perhaps Horace was already associating Atlas with the role of Augustus when, in his epistolary poem, he praises the emperor with these words: "Since so many and such great concerns fall upon your shoulders alone."[25]

As far as the archaic Atlas was concerned, he had indeed resembled a cursed figure; his fate was related to that of his Titanic brother Prometheus, who, shackled to a cliff and tormented by the liver-devouring vulture, had good reason to call himself a "god hated by God." He belongs to the group of eternal sufferers in Greek mythology: Tantalus, Sisyphus and Philoctetes, all bound irreversibly to their torturous overexertion. Barely any traces of this early, tragic view of Atlas remain in the Roman sculpture. The

Farnese Atlas is like a state athlete who has marched into the circus to cheering from the gallery, little different from a gladiator or an oil-glistening Hercules bursting heavy iron chains around his chest with sheer muscle power. When he heaves up the celestial globe, he does so with the routine of the old circus fighters whose skill is suffering. This embodiment of strength performs its duty as if following a mighty patron with his own company of gladiators; he has sensed the air of empire, and knows something about the celebrated pain of heroes in the arenas. His face, blind with effort, listens to the ovations as if witnessing an empowering vision: "Give a round of applause, citizens of Rome, for the Titan, the son of Iapetus, is wrestling with the element!"

The groaning sky-bearer seems aware of his role in the politico-cosmic theater of strength. His body, entirely geared towards effort, testifies to a culture that ultimately discusses nothing but the duty to be strong in a world where there is no relief for the powerful and no tolerance for the weak. We must imagine the gaze of the young Octavianus, the later Augustus, resting on this figure to gain an idea of the interior monologues in which this statue may have had a place. There is no reason not to assume that later on, the philosopher-emperors of the crisis-ridden second century—Antoninus Pius and his adoptive son Marcus Aurelius—also stood before this still image of the suffering of slave and master, meditating on the human condition. We can also be certain that when Hadrian built the dome of the Pantheon, he was seeking to duplicate the globe on Atlas' shoulders on a grand scale—only this time without its mythical carrier, placed directly on the all-carrying soil of Rome. The nudity of the globe warrior would soon represent that of the deified emperors; the figure's cultic athleticism articulates a philosophy of existence and service that found its home at the court of the Caesars. Its solemn kneeling posture and stoical endurance beneath its eternal burden reflect the ban on exhaustion issued for the emperor's life. Like a facet from an imperial mirror, the sky-bearer testifies to the burden character of the eminent life placed at the center of the empire by the gods.

There is still a third relative modernity in the Farnese Atlas that must be mentioned, however, and it is this one that determines its meaning. The figure has rightly been termed a de-mythologized or humanized giant;[26] one could equally call it an intellectualized world athlete, for its shape approaches not only that of the naked fighter, but also the imago of the philosopher. If one takes seriously the suggestions to date the sculpture to late Hellenistic or Augustan times, the nature of its hair and beard become significant for its classification according to the spectrum of Roman types of manliness. Whatever the restorers might have augmented and fabricated, one can say this much: with his almost certainly authentic beard, this world-bearer stakes a claim to membership in the intellectual field of his time. Once the custom of shaving had established itself throughout Greece in the third century as a result of Macedonian rule, and later also in Rome, growing a beard—which had initially been an indication of a conservative, perhaps even anti-Macedonian mindset—became a distinctive characteristic of the philosopher class. The obligation for philosophers to grow beards went so far that in Athens at the time of Marcus Aurelius, the authorities were hesitant to bestow a professorship endowed by the emperor on a Peripatetic with the best academic credentials, simply because the candidate had sparse facial hair; the case was considered so grave that the emperor's personal approval had to be obtained from Rome.[27] As for the Farnese Atlas, he would effortlessly have met the critical requirement to receive the teaching post, for the opulence of his beard offered irrefutable evidence of his philosopherdom. The cloak hanging down from the side, whose presence would be as inexplicable with an archaic Titan as with an athlete whose profession required him to be naked, likewise indicates that this figure belongs to the intellectual class.

Taking into account the unmistakable philosopher's attributes of beard and cloak, the burden which Atlas is obliged to carry appears in a new light. For this world-bearer, understood as a philosophizing athlete, is in reality dealing not with a material weight, but rather a thought of non-physical gravity. As the carrier of the mathematical sphere, the figure bends as if under the weight of a dark theorem. What the statue's observer sees is no less than a logical charade whose wording becomes legible once the signs have been decoded: only the greatest thought can carry the heaviest weight. The massive physicality of the Atlas vividly conveys the effort of this carrying by analogy; for this mental image of the cosmic whole has long since abandoned the massive body known as the sky, which can only be held up through physical strength. The true sky must be held in comprehensive reflections; its bearer or "framing" ["*Gestell*"] is thought itself. The logos becomes the accomplice, indeed the true *fundamentum* of the encompassing, once it understands what contains us. The *periéchon* is the spirit whose lightness causes the universe of heaviness to float.

That is why the philosopher, as Atlas, knows of an effort that is missed by those who seek heights of bodily achievement in the arenas. Athletes and philosophers certainly share a positive understanding of the exertion that makes man in higher culture, and both celebrate *pónos*, the grave burden of life and the effort that forms humans. While the athlete stops at muscular love of effort or ponophilia, however, the philosopher goes further, to the intellectual love of the most difficult thing of all, namely the whole. Thus the *Atlante Farnese*, with its globe feat, brings the basic teaching of ancient philosophical asceticism into view: the philosopher is he who burdens himself with the weight of the world as an athlete of totality. The essence of philosophy as a form of life is philopony, friendship with the totality of heavy and sublime things. The love of wisdom and the love of the heaviness of the one, the whole, amount to the same.[28]

To carry the great weight, the small ones must be thrown off. One can only shoulder the whole if one trains as an athlete of impartiality. For whoever gets involved in small and medium affairs does not have their hands free for the great ones. It is symptomatic that Emperor Marcus Aurelius, himself an authentic philosopher, considered it appropriate to note in the first lines of his *Meditations*:

> From my tutor I learned: not to be a Green or a Blue partisan at the races, or a supporter of the lightly armed or heavily armed gladiators at the Circus; endurance and frugality; to do one's own work and not be a busybody; not to welcome slanderous gossip.[29]

For the philosopher, the reward for such abstinence is the growing ability to view the all-encompassing sphere that cannot possibly reveal itself to the vulgar perception lost in the things around it. Only abstinent and uniform circumspection in all directions can allow the very realest One Orb to become tangible around the reserved witness. It is this orb that is expressed most

Tapisserie des Gobelins, Versailles

appropriately in the image of the mathematical complete sky—the overarching curvature unseen by any empirical eye.

But if the sky carried by Atlas is in fact the sphere of the philosophers, the sensory accessibility of this sublime orb must be a precarious affair. Though the sculpture presents its visibility as unproblematic, further reflection reveals that the circumstance of the orb in its visual depiction can only be a deceptive one. What Atlas bears on his shoulder is a representation of the heavens whose actual counterpart—assuming it existed in physical reality—could never be seen by any human observer from their mortal position. For *who* would one have to be to view the surface of the celestial orb like an object facing one? And above all: *where* would one have to be to see the whole of the existent like a vault from the outside?

2. The Parmenidean Moment

> The world is round around the round being.
> —Gaston Bachelard, *The Poetics of Space*

The peculiarity of the problem posed by the nature of the Farnese celestial globe and its later variants is, from a modern standpoint, so difficult to grasp that it seems justified to reexamine its inherent difficulties from a different perspective. First of all, we must consider that our contemporary understanding of what globes are and mean is now exclusively preconditioned by the model of the earth globe. Our view of the globe as an object is defined almost without exception by current geographical, geopolitical, geo-economic, and climatological interests. It is no longer possible to discover a relevant role in the modern repertoire of ideas and signs for large-scale orbs that neither are nor represent the earth.

That this concentration on the earth globe is a very recent phenomenon—barely older than a hundred and fifty years—is shown by the fact that from their widespread appearance around 1500 until the 1830s, the globes were almost always produced and presented in pairs. They began their triumphal march as an inseparable dyad of celestial and earth globes. Only together could the two orbs fulfill their cosmographic mission, and only together did they symbolize, on the roofs of princely houses and in the entrance halls and reading rooms of the great European libraries between Madrid and Moscow, the universe of knowledge and the knowledge of the universe. Wherever the orb twins were displayed to the educated classes, they pointed together to the privileged duty of the powerful to practice circumspection in all directions. Only in combination could the celestial and earth globes stand for the whole of the terrestrial and supra-terrestrial world. As inseparable dual spheres, they represented the cosmic totality and the telluric sub-totality. They formed the twofold sign of world interpretation in the age of newer metaphysics—or, in Heidegger's words, in the age of the world picture—with the formal equality of the two orbs already manifesting the revolutionary enhancement of the earth's status.

This contradicts the myth, launched by Freud, of the cosmological injury of human "narcissism": on the whole, as will be shown later on,[30] the Copernican revolution in cosmology actually had an inspiring effect on the self-confidence of Europeans, and one cannot seriously speak of a lasting snub through astronomic decentering. Copernicanism emancipated the earth to become a

Library of El Escorial, armillary sphere

Celestial and earth globes from the roof of the former Imperial Court Library in Vienna, c. 1726, diameter c. 400 cm

star among the stars—in fact, as Blumenberg showed, it elevated it to the only star worthy of the name because it now emerges as the transcendental heavenly body that, as the condition of possibility of observing the other heavenly bodies, outshines all others. The regular co- and para-existence of equally large celestial and earth globes is the emblem of this post-Copernican situation: the one earth is worth the entire remaining sky.

After 1830, however, the production of paired globes came to a near-standstill; the earth globe began its triumphal march as the sole representative of the principle of large orb depictions. The celestial globes became curiosities and were increasingly forgotten. Looking at this caesura, it is impossible for the historian of ideas to avoid thinking of the end of classical metaphysics, for if one can describe the celestial globe as the quasi-mass medium of metaphysics, then the extinction of this cosmographic tool corresponds significantly with the perfection of the Old European metaphysical tradition in the Hegelian system. Through the dissolution of the world-whole into sober knowledge, the sky—

Earth globe factory in Paris (1954)

as the last bastion of an objective cosmos—finally also lost its
remaining naïve representative, the Uranian globe.

This constellation enabled the solo earth globe to rise to an
identifying symbol with mass impact for the Young Hegelians. In
the image of the earth, it presented the ineluctable foundation of
all human affairs. Henceforth, anyone speaking of the earth could
believe they were invoking the ground of all grounds. And indeed:
had the nineteenth century not made the descent from the concept

of a fictional sky of ideas to the regained, real earth its epochal task? Had "immanence" not become the keyword in advanced philosophical thought? Had the breakthrough to the things themselves, the descent from false heights to the true foundations, not become the core logical and kinetic figure of all "critique"? The age-old exercise of looking up to metaphorical and metaphysical heavens lost its plausibility when the aim was to re-conquer the solid ground of human facts—which is to say, of genre practice.

The burgeoning age of cumulative technology and self-assured anthropology was no longer interested in transcendences or celestial globes. With the astronomic, visual and philosophical destruction of the sky, its representations too were condemned to pointlessness. Henceforth, the word "sky"[31] would no longer refer to anything more than an optical effect that appears in the medium of a planet's atmosphere when the cosmos is perceived through human eyes. This sky proved metaphysically empty and anthropologically indifferent. Suddenly humans were the creatures that had no business up there, but much to lose—namely themselves. Consequently, the sky at best constituted an aeronautical task, not a metaphysical or a globographic one.

Thus the riches of humans should no longer be wasted on imagined heights. With general alphabetization, the constellations faded into obscurity; the image script in the sky no longer found any readers, and it was only in astrology-addicted subcultures that Cancer, Virgo, Sagittarius and the like lived on in humiliation. The singular earth globe, on its artful stands of wood or metal, became the signifier of the post-metaphysical position in which humans, as inhabitants of the earth's surface, find themselves on the orb that carries them in the cosmos, condemned to self-recovery in the shelless space.

This reference to the crisis of the sky in the recent history of ideas brings the strange, and for the moderns almost incomprehensible, character of the oldest globe into sharper relief. For what the Farnese Atlas carries on his shoulders is precisely that *other* globe which we, as heirs to and participants in the modern world, can no longer understand at first sight: the celestial globe, which represented the cosmos as a whole and was intended to show its viewers the *imago mundi* in its sublime and irresistible roundness. Despite its seemingly plain, manifest givenness, this star-adorned marble object remained a simultaneously real and virtual construct full of cryptic preconditions. It constituted an image in the philosophically demanding sense of the word: a given observation of the non-given. If, to adapt Karl Marx, one could ever attribute "metaphysical quirks" to a man-made medium besides money, it could only be the Old European celestial globe. In its case, we can say that there can be no valid onto-logy that does not require a complementary ontography.[32]

The Greek *sphaira* is thus, as shown above, nothing other than the image or signifier of cosmic totality. Whoever sees the image of the orb sees the orb itself. This immediately raises the question, however, of who would come into consideration as the viewer of the real celestial whole. Its visual representation appeals to a sense of sight not based in natural human eyes, for no pair of human eyes could ever find themselves looking at an externally and objectively present sky, even if they popped out of their sockets. Human perception is always concerned purely with gathering impressions of situations beneath the arch of the sky, never with seeing the sky from without. Thus the celestial globe transpires as a hyperbolic figure that draws on credit from a superhuman vision.

One must put it as eccentrically as the case demands: what the Farnese sky shows is the worldview of God. For an outside view of the sky, as presented by the globe of Atlas, would be a divine privilege—assuming the metaphysical imagination was right in conceiving of God as an eccentric, all-observing intelligence that floats above the realm of finite forms. Such an intelligence should indeed, looking down on the corporeal and transient, see the cosmic whole rising under or before it. The hyper-Uranian divine sight, if turned worldwards, would take in an incessant cosmic dawn and could edify itself in the contemplation of the one thing worthy of it, turning a blind eye to possible uneven details—but where should such imperfections come from, when Uranus is a sky without the possibility of a single cloud?

Standing before the actually existing *sphaira*, the transcendent observer would be looking upon its true cathedral. Faced with the sublime vault, God's narcissism would be satisfied, for the absolute noetic observer should recognize its own being in that most spiritual of all shapes, the radiantly embodied *hén kaí pán*, with ultimate gratification.

The ancient orb constructors and globe sculptors, then, were creating no less than an efficient medium for the imitation of God using the means of geometry and the visual arts. In so doing, they transformed the Egyptian art of earth measurement into the Greek art of celestial measurement, indeed God measurement. Henceforth, all talk of geometry would in fact refer to uranometry, even theometry. As only the god of the philosophers has a worldview worthy of the name, a complete or comprehensive representation of the existent, human beings can share in the divine view—however precariously—by creating a mathematically generated image of the cosmos. The highest image, the *sphaira*, is thus more than an

Carrying, containing, holding, underlying: concerning the whole and its framing

arbitrary sign that stands for the world. This image is not only adequate to the original in the highest sense; it also draws the observer into that which it depicts. The orb transpires as the dynamic true icon of the existent: for by informing and encompassing the observer, it begins to *live* in them as an effective idea. It brings the human eye into the eccentric position which could seemingly only be occupied by a separate God;[33] consequently, it deifies the human intellect that has grasped the rule of orb production. Thus the *sphaira* can be termed the metaphysical thought-image *par excellence*, as its inner dynamic induces and completes the transition from sensory observation to intellectual imagining.

The monstrous element of the orb on the shoulders of the Farnese Atlas has thus been addressed: in this celestial globe, the secret of ancient occidental metaphysics is before our very eyes. Even if it were not the oldest, and virtually the only surviving example of its kind,[34] it would still constitute the most dignified and excessive object of philosophical meditation—for, as a representation of the unrepresentable, it provides thought, which strives to rise from sensory givens to comprehensive views, with its ultimate form. It is the sublime itself, reproduced as a shape and understood as encompassing.

And yet there lies a monumental ambiguity in this globe; for as soon as the shape of the orb had come to light as a mental concept, it had to be decided whether the human spirit saw itself inserted into it or placed outside of it. With the seductive visualization of the whole in the One Orb, the limit and danger of metaphysical imagining are abruptly exposed. The view of the *sphaira* as the imago of totality seduces the seeing party into looking away from their true place in existence and transferring themselves to a fictional observer's life beyond the world. A form of God-deception is thus inherent in philosophizing from the outset. What Heidegger would later term forgetfulness of being [*Seinsvergessenheit*] already begins with the ancient instructions for viewing the orb blissfully from without. The *sphaira*, as the highest form of imagining thought, lured mortals into the game of an initially jovial, then lordly observation of the outside that would one day lead to polytechnical dreams of control and the tyranny of knowledge over concretely interpreted life as a whole. Lordly imagining means grasping the whole as something actually present and placing oneself securely facing it. Would this mean that the metaphysical globalization of the existent already constituted an invitation to forget being and the first betrayal of humanity's existential place?

As far as the Farnese sculpture is concerned, things have not yet progressed far enough to justify warnings of master logic and the rigidity of reification advanced in modern critical theories. An overseeing imagining initially remains the sole privilege of the observer *in front of* the still image. In his strained blindness, Atlas himself—brutally excluded from the whole he bears—stands under his burden, as it were devoid of a world picture. Judging by his bowed attitude, he has not yet gained access to the lightness of theory or any real idea of the object that burdens him. Connected to his orb only through the perception of its incredible weight, he knows only as much about it as his bowed shoulders can understand. His preconception of the world is that which its weight conveys to him. Only the prejudice of its burden character attunes him to the whole of the existent—he philosophizes with tensed muscles, as it were, his neck inclined and his soul squeezed together. It is the weight of the world that illuminates him, the strangest of all philosophers; heaviness grants him access to a dark truth about the whole. That is why this Atlas cannot yet appear as a free-handed master, let alone a technician or experimenter in the Modern Age sense, as his constantly bent state beneath this unshareable weight prevents him from penetrating to the principle of relief.

In this respect the figure of Atlas, even when exposed as a relatively modern likeness, contains a hint of pre-theoretical depth—according to its mythological substance, one can almost take it as a sign from a Presocratic space where wisdom had not yet been subjected to the dictates of scientific culture. In addition, this Atlas is completely unpragmatic by nature, for his deed, the bearing of heaven, is the opposite of technologically setting one's hand to things requiring change or production. Rooted to the spot, he

Farnese Atlas, detail

stands frozen in eternal muscular meditation. Like a pre-Homeric hero, he is an endurer of disasters, not an overcomer of conditions; solving problems is not his affair. At most, the world is ready-to-hand where his hands touch the orb's shell, but this readiness-to-hand is not supported by the knowing or even theoretical eye—thus it is not yet on the way to technology. For to become technological, it would require relief through imagining and attempting, and precisely that is still unattainable for this Atlas.

If, of course, he could one day pass on the orb to another carrier[35]—which would be a logical inner need—or place it on a frame, these same Titanic hands, now free, would also be suitable to work on and distort the whole that would then be present-at-hand. We understand immediately that this would bring Heidegger's concept of technology as a titanoid practice of imagining, producing and distorting into play. For it will be technology that becomes predominant when the world-bearer

Raphael, *The School of Athens* (1510), group of cosmologists

puts down his pictorial burden and conquers the imagined and set-aside world through processing (Heidegger would say: when the underlying is interpreted as a subject and the subject is interpreted as dominating).

There is, at least, one great document of early Greek thought which proves that the choice between theory-less slave suffering and suffering-less master theory does not cover the full range of options in the question of how being and thinking are related. In the fragments from the work of Parmenides that reached posterity, one finds a culture of theory for which the essence of the orb

Giovanni Battista Piranesi, Pantheon Dome

precisely does not reveal itself in frivolous external viewing, let alone in the Titanic slave position.

For Parmenides, the theory of the orb meant nothing other than free circumspection in the interior of an open entity that provides insight into itself. Thus he never considered the notion of a place outside of it. When, at a decisive point in his didactic poem, he proclaims the simultaneously famous and opaque doctrine that thinking and being—*noeín* and *eínai*— are one and the same, this motto is the great leap of the idea into the open center of the world. Only from within, immanently, remaining internal, can the orb of the existent be grasped in thought through observation—not in a gradual circuit, in the regurgitation of commonplace opinions about the things surrounding us, or by combing through the changeful details we encounter all around, but only by suddenly directing our gaze at the undivided, "one-part," unanimous, round, One.

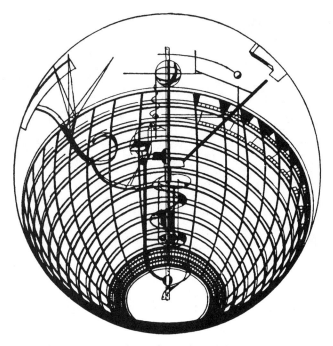

Andreas Weininger, design for a spherical theater (1925/26)

Thus Parmenides discovered the space of the philosophers as the lightened monstrous.

The entire field of the surrounding only becomes bright instantaneously; the gradual is unphilosophical. The whole is illuminated in the floodlight of a simultaneous circumspection which immediately discloses all that surrounds. And precisely this means that the absolute orb is given for the circumspective intelligence, inevitably and eternally from within. This universal synchronous view into the one whole, which vibrates in itself like an illuminated orb-vase, is called for by the goddess as the only true view. It cannot possibly be a distanced, externalizing view of a given whole, but rather points to an ecstatic limit to the primordial understanding of the world from the basic position of being-in-the-world.

The great view into the unanimous, open, surrounding whole is virtually never attempted by ordinary mortals, because they always cling to the current state and the first available thing they encounter; in the midst of the orb, they are blind to it. Entangled in errands, stories and opinions, they fail to enter the exceptional theory-opening state of integral circumspection into disclosed being. Thus they do not "realize" their situation in the immutably unanimous same, losing themselves in fragmenting opinions on this and that. Incapable of collecting their presence of mind for immediate circumspection in the stationary, bright whole, the mortals do not reach the location which the goddess begins to interpret for her favorite, the philosopher, as the true and salvific one.

In the eye-training school of total philosophical circum-spection or all-collecting awareness, the thinker feels and understands what it means to "know" everything, to see every-thing visible, to recognize everything encompassing enclosed by the ring of being, and all of this forever, and always in the same light of perception—if perception or awareness mean here that everything which is can only be reduced to the unanimous common denominator "that it is."[36] This and nothing else is the meaning of the measurement of the orb of being in the original meditation, carried out in a single blow; everything that is dictates the shared characteristic of "existent/being" [*seiend*], *eón*, to it. The existent as a whole is sovereignly determined through "disclosedness for the mental circumspection into precisely this existent." That is why being, in this case, amounts to connectedness in the homogeneous clearing of the orb that is

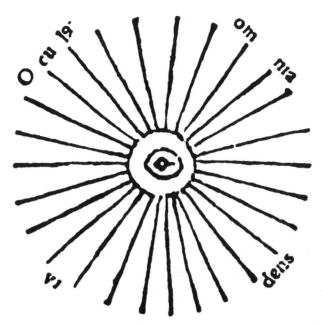

Oculus omnia videns, illustration for Carolus Bovillus, *Liber de sapiente* (1510)

disclosed from within through circumspective perception. "For it is the same to perceive and to be."[37]

> Nor is it divisible, since it is all alike, nor is there any more here, which would keep it from holding together, nor any less, but it is full of what-is. Thus it is all continuous, for what-is cleaves to what-is.[38]
>
> Yet since there is a final limit, it is complete from every direction, like to the mass of a well-rounded ball (*eukýklou sphaíres*), equally resistant from the center in all directions.[39]

Here too, with this ontological quasi-orb that is designed not with the compasses of the mathematicians, but out of a circumspective

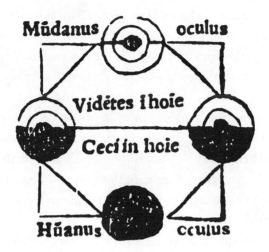

Humanus oculus: illumination, half-sight and blindness

feeling for the common "it is" denominator of everything existent—which is why its extension always has an inauthentic sense
to it, though what sense exactly?—the question arises of who
can perceive it, and where the seeing person would have to
position themselves in order to "realize" it. While the celestial
globe, as shown above, would only become visible as an object of
imagining for a metaphysical observer or an eccentric usurper
imitating the worldview of God, the ontological globe of Parmenides could only reveal itself to an ecstatic who, as an
absolutely contemplative intelligence looking around in a de-
selfed state, would transport themselves into the "untrembling
heart of truth."

Whoever adopts the outside view of the celestial whole is
already looking at the very epitome of objectivity: the world-whole
as the super-object that does not contain the super-observer.
The Parmenidean orb, on the other hand, is the epitome of a

universally immanent figure of disclosure, and as it is only formed with a single predicate, namely "that whatever is covered by circumspective awareness *is*," it has the structure of an intellectual fact, not a thing—a panoramic view of a vault, uniformly illuminated and, as it were, ensouled from within.[40] While an observer of the sky has to assume an absolutely eccentric position, the viewer of the Parmenidean orb of being would have to center themselves absolutely—so much so that they would have to distance themselves radically from their ties to sensory impressions and hearsay in the human community: to lose their mind for the center.

If the outside view of the world already brought into play a certain eccentricity or cosmological madness, the concentricity of Eleatic thought depends on a counter-madness: the ability to place oneself in the absolute center and be surrounded in ecstatic contemplation by stationary, "one-part" abundance. In its lightning-fast circumspection, the Parmenidean spatial eye records the one and only continent of openness to being, which freely provides information about itself. Although the philosopher does not state undisguisedly in his didactic poem that the orb of being is the true God and his clear sight, his entire ontology is directed towards making the philosopher an abettor of the divine panoramic view into the stationary One and Own. Only he, the super-madman, can be granted privileged insight into the world-view of the round God from the innermost perspective. For who but a God looking out of and into his world from within could meet the requirement of capturing the static orb of being as a whole in full amphiscopy?[41]

This raises the question of whether, in the two cases of orb viewing—in metaphysical-globalizing eccentricity as well as ecstatic-

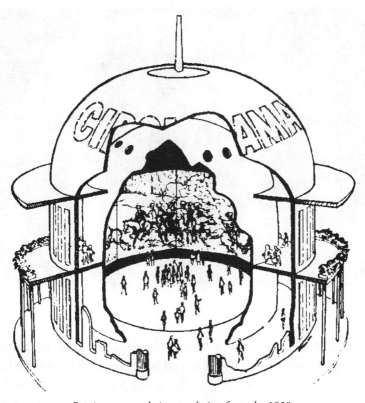

Russian surround cinema, design from the 1920s

circumspective concentricity—one simply finds two different styles of philosophical theology in competition, an exo-theological and an endo-theological one, as it were; one that *contrasts* God and his intelligence with the totality of the concretely existent, and one that places the intelligent God *into* the center of being and grants him insight into his own universal orb from within. It goes without saying that this second path, because it can be directed through the interior of the human self-relationship, has remained the more fruitful and mysterious one by far; and it alone can, perhaps, shake

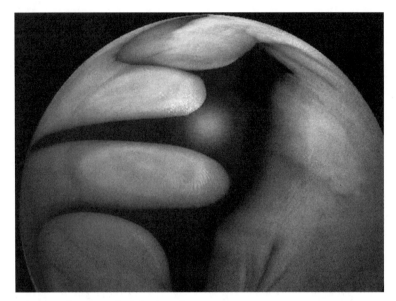

Masaki Fujihata, *Impalpability* (1998)

off the modern suspicion towards "archaic" thought based on universal unity. Its offshoots extend into late medieval mysticism and German Idealism, even as far as Heidegger's aloof interpretations of being-in-the-world, which purport to leave behind all traditional metaphysical conveniences, yet cannot conceal their crypto-Parmenidean structure. Even the ontology of Gilles Deleuze, with its sharpened Spinozist pathos of immanence, is manifestly still located in the Parmenidean continuum.

The Eleatic impulse, however broken by Plato's intervention, dictated the task for later thought to view, from the position of ecstatic concentricity, a circum-existent organized as a close-distant surrounding world: the highest philosophy is the amphi-theory of the amphi-cosmos. How could that succeed if not through a second form of theological madness?

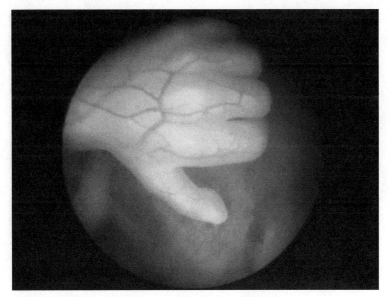

Fetal hand (photograph: Lennart Nilsson)

Perhaps it was Nietzsche who formulated the most incisive commentary on Parmenides:

> Around the hero, everything turns into tragedy, around the demigod, everything turns into a satyr play; and around God everything turns into—what? Perhaps "world"?[42]

3. Carrying God

In the following, we shall make it clear how the basic phenomenon of the microspheric world—the mutual evocation of the two, unified in a strong relationship—repeats itself in the macrosphere, the orb-shaped universe. For the couple, the absolute orb

Halo at the South Pole on January 2, 1990 (photograph: Walter Tape)

too must be won over. We have already hinted that where thought takes place from a single dominant center, the question of the role and significance of the epicenters inevitably comes up. In addition: if a largest finite orb is supposed to contain the existent as a whole, what about its exterior and counterpart? How should we evaluate and place the remainder which it does not encompass (if it exists)?

And it does exist: the remainder is conspicuous. The Farnese Atlas figure vividly showed us the paradox of the all-inclusive sphere. If the celestial globe is genuinely to represent the self-fulfilling symbol of absolute inclusivity, what happens to the ill-fated Atlas, who is so obviously not contained in that which he holds in his hands? What of the quality of totality in an all-inclusive whole figure, outside which a banished, lost, and excluded creature leads its existence? In his statuary misfortune, Atlas embodies the question inherent in all harmonistic orb metaphysics from the start as unease: in a round inclusive world where all power emanates from the center, what is the weight of the eccentric points? What is the significance of the places which seem to have fallen outside the dimensions of the whole, and are located in an eerie and insubstantial outside?

One glance at the situation of the miserable Atlas who must serve as the support for the whole is sufficient to understand that every centristically constructed finite world is targeted by an inevitable eccentricity; for if the whole is a gigantic, yet finite orb, it cannot be avoided that it will be questioned from the position of a leftover outside. The mistreated position of the cosmophorus already suggests that the well-rounded whole could be endangered by a servile insurrection among the outer and lower forces, and that certainly the whole in its geometric euphoria can only last if it manages to keep the eccentric under control from the center. It is precisely this relationship that the Greeks depicted in the Olympic dictatorship over the outwardly and downwardly displaced old gods, the Titans; it stands for the taming of chaos through the cosmicizing form.

One might object that our Atlas figure, in its inevitable sculptural naïveté, cannot help paying twofold tribute to mythical pictoriality and imagining thought. But did Parmenides not show a way to avoid disconcertment by external observation and gaining an immanent in-sight, acquired radically from within, into an absolutely outsideless orb? Would this not establish the dominance of the center perfectly, untainted by eccentric leftovers?

Now the Parmenidean view of the orb can be used especially well to show that it too is befallen by an irrepressible, albeit entirely

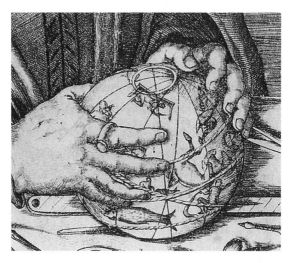

Celestial orb in the hands of the cosmographer Gemma Frisius
(1508–1555); detail from a posthumous portrait (1557)

different eccentricity. This eccentricity does not, as with Atlas, establish itself through a position away from the whole, but through the difficulty—insurmountable for ordinary mortals—of assuming the position of an absolute center. One cannot view it merely as an arbitrary, peripheral condition of Parmenidean doctrine that it was conveyed to an enraptured philosopher through the mouth of a goddess—far from everyday dwellings, after a stormy ascent to a place of superhuman autonomy. For what the goddess taught, namely the ecstatic amphiscopy into the eternally stationary "that it is," established a standard for philosophical sight that simply could not be attained by mortal eyes. For they, clinging to the illusion of active, changeable life, never reach a position of the ecstatic-panoramic center, the only place from which ontological circumspection—ontoscopy as amphiscopy—can be carried out. Consequently, it is ordinary human living and

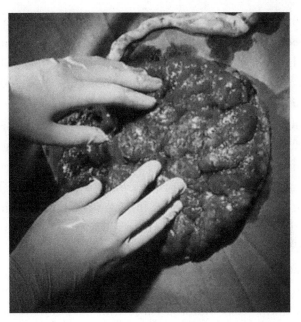

Examination of the placenta (photograph: Lennart Nilsson)

seeing that proves eccentric in relation to the center from which the circumspection of God and the philosopher into the unanimous is meant to take place.

This proves the existence of a second eccentricity with far more intimate and persistent consequences than the first; to set it apart from the externality of the observer, I shall refer to it as "epicentricity." Philosophy approaches the ordinary human intellect with the imposition of understanding the following: I do *not* see the world from the center, as I would see it if I were able to let God see into his world through my eyes; for I myself, as I am, am a cloudiness in front of the absolute view; I look into the world from an epicentric point, and therefore see no lasting whole, only the colorful reflection of an invisible totality. Through the veil of opinions, images and situations, I only ever grasp fragments and partial views of the dark machine of becoming.

While we found a tension in the Atlas sculpture between the world orb and its impossible eccentric outside view, an examination of Parmenidean orb observation produces an irresolvable tension between the absolute, fundamentally centered view into the ontological sphere and the epicentric understanding of the world from the existential perspective. Seeing the world sensually, then, means *not* looking into it from the true center. Thus a significant verdict is passed on the cognitive human condition: assuming they do not attain the ecstatic state of exception of philosophical-godlike amphiscopy, humans are condemned eternally and unreservedly to exist on half-blind epicentric points. They are, to draw on Greek mythology, no longer simply the *brotoí*, the mortals, but also those who have shifted from the center, taken away into circumstances; the situatively dazed peripheral beings. Humans are God's marginal creatures, and as such they are incurably epicentric, half-sighted and half-clear. This early result of Greek philosophy was a major event in the clarification history of human self-relationships, for humans in advanced civilizations, despite their immemorial ethno- and egocentrism, subsequently had to understand themselves as non-center beings.

Classical philosophy was the imposition of having to understand that the center is elsewhere. Certainly humans, when they are themselves, are utilized by the center; but they do not constitute it. From the perspective of enlightened mortals, what was termed the "loss of the center" in the twentieth century, especially in the discourses of Catholic anti-modernism, is an event that took place an epoch ago, conditioned by the new metaphysical interpretation of space. This leads to the notable twist that humans now moved away from the center because a point located outside them forced itself on their thought as the absolute center "opposite" them. Henceforth, being human meant existing in an epicenter of the absolute. Epicentric existence in turn meant feeling breathed upon and affected by the encouragements of a highest center, but being obliged not to confuse it with oneself.

And that is precisely what implements a relationship in the space of developed conscious life that exactly repeats intimate microspheric relationships on the macrospheric level. For the tense relationship between the human epicenter and the divine center replicates the original mutual evocation of the two unified in a strong relationship—but now in keeping with the logically and practically maturing conception of the world. Thinking metaphysically in the classical sense thus means meditating on the magical effect exerted by the center on the epicentric points surrounding it.

The relationship between the stone Atlas and his celestial globe does not yet display any of this sublime metaphysical epicentricity. His externality in relation to the largest sphere and its center has an eccentric, not an epicentric quality. For this reason, one does not see what his carrying of the whole might contribute to the survival of the orb on his shoulders: one could give it a different stand without any noteworthy changes. Thus one cannot claim any essential or intimately co-conditioning relationship between Atlas and his celestial burden, and there is nothing about the whole sky itself that would necessitate support by an external carrier in order to be realized. (For the moment, I shall leave aside the suspicion hinted at above that the sky's ability to be whole could in fact be co-conditioned by the resilient thinker's love of effort.)

The situation is very different with the carrying roles that devolve upon humans when they are assigned to a center as epicenters, and are used and attracted by them. The clearest prototypes of such intimate uses of humans as carriers of the absolute can be found in Christian salvation history, wherever human individuals were placed in a strong relationship with the divine center and appointed as staff for the self-consummation of salvation. In that sense, all Christian practice, in so far as it seeks to achieve the dissemination of salvation, is theophoric—that is, founded on the bearing of the absolute by finite forces. This relationship is embodied especially clearly in the God-pregnant Mary and the legendary burden carrier Saint Christopher. The fame of both figures is based entirely on their theophory, or God-bearing. Both cases make it clear what it means in the new metaphysical order of spaces and roles to use oneself, and allow oneself to be used, for the action of the central divine subject as an epicentric human subject.

The case of Mary is particularly expressive, as it initially seems to present no more than the basic situation of the *micro*spheric creation of intimacy: through the intimate resonance between mother and child, the two partners are evoked—as in every dyad that develops in an ordinarily favorable way—as the poles of their field of closeness. Here the mother inevitably takes priority, as she is the host of the new life and acts as the site, as it were, at which the mutual approach of the two poles takes place. For the natural mother-child scene, then, it would be logical to assume a hierarchy of ensoulment from the mother to the child, which is precisely how Hegel viewed the original process of ensoulment in his lectures on psychology: "The mother is the genius of the child."[43]

Lesser Polish master, Mary with infant (Krakow, 1420–1430)

The metaphysical order of relationships, however, overturns the psychological matriarchy. In the case of Mary, this negation goes so far that the mother can no longer understand herself as the child's producer—and even that her pregnancy is not based on a natural causality of conception. In this manner, the child-bearing Mary becomes a form of intimate Atlas, for her child, as a God-man who has entered her supernaturally yet requires human birth nonetheless, assumes such an overwhelmingly central role that the mother—over and above her natural duties of

Monstrance of *Maria gravida* with mirror: self-recognition while regarding the mother's womb, Vienna, Ecclesiastical Treasury

patience—becomes no more than a marginal condition of divine self-consummation. What she carries in her body, while not the absolute itself, is the intermediary of the absolute. Richard Dawkins' biological definition of the mother can therefore also be applied to Mary: "I am treating a mother as a machine pro-grammed to do everything in its power to propagate copies of the genes which reside inside it"[44]—with the qualification that Mary places herself at the disposal of a divine gene that is only to be copied in a single specimen. In the spherological context, however, "mother"—as we recall—is the most powerful synonym for non-technological immunity, though one must acknowledge that the mechanization of maternity constitutes the manifest program of post-theological civilization.

The role of Mary is paradigmatic for the state of human sub-jectivity in the Christian-metaphysical schema in the sense that it shows more instructively than any other model how the epicentric human is to respond to the call from the center. "I am the Lord's servant; may it be as you have said" (Luke 1:38). As the Hand-maiden of the Lord, the conceiving woman abandons all thoughts of a personal choice for or against and submits to the order from the center: may it be as you have said. This shifts mother-child intimacy to the salvation-historical stage, and Mary's pregnancy becomes an act of the absolute through the woman's uterus. The macrosphere used the microsphere entirely for itself; the highest transference seems to have succeeded. Here the pregnant woman is transformed into the opposite of a Great Mother, and it would seem that one can no longer speak of a primacy of the bearer over the born. In the case of Mary, the slogan "My belly belongs to me" would be Satanic in the extreme; from the beginning and forever after, the Christ in her is more God's son than a mother's child.

Terra nutrix, from Michael Maier, *Atalanta fugiens* (Oppenheim, 1618)

Thus the mother is suddenly more dependent on this child than this child on its mother. In other words, the God-bearer has become merely a marginal condition for God. In the deep structure, He carries her so that she can carry him. Consequently, Mary is not simply the other natural-human pole of ensoulment and the intimate-adequate other for her own child. Rather, she herself virtually shifts to the periphery of this child's genesis, as it is the God-man realizing himself in her. Intimately involved, Mary remains on the threshold of events. She finds herself on the lower end of a majestic relationship, and from this position she can only contribute in the mode of submission. Hence Mary, like Christ, has two natures, for she is simultaneously the natural

José de Ribera, *Saint Christopher* (1637), detail

mother and the surrogate mother of God; this is emphatically stated in Catholic Mariology. This means that she could only— by parental mandate—castigate or pamper the Child Jesus to the extent that her blows or caresses were part of the anthropological script for the God-man's days on earth.

If we turn our gaze from the Marian case to the general, we can say that the epicenter always has to do its best through its complete integration into the actions of the center. The epicenter becomes worthy through devotion to the center: this is the utopia of the strong relationship between the point and the middle in the metaphysical paradigm. One could therefore speak of a macrospheric formation through an anticipatory integration of human episubjectivity into divine full subjectivity. What this latter really demands, however, is only revealed by authorized representatives.[45]

This gives rise to the decisive cooperative model in large-scale worlds: the metaphysics of collaboration—service to the center. The calm epicenter accepts employment everywhere as a worker in the vineyard of the middle. Such a thing cannot take place in the mode of cadaver obedience; for where the subject is only passively involved, God himself would have to provide the entire drive for the action of the serving party. But the tool itself is meant to be actively helpful, which is why the spontaneous forces of the human epicenters are invited to set themselves in motion for the intentions of the center, as if they somehow had a share in the central power after all. In this scheme of things, the obedience of the human episubjects should never be understood merely as an enduring of impulses from the center; rather, it must actively enter the central project as a form of intelligent co-spontaneity. Nothing short of this is Mary's lesson for the Christian-metaphysical epoch: the secondary center strives towards the middle through active submission. In truth, Christian mysticism has often taken Mary's pregnancy as a model, extolling it as beneficial for every soul to permit the pregnancy of the center within itself. The path of Modern Age subjectivity leads to mystical equality via cooperation with God, and from there—after the death of God—to the triumphant awkwardness of remaining behind alone as the universal worker.

Even if Mary's gravidity represents the most radically and most deeply intimized model for the strong relationship between the epicenter and the center in a metaphysically geometrized large-scale world—and thus reveals the matrix of all mysticism of service—it has remained neither the only one nor, at least in certain periods, the most popular one. With the legend of Saint

Christopher, the *Legenda aurea* by Jacobus de Voragine presents a second suggestive pattern for human God-bearing. Christopher, a hulk of a man from the land of the "Chananeans," twelve feet tall and terrible to behold on account of his wild face, had converted to Christianity, driven by the wish to serve none but the highest lord. But which lord should be considered the greatest? Christopher had noticed that his first employer, a king, feared the devil as a mightier figure, whereupon he lost his faith in the king's sovereignty and defected to the more impressive Satan. But his second lord too, the devil, fled from an image of Christ—which, for the hero of the legend, was irrefutable proof that none other than the depicted was the highest of all sovereigns, even if he remained invisible in this world and only showed his presence through signs and wonders. A pious hermit introduced him to a service he could perform for his new lord: he would carry people through a deep, rapid river. One day he heard the voice of a child asking him three times to carry him across the river.

> The child begged him to carry him across the river, and Christopher lifted him to his shoulders, grasped his great staff, and strode into the water. But little by little the water grew rougher and the child became as heavy as lead: the farther he went, the higher rose the waves, and the weight of the child pressed down upon his shoulders so crushingly that he was in dire distress. He feared that he was about to founder, but at last he reached the other bank.
>
> Setting the child down he said to him: "My boy, you put me in great danger, and you weighed so much that if I had had the whole world on my back I could not have felt it a heavier

burden!" The child answered him: "Don't be surprised, Christopher! You were not only carrying the whole world, you had him who created the world upon your shoulders! I am Christ your king, to whom you render service by doing the work you do here."[46]

We recognize our Atlas quite easily in the Christian giant by the river. But he no longer carries the sky as a punishment for his participation in the revolt of the ancient powers against Olympus. The exiled Titan has changed into God's retainer, who comes to the aid of travelers and pilgrims. In the scene at the river, the recasting of the Atlas schema becomes obvious: the solitary weight-lifting role is replaced by a strong relationship with a master. For the Christian Atlas no longer carries the world-whole on his shoulders; the legend inserted a God-man as a midpoint between the heavy whole and its bearer, namely Christ himself in child form. Thus Saint Christopher—*Christophoros*—bears on his shoulders the child that has become the true *kosmophoros*. By bearing the cosmos-bearer, however, the Christian Atlas takes the undiminished weight of the world, now augmented by the light burden of the child lord, upon his shoulders.

One can see in this image how the Christian tale thaws the ancient figure and transfers it from its statuary rigidity into the terrestrial and supra-terrestrial river. Atlas' decisive metamorphosis occurs through his transformation from an obstinately philosophizing athlete-slave to an intimate vassal of God; this change turns the archaic act of strength into an impassioned relationship matter—or, in the language of the reflections above, an employment relationship between the center and secondary center of being.

Master of Messkirch, *Saint Christopher* (17th century), Basel Art Museum, detail

The great popularity of the Saint Christopher legend—
which was depicted over centuries in countless artistic
versions—comes not only from the fact that it makes a rich
mythological overtone series resound; its magic is based most of
all on the fact that, in a simple and profound way, it embeds the
Christian's connection to the world-whole in a strong relationship with a personal counterpart. Thus the pre-human curse of
Atlas is lifted: with Saint Christopher's work, externality and
slavery under foreign circumstances were defeated. From now

The political Atlas: O, how great a burden, from W. J. von Wallrabe, *Neue historische Beschreibung des Lebens Karls V.* (1683)

on, the game with the ball of being would always be an intimate affair. The carrier enters a direct personal relationship with the center of the orb, and only an indirect one with its periphery and weight. The heaviness of the world no longer rests on a solitary Titan as a dead weight, but rather becomes part of the love story between the human epicenter and the divine center. As it is the divine child that directly bears the world orb, Saint Christopher's effort takes on the character of collaboration—and because he only has direct contact with the child, and only indirect contact

Greater than Atlas: world orb on the shoulders of Amor, 17th-century emblem

with the weight of the world, he takes part in divine pantophoria. He, the exemplary servant, bears the all-bearing bearer: in this way he experiences what it means to become God's vehicle.

One can therefore see how a form of inter-intelligent thaw came over the thought-images of myth and ancient physics. The sphere that meant the world no longer stood before the observer as a geometric figure, nor was it merely a universalized environment any longer: it became an emblem of the strong relationship between humans and the center. Now even virile Titanic forces, freed from phallic autocracy and rebel defiance, could even become useful for the monarchy of the center; what was once unruly force was transformed into subservient strength. Thus Christianity, beyond the basic teachings of the Gospels, established a principle of solidarity rooted in the dual space, for it conceives—naïvely and thinkingly at once—of solidary action as the

Atlas at the Rockefeller Center, New York, by Lee Lawrie (1937)

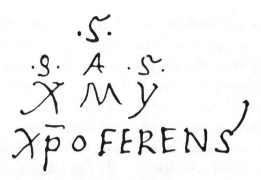

Signature of Columbus

collaboration of the epicenter in the project of the center. It may be that some of what is perceived in the present day as a crisis of solidarities in society and a weakening of the social bond ultimately stems from the decline of this metaphysics of collaboration. Any attentive observer can easily recognize that contemporary team philosophies are far from closing this gap.[47]

The massive effect of the Christophoric model of collaboration on the fates of humanity in recent history can perhaps be illustrated using the greatest Christopher of the incipient Modern Age, namely Columbus—the seafarer, the exemplary exponent of manic Modern Age risk culture who, after his first landing on the West Indian islands, viewed himself ever more openly as a savior and nautical apostle. In his later years he unabashedly signed his letters with the quasi-apostolic name "Xr ferens," as if he had turned his first name into his spiritual program and interpreted the Atlantic crossing as a continuation of Saint Christopher's service in the oceanic ford.

The name magic of Columbus betrays something of the psychopolitical secrets of the European success story after 1492: it points to the operative unity of serving and ruling without which the dynamics of lust for power and level of corporate influence in the neo-European form of subjectivity cannot be understood. Barely fifty years after the discovery of America, the new psychopolitics would take form in the Jesuit order, fully recognized in 1540. The *Compagnia di Gesù* is a radically christophoric order of religious entrepreneurs who do not wait for God to carry them to success, but instead rely entirely on their own initiative. They are the activists of globalization in the Catholic style. In fanatical irony, they bow beneath the greatest weights, inspired by the certainty that only their acceptance can grant true power.

4. The Morphological Gospel and Its Fate

For the moderns, whose thought was shaped from the days of dissident Hegelians onwards by decenterings and existential eccentricity, there is barely any way left to access the forgotten worlds of metaphysical orb splendor. They can no longer truly comprehend—unless they go against the decentering trends in civilization and subject themselves to a remembering process— how far the intellectual history of the last two thousand years constituted the triumphal march of an all-surpassing morphological motif. Even if the philosophy textbooks, and even the archivists of the Perennial Philosophy refer to the old orb ontology only with hints, if at all,[48] and the average agents of the profession, including its Young Turks, have long lived as if behind a wall of forgetting that no ray of memory can penetrate, this does not change the fact that Old European metaphysics, where it was most "itself," constituted one great exuberant meditation on the ensouled orb and cognizant existence within it. Classical thinkers were thus never concerned with what, in a false (anti-)Cartesian turn of phrase, one today calls "ultimate justification," but rather with ultimate encompassing or, as I shall also say in the following, ultimate immunity. One can say, almost as a definition, that classical metaphysics—understood as ontotheology and philosophical cosmology, was nothing other than an immeasurably roundabout and complex theory ritual in honor of Her Majesty, the round form within everything. Only those who descend deep enough into the archives of the One (and, as we saw in *Spheres I*, the discursive archives have annexes in the form of primal scenes in front of them), can begin to appreciate the scale of the monosphere cult. Its function was to allay human unrest in a dangerously opened, unfathomably widened world through initiation into the most edifying, encompassing immune form, namely the universe—literally, that which encompasses everything with a single turn. The message presented by the gospel of being in roundness was that every point in the cosmos, no matter how distant from the center—even my own forlornly trembling existence—is potentially and actually enabled and reached by a beam from the center. And because everything that exists does so from an all-causing, good center (*omne ens est bonum*,[49] so everything good has immune strength), my own shaky life-light can assure itself of being held in a spirit-infused, animated, ultimately immunizing whole.

There is only one precondition for this: I would have to admit and grasp that everything existent, including myself with my ominous depths and denials, is something that lies eminently *inside*, in the catchment area of an organizing form—which means that everything that exists is enfolded, contained and located by a periphery of the greatest size. The gospel of total inclusion spreads through the image of the orb: nothing real can truly be outside, no thing exists severed from the body and continuum of the One. Philosophical meditation on the encompassing ensures that a universe, however great one supposes it to be, can be imagined at all times as an interior, and thus a shared sphere of force and meaning. What looks like esotericism is merely esospherism.[50]

Where all power comes from the center, there is no absolute outside, no lost point, no entity that would absolutely have to stand apart—unless it placed itself there with rebellious intent (and even then, a real exteriority would be problematic). Because the centered whole brings everything inwards by relating every distant point around it to itself as the center, the totality of the orb never constitutes merely an inert block; it pulsates with the relationships of the center and the overabundant correspondences between the epicentric points. That is what the followers of the principle of abundance euphorically profess: the intelligible orb is alive. And, in so far as it lives, it does so through the center's radiating power and eagerness to form relationships. This center, in an incessant bursting, incessantly sends out its radii and continuously re-produces its wholeness by drawing the epicentric points back towards itself. The middle—occupying the divine role in the absolute circle—always assures itself of all points in the space around it by producing and recognizing them; it forms a whole around itself by constantly augmenting itself with every point, however distant. That which has the power to overexert *and* collect itself is whole. Hence the living center does not let go of the points on the radii; it holds them all around itself in a flickering assembly, and just as God counts the stars in the children's song,[51] thus too the center has counted the points to ensure that not one from among their unfathomable multitude is missing.

The ontology of the orb—the basic doctrine of occidental metaphysics, which seemed more secret the more it was openly uttered, and more powerful the more it remained latent—is in its essence a meditation on the impossibility that anything could be lost to being. Being, like the house, loses nothing. Where the whole is viewed as an orb, each individual element can—and, in case of doubt, must—add itself to its total, a situation in which consolation and coercion become indistinguishable. Where the individual element can find happiness through sharing in the whole, remembrance of the orb's center becomes a therapeutic, even saving exercise in itself; for revealing the orb then means no less than spreading the good news that the scattered points belong to the organizing center. When Augustine wrote, "Our hearts are restless until they rest in you," it was part of a dialogue between epicenter and center, motivated by the longing of the point, thrown into the world, to be brought home by the harboring center.

Here metaphysics borrowed from an overblown idea of meaning and brought into play an exuberant conception of ensoulment via the center. Did Plato's myth of the stonemason not already show how ruthlessly such thought could proceed if the concern was to achieve its immunological aim—the totality of the existent under the banner of psychism? For who could fail to see how the spheric and the psychic converge here? The concept of the world soul—whose career extended from Plato to Schelling—proves how much was once expected from the transference of the psychic to the cosmic; animism lives on in it as rationalism.[52] Nietzsche was not wrong to suspect that the metaphysics founded by Plato contained a pious, edifying tendency that persuades to higher deception with closed eyes; and it can scarcely be denied that with Platonism, reflection had been set on a trail that would lead to the intellectual rounding of uneven things, the over-interpretation of the dead as the living and the eccentric as the concentric. The school of all schools itself, his Academy—what was it but a seminary for breeding subsequent generations of circle- and orb-worshipping macrosphere preachers were bred?

With the increasing philosophical alphabetization of Christianity in late antiquity, theologians inevitably discovered the compulsion to pour their discourse on the relationship between humans and God into the molds of the academic metaphysics of the center and the orb. This brought to light, however concealed, the truth that a morphological gospel had enchanted the intelligences of the Old World long before the personal good news. Even if Christ, like the Roman emperors, was given the title *sotér*, "savior," by his theologians—the orb had already been subsumed by thought even more salvifically, and for equally profound, yet older reasons. The god of the morphologists who relates all points back to himself is older and deeper than the god of the basilicas who gathers up the lost souls.

Working out the cryptic identity of Christology and orb metaphysics: this was, in terms of its deep structure, the program of Christian intellectual history. Theologians, admittedly, barely ever realized that they could only achieve their successes as agents of an epochal immunization project in which salvation came from the form become world. Christ saves, as the orb had already saved—but if the orb was able to save, it was because its center constituted the anonymous source of all salvation and all retrieval to the integral. It would take until the mid-fifteenth

Nicolas of Cusa's playing ball

century for this relationship to be written down in a calm tone by a thinker. Nicolas of Cusa brought the philosophical doctrine of the immunizing orb to its bright goal:

> Since he was similar to us, Christ moved the sphere of his person so that it came to rest in the middle of life [...]. And our sphere would follow him [...].[53]

I shall seek to illuminate what remains opaque here in Chapter 5 of this volume, which deals with the explicit orb theories. The latent thesis of Cusa's reflection already becomes apparent here: that all secrets of what Christianity calls "salvation"—philosophically speaking, the retrieval from abandonment in the external, non-round, incoherent—lead to the question of whether the epicenters, the human souls, can overcome their distance from the absolute center of life, that center which, for the Christian metaphysician, can only be the over-simply self-enfolded (*simplicissimus*) yet all-inclusively unfolded God.

All this indicates that the affair between God and the soul is based on an exuberant spherological precondition: the two are only connected in a strong relationship when they belong to a shared interior—with God as the center and the soul as a point outside the center, though undoubtedly on a line extending from the radiating center. If the soul were not positioned on a beam sent out (or, as Kepler would say, ejaculated) from the center, it would be literally eccentric—utterly severed from the core, drifting in an absolute outside, neither capable nor in need of rescue and only "at home" in self-relationships and their additions from the "environment."

In the metaphysical worldview, the only candidates for such eccentricity are Satan and the proud mortal sinners that follow him—that is, those "existences" that have willfully embraced an anarchic, theofugal, salvation-despising mode of being. In the philosophical field, the closest thing to this attitude was found among those ancient atomists and materialists who were the first to consider the possibility of an infinite void with no center. This position is unacceptable within the framework of classical metaphysics, and the fact that it considered it depraved expresses the immune reaction of the self-harboring spheric world against the atheistic claim of externality. For acknowledging an eccentric existence as a legitimate mode of being-in-the-world would mean denying the necessity of the relationship between the center and the epicenter. This would rob the sacred orb of its encompassing power; the difference between existence in it and outside it would be rendered insignificant. It would mean freedom of religion in relation to the One Orb: the license to morphological indifference. Consequently, being-in-the-orb would no longer be the condition of rescue for all beings; indeed, there would be no rescue, no salvation, no retrieval from externality, and even the absence of the universally salvific would not be universally lamented. One could only

Creator of the sphere from the Freiburg Minster, main entrance, early 13th century

Lucas Cranach, *Melancholy* (1532), National Gallery of Denmark, Copenhagen, detail

distinguish between successes or failures among self-referential players between eccentric points, beyond salvation and perdition; thus modern conditions would obtain. Their criteria are the abstention from the coexistence of all in a shared interior and the positivization of externalized traffic as universal "communication."

It is not the large number of rooms in the house of the only father that lends the diversity of worlds in modernity its unifying quality, but rather the large number of stalls, brands and addresses on the global market. Just as the house is the symbol of the good interior, the market is the model of the passable exterior. As long as the orb of being was valid as the ultimate force of inclusion, the fundamental experience of modernity— the concert of countless self-referential eccentricities—would have been taken as a characteristic of hell. The purpose of being-in-the-orb was precisely to separate the point-individuals from their egotistical self-referentiality and relate them to the universally shared center in a great moral and ontological extraversion. In this way, each one would become a vassal of the center; it would find happiness in the liberation from the Satanic and all-too-human error of choosing itself as the preferred point of reference.

Thus the orb is more than a geometric symbol and a cosmological thought-image; it simultaneously introduces individuals to the position of altruistic ethics and eroticism. Where the center keeps the epicenters in a state of tension, the points look towards the center *a priori*—for it is the center that insists on the priority of the other for all points. This means that theocentrism and altruism are structurally identical. In the greatest orb, however, the individual points are not tied to the center alone; the energy of the theocentric pact radiates to each point and enables it to feel solidarity with adjacent points in the widest radii. Therefore the reflection on coexistence in the orb induces the power that Nietzsche's Zarathustra would later call "love of the most remote" [*Fernstenliebe*].[54] As the commitment to love into the distance, the sphere of the theologians is the most powerful ontological figure of alliance. Through the fluctuation common to everything existent outside the center between centrifugal (egotistical) and centripetal (altruistic) tendencies, all finite intelligences are in a state of existential resonance with one another—each one knows, or could know, what it means *not* to be the center of everything while nonetheless considering oneself thus. What unites them, despite all competition, is their shared attempt to be—that is, to assure themselves of their ability to be. In this sense, shared being in the orb provides the ultimate justification for solidarity between the points.

From this perspective, one can understand very well why Europeans were obsessed with shell-cosmological notions for two thousand years. The billennium of orb metaphysics is equal in extension to the age of heavenly sphere doctrine: those cosmological models which located the earth at the center of a system of massive round skies could only flourish under philosophical patronage. These layered planetary shells, all overarched by an outermost firmament, the sky of fixed stars, with nothing higher except the residence of the Blessed with God—all these, beyond all formal justifications in astronomical discourses since Aristotle, only make sense in worldview-historical terms if one also understands them as cosmological projections of a long-insurmountable morphological need. They serve to seal off the world in the sense of a universal immunology. Shell cosmology uses physical means to seal the pact between the center and the universe of points: it shows with almost crude vividness what it means to be in an inner world and to wish to remain there at all costs. Parmenides had set the tone:

> [...] for mighty Necessity holds it in the bonds of a limit, which confines it round about. Wherefore it is not right for what-is to be incomplete.[55]

Plato and Aristotle developed the motif of the good formal limit further; they brought the idea that totality can only endure in spheric economy to its tradition-worthy completion. The Middle Ages took the shell deliria to the extreme, enclosing the earth and the human souls upon it in numerous layers of varyingly massive firmaments, as if this lost, yet chosen place in the cosmos where God deigned to take human form needed to be

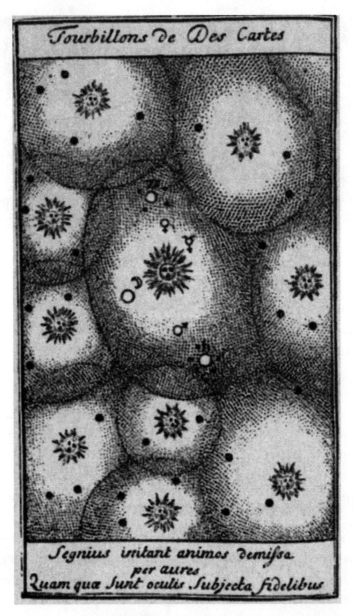

The multiplicity of solar systems: 17th-century illustration of Cartesian cosmology

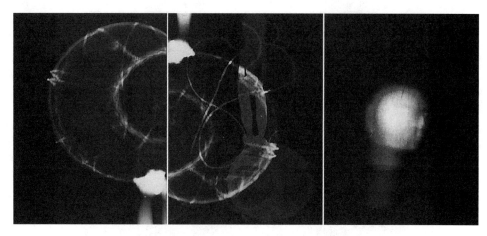

Jurgen Klauke, *Grosses Weltbild II* (1991), three parts, Cologne

shielded from the slightest hint of the outside. Surrounded by eight, ten, twelve or fourteen cosmic walls and ditches, the world of humans on earth enjoyed the humiliating privilege of dwelling in the Interior Castle of being.[56]

Because each human is themselves a small world in the metaphysical paradigm, however, this multiple walling-in of the interior repeats itself within them, so that they transpire as a network of shells and walls around the numinous innermost point that forms the center of human self-being: it is no wonder, then, that *homo metaphysicus* barely ever reaches the final center in himself—for he only lives in the suburbs of his densely layered soul space and knows, like Augustine, that the great other is closer to him than he is himself: *interior intimo meo*. In tireless efforts of the imagination, the retrieval of all epicentric points through the absolute life of the center is affirmed both outwardly and inwardly by means of an all-pervasive delirium of vaults, shells and hollow orbs.

In morphological and immunological terms, one can claim that God's most important act in the metaphysical age was to secure the border against nothingness, the outside and infinity. This most sensitive of all lines could only be defended through the construction of shells. This meant—even if it sounds unacceptable from a theology-immanent perspective—that God could only keep himself "in force" as long as those representing his interests succeeded in interpreting him as a gigantic, but finite self-harboring orb. As soon as theology became serious about the devastating attribute "the infinite"—which, in terms of metaphysical history, was the endogenous process that initiated the Modern Age—it destroyed God's spheropoietic function, as the metaphysically explosive and immunologically decisive difference between inside and outside is lost in an infinite orb. In an orb of infinite radius and infinite circumference, everything would be scattered in the somewhere, and thus suddenly universally externalized. This and nothing else is the result of the Modern Age's infinitization of God and the universe.

It was the cleverest theologians who killed God when they were no longer able to conceive of him as presently and extensively infinite. The statement "God is dead" primarily indicates a morphological tragedy: the elimination of the imaginarily satisfying, tangible orb of immunity through relentless infinitization. Now God becomes entirely intangible, dissimilar and formless—a monster for the human perceptual apparatus, an anti-container, an absolute hole and *Ungrund*. Suddenly one can no longer recognize the advantage in being *in* this God of infinity, as the barrier between inside and outside has fallen.

Undoing God's immunity initiated the atheistic crisis of modern times. This morphological dysangelium spread through the illuminated circles of the late Middle Ages in a hushed tone, with only few of those who fervently passed it on understanding its meaning and effects. For, in the belief that they were communicating something mysteriously inspiring and ecstatically paradoxical, they clandestinely announced: "God is the infinite sphere whose center is everywhere and whose circumference is nowhere."[57] This everywhere introduces the agony of the centered form, and this nowhere introduces the crisis of the metaphysical project of encasing everything existent in the spiritual. As soon as the orb is assigned the attribute of infinity, it dies of overextension into the intangible. The rest is orb posthistory. Now the death of the good, harboring, majestic-finite God sphere need only be comprehended by those affected—a process that spans over half a millennium of European thought and still cannot be considered complete. In truth, positing the orb as infinite meant taking away its collecting power and cutting it off from the interest of the living, thus rendering the greatest devoid of salvation.

The death of God was first announced in a morphological obituary: "The orb is dead." Its expiry results in everything else concerning the decease of God and the administration of his estate—loss of the edge, inflation of the center and wandering of the points. Where the orb perishes as a result of being posited as infinite, then, the previously epicentric points are forced either to choose themselves as the center of all relationships or, beyond the familiar obsession with the central point, to surrender to a masterless game of decentered streams of events. The first option gives rise to modern systems theories, while the second possibility has so far been the prerequisite for a contemporary,

Antonin Artaud (1926)

post-monospheric philosophy. As Foucault rightly noted, "The world, the self and God (a sphere, a circle and a center): three conditions that prevent us from thinking the event."[58] What the nature of thought in event terms could actually be, beyond the macrospherological excess standing behind us as classical metaphysics, is as much of a mystery to the postmodern public as it is to the majority of philosophers. Only as an atmosphere or an inkling does one encounter, here and there, understanding of the fact that the event character as such can only attain its thought outside the One Orb in which everything was meant to find its grounding and ensoulment—that is, in a radicalized outside.

The reason why it is now the *event* rather than the *essence* that must be thought at all costs, however, cannot be sufficiently understood within the framework of the arguments published thus far. For even post-structuralist event thought is unmistakably still beholden to Modern Age metaphysics, as it continues the latter's infinitist frenzy with varying agendas—whether in the name of the libido, commentary, deferral, dialogue, or creativity itself. These are all forms of naïveté that one loves because their naïveté is that of philosophy itself. What is necessary after becoming weary of post-structuralist infinitisms is to work on an ontology of the finite, inchoate, monstrous world; this means creating an equilibrium between conservative and explosive elements—one could also call them psychological and technological interests—both in their respective radicalisms. "Where are we when we are in the monstrous?"[59] The thought of the future—perhaps a transgeneous philosophy—starts from the perception that the metaphysical project of universal ensoulment—monospherism—has failed, albeit without necessarily

Daniel Libeskind, Never is the Center, Mies van der Rohe Memorial, project, 1987

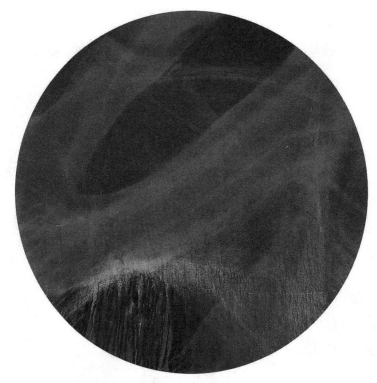

Arnulf Rainer, *Cosmos*, panel 20: *Beam and Flow of Light* (1994)

denying the existence of the spiritual on its willful scale. This remains to be proved.

For the time being, the philosophical situation of modernity is characterized by the decease of the perfect orb, whose crisis-ridden beginnings, as hinted above, extend much further than intellectual historiography has so far been willing to consider. Indeed, an infinite orb whose center, according to the late medieval thesis, were everywhere, would already have rid itself of an effective center; mystical de-selfings would be falling out of it everywhere, none of them distinguishable from the utmost egocentrisms. Consequently

Hans Haacke, *Location Merry-Go-Round* (Münster, 1997), boarded merry-go-round next to the rotunda of the War Memorial in Münster

the core theme of modernity—self-referentiality—had to irrupt into thought as an inevitable consequence, however belated and suppressed, of the mystical *centrum ubique* thesis. The last remaining chance of centering in the infinitized world, after all, is the egotism of points. In this view, everything that is not the monad itself, that is to say the control center of a system of self-reference, belongs to the "environment." "The greatest gift we have received from God and nature is life, the rotating movement of the monad around itself, which knows neither rest nor repose."[60] Anything that is a self or a system must therefore care for itself, whether individuals or states, families or businesses. They are all holy egotists; their asceticism is self-reference.

Thus the epic of the divine orb ends at the threshold of the Modern Age in a general decentering and self-centering—and in

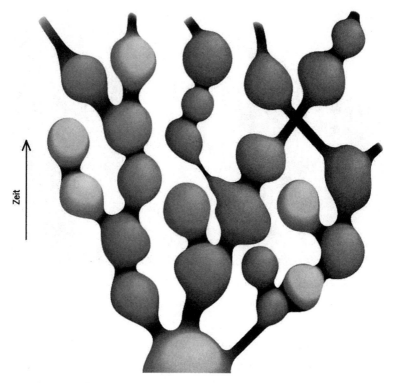

Model of the self-reproducing cosmos as a tree diagram showing a web of infla-
tionary bubbles. Each bubble corresponds to an assumed big bang system.

the indifferentiation of space. The continents and oceans of the
earth have been made accessible by current traffic and communication routines; every point in the neutralized space is now a
potential location, that is to say a relay on the circumnavigated
surface of the earth for money that passes through.[61] In the
general externality, no point can make itself inaccessible to the
others. One could define the essence of modernity in morphological terms as non-Satanic eccentricity—whereas the schema
of center and secondary center, which had underpinned the

The Futuroscope theme park, near Poitiers

metaphysics of collaboration in God's project, is only preserved in religious subcultures. I shall refer to the accumulations of self-referential eccentric points and their environments in centerless structures as *foams*; they will be examined in the third volume of these spherological studies.

The present book, a mausoleum for the idea of all-encompassing unity, belongs to the two-thousand-year empire of the monosphere or the integral globe. Can we still learn anything about mausoleum building from Stalin? Very much so; as we intend to present metaphysics in a glass coffin, it is only proper to display the departed as if it were merely asleep.[62]

As no time is lost waiting in line to see the monument, we can spend more in front of the display cabinet. There we view the universal one in its embryonic stages, its growth (Chapter 1) and its cosmic completion (Chapter 4), observe its external securing and border politics (Chapters 2 and 3), admire its theological triumph and mystical hubris (Chapter 5), follow its politics of signs (Chapter 7) and its negative excess (Chapter 6), and finally become witnesses of its catastrophe, which is followed by its metamorphosis into a mere terrestrial globe (Chapter 8).

By the end of such divine lengths it should be clear why contemporary thought can only arrive at a new non-theological or post-theological, post-metaphysical or differently metaphysical configuration of human immunities in the Second Ecumene, which is initially no more than the sum total of all isolations,[63] by rejecting the one-and-all of the monotheistic-metaphysical world project.

Anthropic Climate

The world bubble has to swell before bursting.
— Alexandre Koyré, *From the Closed
World to the Infinite Universe*

Our probings in the microspheric field showed that humans are beings which initially cannot *be* anywhere but in the wall-less hothouses of their closeness relationships. In this respect, microspherology is nothing other than a proxemic anthropology. The core of personal proxemics is what I have called the strong relationship. From this the autogenous vessels of the primary solidarities, which I ironically explained without irony using the paradigm of the trinitary union of father, son and ghost, form themselves.[64] These surreal relationships are "their own place." Whoever takes part in them lives *inside* in a topologically eminent sense.

As creatures that—under all circumstances—initially live towards one another, house and discard one another, and are nothing else beyond this, before possibly and much later, as so-called individuals, becoming self-augmenting solitary dwellers who cultivate outside contacts (addresses, networks), humans are universally reliant on the supportive microclimates of their early internal worlds. Only within these, as their typical growths, do they become what they can be, whether it is beneficial or harmful to them. There they collect a store of creative, ambivalent and destructive undertones or emotional prejudices about the existent as a whole that stubbornly assert themselves in the transition to larger scenes. It is from this collection that all transferences initiate themselves.

There is no weather forecast to inform us about the first climate; we learn whence the inner world's wind is blowing and which low pressure zones are moving over the interpersonal efforts through the atmospheric sense's power of judgment, and initially nothing else; it is more primal than the oral intimate sense, namely taste, and simultaneously more public. The sixth sense is always the first, it immediately tells people, without inductions or indirect research, where they stand—in relation to themselves, others and everything. They are immersed in atmospheres, and the manifest speaks to them from atmospheres. Immersion in the conductive element makes them originally *there* and open for environments. Space as atmosphere is nothing but vibration or *pure conductivity*.[65] In this sense it is genuinely, according to Plato's beautiful and opaque theory of *chóra*, the "nurse of being." How is one to approach such holistic relationships using a clumsy communications theory? Sender, recipient, channel, medium, code, message—these distinctions come too late for the fundamental opening. They gain significance when the concern is to learn something about something; long before then, however, that being-in or being-in-something must take "place" which is read by the fundamental ontologists as being-in-the-world, being-with and being-attuned. The climate, the mood and the atmosphere: this is the trinity of the encompassing, in whose continuing revelation humans live at all times and in all places—though one cannot say that these epiphanies each comprise a message and a messenger, despite the fact that the moderns have made even the weather a matter of discourse; first the forecast, then the look skywards. This illusion is countered with the memory of the climatic pleroma: the In as the dye bath in which all discrete acts of imagination, will and judgment are immersed.

Because atmospheres are non-concrete and non-informative by nature (and did not seem controllable), they were passed over by the ancient and modern European culture of reason on its long road to the objectification and informatization of all things and facts. Where the discourses developed wills of their own, it became increasingly impossible to waste a single word on the atmospheric exposedness, solubility and disclosedness of existence. Factual sciences and discourse theories alike refused to admit that something could exist apart from the *words* and the *things*, something that was neither of these yet more expansive, earlier and more pervasive than both. The nineteenth century did attempt to grasp this subtle third element when it spoke of *milieu* or *ambiente*, while the twentieth provided its own version by translating it into *Umwelt* and *environment*; none of these concepts succeeded in capturing the atmospheric component, however, and the sole progress was from dull to duller. Superior atmospherologies only came about in the worlds of the great novelists, especially Proust, Balzac and Broch, and they still await combination with fundamental philosophical analysis. Atmospheric "phenomena" as such have, at least, become interesting for aesthetic theory, neo-phenomenology and theology in recent times, particularly in Heidegger-inspired forms, and sometimes even with ambitions to posit fundamental concepts—which can probably be read as a sign of an isolated opening up.[66]

When modern philosophy—fundamental ontology in particular—returned from its two-thousand-year exile in the supersensible and began to re-establish its rooting in being-in-the-world, it rightly described *mood* as the first opening up of existence to the why and wherefore of the world. One could view Heidegger's early work as the Magna Carta of a previously unattempted onto-climatology.[67] It can be plausibly shown why the development of Heidegger's impulses in the phenomenology of moods and in existential psychiatry is one of the most fruitful aspects of his effect. When the string of existence is tightened in an individual, it vibrates with the timbre of a mood[68] or a defining climate. But moods—Heidegger possibly placed inadequate emphasis on this—are initially never the affair of individuals in the seeming privacy of their existential ecstasy; they form as shared atmospheres—emotionally tinted totalities of involvement [*Bewandtnis*]—between several actors who tint the space of closeness and make room for one another in it.

As our microspherological investigations explained, spheres are first of all internal worlds of strong relationship in which the connected parties "live and move and have their being" in an autogenous environment or mutually affecting vibrations. What we call climate thus refers initially to a communitarian element, and only later a meteorological fact. This applies to all human life forms, even those following the principles of distance, freedom of movement and partnerlessness. It is precisely those who live alone that are often especially climate-sensitive, and many

Silver composite amulet with key (Corfu, 20th century)

of those who choose to be solitary do so primarily to reduce humidity. Like tourists who travel counter to the season, they evade the bad weather of intimacies. Humans are not only sensitive to the weather in groups, however; in all that they do in the shared field, they themselves act as microspherically climate-active creatures through the division of their immediate surroundings. The world of closeness arises from the sum of our actions towards one another and our suffering through one another. What has been described in various philosophical contexts—from Augustine via Heidegger to Vilém Flusser—using the pathos-laden term "closeness" is lived redundancy, the abundance of the obvious in which the synchronized parties vibrate. How we fare is determined by how well we match, and how we fare with one another reveals compatibilities and incompatibilities between our lives. In their fields of closeness humans are, without exception, weather makers, casting sun and rain spells at every moment. Their faces are the headlines of their inner states; their gestures and moods radiate both storms and brightening up into the shared.

In the time of the work of art, artists could ascend to outstanding climate shapers of their cultures because attuned communities gathered around their works—which is why it is always a mistake to suppose that producers of art were expressing their inner selves through their works. What we call expression is the collection of formulas from the respective climate-creative possibilities of a group. Heidegger's suggestive language-ontological thesis that the work of art "sets up a world" [*stellt eine Welt auf*] (it was never certain, incidentally, that it should not have been "exhibits a world" [*stellt eine Welt aus*] instead) is thus of primarily spherological significance, and quickly loses plausibility outside of this field of meaning: there was an era in which visual works, religious ones in particular, epitomized the ability to wrap large groups of people in a shared symbolic ether. That is why such works were ascribed the character of truth or revelation: because they marked the center of an openness, a local world-flash. The irony of Heidegger's theory on the origin of the work of art is that it is primarily true of works from *before* the age of art. Hence the decisive aspect of the works meant by Heidegger is not that they are works of art, but that they form cultic sites at which one encounters the exhibition of being.

The one thing that can never be kept quiet because—prior to any representation and exhibition—it makes the manifest shared character palpable is the atmosphere, the encompassing tinting of the space that impregnates its inhabitants. Thus for most people, the weather of their own relationships remains more important, and far realer, than all great politics and "high" culture. The defining feature of ordinary people is that for them, politics and meteorological phenomena have the same status of objective unavailability; one can do as little about bad weather as about high lords, except to speak about them in the manner of higher powers. This speaking, however—and this only comes to light in late reflections—is the ether of societies; hence all groups, from the oral hordes to the advanced civilizations with their writing, printing and broadcasting media, vibrate exclusively in communications about their current reasons for living together: their weather, their local gods, and their group devils. That this vibration in one's own speech is the basal climate-forming function of society, however, only comes into view for theory once the groups have become so fragmented or differentiated that there can no longer be any talk of unity.

For the modern-postmodern sociologists who recently "shifted" from productivism to communicativism (shifting means exchanging one's central error), it would now be necessary to accept that the spherological analysis of societies reveals a "level" situated *before* the distinction between production and communication: the tinted endosphere is the first product of densely dwelling communities, and its mood is their first message to themselves. To seal, round it, regenerate and brighten it is the first human-creating project. Behind trivial place and interior names such as "nest," "room," "cave," "hut," "house," "hearth," "hall," "village," "family," "couple," "tribe" or "city" there will always be an unthought residue that demands to be dreamed further, though it will never be possible to interpret it fully and capture it in representations. This blossoming residue shows that

Inuit building igloo, Northwest Territories, Canada

creations of inner worlds are never complete, and must constantly develop from one "how" to the next. The secret of space production flares up in words that point to the autogenous vessels. *Mundus in gutta*—the whole world in a drop.

Humans have always been committed to the aim of drawing inwards as much as necessary of what they encounter outside, and keeping as much of the external as possible away from the hearth of the good life. That is not least why they set up *images* of the people close to them early on, regularly and stubbornly, and cannot live with integrity in their absence; they fill up their physical and imaginary dwellings with the present signs of absent partners who still remain vital to their lives after they have vanished. The omnipresence of images depicting ancestors and gods, of amulets, fetishes and charged symbols in older cultures shows how great the need is to round off the present world with pointers to substantial absent things, to augmenting and encompassing elements. The necessity of images stems from the coercion of the intelligence by death and absence; and the possibility of images comes from the primordial augmenting function of onto-graphy. If writing ideal-typically means representation in the dissimilar, the image is representation in the similar.

The image-positing urge to round off reveals the human being as the animal that can be missing something. Is culture as a whole not an overreaction to absence?[69] When missing things become conspicuous, morphological pressure ensues: empty spaces want to be filled again, as if the plan of the abundance space did not tolerate lasting vacancies. The compulsion to augment brings inner worlds of self-rounding closer together once more: at first only in the sense of wall-less nest building, where the attribute "round" expresses a pre-geometric, space-psychological, vague immunological quality, but beyond a certain threshold of discursive and political development it also takes on architectural and geometric meanings. For the coexisting, less than one inwardly rounded, interior-providing orb cannot suffice as their characteristic place in the world. Such Euclidean spheres of the group soul only come about, as we know for cooperation-biological and socio-morphological reasons, by sharing the space with first-order closeness beings and their substitutes. At the same time, humans—because they are inner world creatures for whom endoclimatic nest building precedes all other constructions—run a greater risk than any other species of having their wall-less inner worlds destroyed by irruptions from without or endogenous conflicts, for nothing is as fragile as existence in the breathed and built shells of human-specific interiority.

The phrase "climate catastrophe"—the authentic password for our epoch—already formulates the original risk for humanity. Humans are—in a manner of which full awareness can only be recommended with reservations, as the formula "consciousness as doom"[70] can indeed become a reality here—dependent on the favor of internal climatic circumstances, down to the very details of their biological equipment and cultural rituals. That they were able to become what they are today, at least in those procreative sequences that experienced no degenerations, is a result of an unnoticed and unheard-of history of self-benefits through climate creations of their own. As inhabitants of their self-created closeness hothouses, they are at home in a continuum of self-pamperings—which, incidentally, does not influence the degree of hardship, heaviness or failure in their individual lives. Humans live within their pampering; this term should be taken as a provisional reference to the dynamic of refinement in local cultures and individuations. In its evolutionary result, the existence of *homo sapiens* can only be understood as a success story of growing nervous sensitivity and symbolically conveyed, luxuriant self-arousals. The success lines of these stories stand out against a background of merciless selection fatalities in which eradication and failure are the rule.

If one highlights the tension between inside and outside as the fundamental motif of all cultural topology, the insistent return of the inside seems all the more astounding. Have not countless numbers had to experience the outer world as the epitome of sphere-destroying incidents? Is not the outside that pierces, overruns and exposes always infinitely calmer and stronger than any inner world's construction? The bubble image that introduced

Thomas Struth, *Musée du Louvre I* (1989), detail

our theory of intimate spheres evokes the fragility of the spaces inhabited by humans. What can the ability of mortals to look after themselves in their relationship hothouses do against this? The power of the connected to stabilize themselves in primary relationships with one another, even though all endogenous and

Oskar Schlemmer, *Youths Forming Groups* (1928)

exogenous factors seem to be working to burst the spheres that enable humans to exist, is wondrous enough. And yet: this self-harboring in the self-created space—the ability to cast the cloak over oneself and those who are close to one, then withdraw to the invisible glasshouse of perceived solidarities—is the original and never-ending sphere-creating impulse that must prove itself in countless cases, especially after group crises. It is from here that those structures emerge which would later, in bourgeois, urban, theory-spawning times, be called "societies" or cultures. It seems that humans connected to one another have an immeasurable capacity to dispute that they are lost in externality. How else could one bear the risk of belonging to a species of speaking, fear-prone, moribund beings? And how unbearable would the threat from the outside be without a regenerable husk of re-animating solidarity that would oppose disintegrative attacks, as long as possible, with creative resistance.

As a process of growing solidarity complexes, the history of *homo sapiens* in the time of advanced civilization is above all a battle for the integral and integrating hothouse. It is based on the attempt to provide the wider inside, the reconciling own, the more far-reaching common area with an invulnerable form, or at least a livable one that is superior to the attacks from the outside. That this attempt is clearly still in progress, and that—despite immeasurable setbacks—the struggle for ever larger parts of humanity to move into ever larger communal shelters or endos-pheres is still being undertaken, testifies as much to its irresistible motives as to the stubborn resistance to the historical pull into the extended realm of inner security. Struggles to preserve and expand spheres form both the dramatic core of our species' history and its principle of continuity.

If we observe the countless small cultures that arose from the primordial world up until historical times, watching this swarm of shimmering bubbles filled with languages, rites and projects spouting out and bursting, and if we can, in select cases, watch as they float further, grow and rule, one wonders how it can be

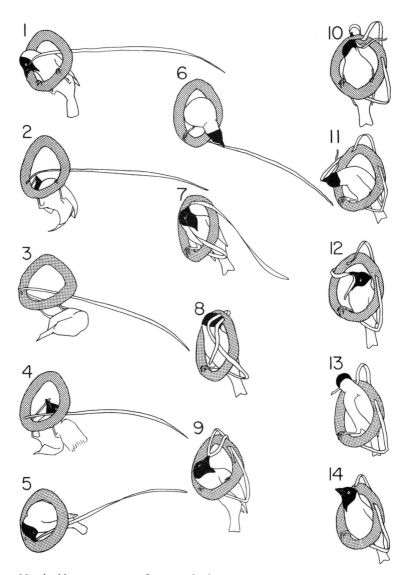

Nest-building movements of a weaver bird

that everything was not blown away by the wind. The vast majority of older clans, tribes and peoples disappeared almost without a trace into a sort of nothingness, in some cases leaving behind at least a name and some obscure cult objects; of the millions of tiny ethnospheres that have drifted over the earth, only a fraction survived through metamorphoses based on enlarging, self-securing, and positing power symbols. It is these that will be examined in this book devoted to macrospheres, and they raise a question: why are large spheres still more likely than none?

CHAPTER 1

Dawn of Long-Distance Closeness

The Thanatological Space, Paranoia and the Peace of the Realm

All history is the history of animation relationships—this was for-mulated in the introduction to the first volume of the present endeavor.[1] The microspherological investigations reveal the scale of this assertion. It encompasses a great wealth of bipolar and multi-polar relationships inside intimate resonant spaces where humans provoke and create one another. Using the image of the bubble—the delicately walled little world billowed by gentle internal pressure—we explicated microspheric forms in comprehensive, bizarre and perilous descriptions, as far as the insubstantial or semi-substantial nature of these constructs permitted. This yielded insights into microcosms of symbiotic, coexistential, bipolar and multipolar constitution whose embedding in larger structures and growth potential could be provisionally foreseen. The dynamics of transference in primary situations was only touched upon. The outcome of the first book was the realization that the word "micro-cosm" can only be used for couples, not individuals—a clear break with metaphysical tradition. All history is the history of anima-tions resulting from the division of space by the two.

It is time to develop this overly compact thesis further: in reality, all history is the history of struggles for spheric expansion.[2]

What was traditionally termed the realm of the soul is the dimension in which the tension between the intimate and the non-intimate is experienced. One could formulate the tendency of metaphysical psychism with the para-Freudian motto that where there was couple soul, there will now be world soul. The pathos of classical philosophy is contained in this instruction. The concept of the world soul holds the categorical command to view all events and things in the external in such a way that they can be understood as elements of an enlarged inside at any time. One already senses that this program is synonymous with the demand to stretch the mother-child symbiosis to the edges of the world by geometric means. The capacity for such distensions is the core of what was traditionally termed "faith."

Expansions only take place if previously external elements can be absorbed by the smaller sphere and reinterpreted as factors of its tensile force and superelevated curvature. To consider this plausible one would have to warm to the idea that spheres are adaptive constructs, as it were practicing immune systems and containers with growing walls. Only if the shared intelligence of the participants is not paralyzed through spheric disasters, but rather challenged to perform major repairs, can that which would normally lead to a sphere's death become effective as an incentive to growth. We will see that even the simple reproduction of living spheres can never succeed without a primary reparative intelligence: humans always live in danger of being separated from those who are closest to them by violence and death, and in the early, small human worlds, those left behind have always faced the problem of finding a way to go on living without their most important augmenters. The human space comes about through injection with death.

Silver amulet keys (18th century)

If humans did not possess the frightening and admirable ability to come to terms with the deaths of their nearest, and if they were unable to fill or cover up the gap left by the vanished with substitutes, no individual could ever die alone; people would never go ahead into death unaccompanied, for the death of the irreplaceable one would always be the death of the allied other too. Cultural tradition would never get underway as creative replacement under such dying conditions, and the transcendence of the other would never turn into inner experience, as the irreplaceable would never have to be substituted under such circumstances.

It is those who are scarred by the disappearance of irreplaceable others that become individuals. What we call individuality has its irreducible core in the fact that even those who are intimately connected do not usually die at the same time. Becoming an individual in a society of individuals thus means preparing oneself to be abandoned with the predecease of the irreplaceable other. This results in what one could call the basic hardship of adult individuals; it acts as an insulation against symbiotic

James Cameron, *Titanic*, *Liebestod* (1997)

temptations to closeness. Human societies frown upon the *Liebestod*—for systemically sound reasons (assuming that systemic reasons can be sound), because they denounce the betrayal of the universal human fate by those who die joined: while all ordinary individuals must already live today as those who could be left behind tomorrow, the accomplices in *Liebestod* disable the law that even the intimately connected end their lives at different times. (James Cameron brought about the overwhelming emotional success of his film *Titanic* by making this normally latent rule visible, for he managed to invoke the *Liebestod* in the story of Jack and Rose—"nothing on earth could come between them"—while avoiding its synchronicity: Isolde outlives Tristan by eighty years. This is the fulfillment of the American dream of love, and indeed the modern one in general: to have the *amour fou* and total survival at the same time!) The lovers who die together in reality revoke their solidarity with the basic effort that every individual seems to owe the world, even if it is never declared as an explicit commandment: to continue bearing the weight of the world even when abandoned by the most important co-bearer of one's burden.

The most significant individualization depends on rehearsing abandonment by one's nearest—just as culture can only succeed if it works as a preparation for living on after the death of the masters. (This is normally discussed in terms of a "legacy," which accentuates the positive handing over; one could equally view it from the perspective of being abandoned, and say that the one left behind is damned to take over.) The ego comes about not through an illusory mirroring, as Lacan seductively and wrongly taught; it first assumes a self-referential shape through the anticipation of being orphaned and widowed, and posits itself as

Medallion from the tomb of Thomas de Marchant et d'Ansembourg (d. 1734) and his wife Anne Marie de Neufonge (d. 1734), Tutange, Luxemburg

deserted and deserting. The ego is the organ of pre-abandonment and pre-farewell.[3] Because the ego-forming expectation of abandonment is of an essentially anticipatory nature, it protects those who have braced themselves for being left alone some day from irreparable separation disasters.[4] What we call individuation is preemptive orientation towards a state occasionally named on French gravestones: *Un seul être vous manqué, et tout le monde est dépeuplé*—one need only miss a single person for the whole world to feel deserted. If the world is to be repopulated, the abandoned life should not be fixated on remaining together with the lost part. Let us say, then, that losing someone must be practiced before the loss exceeds the loser's control.

Rings and wedding rings: amulets to ward off separation through death

The most important part of all mourning must be completed *before* the death of the significant other if their loss is not to lead to the petrifaction of the survivor. Pre-mourning manifests itself as distance. In the *amour fou* this advance farewell is revoked, as if the joined wished to forestall any possibility of separation for all time. They make each other accomplices in the resolve to deny the loved one any chance of outliving their intimate partner.

If those at risk of desertion, however, the survivors of the significant deceased, are capable of entering traditions nonetheless, it is because they follow the necessity of replacing their great absentees—those whom they trusted first, and those from whom they acquired the knowledge. Whoever readies themselves for this compensation accepts their share of the weight of the world. If the world is heavy, it is not merely because most people in historical times slaved away to earn their lives; the heaviness becomes most palpable when people submit to the task of succeeding irreplaceable others.

How, then, can spheres grow? In what ways do intimate worlds, couples, families, hordes and small peoples learn to survive their disasters, their schisms and the threat of being overwhelmed by explosive forces from without and within? How can it be that challenged and overwhelmed groups do not all fade away silently in the ahistorical, but that a few of them bestir themselves to integrate that which usually results in destruction? What change in their way of life do small human communities undergo when they manage to bear the unbearable beyond the usual degree? What happens to the joined when they succeed in securing their survival in the face of irreplaceable losses? How do they learn to gather, heighten and harden themselves—to commit themselves so firmly to a vision of themselves that they become forces of fate for others, rather than suffering fates through external circumstances?

Whatever the answers to these questions, they inevitably have a morphological implication, which in turn conveys an immunological and spherological meaning (and *eo ipso* also a uterotechnic one). In each case, the task is to explain how human groups survive their crises of form in spite of external forces and inner tensions.

Microspheres grow into macrospheres to the extent that they manage to incorporate the stressful external forces into their own radius. One could thus describe the growth of spheres as a stress course during which external elements are neutralized by being included in the spheric interior. It is mostly proto-political stressors like enemies and strangers, socio-psychological stressors like collective depressions, and mental stressors like the monstrous and the idea of the infinite that have to be integrated before a small ethnospheric unit can develop into a higher-level world form.

A group that had withdrawn all significant monsters inwards and, in a sense, overcome or enclosed them, would have grown into an empire or advanced-civilized macrosphere. One can therefore only speak of an authentic macrospheric form if the character of an inner world is still evident on the large and largest scale. In an inner world-like large orb, the will to power must show the same expansion as a will to animate the entire space. As far as I can tell, only three advanced civilizations of antiquity developed and thought through such world interiors in their full implications: China, India and Greece, namely those cultures which, according to a relatively broad academic consensus, are the three birthplaces of philosophy.[5] It was in the cosmologies of these cultures that the morphological imperative—round and rule—began to apply without restrictions.

And thus, here too, *geometry* ultimately came on the scene and—who would have expected otherwise—immediately placed itself in the service of imperial political cosmology. The powerful and their exegetes conceive of their world with dividers and legions. As soon as humans attempt to adapt their form of their souls to macrospheric conditions, they must develop into statespersons, either as officials or sages; for where the advanced-civilized state gives food for thought, the meaning of world moves towards an encompassing inclusivity: the whole is the enclosure of the inclusive animal.

It was the achievement of the great cultures to have taken the inclusion of the stressful outside to a more historically sustainable level. The world powers that became more than military improvisations were those that managed to tame the monsters of externality—death, evil, the foreign, the boundless—and transfer these taming successes to subsequent generations as a cultural habitus. Even if none of these forces ever lose their destructive eeriness, they are converted into internal stressors by the great worldviews and enlisted dialectically by the "great whole." Advanced civilizations know how to turn devastating externality into useful negativities: they use the monsters as a form of growth hormones to increase from microspheric forms to macrospheres.

Let us repeat the basic idea of these reflections: the human being is the animal that must expect and survive separation from those closest to it. In the earliest human life forms, the archaic hordes, death already imposed itself as the compulsion to gaze after deceased companions. Where gazing at the corpse and staring into the empty space take on ritual forms, they become organized as commemoration; from this come the funerary and ancestor cults; they induce the original metaphysical stress to which human groups were already subject in the early stages of hominization. It becomes clear that these cults always have a spherological purpose as soon as one recognizes that dealings of the living with their dead are not only—as is customary in cultural studies—a tradition-forming religious practice or a form of organization for cultural memory. Remembering the dead necessarily initiates sphere-creating processes, as the psychological sphere rent open by the disappearance of the important other, the intimate bubble of coexistence, can only be restored through a form of space-creating immune reaction.

It is impossible to repair the closest intimate space without expanding it: if the survivors insist on remaining together with the departed in a certain sense, this can only occur if the dead are located as if in a second *ring* around the sphere of the living. What psychoanalysis described with so brilliant yet questionable a formulation as "the work of mourning" [*Trauerarbeit*] initially,

Joseph Beuys, *Community Spade x 2* (1964)

from a psychohistorical and psycho-topological perspective, means nothing other than the effort of the survivors to transpose their dread from the wounded innermost vicinity to a wider, pacified ring of closeness. This ring is drawn by mourning— that is, the psychological effort to reach a compromise between sorrow over the final distancing of the deceased and the wish to keep them "there" nonetheless in a different form of closeness. Where small archaic groups refer to their deeds, the spheric space is expanded beyond the current relationships between relatives and cohabiters to a larger bubble that encloses both those present and those absent. It provides the minimum scope

Saints Innocents Cemetery, Paris, c. 1550

for a culture—if we rightly understand cultures as spheropoietic structures that preserve memories of significant dead and pass them along through the generations.

Although the place of the significant dead can initially only be the distance, the undefined yonder and the immeasurable elsewhere, the mourners turn to the task of assigning humanly favorable dimensions to this vague and potentially boundless remoteness. Mourning creates the tense closeness that transforms the infinite into a tractable hereafter. It is the first proxemic passion—a spatial suffering that produces long-distance closeness

in relation to the lost. (It is unclear whether Freud was well advised to interpret this suffering with the concept of work, for only objects can be worked on, whereas mourning is concerned with putting something vanished in a new place or seeking a new place for oneself vis-à-vis the person taken away. Thus mourning does not mean working on an object, but rather changing locations in a stretched space.)

In this sense, one can say that de-distancing is the true culture-forming impulse. It does not permit the significant dead to move too far away, instead keeping them in a wider environment that marks off a cultural sphere's space of living and animation—or at least a wider ring within that space. Hence relevant memories are initially always present in the group public space; their signs are the graves, which vividly mark the space of long-distance closeness for the members of the group.

As the monstrous employer in the work of mourning, death is the first sphere stressor and creator of cultures. The mourning communes survive by accepting the task of taming the fury of disappearance through expanded spatial formation. It is the distancing power of the imagination, which embeds the current living space in surrounding spaces of ghosts and the dead, that spawns cultures as self-harboring spatial figments in the first place. The long-distance closeness of the important dead: it enters the radius of the original, actually existing autonomous spheres— that is, the circle of hordes, clans and small tribal societies—and thus creates the first independent world form. Only a system of coexistence including the living and the dead can ontologically possess world character—and ontographically possesses the power to draw a border for its own world picture around itself.[6]

It was more than ethnological sentimentality that induced people in the twentieth century to begin studying the rites, myths and world constructs of primitive one-hundred-person clans in the jungles of Brazil, Africa or Polynesia with an attentiveness that had previously been considered permissible only for great cultures such as the Greco-Roman, Egyptian or Chinese. If the spiritual dignity of a life form can be ascertained from its sphere-forming power, its capacity to keep the living and the dead together in ritual communions within an agreed-upon horizon, then small tribes are no less admirable constructs than empires which force many millions of people into a circle of rule. For whatever the numerical scale and political radius of a culture, every group that masters its generational process of its own accord thus creates, with its native psychological, imaginative and symbolic forces, that ring of distant closeness or close distance around itself in which genuinely human, space-animating existence that is open to the world and to death situates itself. Within these rings lies what some have rightly called the "anthropological place."[7] Place, in the strong sense of the word, is the territorial commitment of a sphere. Such a tie to a terrain would be inconceivable had the spirits of the people's own dead not occupied the earth and the sky above it as their special "lifeworld." The living space of the groups is pervaded by the signs of ancestral and divine presence. These signs are the edges and tips (in Old High German *orte* [modern German for "places"]) extended to the living by the gods and the dead. The age of territorializing ethnospherics begins with the setting up of overarching lifeworlds for the living and the dead.[8] From this perspective, cultures are functions of the crypts above which the active generations settle. Traditions are streams of signs in the thanatological space.

One must beware of the ethnological idyllicism that presents the modern perception with phantoms of an easier death and a more indolent or better comforted survival in early cultures. These are practically always optical illusions based on gaps in traditions, nostalgias and failing introduction. As soon as written documentation begins, it tells of great mourning struggles and describes how survivors struggled with the unbearable ordeal of a separating death.

The second half of the Babylonian *Epic of Gilgamesh*—the earliest document of imperial storytelling, printed in four different languages between the twenty-first and sixth centuries BC—

deals with the futile struggle of the hunting hero, city king and two-thirds-god Gilgamesh against the death of his friend Enkidu, as well as his rebellion against the realization that the disfigured corpse of his friend was giving him a glimpse of his own fate. The world of Gilgamesh already constituted a form of large-scale world in which the dead withdraw to a very distant beyond or a very deep underworld, meaning that the integrative mourning over them only succeeds when the hero advances to the edge of the world to find an antidote to separation and to his own demise. It is metaphysically informative that Gilgamesh's awareness of his own mortality was only awakened through the death of his alter ego. For death does not, as later Greek and Christian philosophy suggested, become a problem for individuals through the prospect of their own end, to which mortals "run ahead," as was commonly said in the last century; death's sting is first experienced through the imposition of having to survive the innermost other, the twin, the indispensable augmenter. At the edge of the world, the goal of Gilgamesh's voyage of mourning, the following dialogue ensues between the disconsolate searcher and the wise helper Utnapishtim:

> Said Utnapishtim to him, to Gilgamesh: [...]
> "Why in your heart does sorrow reside,
> and your face resemble one come from afar?
> Why are your features burnt by frost and by sunshine,
> and why do you wander the wild in lion's garb?"

> Said Gilgamesh to him, to Utna-pishtim:
> "Why should my cheeks not be hollow, my face not sunken,
> my mood not wretched, my visage not wasted?

"Should not sorrow reside in my heart,
and my face not resemble one come from afar?
Should not my features be burnt by frost and by sunshine,
and should I not wander the wild in lion's garb?

"My friend, a wild ass on the run,
donkey of the uplands, panther of the wild,
my friend Enkidu, a wild ass on the run,
donkey of the uplands, panther of the wild—

"having joined forces we climbed the mountains,
seized and slew the Bull of Heaven,
destroyed Humbaba, who dwelt in the Forest of Cedar,
killed lions in the mountain passes—

"my friend, whom I loved so dear,
who with me went through every danger,
my friend Enkidu, whom I loved so dear,
who with me went through every danger:
the doom of mortals overtook him.

"Six days I wept for him and seven nights:
I did not surrender his body for burial
until a maggot dropped from his nostril.
Then I was afraid that I too would die,
I grew fearful of death, so wander the wild.

"What became of my friend was too much to bear,
so on a far road I wander the wild."[9]

This reflection on death shows no trace of holistic idyll. The wide radius of Gilgamesh's mourning voyage shows the extent of his wound; his failure to bring home the herb of immortality marks him for all time as a metaphysical loser who now, convicted of his own mortality, must respect the difference between him and the true gods. Only the fact that he returns after his voyage to Uruk, the city he rules, rounds off the epic in a way that amounts to consolation through the form itself. Gilgamesh's journey frames mourning in a full circle. In the Babylonian empire, of course the king's double, his dead intimate friend, can no longer be buried under the middle post of the community center to witness the lives of his loved ones as a household spirit. The taming of his disappearance no longer occurs through animistic local traffic with a convivial hereafter. To follow the dead Enkidu into his radical distance, Gilgamesh must go as far as the Babylonian conception of space and size allows: to the limits of the world. The separated parties are now worlds apart; the long-distance closeness of the unlosable lost one has taken on cosmic traits. The hero travels for forty-five days to find the cure for death at the edge of the world. Do we understand what edge he is exploring here? What border waters does the mourning hero cross with his stone oars? Into what hybrid sea must he dive to find the wondrous herb? Through the epic images, the outer extremes affect those of the inner world.

In this earliest of epics, there is no reference to the prospect of reunification with the beloved in the hereafter. Yet Babylonian culture as a whole becomes a resonant space for the tale of heroic friendship, the disaster of loss and a voyage of mourning. For more than one and a half millennia, the drama of the separation of the inseparable and the king's quest for a herb to prevent death was recounted over and over again. Regarding these narrative streams, one can venture the assumption that empires are not only legal, administrative and presumptuous spaces, but that, if they are to last as animated spheres, they must to an extent also act as echoing spaces for civilizing laments and resonant bodies for empathy with exemplary human fates.

One encounters entirely different circumstances of mourning in Saint Augustine's account in the fourth book of *Confessions* of the loss of his closest childhood friend, a youth of the same age with whom Augustine (born in 354) had reveled in shared inclinations and attitudes during a happy year. The incident must have taken place around 376 in Thagaste, a few years after his conversion to Manichaeism. The fact that his friend stood under his influence, and was also close to him as an accomplice in metaphysical experiments and aberrations, partly explains Augustine's devastation upon his friend's sudden death. The breaking of this spiritual allegiance becomes all the more painful when he learns that his friend had chosen to be baptized at the point of death, with no opportunity to discuss the change of heart with him.

This death too, this catastrophic severance of a symbiotic alliance, opened up an intramundane abyss that seemed insuperable from the perspective of life thus far, and here too, the highest consoling reasons the age had to offer were required to interpret one's own survival in the face of the deceased beloved. These reasons have meanwhile reached a high theoretical level; they have been philosophically developed and thought through psychologically; they are founded on a metaphysics that made available a matured monotheistic conception of God and an advanced idea of providence or predestination.

Under the monarchy of God, it behooves the believer to face the unbearable with a strong assumption of an underlying meaning. They must view their own life, including its abysses of separation, wounds and defeats, as a curriculum conceived by God; the Christian must accept being "tossed about in diverse trials": *in experimentis volvimur* (*Confessions*, Book IV, V [10]). Wherever this idea of trial and catharsis appears, it can be expected that even the most overwhelming losses will transpire as gains at a higher level. There seems no reason to be suspicious towards Augustine's account of his state after his friend's death for being overly conventional or rhetorical—not least because the author, a man in his mid-forties at the time of writing (397–401), was recounting events that had taken place almost a quarter of a century earlier.

> My heart was black with grief. Whatever I looked upon had the air of death. My native place was a prison-house and my home a strange unhappiness. The things we had done together became sheer torment without him. My eyes were restless looking for him, but he was not there. I hated all places because he was not in them. They could not say, "He will come soon," as they would in his life when he was absent. I became a great enigma to myself and I was forever asking my soul why it was sad and why it disquieted me so sorely. And my soul knew not what to answer me. [...] I had no delight but in tears, for tears had taken the place my friend had held in the love of my heart. (Book IV, IV [9])[10]
>
> I was wretched, and every soul is wretched that is bound in affection of mortal things: it is tormented to lose them, and in their loss becomes aware of the wretchedness which in reality

it had even before it lost them. [...] I wondered that other mortals should live when he was dead whom I had loved as if he would never die; and I marveled still more that he should be dead and I his other self living still. Rightly has a friend been called "the half of my soul." For I thought of my soul and his soul as one soul in two bodies, and my life was a horror to me because I would not live halved. (Book IV, VI [11])[11]

While ancient Babylonian mourning drives the hero to the limits of the world to seek a remedy for the unacceptable, Platonic-Christian mourning admonishes the adept to learn a decisive lesson at the school of separations. The death of one's closest friend, though the epitome of a microspheric disaster, provokes a spheric leap and urges the survivor to redefine their place in the existent. In truth, the author of the *Confessions* both Platonized and Christianized his sorrow; he Platonizes it by reading the loss as a stimulus for love to rise from the ephemeral to the everlasting, and Christianizes it by shifting his loyalty from his friend, who died of fever, to Christ, who died in order to kill death from the overabundance of his life (Book IV, XII [19]).

Yet both of these—the Platonic ascent from the ephemeral sensible to the everlasting supersensible and the Christian killing of death—are already typical operations to create macrospheres, large interiors of spiritualized vitality that successfully oppose the attacks of the outside. The basic operation of the Christian "work of mourning" lies in replacing the lost partner in closeness with the partner in long-distance closeness, the living God. Whoever does not wish to live on as an abandoned half must find a new augmenter, and wherever metaphysical needs intervene in this difficulty, the augmentation will be of a spiritualizing, transcending and superlative nature. As in the Platonic school of love, the inner twin must first present itself as a beautiful individual, then as the beautiful as such, and finally as the over-beautiful, over-good God.

The manner in which Augustine, writing the *Confessions* in his middle years, looks back at his formerly disconsolate and abandoned self and his friend, taken from life too early, yet at the right time, perfectly illustrates the effort to ascribe sense to the senseless from an elevated position after the fact. The church father unwaveringly reads his progress in the training course of distances as a work of grace. Consequently God, the teacher of all teachers, had to separate the two misguided pupils so that the more talented of them would find the right path; only by removing one of them from life did he induce the other to understand, gradually, his error in clinging to something mortal as devotedly as if it were unlosable. Distancing himself from his own devastation at the death of his beloved friend, Augustine develops a critical theory of love: what matters is to distinguish between objects of love and then choose correctly. "For he alone loses no one that is dear to him, if all are dear in God, who is never lost."[12] Where God's love wins out over blinkered eroticism, it becomes—according to the clergyman—the tensile force in a sphere-stretching of universal proportions.

One can read Augustine's account of mourning as an indirect theory of the church—that is, as the basis of a radically inclusive realm of the heart. This would do away with preferential love, that all-too-humanly selective and vulnerable sentiment, in favor of a non-preferential affection for all (like-minded) fellow creatures. This would simultaneously restyle death as an advantageous stressor; indeed, Christian churchgoers have edified themselves since earliest times with the notion that the living and the dead would sit on the same pews, as a solidary multitude, at the great council that would assemble the entire *communion sanctorum*. The dead, admittedly, would be in the vast majority and one level higher than the living, as their deceased status seems to promote them all to informal Doctors of the Church.

What is particularly striking about Augustine's later interpretation of his youthful mourning from a sphere-theoretical perspective are its autotherapeutic and psychagogic aspects. The author is fully aware that the hole in the existent which was torn open by the death of the dearest other adamantly demands to be closed up again: hence his statement that his weeping for the departed followed his friend, as it were (*successerat*), taking his place in Augustine's soul. The tears are the first, still sensual replacement for the relationship with the object of love, and it is not for nothing that Augustine calls his weeping sweet: *solus fletus dulcis erat mihi*. What had been a relationship of embraces became one of weeping. The tears, for their part, also had to dry up and be replaced by entering a relationship of observation and adoration with a higher partner. Certainly Augustine's tears were no longer those of an animist who maintains a convivial relationship with the departed other beyond the grave, but rather those of a metaphysician seeking relief in sighs, abstractions and distractions. While his dead friend—who, to Augustine's bafflement, converted in his final hour—stays behind in the soil of Thagaste, Augustine moved to Carthage to avoid being constantly reminded of him by their former shared surroundings. This relocation was no epic voyage of mourning, however, but an escape to diversion—a movement of which Augustine would later say that it only reached a favorable conclusion ten years later, with his conversion and baptism in Milan in 386. Nonetheless, this flight would—through his later conversion—take on a healing meaning. For what was the purpose of Augustine's restless survival if not to enable him to speak one day about the torturous false love of the ephemeral, and the sweet true love of the enduring?

After the weeping, then—with a detour via diversion—edifying speech comes to replace the irreplaceable. Whoever is successful in mourning acquires the position of teacher: they gain the mandate to speak to fellow believers about the difference between the temporal and the eternal. At the same time, speaking, speaking, speaking becomes the perfect model for the course of life and a cipher for our replacement by later things in time: to create a meaningful sentence, the words must appear in succession, quickly make their contributions to the sense of the whole and then make way for the next word. If his dead friend was the preceding word, Augustine knows that the present word is his, and that others will have their turn after him.[13] All successive lives are particles in the sentence structure of God: this is the assumption which gives the metaphysician the certainty that the dead, the living and the unborn are all given their positions in the divine syntagma according to a master plan. This attitude later enabled Augustine to endure the death of his son Adeodatus, who died at roughly the same age as his youthful friend from Thagaste, with a degree of inner calm.

The Christian-philosophical project of tranquility would only fail on a large scale once more in Augustine's life: upon the death of his mother in Ostia. He did, as described at length in the ninth book of *Confessions*, succeed in holding back his tears during the funeral rites, causing his companions to admire his composure. In his private chamber, however, far from their gazes, he let his tears flow one last time (*Et dimisi lacrimas*). Subsequently, Augustine claimed never again to have wept over human, all-too-human losses, only when moved by religious and moral impulses. Henceforth he lived—precariously, but resolutely—in that absolute interior of the religious imagination from which one supposedly never be expelled, known in Christian terms as the kingdom of God. And indeed, it seems that whoever has rooted themselves in the sphere of the *pater orfanorum*, the father of orphans, in something like a final system of kinship, will never be left behind orphaned.[14] According to John the Evangelist, Jesus told the disciples that he would never leave them orphaned, and that his departure was merely the external condition for him to stay for good; with its permanent presence, the spirit would offer a substitute for the son who would remain absent until the end of times (John 14:16f.). The maximal inside, taken to its Christian conclusion, forms the spatial holy of holies in which those ideas of the absolute that are redeemable persons come together. Should one still be able to fall out of this convent once taken up into it? If so, this does not become manifest until the final crisis, the Last Judgment, when God—as if taking stock at New Year—adds up his own and crosses out those who are not his own. With the chosen, God then forms the ultimate and greatest possible spiritual soul spheres as a pure gathering of the ever-living. Death is no longer a threat to them, only an irritation that has been overcome—an injection for the eternal life that results from the immune response to death. The most reliable information about this saved society, which only moves in God's best circles, can be found in the *Paradise* cantos from Dante's *Divine Comedy*. They show what happens when the widest inclusivity is combined with the strictest exclusivity: in Dante's heaven, the harboring of the chosen souls in the divine orb has become *a fait accompli*.

If death is the initial sphere expander whose stressor effect is what leads to the formation of cultures or "societies" in the first place—each of them contained in the open ring of their close-distant dead—then the stress injected into the societies by envy and evil acts as a sphere consolidator of the first instance. Through the violent rites with which they warded off evil and sought to drive it out from within themselves, the early groups consolidated themselves as conspiracies against malevolence, massing together as teams to exclude and expel it. Consequently, older societies viewed the outside less as a geographical or topographical fact than a demonic-moral dimension; it stood for the uncontrolled space—the exosphere, in ethnological terminology—to which evil or its human manifestations were to be driven, and whence their return was to be feared. In moral-topological terms, all archaic human communities were enclosed by an unclear ring universe whose predominant character was that of an ambivalent outside. For outside in the uncontrolled space, alongside the countless incalculable factors of favorable, indifferent and undesirable kinds, the ghosts of the banished and murdered who once belonged to us also roam about. The excluded potentially return from the monstrous, that is to say the evil-infested environment, and surround the group lifeworld with a besieging ring of exospheric dangers—which is why all xenophobia, like religion, begins with the fear that the expelled will return. (This extends to the trembling of traditional Christians when imagining the second coming of their lord, whom they believe to be in heaven while fearing that he will leave once more on that most monstrous of all days in order to settle with his children: *unde venturus est iudicare vivos et mortuos*[15]). A contributing factor in the monstrousness of those who return is that the entire outside, the undefined exosphere, is open to them, and that from there—the direction and the hour are unknown—they could attack the community gathered in its round camp.

In addition to the arrangement of the dead in a protective-surrounding long-distance closeness, the basic effort of all social units consists in casting out evil from the inside and securing the borders. The topological difference between inside and outside thus has a moral purpose, just as morality has an immunological one; it creates the divide between the good and internal to the bad and external—a divide that is often interpreted simultaneously as the difference between the pure and the impure, the just and the unjust. To the extent that they follow this schema of exclusion between endo- and exospheric states, societies—whether archaic or modern—always remain primarily communities of effort and intoxication, occasionally vibrating in unanimously shared ecstatic uproars directed at the real and presumed originators of evil. The sacrificial rites that provided ancient societies with cultural or religious continuity, each in its own particular way, constituted routinizations of these solidarity-creating uproars. (In modern, seemingly victim-free societies, they are re-enacted through periodic scandals and exercises in outrage.) Thus the interiors of cultures or original societies are arenas of affect that keep their fellow players inside through participation in the most exciting, binding and infectious of all communal undertakings: the forceful removal of evil from one's own inner realm. Sanctifying the interior and demonizing the surroundings are directly connected processes; by separating the sphere from everything that is supposedly not itself, they produce the first social and ecological facts.

The efforts to exclude evil from the community's interior therefore have a directly sphere-expanding effect; first and foremost, they constitute an attempt to impose a safe distance between the group's immune space and its banished corrupters. Here too, the expansion is inseparable from the reinforcement of the sphere, as the moral walls and ditches that protect the group from its real or purported disturbers are always placed around the integral internal world at a tactical distance.

Central aspects of these reflections effortlessly overlap with René Girard's ideas about the birth of cultures from the spirit of the sacred mechanics of violence. In numerous studies, Girard developed the monumental thesis that all human societies cannot initially be anything other than systems of envy and jealousy, throbbing with compulsions to imitate. For immanent reasons they are under a high endogenous, self-stressing tension and are forced, as if by some group-dynamic or socio-morphological natural law, to cleanse themselves by collectively murdering the supposed originators of their evils in a frenzy of bloodlust. This would make every local culture a clique formed through a founding murder; its central language game in each case would be the collective, unanimous accusation and condemnation of a victim who must take all evils upon themselves, along with the monotonous and consistent denial of personal responsibility for the violence-liberating escalations. The members of a "culture" in this sense of the word are those who participate, actually or symbolically, in the sacrifice of the scapegoat whose expulsion from inside the society allows the calm of a sense of justice and a post-stressal peace to return to the group. For Girard, cultures are constructs that are bound together by the fusionary energies of the maximum stimulation of lynching stress—and which, after the excess, find their way back to the basic line of relaxed order and purified solidarity.

The calmed, edifying communal feelings that followed the orgies of founding murder form the basis of the rites and myths of peoples; the rites constitute the symbolized and restricted repetition of the original disinhibited impulse of shared murder, while the myths provide the justificatory narratives. Thus all cultures or ethnicities, if Girard were right, would be based on fusionary criminal co-operations, then indispensable agreements on joint lies, namely myths apportioning the blame for the violence to its victims. The upshot of these reflections is the sociologically subversive thesis that the scapegoat alone can be the involuntary integrator of their group—for the greatest excitations of all society's members converge in it, and their narratives revolve around its expulsion or its salvific sacrifice and idealization. Both of these, excitations and narratives, act as a strong affective glue for the societies, giving them an unmistakable sense of unity and solidarity. It is only with the exclusion of evil that the self-inclusion of the non-evil in a pathos-charged "we" space becomes possible.

In this sense, all groups with close cultic integration, whether archaic or contemporary, rely on discrimination mechanisms—they cannot exist without enemies or victims, and therefore depend on the constant repetition of their lies about the enemy to build up the necessary degree of autogenous stress for internal stabilization. This simultaneously means that they cannot survive without God and gods, as the gods—based on this deduction—are initially nothing but the numinous and uncanny guises taken by the scapegoats. One by no means has to "believe" in gods at first; it is enough to remember the constitutive festival of murder for us to know how they concern us. It is the uneasy recollection of a concealed crime that constitutes the supposedly deep religiosity of earlier cultures; in their religious mood, the peoples are close to their ghostly foundations of lies. God is the authority that is entitled to remind its followers of their occulted guilty secret.

The community's intimate relationship is constantly reaffirmed by this memory, however mythically removed and ritually muted it might be. For what could belong together more than the collective of perpetrators and its victim, who became its god? It is as narrative communities and communes of excitation—that is, in the cult—that cultures, these guilty groups enchanted by their atrocity, are most themselves. For where excitations and narratives overlap, the sacred is formed—and this is what immerses the groups in their unmistakably own climate of awe, guilt, timidity and willingness to make sacrifices. Thus the sacrificed object is placed at the center of a society's spiritual space. The cultic invocation of the sacrificed god makes the society experience itself as a homogeneous entity that must keep vibrating anew in shared sacred unease if it is to remain internally coherent. The very fact that, as a sacrificial and cultic community, each group has its medium of unity in its own very particular memories of violence, gave the early societies their typically impenetrable character. (One therefore cannot convert to primitive religions, for it is impossible to take part in the constitutive crime of another group, except as a spectator; by contrast, one can move from any cult to advanced-civilized religions such as Christianity or Buddhism, because both have the structure of emancipatory movements that lead their followers out of early complexes of cult and guilt—even when, as in Christianity, the liberation movement becomes stuck in self-sabotaging new debt to a sacrificed god.)

If this is augmented by the phenomenon whose existence in countless sacrificial groups or cultures Girard believed he had proved, namely the elevation of the scapegoat to sacred kingship, then the group synthesis predicated on excitations, narratives, panics and lies, gains additional political consolidation. Thus the internal stress of envy and violence—which, if it escalates, arouses societies to the brink of disintegration and sometimes beyond—simultaneously proves the most important sphere stabilizer, to the extent that the jealous tensions which triggered the violence can be brought under control by ritual means after the crisis. This, according to Girard's model, is precisely the function of cults based on blood sacrifice: their civilizatory function lies in suppressing excessive actual epidemics of violence by carrying out ritual violence.[16] (*Post Christum crucifixum* this leads, as Girard never tires of emphasizing, to the *via antiqua* of the perverse people who still practice sacrificial violence, even though they could have learned long ago that the victims are no guiltier than they themselves, and that this seemingly purificatory violence merely repeats the same wicked game *ad infinitum*.[17])

One could equate the transformation of the pre-human hordes into human ritual and sacrificial communities with an immune response of the sociosphere to its greatest immanent threat. In fact, the stressor—the mimetic plague in which everyone infects everyone else with their desire—is here converted into a religious stabilizer: what was evil shall become sacred. This shimmering sanctity normally appears as an ethnic deity with the mandate of guaranteeing tribal coherence as a sphere guardian and group protector. Thus groups adhering to archaic sacrificial religions possess the form of integristic gangs who, if they do not presently commit crimes together, at least identify one another through the signs of past atrocities. Where this integrism produces stronger symptoms, the hunger to relapse into the acted-out orgy becomes acute. And groups seeking violence usually find their victims very easily, quickly creating the pretexts to practice and celebrate their removal once again.

Such quasi-natural group integrisms, with their thirst for escalations, are not immune to enlightenment. Within ritually pacified societies, especially when these have grown into consolidated realms and can look back on a longer experience of peace, it is possible for critical reflections on violence to develop that reveal the game of arousing jealousy and break the cycle. Some of the oldest evidence of the development of jealousy-dampening, explicitly anti-mimetic ethical codes can be found in ancient Egyptian wisdom books, in particular the sayings of Amenemope, a scribe and supervisor of the granaries from the time of the New Kingdom. The text is a work of moral instruction, written around 1300 BC, whose reflexes are unambiguously evident in Near Eastern literatures, but most of all in the wisdom texts of the Old Testament, not least the proverbs of Solomon. The ethics of the New Testament was also anticipated in this work, as in numerous other ancient Egyptian wisdom reflections. *The Instruction of Amenemope* contains the following axioms:

Do not get into a quarrel with the argumentative man
Nor incite him with words;
Proceed cautiously before an opponent,
And give way to an adversary;
Sleep on it before speaking,
For a storm come forth like fire in hay is
The hot-headed man in his appointed time.
May you be restrained before him;
Leave him to himself,
And God will know how to answer him.[18]

Do not displace the surveyor's marker on the boundaries of the
    arable land,
Nor alter the position of the measuring line;
Do not be covetous for a single cubit of land,
Nor encroach upon the boundaries of a widow.[19]

Do not covet the property of the dependent
Nor hunger for his bread;
The property of a dependent is an obstruction to the throat,
It makes the gullet throw it back.[20]

Do not laugh at a blind man nor taunt a dwarf,
Neither interfere with the condition of a cripple.[21]

And give a hand to an old man filled with beer:
Respect him as his children would.[22]

God loves him who cares for the poor,
More than him who respects the wealthy.[23]

One could read these maxims as documenting a revolution of discretion. Almost a millennium and a half before the Sermon on the Mount, these reflections from the Nile Valley frown on the shamelessness with which the violent have always let themselves go, as if no one worth taking seriously were watching. Egyptian thought already advanced to the decisive question of all advanced cultures: what are violence and rudeness but signs of inconsideration towards the higher witness? The proverbs of the grain supervisor show that in the milder climate of ancient Egyptian middle class culture, the conditions existed to produce an ethos of wisdom resembling a first Enlightenment. It no longer seeks the basis for coexistence in rites that quote distant acts of bloody violence, but rather in the shared state of being sheltered and included by an all-attentive God. The new wisdom teaching reveals, with complete lucidity, the mechanism behind the escalation of envy-born aggression between humans, showing the way to a life in discretion and moderation. The newer Egyptian way of life was an asceticism of de-escalation. It rests on the positing of a space-pervading divine attentiveness that notices even the innermost feelings of the actors.

The belief in the highest observer, who commands discretion, was thus the start of a development that was carried on by the Jewish prophets and Jesuan ethics, finally culminating in the modern formulations of human rights. This moral-evolutionary trend is based on the realization that large spheres in the form of kingdoms and empires (and especially of worldwide churches) are only capable of preserving their form in the long term if they cease to rely primarily on sacrificial violence and divine terror. Large-scale political entities attain their appealing inclusivity by bringing themselves, as attested by the teachings of Amenemope, to formulate an ethics that expressly protects current and potential victims—the weak and strangers. This tendency had already manifested itself around 1700 BC in the Babylonian codex of Hammurabi. The tenor of the new wisdom teachers lies in the admonition to participate in violence-inhibiting escalations. This corresponds to an ethical climate characterized less by the mobilization of the group against scapegoats and outside enemies than by the concern for civil coherence in a pacified large-scale space. The climate of inclusion marked the beginning of the world ethos. It is part of the climate policy of stable empires to promise care for the needy, the endangered and the disadvantaged. (Hence Nietzsche's genealogy of morals from the *ressentiment* of the losers is a sound, but one-sided derivation; it needs to be augmented by an empire-morphological genealogy.) This ethos entails the paradox that it causes new exclusive effects, as it has to declare integristic groups or strong-willed peoples who are unwilling to dissolve into the civilized lukewarmth of the realm of its enemies. Thus it is precisely ethical universalism that comes up against the structural boundaries of pacifying inclusivity on all sorts of fronts. In fact, milder internal climates develop mostly and initially behind reliable walls, and in attempting to export the standards of the mild climate, imperial power breaks more or less crudely through the pacified shell.

The great inclusive religions and wisdom doctrines have had to live with this dilemma since appearing on the world-historical stage three thousand years ago as symbiotic partners of the empires, and simultaneously as their chronic dissidents. One particularly marked dissident symbiont of the empires was historical Judaism, which always had to seek its chance in inter- and intra-imperial gaps. At the same time, from the emergence of Axial

Age worldviews and advanced ethics onwards, empires faced the task of dealing with the seed of the good people who had contempt for the armed peace enforced by states and their finite legal systems, opposing it with the peace of an entirely different kingdom and an entirely different, infinite justice. The distinction between forms of peace set off the true world war: the world-historical struggle over the antithesis between power (rootedness, assertion, apparatus and culture) and spirit (uprooting, resistance, anarchy and art). If there were an "end of history," one would notice it in the expiry of these oppositions.

CHAPTER 2

Vascular Memories

On the Reason for Solidarity in Its Inclusive Form

Believe me, that was a happy time, before there were architects…

— L. Annaeus Seneca, *Epistulae morales ad Lucilium, XC*

It is obvious from all that is fashioned, produced, or created under her influence, that Nature delights primarily in the their nests, and so on, all of which she has made circular?

— Leon Battista Alberti, *On the Art of Building in Ten Books*[1]

> whence the voice that says
> live
> from another life
>
> —Samuel Beckett, *Mirlitonnades*[2]

The human being is a *zóon politikón*: among the many characteristics of the human race, this claim by Aristotle emphasizes that they must first and foremost be defined as animals that lead their lives together. Admittedly, if one looks closer, the attribute *politikós*—which has a biological accent here—is in all respects too weak to indicate the specific quality of human associations. In Aristotelian discourse (especially *Historia animalium*, I, 1), revealingly, it does not stand exclusively for the human mode of being, but equally for that of state-forming insects, or pack animals like wolves and cranes.[3] Greek zoology speaks of the "gregarious" animals as "political" creatures, without giving much thought to what other disciplines will have to say about human beings as narrating, sacrificing, city-building and concept-forming animals.

Thus the word *politikós* aims—without hitting the mark entirely—to pinpoint pre-political, non-urban motifs in human association. It points out that from the outset, humans are those who do not live alone, and that they come together not only for procreation, but also not only for urban trade. Whoever refers to humans as the "political" animals admits that there are binding forces between these creatures which can scarcely be grasped from the perspective of individualistic ideologies. Individualism is a form of thought that reserves the attribute "real" for individuals and acknowledges communities only as secondary, less real and terminable agglomerations of autonomous parts—that is, as "societies" in the contract-theoretical sense. Such an approach prevents any understanding of the irreducible density of human intimate relationships; it blocks out the field of strong relationships from the anthropological perception.[4] But what is the shared "work" that drives the gregarious beings to one another almost *a priori*, interlocks them and gives them shared reasons for existence?

After the microspherological groundwork of the first volume, I shall begin here by developing a number of macrospherological answers to these questions, all of them dependent on an elementary observation: if human groups from Paleolithic hunter-gatherer cultures to the threshold of modernity all tend to display very

Reindeer in the snow desert of the Siberian Arctic

strong internal cohering forces, this is because on all steps of the socio-systemic scale of magnitudes, they are subject to an overwhelming existential form imperative. For species-specific reasons, and long before the life form of the *polis* would dictate to humans their decisive shared ideas, members of that group were interwoven in strong relationships—more so than any communications theory has so far been able to describe, but also differing from the fictions created by the known Romantic, communitarian and organicist views. One need not espouse the hyperbolic doctrine of national spirit to perceive the reality of close-knit communes and cultures in their own right.

Just as Christian theologians argue that the persons of the immanent trinity do not need to set up any wall for each to be entirely itself, yet able to merge into the others,[5] so too the members of primary and primitive society need no physical barrier enclosing and grouping them together in order to realize their strong relationship. For a long time, they would not need walls around their settlements to show that they have something to do with one another in the most radical way. The wall-less community reproduces endogenously from energies of cohesion that cause each group to create their own existential space, as well as the typical form in which it can appear to itself and others. Even without solid architectural reinforcements, every we-group knows how to harbor itself in a perceived form and, through a manner of centripetal pull, to settle in an integrative whole form. All primary cultural units can be understood only as self-triggering morphogenetic processes. The immediate project of every community is the continued self-harboring of the group in its morphological shell: all concrete "societies," whether primitive or complex, are sphero-poietic projects (though we can initially leave aside the geometric meanings of the term "sphere" and restrict ourselves to vague internal spatialities).

It is trivial to point out that the vast majority of sphere formations in the history of the human race did not remain clan-based ensembles within tribal cultures, few of which succeed in developing into medium-scale ethnic structures. In truth, a mere *people* is already a morphological effect that, from the perspective of its horde beginnings, borders on the impossible because it presupposes the cultural—and usually also political—synthesis of thousands of hordes (now: families or houses). Only very rarely did these structures go beyond popular units to grow into macrospheres of the highest order, that is to say city-states and multiethnic empires, and in Spengler's and Toynbee's sense even "cultures" able to give themselves the form of *worlds* politically and ontologically. The term "world" then refers not to "everything that is the case" but rather everything that can be contained by a *form* or known boundary. It could also be fittingly described as an autogenous context.

As far as Western antiquity is concerned, we find the decisive symbol of integration for this concept of the world in the Homeric-Hesiodic image of the *oikuméne* surrounded by the oceanic current, the visible human habitat that lies hidden within the limits of an encompassing divine secret. The ancient Chinese world had the analogous symbol *t'ien-hsia*, "everything under the sky" or "realm." In both concepts of ecumene, the concept of world is tied to the notion that all manifest things are encompassed by an outermost ring of invisible ordering powers.[6] This notion is recognized in thought as soon as critical growth in size subjects the primary groups to a morphological stress that must be dealt with by building walls and through symbolic means of political and philosophical self-affirmation. But long before this too, when small groups of humans still lead the life of nomadic hunter-gatherers and are far from entrenching themselves behind city walls and fortified frontiers, they exist in self-rounding and self-enclosing forms. I shall describe these as the wall-less hothouses of sphere solidarity—which is something entirely different from the imaginary and instigated solidarity of interest groups in modern mass societies, whether those of the so-called working class or the old and the young, who would be connected via the detour of social security in purported (evidently unreliable) generation contracts.

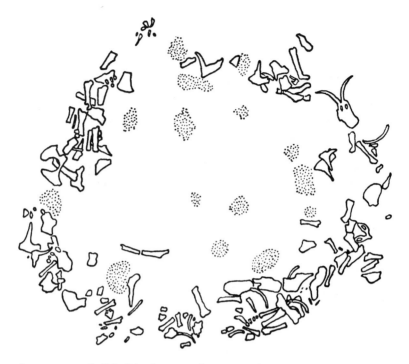

Storage space of a Paleolithic hunter-gatherer group (30,000 BC)

Speaking of solidarity in the form of hothouses is primarily meant to indicate that among those who truly live together, inner relationships take absolute precedence over so-called environmental ones. The earliest hordes in particular displayed this tendency towards the primacy of the inner; in bringing group members to their relative optimum as actually existing relationship hothouses, their foremost aim was self-harboring behind unbuilt walls and unerected barriers. This is why the principle of the wall already came into play in the most primitive of social formations, even where there were no real architectural realizations of the space-dividing inclusion figure. (Heaps of discarded bones were found in the vicinity of tent sites from the Mousterian period, giving the first indications of a magical palisade[7]) when walls—built or unbuilt—divide a space, one is always dealing with physical and mental interior creations: for the first wall is always the one seen from within—the wall for us, the constitutive fence, the self-placed pacification line. The primal topological difference between inside and outside—with-us and not-with-us—initially establishes itself without solid material markings; it is the basis of the magical universe of identities[8] that constantly repeats the law of endospherically dominated space production in the immeasurable abundance of its individual realizations. As a self-enclosing group, the cohabitants cut their own dwelling portion, their peace, out of the space of non-peace.

The self-housing effect results from that *insulation* which Hugh Miller recognized as the most important socio-topological mechanism: through their field of closeness, cohabiting groups develop an internal climate that has the effect of a privileged ecological niche for its residents. Humans are thus not so much niche-seekers as niche-builders; it is characteristic that they themselves make room for the place in which they can thrive. Dieter Claessens highlights this anthropological fact with the necessary emphasis:

> While evolution towards mammals transferred the niche function to a survival-friendly element such as water, then the less ambiguous protection of the egg, and finally the mother creature itself (which thus becomes the offspring's direct patron and develops within itself the artificial internal climate required for more advanced development), evolution towards humans entailed, in a sense, a reversal: now the uterus once

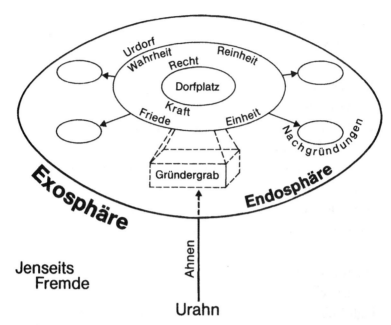

Topological schema of the primitive village space, from K. E. Müller, *Das magische Universum der Identität* (Frankfurt, 1987))

more became a social space, meaning that part of the protective function taken over by the maternal interior was now
shifted back to the outside. This would have been impossible
if such an exterior had not been created beforehand: the
"social uterus."[9]

This means that every society is a uterotechnic project; it must
remove the very protection that enables its existence to a place
outside itself. And yet dwelling, as Heidegger taught, does not
simply mean protecting, but rather distinguishing between
protected and unprotected spheres. Indeed, by lifting the endosphere out of the exosphere in the first place, this distinction

determines what comes to a standstill and what the circumstances are. It causes the non-indifferent, individual light-dark
place to be cut out of the indifferent or cursed extension of the
undisclosed space out there. This pacified, walled-in, self-nurturing
zone often sets itself against encirclements by demons and
robbers—in the sayings of the Roman augurs, for example, one
can still identify traces of an original "fixing" (*effari*) of once-
wild, unpacified fields and pastures requiring consecration. In
the disclosed and freed place for which space has been made, the
world clears up as ours. One's own place becomes the heart of the
existent or the seat of the world soul—though the attribute
"own," as we have seen, has a special character in contexts such
as this. Through our dwelling in it, the chosen, interiorly centered place ascends to a relevant world, distinguishing itself as a
region of greater density and more familiar brightness—but also
of greater jeopardy. Where groups of humans form their dwelling
and living space, self-harboring, self-climatization and self-
rounding establish themselves in the creation of places. The earth
may be strewn with millions of unfamiliar settlements, but
initially and for the time being it is this one here that is incomparable, as it houses us, makes us possible, and is presently open
for us. Here, from the indifferent, immense space, we cut out an
animated orb, the community that we are: this is the place we
will inhabit as our cosmic quarters. Here we know what we mean
when we say we are at home *in the world*. The section is the
message, and the sphere is the meaning of being.

These reflections open up the way back to our microspherological investigations. Now we can ask: where are we really when
we think we are in our place or at home in a region, a landscape
or a city? If this "where?" question is to prove more than a

misuse of the interrogative particle, it forces us to assume that being-in can never be entirely trivial in a public, familiar world. We must make sure once again that joint dwelling in a world-place implies more than an egocentric occupation of space by several people. This was carried out with reference to Heidegger's sketches for an analytics of being-in in the first volume: "In Dasein there lies an essential tendency towards closeness." Through inhabiting or "inning," the world is de-distanced and opened as a space of being-able-to-be-close. As far as the nature and dynamics of world-opening proximation are concerned, they are scarcely illuminated by Heidegger's somewhat formalistic deliberations. Certainly, nothing seems more self-evident that that a group (in contemporary terms, a simple social system) in space is simply where it is, and that, through the simple fact of its being-here, it refers to the space surrounding it (in contemporary terms, its environment). Nonetheless, the being-here of every group in its place is a matter whose character eludes the cartographers and land registrars as much as the field sociologists. Because human ensembles are by nature self-harboring or uterotechnic units, they never occupy only one sector in a given physical or legal space; rather, it is they that produce the space they inhabit in the first place as their sphere of relationship and animation. Wherever they arrive, wherever they settle, they always bring their ability to create their own particular interior and its mood. Spheropoiesis, atmospheropoiesis and topopoiesis occur in one and the same process. They are the formal aspect of local world-creation, in that they produce the section that constitutes the world. From there, reaching out into the open is possible: "The outside is conquered as the image of the inside; the inside is sacralized as the image of the outside."[10]

By settling, those united in their shared world harbor themselves in a circle belonging to themselves as if in a wall-less hothouse, a tent of shape and endogenous sound. It is therefore permissible—even in the case of what seem to be unambiguously established groups—to repeat the bizarre question of where they are when they are where they are. The question attracts fruitful answers to the extent that one succeeds in explaining why the being-inside or being-with-oneself of human ensembles is always infused with a topological ambiguity that places every "here" in relation to an "elsewhere." What does it mean that every seemingly unmistakable, presently valid being-in-there is interfered with by the reference to another inside—a past or future in-there whose presence can never be entirely erased from the current situation? Because interiority always represents itself as a multi-layered state that always also refers to an elsewhere, any talk of being-in-here implicitly refers to the fundamental topological difference that cannot be suppressed by clinging to an immediate or primitive present. Wherever humans exist, their own place refers automatically to other places and positions. With every in-here, there is an inside that was valid elsewhere shining through. Every wall replaces a wall, every interior refers to another interior, and every exit from an interior position brings about other exits.

And it is precisely because this is so that the primitive difference between endosphere and exosphere can become confused from the inside. What Sigmund Freud knew about the uncanny was merely an indication, tainted by psychologizing, of the fundamental pervertibility of the primary spatial difference between the inner-own and the outer-foreign: before all psychology, there is the experience that the inner can occasionally appear foreign, while the outer can seem like the own. Human space-productions must cope with this increase in both difficulty and richness from the outset. An uncanny second inside puts the homely first one in a state of tension, while a promising second outside undermines the meaning of the uncanny first outside. Human spaces are surreal, for the allotopic difference is in effect in each place: we are only as we are here because we, who are always coming from there, have the there with us in the here.

Hence the human being is the animal that, together with its significant others, produces endospheres in almost every situation because it remains shaped by the memory of a different having-been-inside, and by the anticipation of a final being-enclosed. It is the natal and mortal creature that has an interior because it changes its interior. Relocation tensions are in effect in every place where humans exist; that is why their entire history is the history of walls and their metamorphoses.

In the first volume's phenomenology of intimate spheres, I emphasized certain aspects of the original human harboring in a living container—most of all that "retreat in the mother" which imprints the lasting primal scene of being contained in a supportive round cave upon every life that comes into existence. It is from this matrix that most later demands for containers stem—as well as the great container phobias, without which Modern Age individuals cannot say what they want when they declare that they want freedom, with no further epithet. One can define the age of classical metaphysics as that in which the motif of self-harboring in a favorable totality far outweighed that of self-liberation, while modernity is characterized by the precedence of the liberating tendency over the cave need, and through the pull to transcend horizons. Antiquity and modernity differ in their radically opposing insulation procedures.

The shaping of humans through the experience of their immanence in a supportive living shell is undoubtedly the starting point of the evolutionary line. In psychogenetic terms, the space-creating desire of humans for harboring in supportive containers develops from this primordial spatial experience: the intrauterine double life, along with its continuation in the postnatal mother-child field, provides the model for all expansions of the integral situation. It acts as director in later new productions of the space that is meant to grant its inhabitants presence with themselves. (Such self-presence is therefore not a discourse-supported illusion of immediate private inwardness, but rather the primitive ecstasy of being-there-in-the-shared-space.) Being inside is here experienced as being alive within surrounding aliveness. What lies inside in such a way spontaneously makes sure of the advantage of being where it is, as it is affirmed in its own life by the surrounding life. Thus the experience of the first container situation is tied to early evidence of being genuinely harbored in correspondences with the co-living.

The favorable sense of being inside—I shall speak later of infernal inwardness—reveals itself in the light of the first dual aliveness, whose structure is the key to the primary human scene and its inexhaustible translations into all registers of intersubjective resonance. The original encirclement—the floating of the fetus in a containing and contained internal sea—presents all later social geometry or political geography with the formal task of repeating the basic structure of the retreat in the mother with the means of publicized life. The *contentum* can only exist in the *continens*, the satisfied encompassed only in the foundation-providing encompassing, and the well-delivered only in the open container.

What socialized humans initially demand of the others in their lifeworlds, therefore, is quite simply that they join forces in a way that allows them once more to fulfill the first concept of the living space: the living in a ring of the living. One could say that in their simplest modules, social groups are amniotic communes—ensembles capable of enacting the role of the existentially necessary living border for their members. Just as the amnion, as the first uterus-immanent wall, makes the vascular function of the amniotic sac possible for the fetus and its placental twin, so too the sum of cohabitant others in primitive human groups must be able to fulfill the function of a vessel for the individuals and their closest partners. In the earliest evolution of these vessel relationships, however, ceramic, textile or architectural tools are all out of the question; initially, it is almost exclusively the group members themselves who encircle one another, as it were, through more or less chronic physical presence. By constituting the adequately present surroundings of every single group member, they fulfill the basic container imperative: form the shared sphere in such a way that the maxim of being together can at all times be understood as the call to surround the living with other living things.

In the wake of the magnetopathic arts in the eighteenth and nineteenth centuries, psychoanalysis at least realized a partial view by seeking to make the healing of the isolated psyche contingent on artificially staged love affairs. Such affairs are, in a sense, experiments concerning the regression to the wall-less integrity of the primary liaison. What psychoanalysis initially failed to recognize is that what is reactivated in "transference" is

Group Therapy in Pune, 1977

not so much relationship patterns as spatial relationships; not merely individual twistings of the desire for love, but more significantly ways to form a joint primary space with the other. This was identified by Béla Grunberger with his theory of the monad and Otto Rank with his doctrine of the therapeutic situation.

Virtually all group therapy practices—far more manifestly than the face to face situation of individual therapy—testify to the unexhausted power of the oldest model of coexistence: life surrounded by life. Assuming a therapy group does not go completely off course, each new attempt reveals the inclinations and aptitudes of the participants to flourish in conspiratorial euphorias; in this manner they experience the autogenous vessel and, by taking part in a spontaneous spheropoiesis, also experience how the regulating tonic function of the inclusive form makes its presence felt among the members of the field.

To the extent that human groups are self-harboring units, then, they form "circles" around and out of themselves at all quantitative levels. Each "circle" highlights an inside from the outside. Such constructs inevitably possess uteromimetic qualities, as they must enable the self-harboring or self-mothering trait of primitive group formations to come to the fore; it is in them that one must recognize the original socio-poietic process. But more complex, layered societies also tend to stage an order in their hierarchies where the rulers, at least in the imaginary social dimension, present themselves as shells enclosing the people; in his studies on the Indian caste system, Louis Dumont defined the essence of hierarchy classically as the capacity of a relationship pole to encompass its opposite: *englobement du contraire*.[11] The coherence of class societies comes not only from the results of direct and structural force, but also through the binding effects of the morphological unconscious, which embodies itself in the relationship between the encompassing and the encompassed (*englobant-englobé*).

Every organic group is thus a living metaphor for the form-demanding wish to exist in a shared inside. Because groups and peoples, whether traditional or modern, are automatically socio-uterine configurations, every cultural unity rests on a mor-phological constitution that has codified the basic right to shape-like harboring—a right to dwell in the form that is older than any codified charter of gods or humans. Indeed, both humans and gods are probably derived from the experience of the harboring form. The gods are the twins for all, while all are the fetal membrane for everyone.[12]

The group's being-in-form, and that of its individuals, thus derives from primal-scene patterns of integral internal situations.[13]

Child psychologists have provided a wealth of evidence to show that in their "extrauterine early year," newborn children can only begin a promising path into life if they are given the chance to continue enacting the familiar scenes of being-inside with their mothers, in a modified form, in their new outside situation. Alfred Tomatis encapsulated this motif—the inclination of humans, almost to the extent of a natural law, to harbor themselves in metamorphoses of the uterine circle—with his unique and instructive ability to exaggerate:

> The mother remains this expanded uterus, this face that later becomes a hut, an igloo, a house, even the universe. We are always surrounded by walls. We never truly leave the uterus, though it expands in the course of our lives, taking on other forms and proportions.[14]

Leaving aside the matriarchal idealism of Tomatis' system, this thesis provokes a far-reaching insight into the transference dynamics of world picture formations. Even if it were incorrect, one would still have to be grateful for its generous hyperbole. What we call a world picture is in fact unimaginable without an explicit wall and border function, and without the constant readjustment of the edges to match enlarged spaces of experience. Each new world volume requires a new border and a suitable wall thickness. Thus each concept of totality answers, manifestly or latently, the question of how the inhabitants of this whole go about harboring themselves in the inside of a sufficiently expanded and secured world vessel. To the extent that existence [*Dasein*] demands to be interpreted as being-there-inside [*Innen-da-Sein*], it always also means dwelling behind walls and borders.

Making the border of the whole explicitly visible and palpable is therefore a primary function of the "world picture." For what but the highlighted line of encompassment that marks off the outermost can tell the observer that they are genuinely looking at an "image" of the universe? As soon as a manifest periphery is presented, however, the dialectic of the boundary comes into play, where stopping at the line has to compete with the impulse to overstep it. Every boundary simultaneously orders us to stop and to continue—even the one that presents itself as the last. For humans, who are naturally destined for threshold experiences in a dual sense, each new border they reach restarts the drama of changing interiors.

Where world pictures naively fulfill their main functions, namely giving an idea of the whole in stabilizing circumscriptions, the outer contour must not be absent from sensory perception; the world picture inevitably includes the view of the world's edge. This is shown more vividly than anywhere else in the description of the oldest work of world picture art that has survived from the early period of European written culture: the famous description of Achilles' shield in Book 18 (lines 474–608) of the *Iliad*.[15] Homer's portrayal of this object of artifice from the workshops of the blacksmith god Hephaestus—the prototype and showpiece of ancient descriptive literature—pays twofold tribute to the morphological imperative of the well-rounded and well-bordered image. Firstly, the world depicted on the shield is composed like a collection of primal scenes, each and every one with its own rounding-off index—for example the first, the image of the sky with the full moon, the tireless sun and the constellation of the Wagon (or Bear), which turns on the spot yet never sinks. There are also the two scenes from the city in peacetime, first with the round dance at a wedding party bringing about an immanent, morphologically round closure of the scene, and then with a legal dispute that is conducted in a form of legal arena:

> The expert elders sat on smooth stone seats in a sacred circle; they received in their hands the speaker's staff from the clear-voiced heralds; and the two sides rushed over to them as they each gave judgment in turn. Two talents of gold—one from each side—were displayed in the center: they were the fee for the elder who delivered the soundest judgment. (Book 18, 503–507)[16]

The narrator spells out the whole of this world encompassed by the shield's border in similarly self-rounding scenes: the wartime city with the besieging armies centered around it; the fat fields on which wine-drinking farmers lead their yoked oxen back and forth; the harvest scenes around a king feasting merrily; a vineyard overflowing with grapes, encircled by a ditch of blue steel; a herd of golden and tin cattle surrounded by nine dogs; a round dance of veiled maidens and young boys in finely woven shirts, ringed by an enthralled crowd, and at the center, forming a circle through the power of his voice, stands a divine singer. All these scenic units appear in seamless sequence in Homer's text, as if their succession were meant to expound the thesis that an image is that which constitutes the excerpt in itself.

Every authentic "view" is round and complete in its own right: it is this quality of concision that gives the Greek notion of *eidos* its tension. Whatever is an image in this sense can stand in for the world at any time. Homer has Hephaestus, the primal artist, place the overall frame around this accumulation of individually rounded scenes. This frame does not merely add a *parergon* or embellishment to the main artistic matter, as in the modern panel painting—in the manner demanded by Georg Simmel in his essay on the picture frame, where he stipulates that the frame's function is to testify to the ontological rupture between the work and its environment. To make the work a self-referential island, the frame must lead the viewer's gaze around the picture to "flow back into itself" and exclude it from its milieu with the strongest possible "means of closure."[17] In the case of the Homeric shield, admittedly, the flowing border is not an added frame, but rather presents the replica or the view of the objective world boundary in the picture itself. Oceanus flows around the world on his own strength. When it comes to the image of the world-whole, border and frame are very close to the essence of the object. As the ultimate giver of form, the frame of the world picture on Achilles' shield is inseparably bound to the picture's content. Only it, by closing the picture—or rather, by permitting the picture to close itself—can ensure that the present picture truly constitutes the world picture. Just this once, the excerpt that is the message contains the whole. This totality's ability to be whole in the picture, however, is due to a container energy that is itself a function of the picture.

In the world picture, the extraction of the largest from the surplus space spreads the decisive morphological information: that the relevant world, our world, the world of that which lives, is something that can be viewed in the guise of a final container and an outermost boundary.

> Then, round the very rim of the superbly constructed shield,
> he placed the mighty Ocean Stream. (Book 18, 607–608)[18]

Thus the shield of Achilles presents itself as the first manifestation of the work of art that sets up a world by aggregating the large world from small worlds and encapsulating their sum in an overall form. In this sense, the work of art is the complete realization of the ecumenical idea. Setting up the world in the work occurs through the promise made by the form, namely that the collection and union of the manifold into a whole is possible within a beautiful boundary. It is only with the well-boundedness of the total view that the image is given its full due: this is the basic law of Greek eidetics. Everything that is can only be itself within the favorably clear boundaries of its drawn outline. The outline speaks to the eye about the essence of the matter itself.

It is therefore best for vessels that dispense, shields that protect and world shells that encapsulate to be round in shape; what survives as a whole includes a shape of border that, through its own conclusiveness, affirms the heldness of that which lies within. (Quadrangular forms, especially squares—which predominate in Mesopotamian urban construction, and in Asian and Latin American symbolisms of totality—could also perform this function; in Buddhist mandalas, which use both circles and squares, the square often represents the space, while the circle stands for time. They belong to a stage of thought in which royal circumspection in the kingdom provides the dominant spatial schema, which is why fantasies of the world as a palace and the corresponding forms of palace inwardness are depicted in countless mandalas.[19]) Thus the border of the world picture is more than a formal bracket across non-uniform elements, more than an envelope wrapped indifferently around its contents. The round shape of the shield doubles the panorama of the epic overview of a round totality. All remaining objects narratively evoked elsewhere in Homeric circumspection are mirrored in this construct as if in a poetological focus. Thus the shield, as a succinct imago of the whole, displays the entire universe of the *Iliad* once more, including the singer at the center. The shield is the perfect circle of circles, the ring of rings that is led back into itself.

This encompassing figure has a twofold peculiarity evident in its name—Ocean Stream (Oceanus). First of all, the moderns find it strange that Oceanus stands here not for a sea, but rather a river. As a river name, Oceanus recalls the early centuries of Hellenistic culture, when the Greeks—much like the ancient Near Eastern peoples—apparently imagined the inhabitable land mass of the earth as a disc with a broad stream flowing around it. In the Homeric world picture around 700 BC, as in that of Hecataeus from the late sixth century, the lands of the world float in the circular surrounding river Oceanus. Naturally this primitive cosmogram had to be corrected through the empirical findings of seafarers, military commanders and merchants over the course of subsequent centuries. With definite proof of the Mediterranean's semi-enclosed character and the increasing view onto extra-Mediterranean spatial conditions, the meaning of Oceanus changed from the border river of the human-bearing ecumene to the notion of an outer sea surrounding the entire mainland. This process culminated in the earth map of the polymath and geographer Eratosthenes of Cyrene, director of the Alexandrian library from 246 AD, who positioned the Euro-Asian-North African land masses in an open sea that he called "Atlantic." The Atlantic of Eratosthenes, which he claimed could be circumnavigated, thus extended from Portugal in the West to India in the East, and the Ganges had the honor of leading to this all-encompassing sea postulated by a Greek. One should recall that Alexander the Great had already spoken of sailing around the world on the outer sea, which would have amounted to a first geopolitical globalization.[20]

With the concept of a peripheral sea, ancient cosmography established a semantic reservoir on which modern oceanic ideas could draw—for it was only the Europeans of the Modern Age that understood the oceans as real global seas and world media.[21] This lexical history mirrors the historical shift of emphasis that led potamic spaces and river cultures to fall behind Pontic-oceanic power centers.

What is even more notable about Homer's mention of Oceanus is the reference to conceptions of the world dominated by the Great Mother, for, as an all-encompassing figure, the world boundary river Oceanus has unmistakable amniotic qualities. How else could vascular attributes be assigned to a surrounding body of water? Oceanus may be depicted on a masculine-maritime device, but his energy of form testifies to an older world context defined by the precedence of female motifs; it is characteristic of this context that it is not the solid enclosed by the liquid, but the liquid by the solid. If liquid is to be presented as giving stability, it must be accompanied by a specific container energy—a condition that is only met if the surrounding water possesses amniotic morphological powers. This world boundary thus has elements of that original life-within-life structure which, as I attempted to show above, had to provide the self-harboring of the we-groups in the endo-milieu before all architecture or metallurgy. As long as the outermost wall is imagined as a boundary of water, it absolutely possesses the properties of the living that contains the living. (Vascular reversal: it is not the wall of the jug that makes it possible to pour in

Reconstruction of Eratosthenes' world picture

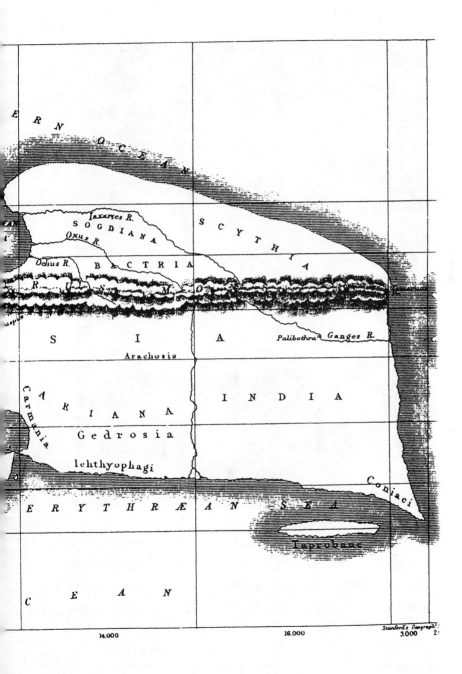

World disc from *On the Properties of Things* by Bartholomaeus Anglicus (15th century)

liquid; rather, because the contents contain themselves, the vessel appears together with and around them.) Here, therefore, wall and border are imagined in terms of the female; being still means being immanent in a Great Mother, in so far as immanence means an inside dwelling despite a change of location. Under these premises, cosmography and uterography can converge.

The schema "immanence despite change" makes memory and imagination possible—indeed, it remains the underlying motif of all great world picture creations in the age of the First Ecumene. Initially, "remembrance" is always merely the experience that our position in this space has been preceded by other positions in other inner worlds. Thus every wall replaces a wall, every interior points to another, every creation of a partition takes up an early harboring idea, and every habitation stems from an older interiority. The greater the dangers of the outside life become, the more the endangered life feels compelled to set up stores in which memories are hoarded as food supplies for times of trial. On the threshold of advanced civilization, humans reached a lucid and almost final definition of what is necessary to survive failed harvests and wrong living conditions: grain and memories of integrity. Storing these two commodities inevitably requires building vessels—granaries in the city center and silos for deities at the center of the soul space—and because each of these commodities is somehow connected to the living principle of the group, the walls of these (built and spoken) vessels that contain such indispensable stores must be guarded with sacred attentiveness.[22]

We note: there is a primary animism of walls and an original division of space in the service of interior-enlivening. To the extent that this principle establishes itself, the interior-producing walls of the community themselves remain living elements, even if they are presented in "dead" material. As long as all significant walls are experienced as native, the building of walls is subject to the primacy of the inside; in this case, the inhabitants—*intramurani*—can move back and forth unimpeded between inside and outside, constantly re-assuring themselves of the advantages of living behind walls of their own. But if the walls become foreign, monumental and impervious to empathy, and only a privileged few succeed in assigning them to an interior of their own, then it becomes necessary to distinguish between walls. The distinction between foreign walls and one's own becomes an elementary function of social reason. Now the walls of the others are experienced as offensive and rebuffing—and they demand a historically new aggressiveness: the longing to prove to the enemy that they cannot even feel safe behind their own walls. This is probably the world-historical prototype of *ressentiment*; creating security advantages for oneself now means making the walls of the others insecure. The prime document of this is the biblical account of how the walls of Jericho were made to crumble by the sound of the Israelites' "trombones" (Joshua 6:1–21). It displays the nomadic people's bitter thirst for revenge on what it experienced, and denounced, as the arrogance of settled territorial lords.

The history of wall-hating peoples remains to be written. In the more advanced civilizations, however, it is not only the enemy walls that can be experienced as foreign and repulsive demonstrations of power. Where hierarchized large societies have established themselves, inevitable processes of estrangement begin—even estrangement from the walls of one's own culture. Estrangement became epidemic in Roman tenements. This was registered by the millionaire-moralist Seneca when he noted in his architecture- and luxury-critical pontifications that "nowadays our own homes count for a large part of our feeling of insecurity." (*Epistulae morales ad Lucilium*, XC, 43) In addition, the loftiness of what is one's own becomes more foreign to many than the lowness of the foreign; hence in many regions of the earth, ordinary people can understand the poor of foreign populations better than their own high-building lords. (An experiential schema that remained current into the trenches of the First World War, and is currently being invoked to set up something resembling a world people's front of globalization losers.) These estrangements from the walls of lords and owners extend to a reversal of the relationship between container and content.

All theories of estrangement are attempts to understand the pre-givenness of repellent outer walls and the purpose of separating inner walls. What is the nature of the wall of the "hut which you did not build"?[23] What theory of the wall underpins the motto of bringing war to the palaces and peace to the huts? Such questions are a response to the increasing acuteness of an architectural difference in class-based society. Only under conditions of great inequality—defined in Marxist tradition as class societies—is it a frequent occurrence for the life of losers to be forced into a *ressentiment*-dominated inwardness. Now building takes place around it in such a way that most people are estranged from their container environment. Then individuals gradually cease to understand their "own walls" and the community to which they are beholden—the crisis of the house form as world form casts its shadow ahead. Once the previously native walls of encompassment have finally died off completely, enclosed life experiences itself radically as no longer with itself; it no longer feels secure in a power-protected expanse, but rather bottled up in a worldwide hopelessness. ("I am in this samsara like a frog in a waterless well." [*Maitreya Upanishad*]) What now stirs is the metaphysics of a panic-stricken immanence that dreams of breaking out. The dualism of trapped, living immaterial souls and dead material dungeons comes onto the stage of intellectual history—and this opposition, acute since Plato at the latest, exposes a basic Gnostic schema that has assisted Europeans for over two thousand years in the articulation of their reserves against being-in-the-world. In the Modern Age, this reservation about the world broke out of the enclosure of religious and philosophical traditions and spread everywhere in countless profane metamorphoses. One of the last great formulations against the hopeless mundanism of modern economic society came, rather revealingly, from sociology, when Max Weber dared to speak of life's captivity in the "steely shells" of streamlined society formation.[24]

Where the matristic animation of the outermost boundary no longer succeeds, as in large-scale political structures that have become cluttered, the imagined world-whole potentially and actually becomes a foreign casing or a dungeon. The world boundary is pushed out to the unempathizable and unimaginable due to an overstretching of space. Consequently, the whole loses its shell nature; now the city dwellers' power of spatial animation is no longer sufficient to penetrate to the outermost edges. People feel under siege from a non-animable, cold outside, and the outer boundary could only be portrayed as productive and advantageous through greater additional efforts by the imagination.

Additional effort: it is only from this perspective that ancient European shell cosmologies, which shall be examined more closely in the following, can be grasped in world picture-economic terms. They are attempts to defend a no longer animable whole-form as a domestic structure despite its monstrously overstretched transcendence. I will reveal—by interpreting the cosmic spheres as the house walls of being—the basis of the intellectual-historically overpowering architectural and thought figure of the house.[25] For the last two and a half millennia, the house has been humanity's most important spatial idea, as it represents the most powerful transitional form between the original human mode of being, namely in wall-less self-harborings, and the modern stay in soulless casings. The history of advanced civilizations was inevitably also the history of house building, as no advanced civilization could have solved its self-harboring problems without the semi-animism of the house. For what are advanced cultures but endeavors to force the impossible equation of house and cosmos against the evidence of imperial estrangement?

People in advanced-civilized times used their own houses to train the ability to animate walls made of dead material. No cities or kingdoms could have been built if the experience of the animated wall had not been easy to call up at any time. City dwellers and citizens of the realm are the classic representatives of a type of person with the precarious psychopolitical ability to think of themselves as unified behind breathing walls, even on a large scale. Such notions of unification assume that the political collective can draw on the idea that the distant boundary walls, ditches and fortifications around them are filled with an unmistakably native, people-specific life. But how do the citizens of fortified cities learn to defend the walls like their own skin? How can the citizens of a state come to view it as their own body? How does the skin of the state become politically ticklish?

The first thinkers of building were already aware of the difficulty of grasping the transition from houseless and wall-less to housed and walled life forms: this is shown by the reflections on the origins of house building at the start of Vitruvius' treatise *On Architecture*. Vitruvius claims, both boldly and plausibly, that untamed fire is the starting point of human gatherings, and that the cultivation of fire was the stimulus for the architectural practice of humans. In an adventurous speculation on the prehistory

Aboriginal Australians: informal gathering in the thermosphere

of humanity, the mentor of ancient European architects portrays the nurturing of hearths, the birth of language and the building of huts as following directly from one another.

1. As was usual in ancient times, men were born like wild animals in the forests, caves and woods [...]. Somewhere or other in that period, the trees grew together densely, and, being tossed about by storms and gales, burst into flames when their branches rubbed together; those who lived in the area were terrified by the raging flames and ran away. Then, after the fire had died down, they moved closer and, when they noticed that being near the heat of the fire was very beneficial for their bodies, they threw wood on it and kept it going; then they called the others over and, showing it to them with sign language,

made clear the advantages it provided them with. In such gatherings, when sounds with many different meanings were emitted when they uttered, men began to form words as they happened to arise through daily use; then by indicating frequently the things they used, they began to talk in a haphazard way and so generated a common language.

2. So when the initial impetus for men's social gatherings, for their contacts and communal life, occurred because of the discovery of fire, and more and more of them assembled in one place [...] it was then that some of them from these first groups began to make shelters of foliage, others to dig caves at the foot of mountains, and yet others to build refuges of mud and branches in which to shelter in imitation of the nests of swallows and their way of building. Next, by observing each other's shelters and incorporating the innovations of others in their own thinking about them, they built better kinds of huts day by day. [...]

7. Then, growing in self-confidence and looking forward with greater ambition on the basis of the variety of the arts, they began to construct houses, rather than huts, with foundations and walls built of brick or stone and roofed with timberwork and tiles [...].[26]

The vital point of Vitruvius' speculations is obvious: building follows a centripetal force that first causes humans to come together, and then results in the necessity of accommodating those who have gathered. At the heart of human gatherings lies a coincidentally discovered and subsequently indispensable convenience, a *magna commoditas*, that demanded to be augmented by a second comfort: the house. Fire pampers humans and makes

Theodor de Bry, *The Towne of Pomeiooc*, engraving based on a watercolor painting by John White from 1585

them dependent on forms of relief; thus civilization could begin as a history of pampering—and a battle for access to the scarce means of pampering. All other pampering and relieving measures, both domestic and urban, followed the first great convenience of the open fire. It is the warmth of the tamed fire that draws people together in a gathering place, as if around a focal point. It would cost no effort to develop Vitruvius' laconic ideas further into a sociology of the hearth, which would identify the first motives of group formation in a doubly irresistible convenience: the soothing thermal radiation itself and the pleasant human conversation about this pleasantness. Vitruvius highlights the decisive point very clearly: the first humans to enjoy that warmth called the next over, then communicated with them in gestures and primitive words about the benefits of the new-found, wondrous central force.

An incipient thermal socialism, then, a primal gathering around a nurtured fire, a ring of people around what would later (with the addition of pots and cauldrons) be called a hearth—and simultaneously the paradigmatic experience that the radiated warmth spreads evenly in all directions around the center of the embers, meaning that those gathered would never come into conflict as rivals for this beautiful *commoditas* as long as they only formed a *single* ring around the fire. If all benefit from the radiation, it means direct solidarity. If someone joins the group, it is in such a way that space is made for them in the ring. If the egalitarian ring becomes so large that no one profits anymore, the magic fades and all become equal in frosty discontent. As soon as candidates for warmth have to wait in line, however, thermal class society is born.

The hut building to which Vitruvius refers begins as a second harboring that augments the first, which is the experience of a shared capacity to be contained in the generous sphere of warmth.[27] It goes without saying that this hearth-like interior itself has implicit uteromimetic qualities, in that the gathering warmth brings those standing close together into a supportive internal situation. Consequently, the architectural conversion of

Mongolian felt hut, from Peter Simon Pallas, *Collection of Historical Information on the Mongolian Peoples* (1776)

this inside would be no more than the material execution of a socio-thermal harboring imperative that is already in effect. Solidarity means sharing the same fire, then later sharing meals while they are still warm, and finally the communization of cooked or fried meat in the large, religiously motivated festivals of redistribution. This corresponds to the almost universal ethnological finding that in early societies, sharing present goods acted as a universal insurance technique against need (the loss of solidarity only came with the advent of reserves). According to Vitruvius, what applied to private buildings in the eyes of the Greeks and Romans also applied to society as a whole: the hearth is older than the house, and a house is above all a converted fireplace. One of the most important acts of humanization takes place at the hearth, as the primal experience of alimentary alchemy—cookery—develops here in the interaction between vessel and fire. Human vessels and cooking vessels form a material rhyme around the hearth. I have shown in a different context why, in addition, the house always had to be a residence for spirits of closeness.[28]

How far the public space of ancient European cities had to be designed according to the model of the hearth is demonstrated by the Greek institution of the Prytaneum, which served both to guard the city's fire and to provide a gathering place for political banquets—civil Eucharistic feasts, one might say. Aristotle made it clear that good city life included shared meals (*Republic*, 1329b, 39ff.); this is where the archaic (protein) redistribution festivals live on under urban auspices. Only at the city hearth, consecrated to the goddess Hestia, could the solidarity-providing primary combination of domesticity and statehood be staged in a manifestly convincing manner.

The most impressive materialization of these basic thermopolitical conditions, however, appears in the shape of the Roman state hearth on the Forum Romanum. For the Romans, the shrine of the hearth goddess Vesta was undoubtedly the center of their *res publica*. Through the sacred fire guarded in her temple, the Romans secured their indispensable equation of house and empire. Whoever desired the happiness of one had to have the prosperity of the other in mind; tending the ever-burning fire implicitly meant looking after the state soul. Without the gathering-power of the sacred *commoditas* in the heart of the public space, political *coetus*—the gathering of many around the shared center—could never have taken place.

Ruins of the temple of Vesta at the Forum Romanum

It was not without reason that the Roman state ritual placed the temple of Vesta at the geometric and symbolic center of the city, the empire and the cosmos. Guarding the fire was deemed the most important sacred duty in the system of Roman worship. Thus the maidenhood of the vestal virgins, who were given the responsibility of tending the state hearth, could become a matter of state interest; public convention saw to it that these young aristocratic servants of the sacred fire (whose number, six, supposedly recalls the unification of six noble families to form the original city), lived in a chaste barracks directly next to the shrine and the Forum Romanum, shielded from any compromising temptations. The untouched vestal virgins guaranteed the aura of utmost intactness, without which the gathering of citizens around the immaculate central hearth would have been unthinkable and unguardable. The priestesses of divine domesticity had to be equipped with extraordinary salvific privileges: if a criminal condemned to death passed a vestal virgin on the way to his execution, he was immediately set free.

The miracle of immunity testifies to the whole-making radiation of the first fire. Because the empire is morphologically dependent on the house, and because imperiality must define itself as the continuation of domesticity by other means, it is imperative that the house's source of warmth, the hearth, also permeates the public world to its limits, however remote these may be. A harboring radiation emanates from the state hearth, warming the Roman-tinged cosmos like a political mother fire. Spengler rightly noted: "The Roman Imperium was nothing but the last and greatest Classical city-state standing on foundations of a colossal synœcism."[29] The motif of synœcism, the decision to live together, means orientation towards a collectively binding central fire; one can view it as the first effort in Roman reflections on power to approach the principle of radiocracy.[30] Even when the Christian cult began to enjoy the emperor's open patronage under Constantine, it would still have been unimaginable to replace the eternal fire at the heart of the forum and replace it with Christian memorial candles, even if its flames were heathen ones.

After all that has been touched on here regarding the political morphology of the circle, it is virtually self-evident that the building which housed the state hearth, the *aedes Vestae*, had to be a round temple. The imaginary aspect of the empire demands a centering inclusivity that extends to the enlivened outer boundaries, as if thermotechnics were the center of politics. It already contains the entire social synthesis—focal politics, inclusion politics, womb politics, immunity politics and form politics. It bespeaks the dramaturgical and cosmological awareness of the Romans that they extinguished the fire in the state hearth for one night every year, ceremonially relighting it on the first day of the new year. This political-religious heat break allowed them to experience the empire and the cosmos holding their breath in a cultically controlled regenerative crisis. As long as there were such regenerations, the empire would not expire.

It is even more telling when the Romans' sacred fire was extinguished once and for all: this event, absolutely unimaginable to the ancients, took place in the aftermath of the conservative rebellion of Flavius Eugenius, who had rebelled against the Byzantine dictates after Christianity was declared the sole state religion and pagan cults outlawed in the year 391. After defeating Eugenius in 394, Theodosius I felt he had cause to attack the relics of paganism with a severity that had been unimaginable until then, and decreed that the state fire be snuffed out. Only then did it become clear to all what the shifting of the main Roman power eastwards meant in religion-political terms. The symbolic destruction of ancient Rome through the quenching of the state hearth was only possible, however, because the empire, particularly in its new headquarters, the Second Rome, had found a different integrative principle and an alternative symbol of social synthesis in the religion of Christ. And indeed, for over a millennium, the Christian *lux perpetua* proved eminently suitable to replace the sacred fire of ancient Rome.

Against this background, one understands why the theologically precarious new Caesar cult, which was launched shortly after the dictator's murder by parts of the Senate and a "people's movement" led by Octavian, had to establish itself in the most prominent place on the Forum Romanum, and why the temple of Caesar—a cult center of empire-age imperial theology—could be erected directly opposite the venerable temple of Vesta. Without proximity to the *feu sacré*, the Caesarean cause could not develop any radiance. Because of her function, the goddess of the state hearth, Vesta, also entertained solidarity with the spirits of private households, the Penates. As gods of the stores (*penus*), they had protective functions for a narrow familial area of life, and were usually venerated at domestic fireplaces.[31] The religion-political ingenuity of the Vesta cult is abundantly clear: through the liaison between the heat source that is sufficient for all with the spirits of the reserves that are not enough for all, the inevitably de-solidarizing effects of housekeeping-oriented thought can at least be kept in check at the imaginary level. The rest must be taken care of through public offerings.

Because the *res publica* was also considered the shared house of the Roman people, however, the collective gods known as Penates,

Round village of the Kraho, central Brazil

di penates populi romani, had to be honored at the state hearth in Vesta's temple in addition as the protective spirits of all Roman citizens. In this way, the heat-radiating state hearth and the space-enlivening spirits of the individual houses joined their sphere-forming potencies to establish a dominant focus, both on the large and the small scale.

It is evident that all cult politics in imperial Rome was indeed the elevation of domestic animism by public means, not least in the fact that from Augustus onwards, the altars of the Lares or protective spirits at crossings (*compita*) were also used for the cult of the emperor's genius. This cult idea rested on the notion that the house spirits accompanied their wards from their own four walls to the streets and crossings, and from there onwards to the inhabited world, which was henceforth animated and secured by none other than Caesar himself. Imperial rule was thus able to combine itself with the domestic imaginary world of each individual Roman. The Roman imperial cult anticipated later Christian psychopolitics, which likewise wanted it to be easy for the God who created heaven and earth to follow each individual soul into its quiet room, or on its longest journey. The secret of monotheism's success (and that of summotheism, which played into its hands) is plain to see: whoever wishes to rule must expand the house into a cosmos and describe the universe as a mansion. That is what the powerful and the wise had in common from the old days of the Stoics onwards: they learned to act as if they could be at home anywhere—or at least that they could summon the world to their home, to eternal Rome.

Vitruvius' intimations regarding the birth of society from gathering around the fire cannot only be read as remarks on the special Roman path to the minimally solidary large-scale state. They contain a valid intuition into the essence of pre-architectural motives for human assembly and their projection into built forms. Yet even where there is no explicit reference to a heat source, societies can find a formal crutch in cultic centering. Using the Brazilian Bororo people as an example, Claude Lévi-Strauss pointed out the identity-providing power of round village structures. The Bororo, a matrilineal indigenous people in the flat wetlands of the Pantanal, lived in cartwheel-shaped settlements with the Great Men's House at the center. This was where the tribe's adult males spent most of their time smoking, chatting, sleeping, adorning themselves with feathers, reciting holy songs and producing sacred instruments. Women were strictly forbidden from entering the men's house, and any girls who came too close to it could easily find themselves being captured and raped by the entire group.

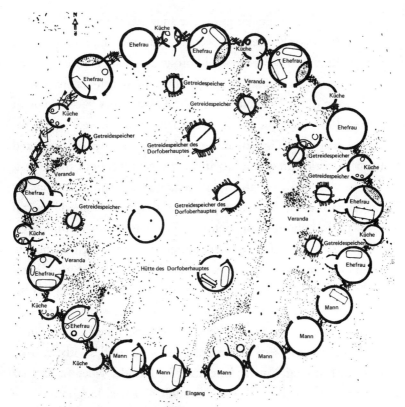

Cameroonian round village, contemporary

That these primitive village societies concealed a morphological secret became clear to the missionaries who vainly attempted for a long time to convert the Bororo. These Salesian monks, who had been sent to proselytize among the indigenous Brazilian peoples, gradually became aware of a connection between the village structures and the inhabitants' psychological resistance to external influences. The round shapes of the villages were the immune systems of this culture, as it were, and as long as the Bororo were able to hold on to their traditional settlement forms, they succeeded in blocking out the suggestions of the European priests. It was only after they were forced to settle in long-shaped villages that their immune shield broke apart, after which they let in the Christian influence.[32] Whether one considers the Christianization of the indigenous peoples a civilizatory necessity or an imperial injustice, the events described can be viewed as a sociological experiment in which the immune properties of a centered form of world interpretation and settlement were put to the test. The result seems to confirm the missionaries' assumption that for the inhabitants, the round village shape contained central information about their identity. To put it in our terminology, the village's round shape actualized collective self-harboring behind a morphological wall. The destruction of this basal endogenous integrity structure made the Bororo receptive to the offer of a different salvific potency announced by the priests. If the circle no longer saves, perhaps the proclaimed Christ can.[33]

Similar round settlements have, among countless others, been identified among Native Americans in Florida, where a circular swarm of round huts is spread around a central longhouse. The whole village endosphere is in turn enclosed by a ring of log stakes with a single corridor-like opening. Existence in such villages must have resembled a constant exercise in centering and orientation.

Analogous building forms from America, Africa, ancient Europe and the Near East show that the construction of round villages and round huts was a motif resembling an elemental idea that spontaneously appeared everywhere. Remains of primitive round houses were even found in very early layers of the ancient Palestinian city of Jericho. In Europe, irregular agglomerations of small, densely packed oval huts have survived from the Neolithic Age, for example in San Giovenale, near Rome, or on the Aeolian

Reconstruction of the Chinese village Banpo from the early period of Yangshao Culture (4800–3600 BC)

island Filicudi.[34] Circular villages have been found in present-day Cameroon whose perimeter consists of larger and smaller men's and women's round huts. These edifices too display a twofold realization of spheric space production. It would be natural to take the inhabitants of such settlements—regardless of their specific religious notions—for geometric animists. The animistic qualities, admittedly, come less from the geometric structure of the buildings as such than from the spherological imperative that the original group structures obey without exception.

All arts of living in the primary units stem from the necessity of forming the group as the autogenous vessel whose content contains itself. The phenomenon of solidarity, as a primal gathering around a microclimatic advantage that can only be perceived from the inside, keeps its morphological secret to the end.

Joseph-François Lafitau, depiction of Iroquois funeral ceremony with a round grave (1753)

Giacomo Leopardi, however, showed in his dialogue *The Copernicus* that this applies not only to the small focal units, but to humanity as a whole, in so far as it is united in latent solar socialism. The poet attributes the Copernican revolution to a decision by the sun to have a rest instead of continuing to circle an arrogant grain of sand called "earth." With the sun's retirement, the conditions of solidarity between the mortals fundamentally change, for they must now realize more than ever that if they could not gain access to the surpluses offered by the sun in the

Women's house in Ghana

new regime, they would be condemned to freeze to death. The sun, for its part, makes no secret of being far from a humanist:

> "Why should I care? Am I, by any chance, the wet nurse of the human race, or the chef who must prepare and cook their food? And why should I care if a few invisible little creatures, millions of miles away, can't see and can't stand the cold without my light? And then, if I must also serve, so to speak, as a heater or a fireplace for this human family, it's only reasonable that if the family wants to warm themselves, they should come to the fireplace, and not that the fireplace should go running around the house. So, if the earth needs my presence, let her go moving around herself and do everything possible to get it."[35]

George Rodger, *The First Meeting of the National Party* (Naples, 1943)

Humans are thus given the task of seeing to their own place by the sun. Who can deny that all political approaches of the Modern Age exhibit the difficulty of gathering humanity, the over-numerous solar family, around that eccentric hearth?

CHAPTER 3

Arks, City Walls, World Boundaries, Immune Systems

The Ontology of the Walled Space

> The city is the repetition of the cave by other means.
> — Hans Blumenberg, *Höhlenausgänge*

The form that allows humans to be jointly "inside" in their own place not only provides immunity in a vague metaphorical sense, but can even be the technical condition for salvation and survival: this is the morpho-evangelical meaning of the biblical and extra-biblical flood stories and the accompanying ark fantasies. The ark concept—from the Latin *arca*, "box" (compare to *arcanus*, "closed, secret")—exposes the most spherologically radical spatial idea which humans on the threshold of advanced civilization were able to conceive: that the artificial, sealed inner world can, under certain circumstances, become the only possible environment for its inhabitants. This gave rise to a new kind of project: the notion of a group's self-harboring and self-surrounding in the face of an outside world that has become impossible.

The ark is the autonomous, absolute, context-free house, the building with no neighborhood; it embodies the negation of the environment by the artificial construct in exemplary fashion. It provides the surreal spatial schema of the autogenous vessel with its first technical implementation, even if it was only a technology of the imaginary. The episode with Noah's Ark in the Old Testament reveals how house building can lead to deliverance from the wet evil. Because the absolute house, if it were constructible, would have to be a free-floating building, it would have to dissolve the relative house's bond with the ground and the neighborhood. A building can only be absolute by completely decontextualizing itself and clinging neither to landscapes nor adjoining edifices. It could only possess the ground that formed part of itself—it would have a keel, not a cellar, and a navigation system rather than a foundation. (One notices that the biblical ark, the paradigmatic ship in the history of human natural disasters, seems to have lacked any means of steering, as if ships whose construction has been decreed by God have no need of a bridge; this would make the ark not so much a ship as an oversized raft.)

Read from this angle, the biblical tale of Noah's Ark reproduces the first de-founding experiment. In its own way it would be unsurpassable, were it not for the fact that numerous extra-biblical, extra-European cultures are equally familiar with the motivic alliance of a flood and successfully floating endospheres. The realization that the outer floor can be withdrawn, and must be replaced with a floating inner world's own floor, has been expressed in manifold mythological forms across the human race. Clearly the idea of de-founding and the repetition of the ground in the endo-foundation is as old as the flood, which probably constitutes the most important shared memory trace in world cultures. Ark building was the start of constructivism. (In phenomenologist manner, Edmund Husserl had evidently "bracketed" the possibility of floods, even regular seafaring, when he formulated his late theorem of the "primal ark" [*Ur-Arche*], whereby the natural attitude in the lifeworld is earthbound.) Discovering the possibility of retreating to a dense inside is not a European privilege. As one example among many, I shall quote a genesis myth that was common among the peoples living around the Gulf of Tonkin:

> The first humans were very imperfect creatures. Their heels pointed forwards when they walked, and they were misshapen in other ways too. They knew nothing of fire, lived in grottos, lived off plants and meat, and mingled with one another without any form of regulations.
>
> Pangu took pity on their miserable state and asked heaven to destroy them. God sent him a seed, borne by a swallow, and Pangu planted it. The plant that grew from it bore fruit in the form of a pumpkin as large as a house. Pangu had barely entered it with his sister before a flood broke out, lasting three days and three nights, that destroyed all people, animals and plants. The warm waters sank once more, and the pumpkin landed on the Kunlun Mountains. As they found no humans anywhere on earth, they put aside their reservations and married. After three months his sister gave birth to a bloody mass of flesh, and Pangu wanted to cut it into 360 pieces. He made a mistake, however, and only 359 resulted. The last piece was therefore augmented by a leaf stuck to the flesh. All these pieces grew into people, the ancestors of the families that populate the earth.[1]

In this tale, the pumpkin takes on the function of the absolute house, albeit with the feature—typical of pre-patriarchal and pre-technological conceptions of the world—that the inside posited for itself is imagined more as a growth than an artifact. The South Chinese pumpkin ark constitutes a clear vegetable metamorphosis of the mother's womb. The inexhaustible provocation of the biblical ark myth, on the other hand, was that, for the first time, it completely extracted the endosphere from the old nature and presents it as an entirely artificial construct. In Noah's Ark we already find a mechanical uterus in which life asserted itself against an unmaternal environment. One could see this as an indication that in contrast to the other ancient peoples, Judaism not only learned morally from the incident of the flood—of which it became aware through its Babylonian oppressors in the sixth century BC at the latest— but above all nature-philosophically, theologically and ethnotechically: in truth, after the flood, nature could no longer be viewed without reservations as the universal mother, whether as the sky or the earth. The reference to the flood acts as a cipher for the fact that it is not nature which makes provision for humans in all things; rather, humans are condemned to care for themselves with God's help. Thus begins history as a technological time; the true time of humans should be counted not from creation, but from "the sinking of the water."

The building of the ark brought about a clean break with matristic illusionism; as a result, humans—having drawn the full conclusions from this myth—would face nature as ontological adults. In the floating house, nature no longer harbors humans— not even seemingly. Rather, it is humans who must invite the animal natures into their saving enclosure if those are to survive. In pairs capable of reproduction, Noah's Ark harbors the wealth of the animal kingdom, which will begin a second chain of life after the annihilation of nature by nature.

"Bring out every kind of living creature that is with you—the birds, the animals, and all the creatures that move along the ground—so they can multiply on the earth and be fruitful and increase in number upon it." (Genesis 8:17)

The box posited for itself, *arca*, reflects a relationship with nature in which it can never again be viewed as an unproblematic matrix of human, animal and plant life. In postdiluvian times, nature is given to humans only in second givenness as second nature, whose form must be a different one from the trusting enclosure and custody of humans in concepts of mother-immanence. After the crisis that annihilated all continua, the reliability of nature is given a new contract-shaped foundation through a *treaty* between God and that which lives. The heart of the nature contract is a storm clause, a convention on the future exclusion of the worst:

"I establish my covenant with you: Never again will all life be cut off by the waters of a flood; never again will there be a flood to destroy the earth."

And God said, "This is the sign of the covenant I am making between me and you and every living creature with you, a covenant for all generations to come: I have set my rainbow in the clouds, and it will be the sign of the covenant between me and the earth. (Genesis 9: 11–13)

This can also be read as a letter of resignation: humanity's right of residence in the primal date of the naturally existent is lost for all time and must be given a new, formal foundation; all that was nature will henceforth appear against a revolutionary ethical background. Its religious-legal shape is the *covenant* between God and the post-Noachic human race. This covenant idea indicates that even nature, ostensibly given in pre-linguistic self-evidence, is now only given as a promise, not like an autonomous pre-world or an autonomous matrix of life processes. The Noachic covenant was the first version of a *contrat naturel*—that is, the integration of the natural into a divine-human legal sphere; no monotheism without an anti-flood treaty.[2]

The covenant reveals the formal reason why the ark principle had to continue existing even after Noah, his family and the animal kingdom had exited the physical vehicle. It is not so much a material structure as a symbolic harboring form for rescued life, a casing of hope. It is therefore an act of archeological folly to search for ruins of the real Noachic ark at the cliffs of Ararat or wherever, as if a formal principle could be grasped with a spade. Whoever wants to find the ark must be able to read; one must observe how people reinterpret their disasters as tests, and how theologians wrap theirs in rites and stories. Arks are autopoietic—loosely translated, self-sealing—floats in which the united make use of their immune privilege in the face of unlivable environments.

The tale of Israel's postdiluvian fates turns into the novel about the monotheistic ark's voyages through the vagaries of the ages. It deals unwaveringly with the triangular, heavenly-infernal relationship between Yahwe, Israel and the others. It unfolds as the great narrative of the sinister adventures experienced by the chosen people on their journey through an age in which the empires are always those of the others. In this era, being a Jew means suffering under empires, maneuvering between empires or seeking the patronage of empires, without ever being able or willing to establish an equally powerful empire of their own. The wooden ark of

Noah's Ark, 14th-century miniature, Flanders

Noah, augmented by the rainbow-sealed first covenant, might have landed somewhere after the flood—if it had actually taken place—and would then have been abandoned by its crew as a tool that was no longer required. As an ethnopoietic formal idea, however, a covenant-theological immunity principle, the ark remained indispensable to Judaism. To disembark from such a harboring vehicle would have amounted to self-destruction.

The Noachic vehicle therefore had to continue its rescue voyage—initially as Abraham's Ark, for which a covenant of chosenness was put into effect between God and the circumcised peoples. In post-Egyptian times, it set off again as Moses' Ark—now manned exclusively by the Exodus people of Israel, who had ended the table fellowship with the other peoples and drifted through the ages in the dream shell provided by their awareness of chosenness. Aboard this ark, beyond circumcision, honoring the Sabbath and observing laws had become the decisive symbols of the covenant. After the apocalyptic crisis of Judaism, it was rebuilt into Christ's Ark, which is how the early Catholic Church viewed itself—made visible to the world in the host and the cross. In this ecclesiastical refitting, the drunken ship of God seemed to be embarking on a triumphant voyage, almost as a second form of world power alongside the still barely containable imperial monsters. As far as the Jewish community is concerned, it gathered up its splinters in a Talmudic box or text ark, whose capability becomes clear when one realizes that it traversed almost two thousand years in the faith that there was nothing outside the text and its virtually infinite commentary.

In all of these versions, the motif of the absolute house—the text that is its own pretext and context, one could say—wins out in the face of different and variously unfavorable "milieus." To the extent that one succeeds in recounting world history as the report of a singular, chaotic, yet continuous ark voyage, it can be represented as the salvation and catastrophe history of a simultaneously exposed and harbored special people. Such a theology of history must therefore culminate in a theology of survival—or, in harsher terms: a theology of selection. From Isaiah's time onwards, the Jewish name of God was the title for the royal right to appear—without providing any justification—to one's own as a savior and to the others as a terminator. Consistently with this,

Saint Peter steering the ship of the church, Lombardic miniature (c. 1480)

covenant theologies, that is to say foundational discourses aboard the ark, can only really be about sheer survival. When theologians speak of the "law," they mean instructions to survive with God—behavioral regulations in the rescue box comprising text and church. And, in truth, survival in non-supportive environments can only be rehearsed in self-contextualizing boxes. Arks are built and sail on their own successfully when the highest principle of alliance, the absolute pole, is among those on board.

Even the one God's own, however, cannot quite explain how it came to pass that he boarded this particular ship. God's arcana are impenetrable at first, and they remain thus to the end; all that is certain is that God's intentions manifest themselves in his respective ark miracles and the corresponding covenants. With each of these miracles, with each covenant, God repeats anew his abetment in harboring his own from the floods. The fundamentally mysterious aspect of this is divine selectivity, which chooses some and passes over others according to unfathomable rules. This *mysterium iniquitatis* is involved in all ark voyages; for every self-harboring in a strong form, that is to say every settling of a community in an endogenously closed shell (in the Noachic version coated with pitch, Genesis 6:14), not only posits the ship's side absolutely, rejecting any real outside—it also no longer hides the fact that only those who managed to acquire one of the rare boarding cards for the distinguished vehicle can find salvation. In all ark phantasms, the selection of the few is affirmed as a sacred necessity; many are called, but few embark.

For those who feel a moral and logical need to envisage paths to salvation in universalist terms, this involves an almost unbearable restriction that must be removed through inclusivist reformulations of the Gospel; church-building has its attendant obligations. It

Boat people, Vietnamese refugees on the South China Sea, 1975

is seemingly a law of universalist language games, however, that exclusivity in general and inclusivist systems can only be dealt with through denial or, failing that, through rituals of outrage. The growth of universalism is accompanied by the compulsion to feign and make noncommittal demands—a rule of which the Christian religion, along with the trail of aestheticized mentalities resulting from it, was the most important application. Even if it was not full, the boat of the One God only had a limited number of seats—far fewer than the number of salvageable humans.

Nonetheless, the Christian ark sailed through the ages spreading its message on all sides, infused with its inclusivist mission; it never ceases to address humanity, as if it wanted to take aboard all the shipwrecked of all centuries from all corners of the earth. It is only because most were unable or unwilling to accept

Noah's Ark on Mount Ararat as a fireworks machine: festive decoration in Rome for the triumph of Innocent X, 1664

the invitation to rescue that there is still room for new arrivals on the boat that promises salvation in all directions. Only if not everyone can get in does everyone get in; but if everyone can get in, not everyone gets in (an age-old joke among pastors, and the first step taken by systems theory towards set theory.) With its exclusivity dressed up as universalism, the ark of the saved—as a ship of many species, as the chosen people and as the ecclesia—simultaneously represents the first model of what one now calls an internally differentiated subculture. The early Christian church was the prototypical trans-ethnic ensemble whose claim to comprehensive inclusivity was, at the same time, militantly asserted as implacable exclusivity; with its merciless battles over the formulation of dogma, church history offers a spectacle littered with systemic paradoxes. It was only with modern society that these paradoxes were generalized and normalized. The manifold subcultures of modern social systems—whether organizations or private contexts—form colorful fleets of arks on every scale that navigate self-referentially in a flood of environmental complexity that will never sink again. But one no longer sends doves to fly from one's own scene so that they can show with a green twig in their beak that things are simple again outside. Postmodernity abandoned the dream of landing after the flood; now the flood is the land. Where only absolute houses are left, each in its own drift, returning to what was once called land has become impossible.[3]

Even if the ark concept is the most suggestive model for the human turn away from the apparent precedence of the environment, as well as the most convincing metaphor for the self-harboring of a group in its radically artificial independent casing, it is not the ark that came to epitomize constructivist gestures of autonomy, but rather the *city*. The city is, in a sense, the landed ark—it constitutes a survival ship that no longer seeks salvation by drifting freely on the waters of catastrophe, instead anchoring itself obstinately on the earth's surface.[4] One could define cities as compromises between the surrealism of free-floating self-reference and the pragmatism of groundedness. Cities and states developed their triumphant improbability from the merging of these mutually counteractive motifs; they gained their history-making power by combining the two to form a morphological machinery. Harboring oneself in magical concentrations of the will behind one's own walls, as if aboard a ship drunk with willfulness, yet also satisfying the territorial imperative and drawing power from temples, walls and stores: in this spatial formula lies the secret behind the spherological success of the city as a world-historical construction figure. Inwardly, the early city had to compact itself like an ark of God, who marks his own with the sign of preference; outwardly, it had to affirm itself through walls of triumph and towers of rule in order to disperse any doubts about its right to stand here, and to reach out into the expansive from this eminent point.—Only when this sphere formula is fulfilled do Oswald Spengler's theses on the convergences of urban culture and advanced civilization fully apply:

> It is a conclusive fact—yet one hitherto never appreciated—that all great Cultures are town-cultures. Higher man of the Second Age is a *town-tied animal*. Here is the real criterion of "world-history" that differentiates it with utter sharpness from man's history—world-history is the history of civic man. Peoples, states, politics, religion, all arts, and all sciences rest upon one

prime phenomenon of human being, the town. As all thinkers of all Cultures themselves live in the town (even though they may reside bodily in the country), they are perfectly unaware of what a bizarre thing a town is. To feel this we have to put ourselves unreservedly in the place of the wonder-struck primitive who for the first time sees this mass of stone and wood set in the landscape, with its stone-enclosed streets and its stone-paved squares—a casing, truly, of strange form [...].[5]

Spengler's call for thinkers to perceive the strange casing as if for the first time implies the intellectual imposition of choosing a location outside of urban edification, hominess and pampering. This is exactly what previous urbanists and urban historians, numbed by the mental and civilizatory comfort of their object, have almost all failed to do. According to Spengler, one can only understand what cities originally are and want if the city dwellers *par excellence*, the philosophers, stand outside the walls and meditate on the phenomenon of the city as if they did not yet have any share in its harboring and seductive power. First of all, then, thinking the city means reversing the pampering undergone through the city and avoiding being deluded by its self-interpretations. Because the mighty city in particular is always an organizational form of the loss of reality or detached control over materials and signs, city dwellers who do not want to be anything else can never adequately understand their own conditions of possibility and reality.

A morphologist of history like the one imagined by Spengler, observing the city as a fundamentally amazing phenomenon, would have to be a phenomenologist who took upon themselves the blessed fear of a thinking from outside; in this, Spengler was the direct predecessor of such revolutionary structural historians

Hans Hollein, *Aircraft Carrier City in Landscape* (1964), Museum of Modern Art, New York

as Foucault, Deleuze and Guattari. When he suggests imagining a reversion to the amazement of an early human seeing the inconceivable giant casing loom on the horizon with its walls and towers, he is following the intuition that the truth about everything that manifests itself in the outside space can only be learned through an initiatic spatial fear. This fear bridges the gap between the archaic world and modernity, as it testifies to the surplus of ecstasy over security that can never be entirely absorbed. Once this surplus is made fruitful for theory, the field of genuinely modern thought is open. To the extent that Spengler thinks from the position of this surplus or ecstasy—or one could more simply call it insecurity—his allegiance to the adventure of essentially contemporary thought is undeniable. The clarity of vision he displays in his phenomenology of cultures comes from the experience of unsecured existence in an overstretched world that can never again be idealized in its

entirety as a home. Spengler's morphology of world history
draws its philosophical momentum from a theory of creative
spatial fear that allows members of advanced civilizations the
revelation of the third dimension as "depth," meaning as the
space of origin of the inescapable.[6] The cool-headed morphologist and his shadow, which seeks to resemble a perturbed
primordial human, should agree on an amazement that is in
truth a state of near-incredulity, of dismay. And indeed, what
would a city of the same type as the Mesopotamian god-king
metropolises be, viewed with the eyes of a prehistoric human, if
not an explanation of the thesis that in advanced civilizations

the monstrous manifests itself as the work of humans? And what are these casings of the strangest form, viewed from the outside, but harboring-machines whereby people have managed their specific revelation of world-fear and erected monstrous monuments to their will to not-being-outside?

Spengler's backward step outside the city thus has nothing to do with modern civilization critique, nor with the anti-Babylonian *ressentiment* of the Jews, which was copied by the Christians and, since the marginalization of Christianity, has floated about ubiquitously as an anonymous ferment in contemporary cultures that have tired of quality. Rather, it means an act of theory-enabling *epoché* regarding a milieu that can barely be kept at bay any longer, and serves to help the thinking distance themselves from the delusions of the life that has always been lived in cities—along with its unthematized demands of self-aggrandizement, overcoming spatial fear, relief and sensory input. The theory of the city can only begin with a weaning from the pamperings made possible by the city in the first place. Thinking the city thus means reflecting on the pampering habitation inside it as if one could be at home somewhere else—indeed, as if the longing to strike roots at all could be bracketed as a whole. Residing as if one were not residing. Living as if there were neither a house nor a city behind one. Thinking as if in free fall.

What would give a phenomenologist pause who had died to their own seeing habits, and was seeking to re-enact the amazement of primordial humans before the first manifestation of a city, at the sight of an early major power's city such as Uruk, Kish, Babylon or Nineveh? They would probably have to marvel most at the fact that the vision on the horizon stands up to a second glance, asserting itself as something that certainly does not mean to be a hallucination. The unpampered view of the city is taken prisoner by the latter's insistence on towering so high; it is confronted with an emphatic will to appear. Here a height has entered the world whose imposing power has not been heaved here by pre-human forces. Everything about the great city, both the early and the late, is human artifice and masterly willfulness. From the second glance on, the givenness of the city bespeaks that it is made precisely for such glances by nature. Everything about it is intention and effect; everything is meant for the appetites of wide-open eyes. When Dostoyevsky described Saint Petersburg in *Notes from Underground* as "the most abstract and intentional city in the whole round world," he only forgot to add that each of the early great cities was the most abstract and intentional at one point. Even if the books of the Old Testament never tire of mocking the city of Babylon as the great whore, this classification—aside from the tone of moralistic outrage—precisely encapsulates the character of the object. What prostitutes and capital cities have in common is that they are packaged and devoted to visibility; they are exhibited and live off their conspicuity. Anyone wishing to get closer to them will have to pay a price, whether they like it or not. And whoever does not bring zeal of their own and lock themselves inside it to avoid truly setting foot on the city's streets, even within its walls (like Luther in papal Rome), will usually enjoy what urban life has to offer.

The early cities were there to capture gazes, to raise and to humble them. Their uninhibited visibility declared war on the harmless eye and demanded submission to the flashing-up, the defiance and the staying of the sight. The primeval phenomenologist seeking to repeat their first and second upward gazes at the towers and walls of Jericho or Babylon would immediately have to take into account that this city, through its unconcealed standing-here, had disabled their entire previous way of seeing. Only someone who had seen a city such as this could say that they knew the meaning of an appearance. The city—and only the city—shows what it means when a construct relies unreservedly on the opposite of being hidden and plants itself at the center of visibility. From the dawn of the cities onwards, appearance meant erection, ostentation and constant revelation. In Heideggerian terms, city-building is a manner of unconcealing.

To be sure, early humans already gathered formative experiences of usually invisible things becoming visible; they knew what happened if the eye was caught unawares by the appearance of a predator, prey or a stranger; equally, they never forgot those moments when they took fright at unusual phenomena in the sky, namely eclipses, comets or falling stars. Grisly prodigies that were suddenly *there*—miscarriages among humans and animals, bloody rain, earthquakes or firestorms—have always demanded to be read as signs of being. But only here, in contrast to the insistently steadfast, irreverent and sublime monstrosity of the universally visible city, do they realize that earlier glances at presences of this kind were mere preliminary exercises for this epochal, revolutionary, inexhaustible instruction by the lasting appearance of urban magnitude.

The city stands there like a building claim to truth, validity and longevity. It seeks to embody an unshakeable being that keeps itself visible in calm magnificence for the second and third glances too; it even wants to remain valid for the final one. This force was transferred from Mesopotamia to the ancient European urban phantasms—to the eschatological city of Jerusalem as much as the Eternal City of Rome. The city does not flash like a

Mural appearance: city wall of Niniveh, restored by the Iraq Antiquities Service

meteor that seeks in vain to capture the eye. Certainly the way in which the city suddenly stands there involves a certain flaring-up, a sublime suddenness; but this flash from below becomes a stationary image, a lasting presence, and however long the eye might stare at the presumptuous mass, it will perceive no flickering in the manifested image, no concession to transience. There is nothing about the splendid, self-imbued existence of these walls that suggests a tendency towards disappearance. What here appears and persists in appearance is the rejection of transience itself. This appearance is replete with the power to remain, and in this will to stay, the phenomenologically illuminated early human has their first experience of a new type of gods.

The city god reveals his nature in the splendidly forbidding walls and towers, in so far as these bring together the constant presence of a power with a constant residence in visibility. This power of walls and towers is pure, stationary Now. Anyone who saw the towers of Uruk and, even earlier, the walls of Jericho, became an eyewitness to a theological revolution. The Mesopotamian royal cities opened a new chapter in the history of revelations; for here God has become wall, and he lives among us to the extent that we dwell in it. Anyone living in such a city inhabits a hypothesis of eternity.

For the outside observer of the city's appearance in particular, this much is certain from the start: whoever lives behind such walls must be not only protected and harbored by them, but also charged and possessed by them. They must have offered their life to these walls—firstly, to erect them; secondly, to desire their continuance; and thirdly, to satisfy their demands of fame and favor. It seems as if one could understand merely by attentive observation of the walls that in the Sumerian religion, humans were genuinely thralls of the city god.[7] The god become wall holds his own tight in his perimeter, waiting through them for distant enemies who must be humbled, visitors who must be deluded, and a constant supply of slave labor that must be used up. Every city of the early, monstrous kind waits for something that comes from afar and leads far, and the principle of its continued existence lies in its power to await the distant and challenge what is even more distant.

Gazing at the "casing of the strangest form," the observer realizes that this proud shell of force holds an inner life which can only be understood in relation to its enclosure. The city desires to stand out so superbly not least because the thought of other cities is alive in it, and because a god inside it longs to raise himself above other gods with the help of his active media, the kings and priests. City souls, like theologies, live off escalations. Every city thus forces out a different one; every urban being-*here* is saturated with a power-laden distance *there* that is co-meant, co-challenged and co-humbled. Without this connection to rival distance and breadth, these walls would not be so high and these towers would not be so threatening. Someone truly facing the looming of an old god-king city with the amazement of primordial humans would also directly see the competition between cities—and also, as the cities are manifestations of people-producing tensions of will, the comparison and competition between ethnic, urban and imperial gods. The heroic city-building of Mesopotamia revealed to humans the fitness of the gods—for what are revelations but proofs of the fitness of higher causes? If the god is the final reason for earthly fitness, then the priests, kings and military leaders are the athletic participants in the trial of strength among transcendent powers.

The city is also a shell phenomenon that aims to persuade observers to believe their eyes, so that they believe what they still do not really see: the flash of empire-theological lightning that struck the mental city center. Let us not forget: with the height of its most eminent buildings, the city gives a sense of its intentions in the horizontal. As soon as a will to power becomes manifest, it characterizes itself by imagining formats. With the early city, an ambitious reformatting of the imaginary began—politically, ethically, geographically and cosmologically. This initiated the rise of the great-soul forms that would one day grow into the highest philosophies and cabbalisms and, in our times, metastasize into problems of globalization. The monstrous

Partial model of Babylon in its state during the 7th century BC, scale 1:500, Bible Lands Museum, Jerusalem (1996)

nature of the ancient Mesopotamian royal city was evident in its confidence that it could set up its entire fortified space as one great animated interior and maintain that shape. This was the technological beginning of the world-soul experiment.

Thus, if the city is meant to be the world, anything less than the wall-becoming of God is inadequate for so ambitious an enterprise. The Mesopotamian gods were the prototypes of a new kind of ontological sovereignty for builders; here, divine power manifested itself as the capacity to erect a political construct with the size of an encompassed city and an enclosed empire as a coherent immune system. From that point on, politics, architecture and theology are merged into a shared macro-immunological project. The large-scale body politic appears as the builder of a world interior. As late as the sixteenth century, Martin Luther would formulate his reformatory battle song "A Mighty Fortress Is Our God" entirely in the tradition of ancient Near Eastern and ancient European mural phantasms of immunity. In this respect, one can view the Mesopotamian city buildings—alongside the Egyptian temple complexes—as the most important laboratories of the rising imperial psychology and theology: more than in any other part of the world, people experimented here over millennia, in ever new arrangements and from ever new centers, with the production of large-scale interiors with their corresponding construction forms, world picture forms, soul forms and immune structures.

All of these experiments were concerned with resolving the city's psychopolitical paradox—searching for the most resolute self-securing of existence in, of all places, the most visible, exposed and provocative form of life. How must one build for the most exposed building to become a "mighty fortress"? What habitus of dwelling will enable such imperial houses to be appropriated by their residents? These questions respond to the fundamental contradiction in the early examples of charismatic rule over cities, for they all relinquished the protection of life offered by inconspicuousness, instead seeking that protection anew in the greatest conspicuousness. In subsequent historical eras, not being noticed would only remain a possibility for the unimportant, an option among nomads, fringe figures and private persons for whom it occasionally remained true that living hidden and living well converge. The important, on the other hand, had to expose themselves and be noticed.

The field of this dangerous conspicuousness would one day be called history: it is no coincidence that early historiography dealt almost exclusively with the vagaries of the conspicuous, all too conspicuous cities and their hinterlands, which were entangled in the fates of the cities as affiliated imperial territories. Through the political behemoths, the intelligence of peoples learned the most suggestive figure of reflection in burgeoning thoughtfulness, which would initially appear as a culture of wisdom proverbs and later as philosophy: the strict, melancholy schema of the rise and decline of powers, for only what stands out can fall down. Where supremacies, arrogances and conspicuities had come and gone, there was an aftermath of cynicism, *ressentiment* and its milder distillate, wisdom. The perception that the past was full of the collapses of the seemingly indestructible led to contemplative thought, which emancipated itself from priestly commitments by pointing beyond the affirmation of current powers; its guiding intuition was reverence for the supremacy of time, which carries away all local manifestations of divine builder power. The ruin romanticism of saturated power and the ruin sarcasm of the surviving victims grew from this in equal measure. Now storytellers in the subsequent cultures could think of claiming that the well of the past was deep—and that because of its depth, in which what has been flows together with what is yet to come, it was important for every present time to keep drawing from it.

> Thus everything in history is transient: the inscription on her temple is, evanescence and decay. [...] Egypt, Persia, Greece, Rome, flit before us like shadows [...].[8]

The essence of the early metropolises remains inaccessible to contemplative retrospection, however, because the miracle of the first towering cities and walled-in interiors cannot be called to mind in retrospective observation, whether spiteful or melancholy. Anyone seeking to understand the ancient city *in actu* must not poke about in its ruins, but rather simulate a situation in which they prophesy it again after the fact. It is not the exanimate, ruined city that makes us think, but rather the one to be built, organized and established—the city as impossibility that is about to become reality. Only here does the macrospherological challenge come to light without which effective city-building would never have taken place. To understand the initial constructive courage and utopian élan that led to the Mesopotamian building excesses, one must therefore attempt above all to understand how the first city lords arrived at their building ideas, and what status in the world they conceived for themselves upon realizing that they could position themselves in towering cities. How could they possibly have thought that they would find harboring in the utmost exposure? What formal imperatives, what guiding phantasms must have informed their actions when they were seized by the sublime illusion of seeking a safe haven in constructs of unprecedented conspicuousness and artificiality? What was the magic not used by the early city lords to bind their helpers to them, in order to entangle them in the project of a shared regal and spatial delirium?

The answer can be found in a threefold reflection. The first part concerns the religion-phenomenological achievements of the city—most of all its interior-creating effect and its role in the reordering of relationships between immanence and transcendence. The second part devotes itself to its monumentalism and its immunological design as a magical polity and uterotechnic extension, while the third considers how to envisage the intimate augmentation of individual citizens' souls through joint city geniuses.[9]

We are shown the first key to the phenomenon of the city by a reflection on the novel relationship between urban power and urban religious structure. What seems to have emerged in the early Mesopotamian cities as the world-historical opening of a continuum of the will to power is based on the revolutionary experience of the capacity to define, through one's own marginal constructions, a world form whose interior has literally grown through power and violence. The builders of Uruk, Niniveh and Babylon were not motivated by dreams without resources when they gave the orders to erect their towers and fortresses; practical experience of a skill with the authorization to radically transform the visible world was already present in them. They already enjoyed the architectural intoxication that employed bricklaying to build the imperial inner world, the ruling cave, anew. The city came about as the project of creating the residence for a settled god—not merely as an isolated throne, but accompanied by the only fitting environment: the cosmos to go with the palace, and the kingdom to go with the god-king. The establishment of a temple, a palace and the accompanying districts for artisans, workers and slaves inside and outside the walls is no less than the realization of a world interior for the present god, a macrosphere in which his god-kingly demand can be fulfilled: being-always-inside-with-oneself—even when giving orders that are to be followed no less than forty-five days' journey away.[10] For the city god to take human form, he must define himself by his wall and reveal himself in it—inwardly as well as outwardly. His sovereign residence in the city is analogous to his ability to cross freely between the territories around it. As well as the Mesopotamian god-kings, the Egyptian princes also presented themselves as living walls around their subjects. In the fourteenth century BC, a pharaoh was addressed in a hymnal tone by a vassal: "You are a sun that rises above me, and an iron wall built for me." At the same time, the heretic king Akhenaten praised the sun-disc Aten, which had been proclaimed the one god, as a "wall of a million cubits."[11] It would seem that the hour of mural theologies had struck in the early empires.

The revealing of the god-king through the wall introduced a new reflection into existence: it allowed observers to witness the appearance of an intelligence that penetratingly recognized this world in its outline. The entire idea of *transparency* probably originated from the entrance of the wall-creating spirit; for undoubtedly, anyone who surveys the built world around them from a wall or cult tower not only enjoys their own circumspection, but also shows their environment and circumstances that they are pervasively seen. First and foremost, every city power must let people see that it is looking around itself; it must ensure everyone knows that it knows everything. It would therefore be mistaken to view the Mesopotamian ziggurats, of which the Babylonian specimen attracted most attention, merely as "observation towers": rather, they were part of a revelation of power before itself. Revelation here means the demonstration of penetrating attentiveness; this would one day lead to the claim that nothing is concealed from the all-knowing God. Until then, however, the rule was this: the wall looks at you, and the tower looks down on you (much later, Napoleon still tried to impress this upon his troops before the Battle of the Pyramids and had little success, as we know—probably because the millennia looking down upon Napoleon's army from the tips of the pyramids belonged to the other side.) Henceforth, no one with power could escape the duty to let others see their own ability to see—for all the millennia that followed. Until the twentieth century, the construction of towers and skyscrapers was considered a characteristic signal of power and far-reaching sight.

To the extent that the clear-sighted god shows himself in the walls, however, he also retreats behind them. The inception of the revealed walls is simultaneous with that of the secret of power, which seems to be inward, locked-up and as inaccessible as a sunken treasure. An inner temple and palace world, dreamed of by the faithful in the atriums and shifted into the distance by walls and gates, begins to flower. The walls multiply, and passing through one gate is certainly not enough to reach the goal. Further walls, additional gates and a reinforced guard move the inner far away and make it difficult to come close, for friend and foe alike. Herodotus recounts in his *Histories* how the hillside fortress of Ecbatana (modern-day Hamadan, Iran), which acted as a summer residence for the Persian Great Kings of Susa, ensconced itself in an over-enthusiastic system of fortification in the seventh century BC:

> [...] the place which is now known as Ecbatana—a huge, impregnable stronghold consisting of concentric circles of defensive walls. This stronghold is designed so that each successive circle is higher than the one below it just by the height of its bastions. [...] There are seven circles altogether, and the innermost one contains the royal palace and the treasuries. The largest of the walls is approximately the same size

as the wall around Athens. The bastions of the outer five circles have all been painted various colors—first white, then black, red, blue, and orange. But as for the bastions of the last two circles, the first are covered in silver and the second in gold. (I, 98)[12]

This caprice, which was only seemingly military in its motivation and dreamed of the inaccessible depth of a royal interior, perfectly illustrates the epochal phenomenological paradox I cited as underlying these cities: security within the most spectacular appearance. The builders of this complex obviously discovered the form of the fortress as an aesthetic offensive force and developed the surplus of pure appearance over military function as a charm to be cultivated; this architectural hubris creates an additional immunity for the heightened, deepened, deferred inside.[13] This explains why some military commanders, like God-seekers, were obsessed with finding happiness by advancing into near-impregnable, multiply walled-in citadels. Often enough, the dreams of looters and mystics move in the same direction; God is where the gold is. And even if God were the non-distant, as His intimates would tirelessly claim in later times, and everything were filled with him, there would always be many arduous steps ahead for those in search of him; in monastic times, when immersion was given a procedural framework, mystics would write itineraries dealing purely with sequences of steps—through, up, inside—via three, seven, nine, fifteen, twenty-five or however many stations, levels or resistances. As late as the sixteenth century, Saint Teresa of Avila would adhere to the late Persian thesis that the highest union of the soul with God possible during one's lifetime was to be attained in the seventh and final chamber of the *castillo interior*.

No religious person on the first level can discern the primal fact of all religion as crypto-architecture and crypto-grammar. Only the walling-in of the god creates his specific secret; only the codification of the divine removes it from public cognizance; and only the competition among the chambers for the deeper internal position results in what claims to be a greater proximity to the god. Hence the crypt must be sought in both the horizontal and the vertical, for "depth" is not a fixed ontological dimension, but rather a measurement range for encryptions and wallings-in. Going inside means penetrating to what lies deeper within—all psychologists and theologians of premodern millennia developed this comparative. For them, being inside *eo ipso* means being further inside than any worldly and superficial individual could initially suspect. Only those who are willing to pass through many antechambers are admitted to an audience in the cella of the divine city. Whoever wishes to proceed further must break codes and walls; for the truth inhabits the "inner human," as the profane human in the deep-set self naturally resides further outside. The ordinary worldling thus cannot reach its own secret, for its psyche, as one now understands, is constructed like an inner Ecbatana—as a series of ditches and walls around an almost unattainable *nunc stans* that is a stationary "we": the interiorized soul and its allied god.

It was only with code-breaking modernity, which found everything out, dug everything up and deciphered everything, that the deep metaphysical space was dissolved and its concealed folds of meaning smoothed out; it placed what was once internal and external into the same surface, the same public disclosedness; it postulated the same level of accessibility for everything that is. Augustine, on the other hand, who was not yet affected by modern smoothings-out of space, could remain coherent with the model

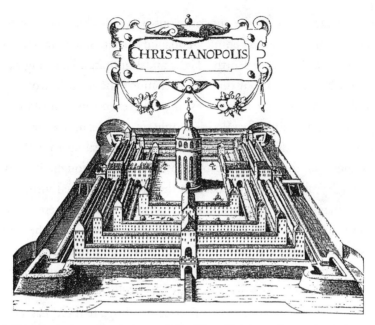

J. Valentin Andreae, frontispiece to *Rei publicae Christianopolitanae descriptio*
(Strasbourg, 1619)

of staggered interiority in describing God as closer to him than
he himself: *interior intimo meo*—the comparative sense of *interior*
is unmistakable in this context. Yet if subjectivity—or, traditionally
put, the human soul—is a complex edifice, or a nested palace
complex where a remote, high and deep god resides, then it is
clear why most individuals only inhabit the forecourts of their
innermost essences, only gaining audiences with their selves in
exceptional states of existence.

One could even go so far as to claim that what monotheistic
religious tradition called faith was a psychological side effect of
Mesopotamian wall-building (and probably also of Egyptian temple architecture). The typical advanced-civilized faith came about

at the same time as the subconscious-occult—which can by its nature only be a place behind an opaque barrier. Since the days of the city-empires between the Tigris and Euphrates, believing has meant being convinced that however much the miracle-working walls might show of themselves, there are even more substantial parts that remain concealed—if only, at first examination, the next wall, which in turn reveals that it is concealing something momentous. Before faith moved mountains, it thought its way through walls and unified itself in the mode of touched intuition with that radiant wisdom which managed to erect these testaments to its power from its invisible innermost cell. Thus the wall itself was already an epiphany; it was the built vision, the obverse of an emanating inside. Anyone receptive to the appearance of the sacred would spontaneously find the sight of it numinous, tremor-inducing and genuflection-demanding. If there has ever been an effect that pointed directly to its cause, it is the stationary wall, which naturally implies the power to build it. Whoever favors the idea that God is something which occasionally deigns to reveal itself as the principle of a presence will get their money's worth before the monumental walls. Being actually present, the wall leaves no doubts as to the reality of the power that built it— an experience, incidentally, that still captivated European archeologists and art historians in the nineteenth century, as for them too, any authorship, not least that of cities buried by rubble, constituted an encounter with the sublime in builderly form.

Mesopotamian wall-building ushered in a religious and psychological regime that pointed to a new, faith-shaped participation in the simultaneously concealed and unconcealed divine: mural presence, transmural transcendence. The presence of God in the symbol of the wall and the otherworldliness of

Heinrich Schliemann with his wife and staff at the Lion Gate of Mycenae

God in a wonderfully remote palace interior. (The corresponding form of enlightenment entails proving that however venerable and massive the wall might purport to be, there is nothing behind it; breaking through if necessary, showing that one finds exactly the same thing behind and in front of it; and exposing hierarchical validity claims from beyond the wall as unfounded.)

Nonetheless, the proof of God's existence was given for ordinary observers wherever and for however long the wall stands. This affected the increase in the rational factor in later conceptions of the world, as God would henceforth be imagined as the builder of all builders and the artisan of all artisans. A lucid producer god of this kind offered people a chance to perceive themselves in a new light; they must have felt that a royal engineer or divine ceramist had also produced them, and that they belonged to him more intimately than to their own mothers. They familiarized themselves with the notion that they ultimately came more from a workshop than a maternal cave.

Perhaps this is where we find the technognostic origin of Near Eastern salvation religions: whoever can produce humans must also know how to repair them. (Mothers, on the other hand, can at best re-swallow their children, which is unconvincing as a form of repair in the long term. If, on the other hand, the gnosis of late antiquity distinguished so passionately between the creator god and the savior, it only showed that being wise customers, humans seeking repairs would not go to the original bungler who had made the physical part of the world, but only where ability and will were still one: the unconditionally otherworldly god who is not compromised by the botched creation.) In the experiential circle of building and forming with clay, those who believed in the god and builder discovered the irresistible cognitive comfort of feeling understood by their producer—and only through this comfort were they able to distance themselves from the irrational astral gods who thirsted for blood sacrifice. The bright engineer-gods gained the upper hand over opaque demons: this was the world-historical achievement of the Mesopotamian building empires.

(Next to Adam, the golem is the foremost thought figure of technical anthropology, as it interprets humans themselves as wholly artificial; it is the emblem of a will to ability that spans the history of human relationships with encountered circumstances.)[14]

Even before the clay man, however, it was the brick city wall that could say to its creator: "Only you understand me fully, Lord, for you made me; through your *savoir-faire* you understand me better than I do myself." The creation idea borrowed from the city wall, with the creation piety implicit in it, is the lesson learned by non-city-building Judaism from its hated oppressors, the Babylonians with city-building power, and generalized during its enslavement, "weeping by the rivers of Babylon," between 586 and 537 BC—the period in which it took "the first step from a tribal to a world religion,"[15] or rather a world-claim religion. As a result, the convergence of making and understanding became plausible for complete worlds too. It was only the experience of building walls and cities that cleared the way to the theology of one god who knows everything because he made everything, and who made everything in order to ontologically outstrip other pretender-manufacturers. Only thus could the element of reverence for the all-capable and all-making god gain significance in Near Eastern, and later occidental, religion. It is this idea of ability, coming from the competition between different imperial gods, that governed the Jewish Genesis narrative redacted in Babylonian times or immediately thereafter. The monotheism of ability had already formed the substance of Mesopotamian city-building, and its dynamic location was the competition between abilities; it was generalized and released in Jewish thought, which went even further.[16] It is faith in a knowing doer whose revealed deed is this city—or, if one does not have a city oneself, then simply the whole world.

As far as the wall that stands there is concerned, it claims truth in the form of overwhelming evidence; whoever surrounds their capital with walls ninety feet thick and forty feet high is in the right. The Yahwist theology of one-upmanship does not stop here: the one who has the last word is the god who commanded the world into existence in the first place. Relying implacably on outdoing others, the authors of Genesis made their lord build the creation day by day in the mode of arranging through commands, with only occasional direct intervention—to make the balance of power quite clear to the Babylonian city and tower lords. Undoubtedly, practicing theology means participating in escalations. In the Near East in particular, where empires and their gods have frequently collided, any talk of God automatically becomes a competition in talking about God.[17] Theology is by necessity a competitive science, as it aims to be the ascertainment of the Highest that invalidates other such ascertainments—if, that is, something ascertainable can be the Highest (a qualification belonging to a later escalation that became known as negative theology). Anyone who reads the Jewish account in Genesis inevitably gains the impression that this god must have won: whoever created in this way is leading the field. But the fact that the god of the Jews took a Babylonian week for his creation of the world has a treacherous implication, for it indicates that while he successfully strives to produce his own universe with all creatures, he yielded to the working rhythm of the hated false gods: he created his world according to the almighty Babylonian calendar scheme. The week is the Babylonian monopoly that thwarted the precedence claims of the later one-upmanship monotheisms. In cultic terms, Jews and Christians remain Eastern septemtheists through their use of the week; ultimately they believe more in the

Cornelis Anthonisz, etching (1547)

seven than the one, and make their pilgrimage four times a month—bored, but absolutely convinced—through the avenue of weekday gods before raising their hats to their Sunday lord.

The architects and builders were consequently the spiritual creators of the archaic city-state—for it is with them that magic was wholly converted into technical expertise for the first time— just as the military fortune of the Babylonian commanders was expected less from the perfectly executed rituals than from a professionally handled war technique. Upon closer inspection, then, the miracle of presumption as which the early, heroically walled cities of Mesopotamia towered before the eyes of our hypothetical primeval human was due to the opposite of a simple arrogance. Thanks to a brick building method developed over millennia, the construction of even the greatest complexes had become entirely routine, cold-blooded and virtuosic in the ancient land of two rivers. Anyone who could build in such a way was obviously capable of achieving great effects without sorcery and merely relying on their profession.

This ability-based calm, however, unleashed an unprecedented exuberance of volition; building expertise continued to dream, and awakened amid theological extravagances. Hence the biblical account of the Babylonian tower-builders' hubris can—despite its marked anti-Babylonian inclination—be considered accurate in its content, as it reflects the theological point of the hated enemy's large-scale building ambitions quite accurately. It is true that a far-reaching theotechnics manifested itself in Mesopotamian tower- and wall-building: it expressed the notion that skilled humans can share in the skill and will of their god. Or more precisely: what their gods were able and willing to do, they were able and willing to do through the humans who are assigned and subordinated to them. This *through* is the central idea of every imperial theology as an autogenic training of power; throughout the entire metaphysical era, the builders, commanders and princes would explain their successes using the schema "It is not I who act, but God who acts through me"—which inevitably also means "He subjects himself to representation by me."[18] (Europeans would have to wait until the fifteenth century for the idea of God's deeds through humans to receive its most precise formulation in the work of Nicholas of Cusa; here archaic mediumism, in which God's agency uses up the entire human being, was given a subtle and subject-ennobling clarification:

possession by the power-giving God would now become a motivated freedom in the absolute.[19]) As far as Mesopotamian conditions are concerned, one had only to look at the great city layouts to understand that the new builders were completely serious about their new technology, and no less so about the accompanying theology. Anyone who builds in such a way abets the appearance of gods.

Naturally the complex of architecture, religious celebration and self-aggrandizement would have struck all outside observers as the epitome of all arrogance, indeed the essence of the unbearable—just as the advanced ability of those possessing competency is always viewed as repulsive hubris by those who are unable to compete. The Babylonian complex of ancient Judaism rubbed itself raw on an indelible humiliation: that the god of Israel, Abraham and Jacob was not leading the field as a builder of cities and towers at that time (or any later one). Should it nonetheless be claimed that he was the One, the Almighty, his followers would have to find a way of outdoing the Babylonian demonstrations by non-city-building means. The Jewish god would subsequently specialize in predicting and awaiting the demise of self-aggrandizing foreign cities—whether by conquest from outside or as a result of construction errors or ecological disasters. Yahwe conceded that the walls were built by misbelievers who looked up to false gods as they worked, but he made it unmistakably clear that their fragility originated from him. A new way of speaking the truth could now be developed: the prophetic exposure of cracks in the walls of the others. This is the essential feature of Judaism's anti-Babylonian theology— *deconstructio perennis*. It proceeds as a prophecy from the crack in the wall—a forecast of the inevitable end of every totalitarian,

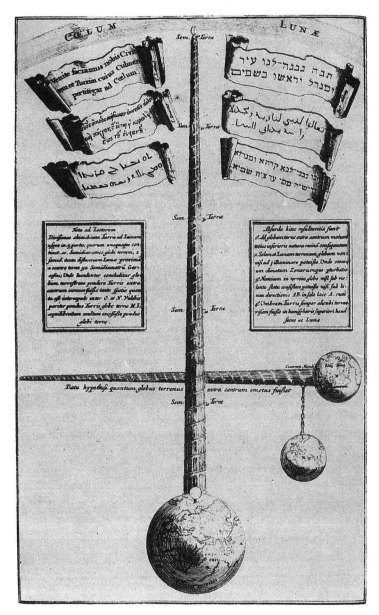

Athanasius Kircher's demonstration of the hypothesis that the tower of Babel cannot have reached the (lunar) firmament due to gravitational conditions, from *Turris Babel sive Archontologia* (1679)

yet fallible power through a knowledge of its building errors and internal contradictions. The god of the Jews, who is concerned with His transcendental sovereignty over the empirical sovereigns, acts like an observer towards the building trade of the others, one who refrains from construction of their own for the sake of critical (or eschatological) distance—with a single exception: the second temple in Jerusalem, where a Jewish feeling of also being able was temporarily incarnated. (This corresponds to the modern state of Israel having its own semi-secret nuclear weapons.) To assert himself as the Lord of Lords beyond all world powers, God must not participate in the self-glorification practiced by cities through their building frenzy and historiographies. He eternally transcends the constructed city, the constructed empire and the constructed Grand Narrative. In exchange for this abstinence, he can make the risks of collapse that are latent in all large constructs work for him. If towers are erected to the false gods, the true god will appear in their cracks; this would become significant once again in the so-called de"con"struction of the central edifices of absolute knowledge.

On a side note, one facet of the history of monotheism is a struggle between the sadistic (acting) and masochistic (observing) position for privileged access to the truth. Undoubtedly Christianity, following the Jewish model, put the masochism of the non-able ahead of the sadism of the able, at least rhetorically and pedagogically; accordingly humility, even without works to show, gained the reputation of leading closer to God than pride, even when the latter shone with God-pleasing works. That is why no contributions to a positive theory of the power city can be expected from Christianity or Judaism, as there is no access to the

Mark Tansey, *Doubting Thomas*

manic affirmations of tower- and wall-building ability from resentful positions. Consequently the Christianized imperialisms of Old Europe always drew on non-Christian, primarily Roman sources; the Christian masters had to go to Virgil to find whatever they could not get from Paul, and borrow from Alexander's exploits whatever the Acts of the Apostles could not provide. It was Augustine who gave the Christian reservations about the narcissistic city their decisive, albeit not their final form in his doctrine of the *civitas terrena*: the earthly city must always refer only to itself, but whatever favors itself bypasses God with its love. Whoever refers to themselves spends their libido in a cursed fashion. At the same time, the Bishop of Hippo gave the difference between the ark and the city a solid historico-philosophical basis and showed why the party supporters of the true religion could perhaps be harbored in God's security in arks, but never in cities—and this only by God's grace, not through their own magical or technical abilities. Augustine has to admit, at least, that arks are no less fallible structures than cities, which is why the fragility of the earthly city does not arouse feelings of triumph in him so much as creaturely sympathy; he recognizes that there is only a gradual difference between the open ruin of the city and the pious uncertainty of salvation aboard the ark. Had not the Visigoths' plundering of Rome in 410 reduced the queen of all cities to a mere raft on which the shipwrecked of this world huddled together? And had dubious figures with questionable chances of salvation not been seen aboard the ark of the church—indeed, did Augustine not experience himself, until his final breath, that humans can only apply for salvation, but never gain certainty thereof?

The second key to understanding the paradox of the city, namely that of seeking the utmost security in the greatest conspicuity, can be found through a closer inspection of the ancient Mesopotamian walls in terms of their scale or volume. Here we encounter that lordly monumentalism which Jewish observers had found so offensive and the Mesopotamian rivals so worthy of emulation—the tendency towards the excessive that can no longer be easily erased from the history of building world powers

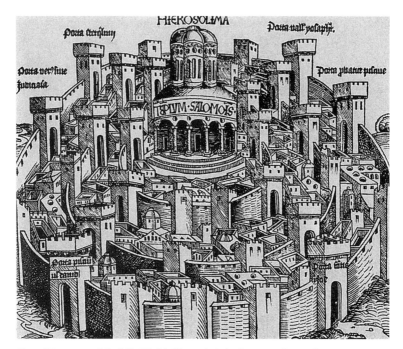

From Hartmann Schedel's *World Chronicle* (1493), view of Jerusalem

(in so far as they appeared as hardware powers). In its beginnings, monumentalism resulted from a theotechnic gesture: the builders felt they owed it to themselves and their god to pile up the sublime as high as possible with their own hands—or to offer their services for the self-fulfillment of the divine, which amounts to the same thing.

The first to master this gesture were, as noted above, the builders of the monstrous walls erected to give the new cities and their populations security in exposure. Mural theotechnics produced the first "political" large-scale interiors. As early as 2700 BC, the southern Babylonian city of Uruk was surrounded with a double ring wall over twenty-five thousand feet long with nine hundred fortified towers rising above it; it was said to be the work of King Gilgamesh, the epic hero. Alongside the two temple districts for the deities Inanna (goddess of stored fruits) and Anu—complexes of monumental dimensions and hermetically layered spatial depth—this "first metropolis in world history" had enough space to house at least 50,000, perhaps even over 100,000 people. Here the theology of monumentalism demonstrated, for the first time, its alliance with the idea of the absolute self-harboring of humans in impregnable large-scale constructs. That a king of this particular city, Gilgamesh, became the hero of a great tale of human failure in search of immortality can be read as an Urukian version of the later European motif "enlightenment through myth." The commentary on Gilgamesh's futile endeavor seems to have been formulated—at a remove of over two millennia—by Epicurus, who noted that humans can take refuge from most things, but in the face of death they all live in a city without walls.

Nonetheless, the formal motif of life behind impregnable sacred walls established itself inexorably in the entire Near East—as if the walled city were, at that time and in that region, the most advanced idea of what philosophers would later call the world spirit and the zeitgeist. Around 2500 BC, the royal Canaanite city of Hazor (known today as Tell al-Qadah) surrounded itself with a brick wall twenty-four feet thick, built on stone foundations. Over a thousand years later, when the spies of Moses went ahead to the land of Canaan to scout for settlement possibilities for the wandering Israelites, they found cities there—"the cities are large, with walls up to the sky" (Deuteronomy 1:28).

Since the early third millennium BC, walls of monumental thickness have belonged to the elementary vocabulary of life forms in the Mesopotamian and neighboring areas. When the Assyrians built the magnificent city of Nineveh on the Tigris around 700 BC, they considered it obligatory to make the wall thirty feet thick and ninety feet high. The motif of multiple walls also spread throughout all the early fortress- and city-building cultures—from Tyrins in the Peloponnese via Troy to Susa and Persepolis. It reached its culmination in—alongside the afore-mentioned Persian fortress of Ecbatana—the fortifications of Babylon that were erected around 600 BC. Nebuchadnezzar enclosed the giant square-shaped city with a fivefold protective ring; according to Herodotus, the outermost line would have been a colossal wall four times fourteen miles long; the numinous city center comprised a monumental double ring wall—the outer wall twenty feet thick, the inner twenty-five—with 600 towers overlooking it. Considering that the thirty-five-foot space between the two walls was probably filled up with packed earth, then this complex of 1.5 square miles, which encompassed only the old city center with the temples, was surrounded by a wall no less thtan eighty feet thick—which corresponds fairly precisely with the figures noted down by Herodotus, whose information about the dimensions of Babylon was considered mere fantasy until the excavation of the city ruins by archeologists in the early twentieth century.

The excessively thick walls of the fortresses, palaces and cities in the early urban era have usually been taken as expressions of a hypertrophic need for security—as if these orgies of fortification had a primarily military purpose that could be explained by the typical chronic frictions between aggressive nomads and defen-sive, settled urban and provincial peoples at that time. If one accepted this explanation, one would have to augment it with an elucidation of why the defensive complexes went far beyond what was militarily productive in so many cases. Simple reflections show that the security of city dwellers does not grow proportionally to the thickness of their fortifications; even protective walls are subject to the marginal utility effect, and beyond a certain relatively modest thickness, further increases are no longer conducive to security. Wherever city walls were built in the ancient Mesopotamian monumental age, massive expressive surpluses beyond what was militarily necessary went into their volume. It is clear that the early city dwellers carried out frenetic building projects that exceeded any pragmatic use and showed almost no regard for human or material costs. And the particularities of brick architecture, which suggested thicker walls to combat the danger of sinking roof beams, do not offer any sufficient reasons for the ancient kings' mania of construction and scale.[20]

Historians have usually attributed these excesses to early imperial megalomania, using this madness as a sufficient explanation for disproportionate actions. If one adds an excessive fixation on security to a hypertrophic craving for admiration, their sum should be identical to the proto-political paranoia that would later justify the monumental tendency of ancient Mesopotamian and Persian city cultures. Most historians who argue this overlook the fact that the explanation is too convenient to be true. It introduces modern psychiatric concepts directly into ancient history, giving such notions as megalomania and paranoia the role of decisive behavioral reasons without closer inspection. But whence is the paranoid megalomania of the ancient city builders supposed to have sprung all of a sudden, and whence could the early wall-obsessed peoples have drawn the decisive additional fear and maddeningly increased craving for recognition that seems to have been an indispensable motivation for their monstrous acts of construction? Even if we took the paranoia of the ancient Mesopotamian city regimes as given, the psychohistorical task of specifically thinking through the genesis of this illusory reason would remain. What was it that guided the first city rulers onto their para-noogenic path? What supplement of error and immoderation tainted their efforts and led them onto the slippery slope of untenable exaggerations? Which reasons for their behavior were apparent to themselves, and what divine imperative gave them the certainty of doing exactly what was right in their situation?

I suggested an explanation for the phenomena of early monumental architecture in terms of macrospherological and politico-immunological considerations above. The enormous walls of ancient Mesopotamia testify to a change of imaginative scale that was articulated in both city-building and in the demographic structure of early god-kingdoms. Mural gigantism is thus a symptom of ontological crisis—the hallmark, as it were, of the morphological puberty of societies on the threshold between small-scale and large-scale modes of being. It constitutes an immunologically significant first reaction of the spatial imagination to injection with the great. It is not the escalation of private megalomaniacal ideas that precedes monumental building projects; rather, the experience that something genuinely great is looming on the horizon and demanding a response forces the rescaling of souls and their settlement sites to unaccustomed measurements—with the ever-present risk of megalomaniacal transgressions.[21] For the first time, the large-scale outside infected the domestic world bubble in which all humans had previously been able to spend their existences, forcing an immune reaction where what had been external was dimensionally incorporated by the internal.

This would mean that the early cities were processual forms of a psychosis of scale—brick-built agonies of the magically sealed tribal world interior in which human existence had been accustomed to securing itself since primeval times. The reason for the cities suddenly walling themselves in to such a degree was not that their residents suddenly became much more afraid of real and imaginary foes in the distance than before, but that the outside entered them as large-scaledness, as divine terror, demanding its correct proportions and presentation. The walls were psychopolitical responses to the dimensional provocations of the emergent large-scale world, which included its own expanding gods. They were the achievements and self-exhibitions of a reformatted internal spaciousness—not mere dictates from fear of the external enemy. The massively and multiply walled-in city helps its residents, the god-kings and their surroundings, which share in conceiving, building and elevating god-kingship, to endure infection by the outside. The gigantic wall supported the city residents in their attempt to overcome their soul infection through the internally understood large-scale space. The true purpose of the walls was to show their inhabitants, who were forced to adopt large-scale thought, the state of things. By looking down on the population inside them, the monumental edifices informed them that great thoughts and great dangers would henceforth be an immediate reality. At the same time, they provided an unaccustomed memory exercise, for they made it easier for residents to continue living "with themselves," even though circumstances on the inside would henceforth be more like those in an outside world—exotic, complex, unclear and polyvalent. The walls provided a clear view in the face of that which can no longer be viewed so clearly. In this sense, they were the first agencies of a relative globalization. Their task was to defend the utopia of a close-knit community in an imperial world form—precisely in a time when peoples were beginning to have disturbing experiences with the vulnerability of their border constructs.

When the Jews were deported to Babylon in the early sixth century BC, they encountered a city in which foreign gods were worshipped in over fifty temples and at 1,300 altars; twenty languages were reportedly spoken in Babylon, though this did not cause any long-term complications on large construction sites. The concern of the ancient megalopolis was not so much safety from outside enemies as self-order in the face of the inward-drawn complexity of the world. It was meant to impress itself like something built for eternity according to the will of the gods, even though the likelihood of its sustainability was unmistakably small.

What appears to any observer from a small or small-thinking background as megalomania is essentially nothing other than the confrontation of city dwellers with a real quantitative task: what should one do if genuinely expansive dimensions, real diversity and provocative complexities force one to redraw one's inner maps? How should one behave if a clear-sighted deity has settled in our exact location and will not content itself with less than a complete world as its residence? How can one live up to world-demand of this god, the inner twin of the king and all who follow him, if not by setting up an elevated and widened world interior by architectural means? To the extent that intelligence advances as a view from above, it implants superhuman views into human visions: humans contribute to the conception of their gods' worldview and share the burden and euphoria of great vistas with

Uriel Birnbaum, *The Apparition of the Heavenly City* (1921–22)

them. The scale is the message, the dimension is the god. At the right time, wall-building is the piety of thought. Had the large-scale gods not seized power in Mesopotamia, the people of these cultures (and the cultures that followed them in Israel, Greece and northwestern Europe) would never have joined the path to historicity—logically, psychologically, or technically. The act of thinking one's way into the god who bears the glory of the great as such, and suffers the cosmic passion, turned the people of early times into citizens of the large-scale world—that is to say, into ecumene-compatible individuals who succeeded in moving from caves that were poor in images to high-vaulted macrocosms. Humans would not have expended such effort on the great periphery projects if sharing in the center and its projection of the world had not tasked them to the utmost level. Only because the god, the shining twin of the moved individual, grew into a large-scale god, a world-pregnant city and imperial god, did the human halves of this pair of twins have to follow their intimate other into its adventurous reachings-out.

It is also in the face of the unaccustomedly large too, however, that the morphological imperative for the city-world dwellers can initially only mean one thing: remember! Like all memories that help to understand the present, those of the new power city dwellers drew on *stores* in which old immunity experiences and morphological ideas are preserved. In this way, the monumental city walls became the walls of a vessel that brought forth the archetype of all integrity even in the gigantic. Here the concrete shape of the wall—whether oval, round or square—was secondary. At this level, the correspondences between geometry and uterotechnics were still ambiguous and variable; the circular form, which took the leading role in the Greek geometrization of the existent, had not yet outstripped all other architectural possibilities. What is decisive is that wall-building marked the start of the great introversion. The outside world increasingly ceased to be an ungovernable environment, opening up more and more as the private world of the first lords who touched, explored, described and comprehended it.

In morphological terms, the early megalopolises were walled-in soap bubbles—petrifactions of a large-scale form of fragility. There were many things for humans to remember inside them; they had to process an increasingly powerful flood of current experiences, using categories that were drawn from ever deeper within them, yet also increasingly general.[22] Large volumes of experiences appeared on the horizon, demanding to be taken in and co-known, until one day, at the maturing point of meta-physical thought, the whole of this internalization process could be recounted as the phenomenology of the spirit and the philosophy of history. At the point of narrative fruition in the metaphysical age, with a sufficient mass of retrospection, Hegel produced his epic on the subject of how the spirit succeeded in reabsorbing externality itself. What had started between 12000 and 8000 BC in Neolithic villages with the appearance of *reserves* as a thought and behavioral form now sought completion in a final, self-reflexive text container. On early Sumerian accounting tablets, the notion of the granary is represented by a square inscribed with an ear of corn; in Hegel's metaphysics the spirit, as the store of all stores, would present itself in the image of a circle of circles. This immune and memory system, matured through its many trials, collected everything that could ever be archived as a reserve or objective spirit and redistributed: grain, law, religion, science, technology and art.

As we have seen, the ancient Mesopotamian walls belong to the start of this history; they show that their inmates had learned to overcome a previously unknown problem of demarcation: they do not so much fortify their habitat, the mere sum of accommodations—for groups of houses, as countless villages and many cities show, can stand together in morphological and political integrity without any massive walls. The Spartans famously prided themselves on their lack of walls, relying entirely on their laws for protection, and the city of Rome too, along with the Italic cities in the time of greatest Roman success, were likewise proud of their wall-less self-assurance. The reason for the existence of the ancient Near Eastern giant walls was rather that the elite of the residents had to redraw the outer boundary around an expanded world interior. One could say that they did much the same, with an excessive outlay of bricks, as the blacksmith god Hephaestus would do much later in Homer with the border of Achilles' shield—and, later still, the philosophers after Aristotle when they imagined the cosmos as a system of massive ethereal spheres: they created the explicit city border as an image of self-closing totality, and allowed this heroic opulence to emerge sharply within the limits of its outline.[23] Hence they built an idea of totality; they opted for a large-scale inclusion of humans in an animated world body. All the energies of these cultures, it seems, were invested in the construction of the perimeter; indeed, one is inclined to believe that the reason for archaic states or proto-empires to build border walls was to provoke the outside world and repel the counter-provocation of rival systems. The walled-in majestic interior seeks to assert the primacy of the inner through its real existence: from now on there were only chimeras floating around outside, while true substance resided on the inside, in its own framed space. There humans incubated themselves as if in the artificial uterus of a power that can do what it wants, and wants what it can do.

In philosophy-historical terms, these monumental architectures reveal the first stirrings of what would, in the distant future, be called the transcendental subject. The city comes into itself as an autonomous condition of possibility for a grasped, self-governed, self-sufficient and self-nourishing world. To understand the aim of this, one must call to mind the scale of the physical and mental efforts that contributed to this uprising of the city spirits. In every generation for millennia, armies comprising hundreds of thousands of brick workers were used time and again for no other task than working on the border of the totality container. Their mission was to expend their lives on the sacred contour of the city, whose purpose was to testify that all that is can be contained in a form.

What gives the Mesopotamian wall-states such far-reaching historical significance is that they articulate a politico-social formal law that would remain in force everywhere until the twentieth century: behind the giant walls by the Tigris and Euphrates, those massive container societies grew whose central principle was expressed in the erection of strong-walled boundaries around themselves. As shown above, however, these containers primarily had self-container functions resulting from the necessity of animating large numbers of people inside a sphere of meaning with shared motifs and solidary notions of space. Over millennia, this basic relationship would come to be taken for granted to such an extent that until the twentieth century, the strong-walled self-container group on its territory would be understood without further analysis as one of the units of the historical world, the peoples. It was only with the entrance of First World nations into the post-national horizon, which barely occurred before 1945, that the world-historical novelty of a *thin-walled society* came into view.[24] This novelty is the focus of current globalization discourses among sociologists who believe that they can manage the new situation theoretically with the

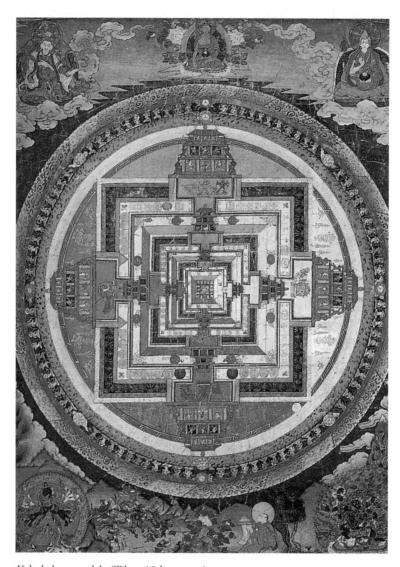

Kalachakra mandala (Tibet, 18th century)

unsubstantiated terms "global" and "local," as well as naïve combinations of the two. In reality, the revolution of political morphology in the twentieth century cannot be conceived of using sociological means, as the motive for the process—the reformatting of political and existential immune systems from strong-walled to a thin-walled nature cannot be perceived from the perspectives of sociology.

According to these reflections, then, ancient Mesopotamian brick structures were neither militarily necessary fortifications nor mere expressions of megalomaniacal confusion; rather, they were morphological experiments testing the possibility of creating a large-scale world as a self-incubating inner and private world. From this perspective, the disproportionately thick walls can only be understood as immunological phenomena and political phantasms of abdominal cavities; in their historical situation, they were productive and necessary, perhaps even prophetic exaggerations. They anticipated that humans would exist in secure cohabitation to a previously unimaginable degree. That the excessive Mesopotamian walls were sooner formed immune systems than military necessities is evident not least in the fact that in later large cities, fortifications could become almost meaningless once more if the city's immunological definition was made sufficiently clear by other means.

The Roman example illustrates this best of all. The earlier Romans only managed to build an authentic defensive wall after the severe ransacking of their city by the Gauls in 386 BC. The anachronistically dubbed Servian Wall (named after King Servius Tullius, who had ruled in the sixth century BC) became increasingly obsolete in the later part of the Roman success story, and never attained city-morphological authority; following the Punic Wars, the architectural development of the growing world city pushed far beyond the old lines. It would take over 600 years before, initiated by the emperor Aurelian (d. 275), a new wall was built around the expanded urban area between 272 and 279—once more with acute military motives, to protect it from what historians call imminent barbarian invasions.

The fact that the wall issue remained not irrelevant, but certainly of secondary significance for the city of Rome during the height of its success story cannot simply be explained by the absence of real military threats. For centuries, the Hannibal trauma remained sufficiently vivid to provide a motive for extravagant fortification efforts. That this did not happen was due—aside from the actual historical pretext, namely the suppression and destruction of Carthage in 146 BC by Scipio Africanus minor—to the unique morphological constitution of Rome's urban space. The self-concept of Rome as an inwardly calm, power-radiating city rested on the notion of the sacrosanct city border known to Romans as the *pomerium*, which itself possessed all the properties of a well-bordered immune field equipped with numinous privileges. The *pomerium* was a magically charged territorial immune system, a spatial structure whose untouchable nature was irrevocably inscribed in the imagination of every Roman. It was the most pointed manifestation of the universal Roman fetish for boundaries and margin magic. Through this internalized idea of the city boundaries, the Roman urban area as a whole was set down like an indelible entry in the land register of the heavenly gods, and accordingly a physical wall could only have made a supplementary contribution to its protection.

One of the peculiarities of Roman urban culture was the fact that the line of the *pomerium* was rather inconspicuous, and would barely have been perceptible to a stranger; it went generously around the built-up city like a form of no man's land, an undeveloped strip only hinted at by an old plough furrow and marked by a thin row of boulders. Nonetheless, this line had the status of an *ens realissimum* for the inhabitants of Rome—it showed the gravediggers and military commanders the point at which their jurisdiction ended. It gave the Roman citizens an awareness of being on chosen ground, on maternal-sacrosanct terrain. The space within the Roman city border was too holy for bodies to be buried in it, so burial spaces had to be placed beyond the line; but it was also too much a space of civil consensus for the commanders-in-chief of the Roman army to set foot on it. Departing officers therefore had to consult the auspices at the border, while those returning had to perform a demission ritual at the *pomerium* before they were admitted to the city, relinquishing their *imperium*, their power of command over troops, before crossing the line. Needless to say, it was forbidden for regular combat units to enter the protected urban district; hence the Campus Martius was considered outside the border. The jealously guarded precedence of the civil over the military among the Romans expressed the religiously motivated concern for excluding the power borrowed from weapons from the inside of the citizenry.

This immune concept originated from the Roman founding myths and their preservation in sacred ritual. In earlier periods of the city's history, it had been the task of the *luperci*, the wolf expellers or wolf priests, to bestow a magical blessing on the city's oldest area every year with a run around the Palatine Hill; dressed in the skin of a freshly slaughtered goat, they drove away evil spirits and contributed to warding off harm from people and live-stock within the city's outline. This custom was repeated until late antiquity at the festival of Lupercalia, on February 15, even after Rome's urban zone of immunity had long expanded far beyond its original boundaries. The thought of the founding furrow around the Palatine Hill (the *sulcus primigenius* dug ceremoniously with a plough at later foundations of colonial towns, usually as a circle, in such a way that the first clod of earth fell neatly inwards) combines with the memory of Rome's founding murder—the killing of Remus by his twin brother. Romulus struck his brother dead after Remus jumped over the first furrow of the field—in other accounts the rudimentary city wall—to mock the city's founder. After the deed, Romulus is said to have prophesied that the same would happen to anyone who dared harm Roman soil. Thus the *pomerium* concept was also shaped by a taboo originating from a founding crime. In view of these mythical foundations of the political space, tampering with the *pomerium*, even in the sense of its expansion and reinforcement, could only be permissible for personalities who, as revenants of Romulus, had proved their founder qualities, acquired primarily through the military expansion of the imperial borders. In the history of Rome's growth, the *pomerium* was expanded a total of six times—by Sulla first and Hadrian last—and the Claudian extension, which lead to the integration of the Aventine Hill, became even more important for the history of the "whole city" than the corrections of the outer lines under Caesar, Augustus and Vespasian.

That the immunological purpose of city demarcations was often far more important than its military functions is also shown by many imperial constructs in non-European cultures. In the history of China in particular, walls and ramparts took on a psychopolitical significance that cannot be overestimated;[25] some of the empire's most advanced city layouts, such as those of Tartar Beijing and the designated Ming capital Linhao (known today as Fengyang), were born from orgies of self-enclosure in a densely layered system of walls, as if one condition of Chinese life had been that it could only assure itself of its integrity in boxes and multiply sealed hidden courtyards. The example of Linhao is significant because its complex remained a ghost town: only the outer walls were built, and the city as such never followed. In 1369, the founder of the Ming Dynasty decided to elevate the insignificant provincial town to the middle capital of the empire and equip it with magnificent representative architecture. In a mere seven years, a giant army of workers mobilized at short notice created an encompassing outer city wall roughly five by four miles. This enclosed a forbidden city whose wall was some one and a quarter miles on each side, and this in turn held the palace city, whose walls were approximately 3,100 by 2,900 feet. This plan was obviously inspired by the model of Beijing, built in the thirteenth century by Kublai Khan, which was likewise a nested city afflicted by giantism, comprising the Tartar city, the imperial city and the Forbidden City—a surrender of the initially anti-urban nomad princes to the immune magic of the multiply self-interlaced cities.

These nesting orgies of China's real and virtual capitals were surpassed only by those of the imperial tombs, for example the tomb of Qin Shi Huangdi, the First Emperor (famed for its terracotta army), who was "buried" in 210 BC in a monumental subterranean complex on which up to 700,000 workers supposedly worked for thirty years. (The figure of 700,000 workers also appears in descriptions of Mao Zedong's mausoleum, on which people from all imperial provinces worked in order to avert the danger of a political collapse after the Chairman's death.[26]) The monarch's body lies under an artificial mound, enclosed within over a dozen massive concentric squares of which the largest measures some 8,200 by 3,300 feet, and where each box can be considered an independent fortification. To this day, Chinese archeologists have still not physically unearthed the complete structure of this hermetic inner world (only probed it by sonar and other methods of "soft" archeology, with occasional isolated digs), as if they were hesitant even now—despite superficial modernizations through communism and post-communism— to interfere with the still effective cosmological-imperial legitimization system of their culture. As far as the city of Linhao is concerned, it was never completed and never populated, so nothing has remained of it save the empty lines of an imperial decision. Its tremendous gesture speaks a spherologically clear language: it conveys that the later inner life was intended merely as a function of its outer encompassment from the start. As that life failed to ensue, all that remained of the imperial design was the casing—a monstrous immune-technical speculation ruin.

That Chinese classicism already had knowledge of the risks and weakness of an ideology of self-immurement is shown by Confucius' vision of a future in which the complex of xenophobia and claustrophilia among his fellow countrymen had disappeared:

> When the Grand Course was pursued, a public and common spirit ruled all under the sky; they chose men of talents, virtue and ability; their words were sincere, and what they cultivated was harmony. Thus men did not love their parents only, nor

treat as children only their own sons. [...] Robbers, filchers, and rebellious traitors did not show themselves, and hence the outer doors remained open, and were not shut. This was (the period of) what we call the Grand Union.[27]

Here, as everywhere in the ethical system of advanced civilizations, the concern is to make the transfer of solidarities and reserves of sympathy from the small social units of the horde and tribal age to the highly inclusive imperial structure plausible. This can only be expressed through preemptive fantasies of a universal commune devoid of enemies or environment—in images of a universal society with no non-members.

Once it is clear that a city of an ancient type is first of all a spatialized immune system, and hence a socio-uterotechnic construct, one can then inquire as to the procedures of "psychological city-building." This brings us to the third group of reflections on the psychopolitical possibility of citizens' communes or solidary "populations." Early Greek sources reveal that living "in villages" came to be considered inappropriate, leading adjacent rural communities to join and form the cities in a *synoikismos*, the decision to settle together. To comprehend what a massive effect this morphological compulsion to the polis must have had, one must consider—in agreement with Jacob Burckhardt—that for most of those concerned, this entailed a relocation that would have been a bitter sacrifice for people with "the strongest sense of place" and "the greatest reverence for place." The security of such new cities was as much a matter of swearing by shared symbols as one of fortifications; the town of Tegea claimed to be impregnable on account of possessing a few hairs of Medusa, while others carried out the ritual slaughter of young girls and sought their magical immunity in the shadow of sacrificial stress.[28]

Ancient Roman sources prove that the city-founders and wall-builders from the time of Romulus onwards were aware of the precedence of the immunizing or religioid functions of city walls over their practical military significance. Hence they could begin to dispense with the mural excesses that had appeared in ancient Mesopotamia, and also in the Mycenaean Cyclopean period, as indispensable self-displays of stationary power conglomerates. They understood that even a non-hypertrophic wall was still capable of performing its task, as long as it was cherished as a morpho-politically sacred thing and considered a privilege granted by the gods, namely to live as *intramuranus*, connected to identically animated fellow citizens, in the freedom of such a numinously charged city territory. In his major architectural treatise *De re aedificatoria* (c. 1450), Leo Battista Alberti attentively summarized the ancient views on this matter:

> The ancients, Varro and Plutarch among others, mention that our ancestors used to set out the walls of their cities according to religious rite and custom. On an auspicious day they would yoke together a bull and a cow, to draw a bronze ploughshare and run the first furrow, which would establish the course of the town walls. The fathers of the settlement would follow the plough, the cow on the inside and the bull on the outside, turning any uprooted and scattered clods back onto the furrowed line, and piling them up to prevent their being dispersed. When they reached the point where the gates were to be, they carried the plough by hand, leaving the threshold

of the gate untouched. By this means they deemed the whole course and fabric of the walls consecrated [...]

Elsewhere, I find that it was customary to mark out the line of the intended wall with a trail of powdered white earth, known as "pure." When Alexander founded Faro, for want of this type of earth he used flour instead.[29]

These founding rituals, whose morpho-political and immune-technical purpose is clear enough, would have remained incomplete if, in addition to securing the periphery, the animation principle had not been activated from the shared center. Only both gestures together, the defensive and the inspiring, combine to result in a macrospherologically complete act of state-founding. Only if the dual-psychological precepts are transferred from the microspheric dimension into the large form can a macrosphere take shape as an adequately animated space. Alberti had an inkling of this too when, in the seventh book of his "architectural matter," he reminded the reader of the necessity of placing a city's population under shared divine custody or the care of a guardian spirit:

> The ancients would set out the walls of their cities with great religious ceremony and would dedicate them to some deity for protection. They thought that no method of government could be devised to resist changes that result from violence and treachery between man and man; and they compared the city to a ship on the high seas constantly exposed to accidents and danger, through the negligence of its citizens and the envy of its neighbors. This was, I imagine, why legend has it that Saturn, out of a concern for human affairs, once upon a time

appointed heroes and demigods to protect every city with their wisdom; because we depend not only on walls for our safety, but also on the gods' help. [...] Others credit the providence of the great and good God with the allocation of guardian spirits not only to individual souls but to nations. The walls were therefore considered particularly sacred, because they served both to unite and to protect the citizens [...].[30]

Alberti's description here touches, albeit somewhat schematically, on the sensitive point where the question of the necessary and adequate animation of the city is decided. If, as in the ancient Mesopotamian city, a present cult king embodies the metaphysical city center, it is evident what connection the individual city dwellers have to their animating focus; the king himself figures in the role of the intimate second for all who are spatially and mentally close to him (the psychopolitical miracle of this structure lies in the amalgamation of intimacy and majesty from which the figure of the Great Other emerges in the first place[31]). The main reason for the coherence of the archaic city is the competition among the inhabitants for empathy with the reigning god who dwells among them, yet on whom they barely ever lay eyes. As long as the royal emanation is effective, such cities have sufficient centripetal forces because the shared is at once that which is close and difficult to grasp; they live off the functionaries' taste for being charged with the mana of the high pole. As we know, archaic class societies in particular are held together less by repression than by an adequately broad distribution of chances for sharing in majestic privilege. All empires, ancient and modern alike, rest on the proliferation of chances to enjoy power.

The Greek polises—as noted pointedly by Jacob Burck-hardt—already had the structure of local religions, as the true emblems of each city were its gods and their cults. Psychological city-building everywhere succeeded only through varyingly discreet forms of possession by the polis, of which lifelong military service for male citizens remained the most visible expression. Before the Macedonian leveling-out broke up its cities, then, Greece was a patchwork of rigorous local orthodoxies that bound themselves up in rituals to remain magically in shape. Individuals everywhere knew that they were utterly tied to the fortune and misfortune of their cities. It is therefore no surprise that when the polises and the belief in the old gods declined, a new cliché of the city god appeared: Tyche (roughly equivalent to the Roman goddess Fortuna), who was symbolized by the mural crown and in whom citizens, for example those of Alexandria and Antioch, worshipped the principle of being coincidentally on top. In such times, one could enjoy a sense of power by pushing one's way towards fortune's favorites.

Residues of this psychodynamics have remained potent to the present day despite, or perhaps because of, the political disempowerment of kings—as the magnetizing and hysterizing effects of the star system and the celebrity class in mass society reveal. In truth, the god in power is always close at hand and elusive; his charisma may be based on delusion, but it makes people willing. As the Greek cities, and later Rome, defined themselves by the fact that—except in their earliest periods—they were unwilling to tolerate the rule of princes, let alone god-kings,[32] they had to fall back on a different principle of unity, one both cosmically founded and locally efficient.[33] One way of achieving this, as Alberti hints, is by synthesizing the geniuses of the individual souls into a collective genius. The personal genius, as we have seen, was a prototype of the spirit of augmentation that formed an integral microsphere together with the individual.[34] If one assigned a shared genius to an entire citizenry, each of the many individuals in the city could experience themselves as the soul sibling of their city spirit, and the latter as the intimate other of everyone. This psychopolitical bridge between the structures of micro- and macrospheric spatial formation enabled what is still praised and demanded in the republican community to this day as "public spirit" or *concordia*: a deep-level solidarity among citizens who seem to possess a shared ground of life that is simultaneously intimate and public.

It causes malign confusions, however, when those searching today for the lost public spirit call up the ghosts of Old European political holism once more in order to treat the current, individualistically centrifuged societies—for the collective geniuses that were meant to present the metaphysical basis for the connection between citizens have irretrievably disappeared, along with the ancient Near Eastern and European urban and imperial culture, and no one can say how a non-fascist renaissance of totality-based rule might be achieved.[35] In political matters, there is no returning to the "Euclidean feeling"—a phrase with which Oswald Spengler aptly described the complete absorption of ancient humans by their gender and city spirits. When, as in modern society, political holism no longer offers any substantiated hope and individualism relinquishes the public and communitary space, the spherological path is—in questions of social synthesis too—the only one left open.

Dying Later in the Amphitheater

On Postponement, the Roman Way

sine missione nascimur
— Seneca, *Epistulae morales*, XXXVII[36]

Closed place. All needed to be known
for say is known.
— Samuel Beckett, "Fizzle 5"[37]

That the Roman arena could advance to a metaphor for the world stemmed from the fact that the central tenet of ancient fatalism attained concretion in its construction: no one escapes the grasp of this world alive. Everyone in it must fulfill their destiny to the end. The only concession offered by this place is that, with a little luck and diligence, our failure can be postponed.

The Roman-style theater of cruelty acted as a destiny generator in which the masses observed the last relevant difference between humans—the distinction between those who die sooner and those who die later—in the form of a sporting divine judgment. The gladiatorial fights created a popular form of philosophical theory that demonstrated how this decisive difference comes about. In the sporting drama, the separation of the living from the dead could be observed in a state of impersonal excitement.

The spectators were not abandoned when the losers were left lying in the sand; they were spared the imposition of grief when the vanquished were dragged out. They watched the decisive difference take effect in a state of detached arousal: some die now while others die not now, but soon enough—a round, a season or a few arena years later. Only rarely was there opportunity to give a veteran gladiator the wooden sword upon his retirement. Postponement was everything; depending on their own fighting prowess, the death of the victorious fighters was delayed until an unspecified point in time. Certainly this point would come in the not-too-distant present, but the circumstances of its arrival would remain concealed until then; what could be enjoyed as a victor's life was no more than this ongoing concealment. Whoever was still alive in the arena come evening could relish the privilege of leaving the date of their own death open; for the losers, however, the day and the hour were precisely determined.

Thus the lesson of the arena is that a human life can never be more than saving up to die later. "This is the state of things, Roman: look at it. If you are among the living, it is only because you have managed to remain undefeated to this hour; but you are still subject to the law of the arena, and remain bound to the gladiator's oath until the end." When the fighters vowed before the games commenced that they would not resist their fate in the arena, even if they were hacked to pieces or burned alive, they concluded this pledge to hopelessness with this formula:

> What difference will it make if you gain a few more days or years? We are born into a world in which no quarter is given.[38]

Continuing establishment of the difference between lying and standing: *Vic(tor):*
Imago et Victoria convertuntur. Floor mosaics from a villa near Tusculum (3rd century)

Yet it was this difference, and this alone, that gave color and
body to life as understood by the Romans. It was not for nothing
that Seneca, in his famous 37th letter to Lucilius, said that even
the wise man can never do any more than repeat the forced,
shameful oath of the gladiators in the form of a voluntary, and
thus honorable vow; for even the best life can be no more than

an upright acceptance of the fate that awaits us in the world arena. Even though Augustus banned gladiatorial fights to the death for a time, the bloodthirsty habitus won out in the long run. Wisdom is consent to a life that must be led *sine missione*: one cannot apply for release from the coercion to exist.

What Jacques Derrida called *différance*, the distinction that is also a deferral, could already be observed in the Roman arena as the simple result of qualifying tournaments in theoryless theory. The Roman games simplified First Philosophy and replaced it with a crude rule of thumb. Whoever went to the amphitheater for gladiatorial games could contemplate the basic Roman truths like an introductory philosophical seminar financed by emperors and magnates—after which advanced seminars were no longer necessary. It was the Roman enlightenment to uncover how the victor's life prolonged itself at the direct expense of the loser's. The attractiveness of this procedure lay in its bold intensification of primal observations about biological selections. From the perspective of these observations, all mortals carry with them a dark knowledge of the fragility of the human condition; they know, usually without wanting to learn any further details, about the difference between those who depart sooner and those who do so later. They also understand that their own position in the process of life is connected first of all to their age roles, which define the general character of their relationship with the end. It was only with the Roman games that a causal bond between the earlier death of some and the later death of others was methodically established: because from then on, the victor in the serious game won out against the loser as the cause of his death.

With this step, imperial thanatology entered its critical stage. The games, like imperial politics in general, organized themselves as an outdoing and acceleration of natural selection through martial art as a duel of extermination. Where this habitus takes root, a craving for elimination dramas and end games seeps into the audience, as the now-visible end of the one group heightens the feeling of survival in the other. Hence the fascination with tournaments: analogously to animal breeding, the elimination process becomes a man-made selection. Him or me, us or them: this is rehearsed in the arena as if in an experimental set-up for artificial selections. It is quite obvious, then, that the fascism effect was invented with the Roman gladiatorial games, assuming we define it as the political enactment of selection or a theatricization of *différance*.

The truth about Roman biopolitics came to light in the arena. The city of Rome had cast down all enemies around it as the gladiator of the cosmos until the entire world around the *mare nostrum* could look upon the victorious Rome like a universal crowd of spectators, and it was in much the same way that the masses in the amphitheaters of Rome and its dependents watched the fighters in the bloody ring of decision settle these questions: who will be left? Who rules the sand? Who will keep his life so that he can confront renewed attempts to shorten it? The underlying thought figure of the amphitheater was the naked postponing distinction: the not-yet-dying of some was itself the presently necessary and sufficient reason for the dying-now of the others. Admittedly, this difference has been familiar as the universal law of sooner-or-later mortality at all times and more or less all places, as the living always identify themselves imprecisely as the not-dying-so-soon. In the arena, this difference is made precise and driven to an artificially precipitated apocalypse; it stages the separation, resembling a divine judgment, of

Giovanni Battista Piranesi, *Interior of the Colosseum with Niches for the Via Crucis* (c. 1750)

those who fall today from those still standing. Viewing this drama of distinction, the diffusely living are given the possibility to feel their membership in the group of the not-yet-dying with a hot surge of currentness. When the stadiums scream, the masses celebrate their own success in postponing death. It is implicit in the cult of victors that the crowd shifts its allegiance from the camp of those lying in the sand to those who are left standing upright after battle.

Anyone seeking to understand the Roman games (and their modern derivatives) must be aware that the round form of the amphitheater articulates a lesson in worldview. The roundness of this circular theater is not only a symbol of the world for the average intellect, not only the Roman response to the sphairophilia and philocyclism of the Greeks; most of all, it characterizes the impossibility of escaping the whole in any direction. Whoever wants absolute immanence must also affirm the Roman theater of death. Its architectural form was that of a closed circle or oval, like "two Greek semicircular theaters put together."[39] In the arena, the spectator lost the view of a stage *opposite* them; no gods were presented appearing from the other side. All actions were drawn into the middle and the mediocre, attaining completion in the immanence of the stadium. The tragic plot was taken back to the level of butchery—Roman pragmatism always demanded the real thing, and would only tolerate as much staging and metaphorical ornamentation as was possible without impairing the pure massacre. The actors could only act if surrounded; if one of the tormented, as a last resort, attempted to leave their role, armed men at the edges of the arena ensured that the fugitive returned to his position in the game of slaughter. What spectators gazed on in this cauldron was not only the closed totality of the scene; they also saw the fatally limited view of the fighters, and in particular saw hopelessness become actual present for the losers. The observer enjoyed the privilege of seeing that the other's death had a highly current date: now. But they also saw that the victors, or their part, saw no further than the next fight—in this sense, there was solidarity between them and their cheering audience.

> The tiered ring of fascinated faces has something strangely homogeneous about it. It embraces and contains everything which happens below. No one relaxes his grip on this; no one tries to get away.[40]

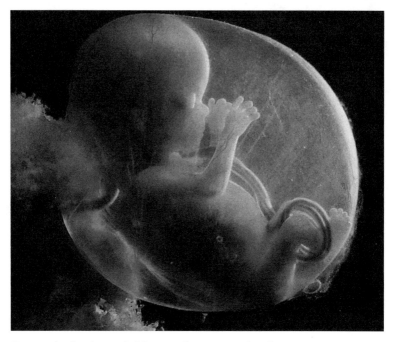

Fetus in the fourth month (photograph: Lennart Nilsson)

That is why Roman theory is no philosophy of jovial circumspections; it knows no *epoché*, no relieved observation freed from practical considerations—only meditation in the sand, the brooding view of the situation during pauses in the fighting. If the Greek watchword was "Know thyself," the Roman one was "Know the situation." The gladiator understood what the situation was when he looked up from the arena to the seats. He knew that there, the mood of the mob passed divine judgment by thumb.

The Roman amphitheaters rehearsed the maxim that people with a sense of self-preservation should ensure at all costs that they are among the victors. As a theater of selection, the Roman

Jean Léon Gérôme, *Pollice verso* (c. 1859), detail, Phoenix Art Museum

games methodically appealed to the necessity of acknowledging that cruelty is always right. In them, this going along with the results of the fights turned into a para-religious genuflection before the stone mask of violence. Were even Roman-style victories and triumphs, then, not merely desperations in a different state? The Stoics had analogously declared, with good reason, that wisdom consists in the imitations of stones. The gods themselves are damned to opportunism; their believers must learn to yield to the results of games, on the small as well as the large scale, like revelations. This is exactly the point of fatalism as a religion: the readiness to see the will of the gods involved in the most vulgar coincidences.

From Heinrich Khunrath, *Amphitheatrum sapientiae aeternae* (1602): at the center the narrow gate of wisdom as a flaming point of light

The origins of mass culture undoubtedly lie in the entertaining excesses of the Roman theaters: they constituted an early and complete form of fascination industry that supplies agitated or decadent societies with arousals and binds them with enchantments. In functional terms, the ancient fascism of amusement (whose last direct descendant is Spanish bullfighting) anticipated numerous attributes of modern control over the masses via media of arousal. In both cases, the mass culture organizes the coercion to look: its element is social synthesis through fascination with violence. And indeed, who could have shown the onlookers at the climax of the games any other object strong enough to tear away

Bartholomeus Dolendo, *Theatrum anatomicum* of the University of Leiden
(1610): a scientific prefiguration of horror literature

their gazes from the spectacle of the fundamental distinction?
Humanist intellectuals, and later on Christian authors, polemi-
cized in vain against the intoxicating, fatalizing and hardening
games. The Christian prohibition of *curiositas*, the enslaving
service of the eyes and centrifugal, soul-eating curiosity, was motivated primarily by the fight against the eagerness to see death in
the Roman games. For seven hundred years it was this theater of
fascinations that conveyed to contemporaries the Roman instruction: kill now, die later, and force the crowd to watch.

Now we can explain why the early Christians fixed their gazes
on the Roman complex: in the light of the Roman cult of life and

death, one can understand how Rome inevitably became the undoing of its Christian dissidents. If Rome merited a mass, it was because the Christians only learned from the Romans what the *vera religio* ultimately rebels against. Christianity found its historical identity as the inversion of the Roman fatalism of survival. It had to oppose the doctrine of the amphitheaters and the religion of victory on their own soil, as it was only in the capital of political biology and the selection games that the counter-thesis could be posited: survival alone is not the truth, and outward victory alone is not the sign of success with God. Christian criticism gave success a second face turned away from human judgment, and the emancipation of the European spirit from fatalism only became possible through this discovery. The architectural symbol of this turn only took shape between the fifteenth and seventeenth centuries, when St. Peter's Square was conceived as the true anti-circus, the evangelical counter-arena.

That the Romans worshipped success in all areas—not only in the theaters, but also in the cult heart of political power—became clear through, among other things, the fact that throughout the imperial age, the Roman Senate regularly opened its sessions with a sacrifice at the altar of Victoria; it was not until the reign of Constantius II, Constantine's successor, that the altar of victory placed there by Augustus was removed from the Senate building. For an entire age, Rome's political class had worshipped the principle of its survival at that altar. (It took substantially longer for the church to triumph over the bloodlust in the arenas: in the Colosseum, the gladiatorial games continued—despite intermittent bans—until 405 AD, and animal hunts until 526.)

Therefore, once implanted in the Roman world, Christian dogma no longer taught only the overcoming of death through a

The Roman circus floating on the globe; medal owned by Wilhelm V of Bavaria (1715), with the motto *Agnosco. Dole. Emenda*: recognize, grieve, improve.

higher life; had it relied on this thesis alone, Christianity may have remained the peripheral religion it initially was. Proclaimed from the Rome of the amphitheaters, however, the Gospel declared that those who died sooner were not always the losers; merely dying later could no longer replace salvation. Christian theology opposed the fatalism-rehearsing selection of the stronger in the theaters with selection by God. God also made a distinction that separated his own from the lost masses, admittedly; but God's distinction did not share the structure of nihilistic *différance*. It appeared in a flash as an eschatological judgment that recorded the only decisive result of human life: belonging or not belonging to the divine love sphere. The distinction between empire and church that was so momentous for Europe originated from this difference. If the empire was the power of command, resting on faith in the

Medieval Arles in the outline of the ancient amphitheater

vocation to triumph, then the church, ideal-typically speaking, was the key power that guarded access to the community of love.

These definitions enable us to identify more clearly the foundation of the Modern Age with regard to salvation: it began with the realization that it would forever remain impossible for individuals to decide with certainty whether they themselves were closer than others to the *communio* of those loved by God. What community of love could rightfully claim itself objectively superior to the unloved, the loveless, and people with strange preferences? Today, distinguishing between parishes and egotisms is a matter of personal discretion—and the self-praise of the chosen is merely one vote among many. Indeed, the very notion of a community of love has become a subject of unease, as if, without any explicit discussion, the realization had spread that the unattainable is equally remote wherever one stands.

Excursus 2

Merdocracy

The Immune Paradox of Settled Cultures

And holding my nose, I wandered disgruntled through
all of yesterday and today…
—Friedrich Nietzsche, *Thus Spoke Zarathustra, "On the Rabble"*[41]

The phenomenon of the Roman games clarifies the risks involved in the regulation of affects in large-scale imperial bodies: inurement to arousals in the masses produces a dependence on violence-induced stimulations whose abolition demands no less than a culture-revolutionary shattering of the entire paradigm. The Roman entertainment massacres had established a standard of mass incitement that could no longer be moderated or sublimated immanently, only eliminated through a radical break with the existing system of affective ventilations. The transition to Christianity indeed established a completely different affectology for the populations of the Roman Empire and its cultural successors, until the culture industry of the twentieth century once more spawned phenomena that can be interpreted as taking up the ancient level of atrocity consumption once more.

The Roman *ludi* [games] and *venationes* [animal hunts] belong to a behavioral complex I shall call "active self-climatization." This refers to cultural techniques used by a given population to adjust the atmospheric constants of their existential space according to their own options—in the Roman case, it was a climatic paradox that can be summarized as "pampering through bestialization." A tonicization and climatization of the "lifeworld" is clearly unachievable in large-scale bodies politic like the ancient metropolis without a high level of self-intoxication. In this respect, societies would always also be communities of exhilaration, pampering and poisoning. The functional effects of such mechanisms on the reduction of metropolitan crime cannot be directly proved after the fact, but must, in the light of everything we know about these connections, be postulated for systemic reasons. And the fact that modern entertainment culture's obligatory association of sexuality with violence was almost entirely absent from the affective world of the Romans can undoubtedly be attributed to the intensive consumption of pure, pretextless scenes of violence in the theaters.

More than such active techniques of self-stimulation, however, the social synthesis of early settled groups depended on passive and undramatic self-climatizations. Since the question of stationariness arose for humans, their own excretions and perspirations gained culture-defining significance as endogenous climate creators. From a culture-climatological perspective, a settled ethnic unit is above all a group that smells itself and finds a spherically extended criterion of identity in its own smell. In cultural historiography, little attention has so far been paid to the fact that the transition to sedentariness not only brought humans the achievements and hardships of the agrarian age—the plough, the sword and the book, to cite Gellner's formula; more importantly, the sedentary way of life brought about an endo-climatological problem of epochal proportions for which—after the canal systems of the early world cities—only the hygiene policy of the nineteenth and twentieth centuries in the industrial states appears to have found a systematic solution.[42]

The atmospheric dilemma of sedentariness manifests itself in the fact that groups of people who have bound themselves to houses and grounds can no longer evade their own excrement and its olfactory-spatial emanations to the degree that had seemed naturally given for prehistoric wandering tribes. Settled culture is subject to a heavy, self-created basic sanitary strain, as it pays for the advantage of living close to fields and granaries with the disadvantage of having to remain close to its own latrines. As far as the excretory practices of nomads are concerned, they are still free to pursue disseminative behavior—which casts the matter somewhat anachronistically, as these carefree disseminators have not yet seriously discovered the principle of sowing—and only occasionally enter binding relationships with grounds, properties and latrines.

Thus, while the nomads preserve the fecofugal dynamics of movement, farmers and especially city dwellers are fatefully condemned to a latrinocentric style of existence. For them, the spirit of the place and the law of the latrine converge. One could give credence to the assumption that it was only the settled human being that became disposed to the idea of retributive causality, after the near-universal evidence of latrine emanations had proved the impossibility of a secret act with no consequences. The infamous smell brings it to light, and the return of the smells to their creators imposes the idea of a miasmic karma or olfactory nemesis on the humans who cannot evade them. What phenomenologists, following on from Husserl's late work, tend to describe with the term "lifeworld" should be viewed primarily as an olfactory phenomenon before the deodorizing revolution of the last two centuries—on a scale that modern subjects lack the criteria to "grasp." The being-with-oneself of the early groups in settlement collectives cannot be described without reference to a constant presence of ominous native vapors. Lifeworld is breathworld—nicely said, but what is the point of breath as long as the shared air of the settled lies under the spell of the sewer?

The actually existing village, the actually existing city: in historical times, by premodern standards, these were always and primarily atmosphere-based odorous architectures that built up around the olfactory emanation centers of the communes—first of all the latrines, the sewers and the stables of large pets, and secondly, the domestic hearths, the knackeries and the garbage pits. Numerous literary documents show that in terms of their sanitary and odor standards, medieval European cities could only be called populated cesspools, and well into the time of Goethe and Beethoven, the sanitary policing measures of the territorial state were capable of lessening the smell, but not neutralizing it. Michel de Montaigne noted in the sixteenth century, "My liking for those fair cities Venice and Paris is affected by the pungent smell of the marshes of one and the mud of the other."[43] The breath of the latrine dominated Old European urbanity like an iniquitous city deity. Odor sources of this kind are actual emanation systems, for here too, all power issues from the central substance that, in spherically overflowing fashion, wastes itself on its surroundings in the mode of self-communication. But while the noble emanations articulated by Neoplatonism serve the out-pouring of light into the public sphere of being, the suspicious emanations of the latrines always result in a form of olfactory cave effect and the exclusion of more remote persons from the established totality of odors—a fact to which some ethnographers have attempted to draw attention as discreetly as possible, noting that intensely odorous peoples are particularly unlikely to register their own smell or that of their habitat in general. What the new arrivals notice most of all in such cases is the fact that the locals do not notice anything. Sewer emanation too undoubtedly constitutes a case of substance domination—that is, the self-spreading of a presentist force over an included area. As long as the destiny of the dominant element only concerns the sublime or violent manifestness of power, however, which is the norm in an atmospherically blind (but all the more object- and event-fixated) culture of theory like the European one, then the dominant element, which presents itself as an extended odor bell, or more precisely an inhabited volume of stench, can hardly ever be mentioned explicitly—aside from a few clever turns of phrase in popular scatology ("shit happens").

Opinions and noses differ regarding these circumstances, and all reliable methods abandon us on the threshold where the humane sciences must really become the gas sciences. The only certainty is that all modernisms and cosmopolitanisms lead us astray here; for while the modern notion of society implies the interactions among the deodorized in the olfactorily neutral space (human rights are preceded by the zero smell hypothesis), any examination of premodern forms of communality must address highly obsessive and highly invasive odor-auratic modes of an "existence [*Dasein*] as being-with [*Mitsein*]."[44]

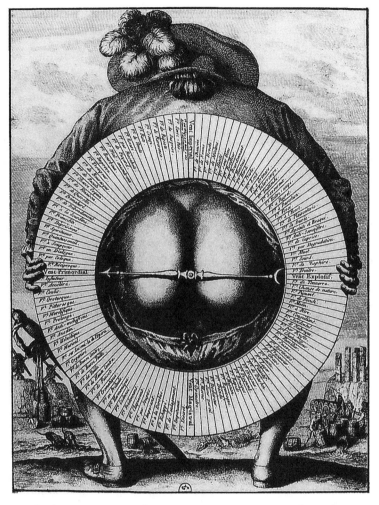

Bombardoni, *New Compass for Sensitive Noses*, Paris, Roger Viollet Archive

I spoke further above, probably with too many concessions to sentimental needs, of the basic characteristics of a thermal socialism—that is, the sharing of warmth advantages from the same radiation source.[45] Since then, we have encountered reasons to consider the possibility of an almost equally originary latrine socialism. If we take this directly community-forming power as a presence of currently inescapable spheric structure—a microclimate, a local spirit, a house atmosphere, a breathable element—then it is obvious why the aromasphere of a group is the first of a given collective's effective sensually shared principles of coherence. Different people experience themselves first of all as different odors. The etymological kinship between the Latin words *odor* ("smell") and *odium* ("hatred") points from a distance to the nasal clash of civilizations—though this only ever means encounters between stinking groups or their representatives, not an actual collision of two miasmic landscapes, as the actually dominant stench sources naturally remain stationary, almost possessing the stability of holy places. Like the temples, the sewers have a specific space-disclosing power; it is only the *stabilitas loci* of both that expresses the full gravity of a land appropriation and a marriage between the people and the ground. In this respect, all settled cultures before the hygiene revolution of the late eighteenth century were subject to a bifocal system of place consecration and ground definition—perceptible in the homely twofold aura of pleasant smells and miasmas, which mingled from the start.

Every merdocratic space, every here, everything ours, is a kingdom of its own; it forms an auratic monad that catches its inhabitants in a particular underlying mood and impregnates them with the whiff of the smellscape. What came to be thought of— somewhat willfully, speculatively and tendentiously—as national spirits in eighteenth-century Europe are therefore, initially and mostly, national smells or gases (which are evidently credited with the ability to penetrate the literature and folklores of nations—a mental pendant to smoked foodstuffs). It was only a later variety of xenophobic theory that sucked these scents from their endoclimatic spaces, condemning them as foreign, offensive auratic elements. In Japan, books were written around 1900 about the disgusting smell of male and female Europeans, whose odors caused convulsions of discomfort, while Germany saw the emergence of relentlessly exact dissertations on Jewish and Negroid smells.

What was regularly overlooked in these odor-xenophobic exercises was that for everyone, no matter whence they might originate, no place can ever stink as pervasively as their home. The olfactory dilemma of settled existence comes to light not so much through the foreign smell, but rather through one's own, to which one constantly contributes and which constantly blows back. What one calls home is the place whose stench one views as a merit. A patriot is one willing to forgive what is ours for certain smells. The only homely miasm is that which disarms; it is the point of reference for the atmospheric world ties of the settled who breathe together. When Heidegger emphasizes that "In Dasein there lies an essential tendency towards closeness," the approving exegete can only add that this closeness must, like it or not, include proximity to the constitutive latrines. Adjacency to one's own excrement and its collection, its gleaning, is the first law of proxemics. If a physiologically privileged sense of proximity exists, it is the one updated by the odor. Not the night, which Heidegger praised in factually and linguistically problematic formulations, is the seamstress of being; it is the common sewer that connects the village and the city quarter self-inclusively to itself, and makes them inwardly round, as a self-malodorizing "undivided world-whole." It is this that once enabled local life to gain the attunement of a primary world safety.

It is also understandable, however, why the traits of auratic familiarity associated with "world" as such had to be increasingly privatized, marginalized and neutralized in the process of a deodorizing modernity. If one calls to mind the significance of odor-auratic elements for primary social synthesis, as well as the world housing of the individual (though what exactly does it mean to call to mind lost smells?), it becomes clear why some peoples had to undergo particularly difficult crises on their way to modernity, which here means the transodorization and deodorization of the lifeworld—not least the Germans, who expressed their longing for sensory evidence of a home more vehemently than others, without considering that the original latrine security of existence cannot be brought back through patriotic parades and forced national efforts.

If settled life's connection to the world prior to the age of deodorization policies was inevitably influenced by the latrinocentrism of domestic, village and urban atmospheres, it is clear why a new ecology of odor identities took shape with the advent of modernity. Not only did industrialization and motorization significantly change the odor-auratic functions of the lifeworld; the constant hygiene revolution from the late eighteenth century onwards also liquidated the old system of olfactory local spirits almost entirely, in cities and the country-side alike. In Bavaria, experts are producing a report assessing whether there is still a sufficient legal basis for open-air storage of manure heaps. Because the equation of odor-auratic rooting with existence's attunement to home ground still retains residual validity for settled populations, even in the modern world, those who create the climate in national societies are faced with the serious problem of how to immerse large populations in community-forming miasmas by a system of metaphorical national odors.

This is the systemic location of the modern mass media, in so far as they function as transporters for symbolically coded secondary smells or metaphorical vapors of large groups. Here we find an opportunity to recall the kinship, not only an etymological one, between smells [*Gerüche*] and rumors [*Gerüchte*]. The rumor is the spoken smell—it is no coincidence that rumors are imagined as winged creatures that infiltrate social biotopes with demon speed.[46] Rumor is as infectious and rapid as ill will. With the implementation of a system for the text-assisted spread of smells, the mass press' that has been successful since the nineteenth century makes a contribution to the current social synthesis that is impossible either to overlook or oversmell. It does so through semiotically transmitted, highly macroclimatically effective and sustained, nationwide self-contaminations. What was achieved through the hygiene policies of the municipal works and waterworks at a local level, namely the extensive neutralization of fecal emanations—whose microbic risks also began to be noticed in scientific discourses in the nineteenth century—was abundantly offset in functional terms, likewise locally based but with nationwide effects, by the mass press' "mission to inform." The paling odor-auratic local mood is replaced through the establishment of a national informatic climate system whose purpose is to ensure the large society's affective, thematic, toxic and thus domestic political self-ventilation. (It is clear, incidentally, that the interior secretaries cover the structured side of the merdocracy, while the media exploit their leeway as indirect merdocratic forces.)

It would be easy to show that what the initially press-supported, then later radio-supported national climate creators do is, in many ways, nothing but a transposition of the communes' latrinocentrism to the national and regional level. The system of nationalizing secondary smells gets running primarily via infectious communications of disparagement or incitement—its favored topics are disasters, criminal cases, political intrigues and the private lives of celebrities, and its most important mechanisms the provocation of waves of outrage and the capturing of attention through scandals. The mass media latrine organizes, to paraphrase Nietzsche, the odor context of general *ressentiment*. It was the author of *The Gay Science* and *The Genealogy of Morals* who, keen-eared and keen-nosed like no one before him, reported to what extent modern mass societies are organized as collectives of self-incitement and self-malodorization—which is why for him, even the subtlest aspects of enlightenment would remain a primarily nasal matter. What has entirely unjustly been termed his "hermeneutics of suspicion" was in reality a precise oversensitivity to the nefarious emanations spreading through modern societies beneath the masking odors of philanthropy, egalitarianism and the duty to remember. His nasal hermeneutics is virtually never concerned with insinuating motives, only detecting them. Nietzsche shows that the deodorization project is doomed to failure as long as the basic macroclimatic process of democracy, the mass media production of self-stressing (verbal, pictorial and local-musical) miasmas that induce feelings of "we," is allowed to take place uncontrolled.

The discovery that the soil-bound communities subject themselves to atmospheric endo-stress through their forced proximity to their excrements, waste, carrion and dead is not an exclusive prerogative of modern social critique. In Europe, one can find indicators of a burgeoning legal engagement with the dynamics of physical self-contaminations in cities as early as the thirteenth century. I would not have dared to mention excrement, waste, carrion and dead in the same breath if an eminent document from the dawn of the ecological consciousness had made this precarious connection explicit: the air conservation law of Frederick II of Hohenstaufen from the Constitutions of Melfi. In the third part of this body of laws from 1231, the Holy Roman emperor decreed the following for his Sicilian estates under Title XLVIII:

> De conservatione aeris
>
> We intend to preserve the healthfulness of the air (*salubritas aeris*) insofar as we can, for it has been reserved to the attention of our provision by divine judgement. Therefore, we order that no one should be permitted to soak flax or hemp (*cannabem*) in water within a mile of the city or near a castrum so that the quality of the air may not, as we have learned for certain, be corrupted by it (*aeris disposition corrumpatur*). If he does this he will lose the flax and hemp which has been put in the water, and they will be brought to our court.
>
> We order that burials of the dead which are not contained in urns should be as deep as half an ell (*mensura cannae*) extended. If anyone acts contrary to this, he will pay one augustalis to our court. We order that cadavers and filth that make a stench should be thrown a quarter of a mile out of the district or into the sea or river by the persons to whom they belong. If anyone acts contrary to this, he will pay to our court one augustalis for dogs or larger animals, ½ for smaller animals.[47]

Frederick's air conservation law crossed the threshold of modernity with two realizations: microclimates and lifeworld atmospheres could become legal and political factors, and not every stench emission could be defended by recourse to the natural right to inevitable miasma formation classifiable as latrine emanation. Even if Frederick's decree concedes that the healthfulness of the air (*salubritas aeris*) can ultimately only be secured by God, its energetic style—leaving aside the precarious carrion paragraph for a moment—shows how clear it had already become to its authors that in a dense, business-intensive, high-waste society, a far-sighted administration would have to lay down rules for man-made taintings of the atmosphere. The requirements for modernity are fulfilled when immune relationships are exempted from religious submission and converted into technical, legal and political structures. As an atmopolitician, Frederick II of Hohenstaufen is our contemporary. His directives reveal that every genuine concern for actual society presupposes a miasmology: a critical theory of air and a positive concept of the atmospheric *res publica*. It is no longer politics *sans phrase* that is destiny, but rather climate politics.

CHAPTER 4

The Ontological Proof of the Orb

Can anybody admit all this and still put up with people who
deny that "everything is full of gods?"
— Plato, *Laws*, Book X, 899b[1]

Do not say, "I am hidden from the Lord; who is there in
heaven to give a thought to me? Among so many I shall not
be noticed; what is my life compared with the measureless
creation?"
— Ecclesiasticus 16:17

The fate of all metaphysical immune systems is decided by the
question of whether the beings open to the large-scale world,
namely the people of imperial and urban times, succeed in
making the leap from collective self-harboring in fortified
urban communities to individual self-securing in the whole—
beyond their coincidental fatherlands. It is of existential
interest to them to ascertain whether they would still be capable
of a life of integrity in the most remote, unfamiliar places—a
question that encodes itself for them in the reflection on

Joseph Cornell, *Soap Bubble Set, Lunar Rainbow, Space Object* (c. 1936)

whether they, the mortals, familially dependent and locally attached, could become friends with the world's outer space itself. How much exile can humans endure? How much weaning from the first places does the intelligent require to come into itself? How much uprooting is necessary to become wise, meaning resistant to fate?

It would be trading, war-waging city subjects marked by travels, defeats and expulsions, literate and experienced in argumentation, that cast their pondering gazes beyond their own walls. They, the first "civil people," knew better than anyone else that people like them lived in other places too, and that it would only take a few trivial twists of fate to end up in foreign lands; powerlessness follows the self-assured life as the shadow follows the illuminated body. A storm at sea, a failed journey or a lost war could change everything. Should what we call foreign parts, then, only be supposed to exist outside? Have death and externality not long since taken root in the native, in what is ours? The more experience mobile individuals gain of life in fallible cities, familiar and unfamiliar alike, the more acutely they realize that even their home town will no longer satisfy their longing for a fulfilled rootedness. If you are miserable in foreign cities, that should not surprise you under the circumstances; if you are miserable in your own city, it is time to think about existence in cities and about being-in-the-world itself.

Nowhere in the Old World did this reflection take place as radically and momentously as in post-Socratic Athens—the shattered city that emerged from the ordeal of the thirty-year war against Sparta humiliated, broken, confused and lastingly poisoned. The city walls were disenchanted. The people sensed that after the endogenous terror that had raged during the dictatorship of the Thirty Tyrants in the polis, the cardinal difference between inside and outside had also lost its significance. By comparison, the reinstatement of democracy meant little. The trial of Socrates had exposed the city's unstable and seditious nature, and the case of Alcibiades, who had defected to the Spartans out of spite for his own people and even fraternized with the Persians, had made it obvious that the city could hold on to its most brilliant children least of all. Where the plague had ruled—first the bacterial and then the political (or was it the other way around?)—the polis was broken as an immune system and invalidated as a world form. How could the defeated, the self-flagellating and self-poisoned build, dwell and think in future? What, if it should ever exist again, would be the fruit of the urban disaster?

Now it becomes apparent how this city without precedent managed to rescue itself through a forwards breakdown—one could also say in an act of progress, or a prelude to what would one day be termed the "dialectic of enlightenment." Desperation leads to boldness, and the memory of the catastrophe released all constructions from what was fundamental. For what if one could prove that beyond the city and the state, the cosmos itself formed a self-enclosed sphere that lost nothing and could withstand all attacks on its immunity? If, at the highest level, everything stood in its place, "true as the circumference to its center" (Hermann Melville)? Could the city-sore mortals not then embrace the dream of being at home with themselves even in de-restricted cosmic dimensions, and precisely in those, in a new, fabulously invulnerable fashion? Indeed, who could live in outer space? Who could strike roots in being itself…? Who settled at an altitude local vapors would not reach, and where political miasmas would have lost their infectious power? Who would be able to keep the planet company? Who would reach the point of breathing the scent of pure being? Who would succeed in going on holiday in the absolute, far away from all proximity to quarrelsome dull-mindednesses? Who would discover a place where souls could recover from the local plague, the irreparable maliciousnesses and the self-seeking cliques?

The emergence of such eccentric and cathartic speculations, where wishes and knowledge enter a new alliance—sealed by the both artistically and evangelically resonant word *philosophía* set off what has been called the Greek miracle in the narrower sense: the transformation of a regional wisdom tradition into a universally oriented knowledge culture. In this culture, geometry entered an unheard-of liaison with immunology. In Plato's Athens, practicing philosophy meant one thing above all else: expanding the immune principle of a vanquished city beyond its borders more powerfully than ever. Without the Athenian catastrophe, ancient Europe would perhaps have taken entirely different paths from pre-scientific wisdom to the philosophical concept. Only there and at that time, in the immune reaction of the most intelligent city to its most severe politico-atmospheric defeat, could the way of thinking develop that ultimately led the world concept of the Hellenic intelligentsia in the early occidental direction.

In the moment of its foundation, philosophy was a purification plant for traumatized intelligence. With its establishment before the gates of Athens, a technique for filtering spoiled atmospheres was created. Like a doctor prescribing diets and exercise, Plato recommended logical investigations and upliftings of the soul for the perjurious city. Remembrance is the great soul cure—not remembrance of what moderns call experience, however, but rather a Uranian knowledge that points further back than all histories and fatherlands. Plato's psychagogic genius lay in cheering up the young souls that rushed to his dialogues by involving them in unprecedentedly serious clarifications. There should be no doubt that the Academy was the funniest and most serious place in the city; within its walls, comedy and tragedy were transposed into a logical key. This brightening of the city's atmosphere would make history, or rather counter-history— until things one day reached the point where the utopian institution of school itself became no less stuffy than its environment, which had been poisoned earlier and differently. As a result, the free spirit had to search for places to breathe beyond the two options of school or society.

First of all, however, it is a matter of correctly emphasizing the leap into the development of the first academy effect: one must judge what it meant that the Athenian down-to-earthness and its wisdom had imploded, and that nothing less than the very colonization of being would satisfy the habitation needs of an intelligence that felt uprooted from the secrecy of the city. A new formula for habitation had become necessary. In future, after the catastrophe of the polis, only the hyperbolic philosophical faith in the identity of house and cosmos would protect the city dwellers from invasions by the coldness of estrangement. The prime concern for the philosophical founders of the polis was warding off political depression: they had to keep the community safe from the paralyzing suspicion that the gods were too far away to be interested in humans.

One must place the event that was Plato before the background of the political and biological polis catastrophe in order to understand how much of a change later Hellenism brought about in the lifestyles of the educated. It radiated a suggestion that would remain characteristic of philosophical life for an entire age: as a broker for the new ontology, the philosopher tries to convince his fellow citizens to participate in the transition from dwelling in the city to dwelling in being. This and nothing else was intended by the project of the love of wisdom. The time was clearly ripe for it; a stronger, perhaps desperate preconception of wisdom is to be assumed if the adept pursues the task of acquiring the most beneficial knowledge of the whole—within the brief span of a human life. Plato's wisdom was a fire into which *one life* plunged in order to save itself and its dream of immunity. Yet even those who did not wish to be burned, only to edify or warm themselves from a distance (like the average client of *paideía* in Hellenistic times), would soon have no choice but to bow to the authority of this new source of meaning and heat.

Injecting life with the madness that calls itself being: through this operation, the philosopher claims the future right to present himself as a doctor and relocation assistant for surrounded life; behind the mask of an expert in other places as such and other dwelling in general, the philosopher offers his services to alienated societies as a specialist in illnesses of culture, meaning and place. It is, according to Socrates' parable in the *Theaetetus*, his mission to release good ideas from bad circumstances. Just as post-Babylonian Judaism had learned to live fundamentally beyond its means in theological matters—returning from exile and trembling with anger, weakness and amazement, it nonetheless elevated its God above the imperial gods of the surrounding major powers—so too the Athenian genius gained the utmost philosophical potency after recovering from its own fall and colonizing being itself as a cryptic *Magna Graecia*. From that point on, philosophers resided in their host cities as if they no longer lived there; the Academy, located outside the city walls, grew into the school for a metaphorical and metaphysical exile. In that school, transference and transcendence were trained as primary movements of the conscious life. This gesture, along with its replicability, was the basis for the immeasurable export successes of Athenian scholasticism.

From that point, to think meant moving into the space from which no further uprooting is possible.[2] Just as every life crosses over from its initial abdominal cavity to a social container, so too the philosophy whose aim is to be a midwife into brighter clearings now practices relocation from the political container into a cave of pure light. This, to reverse Gaston Bachelard's formulation, no longer provides "the great securities of a belly," but it offers "the rational beauties of geometric volume."[3] The example set by

Diogenes in his notorious *píthos*, the tub-abode, would be followed in the next millennium and beyond by all authentic members of the profession: they no longer lived in the empirical city but rather in a luminous tub, namely the cosmos. The tragedian Euripides is said to have made the following statement, already fully marked by the spirit of academic semi-exile: "As the whole sky can be crossed by the eagle, so the entire earth is a fatherland to the noble man." Even where philosophers have citizenship as political persons, they live in their host cities like metics or *peregrini*, as incomers and passing travelers in an only coincidentally existing, stuck-together and intellectually hopeless commune. In this respect, even the sharpest antipodes of classical philosophy, the Platonists and the Cynics, did not differ. While the Platonic soul insists on its right to roam freely, both "under the earth and above the sky" (*Theaetetus*, 174e), the cynic claims to be invincible as someone "whose country [was] disgrace and poverty."[4] Both placed irony between themselves and the city. Indeed, what use are heroic walls when they no longer protect the conviction that the best life is at home behind them? Comparisons and defeats shattered local naïveté. Why continue to build if walls can no longer ward off the fear of soulless depth? It is not only in the face of death that all humans, as Epicurus would go on to say, live in a city without walls; in addition, the inhabitants of the fortified cities can no longer find safety from the feeling of having ended up in a space abandoned by all bright communal spirits—put in modern terms, from depression, de-solidarization, neglect. This makes it all the more urgent to ask how one can succeed in acquiring citizenship to dwell in being.

The political concern for space among humans on the threshold of the imperial state is marked by a motif that, drawing on Oswald Spengler, one could call an archaic cosmological claustrophobia—a fear that Spengler wanted to view as a hallmark of all alert and freely mobile life. "This world-fear is assuredly the most creative of all primal feelings."[5] It is this that every original "symbolizing of extension, of space or of things" seeks to avert. It seems more plausible to assume that the specific fear of the interminable expanse of the terrestrial and celestial space is only broken up as a side effect of spheric disturbances—in the violent absorption of groups and tribes into larger imperial structures, and in the de-securing of cities. It is not necessarily the naturally experienceable vastness of the cope of heaven that gives humans the feeling of being lost in the overextended space. Cultural anthropologists and characterologists have shown that some cultures and individuals know little about claustrophobia; Frobenius celebrated the world experience of expanse-seeking cultures, and Michael Balint provided the individual-psychological counterpart in his analysis of the philobat. The cosmophobic mode of feeling is more of a derived phenomenon whose prerequisites are failed immunizations and collapsed narcissisms. From time immemorial, people with minor residual traumas have associated the sight of the blue sky most readily with images of tents and magic cloaks, and in the time of architects also domes, vaults and palaces; they recognize its expansiveness as an accomplice of their courage and its altitude as a prefiguring of the possibilities of their intelligence. The experience that the cosmos is not sealed, on the other hand, and invites mortals to fall out of it, or that feeling of a serious and terrible *depth* which Spengler described so unforgettably in his theory of space—or the angry awareness of seeing the edge of a walled-up desert when one looked up at the sky—are among the psychopathological achievements of times in which more and more individuals experienced themselves as exposed and lost, rejected by humans and forgotten by the gods. Perhaps this mode of experience also contains admixed remnants of an archaic religion of panic that may have formed under the impression of cosmic disasters.

The modern atheistic sentiment characteristically invoked by Pascal—"The silence of those infinite spaces terrifies me"— which escorted beautiful souls from the seventeenth century on, has a complex background that could, in its outlines, be reconstructed with the tools of a theory of spheric disasters and acquired psychocosmological immunodeficiency. The difference between the history of empirically acquired world fears and a general history of injured life would be that the former would be concerned with the disturbances in psychocosmic immune systems: it deals with deportation, exile, estrangement and existence in the Interior Castle of separations, whose inmates seem condemned to a deviant life in deathlike dungeons. At the same time, it differs from the history of unease in culture[6] in that it thematizes not so much an abstinence from drives as a withdrawal of form, and deals less with libidinous privations than spheric ones. Fates of spatial feeling, not of drive, should be seen here; illnesses not of relationships, but rather of the soul. The weakness of the object relation appears as an aspect of a weakness in the world form.

At the same time as these disturbances in existential-political immune systems, this history would also have to involve showing the healing methods introduced by the ruling exegetes of world forms—kings, religious founders and priests, and finally also philosophers, albeit informally and without any office—to close gaps in the psychological city walls and mend cracks in the shells of lifeworlds. This would yield a history of macroscopic concepts, wisdom teachings, and finally philosophical doctrines of being under therapeutic-immunological auspices. It would have to show that the concept of world as such only gained its metaphysical overtones through all-healing arts of interpretation.

Aggressive repair work on the older mythical-animist and religious concepts of the whole resulted in the "world pictures" of advanced civilizations. In their basic spiritual features, all of these constitute therapeutic ontologies, in that ultimately, they dealt with one question alone: how could endangered individuals in the potentially and actually unsealed communities of the confusing large-scale world still somehow be held safely in a form-giving container of the highest order? The great socio-cosmological models of ancient cultures, from China to Greece, revolve around the question of how the restless, isolated humans in the turbulent urban and imperial times should go about making the transition from fallible human communities to the irrevocable citizenship in the universe.

The great doctrines of order that present themselves as philosophical schools of life and political ontologies define, in general terms, what people must consider if they wish to elevate themselves above tribal, urban and national history and its vicissitudes to rise to the orderly cycles of eternal nature. But because these edifying regularities that humans are to take as their yardsticks— the constant celestial phenomena, the orbits of the sun, moon and planets—supply the suggestive paradigm, nothing seems to have been more important for the classical ontologies or onto-immunologies than clarifying the relationships between the most restless creature and the calmest form of order, between unstable humans and the heavenly constitution. (This presupposed that among the people of the incipient philosophical age, even the slightest trace of a potential memory of larger astral irregularities, if indeed these existed in historical time, had been eliminated. In order to see planetary movements as the archetype of eternally uniform concentricity, it had to be given that they are not affected by any offshoots of astrophobic psychoses, which can be supposed in some Near Eastern, Asian and Latin American religions. Only then could an allied sky be deified as a guarantee of universal implementations of order.[7]) The stirred-up, released, fear-ready people in the times of warring cities and states had to become convinced that they could at no time stand outside of valid forms of order, indeed never far from a sealed and full whole, if they only accepted this novel, exact definition of their cosmic condition through philosophical thought.

Once mortals recognized their situation in the universal container of being, they would always succeed in coping with personal divestments and the losses of form in local politics. If the Persians wiped out your relatives or Macedonian pirates sold you at a slave market, even if Scythian riders roasted you over a slow flame—there would always be a position from which this, even for you, would appear merely as the rippled surface of unperturbed depths. That is the consolation of philosophy, in so far as it sustains its mission of harmony to the utmost: it gives its own the key with which they recognize that as far as we are concerned, everything happens as it can and should. It is the art of changing perspective according to each incident, such that denial can become affirmation, the foreign can become one's own, and annihilation can become a contribution to the eutony of the whole. The wise man always understands good fortune and misfortune

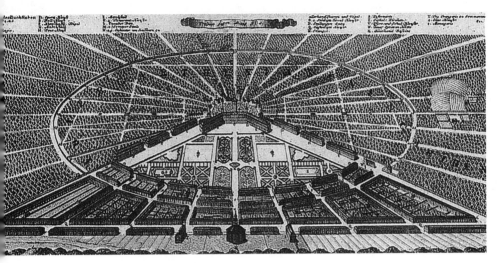

Heliopolis, also known as Karlsruhe, 1715

merely as lessons in a course of adjustment to the universe; he is
the human who has refuted the outside. His method is a Uranian
structuralism. Faced with the utmost, existentially and cosmologically, the edifying schools enforced the central holistic tenet
that for heaven, externality is impossible. One need only assume
the position of the cosmos to gain a share in its invulnerability.

It was obvious to all interested parties in ancient times that
this shift of standpoint to the more than human would be
impossible. A practicing life therefore became obligatory for all
thinkers who were serious about refuge in philosophy. Schools
are rationalist and ascetic orders; they seek to turn mere
humans into interfaces for the cosmic logos. Certainly you
yourself, as a fragile individual, may be too weak for insight
into the whole; but this does not absolve you from the task of
assimilation into the greatest of all immune systems: the perfectly smooth, shining periphery of heaven, which cannot

collapse, even when all securities of the human world start to come undone. The uppermost sphere remains untouchable by disturbances—firstly, because the edge of the whole circles calmly around itself, and secondly, because the seeds of evil, the outrageous unevennesses of incidents in the lower realm, never reach up to the highest heights. The ether feels nothing of the sublunary miasmas; the sphere of ideas rests timelessly in its light. That is why meditation on the outermost, invulnerable containing ring of the existent in the whole was the decisive mental exercise of post-Platonic philosophy.[8] All practice serves to strengthen this mental immune system. In their practical purpose, the ancients' contemplations on order were never anything but individual continuations of the now-meaningless building of city walls by logical means.

"The chisel, in this second sculptural art, is the compass."[9] Its aim is to prove that in all circumstances and at every point on the earth's surface, the soul can invoke its inalienable privilege of being a citizen of the nurturing cosmos. Citizenship in the absolute city remains the property of the wise man, even when everything else brings him upheaval, plague and exile. That is the cosmic cogito which must be able to accompany every human situation: the universe is a house, and the house loses nothing, not even me, no matter how perplexed and lost I might feel.

It was Plato, of course, who set the standards for the glorification of the completed world in his late work. The *pater philosophorum*, as the neo-academic Marsilio Ficino usually called the founder of the Academy, made a personal effort to explain how any refutation of the outside is to be carried out. For this purpose, following on from his nature-philosophical elucidations from the *Timaeus*, he introduced the new argumentation genre of the proof of God's existence in the notorious tenth book of *Laws*; in essence, this entailed the refutation of the assumption that there are bodies which are not encased, fulfilled and governed by a soul.

It is immediately clear that theology—the new philosophical kind no less than the older priestly one—was political from the first moment on, for the defense of God always takes the form of a defense of the community of his followers against the external deniers. It is equally clear what the atheist attack comprised, as the doctrine of the non-being of the gods had always been able to join forces with the antisocial tendency and political materialism, that is to say the doctrine that might is right. If, as the deniers of God's existence preach, there were indeed only mere bodies not infused with any harboring and guiding divine soul, one could rightfully say that these were outside in both an absolute and a relative sense. If the bodies were external and exanimate, however, it would be humans who were themselves bodies among bodies, no less. Furthermore, the bodies of wandering stars, if they were not gods but merely hot piles of rubble and rock, could not possibly look after humans with wise caring. If the great celestial bodies were no more than glowing deserts far away in the cosmos, the cosmic solitude of humans would be a *fait accompli* and would inevitably be followed by social loneliness. Then the atheists would be right to poke fun at the pious fictions of the well-intended who imagine they were surrounded by gods, and that the course of things is governed by wise foresight. Suppress the gods and deny the souls: then the stones are our closest neighbors, and the difference between animated and lifeless bodies no longer means much.

For humans thus disenchanted, the heavens would become a school of indifference. Among city dwellers, the indifference of all towards all would have the last word, for lacking a unifying principle, they could not acknowledge one another any more than one stone acknowledges another. Without fear of punishment in the hereafter, they could also do to one another whatever they wanted. In emptiness, there is no higher authority that would come to the aid of victims and avenge injustice. The right of the stronger body would remain the *ultima ratio* in the regulation of relationships between forces in the external space. At most, the weaker bodies—provided they became temporarily accustomed to one another—could hold on to one another to form coalitions against stronger bodies and thus evade loneliness for a deceptive while. There could never be a substantial or animated community between them, however, because unifying field souls or communal spirits are negated from the outset. The cheerfulness of the unpunished criminal triumphs over philosophical contemplation—a possibility which post-de Sade modernity, with its cult of the artist-criminal, knew how to utilize. Plato's conservative caution is evident in the fact that he expected no good to come of the political apparatus of democracy, with its superstructure of contract theory, conventionalism and anthropological optimism, and sought a more solid basis for the foundation of the body politic.

The premises of Plato's intervention are thus clear: the philosopher understands what opponent he is facing. Entertaining no illusions, he observes the spectacle of political atheism preparing to attack the heart of the commune. When Critias described the gods as the invention of a clever man in his (lost) comedy *Sisyphus*, when Anaxagoras termed the sun a glowing mass of rock, and when Aristophanes portrayed the heavens as a weather machine devoid of gods in *The Clouds*, Athenian lovers of words and wit may have enjoyed these liberalities together with friends who were in need of laughter; they formed part of *agorázein*, the free men's life on the market. But the truthful philosopher reflecting on being's conditions of possibility had to conclude that such talk advanced the death of the commune inside its citizens. Indeed, even if the truth about all this were exactly as those who deny the soul and dispute that the world is full of gods claim, one would have to be doubly wary of advertising such doctrines in public. It is disastrous for the spirit of the community if the opinion spreads that people can be no more for one another than manipulable bodies in the exanimate space. Such convictions would not only disinhibit the strong to enforce their own concerns even more unscrupulously over others; they would also disempower the alliances of the weak and corrode the religious awe that sustains civil solidarity. In addition, any philosopher who has witnessed the mistreatment that takes place when people view one another as bodies in the emptiness knows only too well that humans who are left to their own devices are no consolation for one another—not in peacetime, much less in wartime. Only those who have experienced the "appalling bitterness with which these petty towns strove to destroy one another"[10] can comprehend what the panic of soul loss can trigger between humans who wish to save themselves at the expense of others.

If one wishes to save the citizens from acting towards one another like a random mass of unreasoning bodies fighting for survival, conservative concern tells us, then the atheists cannot be given a say in the polis. Resisting our beginnings—this applies to erotic infection, but even more to the atheistic variety. It holds, as Plato—pioneer of all avant-garde conservatives—thought he had recognized, the seed of de-solidarization. If someone does not advocate a form of *a priori* bond between people living together, are they not encouraging isolation and political neglect? Are those who are unwilling to believe in a communal spirit not driving the dangerously present loss of spirit further? Plato, whose early life was filled by the thirty-year war between Athens and Sparta, had convincing reasons for wanting to advance the New Science of polis animation in the face of the physical and psychological ruins of his home town. It was in the nature of things that this science also had to become a new conception of the doctrine of the gods—and even more, namely the first explicit theoretical theology. Whoever wanted to rescue the community more thoroughly than democratic agitators and market liberals could ever dream had to find a new way of inextricably intertwining the city, the souls of its citizens and the gods in a new way. For only then—just as the divine soul can animate and govern a body if connected to it—could, according to Plato, the presence of a divine organ of reason in the city illuminate and control it in the most beneficial way.

In its tendency, Plato's political theology amounts to a cosmically assisted communitarism: it states that urban communities can only turn out well to the extent that they can be moved by an actually present principle of reason as animated bodies. If they correctly understood themselves, they would resemble logical churches or theonomically constituted units, which would ideally be managed by the true and real philosophers. For ordinary people, this salvific noocracy would be represented by the traditional cult of the gods for the time being, in so far as this cult could still be practiced in good faith without excessive concessions to the old abominations of blood sacrifice. With the new philosophy and the old piety, social synthesis would be adequately supported from above and within; in each case it would be regionally evoked, individually embodied substantial spirit souls, city gods, numina and Tyches that kept the empirical community in shape. (This holistic rule would remain in force for millennia, though broken through countless setbacks; it was not until "internally differentiated" modern society, which managed to create non-theological, primarily welfare-state harboring systems, that someone undertook the experiment of attempting its synthesis without any unifying gods—on the assumption that the political suspension of the divine was possible without immediately provoking the rule of wolves. Because mere sociotechnic bracketing systems are clearly insufficient to animate a good society, however, there are once more calls for "values" in modernity too; yet what would these "values" be but the old polis gods in exile?)

If everything is full of gods, however—Plato adopts Thales' saying *pánta plére theón* at a key point in his demonstration—then bodies, including those of the polis that are primarily at issue here, are always connected to reasonable souls, and the straying of isolated bodies in an empty space and of souls in an uninhabitable world would become impossible. This impossibility is Plato's *demonstrandum*—the beginning and end of his efforts to ground the community in actually present, effectively encompassing, divine essential forces. Where the soul of reason created a body politic, the first deductive city, one could—perhaps for the first time in human history—eliminate the forces of greed and *ressentiment* from the regiments of citizens and replace them with a noocratic regime.

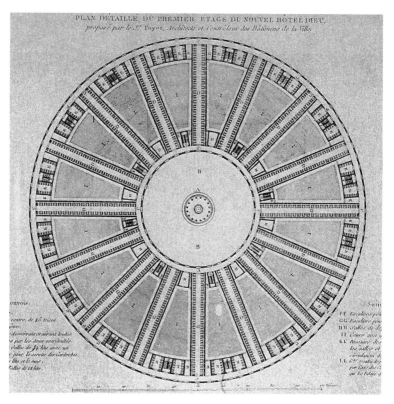

Plan of the second floor for the surveillance clinic designed by Bernard Poyet (1785)

If one subjects Plato's arguments—which I shall consider more closely in a moment—to critical examination from a greater distance, it becomes apparent how quickly, even precipitously, he reached the goal that he would under no circumstances have been willing to abandon. Should one have suggested discreetly that he take a little more time over his demonstrations? Could one have advised him to hesitate longer before reaching his conclusions, and to place less faith in his experiences of evidence? These questions are obviously of a rhetorical nature, as we have no advice for the greats of tradition after the fact. On the contrary: it would seem that thinkers who know their results from the start always and seemingly necessarily rush their thoughts (especially under the pretense of slowing down their argumentation, and with great respect for logical sequences of steps). This is because for them, the reward lay not in the journey to their goal, which was rather their starting point and required the illusion that it had been found in the course of investigation and would be generally and reliably accessible to all benevolent and reasonable people. We moderns are simultaneously suspicious and envious of anyone who enjoys the privilege of being allowed to begin at their goal (for those who eventually realize that they are already where they want to be can consider themselves illuminated, whereas there can be no illumination for the goal-deprived and indecisive, only ecstasies of skepticism). The logical situation of the present is characterized by the fact that it explicitly advises leaping if walking will definitely not lead to one's goal. Perhaps one needs to have lost that classical certainty of one's goal to understand what a privilege it was when the goal-assured of former times flew towards their results with joyful haste—or approached them with beneficial delay. Then one realizes that one expected too much of the old masters in seeking to make them accomplices of modern doubts and depressions. Can the result be left open at all when dealing with urgent matters? Does it not become possible only when nothing is at stake anymore? Has the famous "Cartesian doubt" not always been a farce, serving merely to conceal the manic-resultative or depressive-indecisive dispositions of authors? (In contemporary thought it was Jacques Derrida who experimented most with forms of a radically undecided discourse—where philosophical argumentation is transformed into an exercise in non-arrival at a positive result. But this always-already-not-arriving merely reveals the other side of classical metaphysics' always-already-being-at-the-goal.)

Be that as it may: anyone still attempting after Plato's proof to claim that there are no gods, and human bodies are placed loosely, arbitrarily and always separably in the godless space will, according to the saying of the school and the temple, simply remain in error initially and the rest of the time. For the true thesis whose consolidation is the concern here is, once and for all, that everything is full of gods.

But because the godless human, especially if they are an impetuous young person under a bad influence, can only be mistaken at first, they have a right to instruction. No one enjoys being in error, and every misguided individual is entitled to be corrected through better knowledge: these Socratic axioms follow the basic rule of the Greek urban mentality, namely treating even the highest cultural treasures not as esoteric, but rather bringing them to the center of communal life, *en méso*, between witnesses and orators. This was successfully demonstrated by the tragic plays of the Athenians, and the new theology, whose aim was to outstrip the Dionysian theater, could not differ in this respect. Before Plato approached the question of whether and how one should punish the godless, therefore, he believed it right and necessary to attempt a socio-pedagogical application of his divine proof in order to rehabilitate atheists deserving punishment. This is where the thinker obliged to methodic patience parts ways with the priests, who are quicker to curse whatever does not swear by the same things they do. Only in the case of an obstinate insistence on their crimes, Plato ultimately argues, is it right and necessary, with a certain regret, to make delinquents feel the severity of the law. But in both matters—the proof of God's existence and its therapeutic application—Plato makes it clear that the question of the existence of God and gods (the difference between singular and plural is less significant here than generally assumed) is not a mere dispute over a theoretical viewpoint, to be practiced behind the Academy's walls as a contest of argumentation. Affirming or denying the gods: these are not competing, symmetrical positions in a wrestling match that one could watch with a sporting interest. Regarding the thesis that there are gods, and that these, though existing on the largest scale (*mégiston*), also concern themselves with the small scale (*micron*) of human affairs, there can—if philosophy is to be of any use to the community— be no freedom of opinion, and thus no license to deny. If the polis is to be, then gods must be; it is because the gods are that the polis is possible and real—and if life in the polis is in a sorry state nonetheless, it is primarily because forgetfulness of the gods has already spread among the citizens in an alarming fashion.

In this situation, the philosopher puts himself forward as the cultural doctor against forgetting. He certainly does not become involved in the undertaking of proving the existence of the divine by revealing hidden evidence in order to participate in discursive shadow-boxing. The aged Plato had no affinity for the athletic sadism with which talented students strangled the opinions of their forefathers in mid-air as Hercules strangled the snakes. His argumentation is conservative and mournfully constructive. He knows that no society can actually put its effective immune systems, its life-giving shared convictions, up for negotiation without destroying itself. His proof of God's or the gods' existence does not have the purpose of providing the arguments for the more probable option in an unresolved matter. The matter has been decided at the highest level, and a judgment has been pronounced for human and divine reasons. The gods are alive, and their reality and presence must not be challenged by any serious counter-thesis. When Plato argues nonetheless, pondering for a moment whether argumentation is even appropriate here, his concern is to provide additional security for the indispensable result—the doctrine, confirmed by thinkers of all eras and intuitively approved by the healthy minds of all peoples, that there are good and wise gods interested in humans—in the face of the atheist provocation.

We are thus dealing with an Athenian prelude to the medieval *fides quaerens intellectum* [faith seeking understanding] thesis, but now under the leadership of philosophy, which claimed the key new theological competency for itself over popular and priestly belief. Consequently, the decision to argue was not without idea-political pitfalls: if the gods became dependent on proof, then the legitimizing foundations of communal power and order shift, at least hypothetically, in favor of those who advance the best arguments for its theological grounding. Plato's introduction of the proof of God's existence provided the model for a conservative revolution in favor of the substantiating class.

Of course, the polis had always lived off the conviction that its survival was guaranteed by attentive, geographically loyal gods present in the souls of citizens. In future, however, it would also have to make sure that the city order as a whole, as a harmonic joining of parts, shared by analogy in the divine-geometric order of the tiered and rounded universe;[11] this is where the specifically new contribution of philosophical cosmotheology came into play. The city had to become round like the cosmos and be

House for a Cosmopolite by Carl Peter Joseph Normand (1802) (engraving after Vaudoyer, 1785)

hierarchized like the cosmos, from the best down to the less good. The conventional cult experts, the priests, were no longer competent to speak of this divine geometry—unlike the mathematically educated new philosophers.

Thus, in his attempt to ward off the opinion crime of atheism, Plato, immunologist-in-chief of the metaphysical age, laid his cards on the table: in the light of all his observations, a true doctrine of divinity, and hence also community, was now—once and

The utopia of the factory city: Claude-Nicolas-Louis Ledoux, project for the city of Chaux

for all—only possible philosophically and spherologically. The rhapsodists could happily go on recounting their myths, and the priests would retain their ritual responsibility—but it would be the philosophers, as the only group holding the proof of divine existence, who were entitled to claim the adequate spiritual representation of the community.

Thus, at a single blow, it was revealed how the new philosophical theology would be integrated into the immunological and institutional reconstruction of the better city. In his proof of God's existence, Plato was concerned with a proof of universal ensoulment. How peculiar: God could be considered proven if it were made evident that the cosmos was orb-shaped, and that this all-inclusive orb was homogeneously ensouled in its whole extension. If this were attainable through argumentation, every externality would be refuted and the intelligence endangered by

O. E. Bieber, competition entry for a skyscraper in Cologne (1925)

cosmic and social isolation could breathe a sigh of relief once and for all. The world was not governed by arbitrariness and chance, then, as the austere teachers of natural law claimed with their doctrine of the rule of the strong; rather, the existent as a whole, whether humans understood it or not, was controlled by the encompassing divine law, which simultaneously manifested itself in geometry and ethics. Philosophical mathematics would thus shatter the illusion of the privilege of the strong: it showed there was a strength that was iniquity and weakness. If animated wholes were the true realities, however, then life in the cities—even in Athens after its deserved ruin—could and should become good once more.

The fateful question for the political community was therefore how it would arrive at an anti-atheistic constitution, as well as an educational system that fostered solidarity. Here philosophy put itself forward as the first constitution-protecting science. On the one hand, Plato's case for God and the gods countered the currently more dangerous atheism towards the city gods, which had always been condemned as the crime of godlessness (*asébeia*)

The settlement of Leipzig-Lössnig, c. 1925

in the polises—the case of Socrates remained unforgotten. On the other hand, it opposed nature-philosophical or cosmological atheism, which argued for a world without God, and thus a universal outside: a thesis whose inception shows how remote freelance sophists could become from the traditional duty of priests and sages to foster native mentalities towards political and physical communities. In a cultural situation where the cities were dependent on a constant regeneration of communal mentalities, both varieties of atheism—the regional and the universal—had a highly corrosive effect; they amounted to a form of communal and ontological desertion. Denial of the city gods was a more immediate danger, as it directly tempted people in the polis, whether educated or uneducated, to act without regard for the laws and the legitimate interests of fellow citizens, whereas absolute or cosmological atheism only attracted the clients of various all-too-clever sophists. As long as they had no other choice than to articulate the basis for their unity in theological words and rites, however, both forms manifestly attacked the mental immune systems and animating phantasms of shared bodies in political collectives. If the gods were the effective hypostases of the public spirit, and if cities lived off the fact that their citizens consider the community's life force more real than that of any individual life, then doubts as to the gods' existence could on no account be uttered in public; and it was all the more important that speeches denying the gods, authored by seemingly wise men, should never circulate as debatable opinions.

Plato's fervor against the deceptive appearance and its producers and middlemen, the sophists, stemmed primarily from one vexation: how easily atheistic and antisocial arguments could adopt the semblance of plausibility. Destroying this façade was the critical purpose of "true" philosophy, which for the time being meant Platonic philosophy. In the cultural conditions of antiquity, atheists could be viewed as semantic terrorists aiming to erode social synthesis with arguments. If philosophy meant to become indispensable for the grounding of communal life, it therefore had to begin proving something it had previously seemed unnecessary to prove: the reality of the gods—and even more, the infusion of everything existent with a delayed divine presence.

It was only this new enterprise of proof, which seemed procedurally revolutionary while retaining a conservative outlook, that gave the central principle of these investigations—the concept of the *sphere*, or the actually existing, meaning-filled, all-ensouling and all-harboring orb—its epochally outstanding position. The Platonic proof of God's existence enthrones the orb, with due formality, as the final morphological principle of the existent in general. Whatever may have been hinted at by Anaximander, Anaxagoras, Parmenides, Empedocles and above all the

The Pantheon, total view of the dome through a fisheye lens

Pythagoreans about the spheric structure of the world-whole, it was only with Plato's complete and masterful argumentation that the theology of the orb was promoted to an unforgettable paradigm. It was his arguments in the *Timaeus*, the *Phaedrus* and the *Laws* that set in motion the geometrization of the existent as a whole, with almost incalculably far-reaching consequences. One cannot overestimate the significance of this event for the history of thought: not only did the proof of God remain the supreme discipline of edifying philosophy for over two millennia; for almost equally long, Platonic arguments would assert their validity in the discourses of cosmology and noology. It was only when the younger Europeans learned to seal up their communities with non-religious binding agents—market economy, parliamentarianism, welfare systems, mass media, law and the art world—which means not before the eighteenth century, could they afford to forget their Platonic legacy almost overnight. *Voici le temps des esprits forts*: an infernal racket from all free spirits. Yet did Hegel not already voice the suspicion that mockery of the philosopher-kings only managed to become a vulgar entertainment, especially among the respectively newest philosophers, because the modern state was itself the realization of Platonism, the reign of principles?

In Plato, theology fully became morphology. In revealing God as the highest matter of form, it made itself possible in the first place as the art of speaking reasonably about God. With the proof that God possesses and grants the best form that is possible in the realized whole, it entered its rationalist or constructivist period; from that point on, anyone unwilling to speak of the orb would also have to remain silent about God and the gods. It was, admittedly, characteristic of the spirit of the old West from Ionia to Jena that it now *constructed* God, but had to pretend it was submitting to a revelation. What we call the age of metaphysics was essentially the time of a constructivism that was forced to deny its own existence. Its primary architectural and thought figure was the spheric God as an unsurpassable guarantor of ontological immunity. If the religious theologies have treated that basic realization with outrage to this day, however, dismissing the constructible god as a fetish or an idol, it is only because they think of constructs and their safeguarding functions in small terms, clinging to the notion that higher immunity can only be found, not made.

This holds a practically wise insight, in that it relies on a God who holds His hand open when everything is slipping out of human hands. It is theoretically half-hearted, however, because it closes its eyes to the power of constructed immunities. Perhaps this half measure is psychologically understandable, for even theologians, in their discursive dealings, do not want to be without the certainty of being allowed to drop themselves into an encompassing shell if necessary. Hence they stop short of that threshold beyond which theology would, through the internal logic of the matter itself, turn into morphology and immunology.[12]

The new science of the constructible god hinges entirely on Plato's epoch-making argument that the divine universe must be a single ensouled orb for two reasons: firstly, because the soul, as the moving element, universally asserts its precedence over the body as the moved one; and secondly, because the creative divine spirit, because of its own bestness and lack of envy, or paradoxically put its "eternal product," can only provide the best movement, namely the circularly self-propelled one. As the wealth of the good includes the full number of primary and sensually experienceable dimensions—the three—the circle must be elevated to undeprived abundance, namely the spherical form.

One cannot marvel enough at this argument, which constitutes the logical cell of metaphysical globalization; it not only reveals what phantoms celebrated their rise in the pale light of evidence, but also depicts in almost caricature-like purity to what conclusions the pretension of gaining "truth from the concept" can lead. If one reformulates the Platonic idea with an emphasis on its logical form, its peculiarity becomes even more striking: the cosmos *must* be an orb, for God must be adequate to His concept! Firstly, God's conception of himself requires, with a violence that demands consequences, that the world not be left uncreated, as this would be a form of economy unworthy of God (God and the sun are the great providers of the metaphysical age; they act as ontologized kings of wastefulness whose generosity buys the allegiance of everything that is—except for gratitude-withholding rebels). Secondly, it also requires him to craft the world in a literally godly, or at least godlike fashion, for any less than the formally and materially best cannot express its maker (God's *modus operandi* is inevitably expressivist-perfectionist). The spherical shape of the whole expresses the necessary convergence of the maker's bestness, the process' bestness and the result's bestness. Roundness is the revelatory form of the world's ontological *aristeia*. This brings us to what was intimated in the prologue regarding the exact optimism of ontology: a theory of the whole *can* only be a theory of the best.

This unmistakably creates a relationship between God and the world that is analogous to what, in the biblical genesis, is termed the "image of God"—though Plato's god behaves more generously in extensive terms, as he already places the morphological optimum "outside" himself with his first action (the work of the demiurge, after all, is not a gradual creation in the Judeo-Christian manner, but rather a protuberance that grows weaker as it moves from the center towards the periphery); Yahwe's generosity, by contrast, is more an intensive and culminating one: he begins with the crude divisions, saving the best investment till last in the form of Adam, the last-created, and his descendants. It is obvious, then, that the two thus constitute radically different theologies that could be termed cosmotheism (Greek) and ethnotheism (Jewish), or perhaps morphotheism and nomotheism.

With the forcefulness of the first time, Plato thus makes the gods—the moving souls or principles of the bodies—and the manifesting God—the self-propelling universal body, the heavens, who is the whole or the cosmos—contingent on their intelligibility and constructability (one could also say their rational manifestability and disclosedness), and hence their logical and geometric, or rather uranometric properties. Now is the time when comprehensibility, roundness and bestness converge, and in philosophical terms, the focal point of this convergence is called truth. Thus the proto-constructivist situation is reached; rational theology, also known as ontotheology, has become possible.

Proving God; geometrizing (or rather uranometrizing) God; ascribing to God, along with his bodily analogy, the cosmos, the most sublime shape and movement; making God return into himself, without beginning or end and endlessly circling within himself—it was the concomitance of these purposes that constituted the primal act of European philosophical rationalism. It made geometry, the only discipline competent to deal with circles and orbs, into the underlying science of theology—and, through the latter, of political theory too. (The alliance of geometry and political science would be affirmed until modernity, most of all in the phantasms of a "geometric community" from the time of the French Revolution and the socio-architectural constructivism of modern construction from Bauhaus to Le Corbusier.[13]) The god of the philosophers was now no longer responsible for lifeworldly self-harborings and interior-sealings in merely a vague immunological sense; as an exact god, he created himself and his space according to the model of the noblest movement and the most stately shape. From that point on, spheres were to be understood as *orbs* in the precise sense—no longer merely pre-geometric, psychocosmological outlines of the world of closeness, with its morphologically indistinct architectural extensions. With the help of the compasses, the older village and urban world interior was renovated as a perfect cosmic form. Those in the know would henceforth live under a subtle *dome* that becomes visible when, after the disenchantment of sensory perception, the new enchantment of formal observation comes into effect.

The mathematical modernization of the cosmos would have fallen short of its purpose had it not been obvious to adepts of philosophy that in this round dome of being, the reasonable soul is with itself everywhere, and cannot possibly stand anywhere outside of the good whole. This raises the question of how individuals understand their own standing within the absolute shell. Can they draw conclusions about their duty from their place in the whole, about their fate from their achievement, and about their immunity from their circumspection?

The most important part of Plato's proof of God's existence for the large-scale political creation of spheres is the doctrine asserting the non-indifference of the gods to humans. What good would it do to recognize that God is an all-inclusive orb if one could not simultaneously make it plausible that this orb not only contains humans along with the totality of elements and things, but also looks after them? If God were no more than a large container, how could he be interested in his own contents? What does it matter to the orb's circumference what it encompasses? If it were merely an external border, in what way could the *sphaira* communicate with the scattered logical points inside it, with individuals and all other ensouled creatures?

Plato's answers to these questions impressed European thought for more than two millennia, and if classical doctrines on the connection between the meaningful whole and its intelligent parts seem more or less obsolete today, it is less because they have genuinely been refuted—for what does refutation mean in the field of exuberance?—than because they have fallen prey to the culture-revolutionary change of subject in modernity. In logical terms, modernity is the self-fulfillment of the analytical myth that gives the smallest parts precedence over their composites. Sociologically too, the precedence of individuals over their associations and of systems over their environments is dominant. Thus market society no longer has any use for the hierarchical schema of the whole and its parts for its routines; it is only kept in reserve for times of war, when modern social systems are re-converted to military-holistic standards (with a totalitarian division of stress, or total mobilization).

As is scarcely avoidable with problems on the threshold of the utterable and justifiable, Plato cloaked many of his critical insights in mythological parables, offering a suggestive appearance for the most unfounded speculation. When the concern is to show that the cosmos is not indifferent to the humans within it, Plato galls back on the stonemason myth already developed in the *Timaeus*, with which he can easily show why the parts are highly significant for a whole in an intelligent plan: "even masons say the big stones don't lie well without the small ones." (*Laws*, 902d)

The co-operation between human and cosmos was initially conceived using the analogy of a great machine or thoroughly rationalized city in which all parts act in concert according to a detailed master plan. Plato describes the binding of the individual human into the architecture of the world as follows:

What we say to the young man should serve to convince him of this thesis: "The supervisor of the universe has arranged everything with an eye to its preservation and excellence, and its individual parts play appropriate active or passive roles according to their various capacities. These parts, down to the smallest details of their active and passive functions, have each been put under the control of ruling powers that have perfected the minutest constituents of the universe. Now then, you perverse fellow, one such part—a mere speck that nevertheless constantly contributes to the good of the whole—is you, you who have forgotten that nothing is created except to provide the entire universe with a life of prosperity. You forget that creation is not for your benefit: *you* exist for the sake of the universe. Every doctor, you see, and every skilled craftsman, always works for the sake of some end-product as a whole; he handles his materials so that they will give the best results in general, and makes the parts contribute to the good of the whole, not vice versa. But you're grumbling because you don't appreciate that your position is best not only for the universe but for you too, thanks to your common origin. […] Seeing all this he contrived a place for each constituent where it would most easily and effectively ensure the triumph of virtue and the defeat of vice throughout the universe."[14]

Positive spirits would take the oppressive sublimity of this argument as an example whenever they needed to thwart the demands of dissatisfied, rebellious—in modern parlance, dissident—individuals. One can hold the opinion that Plato here finishes by argumentative means what the ancient Mesopotamian city-builders had begun with architectural methods: the closure of extended power to form a homogeneous world interior, and even more the binding of the individual into the total edifice. Only as such can this outsideless inner world become the territory of a divine subjectivity that determines everything because it calculates everything.

That the marvelous is close to the dreadful in the meticulous construction of the absolute inside becomes clear from Plato's indications that there is no escape for ill-disposed, obstinately self-willed individuals from the all-attentiveness of the gods. No one can boast of evading divine retribution—for the gods will find you everywhere: "make yourself ever so small and hide in the depths of the earth, or soar high into the sky: this sentence will be ever at your heels" (905a). In the Platonic space, the rule-breaker is always hunted down—the investigative success rate of eternal justice is 100% (by comparison, the Bavarian police proudly reported that a near-sensational 65% of crimes were solved in 1997, with a national average of 52%). Only the ill-disposed view this as a threat, whereas well-meaning souls could not possibly want to be anywhere other than these transparent conditions. (God's omniscient executive was similarly well developed among the Jewish prophets: "Though they dig down to the depths of the grave, from there my hand will take them; though they climb up to the heavens, from there I will bring them down." These words are from Amos 9:2, and we find an analogous passage in the ancient Indian *Atharva-Veda*: "He that should flee beyond the heaven far away would not be free from king Varuna.[15]")

In order to mute the potential and actual terror of this hyper-transparency, Plato introduces his second mythological construction, which helps us to understand why humans are not

Inmate in prayer before the central building of a panopticon prison

merely placed in certain positions by a higher power like small stones in a great construction or figures in a board game after all—and conversely, why freedom lies not only in wrongdoing. The heteronomic factor in such holistic considerations conveys an extravagant mentality of order that does not so much edify as outrage, for individuals are being controlled as if they were not free but rather tools, not reasonable creatures choosing their own purposes but rather erased enforcement officers in the totalitarian service of being and God. (This heteronomism accompanied political holisms until the nineteenth and twentieth centuries, when there were attempts to politically implement the ideas of totality from political Platonism, also known as German Idealism, and the naturalistic systems that followed it.) If one wishes to turn on the charm of the doctrine of the divine regiment, one should not spoil it with arguments that counteract notions of freedom. It is therefore a logical step to reformulate this harsh idea of heteronomy in the direction of autonomy, which can only occur through a reflection that turns the prudent human into an independent employee of the gods.

At this hazardous juncture, Plato falls back on a second mythological reserve: the legend of the kinship between the human spirit soul and the gods. After all, Prometheus' thefts gave humans "a share of what was allotted to the gods," as Socrates explains in the early dialogue *Protagoras*. Thus, if the universe is controlled by divine powers or principles according to con-summate structural wisdoms, humans cannot remain entirely excluded from this ability. If they make good use of the power of reason that was stolen for them, they will not discover the given order merely in the attitude of acceptant submission, but have a share in it with a form of intellectual co-spontaneity. They would by no means be mere prisoners of the cosmic domes, as later Gnostic enemies of the world would claim, but rather co-producers and shareholders of the well-formed totality. By sharing in the production of what matters, they preserve their kinship with the gods. As members of the intelligible aristocracy, then, humans are well-advised to feel *absolutely* at home in the great orb. Just as the high nobility have relatives in all corners of the world with whom they can reside on occasion, the intellect recognizes at any given location the goodness of the immanence that is ready to receive it.

That this sublime system of inclusion, which grew from the conversion of the city to the cosmic orb, cannot be defended without paradoxes and new, precarious exclusivities is demonstrated by the unpleasant fate of those who insist to the last on their urban or absolute atheism, and even (like the notorious Alcibiades) take the liberty of celebrating heretical or parodistic private mysteries that help them to "wreck completely whole homes and states."

> If one of these people is found guilty, *the court* must sentence him to imprisonment as prescribed by law in the prison in the center of the country; no free man is to visit him at any time [...]. When he dies the body must be cast out over the borders of the state unburied. If any free man lends a hand in burying him, *he must* be liable to a charge of impiety at the hands of anyone who cares to prosecute.[16]

The subtle argument culminates with amazing blatancy in a crude practical suggestion. The expulsion of the godless from the good whole opens up paradoxes that would have devastating effects on the rational soundness of the construction if they could immediately be made explicit. For an explication it would be sufficient to ask where—in the topics of the existent as a whole—the corpses of the God-deniers would end up once cast out of the country, and what topological purpose their non-burial would serve. For either the orb is inclusive, in which case even atheists cannot be excluded from it, or it is non-inclusive, which would prove those right who assert the existence of soul-less bodies and a godless outside. The irony of the drastic excommunication, after all, is that it casts the false teachers into the very outside which, according to their theistic opponents and judges, cannot exist. Refusing to inter atheists who are unwilling to change their opinion despite the proof of God's existence in their native soil, in violation of the sacrosanct Greek custom—would this not mean using them to demonstrate that some bodies do indeed end up in the exanimate space? Their unburied corpses would not cease preaching the impertinent doctrine of the outside—if only someone could approach them to hear and carry further these sermons from the cold.

It is clear from this passage and numerous others from Plato's body of work that his collected utterances are far from systematic; even the fundamental opposition between monistic and dualistic tendencies in his thought is not brought into any sort of equi-librium, and one certainly cannot speak of any unity in his final vocabulary or basic conceptual field. The present case speaks for itself in every way: excommunicating the denier of the ensouled universe from the ensouled universe—this paradox is disastrous enough to refute the all-inclusivity of the divine orb (which points to monistic options). One realizes immediately that it is not simply a matter of theoretical truth here, however, but more: the immune functions of a large-scale worldview. Just as the city could not live without the right to excommunicate irredeemable enemies of the polis *ultima ratione*, the all-containing orb could not stay in shape if it were unable to discharge *in extremis* what it failed to integrate. Even the One Cosmos cannot be conceptually rounded without discriminating against the other.

At the critical point where the paradox could break open, the theologian-lawmaker issues a ban on thinking—here in the form of a harsh admonition against siding with the godless man after his death. Whatever objections the dead outcast might present to the theologian must under no circumstances be articulated by another in his stead, otherwise the calmed dispute between theists and atheists would be revived. In procedural terms, the ban on burying atheists is equivalent to the directive of withdrawing the atheist cause as a whole from discussion. Thou shalt have no dealings with advocates of the soullessness thesis, and thou shalt ask no questions that aim beyond the One, the good, the whole and the inner. To prevent the analytical monstrosity from growing new heads, those who grant deceased God-deniers the honor of burial in their native soil must themselves be charged with *asébeia*. (One might, furthermore, recall that atheism was deemed punishable by death in the Body of Liberties established by the theocracy of Massachusetts as late as the mid-seventeenth century; in Europe, atheistic views were a reliable pretext for excommunication until the late nineteenth century, and later in some areas—not so much from church communities as from respectable society.)

If one needed proof that universalist discourses are creatures which easily catch cold in the draft of their immanent paradoxes, one would find it in the object lesson Plato gives in the practical part of his proof of God's existence. There is no need for such evidence where, as in our spherological investigations, the immunological quality of totality formations and inclusion figures is emphasized from the outset—whether these are ritualistic (as in traditional cults), architectural (as in ancient Mesopotamian wall-building) or argumentative (as in the new Athenian ontotheology).[17]

Like Plato, his successor Aristotle also gave circular movement precedence over all other forms (linear, curved or compound). In keeping with the rapid expansion of post-Platonic discursive games, however—or because of scientific progress, some say a little hastily—he had to dissolve the mythological shell in which the founder of the Academy had clothed his cosmological teachings. While, in the *Timaeus*, Plato had still made a divine demiurge responsible for the spherical constitution and circular movement of the world body, Aristotle was forced to abandon the producer myth and discover an immanent, structural or material reason for the world body's round shape and rotation. That was no easy task in his situation, for none of the elements defined since Empedocles—earth, water, air and fire—which seemingly composed all natural bodies, displayed rotation as an inherent kinetic characteristic. All of them exhibit only movements along straight lines—either rising from a given point like the weightless elements air and fire, or falling from a given point like the heavy elements earth and water. The rotation of the heavens, seemingly proved by simple empirical evidence, cannot possibly be explained from the properties of the canonic elements. Aristotle recognized very soberly that one cannot fashion a state cosmologically using the trivial base material of nature. None of these are capable of more than finite, linear, exhaustible movements; heavenly movement, by contrast, must be infinite, rotative and inexhaustible if it is to fulfill the expectations of cosmologically interested reason. Neither from earth nor fire, neither from water nor air, is there any physical path to the sublime observation of the rotating, perfectly rounded sky.

To explain the sky in its shape and movement, then—by means that respect and exceed Plato's directives—Aristotle took refuge in one of the most violent and suggestive hypotheses ever advanced in the history of scientific thought: he postulated the existence of a fifth element or fifth body, whose nature would include the circular motion essentially absent from other bodies. Taking up older traditions, Aristotle called this circling, inherently rotative and spherogenic body the *aithér*.

The ether was already known among the earlier poets as a subtle sky-filling substance—"derived from the fact that it 'runs always' for an eternity of time (*aeí theî*)."[18] Plato himself had, in his late treatise *Epinomis*—a form of astronomical postscript to the twelve books on laws—presumed a fifth element, a *quinta essential*, likewise called *aithér*: a clear region located above the air and inhabited by demons and divine intermediate beings. With Aristotle, however, the ether would become the First Element, *próton sóma*. This was the stuff of which perfection was made, the substance of the sky and stars, *prima material* of all everlasting circulations. Naturally a direct observation of the ether was forbidden for mortals, as their sensory organization restricts their empirical dealings to the four earthly elements. It is of these that the lower world is made, the darker core of the cosmos beneath the moon, while the ethereal orbs, far removed from human touch and observation, fill out the monstrous heights of the moon, ascending above the planetary globes up to the outermost vault, the sky of fixed stars.

In quantity and dignity, therefore, the ether is by far the first substance in the cosmos. It is difficult to envisage its consistency from a sublunary perspective, as humans can hardly lay hands on more than what reveals itself in the flickering of the stars. It is finer than fire, breathier than air, subtle as gold frothed with sunlight and glistening like morning mist over Olympus. Most of all, however, it possesses the required cyclophoric property: it is the natural carrier of circular movements, and in this sense comparable to a divine thought that returns to itself. If it is fitting to understand Uranus as a universal body, then, its uppermost layers can only have been woven from the first element, this living, internally rotating wonder substance.

Because of its immense extension into the sublunary dimension, the ethereal world of Aristotle encompasses virtually everything that is the case—which is why the cosmos has suitably dignified properties almost everywhere, not only in the area close to the earth. The rotating ethereal body of the sky can "neither grow nor diminish";[19] it must therefore, according to Aristotle, also be unchanging, uncreated, eternal, ageless, simple, untouched by oppositions and effort, and must exist invulnerably from within itself.

Though a part of physical nature, the newly identified first or fifth element shines with a comet's tail of metaphysical attributes— as if the divine, if it is not yet meant to become human, is most appropriately embodied in the ether. Once the existence of the fabulous element has been conceded, the spherical shape of the cosmos-Uranus is automatically explained, because the ether's property of carrying out rotating movements means that it takes over the entire business of spherogenesis itself. If one has the ether one also has circular motion, and with this in turn the orb—just as, to use an analogy, one need only have capital to arrive at the circulation of money-commodity-money, and with it terrestrial globalization. The Aristotelian ether mythology impressed posterity with its paraphysical purity, which now allowed it to motivate cosmic relations nature-philosophically rather than theologically, as Plato had in the *Timaeus* when he ascribed the most godlike form of movement to a God-made world.

In his momentous treatise *On the Heavens*, Aristotle draws on great ingenuity to prove the thesis—already supported by Plato—that there can only be a single sky or cosmos. Supposedly this is not self-evident, because "sky" is a general concept that could apply to several concrete objects bearing this name. Thus there are iron and golden orbs or iron and wooden circles; the only circle and the only orb are certainly logically different from circles and orbs in general. This sky we see is likewise, judged from the logical perspective, not identical *a priori* to the sky as such—yet is one with it, for the sky as such that we envisage and the sky over there beneath which we live must, for logical and ontological reasons, be one and the same. This, however, must now be proved. Aristotle uses the argument that the sky over there is at once the sky as such—because there can factually only be a single real one—to develop a specific proof of the coherence and unity of the world-whole. If the sky encompasses everything that is physically the case, all reveries about a place or body *outside* of the whole must be rejected. Thinking the sky as singular means demanding the immanence of all that exists in it.

> Now the world must be counted among particulars and things made from matter; but if it is composed, not of a portion of matter, but of all matter whatsoever, then we may admit that

its essential nature as "world" and as "this world" are distinct, but nevertheless there will not be another world, nor could there be more than one, for the reason that all the matter is contained in this one. [...] Therefore it is impossible that any of the simple bodies should lie outside the heaven. [...]

It is plain, then, from what has been said, that there is not, nor do the facts allow there to be, any bodily mass beyond the heaven. [...] we may conclude that there is not now a plurality of worlds, nor has there been, nor could there be. This world is one, solitary and complete. It is clear in addition that there is neither place nor void nor time outside the heaven [...].[20] Again, since it is an observed fact, and assumed in these arguments, that the whole revolves in a circle, and it has been shown that beyond the outermost circumference there is neither void nor place, this provides another reason why the heaven must be spherical. [...][21]

Our arguments have clearly shown that the universe is spherical, and so accurately turned that nothing made by man, nor anything visible to us on the earth, can be compared to it. For of the elements of which it is composed, none is capable of taking such a smooth and accurate finish as the nature of the body which encompasses the rest.[22]

In our context, it is easy to see why Aristotle not only articulated the state of cosmological theory-forming skills in his time with these arguments, but also fulfilled his duty as a citizen of the world. Though he, the metic who never struck roots in Athens, had become alienated from the city-founding extravagances of Plato, even the Stagirite had to stand his ground as an apologist for the fortified universe. If the worst came to the worse, he too could not evade the task which, from antiquity onwards, remained obligatory for all thinkers who were loyal to being: to defend the walls of the full cosmos against emptiness, the outside and nothingness. The uppermost heaven, to which the fixed stars were attached—the firmament that was still present in the children's faith and poetry of the nineteenth century—does not exhibit the properties of a solid outer limit for nothing, and when Aristotle insists passionately on the thesis that the giant dome of heaven is a single finite body, this argument is affected not only by physical and geometric reflections, but also decisively by consideration for the immunological and uterotechnic mission of cosmology. How could humans inhabit the cosmic city if it were a diffuse monster extending into the formless, the infinite? An infinitely large body would be an amorphous absurdity with no more real-world sense than an infinitely large foot (which no one could use to walk) or an infinitely large womb (in which no child could come into being).

Only the finitude of the greatest orb guarantees its harboring quality, just as only its supernaturally perfect sphericity secures its intelligible character. Even the gods could not build in the infinite; they could not gather around their blessed tables in the formless. According to Aristotle, furthermore, the orb's finitude does not contradict its divinity, as its finite extension is superbly compensated for by the infinite nature of the rotating motion that, in the highest body, returns into itself without beginning or end. For this reason, even the world body encompassed by a good border need not forego the divine attribute of infinity. Good circular infinity demands well-defined morphological boundaries, while a bad linear infinity would lose itself in the boundless, formless and baseless—Hegel would still use this distinction to support his defense of the all-grasping circle of the spirit (and *eo ipso* rationalize his aversion to everything unconnected, open and fragmentary). In a sense, the uranometer-philosophers of Greece thus continued the project of the Babylonian politics of inclusion by argumentative means; but while the ancient Mesopotamian god-kings had hypertrophic brick walls built around a power-heavy city-world interior, the philosophers constructed the edge of the cosmos as such from ethereal bodies of rotation.

It would be the Stoic philosophers who articulated the architectural or urbanistic purpose of philosophical cosmology by openly declaring the metaphysical equation of world and city, which had so far only been latent, their program. With refreshing candor, they gave the name "Cosmopolis" to the city that meant the world, and they made citizenship in this residence an inexhaustible ethical ideal. This moral world-city took on more palpable contours after the time of Alexander, when the mobile classes of the circum-Mediterranean ecumene had become more numerous and began to look around for a plausible logic and ethics of mixture. After his victory over the Persians, Alexander had emphatically advanced melting pot politics, the practice of shaking the "crucible of peoples"; he commanded his subjects to enter mixed marriages, furthered the transfer of customs and knowledge in all directions, and thus created the conditions for Zenonian Stoicism to become the universal language of a mestizic and migratory international.[23] Demand arose for patterns of sovereignty that would help individuals to stay on top in chronic upheavals. Even the first philosophical states sprouted from the war-ploughed soil; warlords and utopians lived border to border; around 300 AD, the ideal state of Uranopolis grew on the peninsula of Athos, ruled by a prince who appeared as a sun god, and whose subjects called themselves "the heavenly ones." Under the Roman administrators too, the plausibility of the idea that humanity between Spain and the Euphrates was a single family in a single city increased continuously, such that the rhetorician Aelius Aristides could proclaim in his great oration in praise of Rome (150 AD): "The entire universe is a single city." In philosophical escalations such super-urbanisms also had temple-storming consequences, as the free-floating wise men could no longer accept that the gods were imprisoned in houses when the whole of heaven was one great pantheon.

This urban-humanitarian impulse awakened to idiosyncratic currentness, albeit highly altered in its meaning, when the Europeans embarked on their epoch-specific adventure of terrestrial globalization around 1500. If philosophy, along with its humanitarian pathos, gained new citizenships in modern democracies—and finally won its emancipation from theology and the church—it was primarily because compared to all positive fatherlands, it had a cosmopolitan plus of which to remind people, and barely concealed within this an egalitarian and communicative gospel. The modern cosmopolites were no longer aware of what the concept of Cosmopolis had meant under ancient conditions, however, and when they presented themselves with the cockade of world citizens, they were confusing the ancient cosmos with the modern earth disclosed in colonialist world traffic. In the present talk of cosmopolitanism, the non-distinction between metaphysical and terrestrial globalization can run free with a clear ideological conscience.

Nonetheless, an authentic spark from the ancient world-form enlightenment did manage to reach the Modern Age: the Old World had already codified experiences of freedom that would become unforgettable for Europeans. Thus the moderns could no longer bear any form of life that did not accept the open, the other and the comparable as its critique. What had been considered the worst fate in earlier antiquity, namely forced exile from one's home town, was positivized by modernity as the human right to travel and emigrate—and simultaneously combined with the right for free trade to invade all not-yet market societies. While Hellenistic cosmopolitanism had constituted an attempt to make the soul capable of unlimited exile through pre-emptive weaning asceticisms, the modern variety was the enterprise of demanding the same comfort level everywhere for tourist bodies. To describe the human being merely as the emigrant-immigrant animal, however, is to risk championing, out of apolitical recklessness, a harmful openness that fails to recognize the actual communes' morphological imperative. Postmodern cosmopolitanism is usually no more than the philosophical superstructure of cheap flights between European and American capitals. Anyone who is serious about the motif of the wider world's irruption into local lifeworlds must occupy themselves with the spatial crisis of "open societies." When seeking a formula for the best cosmos policy in the age of the Second Ecumene, it is advisable to follow the maxim that what counts is finding the right mixture of mixture and non-mixture.[24]

The epochal success of the Platonic-Aristotelian impulse in sphere cosmology indicates that the grandmasters of Greek thought had succeeded in formulating a highly effective new immune design for humans in the age of the rationalized world picture. Evidently the re-securing of the outer cosmic boundary through the doctrine of the celestial orbs was ideally suited to the deristrictions of the horizon through ecumenical communications and first natural sciences. When later generations used the Greek term for the world-whole, the *cosmos*, it was already charged with the magic of the philosophically molded piety of circles and orbs. That the words for "world" (*kósmos*) and "heaven" (*uranós*) had become synonymous since Plato cast a light from above on all future discussions of the world. Henceforth, the word "cosmos" itself henceforth sounded like a geometric credo—a *symbolon* of final suppositions of order and a password that confirmed the authorization of mortals to enter the best circles. It is a testimony to the overwhelming authority held by Platonic spherism for entire epochs that when Copernicus formulated his arguments in favor of the heliocentric thesis, he was still afraid to question the philosophical lesson of circular planetary orbits. Kepler only did away with the discrepancies Copernicus had left behind after bringing himself to consider the metaphysically disappointing, yet mathematically and astrophysically convincing ellipse as the orbital shape of the planets "circling" the sun.

That the doctrine of the ideal circle was always concerned more with the immune-morphological virtues of geometric idealism than the scientific merits of the orb models had become evident very early on, when the Platonizing astronomers, most importantly Eudoxus of Cnidus, who collaborated collegially with Plato, encountered truly insurmountable difficulties in the rational reconstruction of obviously non-circular, real planetary movements. These were not overcome by revising or abandoning the mechanically implausible sphere model, but through slightly desperate auxiliary structures based on Plato's directives. Eudoxus already felt compelled to increase the number of orbs to 26 merely to explain the irregularities in the paths of the seven main orbs: as well as the orbs in which the wandering stars were thought of as being moved in fixed positions, one also had to imagine a multitude of additional orbs in displaced rotation—four each for Saturn, Jupiter, Mars, Venus and Mercury, and three each for the sun and moon. The sole reason for all these to exist was so that the stars' deviation from the idealized simple circular path on their carrier orb could be interpreted in accordance with spherist dogma. Aristotle went far beyond this, ultimately presenting a system that required fifty-five spherical shells complicatedly rotating against one another to do at least partial justice to the empirical findings.

The epistemological satyr play that was authored by Plato and became known as the "rescue of phenomena" was in fact meant to rescue a psychocosmological immune system that had rapidly become indispensable, and whose most important asset was the geometrization of the outer border of the existent. This comedy of theory, which managed to stay in the academic repertoire for an age while subject to a strict ban on laughter, was outdone only by Christian hermeneutics, which had to fulfill analogous immunization tasks as the "rescue of the sense of scripture." The successes of philosophical enlightenment had turned the circle and the orb into the decisive onto-immunological figures, without which no questions about the world picture— let alone the world edge picture—could be adequately answered, even if the additional epistemological expenses of this world model, at least in the eyes of experts, soared disturbingly high. Aristotle would have had good reason to direct the sarcasm he showed towards the bizarre theories of his predecessors and physicist colleagues at his own presentations:

World cartwheel, Konark Sun Temple (India, 13th century)

one might be surprised that the solutions concerning these things do not seem stranger than the difficulty.[25]

King Alfonso X of Castile, a patron and connoisseur of medieval astronomy who reigned from 1252 until 1282, thus had good reasons for his well-known witticism, "If God had consulted me before embarking on the creation of the planets, I would have suggested a simpler system."

The triumphant history of the philosophical-cosmological celestial orb model shows very clearly that questions of cognitive expenses bore little weight alongside the outstanding morphological utility value of the sublime construction. For the general public in particular, for whom rescuing the phenomena was not a concern, the notion of a universe comprising many concentrically nested orbs with the earth at the center seemed irresistibly plausible and, to a certain extent, also psychologically attractive. It permitted those living between late classical antiquity and the early Modern Age to attain the indispensable level of homely acclimatization in a universe that already seemed to have expanded to unsettlingly gargantuan dimensions. For two thousand years, this notion proved itself as European culture's decisive technique for befriending the world; it interpreted the cosmos as the city in whose invulnerable walls mortals led their existences.[26] They recognized it as the utmost that could be achieved in the transference of their urban uterotechnics into the universe.

The autonomous hyper-orb offered a view of the form of cosmic totality that, after consideration of the advantages and disadvantages, was largely satisfactory, as well as a suggestive, albeit problem-laden answer to the question of the earth's location. In fact, it could not be positioned anywhere but at the center of the concentrically layered shells. Despite various non-geocentric hypotheses among the Pythagoreans, who had presumed the existence of a cosmic central fire, and despite the isolated breakthrough to heliocentrism by Aristarchus of Samos, the greatest astronomer of the third century BC, Aristotelian geocentrism established itself unthreatened. It is he who, using the catchword of the Ptolemaic world picture, set the guidelines for European cosmography for almost two thousand years—minus the half-hearted medieval return to the concept of a disc-shaped earth. But even in the millennium between the decline of the Western Roman Empire and the research of Copernicus, the memory of the earth's *globositas* was never completely eliminated. The medieval fate of Aristotelian cosmology and its unstable compromises with both the biblical Genesis and Saint John's account of the apocalypse need not concern us in any detail here.[27] It did not, incidentally, impair the triumph of the Aristotelian-Ptolemaic system in the slightest that many of the alleged measurements on which the system of Claudius Ptolemy (c. 100–170 AD) seemingly rested were no more than convenient forgeries and adaptations of earlier authors. Rather, the success story of Ptolemaio-Aristotelianism shows that world pictures and cosmographies, particularly those appearing as scientifically consolidated doctrines, are first of all auto-suggestive systems of convictions that only receive widespread approval if they prove themselves in the imaginative ecosystems of their societies. From this perspective, the shell belief of the ancient Europeans established itself as one of the most successful cognitive autohypnoses in the history of theory and culture. For an entire age, the ontological icons of circle and orb kept empirical astronomy in a state of pious torpor, with the silencing of research ensured most effectively by faith in the results of supposed earlier research. It took a complete revolution in the world picture, and with it a radical reformatting of psychocosmic immune relationships and dynamics of faith among Europeans from the sixteenth century on, for the natural sciences and religious concepts of space to break away from the immemorial spherism.

The dogma-historically active surface of this transition has been described in exemplary fashion by the historian of ideas Alexandre

Koyré under the programmatic title *From the Closed World to the Infinite Universe.*[28] As far as an exposition of the change of world picture from a systemic and immunological-spherological perspective is concerned, the like has never been attempted, and the laconic intimations in this direction given in the present book can in no way replace a detailed discursive and systemic history of the great extraversion. In such an investigation, the project of modernity would have to be rendered intelligible as a large-scale experiment concerning the harboring of mass societies in non-theological immune structures and salvific technologies. For such a characterization to do justice to its topic in the decisive point, it would require a specific examination of the takeover by the outside as the central event of what Heidegger termed the "age of the world picture." In the final chapter of this volume, which deals with the Last Orb—that is, the circumnavigated, mapped, occupied and used earth—I will at least attempt a general outline of how this revolution in the external way of thinking combined with the globalization processes of the Modern Age.

One of the precarious side effects of geocentric shell cosmology, aside from insurmountable complications in the empirical application of the model, is a fundamental, not to say ruinous ambivalence in the definition of humanity's place and standing in the cosmos. After all, placing the earth at the center is only seemingly a concession to the purported cosmological narcissism of its human inhabitants. For the circumstance that the Copernican revolution decentered the earth at long last, after being fixed at the center of the world picture for millennia, was by no means a cause of narcissistic injury for humans, as Freud and his parroters suggested without any knowledge of world picture-historical conditions,[29] but rather occasioned the long overdue liberation from a cosmological anxiety that had become stubborn and pointless. Thus heliocentrism enjoyed a public support that fluctuated between enthusiastic agreement and indifference, and where it was explicitly rejected, as in some circles of official Roman Catholicism, it was more because of a reluctance to abandon the central earth as the location of *humilitas*—but most of all because, in a Copernican world, one would no longer have known where to locate hell, without which the psychopolitical regime of counter-reformatory Catholicism (and indeed the entire Christian three-layer world picture comprising inferno, earth and the world above) would have become untenable.

Many reasonable contemporaries even thought that the elevation of the earth among the stars, a conclusion that could be drawn from Copernicus' book about the heavenly orbits, was a step too far. Philipp Melanchthon's outcry against the heliocentric innovators, six years after *De revolutionibus orbium celestium*, was typical of a critical reader's bafflement at so bold an overvaluation of the earth: *Terram etiam inter sidera collocant* ("They even place the earth among the stars!")[30] The Freudian myth of injury is thus empty in world picture-historical terms, and is purely an element in the self-aggrandizement strategy of the psychoanalytical movement (even if Goethe paved the way with his splendidly naïve remark that the revolution in the world picture forced humans "to forego the immense prerogative of being the center of the universe"). This little fabulation is notable nonetheless, as it can—from non-Freudian perspectives—be productively developed further towards a general ecology of injury that addresses the socio-psychological side effects of theory inventions and introductions of techniques. In truth, every innovation creates losers who must be spoken to. The successes of psychoanalysis too, and all other "I see something you don't see" systems—where are they achieved if not on the free market of injurious asymmetries between those who claim to see something new and the correspondingly blind others?[31]

As far as the injury of a supposed narcissism on humanity's part is concerned, it did not—assuming there is any to speak of—take place through the Copernican ex-centering of the earth, but rather through Aristotle's centering two thousand years earlier, which developed a precarious secondary anthropological meaning. In reality, after all, it was the earth's central position that brought about a fateful onto-topological devaluation for it and the humans on it. The reasons for this, which have been summarized above, were only accessible to a very small educated minority, while the general public in the Middle Ages only felt the atmospheric consequences of this demotion: for an epoch, it paid the price for the all-pervasive "vale of tears" rhetoric that shaped Christian miserablism. In cosmological terms, however, this miserablism was an entirely legitimate consequence of the Aristotelian world model. Christians did not usually realize how they had arrived at the inevitable depressive view of humanity's situation in the universe, and it was mostly associated in a muddled fashion with the consequences of original sin. Such a link may be anthropologically and morally significant, but in world picture-historical terms its outstanding feature is blindness. Original sin is not to blame for the degradation of the earth by ancient philosophers and cosmologists. The cosmological disparagement of the earth is not solely the domain of Christian teaching, let alone a typical invention thereof, but rather an inescapable consequence of the idealization of the ethereal periphery in Aristotelian cosmography. For if the perfect and encompassing is to be found above, then—as bizarre as it may sound—the center is inevitably below, and that is where the earth, with all its mortal, error-prone dwellers lost in ambiguity is situated. If the cosmic orb's center were an excellent place, its merit would be a dismally ironic one: the inhabitants of the middle would have the negative privilege of residing at the darkest end of the whole. Because the best must be located at the upper edge, as we have seen, the worst inescapably gathers at the center below.

Anyone looking for the weak point in Aristotle's grandiose world conception, then, need only make the effort to keep an eye out for the earth that is privileged through its central position: this planet tinged by death and error is the miasma of the cosmos, the dark spot on the clean slate of the heavens. Only the subterranean parts of the earth can surpass the human location, namely the earth's surface, in lightlessness and remoteness from God—which is why the regions of Hades and hell were genuinely presumed to lie beneath the earth's surface in the shell-cosmological world picture, in the final sediment and privy of the universe. This sums up the sad cosmopolitanism of the Stoic Aristippus when he declared that the journey to Hades was equidistant from every point on the earth. The innermost center of the corporeal world is the heart of darkness—and humans are its endangered neighbors. This is precisely what Dante encapsulated visually and conceptually in his nightmarish visions of hell. The Christian cosmos is infernocentrically constituted—in the same way that the primitive lifeworld of settled peoples could only be latrinocentrically constituted. But just as all Western onto-cosmologies display a bifocal structure—a high center in God and an infamous center in the terrestrial-subterranean—the spatial orders of settled civilizations in the agrarian age also paid tribute to bifocalism with the dichotomy of a splendid center (temple and palace) and a miasmatic center (latrine, knackery, dungeon).[32] If one acknowledges these basic topological conditions of Old European world picture constructions, it becomes evident that any talk of a Copernican injury must be either a misunderstanding or an interesting misdirection.

In his book *On the Heavens*, Aristotle undauntedly addressed the inevitability of devaluing the physical and geometric center of the shell cosmos—not without setting apart the depraved physical-material center from a noble, incorrupt *other* center:

> The Pythagoreans make a further point. Because the most important part of the Universe—which is the center—ought more than any to be guarded, they call the fire which occupies this place the Watch-tower of Zeus, as if it were the center in an unambiguous sense, being at the same time the geometric center and the natural center of the thing itself. But we should rather suppose the same to be true of the whole world as is true of animals, namely that the center of the animal and the center of its body are not the same thing. For this reason there is no need for them to be alarmed about the Universe [...]; they ought rather to consider what sort of thing the true center is, and what is its natural place. For it is that center which should be held in honor as a starting-point; the local center would seem to be rather an end than a starting-point [...]: but that which encompasses and sets bounds is of more worth than that which is bounded, for the one is matter, the other the substance of the structure.[33]

Intellectual Catholicism lived off this argument, which mixes ontological distinction and a cunning excuse, for over a millennium.

For if the earth, precisely because it sits at the mundane center, is irredeemably condemned to endure existence in the lowest and most ungrateful place—in a *favela* of the cosmos, one might say—then its inhabitants will feel the effect of this world model's faulty immunological design sooner or later, whatever promises of salvation theologians might offer. The Christian reception of the Aristotelian-Ptolemaic schema makes this clear, for it highlights the *humilitas* of the human position by all available means—not only in a religio-anthropological sense, but also from a cosmological perspective. As Alain de Lille wrote: "Man is like a foreigner who lives in the suburbs of the universe."[34] It is precisely this seemingly excellent inner position at the core of the strictly hierarchical system of cosmic shells that puts humans at a locational disadvantage which medieval Christendom tasted in all its bitterness, and which only a radical shift of position by new cosmological means managed to alleviate.

Bringing this about was the immunological and world picture-historical purpose of the Copernican revolution. For what was seemingly the ideal position in a fabric of massive, albeit subtle and transparent walls hermetically sealed off from the outside transpires, in onto-topological terms, as a fatal and irreparable defect for its settlers. The perfect enclosure of the earth and its dwellers at the gloomy center of the cosmos had to deprive them of proximity to the existentially higher and highest. For Europeans, it already became clear in antiquity that the metaphysical risks and side effects of geocentrism were so grave that they could only ensure their spiritual survival by setting up escape routes from the dark zone of the cosmos.

That is why the ominous word "cosmopolitanism," which Diogenes of Sinope supposedly inserted into the ancient debate,

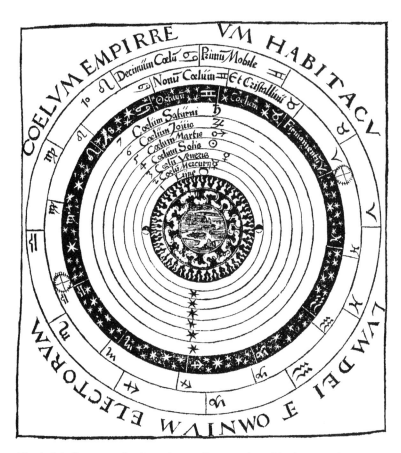

Classical shell cosmos after Peter Apian, *Cosmographicus liber* (1525). The circum-
scription gives greater emphasis to the immobile *Empyreum*, which lies at the outer
edge of the stepped cosmos, compared to the ten rotating heavens, of which the
eighth (the sky of fixed stars, or firmament) is highlighted: it underlines the notion
that the chosen (*electi*) will find their final immune form or dwelling (*habitaculum*)
in the peace of the highest height.

had a sarcastic undertone, even if the Stoics would later endeavor to use it without irony. In the city known as the world, the most important thing for the wise men was to ensure that they did not live in the dilapidated city center, but rather on the distinguished outskirts where the better ether circles had their villas. Whoever speaks of Cosmopolis always has an exit from the concrete terrestrial locale, or at least the aestheticization of the space of width, in mind to a small degree. Even Hegel still had distant memories of these Old European-Aristotelian spatial conditions when he described the spirit coming into itself in the *ether* of the concept—though this meant less a procedure for being unfaithful to the earth through spiritualist evasion upwards than a program for implanting the sky into the conditions on the earth's surface through state and culture.

That Stoicism, Platonism and Christianity were, in certain cases, able to develop shared strategic interests within their respective psychagogics was due not least to the fact that all three of them offered to eliminate the human disadvantage of residing in the malign center of matter through attractive programs of transcendence. Indeed, perhaps the susceptibility of late antique, medieval and early modern Europeans to every possible form of idealistic evaluation aid and philosophical doctrine of transcendence can be explained by the necessity of looking for emergency helpers against the geocentric injury.

It was only long after the celestial orbs had been burst and the earth had ascended to the same cosmological rank as other heavenly bodies that Nietzsche's Zarathustra could have the striking idea of preaching loyalty to the earth among his friends. In the two-thousand-year empire of Aristotelianism this would have been an absurdity, for it would have meant a direct renunciation of one's share in any higher spheric life; under such conditions, loyalty to the earth would have been as productive as the loyalty of a prisoner to his dungeon.

But Aristotle, like Plato before him, had given a precise description of the main escape route from the central sublunary area to the higher and better: the way to precisely that *other* center discussed in the passage from *On the Heavens* quoted above, which means no less than that the utopian topos of the supramundane God, whose mental reflex—the world soul—had been implanted in the *center* of the cosmos by the demiurge. Only through the use of their own spirit souls can humans attain the vicinity of that good, sublime, other center, through the circumspect thinking that, if it understands itself correctly, recognizes itself as an emanation of the first good.

This is a concession that the center of the corporeal world and the center of the good do not coincide. The basal game of all spirituality—find the center!—holds a spherological ambiguity that the metaphysical age was unable to clarify. In the question of the central point, the masters of Greek philosophy bequeathed a pathos-laden confusion to posterity; in the following I shall describe it as the Old European two-center system, with such exaggerated clarity that it will dissolve through the light cast on it, as it were—just as some tomb paintings supposedly vanished under the torches of explorers. This will reveal once again, and in a different way, what was already known from other sources: even when it attempted to maintain its cosmotheist appearance, Greek metaphysics in fact became a varyingly precise theology of transcendence.

Transcendence-based thought is the formal indication that the lower center has been joined by an upper one. *Nota bene*:

even after the lower center's loss of value in geocentrism, a monarchic idea of the central point remained in force—though it could only be defended with theological and spiritual arguments, and only retained its meaning in non-physical, non-cosmological contexts. Useless for human narcissims, it refers to the center where mortals, those who are-in-the-world, precisely are *not*. This leaves the problem that in the geocentrically constituted world, the good center must be taken as extramundane and supramundane, hence transcendent, spiritual, and—if one can speak in spatial terms—located on top, even if Timaeus claims with metaphysical tact that the world soul (equipped with the *nous*) was implanted in the center of the world body. One understands that this turn of phrase was a polite code for supramundanity, conveying that it would be highly unwise to look for the soul at the physical center of the world where, according to Plato's ambiguous description, it resided: for this center, consistently enough, is located in the earth's core, because the earth is at the center of the shell cosmos—and that is precisely where the medieval infernologists, who understood the difference between the divine and earthly centers rather better than the devotional philosophers, presumed with complete topological accuracy that hell was situated. The convergence of being-in-the-world and being-in-hell will be explicated further below, in the chapter on "anti-spheres."

There are essentially two ways to maintain the connection between humans and God in the classical metaphysical interpretation of space: either humans must ascend into the open from their central dungeon on an intelligible ladder connecting them to the world of the living, or God must descend to them—presumably using the same ladder, whether through signs and wonders or by assuming a bodily form. Transcendence and incarnation thus constitute symmetrical vertical movements; both serve to keep open the endangered connection between the bad center (of the quantitative existent) and the *other center* (of the essential existent).

These vertical tensions show that humans in the "age of the world picture" cannot be helped through integration into a spatial vessel, no matter how well-insulated. Thus all holistic arguments are condemned to helplessness, because humans do not simply wish to be preserved in a wholeness container, a metaphysical *continens* ring, but also to encounter in living inner experience the countercentric Great Other that makes them possible through intimate augmentation. Certainly, the life of societies in the expanded reality spaces of the imperial age cannot survive without effective immunizations and fortified borders; as far as the microspheric integrity of humans is concerned, however, it can only be achieved through harboring in sociopolitical and cosmic large-scale containers. Intimate psychogonic augmentation continues to be more important than shielding the soul field from the outside. Only this augmentation can ensure that the stay in a large-scale world does not end in bitter soullessness or bland surfing.

That is why macrospheric immunization—one could abbreviate this to philosophy, or more precisely the philosophy of transcendence—is not everything. The certainty of being contained in something extremely large may provide calm; the traditional wise men, if their promotional writings are not purely lies, occasionally achieved this. But inner peace would be a misguided goal if it were separated from the exhilaration and spontaneity that arise from communion with the inner other, regardless of whether it is imagined as a presently close, inseparable partner or a sublime and distant counterpart. In advanced-civilized times, then, it is not only the cosmic containers around the political communities that require reformatting. The intimate other of each individual too, the divine close-distant twin, must be defined with more powerful outlines. Where it enters the scene in timely versions, humans can shift their focus from the search for calm in the highest container to eventful love affairs with the absolute. These and other matters will be discussed when we open the long-unread book of Old European gestalt theology in the following chapter. In its pages we find the necessary elucidations of that *other center* which Aristotle was able to postulate, but not develop convincingly by his own means.

Excursus 3

Autocoprophagia

On Platonic Recycling

There has been much ado in the history of Plato's reception about the master's bias towards the geometric figures of circle and orb; it has scarcely been noted, however, that at one point he presented a circulation argument which left behind the abstract mathematical idealism of spherophilia and ventured the leap to a biology of the whole—today we would call it a general ecology. While the modern life and death sciences can only ever take parts of circular process as objects of study against the background of environments that remain outside the circles, Plato touched in a moment of risk on the question of the conditions for an ecology in the absolute. This is an ecosystem of being that would have to be a closed circular process of such a kind that there could no longer be an environment or an outside world forming the background to the circle of life. This absolute ecology can only be realized as an absolute biology, and this latter in turn only as the description of an absolute animal that is a singularity answering to the name "cosmos," assuming anyone wished to call it. The chief passage is at the start of Timaeus' speech, dealing with how to explain why the demiurge had made the entire world orb "perfectly smooth" on the outside "for many reasons":

It had no need of eyes, since there was nothing visible left outside it, nor of ears, since there was nothing to hear either. There was no air around it to require breathing in, nor did it need to be equipped with organs for the intake of food and, once the goodness had been extracted from it, its subsequent evacuation. For there was nowhere for anything that might leave it to go, and nowhere for anything that might come to it to come from. Rather, it fed itself from its own waste and was so designed that every process and action happened within it and by its own agency [...].[35]

Thus is the price of perfection named: the absolute animal must be an autocoprophagist, an eater of its own excrement. Beyond that—and this is what distinguishes aforesaid artful training—the difference between mouth and anus, which is productive and necessary for animals with an environment containing eating places and latrines, must be annulled in this super-creature, such that the body orifices through which the metabolic dramas take place are transferred inwards and directly connected. This results in the ecologically impressive, though psychoanalytically and gastronomically somewhat confusing structure of an integrated oro-anality. (This super-animal naturally lacks genitality, as its mode of being means that it is neither begotten nor begetting in its constitution.)

The creature that endures everything through itself and does everything through itself realizes a divine attribute that, in the period of the Doctors of the Church, was termed aseity (*aseitas*) or "from-oneself-ness," even if none of the scholastic theologians would still summon the Platonic cold-bloodedness to investigate the metabolic details of the divine animal—an omission that

Ouroboros: The Universal One

seems forgivable if one considers that for learned Christians, the cosmos was not an absolute animal, but rather creation. Because, however, Christian doctrine credits the absolute with becoming flesh but not with becoming world, the critical point in being is merely shifted, for the advent of Christ was the appearance of a divine entity that had taken human nature upon itself and hence consented to live with the difference between mouth and anus. Accordingly he began his career with metabolic embarrassments (Luke 2:12: "You will find him wrapped in swaddling clothes.")

And yet he cannot evade the question of whether he will absorb and evacuate the external or live with no environment, subsisting only on what is his own, in the long term: being the true God, he is by necessity a non-metabolizer, just as, being a true human, he by necessity ingests food and excretes feces. Two reception-historical facts in particular show that the true God in him won out over the true human nonetheless, despite the two-nature doctrine: firstly, that the Lord's words were recorded but no physical excretions mentioned or preserved, and secondly, that his transfigured body ascended to heaven, but there are no references to transfigured fecal matter. Hence the God-man is decidedly subject to the difference between system and environment, unlike the Platonic cosmos, which is a system with no environment.

The difference between the Greek and Christian paths to an ecology of the absolute emerges in a clearer light against the background of these reflections. While God's world-becoming produces an absolute animal that goes through a life process devoid of any outside by virtue of its autocoprophagia, God's incarnation results in a metaphysical hybrid whose one side, coming from eternity, neither eats nor drinks, while the other, through earthly food and drink, creates the conditions for the corresponding excretions, which may not be spoken of culture-immanently. The Greek world-animal is thus a creature that neither ingests food from the environment nor ejects waste into the same, for it has no environment—in other words, because it dispenses with all externalization for the sake of its autonomy—whereas the Christian God-man castigates the world, yet undoubtedly leaves behind the aforementioned unmentionable waste products. (The objection of some medieval theologians that Christ did eat but not defecate is perhaps worthy of mention, but not discussion.) The world-animal is the subject-object of an absolute ecology that uses up everything, leaving nothing behind and letting nothing reach the outside (just as—to cite an almost current example—in Tibetan Buddhism until the start of the twentieth century, dried pills made of the Dalai Lama's feces were highly revered as medicinal amulets, perhaps even swallowed as a last curative resort, because waste from the living God cannot be waste), while the God-man dedicated himself to a partial ecology in which the lost remainder is taken on board and waste products are emphatically externalized.

This highlights the difference between Greek and Christian recycling quite clearly. While the God-world is inevitably structured autocoprophagously (that is what the holists ultimately believe, even if they are unwilling and unable to say so), the God-man must either be an anorexic ("not by bread alone," hence as little bread as possible) or a dualist (the communion table and the latrine do not stand in the same world). In Platonic recycling, everything becomes food of the gods: this means that in the cosmic anal-oral system, either the excretions themselves have the character of *haute cuisine* or the mouth of the divine orb is sensually indifferent, making no distinction between ambrosia and feces. What is more important than this indifference, however, is the immunity of the cosmos (its absolute smoothness on the outer arch), which permits no opening through which anything could be ejected into the void. On the Christian side, the God-man comes into the world as if into an embarrassing exile, but not in order to show how one builds eco-houses and fertilizes fields with human and animal dung. His recycling mission applies exclusively to souls. He descends to prove that world-fasting is possible; according to his teachings, metabolism and waste separation are not the calling of humans, let alone an existence as omnivores, whether the autocoprophagous or the heterocoprophagous variety. The Christian connection to what makes beings healthy and round is not cosmologically, but rather pneumatically oriented. Pneumatics share the nomadic privilege of following a fecofugal way of life in the midst of settled populations; they avoid the obligations that bind humans to fixed dwellings; they keep their distance from the atmosphere of latrine fidelity. (Indeed: a Christian should live in such a way that they never need to use a toilet *of their own*; let the waste dispose of its waste.)

Pneumatic ecology contents itself with bringing souls (possibly also counting resurrected bodies) back into the supranatural parental home; it externalizes the rest without remorse. Cosmological ecology, on the other hand, is so interested in internalization that it only permits the absolute animal to feed and excrete inside itself. Thus neither of the two great household doctrines can help the real earth: the one because it is only interested in harboring souls and views the world as mere scenery and waste, and the other because it posits the world as absolute, and thus denies the possibility of waste at all.

The discrete ecological recycling concepts that have claimed to help the earth since the hygiene revolution of the nineteenth century will remain fragmentary, however, because they lack the courage and strength to demand the total circuit. Eco-society will be sabotaged for all time by a humanism that insists on the insuperable difference between mouth and anus.

Excursus 4

Pantheon

The Theory of the Dome

> Splendor's roundness: noon.
> All being is cupola.
> — Jorge Guillén, "Perfection"[36]

There are no great technological developments that have not previously appeared in metaphysics: the culture-diagnostic scope of this claim, which makes technological theory philosophical is demonstrated by the most significant circular building of the ancient world, the Pantheon in Rome. It was discussed between 115 and 125 AD in the reign of Trajan (98–117) and completed during that of Hadrian (117–138), a world wonder of architecture in the precise sense of the word whose dome, with an inner diameter of 142 feet, was the first authentic spherical construction on the earth, and for an entire epoch also remained the largest—not even the architects of St. Peter's dared to surpass the diameter of the gigantic ancient dome.[37] That the Pantheon was a temple construction with a sensitive, indeed overblown cosmotheological connection is demonstrated by the history of the ill-fated predecessor buildings erected in the same place: the temple of the seven planetary gods named by Augustus' brother-in-law Agrippa, dating from the start of the first century, had fallen prey to the great fire of 80 AD, while the reconstruction made by Domitian was destroyed by lightning in 110. If Trajan and Hadrian made a third attempt to renovate the central cult site for the theology of the Roman gods of fate so short a time afterwards, there would have been a resolution in the air that this time, they would create a building which resisted the whims of the elements more successfully than its predecessors, and which forced the universe's consent to its construction and preservation more convincingly than the earlier edifices.

Thus the location, the purpose and the history of the Pantheon, surrounded by dubious omens, provided the ingredients for an exceptional architectural and theological program. The result itself overwhelmingly expresses the fact that imperial monumentalism was here seeking to memorialize itself, and the agreement of the two imperial builders with their architect, the Apollodorus of Damascus, meant that the building was also intended to stand before the citizens of the ecumene as a politico-theological lesson and the revelation in stone of an unsurpassable world idea. Operation Pantheon profited from a favorable historical moment in which architecture and theology wanted to embark on a joint endeavor to create something unheard-of.

The general premises for this present project extended far back: the Greeks had mathematized the sky and woven it into the interlinking symbolism of a precise sphere geometry; the Romans had grouped the planetary gods together and declared them patrons and guardians over the assignment of each mortal's individual fate; and the emperors had finally added a layer of mist, rounding off the *mare nostrum* with a *coelum nostrum*. The synthesis of these interventions in the encompassing gave rise to the architectural event of the Pantheon, which must still be taken as the most conclusive introduction into the nature, problem and achievement of the Perennial Philosophy. It constitutes a case of what—in the apt formulation of a contemporary author—deserves to be described as "Roman solutions to Greek problems."[38] In the Pantheon the *translatio philosophiae ad romanos* became a credible *fait accompli*, even if Heidegger still felt entitled to deride the Roman contribution to the history of thought, and even if the vast majority of those in the trade like to believe that one can pass over the Pantheon and remain a philosopher nonetheless. It is easy to demonstrate that this is an error, as one need only prove that the philosophical idea of the whole can be explicated not only in writings, but also in the form of buildings. Until Plotinus' innovation of Platonism, Roman pantheology, as an immanent theory of the singular building, embodied the highest conceptual rank in its time.

The Pantheon resulted from the encounter between two ambitions of sovereignty, one Ceasarian and the other academic. As far as the aim of the philosophers to consider the whole in the outlines of a clear, invulnerable and irresistibly beautiful shape is concerned, both Plato and his successors and rivals extending to the Stoics said what was necessary. Even in their times of greatest political success, the Romans had to take lessons from the circle- and sphere-based thought of the Hellenes. As for the Caesars, who had come into the inheritance of the victorious, all too victorious Roman republic, the spirit of their office forced them to reflect on holding together an enormous periphery through a collecting and power-emanating center, and the result of these

Caesarian meditations on the correspondence between city and world was a growing willingness to adopt the perspective of the sun and the God who is at work all around, animating and taking responsibility for everything.

The Pantheon formed the center between these two formulations of sovereignty. For if the one side of this extraordinary building is that it expressed something of the secret of philosophical space-production by geometric and macrospherological means, the other side is that it was devoted to an imperial-urban creation of space that still understood world rule as a success of domestic extension, and which saw the Caesar's life as guarding the Roman-occupied world.

Where Caesars discussed the greatest possible symbol of the world with philosophers on these premises, a third force had to come into play, one whose task was to offer both parties acceptable sensualizations of their onto-political and space-theological pretentions. This force could only be architecture, which not so much puts its time into thoughts as the thoughts of the time into buildings. The military engineer and builder Apollodorus of Damascus enabled the finest hour of thought-in-building when he convinced Trajan, and even more his successor Hadrian, to support the concept of an unprecedented spherical temple complex. Hegel's statement that what is reasonable is real, and what is real is reasonable, is truer of architecture than of any other field, for it is here that the ordering ideas of logical and ideal-geometric structure first gain material concentration. The spheric concept experienced its *concrete* realization in the Roman concrete (*opus caementitium*) with which the Pantheon's dome and the core of its wall were built. Beyond all Roman nationalist sentiment, the philosophically educated Easterner Apollodorus

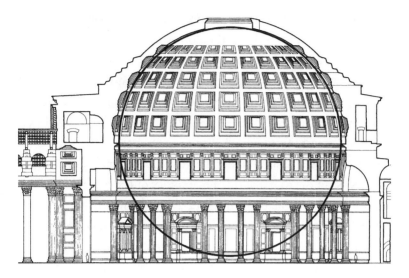

Cross section of the Pantheon

had understood that after the imperialization of the world, the time had come for the edifization of the perfect orb, and that the imperiality of the empire could only attain its full expression in this logico-architectural act. In his alliance with the Hellenophilic Hadrian and the employment of architectural means, Apollodorus thus achieved the same thing Virgil had accomplished for Augustus with his epic a century earlier: the symbolic reinforcement of a large-scale political space that had consolidated itself militarily before any Roman could say what this power monster meant in metaphysical terms.

Thus the architect's art provided the forum for the bilateral summit meeting between Caesarism and philosophy. Thanks to the daring of his construction, which is still impressive after millennia, Apollodorus ventured the thesis that architecture had now come far enough to meet both peaks of the world idea at once as an equal. He satisfied the Caesarian side with a building project that accommodated the domestic concern of the empire and its guardian in strict, monumental forms, and addressed the philosophical concept by accepting the bet that the sphere could no longer be produced merely as a ready-to-hand model for mathematical and astronomical studies, but also be realized as a large-scale temple and a built formal symbol of cosmic widening. Apollodorus was undoubtedly the genius of the enterprise, for he understood how to make the metaphysics of the orb accessible to the lords on the Palatine Hill, and also encouraged his emperor Trajan and his successor to make the unprecedented gesture of having the universe and all its gods brought to Rome. (There was supposedly some friction with Hadrian, who carried out and completed the construction—which seems understandable, considering that the emperor identified with the project to such a degree that he wanted to be considered its true architect. Cassius Dio even claims to know that Hadrian executed the great builder after the Pantheon's completion; other sources seem to contradict this version of events, however.) Apollodorus would not have summoned up the requisite cold-bloodedness for this suggestion if he had not been able to assure the emperor that it was now technically possible (using concrete construction and an advanced cladding technique)[39] to build the heavens themselves, provided they were of the shell variety.

Considering the overall structure of the Pantheon, one must take the formulation "build the heavens" literally. Apollodorus not only realized the most perfect hemisphere that had ever been attempted on such a scale; in addition, he marked the invisible lower hemisphere of the heavens, whose southern pole precisely touches the floor of the hall, on the building's interior, meaning that the dome's diameter of 142 feet also determines the height of the space. The philosophical essence of the building manifests itself in these proportions: the Aristotelian concept of Uranus or cosmos is likewise reached by abstracting from the observation of the light blue hemisphere above our heads and expanding it into the notion of the complete world orb, viewed from the perspective of an external god. This is precisely what happens in the Pantheon through the combination of the visible, constructed upper dome and the invisible, unconstructed lower one; on its own, the first signifies the sky of naïve observation, while the two together represent the sky of the philosophers, the universe. To understand the Pantheon one must grasp *both* domes at once: the difference between them must be taken into account, but simultaneously viewed as overcome. Then the mind's eye will achieve the perfect spheroscopy in this temple of onto-geometry.

As far as its interior view is concerned, then, the Pantheon is nothing other than the globe borne on the shoulders of the Farnese Atlas, translated into a format in keeping with the idea that the divine cosmos is a place of its own which carries itself—and us within it. The naïve constellations of the Greek *sphaira*, which was designed for exterior viewing, now give way to a thoroughly geometrized, graduated sky whose observation takes place, in true Parmenidean and amphiscopic fashion, from within. A world that produces architects and emperors with such ideas and means has no more need of mythical Atlases: the orb that is the whole is now integrated into the sacred form of the house; and according to the will of the gods, who speak to humans through their successes, the Caesarian name for the house that is the universe was *Roma aeterna*. As for the oculus, the bold round opening thirty feet across at the crown of the cast dome, it brings out a triumphalist Platonic aspect: by day, it lets a floodlight into the sphere from above and outside that must be perceived as the perfected symbolism of transcendence. This *opeion* does not wish to be a mere window through which humans gaze out securely into a framed world; it is itself the clearing[40] of the space that means the world.[41]

The Pantheon is more than a monumental thesis containing the result of ancient cosmotheology; it also points both clearly and discreetly to the difference between esoteric and exoteric, without which there could be no wisdom or true knowledge in the ancient world. One aspect of the Pantheon's marvel is that from the outside, one has no intimation of what it shows on the inside, because—like every free-standing building—it presents an exterior view, but one that keeps silent about the inner formal principle, while not going quite as far as camouflage. The Pantheon presents itself to the outside observer as a stout circular building whose flattened dome sits atop a cylindrical base, marked by seven step-rings at the intersection of side wall and calotte; encountering this number, it is not forbidden to be reminded of the planetary gods, to whom the preceding temples were devoted in the same place. One must concede that the exoteric view does not lie and is valid in its own right too, even if it is not corrected by the true counter-view that shows itself from the inside. Apollodorus' building paid tribute to the fact that in Rome, as previously in Athens and everywhere, the vast majorities during the time of thinking were content to walk past places of truth, pose no questions to mouths of truth and miss hours of truth. Plato's notorious inscription above the entrance to his Academy, which stated that anyone who was not a geometrician should keep away, is reformulated in a profound manner in the

Pantheon's inside-outside difference. But here it is sufficient—perhaps in contrast to Plato's garden—to enter the building with open eyes in order to be converted by this unprecedented event of roundness to a life under the banner of world geometry.

From the outside, one simply cannot recognize that something happened in the interior which would fundamentally change the status of the upper limits of buildings, indeed the meaning of roofs, ceilings and vaulted spaces for all time. What took place here is no less than the total metaphysicization of roof and ceiling; with the dome, a serious rival to the genuine sky now emerged. Only those who entered the vaulted temple would learn that the dome had become the message. In early circular and vaulted-roof buildings from the Near East, the motif had established itself that roofs can and demand to become more than mere ways of sealing the tops of constructed spaces.[42] The motif of self-encasement through uteromimetic harboring forms is, as numerous paleo-architectural monuments prove, almost as old as the roof idea itself. The fact that houses always additionally constitute metamorphoses of the maternal space is what gives architecture such an eminent position in the historical development of spatial transference forces. It was only with the Pantheon's dome, however, that the breakthrough to the rational poetics and metaphysics of the vaulted space took place in so triumphant and final a manner that no one could still claim to know what the height of a constructed space could mean if they had not viewed and understood the coffered sky of the Roman cosmos temple.

All later dome constructions in European culture, from Brunelleschi's cupola to the cathedral in Florence, from the domes over St. Peter's Basilica in Rome and St. Paul's Cathedral in London to the vaulted reading rooms of the Bibliothèque Nationale and the British Library, can only be understood as commentaries or counter-claims referring to the space-philosophical thesis of the Pantheon dome. It is no coincidence that the most intense dome-based discussion in the history of the human race—the dispute over the crown of the new building at St. Peter's Basilica, whose construction began in 1506 with the laying of the foundation and (as far as the dome is concerned) was completed by Giacomo della Porta and Domenico Fontana in 1592, using plans developed further by Michelangelo (1475–1564)—started with the antique-styled designs of the first builder, Donato Bramante. These reveal a direct replica of the massive Pantheon dome, resting on pillars, which would have been unfeasible because of the weight. The problem story of the dome of St. Peter's Basilica was the test run for modern constructive rationalism. From the perspective of modern space-production, it is no less interesting than the simultaneous Copernican revolution in cosmology. For the outward de-restriction of space is not an iota more dramatic than its vaulted integration into the grandiose spatial symbolisms of the incipient Modern Age. While the old Pantheon dome could still rest on a brick cylinder of almost telluric proportions, the domes of the Modern Age had to process the difficulty of not being supported by solid walls close to the ground, rather having to ascend to great heights, remote from the earth and artificially, with the aid of daring pillar constructions. This is a measure of the difference between the demands placed on ancient and modern constructivism.

What antiquity and the Modern Age have in common when it comes to large-scale buildings at the limits of possibility, however, is the experience that nothing sublime can exist without

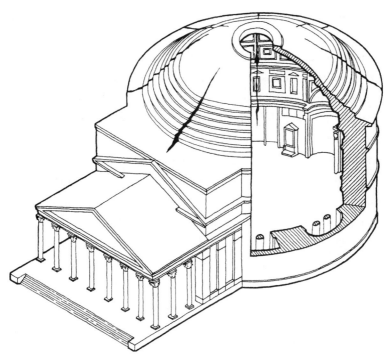

Ancient cracks in the dome of the Pantheon

cracks and risks of breakage. Only a few years after the Pantheon dome was cast, broad meridian fissures had to be filled in; and the history of the dome of St. Peter's Basilica is one of buttressing attempts from the seventeenth century to this day. This experience is less confusing for architects and immunologists than for philosophers, as the former already know that precisely a successful attempt to build the heavens will lead to the problem of having to support the constructed sky sooner or later. (This is the central pragmatic principle of counter-reformatory Catholicism: if God wants the church to continue existing, he will see to it that the Roman edifice does not collapse, in spite of its cracks; if he does not, however, the sign will be that we can no longer master our hypostatic problems.) In its early days, the science of structural analysis developed as a mathematical Kabbalah for the treatment of imperiled domes. Philosophers, on the other hand, since no longer being builders themselves, have often been led by the specific frivolity and marginality of their profession to draw de"con"structivist rather than conservatory conclusions from cracks in the cosmic edifices of other builders.

If one understands the Pantheon in terms of its esoteric program, it becomes plausible that the pathos of Greek philosophy in imagining the cosmos as a whole from a domestic angle only attained its practical realization in Roman architecture, which made the house match the cosmos in ways that had exceeded the means of the Greeks. If the Greek genius—as Hegel praisingly remarked—achieved the domestication of the cosmos, the Roman builders of imperial times achieved the cosmification of the house. In the Pantheon, every visitor can meditate, with no prior ontological training, on the basic principle of ancient philosophy: that the wise person's existence means moving from the local house to the universal one. With the same clarity, the basic logical doctrine of antiquity that knowing and classifying are the same thing shines forth from the coffers lining its dome.

With the construction of the Pantheon, Apollodorus and Hadrian offered their own explanation for the riddle of the Roman success story. The world domination of the Romans, as experts on ancient conditions have frequently emphasized, was not an expression of an offensive imperial instinct but the result, reluctantly taken on board, of a hypertrophic awareness of security and domesticity in combination with a hysterized will to loyalty (*fides*) towards allies at the empire's edges (Cicero writes in

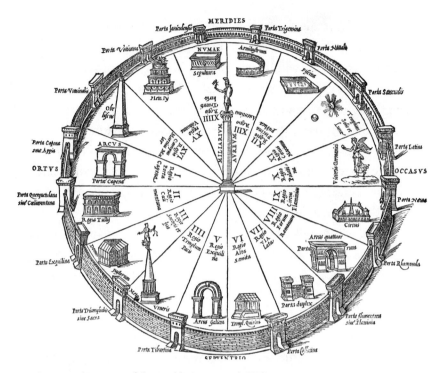

Rome as the center of the world, engraving (1527)

Republic, III, 35: "our people by defending their allies have gained dominion over the whole world"). Hence the empire arose from an orgy of domesticity and defensive moral rectitude—like a system of philosophy that only engages with the wide world so that it will keep quiet amid all the talk. Among the Romans, imperialism was the symptom of a general exophobia that treats itself by internalizing anything external that might disturb it.

Similarly, the Pantheon wanted to deal with the numinous powers of foreign peoples by giving all significant gods from the outside a Roman passport. Long before European and American universities had invented the title of "associate professor," the head theologians of the Romans had discovered the function of the associate god. It was given to those interreligiously recognized numinous powers with which Rome's inventory custodians considered it advisable to be allied. Like the Mesopotamians earlier on, the Romans became aware of the necessity of a religious diplomacy that would mediate between different variations of the world of gods. The Pantheon was made heaven-shaped and ecumenical like an assembly room for all of them, in order to ensure that all powers worthy of being called "gods" swore allegiance to the Roman house idea.

This world-building changes the meaning of immanence with lasting consequences, for it shows how far imperiotechnics as cosmotechnics will go. Such construction into the large and largest dimensions did not yet have any connection to the architectural ostentation of capital cities in later European nation-states, which simply piled up facades where they lacked any genuine world idea or effective world power techniques. The Pantheon offered proof that after the house had managed to adapt to the shape of the universe, the universe had in turn consented to be house-shaped. From that point on, totality became current as the subject of a technological world history; that is precisely what is discussed in the present under the heading of (terrestrial) globalization. This word holds the question of whether the globe "is" or "happens" or "is made."

Following on from these reflections, the cosmotechnic meaning of the Old European dome can be concisely formulated: it gives architectural contours to the idea of universal immanence and lends the immune motif of classical metaphysics—the view of the great encompassing, the all-attentive and all-binding—a place in visibility. The dome bears the statement that human life unfolds according to a cooperative principle, and that the heavens have an interest in the phenomena they span. In domes, the powerful build the utopia of the attentiveness with which the clear upper realm turns towards the murky lower one.

What triumphed in the Pantheon's dome, admittedly, was an idea of world, order and immanence whose high ontotheological tension would soon come into intense conflict with the neo-religious moods that were increasingly encroaching on the center from the empire's periphery. While the emperor was still building a temple for all the gods in which every mere regional god and divinized force of nature would be integrated as a form deity of the highest order, people all over the empire were breaking free of the philosophical religion of transparency (one could also say from the rational general assembly *sous l'œil de l'empereur*[43]) and dedicating their lives to the new religions of opacity.

That is what incorporates the Pantheon, in its own way, into the protracted failure of late antique philosophy. For with its bright faith in spheres, its jovially ceremonious totalism and the subtle coffered structure of the dome's interior, which seems to anticipate the Pseudo-Dionysian concept of hierarchy, the Pantheon constitutes a veritable emanation system in concrete that contained more realized intelligence than all its later visitors could muster together. Only a short while after its completion, the building stood before the cult participants like a meaning machine that one could ritually use, but not build a second time.

Oswald Spengler captured something of the aura of esoteric loneliness surrounding this splendidly high-minded, yet unlimitedly accessible building in his ingenious remark that the Pantheon was *"the earliest of all mosques."*[44] This formulation was connected to Spengler's obscure thesis that in 125 AD, Rome had long been in the process of exiting the circle of ancient "souldom" and being drawn in by the "Magian culture" that was starting to spread in the Near East in numerous pseudomorphic adaptations to foreign ethnic and cultural bodies. (Those familiar with Spengler's principal text know that under the heading "Problems of Arabian Culture," the author presented a book within the book which it would not be an exaggeration to term the culmination of speculative cultural philosophy in the twentieth century.) It was, he argues, the shift of emphasis from ancient to Magian souldom that brought about the penetration of the Roman Empire by a pseudomorphic religion, namely early Christianity in its Hellenized form (which was, for its part, a kindred spirit of the later Islam, that prototype of a religion of submission-demanding and devotion-granting opacity). Spengler's words are at least true to the extent that the meaning of immanence changed in Rome during the Pantheon era, and that the mode in which the gods revealed their intramundane presence was subject to far-reaching alterations.

There is every indication that the late antique masses entering the Pantheon did not yet experience much of what had been considered and realized at the summit meeting between Caesarism, philosophy and architecture. The time belonged more and more to the mystagogues and apostles practicing a de-mathematization of the heavens—today one would call it a re-enchantment of the world. It was due to these agents of a completely changed, openly alogical, telepathic and miracle-hungry feeling of immanence that the later domes, especially those of the Byzantine East, no longer repeated the pantheological construction—whose purpose had been to memorialize the noetic participation of humans in the morphological optimum of the world house as enduringly as *opus caementitium*—but increasingly testified to the complete enclosure

Ceremony in St. Peter's Basilica in the Jubilee year 1700

of the human space by an impenetrable world secret. Oswald Spengler explained it suggestively using the space-philosophically relevant central symbol of Magian culture, the world cave mentality. This change perfectly clarifies the difference between the

Pantheon and the church of Hagia Sophia in Constantinople. While the Roman orb temple had helped the world idea attain its ultimate self-explanation in edificial crystallization (in a building that one entered as a worldling from some province or other, and left as a Greek and neophyte of philosophy), the church of Holy Wisdom implemented a feeling of numinously illuminated and Magi-surrounded immanence (making it impossible to set foot in it without becoming an Arab *ante litteram*, an ecstatic debutant in matters of divine magic).

In the later fates of the Pantheon, the motif of the round heavens would see a new interpretation that seems like an ironic-psychognostic attribution of the orb to the mothers: the Byzantine emperor Phocas made a gift of the Pantheon to the Roman Bishop Boniface IV, who could certainly do nothing better than to consecrate the building as a Marian church under the name *Sancta Maria ad martyres*, which took place with due ceremony one day in the year of our Lord 609. It was only later, however, when the church was rededicated under the name *Santa Maria la rotunda*, that the brightest hour in the history of the world symbol arrived: now the public and exact sphericity of the metaphysicians was merged once again with the intimate organic rotundity of the sky of immanence in Our Lady of Last Month.

The cosmotechnic peculiarity of Hagia Sophia, like all later authentic mosques, lay in the fact that it was no longer interested in the philosophical convergence of house and being, but rather the magical equation of bright world and magic cave. This presented Eastern builders with a creative absurdum under whose influence later Islamic architecture would have to develop into a school of miracles. For just as the technological-theological meaning of the Pantheon lies in the phrase "building the heavens,"

Dome above a teaching room of the Shir Dar madrasa in Samarkand, Uzbekistan

that of the Byzantine large-scale church and the mosque lies in the concept "erecting the world cave."

The late antique re-enchantment of the world also drew building into a re-mystification of the space, though this did not allow architecture, as artistic knowledge of the great building, to stop pursuing its constructivist calling. But the house-becoming of the universe now no longer corresponded to the universe-becoming of the house—rather, the house itself embarked on pseudomorphic travels and transformed back into the walled-in magic tent and the built cave. In the process, architecture entered the service of a counter-architectural spatial idea: first it became the art of building floating miracles and of God's restored incomprehensibility, and then it ended up in stasis, trapped within itself as the witness to a magical stagnation and a technical and cultural helplessness—and as the symptom of a cosmophobic powerlessness that still asserts its injured presence on the world stage under the problem name of "Islamic nation." Where the dome is forced to serve as the building form for cave immanence, advanced technology is placed in the service of a spatial idea of unequal rank. For a while, that can have the most enchanting results; in the long term, however, the orientalized dome becomes the guardian over the half-sleep of an immobilized reason.

Where, however, the dome was raised to tower over modern Western church buildings that agreed to the demand of the oceanic Modern Age, it remained in force until the turn of the twentieth century as the almost universally usable emblem for the neo-European spatial problem: depicting the eccentrically moved world inside centering large-scale buildings. With their domes, which are designed to offer exterior and interior views at once and rise up like triumphal towers, the gigantic projects of San Pietro

Hagia Sophia, lithograph by Louis Haghe (1806–1885) after a watercolor by
Gaspare Fossati

Reading Room in the Library of Congress, Washington

in Rome and St. Paul's in London absorbed the impetus of the Modern Age's outreach into the gargantuan. They reveal the meaning of classicism after the "age of the discovery of the world and of man." In power-stylistic terms, the Modern Age was the attempt to express the world volumes of the oceanic situation in the formal legacies of antiquity. This rule was followed by virtually all state builders of the Modern Age—from Louis XV, in whose reign the construction of what would later be called the "Parisian Pantheon" ("both ancient and Jesuit," in the words of Julien Gracq) to St. Nicholas' Church in Berlin and St. Isaac's Cathedral in Saint Petersburg. And naturally the Capitol in Washington (to say nothing of the tiringly numerous capitols in individual states of the USA) owed itself its own coronation with a dome in the

Lying in state in the rotunda: state funeral for General Dwight David Eisenhower beneath the dome of the Capital from March 30–31, 1969

maximalist style—after a dome debate, incidentally, that almost took on the scale of a constitutional one. With the dome of the Capitol (which responded directly to that of St. Paul's in London and indirectly to that of St. Peter's in Rome) completed in 1864, while the Civil War was still in progress, the *translatio imperii* from the Europeans to the US Americans was already a stylistic *fait accompli* that now only needed to be realized politically; the occasion arose with the USA's entrance into the First World War

Dome of the Washington Capitol, interior view

in 1917. That it was already an architectural fake, a mere stone façade over a concealed iron frame, is characteristic of Washington classicism as a whole.

The decisive metamorphosis of the dome did not, however, take place under the political builders of the countless, varyingly talkative paraphrases of the central-plan building in the Old and New Worlds that were continued well into the twentieth century (the inflated plans of Hitler and Speer for buildings marking the final victory in Berlin were located on the same line). From the 1820s on, it took place under private and economic direction: with the generous, roofed arcade constructions in Paris, Milan and Rome, in which, as Walter Benjamin showed, the spatial productivity of modern capital asserted its most suggestive idea yet. The arcades realize an idea of the interior that no longer expresses the immanence of the world-whole in an immunizing divine encompassment, but rather testifies to the circumnavigation of the earth through the traffic of commodities and the penetration of all life contexts by the flow of money. In the arcade the piazza, the shopping street and the salon merge in the name of the "commodity" or "lifestyle." Anyone with sufficient means can fulfill their need to negate the wall character of the built sky in favor of simulated transparency. This is the immunological purpose of the material glass, whose great career began with the arcade roofs and with which money, which builds its spatial ideas, has an affinity as deep as it is self-evident.

It was only with the built crystal utopias of early constructivism and the revealing, ingenious indoor architectures of the later twentieth century that the space-productive activities in the heads of architects, philosophers and climate designers took a decisive step beyond Old European models. This cleared the way for large-scale built-up spaces that had left behind the difference between exoteric and esoteric and between centrality and decentrality. The new spaces articulated an "unround" idea of the

Central dome of the Galleria Vittorio Emmanuele II (Milan, 1865–1867), under construction

sphere that had freed itself from the dogma of the Old European central space.[45] The twenty-first century would finally design its world roofs entirely beyond the old morphological models of heaven, house and cave.

The modern human, who de"con"structed the firmament and dismissed the sky from its traditional immune function, is

New trading rows (Moscow, 1888–1893); known since 1917 as State Department Store (GUM); central arcade arm

a differently immunized being that therefore lives and builds differently. It designed its roofs and side walls anew and took out insurances that dramatically changed its attitude towards the world's risks. As a creature that thought differently, it also had to become differently thought; being more highly insured, it also had to be able to afford an unprecedented openness to the world.

Model of the dome over the Berlin Reichstag, Norman Foster (1998)

In the coming age, the dome would come to symbolize the insight that even emptiness must be built around. God may be dead, but the dome-building continues—and with it the dispute about the suitable roof over the heads of contemporary humans. The roofs of postmodernity were no longer cosmological dogmas, but rather working hypotheses for provisional communities. It seems today, built emptiness retraces that horizon within which the natal-mortal beings must look after themselves and their meetings. Even the *prima facie* megalomaniacal Millennium Dome built by Richard Rogers in Greenwich, south-east London, which served to celebrate England's entrance into the third millennium, testifies to the intense thrust of these symbol-political spatial demands. An entire country vibrated under the impression of a timely, yet difficult-to-interpret spatial idea: according to British newspapers, language statistics in 1997 showed that

Millennium Dome on the Greenwich Peninsula (London, January 1999)

"dome" was the most-used word that year (after the name Diana).[46] Dome debates are still indicators of collective spatial sensibility. As has been the case since the city walls of Jericho and Uruk, the advanced skill of builders and architects today serves to emphasize the proto-communitarian thesis that even on a very large, indeed a global scale, the primacy of the inside must still apply. To paraphrase Leibniz, there is nothing in architecture that was not first in the immune ideas.

CHAPTER 5

Deus sive sphaera
Or
The Exploding Universal One

The sphere of the soul is true to its own form.
— Marcus Aurelius, *Meditations*, XI, 12[1]

In every now Being begins; around every here rolls the ball of there. The center is everywhere.
— Friedrich Nietzsche, *Thus Spoke Zarathustra*

Where it understood itself best, Western theology was a meditation on the surreal center. It dealt, with an insistence bordering on desperation, with a universal center that could not possibly be out of the world. Because God and the world were separated by the first difference in the design of classical metaphysics, the center of the real world, the light-deprived earth and the wayward humans on it and the center of the world above, the divine center of abundance and the blessed spirits around it, were destined to fall apart forever. Hence the theory of the whole could therefore only turn out bipartite, even bilingual, and ultimately fully dichotomous. As cosmology or the science of the natural whole it dealt with the "universe," and as theology or the science of the spiritual whole it addressed God as the ground or secret of the world. That is why the idea that suggested itself, namely that the two viewpoints could be joined to yield a uniform overall theory, as if nature and the spirit-God were two complementary aspects of the same continuum and their theories merely different projections of the same internally coherent total reality, proved unfeasible—despite boundless protestations and their increasingly refined repetitions.

From a modern position, there is a good chance of understanding that the Old European cosmologists and Judeo-Greco-Christian theologians, though both experts on totality, were never speaking about the same thing when discussing what they called the one and the whole, no matter how obstinately they tried to force the convergence of their discourses. They could have found a formal reason for the harmony between the theory of world totality and the theory of divine totality in the structures of the respective totalities, the kinship between their basic morphological positions—for both, according to their decisive interpretations, should be envisaged as a single ineffably perfect orb, and it seems reasonable to expect two different projections of a largest orb to refer ultimately to one and the same thing. This assumption proves a deceptive one, however, and examination of the two maximal orbs will show that they cannot possibly be the same, indeed that their interconnection—which both the Perennial Philosophy and speculative theology incessantly attempted—cannot follow without absurd implications. The god of the morphologists clearly felt like making fools of the theologians and the cosmologists together by having the idea of presenting himself in two incompatible totalities, as if he wanted to snub the self-evident axiom *maximum est unum*, which states that there is one and only one greatest, the unparalleled and singular one-and-all.

We recall: Plato and Aristotle initially had great success with their attempt to prove that of the many possible orbs, there could only be one that is currently all-encompassing. Plato had taught emphatically that the demiurge produced not two or countless cosmoses but only one, which, in its abundance and completeness, constituted a single-born (*monogenes*) and lonely (*éremos*) singularity. The founders of the Athenian school developed the fateful argument that the maximum could only be one, and that therefore all physically existent things were collected in a single maximum width, that of the real vault of heaven: *the greatest is singular*—a theorem whose dignified formality gave it authority from antiquity onwards, via Cusa, to the modern idealists. If the world is the epitome of that which it encompasses by an outermost boundary, it can accordingly only be the one and only, as the concept of the greatest necessarily includes the integration of everything. The logos-generated and soul-infused cosmos of the philosophers is thus elevated to the greatest of epitomes and the epitome of the encompassing. In cosmological terms, integrity and universal integrity mean the same thing.

Nonetheless, theologians after Plato considered it a clear fact that God must exceed and reach over the world and everything about and inside it. He was the originator of an even more powerful universal orb, albeit one of an entirely different kind— a hyperphysical, noetic, energetic and erotic sphere of all spheres that can only be termed spatial in an inauthentic sense, and in whose center (though what does "center" mean in a hyperspatial domain?) All-doing and all-knowing, he enjoys himself without measure or opposition. God circles everything and is circled by nothing, Pseudo-Dionysius tells us—which clearly articulates his preference for size, both spatially and hyperspatially. If there are sufficient grounds for this claim by the idealistic theologians—and from an immanent perspective, there is much to support this concession—then the orb of the Aristotelian *Naturalia* doctors, the world-heaven that tolerates the earth at its center, and the mathematical-mystical God-"sphere" that releases everything from itself and holds everything within itself are not the same thing after all. Indeed, even the famous auxiliary construction of the metaphysical idea of unity, the *analogia entis* that allows the world, similar in the dissimilar, to follow the immeasurably exceeding God at a humble distance, could not do away with the disconcerting opposition between the two maximal projects.

God theory and world theory remain fundamentally different projects in their starting points and their results, even if both—deceptively similar in their advertised forms—are *de facto* practiced as sphere doctrines of the highest order. Not until Spinoza's *deus sive natura* approach was it shown how one could remove the Western comedy of dual theory from the program, provided one was willing to sacrifice transcendence. However great the temptation to equate the two orb constructs—the cosmological-immanent and the ontotheological-transcendent—they do show substantial dissonances that damn any attempt at unification to failure. Only through an institutionalized interest in consonance and convergence has it been possible to create the impression that Greco-Christian scholasticism produced a unified theory encompassing God and the world, and thus achieved what can be termed a coherent overall picture of the existent and supra-existent, or an integrated metaphysical system. One need only read the relevant texts a little more slowly than usual to

Pseudo-theocentric world picture.—Nicole Oresme, *Livre du ciel et du monde 1377*, manuscript of an annotated translation of Aristotle's *De coelo* for Charles V. The illustrator of this volume inverted the Aristotelian cosmos, such that the seven planetary shells curve, in a cosmographically irregular fashion, around God rather than around the earth, with the orbs of Saturn and the fixed stars inside and the moon in the outermost position.

realize that no such thing can be claimed. In reality, the supposed onto-(cosmo)-theology of the metaphysical age, to whose deceptive homogeneity Martin Heidegger still paid tribute with his essentially superfluous attempt at its "destruction," was fundamentally split. What manifests itself at its basis is the irresolvable difference between two willful and never concentrically practicable models of spheric totality in whose connection to the

Geocentric world sphere from a work by Cecho d'Ascoli (Vienna, 1516)

complex of "metaphysics," viewed in the correct light, there is nothing to destroy, because it already fails as a construct.

All attempts to make the centers, perimeters and inner rings of the two sublime total spheres match were doomed to failure for fundamental reasons, even if the parallelism between rhetoric about God and rhetoric about the world contributed to concealing the factual discrepancy. Hence classical metaphysics neither requires nor permits any *de*struction or *de*"con"struction, for it is precisely a well-meaning, though not dizzy *re*construction that exposes the unfeasibility of the metaphysical project, namely the seamless concentric integration of the world sphere and the sphere of the world above, with dazzling—or tragic, perhaps—clarity.

What would be required is therefore not so much a critique of centrism as such, but rather a sufficiently attentive distinction between the centers and the corresponding peripheries. It would make it clear that the entire metaphysical tradition rested on an interested confusion of transcendence and immanence spaces, that is to say on swapping around two completely different centers and their circumferences. One must concede that this differentiation would be difficult to make for thinkers under the spell of tradition, whether affirmative or subversive in their stance. Even Cusa was content to be dazzled by the constitutive illusion of his era, which had to dream of heaven embracing the earth; that is why he taught the impossible with equal formality and futility: the con(ec)centricity of the cosmic and terrestrial orbs, or the round inclusion of all immanence in an encompassing transcendence, which here amounts to the same thing.

The one, therefore, who is also the center of the world, namely, God, the ever blessed, is the center of the earth, of all spheres and of all things that are in the world, and is, at the same time, the infinite circumference of all.[2]

Such a thing can obviously be written, but is impossible to think—for a reason that will emerge in the following with a clarity not found in any previous philosophical historiography: the discrepancy between the theoperipheral and theocentric interpretations of the world—one could also say between the Aristotelian ontology of majesty (God above) and the Platonic-Plotinic doctrine of emanation (God at the center)—is made of harder stuff than any longing for a harmonization of systems. One cannot construct the whole from the position of the earth *and* that of God simultaneously, and whoever attempts it nonetheless must feign concentricity where there can be none. What or who is genuinely the "center of the earth" in the space of the medieval world picture will be revealed below in the chapter on "anti-spheres" with a fundamental Satanological investigation; and the deceptions that are required to envisage God as the "center of all spheres" can be shown in detail in Cusa's own work, namely his treatise *De ludo globi*.

In high medieval thought, confusion as to the meaning of the center extended to the last layers of the interpretation of God and the world. Without a dense and elastic fabric of pious autohypnoses, supported by a system of institutionalized pseudo-ideas precisely analogous to what are now called "discourses" (in Foucauldian terms, routines of saying things), "Western metaphysics" would never have been able to justify its existence in the decisive question. The price of medieval freedom of thought, which was only possible as a license to theorize within the boundaries of the dogma, was that the bifocalism of the "world picture" had to be kept latent, and that there could be no explicit dialogue about the contradictions between the geocentric and theocentric locations of projection within the illusory bubble of the Perennial Philosophy.

One sign of the depth of devotional confusion was that even Nietzsche's madman, who thought he was proclaiming the death of God, fell prey to the confusion of centers with no inkling that he should have distinguished between two radically different concepts of the one-and-all upon his appearance. When the madman poses his eccentric questions in the ominous paragraph 125 of *The Gay Science*—

> "What were we doing when we unchained the earth from the sun? […] Is there still an up and a down? Aren't we straying as though through an infinite nothing?"[3]

—his tone and content unmistakably speak of the *loss of the periphery* that accompanied the abandonment of Aristotelian cosmology for post-Copernican humanity. Here this is mourning over the evaporated heaven of fixed stars, whose elimination triggered the infinitism shock. The pathos of Nietzsche's questions reveals how the decentering of the earth and the liquidation of the shells undermined the psychocosmic immune system of Old Europe: "Isn't empty space breathing at us? Hasn't it got colder?"[4] Such talk makes it seem as if nihilism were now strolling from one corner to the next; the earth's rotation is interpreted as a fatal centrifuge hurling us into an eternal cold, and the absence of the sky's final canopy is assumed to bring about the de-securing of life. The agitated message is easy to understand: the desert is growing, the point of orientation is lost, the outside is taking everything, and sense can only be found in radically artificial self-harboring systems designed to counteract the objective bottomlessness (in a second-degree act of ark-building).

And yet: when the madman proclaims the death of God in the same breath, he is speaking about something else, namely the *loss of the center* that followed the retreat of modern theology from Platonic-Plotinic positions. Nietzsche's choice to portray this second loss as a consequence of the *murder* of the highest, best and greatest may be a hysterization that one tolerates because it shows an awareness of how acute the successor question is. Yet the deed as such remains problematic, for what compass spike could one have used to stab the absolute center to death? Doubled attention is now required: letting the earth roll out of the center of the Aristotelian-Ptolemaic cosmos and extinguishing the origin of all light at the center of the God orb are two fundamentally different operations, and failing to distinguish between them can only lead to muddled views on all related matters. Not least, this question also determines the meaning of modernity: is it a post-metaphysical age, as is proclaimed from every corner of academia, or a differently metaphysical one that does not yet fully understand itself? Has ontology in general become impossible in it, as quick thinkers in the transcendentalist and constructivist camps tirelessly state, or has a historical type of ontological thought merely completed its service? Has philosophical thought itself uttered its last word, meaning that the alienation theorists are right when they stare into what has passed with universal necrological melancholy? Or is not the old love of wisdom already in the process of changing further into a new historical guise, let us say a transgeneous art of reason? It seems as if the meaning of modernity itself depended on how one interprets the catastrophe of the metaphysical spheres, and thus on stating clearly whether the center or the perimeter are to be considered lost, or both—and which center and which perimeter of which orb.[5]

Nonetheless, the conviction that all these possible losses ultimately mean the same thing is one that has been asserted from the Modern Age to the present day in both conservative and modern legends. The origins of this confusion lie far back, extending to Greek classicism, and the entire Middle Ages stood under its banner. If even Nietzsche was still subject to it, this testified to the immensity of the Old European-Catholic illusion, which had to sustain at all costs the assertion that the world orb and the God orb were, on a higher level, somehow concentrically built after all—not to say one with each other, exactly as Cusa's very catchy, yet logically and objectively completely desperate statement sought to suggest. In fact, the identity thesis would have to be correct for it to be asserted with any chance of success that the earth's removal from the center of the cosmos was metaphysically synonymous with the evacuation of God from the center of being.

This is no more than a suggestion without a factual basis, however. In truth, there are two *toto coelo* different decenterings here, each corresponding to completely different re-occupations—or omissions—of the central point. Modernity had no shortage of candidates for these two vacant centers of the whole: matter, man, the species subject, the avant-garde, race, structure, the unconscious, capital, language, the brain, the genes, the primordial mass—all this and more was discussed as the foundation and ruling center at some time or other, and every customer on the deregulated market of meaning could decide on their own *a priori* according to their taste. Almost no one ever attempted to understand which of the vacant centers was at issue in the first place.

The history of ideas from the last two hundred years is therefore the age of the wars of succession for the problematic centers of ailing totalities—this understandably leads to pacifist suggestions that one should finally relax in a "culture with no center."[6] Not that one cannot understand why clarification is a slow business in a field so muddled by oversized angles, and why little can be achieved here without a form of orbital outside observation and radicalized over-views. Until better knowledge established itself on a wider scale, the terrible simplifiers and psalmodizing conservators would keep the helpless public in the palm of their hand as they pleased. Some took refuge in an Aristotle, who was equally satisfying to archbishops and social democrats, while others put a new coat of varnish on Baroque relics of the Perennial Philosophy for the nostalgic public. The best-known intervention in this field came from the Catholic madman Hans Sedlmayr with his modernity-critical accusatory text *Art in Crisis: The Lost Center* (1948),[7] in which the author mourned a center of which none could ever say where it had supposedly lain. (At least Sedlmayr illustrates, once again, the meaning and aims of Catholic Aristotelianism in accusing modern architecture of breaking away from the "earth basis"— as exemplified by Ledoux' design for the spherical *House for the Overseer of the River* (1775–1780) in Maupertuis, whose purely geometric form allegedly violated the laws of sublunary existence. Sedlmayr generally sees a tendency in modernity to develop "inhumanly pure spheres," which ultimately boils down to an accusation of self-deification or Satanism.) Whether Sedlmayr or anti-Sedlmayr, however, the confusion over the meaning of the center and its loss in modernity was almost equally great in all camps.

In order to distinguish with certainty between the two classical figures of the all-encompassing, namely the celestial orb and the divine orb, one need only look at their centers: the difference between the geocentric and theocentric sphere projects emerges immediately and irreconcilably. It is this difference that forever sabotages the most sublime Old European theory project: to give a logical form to the *hen kai pan*.

In the first model of the Great Orb, as expounded in the previous chapter, the ontological *pessimum* and *ultimum* is at the center: here we encounter the earth inhabited by mortal men and its subterranean bowels, hell, which is defined as the negative pole of the universe and the place furthest from the God on high. Geocentric cosmography has an inherent structural infernocentrism— Dante's innermost circle of hell at the earth's core, where the tears of a three-faced (counter-trinitarian) Satan fall from six monstrous eyes into his own eternal ice, erected a telling monument to this concept of an absolute central point of the physical world. The fact that tradition also called him the Prince of the World shows a cosmologically correct consequence of the Aristotelian injury of the earth. One can learn from the frost-bound Satan what being-in-the-world ultimately means from a Catholic perspective: the devil did not lose the center; he himself is the center.

Around this depraved center of the world, the subterranean negative pole, the earth's surface does at least constitute a lightened, firm shell that is open towards the heavens, a medium on which human life takes place, endangered by the sticky evil depths, but simultaneously drawn towards higher attractors. Classical

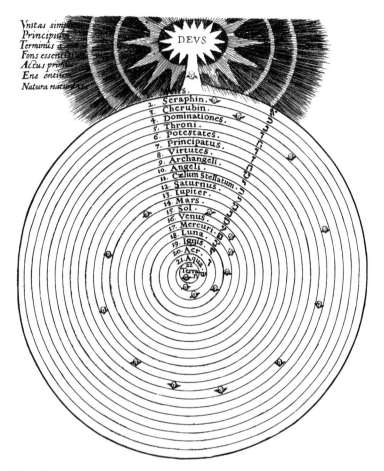

Robert Fludd, twenty-two-step spiral cosmos. The steps correspond to the letters of the Hebrew alphabet. The extremely theoperipheral schema synthesizes the Pseudo-Dionysian system of emanations (the outflow of the nine angelic intelligences from God, 2–10, then the Aristotelian shell cosmos, 11–18, and finally the four elements, 19–22) in a single series. The degradation of the earth (Terra, 22) is strikingly expressed in the hybrid diagram through its ambiguous definition as an element *and* as the central body of the system that is furthest from God. The black sphere implies the existence of a second, this time theocentric construction. From Robert Fludd, *History of the Macrocosm and the Microcosm* (1617).

onto-topology does not cease to repeat its central tenet that the place of humans is the in-between, on which the vector forces work from above and below. Around this globe and its graveyards beneath the moon, formed by the gravity of death and the buoyancy of hope, ethereal regions of higher dignity accumulate layer by layer. In the simplified eight-step scheme: the shells of the moon and sun, then those of the five planets and above them the sphere of fixed stars, with which the planetary ethereal world borders on the Empyrean, the kingdom of the blessed souls that are with God.

Dante's exemplary journey to heaven, which is expanded into a ten-step sequence, essentially corresponds to this geocentric model. It leads first to the heavenly sphere of the moon, which is populated by those souls who were prevented from fulfilling an oath; then to the sphere of Mercury, where the heroes of honor reside, and the sphere of Venus, in which the discreet lovers have found their lasting home; arching over this is the fourth, the sphere of the sun, very fittingly inhabited by clear-thinking theologians who hid their bodies from the light beneath cowls during life, but now compensate by gilding their transfigured bodies in an eternal sunbath. Progressing further upwards, the poet reaches the fifth sphere of heaven, that of Mars, in which the martyrs are gathered as war heroes of faith, then the sphere of Jupiter as that of the just rulers, and finally the Saturnian sphere of the contemplatives. This is overarched by the eighth sphere, that of the fixed stars, which is encompassed only by the final container, the crystal sphere of heaven—which, because of its luminous properties, the Doctors deemed the first *diaphanum*, so that the divine light could flow unhindered into the physical cosmos from above.[8] Above the nine of the most blessed souls, the unutterable ten is hinted at with the heavenly rose and the seat of the Trinity.

Dante's paradise is obviously based on a cosmic-supracosmic bastard model that fuses Aristotelian and Neoplatonic motifs very freely by adopting the arrangements of shells from Aristotle's cosmogram and borrowing God's centering in an over-bright point of light from Plato and Plotinus. That Dante's divine central light shines not at the earth's physical center, rather irrupting into the cosmos from its periphery, already hints at the ambiguous role of the light (as *lux* and *lumen*), which oscillates between physics and supra-physics. In Dante's schema, cosmotheology and spirit theology are liberally mingled without fear of incompatibilities. On his ascent, the poet famously acts as if he were *not* moving into increasingly wide circles and sphere domes, as would be cosmologically consistent, but rather strives towards a high endpoint—an outsourced "center," one could say—paradoxically located both at the uppermost edge of the tiered cosmos and outside of it. With great carefreeness, the poet lets the matter of this topological complication of heaven rest; God alone knows how it is possible to be condensed in a single radiant central point and simultaneously present oneself as the outermost wall and most sublime outwork of the cosmic structure. But even non-theologians can at least agree that God, if he exists, knows no weight problems and may be both point and all-encompassing volume simultaneously.

As far as this geocentrically constituted cosmic orb is concerned, the normal human perspective is preserved in it through the distinction between above and below, which is why the center, entirely in keeping with everyday intuition, is localized

Gustave Doré, illustration for Dante's *Divine Comedy*, *Paradise*, Canto XII, 19–21:

> *così di quelle sempiterne rose*
> *volgiensi circa noi le due ghirlande,*
> *e sì l'estrema a l'intima rispuose.*
> even so those sempiternal roses wreathed
> twin garlands round us as the outer one
> was lovingly responding to the inner.[9]

"down here," while the periphery can naturally lie "up there." It is not for nothing that when Dante is almost at his journey's end and is lifted up to the crystal sphere of heaven, he casts a final glance back and perceives the earth, in all its ridiculous and touching minuteness, in the furthermost corner of the universe:

> *Col viso ritornai per tutte quante*
> *le sette sphere, e vidi questo globo*
> *tal, qu'io sorrisi del suo vil sembiante*
> My vision traveled back through all the spheres,
> through seven heavens, and then I saw our globe;
> it made me smile, it looked so paltry there.
> (Canto XXII, 133–135)[10]

With this, the space travel character of the poet's journey through the luminous world of spheres is displayed once again; one of its desired results is to humiliate the earth in the massive extensions of the cosmos.[11] *Deus est res extensa*—Spinoza's proposition already had a certain meaning for the God of scholastic cosmology, in that he posits heaven or the ethereal world as His indirect extension, which of course means that in the spatial schema, he is less "with himself" lower down, and finally ceases to be entirely at the lowest point, that of Satan, at the center of the corporeal world. Consistently with this, salvation and damnation are distributed according to the difference between above and below in this model, such that those seeking salvation cannot doubt for a moment where their path must lead: climbing upwards to higher spheres, they follow God if they suspect him to be above.

Anyone thinking to seek God *within* the world orb, however, can only discover indirect signs of His works—vestiges, relics,

Dante, *The Divine Comedy*, *Paradise*, Canto XIV, 83–84.:

> *e vidimi translato*
> *sol con mia donna in più alta salute.*
> and looking up I saw myself translated,
> alone with her to more exalted bliss.[12]

hints and hieroglyphs (which is why theology easily turns into theo-detection). As long as the seeker remains in immanence, however close they might feel they are to the object of their quest, they must constantly comprehend anew that the true God exceeds everything which can be sensually, spatially and symbolically grasped. The classic model of a futile search for God in a space where he naturally cannot exist as himself was developed by Augustine in the tenth book of *Confessions*, adapting motifs from Psalm 139; as late as the early nineteenth century, Jean Paul replicated this fruitless space flight in the journey of his dead Christ through the God-forsaken world edifice: "I went through the Worlds, I mounted into the Suns, and flew with the Galaxies through the wastes of Heaven; but there is no God!"[13]

Even for those who attain the utmost proximity to him, then, God's address in the geocentric world is *excelsior*, the most sublime; his residence can only be localized in a layer that towers higher than the physically or symbolically highest. Here it is plain to see why in this schema of the world, humans are condemned to climb up and transcend if they wish to find truth or good; at the same time, it becomes clear why theologians train escalation: they are faced with the insurmountable mental task of always envisaging God as greater than the greatest in the realm of imaginable positive quantities. Whoever desires the best must reach the upper edge of the universe and then go even higher; from this lowly world, one can only come closer to the truth in a vertical ascent. That is why there is no redemption in mere horizontal sciences—for all time, at least from the perspective of the vertically challenged theorists.

In the pseudo-Aristotelian text *On the World* from the late first century AD, we find the exemplary sketch of the geocentric

Dante, *The Divine Comedy, Paradise*, Canto XXVII, 1–3:

> *"Al Padre, al Figlio, a lo Spirito Santo,"*
> *cominciò, "gloria!" tutto 'l paradiso,*
> *sì che m'inebrïava il dolce canto.*
>
> "To Father and to Son and Holy Spirit,"
> all Heaven with one voice cried, "Glory be!"
> inebriating me with such sweet sound.

Dante, *The Divine Comedy*, *Paradise*, Canto XXXI, 1–3:

> *In forma dunque di candida rosa*
> *mi si mostrava la milizia santa*
> *che nel suo sangue Cristo fece sposa*
> So now, appearing to me in the form
> of a white rose was Heaven's sacred host,
> those whom with His own blood Christ made His bride[14]

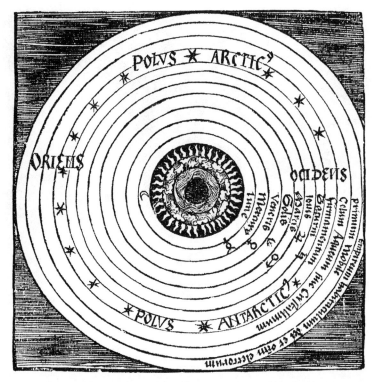

From Gregor Reisch, *Margarita philosophica nova* (1508): classical Aristotelian 10-sphere world picture with the layers 1 Luna, 2 Mercury, 3 Venus, 4 Soi, 5 Mars, 6 Jovis (Jupiter), 7 Saturn, 8 firmament, 9 crystal heaven, 10 primum mobile, and beyond 10 the Empyrean as *habitaculum Dei et omnium electorum* [dwelling place of God and all the elect].

schema on which all Aristotelian-Catholic theologians and cosmographers would base their world picture:

> He hath himself obtained the first and highest place and is therefore called Supreme, and has, in the words of the poet, "Taken his seat in heaven's topmost height"; and the heavenly

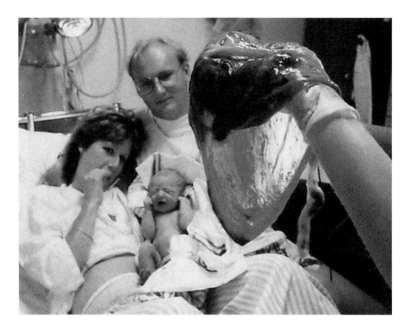

Quaternity (photograph: Lennart Nilsson)

body which is nighest him most enjoys his power, and afterwards the next nearest, and so on successively until the regions wherein we dwell are reached. Wherefore the earth and the things upon the earth, being farthest removed from the benefit which proceeds from God, seem feeble and incoherent and full of much confusion.[15]

A radically opposing perspective must be chosen for the construction of the theocentric orb, whose center is occupied by the *optimum* and *summum*: God. This approach, however, encounters an obstacle that can possibly never be overcome by humans: in constructing the encompassing in relation to God, one can no longer begin from the situation of natural intelligence. The

theocentrists, after all, would have to presume an origin that is—
"initially," say the illuminated—unattainable for human intellects.
What is meant by thinking "in relation to God" can nonetheless
be explained with sufficient clarity under the premises of speculation; after all we know about the attempts that have been made,
however, it is as uncertain as it was at the start whether humans are
the right ones to conduct such discourses. Only by leaping to the
beginning—but who takes the leap?—would one gain the starting
point for the theocentric construction: one would have to begin
with the divine *archè*, that supra-existent, immeasurable rich and
dense primal point from which the wealth of the existent eternally
"pro"-ceeds in a certain mode—by overflowing, emanating,
bursting or unfolding. At the center of the *other* orb, we would
thus find—assuming we can leap there, into the absolutely
implicit—the true god of the philosophers, whom Neoplatonic
infiltration increasingly turned into the god of the theologians
too, especially among supporters of a Christian *theologia mystica*
in the Pseudo-Dionysian style.

If God is assumed to be an absolute point that becomes
world in its eternal bursting, the structure of the distance
between the center and the periphery is inverted: the world and
humans must now be placed at the edge of the God orb—pho-
tologically speaking in the area of the sensually inhibited,
mediated, media-clouded light, and morally speaking in a position of relative *remoteness* from God. As for those humans who
appear in both conceptions of totality as physical-metaphysical
amphibians, their metaphysical desire—the yearning to overcome their remoteness from God—cannot possibly aim in the
same direction in the theocentric and geocentric systems. The
yearning for the best crosses over from the unattainably high to

Matthias Grünewald, *Isenheim Altarpiece*, detail: God the Father with angelic emanation (c. 1512)

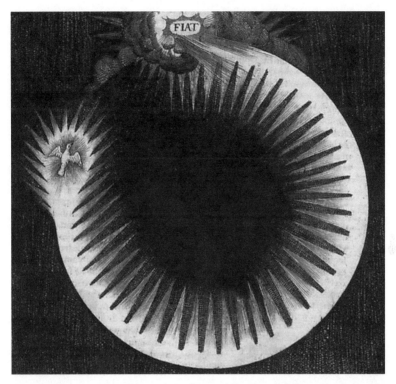

Fiat Lux. The spirit dove issuing from the word "let there be" draws the first circle of light. From Robert Fludd, *History of the Macrocosm and Microcosm* (1617)

the unattainably internal, and the meaning of remoteness changes equally thoroughly. Whoever wishes to leave the murky physical world and come into the light must prepare for an ascent to the highest periphery—Catholic and Islamic orthodoxies never left any doubts in this respect; whoever would reach the divine center of radiation, on the other hand, must learn how to concentrate on an extremely interiorized point in the abyss of their own soul—an interest that is gratified by monospheric mysticisms. What appeared in geocentrism as homesickness for heaven—*superior summon meo*—manifests itself in theocentrism as a longing to return into the enraptured depth center—*interior intimo meo*—of the spirit and soul space.

Forming an idea of the properties and demands of this *other center* was the purpose of the Old European theory project of theology; in its heyday, it could assert precedence over all other disciplines in the monastic and academic culture of reason with its masterful rationalism. Where the participants in this theory game were bright enough to grasp the oddness of their task, they converted to the thinking style "in relation to God," which has been the hallmark of authentic theocentrists since the days of Neoplatonism.[16] Whoever does not accept conversion to a radical-theoretical way of seeing will simply not set eyes on the other, luminous orb. The renunciation of sensual semblance demanded by this comes at a price which experts tirelessly claimed could, with good faith and appropriate instruction, be paid in manageable rates: there are many viable starting points for the journey to the innermost point, they claimed, much like the route to Compostela, edifying resting spots halfway to the goal and a final stretch that is mandatory for all, which must be traversed in an attitude of collected submission. And because this is so, friends of God can and should pursue studies, even if the final examination is far out of view for most of them—deep in the galaxies of an ego-dissolving immersion. As far as the examinations are concerned, they test less for positive knowledge than for an erudite ignorance which responds to the specific non- and supra-conceptuality of the Highest with a specific lack of concepts.

Such long and counter-natural paths as those of theosophical or exact mysticism can only be recommended when the goal justifies the effort—unless the way itself is declared the goal

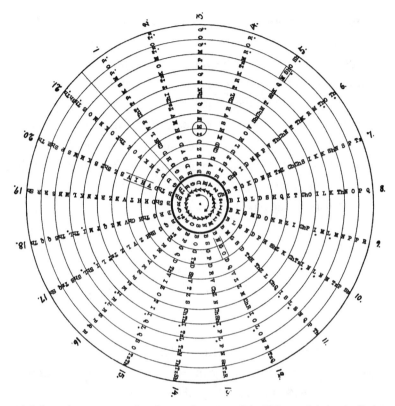

Alphabetical emanation, taken from a depiction of the Hebrew alphabet in *Sepher Yetzirah*

(which always makes immediate sense to nihilists, who believe in means without ends and journeys without arrivals). But where are humans going if their terminus is not the distant above but the distant inside? What are the studies they carry out if these do not bring them positive knowledge, but rather take them ever further away from public objects?

One could compare the theocentric approach anachronistically with the undertaking of entering psychoanalysis with the One and following the motto "Where there was I, there shall be He." Plotinus does not mince words: "One sees oneself.[17]" Later patients of God such as Cusa and Bruno appear as truth-hunters claiming they would finally be transformed into the hunted like Actaeon. Once cured, these sought seekers should be capable of viewing the *arcanum magnum* of being, the luminous God orb, in its glory and transferring themselves to its center. Marsilio Ficino made a respectable attempt at replicating God's original words in his *Theological Dialogue Between God and the Soul*, where his neatly bursting deity speaks thus:

> I fill heaven and earth, I penetrate and contain them. I fill and am not filled, for I am fullness itself. I penetrate and am not penetrated, for I am the power of penetration itself. I contain and am not contained, for I am containing itself.[18]

Thinking from a theocentric "position" obviously rests on fulsome assumptions that can only be fulfilled through a methodically executed de-selfing of the thinkers (which in reality naturally means a deeper selfing)—though it remains unclear to the end whether such a de-selfing is possible, and whether it achieves what the practicing hope for. A characteristic of this approach is a certain superhuman power of intuition and deduction, amounting to an attempt to be as close as possible to the action at the origin or primal outflow of all categories of the existent from the source point. There is no cogito in proximity to the absolute point, only the dazzled witness to the birth from light. If the intellect were able to leap to the beginning, it would become cognizant of unimaginable events: it could follow God's path towards the world step by step (if the pedestrian metaphor

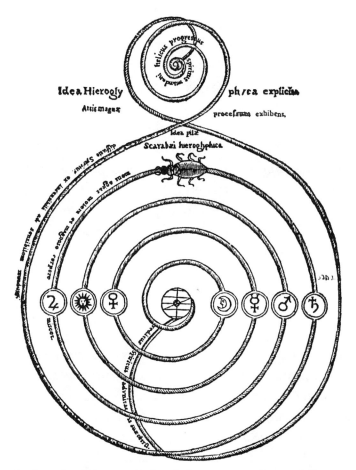

Scarab spheres, from Athanasius Kircher, *Oedipus aegyptiacus* (Rome, 1653)

is suitable here). The eyewitness to divine protuberance would perceive a firework of unfolding principles—a sovereign act of self-deprecation from the absolute that places out, traverses, preserves and encompasses everything, from the light-filled first intuitions in God via nine intermediate links of angels, general concepts and species, to the form of the dust grain at the edge of the universe. The marveling intellect could witness the spectacle of hierarchized light cascades spreading out concentrically in all directions through the outpouring of the first idea rings from the generative center—ring by ring, tier by tier, definition by definition—before finally reaching that zone, relatively far from the center, in which the over-bright outbursts of pure light have been sufficiently weakened to produce the optically accessible cosmos through the connection of the more concrete lights or ideas of species with peripheral matter. Thinking here means letting oneself fall into the roaring of a cosmogonic light explosion.

One must concede that the talk of a theocentric orb retains a strong metaphorical aspect, as the outpouring of the categories of being from the divine *origo* is initially an asensual and supraspatial event, and only develops a connection to spatial and sensual conditions after translation into the language of light metaphysics and light metaphors. It is precisely in these translations and pictorializations, however, that medieval Platonism was in its element, and whoever wanted to discuss how the God of mystical theology created a world in non-biblical terminology at that time had little choice but to join in with the language games dealing with the self-expansion of light in the tiered orb.[19] Here everything was in the realm of the "quasi" and the "so to speak," and yet everything was said exactly as it was said.

Anyone who followed the overflowing of the center towards the edges over all thresholds and tiers—

[...] pollen of Godhead's own flowering;
limbs of the light; paths, stairways, thrones,
realms of pure being; emblazoned delight;
riots of sense's enchantments: and, of a sudden, alone—

you are mirrors: you pour out your beauty
but your faces gather it back to yourselves.[20]

—would directly notice how precariously far from the first center
the terrestrial world, with all its plant, animal and human creatures, appears: a structure close to the outermost edge of the God
orb, still reached and shaped by light yet also powerfully shaped
by darkness and void. For if the material cosmos constitutes a
manifestation for intellects that are designed for sensual media-
tions, it does no more than to realize a darkened "utterance" of the
light flux. The observer of the emanating light gains insight into
the ontological ambiguity of the corporeal world so disturbingly
remote from the center of light: for one thing, only the power of
the center and its continuum keep the bodies in being—every
form-shaped entity extending to the smallest insect of a particular
species, after all, takes part in the outflow of the being-providing
species forms, and thus in the continuum of the best emanating
from the supra-existent point. For another thing, however, the
forms are augmented by obfuscating additions of empty mate-
riality, of a formless primal something, that become denser with
growing distance and become ever heavier, more sluggish and
more opaque until they reach a lightless edge, with a realm
beyond at which theologians dare only make ominous hints. Were
it not unacceptable in the school context to claim expressly that
God's radius is limited, it would be very clear that beyond its
colorful creature-populated periphery, the luminous, essence-
filled orb would have to be surrounded by a night of unanalyzable
remoteness from God. Naturally classical theospherics does not
allow any ray sent out by God to be lost *a priori*; according to the
orthodox theory, all rays only leave the center up to their specific

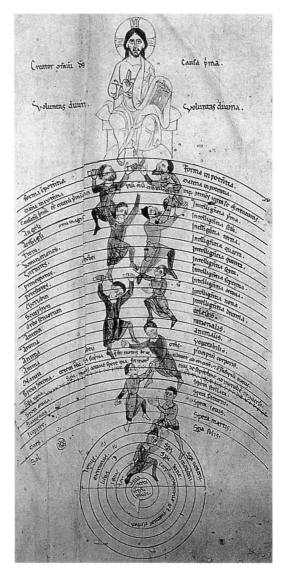

This schema of the *mundus hierarchicus* from a 12th-century Viennese manuscript likewise shows the pseudo-concentric structure of Pseudo-Dionysian intelligences (which supposedly emanate from God in concentric rings) and the Aristotelian world of spheres (which is organized concentrically around the earth).

points of return, from which they hasten back to their beginnings. Reflection, or homecoming of the light, is a high-ranking photo-theological term whose history from Plotinus and Proclus to Habermas, Hawkins and Zajonc remains to be written.

This much is clear, however: not all light reflects or returns home, and for this reason—even if the Catholic spirit is reluctant to look at it—there is a wan outer desert whence no more reflections or retrievals occur. God's outermost edge, or rather the realm beyond His edge, is a ring of almost-nothing or completely-nothing where isolated lost rays, unable to turn back and unwilling to return home, have ventured out. But then the radiating God also has an irrecuperable outside in which the immune system of being fails. With all due caution, the Catholic word for the outside—"hell"—hints at this eerie region.

The peripheries of both orb projects mirror the antithetical relationship between the centers more than clearly: while the world orb's dead end is located at the center and perfection resides on its high perimeter, the God orb is characterized by the monarchy of the center, whereas its extreme periphery—or more precisely its trans-periphery—is only a diabolical anarchy. That is why localizing the hells is so informative in these onto-topological designs. If the lost souls fall out of the *unio* in the geocentric schema, they find themselves in the final below and inside, on the model of Dante's lord of devils; they are mockingly resocialized in hell—the outside which even God does not enter is here the inferno of negativity, where those who have insulted him are stranded. In the theocentric sphere, by contrast, the intransigent rays are lost on a path of no return, behind the outermost turning points for the light that can return home. Their theofugal dynamic takes them to a space from which nothing returns—if one wished to interpret their fate existentially, it would most resemble that of so-called schizophrenics floating through the cosmos bearing an unspeakable pain.

Once the two orbs of totality have been formally distinguished and placed alongside each other using these outlines, even if they are undoubtedly too crude—which, it would seem, was never explicitly carried out anywhere in the European tradition, although both formations are present explicitly enough in the logic of discourses and diagrams and constantly act on and through each other—the notion of equating the two, or even simply placing them concentrically within each other, disappears almost automatically. Only in Islamic philosophy did a few thinkers become aware of the conflict between the theocentric and theoperipheral interpretations of the world, though their attempts at solutions, which generally favored the periphery-based God, did not prove very convincing.[21] The merit of Islamic theosophy lies in the fact that it openly displayed the paradox of a "center" located outside. As far as European thought is concerned, one can say today in a calm tone, far from all ideological polemics, that the God orb and the world orb of classical metaphysics were incompatible due to their opposing constructions, and could not be "reconciled" or otherwise made tolerable for each other.

This makes it all the more interesting to ask how the traditional thinkers set about bypassing this difficulty, and how they managed to keep up a Catholic appearance despite the potentially ruinous schism between the two circulating models of totality. As we have seen, what facilitated this task for them were the morphological analogies between the two systems. In addition to the homely shared sphericity, the decisive factor was the all-pervasive realism of tiers, which was translated in both cases into an obsessive habitus of hierarchical thought. Members of the metaphysical professions could learn from both orbs that Catholic thought and existence were based primarily on discretion of tiers: whether one thought in terms of descent or ascent, whether theoperipherally from earth towards heaven or theocentrically from God towards the world, being always also meant being-in-one's-rank.

The flair of Catholic rationalism remained shaped by hierarchical patterns until the twentieth century; the holy order of the upper and the lower was still in force as the strongest criterion of orientation. In the position of humans within the two orbs of totality too, both the geocentric and the theocentric design shared the pathos of humiliation, for in both cases humans were shown their barely surmountable distance from the optimum, regardless of whether it was interpreted as the distant inside or the distant above. But theocentrism humiliated in a different way from geocentrism: while Catholic-Aristotelian *humilitas* allowed humans a position on the earth and granted them dignity within the undignified, Platonic humiliation spurred on mystic ambition and seduced the adepts to expectations of sublime internalization or transfiguration through extermination; in its followers, it awakened the idea of fusing their own souls with the center of the God orb through self-immersion (in Plotinic terms: *eíso en báthei*, "inside within depth"). Nonetheless, the shared traits of the two classical totalisms are not sufficient to eradicate their fundamental divergence, and even where thinkers attempted to overlook the difference, the real distinction necessarily established itself in their discourses, not to be suppressed by any pious will to synthesis.

Illustration from a 14th-century edition of Ramon Llull's *Breviculum*: prototypes of the ladders that are thrown away after ascending.

The history of the tilted difference between the two Old European super-spherologies, however, begins in Plato's thought. The crystallization seeds for both can be found in geometric idealism or spherism, which—together with number theory—supplies the foundation for the intelligibility of the existent. If there was ever an *inconcussum* that was beyond doubt for Plato, it was that God and the world could only be observed (and exemplarily recreated) in the form of an absolutely round whole. The ancient origins of European globe production from the spirit of philosophical cosmo- or uranography have already been pointed out. That Aristotelian-Ptolemaic shell cosmology constituted a rational continuation of impulses from the superb suggestions in the *Timaeus* is something the modern reader can easily ascertain. At the start of the long speech by the Pythagorean whom Plato gives the role of spokesman in cosmogonic matters, one finds the same almost evangelical formulations about the creation of a round world by a perfect and ungrudging master builder who could not help passing on his own bestness to the best possible work:

> for all these reasons he made for it a body that was smooth, uniform, equal in all directions from its center, and a complete totality... [...] And so he gave it a circular movement, by starting it spinning at a constant pace in the same place and within itself [...] a single, unique universe, capable, thanks to its perfection, of keeping its own company, of needing nothing and no one else, since it was enough for it that it had affinity and familiarity with itself. This, then, was how he created it to be a blessed god.[22]

Aristotle retouched this image with far-reaching consequences by expressly placing the earth at the center of the cosmos-Uranus—next to the Platonic world soul, which from there infuses the whole of the world body beyond its edges; this central position amidst the shell cosmos provided pre-Copernican physics with its millennial form.

(But here too, Plato would take precedence if one read his reference to the earth as "a round body in the center of the heavens" at the end of the *Phaedo* [108 e] as a serious cosmological thesis.)

In the light of this, it seems amazing that it was the same author, Plato, who not only sketched the image of the earth-centered cosmos but also initiated the doctrine of the second hypersphere, at whose center lies not a body but an idea, or rather the supra-ideal principle of all ideas and their connections in a parallel higher or intelligible world. It goes without saying that he means the "good" whose theologians have believed themselves the "true philosophers" since time immemorial. One need not search in remote places to find the *locus classicus* for the theory of the germination point of the doctrine of the spirit orb or God orb, for it is situated at the zenith of Plato's output: at the end of Book VI of the *Republic*, directly alongside the cave parable—as the epistemological peak preceding the final summit of Platonic logopeia. Indeed, one could even claim with good reason that the parable of the sun, in its aloof radicality, was itself the summit for which the parable describing the cave of illusions and the exit from it was merely a supplementary pedagogical illustration. In the very carefully conceived and cautiously formulated parable of the sun, Plato in fact speaks of no less than the currently mightiest object or supra-object of thought, which simultaneously reveals itself to receptive reflection as the true subject of thought: the *ágathon*, which has its unforgettable debut as the god of the philosophers precisely here (after the preludes of the Presocratics). As will become clear, the rising of this super-sun already betokened the turn towards thinking in relation to the absolute, which would subsequently become at once an ideal, a skill exercise and a creed for all theocentrists.

From its very first emergence, this good presents itself as logically unique, indeed as a monster for the vulgar understanding. For on the one hand, it seems—like one problem among others—to stand before the imagining intellect as a theme or object; yet on the other hand, as if shifted inwards through a mysterious shift, it flashes in the eyes of the perceiver themselves and radiates into the world through them. Something is present in a given, appreciable thing and simultaneously provides the appropriate insight for the intellect facing it: Plato can only name one example of this demanding situation from the experiential world. According to his explanation, sunlight is comparably spread between both sides of every visually transmitted cognitive relationship: disseminated via illuminated objects on the one side, present in the perceiving eye as an inborn readiness for light on the other. Thus the physical sun always has a twofold present to offer—the first to the "joyous realm of things,"[23] which flourish and appear under its illumination, and the second to the eye, which stores filtered light and archetypes, as it were, as well as gathering experiences with real visibilities and radiating a second light, a cognitive or intelligible light, onto present objects by combining the two. (Let us recall here that from Plato's perspective, it is not so much a case of the eye being passively affected by the illuminated objects as the objects being "seen out" through an active beam of vision.)

"Then is sight related to its divine source as follows?"

"How?"

"The sun is not identical with sight, nor with what we call the eye in which sight resides."

"No."

"Yet of all sense-organs the eye is the most sunlike."

"Much the most."

"So the eye's power of sight is a kind of infusion dispensed to it by the sun."

"Yes."

"Then, moreover, though the sun is not itself sight, it is the cause of sight and is seen by the sight it causes."

"That is so."

"Well, that is what I called the child of the good," I said. "The good has begotten it in its own likeness, and it bears the same relation to sight and visible objects in the visible realm that the good bears to intelligence and intelligible objects in the intelligible realm."[24]

[...]

"You must suppose, then," I went on, "that there are these two powers of which I have spoken, and that one of them is supreme over everything in the intelligible order or region, the other over everything in the visible region—I won't say in the physical universe or you will think I'm playing with words. At any rate you have before your mind these two orders of things, the visible and the intelligible?"

"Yes, I have."[25]

[...]

"Then when I speak of the other sub-section of the intelligible part of the line you will understand that I mean that which the very process of argument grasps by the power of dialectic [...]. The whole procedure involves nothing in the sensible world, but moves solely through forms to forms, and finishes with forms."[26]

This is no less than the publication of an enormous discovery whose developments spawned the immeasurable asceticisms and discursive galaxies of the Old European metaphysics of spirit and light. The ostensibly simple message was this: forms produce their own contexts, their own textures and their own continents, indeed realms, which are of an entirely different kind than the continua of the sensible world. As soon as they follow the rules of logic, humans can navigate amid the native contexts of forms and see for themselves that forms follow from forms and combine with other forms into conclusive fabrics woven with evidentiary threads. The more experiences the thinkers have garnered through operations in the space of forms, the clearer it becomes to them that the intelligible objects constitute something resembling an idiosyncratic "world" (or should one call it a dimension, a sphere or a contexture, all terms with similar levels of abstractness?) with laws that only apply within it. Thus forms are connective, sphere-forming, context-producing and world-compatible in a way that is theirs alone. Through their own context, they form what idealism, once sure of its basic experience, would later call the *kósmos noetós* or *mundus intelligibilis*.

The novelty of the doctrine does *not*, therefore, lie in the assumption of a second world. Folk beliefs and the pre-metaphysical tradition had always supposed a world behind the world, be it as a hereafter of ghosts or a concealed dimension of transpersonal potencies. That reality is two-dimensional is one of the universal assumptions of popular ontologies and their scholarly continuations.[27] Considering the strong beliefs in the doubling of reality into a manifest and an occult world that are present in all the earth's cultures, Nietzsche's mockery of the "believers in a world behind" found in Christian Platonism seems a little provincial.

The innovation of idealism was that it made the second world subject to a new kind of logical, reason-controlled, and hence somewhat calculable or feasible constitution. From that point on, the "yonder" was one of those rational essentialities characterized by being clearer than anything one could ever encounter in the sensible terrestrial world. Clarity and supersensibility converge to produce evidence: evidence is the mode in which the noetic hereafter manifests itself in this world. The vague ghosts must die so that the precise truths, the forms, the archetypes can live. The haunting must ending for thought—navigation in the logical—to become possible. In idea-political terms, metaphysics therefore appeared as a war on two fronts: it fought both the deceptive terrestrial world and the old, confused world beyond. As soon as the new science of the clear yonder had won its first battles, conventional opinions about any given physical or moral matter would be worth no more than old wives' tales about ghostly apparitions and poets' visions of the gods. The entire phenomenal field had to be rearranged—which is precisely what Plato had called for in his masterful and far-reaching parable of the other sun.

Anyone who has ever experienced the compelling density of the connection between basic principles, corollaries, groups of tenets and colonies of theses—in other words, anyone who has ever argued successfully or calculated profitably—will share the basic affect of the philosophical revolt against triviality: the sentiment that the dependence of thought on loose, ill-founded talk of tradition can no longer be accepted without resistance. The relationships between the forms and sense certainty demand thoroughgoing revision. Thought must ignite its own light—the light of the other context, where everything ultimately depends on the principle of all principles: the first good and its emanations.

Thus began the secession of mathematics from reality; geometry taught how to behold perfect circles and triangles, and evidence planted its flag above the logical level. By going immanently from principle to principle and from figure to figure, thought, intoxicated by its ability to articulate purely internal connections, proves its autonomous power over the world or—which amounts to the same—its aptness to navigate freely in the "true world," consistently and within the framework of consistency. All logical operations, however, even if they begin as direct conclusions, ultimately only trace a single great circle. Every principle that follows from earlier ones receives its light from a logical beginning extending back to the beginning of all beginnings: the good which assigns its light, the brightness of evidence, to all that follows rightly and is concluded rightly.

With this a sun rises, one brighter than any earthly noon. A harsher way of seeing takes over, with a surreal sharpness reminiscent of foehn-warmed days in the south; Plato's genius required it in order to claim, with full consistency, the title "world" for the other side of reality experienceable in thought as thought. And only once it transpires that an autonomous world within what is thought can be posited can a whole world engage with another whole world "in the world."

This friction gives rise to the primal dispute in classical ontology. The envisaged true world throws down the gauntlet before the merely perceived world. It is this provocation that turns Plato's text into the key event in occidental history: it is

Ákos Birkás, *Kopf 55* (1989), oil on canvas 78 ¾ x 64 ⅔ in.

where the ideological and technical rebuilding of the existent begins. It has become obvious that the world itself is not undifferentiatedly simple and unanimous, and that whoever speaks of "world," whether scientifically or not, automatically means world distinction or world war. Once erupted, the primal dispute—which Plato already characterized very realistically as a war of giants over being—does not permit anyone to declare themselves a non-combatant; everyone is a party to this war, even the naïve who claim not to know what is at issue. Not even the most ubiquitous sun can then remain what it always seemed to be, for another sun has risen behind it to challenge the primacy of the visible one. "We recognize... we truly recognize!"[28] The black sun of the other light: its rays glow through human heads when true principles present themselves in thought.[29]

With the parable of the sun, posterity witnesses the intelligible colonies' declaration of independence from the motherland of visibility. Within a single period, Plato proclaimed the United States of Light—a realm that produces itself and was content with itself. With ideas, through ideas, towards ideas, in the medium of ideas: this is how the new citizens of light will live, withdrawn to an indestructible logical asylum, inhabitants of the city on the hill of light, in an elsewhere that is everywhere, yet equally unreachable from everywhere. And naturally these states will export their ideas, and intervene in the troubles of the sensible Old World if need be so as to ensure a new order. It goes without saying that, despite their late discovery after being long overlooked, they will be convinced that their superior evidence gives them the highest rank, and that since the emergence of the New World, the Old will no longer be of interest except as an area of influence and a supplier of metaphors.

El Lissitzky, *Globetrotter (in Time)*; page 5 in the figurine portfolio for the electro-mechanical exhibition "Victory Over the Sun" (Hanover, 1923)

In our context, the most significant aspect of Plato's hyper-heliological spirit model is the central position of the surreal light source, for this is what most emphatically enthrones that *other center* which enabled the second roundness, the spirit orb or theosphere, to emancipate itself from the cosmic orb in the first place. Here lie the beginnings of the later, admirably patronizing theological discourse on the absolute, which, viewed by its own light, would have no need of any world, yet grants itself one—in late Greek times probably through overflowing joviality, and in the Catholic regime through the flowing down of grace. The day on which Plato published his theory of the good was therefore the Independence Day of intellectual history.

With his sun parable, however, Plato created an ambiguity from which Old European devotional thought would gain benefits up to the threshold of the present: the dual role of light, which clearly had to serve constitutive functions on both sides—the cosmosphere and the theosphere—from the outset. If it was possible to discuss hierarchism above as a formal reason for the welcome interchangeability of the two totality models, we can now understand the photological constitution of the two orbs as a material reason for their rapprochement and equation. As a joint between the intelligible and the physical cosmos, the theory of light permitted the necessary degree of assimilation between the two spheric totalisms to prevent the premature disintegration of the cracked metaphysical base (or framework) of European metaphysics. Naturally the early masters of light speculation—not least Plato himself, and even more Plotinus, Proclus, Iamblichus and Pseudo-Dionysius the Areopagite—were aware of the metaphorical, inauthentic character of their heliological, photological and radiological discourses. They did not tire of

Reverse of the Great Seal of the United States of America (1776)

referring to the parable-like, analogical or "parallel" status of
these reflections, though this changed nothing whatsoever about
the homogenizing character of these idealistic rhetorics of light.

As far as the Platonic sun parable is concerned, it exhibits
the figural aspect of the references to light in the awkward
formulations of Socrates, who purports to dislike speaking inau-
thentically—and not merely in passing, for Plato had to ensure
even more clarity than usual here, as he was concerned with
pushing the well-known physical sun to second place behind a
freshly discovered supra-physical new sun. Through this victory
over the sun, the metaphysics of spirit showed where it stood on
the matter of phenomena. Because the true sun was henceforth
termed *ágathon*, and because Helios could now only be interpreted

Stereopticon by Charles A. Chase (1894)

as a projected image and external representation of *ágathon* character, actually shining light—physical and spiritual alike—would always be understood in future as doubled and tiered. After the surpassing of the white sun by the black hyper-sun, the ultimate source of light no longer shines itself, but rather lets another shine. If light shines *realiter*, as sensual brightness or noetic evidence, then only as "light from the light"—in Plotinic terms *phos ek photos*, and in Catholic-Nicene terms *lumen de lumine*. But because real light, whether thought or seen, was now consistently understood as the secondary light of an over-bright primary light, one can attribute a hint of photocentrism or crypto-helio-centrism even to orthodox *cosmo*logy, for the physical light

Odilon Redon, *The Eye Like a Strange Balloon Mounts Toward Infinity*, lithograph (1882), illustration after Edgar Allan Poe

scarcely fares better than the noetic in relation to the super-light of God: it must concede that it is descended not from itself, but *ab alio*. The other center makes both things possible.

Consequently, though geocentrically and ultimately infernocentrically constituted, physical nature too can be represented as if it were ruled by the light—yet not in spirit and from within, but rather by solar means and from above and without. This achieves the best result possible under these conditions: the image of the corporeal world-whole can confidently continue to feign its compatibility with the theocentric observation of the spirit-whole. One can venture to suppose that without this pious fraud, carried out collectively and with unerring instinct, Old European onto-theology—also known as philosophical Catholicism—would have been doomed to failure from the start. Had the light from light not been directly followed by the illusion from the illusion, the theologians could not have unfolded their superb language games at the power center of medieval universities.

The attraction of the second orb lies in the fact that it possesses a form of inner continuity entirely different from all known contexts in the spatial-sensual world of experience. For the light-orb or God orb, one could speak of a continuum of pure inner actions, whereas the cosmic orb is dominated by a continuum of material states and their transformations. This roughly corresponds to the difference between emanation and metabolism. In the theosphere, nothing is significant except operations of noetic light; it spreads within the vaults of its own deeds and ordeals through indestructible immanence within itself. This orb of bright operations is so overwhelmingly attractive for thought because it presents the prototype of a constructivist world-production from a center. Its magic comes from the suggestion that the One at the center of the spirit orb is free to create a complete world through the mere self-realization of its thought, and by further developing first thoughts—in particular, a world that, aside from certain unclarities on the periphery, could not be damaged anywhere by a disturbance from the outside. That light, whether noetic or physical, is not lost in externality but rather "with itself" everywhere in its own space of extension was always emphasized by Platonists, most of all Plotinus:

> Another example would be the sun, central to the light which streams from it and is yet linked to it, or at least is always about it, irremovably; try all you will to separate the light from the sun, or the sun from its light, for ever the light is in the sun.[30]

What applies to the physical continuum of light is all the truer of the self-extension of the *kósmos noetós*, regardless of whether one calls it the good, God, the One or the supra-existent. The light-based continuum principle gives the God orb maximum inner transparency and communicativity:

> for all is transparent, nothing dark, nothing resistant; every being is lucid to every other, in breadth and depth; light runs through light.[31]

This essentially means that every point in the space of the light-orb lies on a radius extending from the spirit center. It follows from this that all points participate in the center, as each one of them can be directly sure of its accessibility through the beam from the center. It is not only between the point and the center

The Platonic dodecahedron (pentagonal dodecahedron) and its derivations, from
Wenzel Jamnitzer, *Perspectiva corporum regurarium* (Nuremberg, 1568).

that there is complete transparency, however; the points are connected to one another in immeasurably numerous, lucid communications. For all lovers of transparency, this constitutes the realization of ideal conditions.

At the same time, it becomes apparent why it was necessary to distinguish between two impulses at an early stage in the idealistic escape to light: an unsociably spiritualistic and a spiritually sociable one, to put it in slightly exaggerated terms. As far as the former is concerned, it is partly to blame for the bad, sect-like reputation of a life from pure spirituality. Undoubtedly, this first constructivism already entailed an anorexic tendency that unreservedly affirmed disgust at moving bodies and their greedy intercourse—the Pythagorean communes probably constituted the first attempt on European soil to re-establish society as an abstinent order.[32] Impulses of this type give nourishment to ascetic, anti-marriage, and generally "bionegative" movements. It seems justified to ask whether there has ever been a form of spirit-metaphysical thought without this supplement of near-autistic abstinence from the all-too-human and all-too-sticky.

At the same time, the discovery of the spirit realm existing for itself also contained a discreet interest in the possibility of a political association of pure spirits. Socialisms were founded in heaven. For if the spirit-soul cores of humans themselves resembled Platonic forms, what could prevent them from forming pure groups, communes of uncompromised light? Then surely humans could imagine that they should in truth be socialized in the other, true world? It seems that considerations of this kind lead to a plausible reading of the peculiar Plotinic formulation that "yonder," in the spiritual world, "every being" is lucid to "every other" in its full depth. The personal turns of phrase imply

Francesco Botticini, *Assumption of the Virgin* (c. 1485), National Gallery, London

that subjectivities which can be equated with "forms" are brought into play here. Then, however, forms and spirit souls (or person cores) are closely adjacent. Such adjacencies are the stuff of which the spirit realms that are interesting for humans are made. Surely over yonder, in the second society, the obvious deficiencies of the first would necessarily be rectified, as only relationships in concert are possible among pure spirits? Does it not seem logical to assume that the socialism of the angelic intelligences and subtle forces is equally in force among those empirical humans who have come to their senses? And should the communicative competency of the pure spirits not also engender that of the embodied ones?

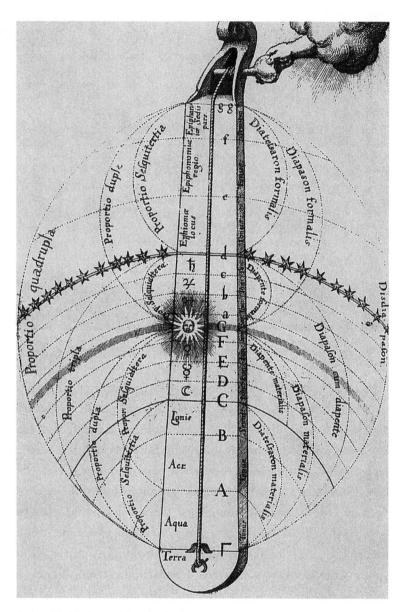

Robert Fludd, *Cosmic Monochord*, 1617.

In idea-historical terms, as we have seen, the doubling of geocentric and theocentric totality is not exclusive to Christian-Catholic metaphysics, but rather a necessary consequence of the basic spherist decisions of Greek classicism. Plato's spherological rationalism—which itself absorbed impulses from Parmenides, Empedocles and Pythagoras—expresses more than simply a forced morphological optimism. It also seals the alliance between totality-oriented thought and geometry, which has had to be watched over since then as the strong characteristic of Old European thought on being. Geometric, or rather uranometric rationalism is the creative answer of Greek thought to the challenge from the large-scale world; it is an answer because the increasingly precise question as to the size and shape of the world precedes it, and creative because it no longer suffers the largeness of the world form merely as an unfathomable fate, but instead co-produces it and infuses it with its own distinctions out of constructive presence of mind. Seen from this perspective, both the spherograms of the Greek nature philosophers and the choral fantasies of the angelo-theologians are emblems of the matured ability to enclose the maximized totality in a clearly imagined shape. In reality, before the cosmos can be placed symbolically under the foot of a commander as a *sphaira* or in the hand of an emperor as the cross-crowned *globus cruciger*, it must be conceived in thought as a cleared, measured and mastered totality. These orbs call out to their constructor by their mere appearance, and any world thinkers and rulers worth taking seriously can now only be found within earshot of this call. Its text conveys an unmistakable message: I belong to the one who can produce me in my true form. The Roman Pantheon is the most powerful testimony to the way in which this call was heard.

Karlheinz Stockhausen at the mixing desk in the spherical auditorium of the German pavilion for the EXPO 70 world exhibition, Osaka

Now we have seen that Plato conceived two completely different approaches to orb creation: the first entails production by the demiurge, who, as a quasi-transcendent producer, creates the world-whole in the form of an ensouled sphere sculpture. The second is reached by drawing the necessary conclusions from the sun parable, which can be understood entirely legitimately as the primal scene of a sphere creation through radiation—for if one considers the matter closely, the Platonic hyper-sun, the *ágathon*, can only flow productively into the subordinate existent surrounding it on all sides through its emissions or emanations.

Both orb creations—the heteropoietic-demiurgic and the autopoietic-emanative—confront humans with a concept of power that releases ambivalent reflections among them. In both cases, humans initially find themselves transferred to the side of the mastered, not the mastering—just as the biblical creation myth places the human being entirely on the side of creatures, a piece of ceramic work molded and breathed to life in a pneumatic feat.[33] This original, passivic, religioid self-finding of the human being on the product side need not harden into a final attitude, however; the humiliation through the creator's mastery, which makes humans feel mastered, does not have the last word in all matters. For *imagining* the highest ability to create, through which I myself have been produced—this in itself is an ability that inspires respect and, if it takes itself at its own word, creates the conditions for extraordinary developments. The idea of God's skill attracts the principle of technology and lends wings to the will to be skilled oneself.

The human capacity to understand the basis of the given, the all-productive power, however vaguely or imperfectly, represents the bright and hot point in the universe: only from here can the logical echo arise of the newly understood fact that all that is made by a central power or its agencies—and it matters little for now whether self-made or made by another. Because round worlds are the works of a highest productive power, as is now known, produced through demiurgic mastery or self-fulfillingly through their own emanation, those humans who have intellectually uncovered out these two facts—the roundness and the craftedness of the world—suddenly find themselves logically affected. This amounts to a loss of technological innocence: they are now caught up in an intellectual provocation incomparable to any other. It is as if one had been drawn into a complicity with the procedures of the gods that could henceforth never be erased; for consideration of the spherical shape of the whole and its craftedness through a principle of ability—in those who truly think, the coincidence of these two ideas causes a sensitivity to totality with which their intelligence recognizes that it is called to share in this all-able ability. Once it has seen this far, the human intellect now sees that it belongs to a close-knit family of knowing and able powers responsible for the thereness and thusness of the world. Indeed, it could even be that the individuals who reach an understanding of such things feel greater kinship with these powers than with those fellow humans who do not attain such insights. Hence this marks a parting of the ways, albeit barely perceptible at first, between the priests and the technologists, because the former interpret the fundamental motto of religious compliance, *non possumus* [we are not able]—while the latter develop the second principle, *dum possum volo*—as long as I am able, I want to.

The knowledge of ability divides societies from the moment when it elevates itself to complicity with the *modus operandi* of the orb-creating God. One could say that there is a new distinction in the world, one that splits the mass of mortals into two groups: those who know that what matters are orbs and the ability that understands and creates orb worlds, and those who continue to concoct their fairy tales without noticing what a large-scale game has begun on this earth that is illuminated by ideas wishing to become practice.

At the same time as the technical difference between the accomplices of the orb and the clueless, a gaping erotic difference also appears whose effects on the dividedness of human societies initially extend even deeper. It splits the communes into the majorities that desire conventionally obvious objects or goals, means of enjoyment, sexual partners, mediums of power and security advantages, and the minority that is moved by the longing for the round *summum bonum*—be it the supra-celestial place located above the cosmosphere where pure spirits associate with God, or that innermost source point of the over-bright theosphere whence the processions of light choirs close to God burst forth.

The difference between the two modes of desire—let us say, natural and excessive love—went on to place the decisive emphases in the development of Christian culture. As later in Islam, the difference between people with normal wishes and people with other wishes would become a culture-defining dividing line. Medieval Christianity established the mode of excessive love as a psychagogic model with broad appeal when it succeeded in simultaneously arousing and nurturing the longing for the most remote in the life projects of countless clergymen and laymen. This was a civilizatory achievement that can be given due credit if one considers how few theophiles in antiquity placed any value on merging with the One, or ascending with one's soul to the supra-celestial realm, for authentically rational reasons. (A relevant Gnostic document refers to "One in a thousand, two in ten thousand.") Explaining or at least shedding light on the secret behind Christianity's large-scale success for the erotic and spherological excess, both vicariously and in its own interest, can be a yardstick for the explanatory strength of general spherology.

If medieval Christianity succeeded in habitualizing the thought and behavioral forms of excessive love among a large part of the clergy and lay society (we recall the organ communion in Konrad of Würzburg's *Herzmaere* from the thirteenth century[34]), it was not because it offered any pretexts for mass eruptions of a love of geometry. It did not preach the virtues of the noetic orb's center from the pulpits, any more than it sang of the attractiveness of the ethereal spaces at the upper edge of the celestial orb. Christian doctrine would undoubtedly have remained theoretically meager and primitive by Greek scholastic standards had it not adopted the central macrospherological principles of classical metaphysics; as has been shown often enough, the *vera religio* only became intellectually satisfactory through its Hellenization. It did not speak of great orbs in its attractive text, however, but of strong relationships; not of curiosity about the center, but of the yearning to return to the integrity of the God-soul space— here openly called *basileía tou theou*, the kingdom of God, or *regnum vitae*, the kingdom of life. Christ is not proclaimed as an ontomorphological principle, but rather as an intimate augmenter of souls—microspherologically speaking, as a genius representative simultaneously holding the position of the highest possible inner other for every individual.

With these suggestions of meaning, which had inconceivable advertising appeal for the moderns, early and medieval Christianity were able to break the metaphysical ice that estranged the ancient masses from wisdom. It turned this cool glance upwards to the hyper-Uranian dimension into a love affair with a passible friend, and the distant tension with the hypostases-spitting center of the orb of being into a liaison with an inner partner god. Augustine's polyvalent apostolic intelligence— which one could anachronistically call religious ingenuity— clearly displayed the distant-close dual nature of the Christian concept of God. With reference to Augustine, the personal charge of the Platonic center of being can be documented in its most lively moment.

The psychodynamic and semantic *Gesamtkunstwerk* of monotheistic high religion must be explained from the perspective of Augustine's writings: the Bishop of Hippo formulated the synthesis of intimate and majestic religiosity with unprecedented clarity and the most accommodating compliance with the necessary demands of both sides. He shows more clearly than any other author that Grand Theory has only ever been concerned with a cosmos-capable and intimist God—that is, a God who does not cease to be the gently shining twin of the individual even after and taking His place as cosmocrator on the imperial throne of the existent (and as a supra-existent entity at the supra-locational center of the ontological reactor).

All manner of spiritually malign delyed effects have been attributed to Augustine's Manichean early period; he himself later tore his former life among the dualists to pieces morally and doctrinally. Nonetheless, no morphologist of religion can fail to notice that the greatest attraction of the Augustinian phenomenon comes from a Manichean legacy in force to the end—the largely suppressed and neglected theology of the twin, which in Mani's teachings had already formed the pivot and turning point of theology from a private genius accompaniment to augmentation by a cosmic god.[35] Augustine must have become acquainted with the figure of an intimate god who remains closely joined to his earthly partner, without ever ceasing to act as the highest principle of the good in cosmic-historical dimensions, in this inner double of the religious founder, described as a radiant twin in the canonical writings of the Manicheans. It was thus through Manichaeism that Augustine came into contact with a god of

Hans Kemmer, *Christ as Salvator Mundi Flanked by Two Donors* (1537), detail

closeness of whom could be characterized more accurately than the Christian God as *interior intimo meo*. After his Manichean impregnation with the twin of sweet closeness, Augustine, as we know, converted to the god of the Platonic philosophers—at the time, carrying out the *conversio* meant devoting oneself to the philosophical life—and it was only after the anonymous grandiosity of the god known as the good or the substance had begun to grow stale for him that Augustine was ready for the synthesis of Manichean intimism and Greek ontology. What resulted was the embrace of extremes.

That is precisely what comes from the system of the *vera religio*, which rests on the balance between God's final closeness and His remotest majesty. In our terminology, this corresponds to the possibility that the intimate-augmenting other in the microsphere, the second pole of the mental dual, is equated with the center of the morphologically expanded macrosphere. From that point on, the soul not only has a secret by its side, it has being itself. That this oath to the absolute should be offered to every thinking individual (or, should that be too much to ask, every believing one) was one of the idea-political bones of contention in the early dogma battles of trinitary theology. It was only because the center of being, as father-son intimacy, was already a relationship, with the spirit as the concluding triadic figure, that humans too could feel they were allies of the whole, not simply contained and impersonally encroached upon. For them, the intimate other coincided with the center of the absolute. Understand this, and you are in the eye of the cyclone.

This superimposition enables the transition from intimacy to majesty and back again: it discloses the absolute for the pair. The epicenter of the small ellipse and the center of the largest orb can thus be merged, or at least brought into resonant proximity—provided the orb is the spirit one—for this operation could no longer be carried out with the center of the material world orb (unless Romantic and neo-pantheist easings licensed the embrace of the universal maternal nature). It is the precise magic of the *other center* that it can be addressed as a supra-With[36] and a supra-you in a personally colored ecstasy of accessibility.

In psycho-structural terms, specific monotheism was never anything but an experimental set-up for this model—undoubtedly the most ambitious in the history of religion—that was spread across cults and cultures and realized itself in a spectrum encompassing the conventional and the unfathomable. In fact, the psychological risks of the acknowledged dual with the One, as one can easily see, are unusually high: the identification of the sublime theospheric center with the intimate soul-space partner makes the serious believers like points immediate to God in the corona of the absolute—and, because the other is simultaneously the encompassing, potentially also ego-deficient mollusks. (As well as this, there is naturally also the non-intimate monotheism, the quiet heteronomy in the every Catholic, every Islamic or everyday Jewish style, just as there is banal intimacy without soul expansion everywhere, the constant exit of pairs from their contexts.)

The close-distant model gives immediate cause to speak of risks. If my twin or invisible companion is simultaneously God, and *ipso facto* the center and circumference of the universe, I can enjoy dynamic euphorias for as long as I succeed in perceiving only the merits of this superb augmentation structure; it is precisely through my intimate bond with the encompassing other, however, that I can easily find myself in the situation of the weakened, forgotten, begging remainder. The immersion of the subject in community with the great other can produce a condition in which religion and addiction converge: Christian mysticism as a form of life is a desired dependence on a shared bloodstream in which the subject can be made fluid by its great other; it stimulates an attentive listening for the heartbeat of a shared world interior.

When one of the most ambitious lay theologians of the twentieth century writes that "God's heart wants to beat through us into the heartless world,"[37] he expressively testifies to the intercordial intimate reality in its contrast with every merely formal encompassment or external aggregation. He conceals the risk of psychosis in this medial position: if the hypertrophic other is beating through me, it is scarcely avoidable that I will lose a sense of more mature symmetries. Certainly, if intimacy were a license to equality, there would be no limits to the integrative heavenly ascension of the subject in relation to the God of monotheism. Intimacy with the distant-close God, however, also means something else: the possibility of finding oneself on the unlivable side of a hyper-relationship with dangerous ease. The frequently attested extreme mental ordeals of those intimate with God confirm the risk involved in an overly close-knit metaphysicized twin relationship. As soon as the inner other is temporarily unreachable, the subject left behind must endure its feeling of being cut off to the bitter extreme. There is scarcely a mystic who is spared the experience of dry, depressive times. Mysticism not only discloses the poetic paradises of flowing presence to the ego, but also—and perhaps most significantly—the prosaic hells of withdrawal.

To avoid misunderstandings: if there were a possibility of the intimized God reliably remaining present in the position of the silent accomplice, continuously attentive to the subject and nurturing it in unproblematic accessibility, the friction resulting from the intimization of the majestic other could be converted into even, mentally well-integrated motivation experiences. This seems to be what a few burning activists of the absolute achieved at the end of protracted transformative struggles, unless an entire library of spiritual accounts is based purely on over-stylization and psychagogic fraud. Because the allied God is the part of a large asymmetrical pair that is normally occupied elsewhere, however, it remains highly probable that I am the one repeatedly finding myself in the darkened position—as God's excommunicated waste product, His black sister, His unspeakable remainder lost in the refuse or buried under a rose tree: the thing that is not allowed to appear and has nothing to give the great other.

It is entirely in keeping with this that one of the most important tasks of mystical literature has been to interpret and contain the mental torments created, or at least made manifest through cultivation, by the mystical culture of intimacy. The tenor of the accounts is this: how much God adorns the soul with suffering. In line with Pauline axioms, suffering is interpreted as co-crucifixion with a crucified God. In Mechthild of Magdeburg's work *The Flowing Light of the Godhead*, this hermeneutics of the mystic's pain is formulated with great variety. Its key principle is this: "When we are sick, we wear wedding dresses; and when we are healthy, we wear work clothes."[38] If one does not succeed in giving the *morbus mysticus* the meaning of a prelude to merging, the symptoms of pure separation depression win out; here the burnt-out souls feel like God's idiots who were denied the premium for self-surrender. It is not only symptoms of isolation that burden the mystically talented in their dark periods, however, but also signs of suffering due to the boundless indiscretion of the other side as manifested in the holy sickness. Daniel Paul Schreber gave a vivid depiction of this in *Memoirs of My Nervous Illness* (1900–1903),[39] which deals for long passages with influence-psychotic molestations by transcendent nerve and idea parasites; the only regrettable thing is that it has so far barely experienced any reception in affirmative mystical research— which, incidentally, is firmly in the hands of the naïve.

However explosive the consequences of the basic monotheistic decision to form the dyad with the absolute, those following the radicalization of the divine attribute of infinity in high and late medieval theology were perhaps even more seismic. One could go so far as to view the theologians' games with the concept of infinity as an experiment whose results sealed the fate of the medieval world model. Perhaps what we call the Modern Age was primarily a reaction of concept-sensitive subcultures to being injected with the infinite.

Through this turn towards infinitism, spatial paradox—and *eo ipso* acute unimaginability—penetrated the theocentrically interpreted light-orb. Consequently, the god of the philosophers also withdrew entirely to the insensible realm, as if unwilling to be outdone by the Christian world ground in the obscurity of his mysteries; he disappeared into an abyss of bizarre definitions that made no sense to the ordinary spatial imagination. Thus the immunological design of the metaphysical world form, the geometrized universal vault as the final level of uterotechnic abstraction and inhabitation of being, found itself in a crisis from which there was no longer any conservative way out. A currently infinite orb—how could this even be imagined? A sphere whose center has no place because it repeats infinitely, welling up everywhere from bursting points—how could one place oneself in relation to such a geometric monster? And how, as a single creature, could one see oneself integrated into such a decentered order? Did not Aristotle conclude his treatise on the heavens by explaining why an infinitely large body was an absurdity, and that clearly the world-whole must be viewed as a well-formed maximum, as this one and only celestial orb?

The decisive source for positing the other center everywhere, the notorious *Liber viginti quattuor philosophorum*, emphatically confirms the crisis finding; here we open the central document of theosophical hermeticism in the High Middle Ages. Theosophy is the thought form that focuses completely on God, merely giving the world the status of a complex fold inside the absolute. Hermetic thought, on the other hand, is part of those terrible secret sciences that seek to make humans accomplices of a boundless ability. The *Book of Twenty-Four Philosophers* may have been compiled a few decades before 1200, or translated from Greek into Latin, by Western editors; perhaps it is even a copy or continuation of an Alexandrian tract from the third century that reached Europe by an uncertain route, and which, according to later hypotheses, contained fragments of an *Aristotelian Theology* that was believed lost;[40] other authors consider the *liber* a compilation of axioms by the Neoplatonist Iamblichus. Around 1200, the book was already widely available in the Latin West. Although it makes no mention whatsoever of Christian articles of faith, it was highly regarded among the elite of the European clergy, as the number of surviving manuscripts attests. Anyone who has ever obtained their literature from alternative bookshops knows what it means to be informed by sources that charge up the reader with very different information. The list of first-rate thinkers impressed or influenced by the book—Meister Eckhart, Nicolas of Cusa, Giordano Bruno or Leibniz—ensures a respectable place for the little treatise in the history of metaphysical speculation. The work, purported to have been authored by the fantastic persona Hermes Trismegistus—the first wise man, according to late antique legend, from whom both Moses and Plato derived their doctrines—leads directly into the highlands of Neoplatonic philosophy, ten thousand feet beyond the priesthood and the catechism.

The introduction succinctly states that twenty-four philosophers—a very suspicious choice of personnel—have gathered to present their answers to the question *Quid est Deus?* with the aim of formulating a joint concluding statement about God (which in fact never happened). This laconic preliminary remark is followed by twenty-four definitions of God that pass by the reader underived, a swarm of meteorites comprising abrupt speculative assertions of unprecedented compaction and boldness. The first, second and eighteenth are of particular significance for us:

1. *Deus est monas monadem gignens, in se unum reflectens ardorem.*
2. *Deus est sphaera infinita cuius centrum est ubique, circumferentia nusquam.*
18. *Deus est sphaera cuius tot sunt circumferentiae quot puncta.*
1. God is the monad that begat a monad and turned it back on itself as a single blast of heat.
2. God is the infinite sphere whose center is everywhere and whose circumference is nowhere.
18. God is the sphere that has as many circumferences as points.[41]

We will show why it is logical to read the three definitions as paraphrases of a single thought that expresses a light-theologically necessary, yet sensually unfathomable notion in the form of a geometric paradox. It is immediately apparent from the shared topic of points 2 and 18, namely the divine orb, that they converge. What is less self-evident, and must be shown through further reflections, is that both are also aligned with the first.

The spherological obstinacy of divine spatial formation can be clarified most easily with reference to definition 18. In any given profane orb, all points can be represented on radii emanating from the center. When the emanation comes from God, however, the principal trait of divinity—its radiating and self-imparting nature—is imparted to all points around God. If this is the case, the trivial geometric difference between the central point and a distant point is initially absent from the divine orb, as the process of emanation can begin anew from every point. It is indeed unique to God that he conveys the gift of his indivisible abundance of essence to every point he touches, meaning that even distant points cannot be poorer than the center, which initially seemed to monopolize everything. Thus what was a point now itself becomes the center, and what received being now itself becomes a source of new emanations of being. This necessarily results in a chain reaction of new formations from every point in the "first" orb; the points all act as centers, casting their light further into new orbs in which all points continue to have a lightening and being-bestowing effect—into infinity (unless, as customary among Neoplatonists, one wanted to take into account a distancing and weakening mechanism that finally results in an edge where the emanation disappears). Consequently, the divine *sphaira* as a whole has as many circumferences as points—an infinite number, which had to be demonstrated.

This eighteenth definition of God, as we can see, has an immanent principle of abundance which ensures that there can be no loss of substance in God, no matter how far His emanations might extend away from the mysterious "first" center. One could equally say that there are no weak points in God, and that, most strictly speaking, regions distant from him are an impossibility (in this respect, as noted above, Neoplatonism is not rigorous, rescuing the primacy of the first center by letting the orb of emanation cease glowing towards the periphery due to distance-related losses). Rather, he is—assuming one had the strength to accept this—present in abundance everywhere as a whole, self-given and self-giving God. Thus the eighteenth definition, at once marvelously simple and complex, provides—in the form of a geometrically paradoxical theorem—the schema that makes the generative principle of self-infinitization vaguely comprehensible to human reason, even if sensory perception is

Thomas Wright, illustration for *An Original Theory or New Hypothesis of the Universe* (London, 1750); every astral sphere possess its own intelligent center. As Wright equated the gravitational center of the universe with God, the world would have had to implode in God if not counterbalanced by an abundance of secondary centers.

rather lost in this theo-mathematical calculation (which is unable, and unwilling, to imagine any point that is infinitely remote from God yet itself entirely God). As God pours himself out into his "environment" from an unidentifiable first center, every point around him is himself, and if the thought of God's gradual mitigation is impermissible once made explicit (and explicitness is the element shared by diabolism and theology), he possesses the non-imaginable talent to be as undividedly himself and overflowingly whole at any distance from His center as at the hypothetical *origo* itself. From every point on his circumference, then, he produces further circumferences in which he is present in equal abundance. *Tot circumferentiae quot puncta.*[42]

All that is missing from this bold assertion is a reference to the centripetal or reflecting forces which would ensure that the light "remained" at its first center. It becomes clear why these retrieving forces are necessary as soon as one casts a look at the cognitive design of the hermetic God. In a pure system of emanations—as with simple perceptible light sources such as suns and lamps—the corona around the shining center would be irreflexively centrifugal; once a beam had left its source, it would already be flung out distantly and irreversibly into constant flight. Each such ray would, at least, be followed by its continual renewal from the source, meaning that even radiated light could, in a sense, be viewed as "remaining in the orb eternally," however attenuated and diluted.

One of the essential features of the divine light, however, is that it continually augments and perfects itself through reflexive or returning beams, which is why every "outward" light journey must have a corresponding, varyingly symmetrical "homeward" journey; this was developed with due formality in Neoplatonic reflection. Hence the primal light not only plunges centrifugally into the immeasurable and irretrievable from its first point of emission, but returns home—in an eternal conservative revolution—from a precisely determined turning point to its source. One could say, slightly disrespectfully, that if the Aristotelian ether can do it, the noetic light can do it even better, for its "reflection" is the continuation of ethereal cyclophoria by higher means. This turning back or homecoming is constitutive of God's being-encompassing, for without it one could not distinguish between the beam and its source, between the first and the second; there would no longer be a rational reason for the hierarchical precedence of the origin over the originated. The first transmitter would be lost in its emissions, and the creator would forfeit His primacy over the creatures; the dissipative God would only have to burst and disseminate eternally, without gathering or recognizing.

As long as one intends to hold on to centrist notions, therefore, the source must have a privilege constitutive of all-encompassing unity, namely that of bringing its emanated beams back home and "uni-fying" them; otherwise it would merely be a chain reaction, comparable to a nuclear explosion, and the light would be no more than the medium of an irreversible dispersal—in contemporary terms, an expenditure with no revenue. If the turn of the light did not take place, the monarchy of the midpoint—indeed the entire economy of the center—would be jeopardized, and once this were abandoned, the whole of speculative theology would come to an end.

It is precisely this law of turns that is meant, in extremely compacted yet sufficiently explicit form, by the tremendous first definition in the twenty-four-philosopher book: "God is the

From Leonhard Euler, *Letters to a German Princess* (1768)

monad that begat a monad." The second half states *in se unum reflectens ardorem*—"and turned it back on itself as a single blast of heat"—with the "it" unmistakably referring to the homecoming rays, the produced monad as a whole, which can be shown to be precisely the sum of the light radiated all around, which is mirrored back from the edge of the light-orb into the center. It is no coincidence that the question of reflection or return-into-itself is already brought up in the first of these definitions of God, for without it God would only be a light reactor, not a process of recognition. But that is precisely what he must be in this omni-science-focused culture of speculation, where God only exists to the extent that he asserts himself as all-creating and all-knowing. And it is beyond doubt that without this harboring reflection, the rays sent out by him would disappear into a homecoming-less "bad" infinity and never return to the point.

That is the only reason why God had to be imagined as an orb, for this form alone could promise the self-harboring of an expanding and free life, whether pan-psychistic, vitalistic or noetic in its disposition, in a curved interior structure. If life were merely a sojourn in the external from the outset, and did not have to provide any immune services or observe any harboring interests on the small or the large scale, there would not need to be any talk of circles and orbs up to the highest level of its metaphysical self-interpretation; for then there would be nothing that needed to seek refuge in the cohesive form. The simple occurrence of things in space is morphologically undemanding, and does not create any problems with the notion that something goes out and does not return. But where thought has been struck by the immunological imperative—one could also say, wherever the concern is to think *a life* in an emphatic sense[43]—the circle motif establishes itself, because it is inevitably assigned the main burden of securing the interior and forming the world's edge *more geo-metrico*. Life wants to reach out with freedom of movement, yet

Paul Klee, *The Limits of Understanding* (1927)

experience the privilege of being able to reside by virtue of an endogenous boundary. (Residing, to quote one contemporary definition, is a "culture of feelings in enclosed space"[44]—an assertion that has the most philosophically demanding consequences if one concedes that the only logically satisfying enclosure can be offered by the *hen kai pan*.)

That is why even a God who plays with infinitist fire is not allowed to go wild; the morphological imperative applies until the end, even in its most expansive internal relationships. Therefore: *in se reflectens*. He emerges from himself and returns to himself—this is what had to be made clear in the first statement of this most excessive of all reflections on God. He projected the blast of heat, which creates an orb all around, out of himself—for that is the meaning of the reference to the creation of a monad by the monad—but this blast must strike back to the transmitter via an arc of light, as it were. With God, as in trivial arithmetic, one time one equals one—the monad that multiplies itself by itself produces another monad, and yet this operation, unlike profanely mathematical ones, is theospherically fruitful because it "explicates" something implicit, namely the identity of the extensionless point or minimal one (I shall leave aside the cosmological impossibility of such an orb for the time being). Coming from the core, the beams surge from the edge of the maximum back into the core. With a principle as protuberant as the monadic god of light, the monstrous retrieval of a monstrous outburst, anything less than a counter-protuberance is insufficient to give this unfettered light the form of unity. God is therefore an orb in a state of calm and explosion at once. It is only because everything which radiates subsequently radiates back that all bursting is balanced out through reflections. Every wastage has a corresponding recovery, every emission an absorption. In the hermetic God too, this is how rotation comes into its own; but celestial orbits have turned into circles of reflection, and ethereal cycles have become orbits of the concept. (This too was anticipated by Neoplatonism in all significant points.[45]) If this were not the case, then centrifugal emanations would tear everything away into the unreflected; the world would be in a chronic state of flight from the origin—which is also the dilemma of contemporary Big Bang theories, which offer a snapshot of the outbreak of a reflectionless initial something from an over-dense, super-hot point as a myth to explain the world.[46]

Unus ardor—it must be one and the same blast of heat that begets the orb from the point and then strives back towards its starting point by turning around spontaneously, unforced and precisely. If the reflections were forced through external resistances, the result would be a coerced God—which is surely the last thing a theosophist would want to hear about. For God to remain uncoerced, the turnings of the light must be free homeward journeys in which there is no place for compulsion through circumstances or opposing forces. The return must be characterized by the same freedom and ebullience as the first departure from the source. Recognition must, in a word, be no less spontaneous (or fruitful) than production.

The light games of the pulsating God therefore include two exuberances, two orgasms, two satisfactions—each an immeasurable fulfillment in itself, yet only as a pair the whole of what pleasure can be after its infinitization in God. The reason for this immeasurable double pleasure is the symmetry of production and recognition, which are related in the same way as emission and return, or ejaculation and self-affirmation of pleasure. The apex of creative extraversion is confirmed and continued by the apex of recognizing collection in a state of endless self-renewal. These movements would not be termed *ardor*, burning and blast of heat, if they did not point to an experiencing fiber interlocking the two climaxes. This is what it means when, in a little-noted passage, Meister Eckhart writes "God is an effervescence that produces an apex from an apex"—a principle that evidently still inspired reverence in Hegel, who, using a poetic quotation in an exposed passage, describes the absolute "foaming" in self-reflection as if in a chalice.[47]

If one takes the explications of the first and eighteenth definitions together, the famous and momentous second principle is also illuminated sufficiently that only a remainder is left unclear—a problematic remainder, to be sure, with revolutionary implications for the world picture.

> God is the infinite sphere whose center is everywhere and whose circumference is nowhere.

One could, with good reason, take the view that this literally eccentric thesis of high medieval hermetic theosophy was the time bomb, possibly one which had been ticking since late antiquity, that would one day blast open the well-rounded, Catholicized Aristotelian cosmos from the inside—a process which the heliocentric turn of Copernicus augmented in an extra-theological setting. Clarification is indeed required in the case of the seemingly conventionally inserted attribute "infinite," which lends the divine orb a peculiarly mathematical iridescence. For how can the notion of an orb, which is only definitively identifiable as such through its finite periphery, still exist if this *sphaera* is unabashedly described as infinite? This attribute still contains an echo of the ancient doctrine in which the orb and the circle possess a good or qualified infinity because, by returning into themselves, they unify beginninglessness and endlessness. Yet one can already hear a more modern concept of infinity making its demands; one cannot quite dismiss the notion that the hermetic orb no longer possesses merely infinite rotation and reflection, but also infinite extension. The sign "infinite" could now already be considered the value of the radius or diameter, and yielding to this temptation—this probability, in fact—would mean the end of Catholic magnificence, with its choirs, hierarchies and immemorial centrocratic habits. As soon as the diameter reaches infinite size, the periphery loses its curved character, as the circumference of an infinite circle must be drawn as a straight line. Thus the inside of the pseudo-circle falls back into the unredeemed. There is no longer an inside; the geometrization of the immune space has failed once and for all; the project of the world soul has reached its end. Everything is outside.

The consequences of the infinitist turn are unforeseeable. The entire transcendence establishment would have to be swept away by the disastrous positing of the center as ubiquitous—for in the infinite, there is nothing to support the sacerdotal notion that certain persons and institutions are "closer to God." To be sure, we are not dealing with a cosmospheric theorem or one critical of Rome, but rather a thesis whose allegiance to a theospheric-theosophical experiment scarcely comprehensible to profane persons is beyond doubt. But because the confusion between the theological and cosmological propositional fields—which is constitutive of the Catholic universe effect—enables and demands the exchanging of individual lessons, it is logical that the hazardous infinitization of the God orb will have consequences for the construction, or rather deconstruction, of the geocentric-cosmospheric system. The Modern Age drama "From the Closed World to the Open Universe"—classified by Koyré in the title of his study—will only reach culmination in its own field and with system-typical arguments, but the infinitist fever spreads from the theospheric dimension to the camp of the cosmographers and cosmologists. The phenomenon of Bruno shows clearly how the spirit of de-restriction simultaneously cast both God and the world out of their old frameworks.

After Copernicus, the universe had to tolerate—with good reason—claims that it could no longer offer the earth's inhabitants the former shell security; the Modern Age and later modernity were unmistakably defined by a radical restructuring of immune relationships. It is not Copernicus, Digges or Bruno who would have to be held responsible for the long-term effects of infinitism in a damages trial, however: long before their cosmological theses, human existence—if only it were correctly understood—had already forfeited all qualities of security in the God torn open by hermeticism. The infinitized theosphere no longer offered protection; it released. The god of the hermetic theosophists had already become entirely uncanny and non-harboring, and one could no longer predict how he could fulfill his immune task for a finite world and finite intelligences. This speculatively elaborated, perhaps fully conceived god had not only relinquished all trace of personalistic tempering; he no longer possessed a single evangelical trait and, unlike Christ, one could not fraternize with him. It was now a mystery, therefore, how the geometrization of the interior could still achieve its immunizing (in Old European terms, edifying) effects on the human observation of the world space.

This god, with a center everywhere and a circumference nowhere, was simply no longer of any use as a morphological fortification against the outside. Thanks to his speculative aggrandizements, after all, he became an ex-centering force of the greatest virulence; the thought of him eliminates the minor residential right of the souls that rely on their salvation in private chapels, landscapes, prerogatives and grandiosities. His kingdom is not of this inner world; his sphere can no longer be inhabited with just anyone as an intimate sphere. Whoever meditates this god finds themselves moving further out into the boundless, the unstable and the extra-human than the coldest thought of the universe's emptiness and the bitterest separation from what is close and beloved could ever carry you. Anyone still wishing to keep their faith would have to approach a god who had discarded the intimate and the round. But who could conceive of themselves in a relationship with this theo-mathematical monster?

Grasping the connection between the death of God and theological infinitism posed problems for subscribers to a more comfortable theology in all confessional camps, and these problems became greater the more they clung to the illusion that the disintegration of religion and the dissolution of homeland through modernization had descended on them like an external, unjust and unwanted catastrophe. They failed to understand that one of the origins of the process of modernity lay in theology itself, for it is theologians who were primarily responsible for infinitism. Theological modernism took place as a struggle between an old, regionally understood god who could be invoked as an accomplice of tribal, ethnic and imperial projections of salvation and a new, ex-centric, unfathomable-infinite and unusable god who did not back up any power or illuminate any earthly metropolis with the light of the otherworldly gloriole—a god who would not forgive anyone for claiming that he existed.

It is therefore absurd to claim that European excentering or decentering in world-political, world-theoretical and world-theological terms began in 1945, a date whose only significance lay in marking the point from which even the last Old European would have to comprehend the situation (to recap: Hans Sedlmayr and the "lost center"). The real decentering process followed impulses extending back to the rise of the mystical wave on the eve of the thirteenth century. Mysticism is the acquired immunodeficiency of regional ontologies; one catches it through unprotected thought intercourse with the stirred-up concept of the infinite. An orb whose circumference is nowhere because its center is everywhere, an orb whose center cannot be found because its circumference evaporates into the infinite—anyone truly interested in the lost center would first of all have made the lost circumference of the infinitized Modern Age god the object of their inquiries. These investigations would have revealed that infinitist theology was the primary source of nihilism. It was responsible for the equation of being-there and insecurity; it was the initial negation of all humane demands for immunity.

Circumferentia nusquam—it was with this nowhere, this negation of finite immune protection boundaries, that modernity's long way to the predominance of the infinite outside began. It decoupled being-oriented thought from the interests of that which is alive;[48] being took on the qualities of homogeneous presence-at-hand and neutral availability. Only through restless reproduction was a faded memory kept alive of what *a life* meant. Existence *in* so ex-centered a god amounts to a stay in the bottomless and borderless outside.

The hermetic end game of theology thus introduced the final transference of microsphericity to macrosphericity—with the absurd consequence that the infinite sphere forfeited its harboring function. Those contained in it lost their immunity and their harboring. With theosophical infinitism, a form of religion developed in which God systematically disappointed his believers. Now he was always the one from whom nothing could be expected—indeed, merely continuing to believe in him became an immunological losing game for those involved. The mystical-mathematical monster always takes more than it gives, and becomes a collecting point for unfulfillable security hopes. This effect is as old as Plotinism, in which the spiritual sphere was assigned the attribute of infinity for the first time. Neoplatonic thought, however, still lived off the transference of the living to the geometric, the projection of a finite vitality into the horizon of the infinite. It exploited the circumstance that humans are very partial to the monstrous as long as they believe it is their ally; they lend to the non-harboring god the immunity which they presuppose in him, yet of which, if they looked more closely, they would no longer find any trace *in him*, because the meaning of being-in vanishes in the infinite. With unshakable naïveté, they even view the infinite as an accomplice in the securing of mortal life as defined by Boethius in his seminal definition of eternity as the "simultaneous and complete possession of infinite life."[49] Life becomes the patron of non-life.

The secret of metaphysics was that it surrounded precisely those ideas in the radiance of the living which abandon it. That is why the theo-mathematical monstrosity of the "endless sphere" could intermittently seem to have a vital glow around it, and that is why Hegel could still teach that the "grand interest of Spirit in history" was "to attain an unlimited immanence of subjectivity"[50]— a program that set up a holistic fake of immunity, which, despite forming an "immanence," would never be a harboring.

For the self-articulation of modern thought, admittedly, the Romantic turn towards nature was more significant than Hegel's completion of metaphysics in the no-man's-life of the spirit. The Romantic philosophy of nature achieved that immeasurably far-reaching conceptualization which, for the first time, made the essence of metaphysics—the longing for the harboring of the subject in an incorruptible ontological alliance—sufficiently clear that it could be disputed, but no longer forgotten. The very point where the demand to harbor the subject merges with the motif of infinity is the birthplace of the explosive concept that forced nineteenth- and twentieth-century thought out of its traditional forms: the unconscious. This concept was an attempt to turn even an infinitized whole towards the protection of life. In the fog of their school, where vision was restricted to distances of under three generations, the Freudians lost the historical dimension and the logical structure of their central concept; they did not know that the unconscious arose from the final transference of the internal form—and thus from the demand that even an infinite totality of nature should continue to provide the harboring function of the former divine shell. Because transferences to the infinite were thwarted by a lack of concrete qualities in the object, however, transference as such finally had to become aware of itself; the Young Hegelians, as the first critics of transference, went through this when they investigated projections of the human onto the divine (and of the artificial onto the found).

Indeed, as a general study of images and spaces of transference, psychology presupposes the death of God, that is to say the bursting of the monosphere and the awakening from monotheistic auto-hypnosis. The unconscious of the early nineteenth century was the medical-ontological hypostasis of an absolute healing power that supposedly manifested itself in the infinite nature as the capacity for good *pro nobis*. It was with this concept of the unconscious that immunity became at all thinkable for the first time—as a threshold concept between biology and metaphysics.[51] Once the pantheistic exaggerations of the Romantic idea of salvation had dissipated, the immune motif was left without any theological dressings. The path was open to an interpersonal immune practice that reached a practicable format in the "analytical situation."

In the field of philosophy, disillusionment at the useless god and the realization of facing a dead infinity empty-handed only found verbal expression towards the end of the nineteenth century. Under the heading "In the Horizon of the Infinite," he writes:

> We have forsaken the land and gone to sea! We have destroyed the bridge behind us—more so, we have demolished the land behind us! Now, little ship, look out! Beside you is the ocean; it is true, it does not always roar, and at times it lies there like silk and gold and dreams of goodness. Bur there will be hours when you realize that it is infinite and that there is nothing more awesome than infinity. Oh, the poor bird that has felt free and now strikes against the walls of this cage! Woe, when homesickness for the land overcomes you, as if there had been more *freedom* there—and there is no more "land"![52]

It was Nietzsche who carried out the immunological turn of thought and began to interpret culture as a whole as a competition between downplaying and escalating vaccination strategies. While democracy performs the serial vaccination of the mass with security motifs, Zarathustra wishes to make the life of the few monstrous once again by transforming thought itself into an infection: "I inoculate you with madness."

The center everywhere, the circumference nowhere—with such definitions, the god of rational mysticism shed the final cave qualities, indeed the most distant traces of cosmic domesticity. If metaphysical border politics had ever been successful, this sublime overstepping of circumferences fundamentally put an end to the use of God for regional and imperial spatial enchantments. After the shift to the presently infinite, the concept of God was no longer edifying for any power, any life context or any regional dominance. All that local powers, holy empires, inviolable precincts of strength, dense magic circles and happiness-providing autohypnoses received from it was the humiliating information that as narrow-minded figures of meaning in a transcendent and oceanic medium, they were always already isolated, burst, ironized and overstepped. This imposed a situation on the thinking in which the subtlest inside was indistinguishable from the most monstrous outside. The god with the circumference nowhere would never again be of use as the accomplice of a finite worldview or world-presumption. Anyone capable of thinking him may have achieved the "view-point" of absolute immanence, but thinking would then mean meditating on the monstrous, on that which leaves us aghast.

The theosophical mysticism of the orb released a centrifugal dynamic in whose trajectories the early modern cult of the

God-analogous, creative genius and later also modern individualism in its most sublime and most vulgar forms would develop. For if the infinitized god lost his central position in the spiritual space in the course of the Modern Age, then his human representatives, the spiritually gifted individuals, had to achieve substantially more than merely occupying a distant place in his interior. The "in" of "in-the-infinite" no longer referred to a demonstrable habitation and participation relationship, after all; rather, the creative humans would have to perform the entire work of the lost form-god from their respective place in the existent if the original aspect, namely taking a life as the starting point, was to be retained. They would have to succeed the center themselves by volunteering for the task of "being" it and representing it.

Catholic orthodoxy knew how to protect itself against such potentially pantheistic excesses or individualisms in its last centuries of exclusive dominance: by banishing the experiments of mathematical mysticism to the limits of what was permissible for true believers. Nonetheless, hermetic individualism remained a characteristic temptation of late and post-medieval thought. It heralded an age in which the absolute was represented by geniuses, not priests. It was Rousseau who laid down the genius rule of the expressivist life from the center of his own soul:

> There is not a being in the universe that cannot in some respect be regarded as the common center around which all others are ordered [...].[53]
>
> "What a disparity," it will perhaps be said. "A while ago we were concerned only with what touches us, with what immediately surrounds us. All of a sudden here we are traveling around the globe and leaping to the ends of the universe!" This

disparity is the effect of the development of our strength and the bent of our mind. In the state of power and strength the desire to extend our being takes us out of ourselves and causes us to leap as far as is possible for us.[54]

Johann Gottlieb Fichte formalizes Rousseau's individual-imperialistic intuitions in his theory of manic environmental creation:

the fundamental image of the autonomy of the mind in consciousness is that of a geometric point which eternally forms and vitally maintains itself. [...] It is thanks to the self that order and harmony have been instituted in the inert and unformed mass. It is uniquely thanks to man that order extends around him to the very limits of his control. [...] Thanks to the self there is constituted the immense hierarchy which runs the scale from the sprig of moss to the seraphim. [...] In this self resides the pledged promise [...] that with man's growing culture, the culture of the universe will grow correspondingly.[55]

Novalis, who turned these principles in an art-philosophical direction, finally presupposed the transformation of classical emanation theology into modern production- and expression-oriented thought when he noted in his sketchbooks: "Every individual is the center of a system of emanation."[56]

More than two hundred and fifty years after the *Book of Twenty-Four Philosophers* appeared, Nicholas of Cusa produced a small sum of scholastic spherology in his late dialogue treatise *De ludo globi* (Part I was written in 1462, Part II in 1463, and the author died the following year), which presents itself on the surface as a light-handed exercise for beginners, even a piece of Christian "philosophical entertainment."[57] Without naming his source, he unabashedly refers to the notorious central principle of the afore-mentioned hermetic-philosophical text:

> After you take note of the saying of the wise man who said that God is a Circle whose Center is everywhere, you will see that just as a point is found everywhere in whatever is quantitative, so God is present in all things.[58]

The way of thinking that I have characterized as theocentric had become second nature to the Cusan to such an extent that he did not permit even an inkling of a growing problem when dealing with the embedding or analogization of the large-scale orbs of God and the world. Thus in the first part of the dialogue, in a reply of the young Duke John of Bavaria to the expositions of the cardinal, the idea is presented that man, as the *small* world, is an analogue (*similitudo*) to the *large* world, also known as the universe, which in turn represents the *largest* world, that is to say the sphere of God. The word "world" could not be used in three forms if the equation of "world" and "sphere" had not already been taken for granted, and if these three ontological regions or "spheres" (*parvum-magnum-maximum*), in analogy to the planetary orbs, were not imagined as concentrically embedded bodies; man is in the world as the world is in God.[59] Thus even a thought that attempted to evade sensible images could not escape spatializations (and needed not do so, for Cusa had not yet fore-seen those moderns who would commit to a "one-sided praising of time," to use a formulation by Max Bense, at the expense of the metaphysically more originary spatial feeling; it was only the chronolatrous one-sidedness of the moderns that led to the disdain for ignoble "spatializations").

Thus the Cusan, or rather his conversational partner, distinguishes between God and the world just as between the *maximum* and the *magnum*, without any reference to the structural difference between the two macrospheres. The large must fit inside the largest—how could it not? Nicholas submits to the Catholic illusion of the reconcilability of the two constructs and has the world absorbed without conflict, like an obedient internal circle within the divine maximum circle. He succeeds all the more easily because his entire discourse is pervaded by rhetorical figures that invoke nothing other than the monarchy of the midpoint and the expansion of the central light from its hyperreal source.

The old cardinal-bishop's centrophilic habitus went so far that he did not hesitate to invent a worldly *ball game* with a deeper spiritual meaning, modifying a "disc" game popular in the Middle Ages, which he recommended to his conversational partners—today we would call them up-and-coming politicians (from the Young Confusion[60])—as a form of boules or pétanque for Christian Platonists.

As one would expect from a sworn theocentric, this game is played towards the middle, which represents nothing other than the true god, the *dator vitae*, who constitutes the goal of all metaphysical wishes. With superb humor—or is it simply ecclesiastical routine?—the cardinal reproduced the God orb in the form of a target painted on the ground with nine rings and a divine bull's eye in the middle. This may, incidentally, be one of the reasons why he tends to treat the concepts of the (two-dimensional) circle and the (three-dimensional) sphere as synonyms in his

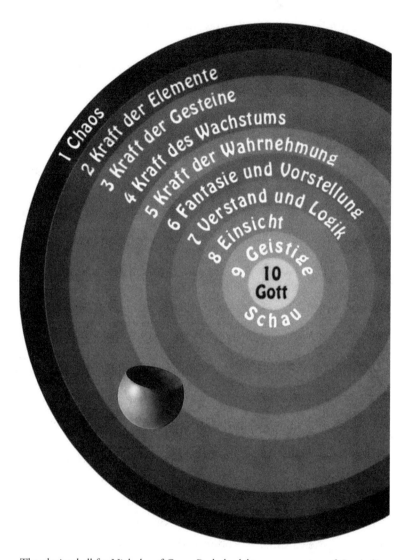

The playing ball for Nicholas of Cusa, *De ludo globi*: reconstruction of Cusa's disc.
1) chaos, 2) power of the elements, 3) power of the stones, 4) power of growth, 5)
power of perception, 6) imagination and ideation, 7) intellect and logic, 8) insight,
9) spiritual vision, 10) God

tract—as we were able to observe in the deformed anonymous quotation from the twenty-four-philosopher book.[61] The Christian boules players thus play a game of illumination, or of coming home to God, by doing their best to throw their balls in such a way that they will come to rest at the innermost center of the divine ten. The Cusan ball game demands a projection of the theosphere into a flat field so that the players standing in front of the disc can relate themselves appreciably to the center and its surrounding rings. One could see in this a certain un-philosophical carefreeness, or at least a very substantial concession to the need for crude visual aids. To hit the innermost ring, the boules players must have a high level of sporting ability and meditative inclinations, for only practice makes perfect with these balls. Thus the search for the center of being becomes a pious shooting match with the God-seeker as the marksman, God as the top score and eternal life as the prize money.

Anyone troubled by the fact that a dignitary of the Catholic church in the fifteenth century was able to present the last secrets of mystical theology in the image of a shooting target—with God as the bull's eye—without meeting any objections should, to put their surprise into perspective, take into account that an analogous form of athletic-knightly spiritualism was developed at the same time in Japanese Buddhism: the art of archery, also known in the West today, which was practiced as an armed-disarming exercise in intentional non-intentionality.[62] Compared to its sublimely martial Far Eastern analogue, which saw the development of a complex subculture around itself, Cusa's bowling game never became much more than a cryptic pre-reformatory amusement—one can still find the balls in souvenir shops in Bernkastel-Kues to this day. Anyone who studies the commentaries in the playing instructions, however, will note that these, especially the second part, are by no means lacking in high tension; and anyone wishing to practice the game on Cusan terms could possibly have been absorbed by it as much as the Zen student by the target, bow and arrow.

The Zen comparison is not merely associative in nature, for it touches on a spiritual characteristic of Cusa's construction. The nub of the game is that throwing the Cusan balls is made more difficult by the fact that they cannot roll straight; this is because, through a profound trick by the inventor, they are notched or asymmetrically hollowed out, as it were, meaning that they do not move directly towards an intended goal once thrown. Rather, they wobble forwards along a crooked trajectory, finally coming to rest by rolling out inwards. (In remote analogy to this, one could point out that the Zen archer does not aim at the target in direct intention like an ordinary bowman, for hitting it is no longer meant to be a function of ego-based wanting.) In a sense these concaved, staggering two-thirds orbs represent the human condition, which, as we know, does not permit us to hasten back to God along the straightest path, instead giving indirect approximations of the absolute through sideways movements and twisting detours. No more than approximations of the perfect are permitted for humans *sub luna*—

> in such a way that at length, after many variations and unstable circular movements and curvatures, we come to rest in the Kingdom of Life.[63]

The purpose of the game is thus to throw the ball, through practice and sensitivity, in such a way that it comes to rest as close to the center as possible despite its curved trajectory. The closer the ball to the divine bull's eye, the more points the player earns with their throw. The winner is the first to reach thirty-four—the number of years Jesus lived, according to Cusa. (Anyone seeking evidence for the psychoanalytical claim that we are not free in our fantasies should remember this case; and anyone wishing to refute Schiller's assertion that man is only fully human when he plays can scarcely ignore the Cusan example.) The winner's reward is no small one, for it promises sanctification during life and bliss *post mortem*.

That the humorous cardinal had devised not only a game, but also a specific game hell[64] is shown in the further course of the text by his reflections on the fate of the losers. For what does it mean to be the loser in this game? At first, this question only seems relevant for those who need longer to reach the full score than their most successful fellow player. One could live with that initially, even if one can already discern ominous undertones here that sound as if the *vita Christiana* were meant to be a living contest with salvation as the prize. As will soon transpire, however, the Cusan ball game—because its theological cargo makes it more than mere fun—can suddenly take a turn for the worse and lead to an existential emergency. This brings into view a losing in the most fatal sense of the word—a losing that especially concerns all those who never even took part in the game for the Christian-identified center. For playing towards the center means aiming for the father—which would be impossible if the son had not revealed the father as a father.[65]

The game of orbs thus reminds us, in a slightly devious way, of the necessity of being a Christian. The circles on the Cusan target represent, in their inventor's opinion, no less than the stages of vision, which can (supposedly) *only* ever penetrate the father-center with the help of the son. Here the game betrays its latent totalitarian character, because it excludes everyone who is unwilling or unable to play towards the center shown or struck by Christ, the place of the "only mediator." Thus a night without vision or hope holds sway outside the ball game; *extra ludum nulla salus*.[66]

> Since the center, which is seen only *within* [each of the] circles, cannot be seen outside a circle: [by analogy, outside the Circle-of-Life] the Life of the living, or the Light of intellectual lights, is not seen.[67]

Whoever does not play by the Christian-Platonic rules is there-fore blind to the center of being itself, and has lost the real ball game, the striving to return to the center supposedly only revealed by the son, from the outset. But this is not all: after ven-turing out this far, Nicholas went the whole hog by presenting Christ as the exemplary player of the game, the only one who managed to throw his ball so that it hit the mark perfectly and came to rest at the center of the ten. What the Middle Ages called *imitatio Christi* was thus translated into the emulation of this incomparable throw. Admittedly no human players, however perfectly they placed their throws, would find exactly the same trajectory and resting point—firstly, because Christ naturally always remains the better player, and secondly, because it is inherently impossible for two different players to reach exactly the same point. For Cusa, being real means being different. Here the mathematical and metaphysical arguments arrive at the same result, which indicates that even a returned Christ could not perform a wholly identical repetition of his throw.

This game, I say, symbolizes the movement of our soul from its own kingdom unto the Kingdom of Life, in which there is eternal rest and eternal happiness. In the Center of the Kingdom of Life our King and Life-Giver, Christ Jesus, presides. When He was like unto us, He moved the bowling-ball of His own person (*personae suae globum*) in such a way that it would come to rest at the Center of Life. He left us an example in order that we would do just as He had done and in order that our bowling-ball would follow [in the pathway of] His (*globus noster suum sequatur*), although it is impossible that another ball come to rest at the [exact] same Center of Life at which Christ's ball comes to rest. For within a circle there are an infinite number of places and mansions. For the bowling-ball of each individual comes to rest at its own point and atom, at which no other ball can ever arrive. And no two balls can be equally distant from the Center; rather, the one ball will always be more distant, the other less distant.[68]

There are two reasons, then, why Christ was the only one who could hit the center of the ten in an unrepeatable manner. The first is a point-ontological one: no two points can be in the same place (a theorem that applies the principle of the non-identity of the distinguishable), which is why the Cusan saw an infinite number of proximities to the absolute center, but never the coincidence of two points. The second is an orb-ontological one: Christ's privilege of being the only one able to play with a flawless round ball (*globus personae suae*)—or should it be said that even the incarnation of God was a wobbling ball?[69] Christ demonstrating the bull's eye (idealistically expressed as *hénosis*, union, or psychoanalytically described as the imaginary fusion):

this was the Gospel, translated into a sporting language. For the Cusan, the reference to hitting the mark is a welcome turn, in that it strengthens the cause of centrism. The image of the target also helps to correct the decentering effects of the hermetic rumor of the omnipresent center.

In old age, Cusa seems to have become convinced that mystical audacities ultimately only produced existential and social unrest, and that with the dangerous subject of spheres, what was important was to bolster the Christological orthodoxy against speculative centripetal forces. Is salvation, in the end, not a question of centering? But how is the soul to aim for the best if the center cannot be shown, sought and found as a fixed element? *Centrum autem punctus fixus est*[70]—that is the tenor of Cusa's reflections, which make no secret of their conservative concern for the logical securing of the center. This center is definitely concealed from sensory and unilluminated perception, as perfect roundness always remains invisible, but well-guided spiritual meditation cannot miss it entirely as long as it bears in mind that God's orb can be observed intellectually in two ways: firstly, based on the idea of the absolute minimum or the pure point, which comprises everything (*omnia complicans*), and secondly, following the image of the maximum or the extended universal orb, in which everything is present in a maximally folded-out state, and whose utter perfection makes it invisible to physical eyes.[71]

On the Cusan target, however, the region closest to the outer edge cannot take up any significant position, as play takes place exclusively towards the center—just as the entire *ludus globi* constitutes a centering exercise: "all power is hidden in the center."[72] Someone who only reached the first ring would virtually be a damned soul; anyone who never scored ten would remain in danger to the end. The most circumspect player, at any rate, would be the one whose throws took into account how the staggering ball traverses all steps of the folded-out existent before turning towards the wonderfully all-enfolding center and coming to rest in its proximity. As strange as it may sound, the nine rings on the Cusan disc represent the choirs of angels or of the steps of being, which, according to Neoplatonic doctrine, spill forth from the super-One and contain the archetypes of everything existent. Hence players of the ball game amuse themselves with no less than onto-theology as a whole. And with each throw, they bring into play the entire system of Catholic discretions, the complete theory of categories. The target represents the existent as a whole, and in basic-conceptual completeness.

> Consequently, there are ten different kinds of distinction (*genera discretionum*), viz., (1) the Divine Distinction, which is symbolically represented as the Center and as the Cause of all things (*causa omnium*), and (2) the other nine [kinds of distinction, which are represented] by the nine choirs of angels. And there are no more numbers or no more distinctions (*nec numeri nec discretion*) [than these ten]. Hence, it is evident why I symbolized the Kingdom of Life as I did and why I have likened the center to the sun's light and have depicted the three circles nearest [to the center] as fiery, the next [three] as aerial (*aetheoros*), and the [last] three, which end in earthen black (*in negro terreno*), as aqueous.[73]

One can perhaps consider it a triumph of spiritualization that the usual black at the center of targets has become white or golden in Cusa's model. With the representation of the rings, however,

Nicholas ventures onto profound and tricky ground. The nine-choir structure of the existent—expounded with significant consequences by Pseudo-Dionysius the Areopagite in his treatise *The Celestial Hierarchy*, then adopted by the Cusan—initially only reflects the three three-tiered orders (*ordines*) of angelic intelligences. Each of these has its own theophanic rank and manifests an aspect of God—from the highest spirits close to God, which comprehend everything at once in simple intuition (*in divina simplicitate simul omnia*), to the less high-performing, but nonetheless truth-serving angels of the discursive intellect, which are closely related to human intellects.[74] In keeping with the conventions of the Neoplatonic doctrine of emanation, the notion that these nine spirit spheres issue from the divine center like luminous rings through a form of wave propagation, yet always "remain at the origin" in a certain sense, can—with a good will to understand—be grasped without any real incoherence or exaggerated preconditions of faith. For the Cusan, however, this descending string of lights alone is not sufficient; the lights sent out by God in ordered progressions must *simultaneously* cover the regions of the cosmologically concrete totality—which is why, as the target shows, this totality must comprise three layers and nine steps, albeit now with a darkened, potentially dis-spirited outer edge.

And it is through this that the systemic disaster reveals itself. For the edge cannot, with the best will in the world, be inter-preted as the lowest level of the angelic and illuminated worlds. Let us take a closer look: the three outer rings on the Cusan target are portrayed as *earthen black and aqueous* to characterize the lack of light in the three *niger* regions with elemental symbolism. The third-furthest of these "terran" zones contains the mineral forces, and the second circle the yet more diffuse, unstructured elemental forces—which presumably means earth, water, air and fire. The outermost ring, which bears the number one and represents sub-elemental substances, is even described by the jovial cardinal as "confused chaos" (*figurat ipsum confusum chaos*): a region in which the emanations of the light center have become so attenuated that they no longer have any formal effects on the substance. It follows from that that the God of light (despite his attribute "infinite") has a dark fringe which his ordering capacity (because he operates from the center) no longer reaches.

The systemic contradiction is now blatantly exposed. If the theocentric principles were genuinely synonymous with the cosmological ones, or at least compatible, this would mean that the ninth choir of the Areopagite and the first ring on the Cusan disc, the confused chaos, would be equivalent. This is entirely absurd, however, for it would be tantamount to declaring the chaos a theophany and claiming that the almost-nothing, the feces, the damp dust, *knew* God in its own way. (NB: to be light means to grasp God at a particular level.) On the terms acknowledged by the Cusan, such a statement is completely inconceivable. Nicholas emphasizes time and again, after all, that only the insightful human soul can ascend and progress from the confused to the distinct.[75] That the formless (*chaos confusum*) should be an intelligence, however, or more precisely the ninth-furthest step of the intelligences radiated by God, could not even be claimed with the most desperate will to systematize.

Regarding the periphery of the Cusan orb system, it becomes painfully clear how the two incompatible sphere constructs—the theoperipheral and the theocentric—are forced together, which results in a powerful, irksome remainder that convinces the analyst of the construct's insurmountable erroneousness. Any moderately inquisitive non-Platonist and non-believer in angels studying the emanation model can be expected to grasp the thesis that the ninth and outermost ring of angelic intelligences around the divine center could still possess the exquisite ability to access valid truths about God by means of the observing and concluding intellect. But the notion that the periphery of the God orb simultaneously—as if it could simply be equated with the physical world orb—includes a confused chaos, like some light-deprived and form-forsaken limbo, is the most severe case of a transition to a different type, caused by a violent leap from theospherics to cosmospherics. Even the greatest thinker of the late Middle Ages was not able to solve the problem, which Plotinus could only cover up with theomathematical riddles and the Arabs through orthodox assurances. Its solution would have consisted in the realization that one can let the impossible rest and must take new paths of thought.

The chaotic dark edge of the Cusan world disc testified to the continued existence of the non-absorbable physical design amid the most generous idealistic fabrications. What had formed the dark center of the standard cosmological model, namely the sublunary space and its hellish lightless core, had been shifted to the periphery in the light center model, albeit not burdened directly with infernological meanings.

This was intended to force something as impermissible as it is impossible: an "edge" of the world that would remain entirely controlled by the center. Once the periphery of the light-sphere has been declared chaos, inescapable systemic constraints make it appear as God's weak, lost, distant place; the outermost edge almost becomes a nothing, an ontological outland where the passports of light are no longer valid. Here light becomes non-light; beyond this threshold, God ruins himself by flowing out into his complete other. He lowers himself so far into the chaotic that from there, he can no longer return to himself in his abundance.

The fact that a system rupture of such elemental force could open up—or rather, be *passed over* in the hope that nothing would open up—amid the most subtle reflections of the greatest thinker of his time proves what was perhaps to be expected anyway: even the most inspired attempts to make the world God-immanent by the integral autism that presents itself as theology are doomed to produce symptomatic flaws. They reveal the systemically conditioned impossibility of enclosing the orb of the world concentrically in that of God. Leaving aside ontological analogies, the *maximus mundus* cannot contain the *magnus mundus* without contradictions. In the Neoplatonic realm of light, as we have seen, the real physical world finds itself in such an outside position that one cannot seriously refer to the world as being contained within God. Through its bleak marginality, the world becomes impenetrable for the central God himself.

Even the shift towards a nature-philosophical perspective could scarcely improve the situation of the Cusan model. Idea-historical studies on the revolution in the world picture during the Modern Age tend to extol Cusa as pioneering the idea of a de-restricted, albeit not infinite universe, without considering that this merely celebrates a different impossibility; as the nature-theological world picture imagines God as enthroned "above all," the great cardinal is essentially praised for having moved God to a place inconceivably far from the world. Had someone mentioned this blasphemous risk to the Cusan, he would undoubtedly have returned hastily to his basic Neoplatonic

SPHÆRA CIVITATIS

From John Case, *Sphaera Civitatis* (1588): the transference of pre-Copernican shell cosmology to political theory; the fixed earth of justice is orbited by the seven planetary shells of majestic virtue; these are encompassed by the sky of fixed stars containing ministers, heroes and advisers. The queen enfolds this sky as God enfolds the firmament.

model—but only to reconfirm the result already described: he would have had to arrive once again at a world that, because of its excessive marginality, would become irrecoverable for the central god himself. Cusa's œuvre thus ends in monumental ambiguity:

conservative centrism keeps revolutionary infinitism in check, as if an explosion had frozen at the moment of ignition. In the light of this finding, it is perhaps understandable why Cusa's effects on posterity have remained almost entirely indirect:[76] the strongest thinker of his age had to exhaust his powers in the most theoretically hopeless situation.

Just as every monism by necessity has its renegade spirits that make the boundaries of the uniform space palpable, so too the One World of the metaphysics of light contains an opaque residue—albeit one almost the size of the whole universe—that cannot be brought home interpretively as a mode of light residing in the regions more distant from the center. The connection between God and the world can no more be regulated through the quantitative relationship of the largest to the large than through the integration of the world-stuff into the divine periphery. As soon as the world comes under view in this sublime system of emanations as an extended, heavy and dense body, a non-assimilable residuum, an unsound, cumbersome, self-governed or rather self-ungoverned outside pushes forwards, denying the immanence of all things in the light-orb.

Thus the *mundus catholicus* undoubtedly contains lost matter, just as there are countless lost souls at the edge of the spirit world that revel in the *massa perditionis*. Whatever is lost is removed from the good orb. And—how could it be otherwise?—when playing towards the divine center, a large number of *a posteriori* losers (who had a chance) and an even larger number of *a priori* losers (who had no chance) are eliminated. Thus the game's evangelical pretense of being a game for all dissolves into a particular and polemogenic demand.

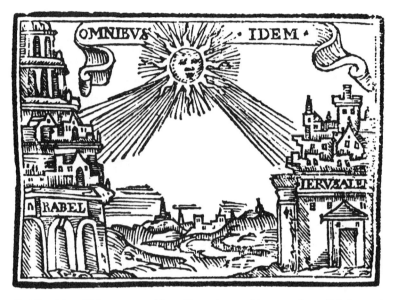

Omnibus idem: 17th-century emblem. The only sun shines equally on Babylon and Jerusalem.

Philosophical Catholicism too, then, never managed to produce more than a system of inclusive exclusivity—which was the cultural norm. Thus it remained merely a regional form, a culture in the anthropological sense, a symbolic order that was the be-all and end-all to some, yet for others simply a wall with a hermetic and provincial drama going on behind it that, depending on one's point of view, could be considered a tragedy or a comedy. If a Catholic form, as the form of all forms, had sought—truly "in accordance with the whole," *káta hólon*—to contain everything existent and encompass the particular worlds in their inexhaustible diversity, it would first of all have had to abandon its own centered mode of being. In fact a totality of totalities, in order to be that as which it wishes to be perceived,

Rose window at Troyes Cathedral (13th century, photograph: John Gay)

must cross itself out and lose itself in the cultures of the others—approximately in the way the Jesuits in China had turned themselves into Mandarins, and the first envoys of Christianity on Indian soil appeared as ascetic Sadhus and learned Brahmans. Even after five centuries of experiments with the globalization of the world form (politically and epistemically) and the production of post-monotheistic life forms (culturally and ethically), it is in no way clear how such a voluntary self-loss could take place on a grand scale. The Vatican's decision in 1742 to forbid the assimilation of missionaries to Chinese and Indian rites shows very clearly how, in its first great test, European universalism chose love for itself over love for others.[77] It is doubtful, however, whether the adjustment of Old European Catholicism to neo-humanistic ideas about human rights could do justice to the holistic impulse of the *hen kai pan*, assuming it even wanted to.

But how should one imagine a "culture without center"? And how to grasp the one that gives us pause as multiplicity without it being subject to the monopoly of a single system? Everything would suggest that the first Catholicity of the Old European ecclesial-colonial complex has long since turned into the second Catholicity of the world market for capital and information. Comprehending this second universalism *in actu* is the purpose of philosophy that diagnoses its time: its vanishing point is an ontology of the money-fluidized world. What this structural transformation of the ecumene means in spherological terms will be touched on in the final chapter of this volume. There, through various remarks on the philosophical reconstruction of terrestrial globalization, I shall interrogate the history and status of the last orb.

Excursus 5

On the Meaning of the Unspoken Statement

"The Orb Is Dead"

The most amazing thing about Nietzsche's parable of the madman who proclaims the death of God is its embarrassing anachronism: who would have thought, without the proof of the event itself, that a thinker on the threshold of the twentieth century would make another hysterical scene because of the Copernican-Brunian hypotheses? Copernicus' posthumous work on the circulations of the heavenly bodies had appeared no less than three hundred and fifty years before *The Gay Science*, and three hundred years had passed since the first attacks of the nature philosophers and astronomers on the venerable notion of the sphere of fixed stars and the crystal sky as the outermost celestial orbs.[78] One could be tempted to assume that cosmological thought in Nietzsche's time had long become the norm, and that the great reform "from the closed world to the infinite universe" would no longer have caused any personal offense.

Indeed, the nineteenth century generally no longer expected much from the physical sky, whose infinite extension was taken as one given among many by the educated and laypersons alike; the memory of shell times had long since faded, geocentrism had shrunk to a distant fable, and the thousand-year doctrines of the spheres were only preserved as world picture-historical curiosities, documents of human gullibility and mementos of the Catholic politics of ignorance. The rupture between religion and physics had become officially irreparable, and the churches had retreated in humiliation from their desire for a position as nature-philosophical teachers. As far as glances at the sky and the temporal horizon are concerned, the enlightened world lived in an infinitism without tears, filled with the belief in the untarnishable convergence of future and improvement. Tomorrow belonged to the more powerful telescopes and the greater social benefits, so what cause for complaint?

It was into these well-oiled optimistic routines, which seemed to bespeak cosmological adulthood, that the madman of *The Gay Science* burst, making an unexpectedly gothic scene before his contemporaries. Nietzsche dredged up the figure of the man in the tub, the arch-Cynic Diogenes of Sinope, from his sarcastic asylum and let him walk across a modern marketplace, once more equipped with his lantern—but this time looking for something other than people. Through a metamorphosis to which Platonism and Christianity contributed, the maddened Socrates of the ancients had given way to an exalted beggar monk, a repentance preacher of the unusual kind: an accuser who wanted to cast his listeners into a state of frenetic, guilty contemplation. He was undoubtedly a disturbed man, who burned in lonely overexcitations and, like all the truly insane, wanted to drive the unmoved others to co-insanity. What could make humans mad better than accusing something they quite simply cannot remember doing? The madman knows where to attack: with the clear sight of the authentically insane, he plunges into his mandate, namely to accuse the stuffy bystanders of an immeasurable atrocity.

"Where is God?" he cried; "I'll tell you! *We have killed him*—you and I! We are all his murderers. [...] How can we console ourselves, the murderers of all murderers!"[79]

The insanity of this intervention becomes clear in two aspects: firstly, it is not immediately clear what should suddenly induce humans to cease explaining God's invisibility not with his natural concealment, but rather as an absence based on an assassination. Secondly, it is all the more incomprehensible why the alleged murderers are not accused, but rather lamented as people in need of consolation. The confused scene can be clarified through a supposition of meaning in the spirit of understanding psychiatry: perhaps there is a core of meaning in the madman's message that becomes visible as soon as one grasps it as a compaction of different mental dramas—an amalgamation of two scenes, for example, the first set in Golgotha and the second in Frauenberg, East Prussia—with Christ as victim in the former and Copernicus as perpetrator in the second.

When the madman makes his proclamation to the world that "God is dead," then, he should not only—as expected—be standing imaginarily at the foot of the cross of Golgotha; he would also be a contemporary of the Copernican-Brunian revolution, and would speak less about the son of God who gave up his ghost on the cross than about the form-god of the occident, the holy outermost sphere, the celestial vault, which had dissolved into nothingness following the great cosmological shift of the sixteenth century. Here one can acknowledge the circle-conservative reserves of the cathedral canon Copernicus as extenuating circumstances, as with Kepler's reservations about the idea of an infinite universe. The madman was thus acting in an inner scene which he was convinced should also be epoch-making in the consciousness of all other people; he would have witnessed the murder of God and experienced a cosmological Good Friday which, unlike in the Gospels, would no longer be followed by a reversal at Easter: "God is dead! God remains dead!"[80]

The statement that "the holiest and the mightiest thing the world has ever possessed"[81] has bled to death under our *knives* is incongruous with this reading: it presents the God-murderers not as a coalition of Jews and Romans who crucified Christ, but as conspirators whose knife thrusts brought the divine Caesar's life to an end. But whether the first scene takes place on the Ides of March or on Good Friday, the motive for the perpetrator's unconscious or uncomprehended deed stems from it: just as Caesar's murderers, who thought they were saving the republic from the dictator, did not know what they were doing, so too the actors at Golgotha little realized the overarching plot they had been chosen to serve.

That the madman did not lose sight of the evangelical paradigm in his deliria becomes apparent in what follows, namely his pathos-laden thesis that this act would be epoch-making, and that all those born after us would belong to a "higher" history because of it—if not *post Christum crucifixum*, then at least *post sphaeram occisam*. At any rate, this performance is a dark parody of Good Friday, for the purpose of the madman's proclamation is not to prepare the truth of a Sunday that follows. This prophet is not mad because he speaks of the death of God, after all, but because he does *not* speak of his resurrection; he is insane because he embraces the belief that he could end the reception successes of the Good News with his Bad News.

"God is dead"—there is nothing new about this statement for Christians, if one considers that they have always meditated on it in their Holy Saturday depressions; the following claim, however—"God remains dead"—heralds a new counter-Easter severity of which it is unclear how it could be integrated into the lives of listeners. The man with the lantern is a lunatic because he wants to force a problem on his fellow humans which they do not know how to experience as their own. Fortunately for them, they do not yet see what the lunatic sees, and as long as they do not, they have actually received sufficient help already. The driving force behind the madman's eccentricity is thus not confusion; it is the unbearable lucidity of one who has lost the ability to participate in the supposedly healthy self-deceptions of the others. His madness comes from an excess of vision; he can no longer lie to himself that he and the world are in a good state. With eyes that are all too good, he sees what makes the new situation special: by bringing down the planetary shells and the firmament, the new cosmologists after Copernicus and Bruno made the earth eccentric and left it at the mercy of a cosmic instability for which none of its inhabitants were prepared.

Nonetheless, one must be a philosopher or a theologian to experience the world picture disaster as a debacle for one's own mental immune system. There is no doubt that according to their evolutionary design, human beings are not made for chilling realizations of this kind; most of them do not catch cold from this new insight, however, because—even in so-called "high culture"—they think and feel in smaller, regional and domestic immunity formats. There is little at stake for the vast majority in the answer to the question of whether there is a firmament; for them, there is no cosmologically determined sickness unto death. After the abolition of the cosmic shell, it is only for the few who use the metaphysical format for their own immune form—the book believers, the brilliant, the overexcited—that the question of whether they can transform into beings that thrive on the new truth arises in an existential form.

The madman is the first endangered, cosmologically alert individual in the Modern Age who can no longer have any illusions about the earth's situation. In his overexcitations he experiences the birth trauma of the exposed planet as if it were his own; he feels the earth falling out of the imaginary shells that had harbored it inside the divine totality during a millennia-long gestation period; he bears witness to their frenzied reeling "backwards, sidewards, forwards, in all directions" as if experiencing it first hand; he personally perceives the cold of being outside, together with "night and more night," consuming emptiness, and the feeling of being desperately lost in a wasteland. He is, in a word, nothing other than the hysterical symptom of a modern, unharbored, shelless and exposed educated humanity. He demonstrates the unity of enlightenment and panic: he lives unconcealment as naked existence, as a brought-forth life out of control and out of its shell.

The anachronistic aspect of the madman's appearance comes, among other causes, from the fact that the age of auxiliary constructions against external emptiness had only ended for the educated in Nietzsche's day: the re-enchantment of empty space as God's extension in Newton's theology had ultimately been foiled by the naked nihilism of gravitation. The attempts of the modern cosmic imagination to garnish the immeasurable with a colorful array of worlds were finally dismissed as literary reveries. It was not until Nietzsche's time, it would seem, that all the enlightening antidotes to cosmic forlornness were tried out and discarded as ineffective. From that point on, the ontological immunodeficiency of modern subjects had to be tackled with new methods.

Taken in its true context, then, the great declaration of God's death means something entirely different from what the vulgar readings of all interest groups customarily claim: understood on its own terms, it deals with the meaning of losing the cosmic periphery, the collapse of the metaphysical immune system that had stabilized the imaginary in Old European thought in a final format. It speaks of the necessity that will apply to all future life, namely to assert oneself against the primal fact of the Modern Age—a metaphysical immunodeficiency acquired through enlightenment—by means of inventive self-help. "God is dead"—what this actually means is that the orb is dead, the containing circle has burst, the immune magic of classical ontotheology has lost effect, and our faith in the God on high, without whom not a single hair on a mortal head had fallen out until yesterday, has become powerless, groundless and hopeless; for the height is empty, the edge no longer holds the world together, and the picture has fallen out of its divine frame. And with this picture, humans too must drift away from the framework of their faith and can henceforth only exist as if in free fall. After the scientific attack on the harboring circle, the personal enchantment of geometry is finished. Now humans are only immanent to the outside, and must live with this difficulty.

But how can the outside guarantee the form of immanence or the inner dwelling? The brilliant seventeenth-century interim solution of deifying infinite space itself and spatializing the infinite God—a path taken by such thinkers as Henry More and

Malebranche—was sufficient to delay the outbreak of the atheist crisis, but not to avert it.[82] In the disenchanted space, individuals can perish from the most trivial colds, the most commonplace injuries, if they fail to harbor themselves in a second immunity that can be mobilized from their own potential, without support from the transcendent frame. If the old religion was the natural amulet of first health, a post-Copernican health would have to draw on higher amulets and more complex immune arts.

This brings to light an objective reason for asynchronies between mentalities in modern societies: while some, as if through some miracle of delay, can still believe in being as an objective and ordering factor, others have already begun to understand that they are doomed to make their own constructions of order. The theologians go, the designers come. Relations between the two are governed by the law of misunderstandings, which inevitably creates schisms between those trying to solve the same (and precisely not the same) problem by overly different methods. That is why the appearance of the madman emphatically testifies to the opening of the mentality rupture: "'I come too early,' he then said; 'my time is not yet.'"[83] For while the few already suffering today from the illnesses of tomorrow put the invention of a second health on their agenda, the majority still live out their lives in first robustness and vague discontent as if nothing had happened, not infrequently in angry incomprehension towards the concerns of those who are condemned to operating with higher complexities. The inevitable friction between the two classes of immunity gives rise to what, from the perspective of diagnosing the time, must be considered the basic tension of modernity—the opposition between offensives of disillusionment and defenses of illusions. Enlightenment economy: the free market of injuries and the free choice between attending illusionists.

The war of immune systems is the reality of the real in the age following the murder of God: it is waged as a deep world war between naïveté and non-naïveté. Who could claim to have true knowledge of the camps in these hostilities? It is precisely because the positions of the old symbolic immune systems have remained almost unattacked in many places that the news of God's "alleged" death glances off them like some outside information. As far as the madman is concerned, he is convinced that even for the naïve of today, the hour will come in which their illusion-based immunity is shattered:

> "the light of the stars needs time; deeds need time, even after they are done, in order to be seen and heard. This deed is still more remote to them than the remotest stars—*and yet they have done it themselves!*"[84]

It is the curse of the insane person to know already at the time of the deed what would only become inner experience for most in the distant future and long thereafter: that God or the immune system of being was destroyed in a joint crime—a crime committed out of intellectual boisterousness, an atrocity resulting from consistency of thought, a crime of curiosity that brought to light a truth with which humans are not, initially and mostly, created to live. It is no coincidence that there are two reminders of the light from distant stars, for the true scene of God's murder is none other than the outermost shell of the ancient ethereal heaven, the sphere of fixed stars that had collapsed beneath the knife thrusts of the conspirators

Digges, Bruno, Galilei, Descartes and numerous others. The dominical saying "for they know not what they do" applies to all these clever perpetrators, as none of them could know that with their annulment of the last harboring sky, they were committing a theological-immunological atrocity that the madman would still have cause to lament thousands of years later.

In Nietzsche's view, the murder of God itself seems like a form of man-made climate catastrophe. The by now automatic use of human intellectual faculties brought about an atheist Ice Age in which the question of how humans can survive had to be posed in a fundamentally new way. This could only happen because European practices of knowledge had emancipated themselves from the Catholic conditions of traditional human existence since the Renaissance, and were now seeking to establish themselves as an autonomous factor. In fact, only a few lines before the parable of the madman in the rambling and escalatory reflections in *The Gay Science*, Nietzsche unabashedly utters this secret of a self-damaging enlightenment with no consideration for old human needs:

> It is something new in history that knowledge wants to be more than a means.[85]

So for Nietzsche, man would be no more than a parameter and medium of an overarching truth process? If knowledge has become an end in itself, then humans must be willing to deploy themselves as instruments serving this superior purpose. In this case, knowing should brush aside human needs and conditions without anyone complaining about unwelcome consequences of this knowledge. If knowing humans are a means to something that leads beyond themselves, their self-endangerment through the destruction of their old immune needs could plunge them into a creative crisis from which they might emerge as higher creatures—beyond the sheltering illusions of their first nature. This great "if" transforms all life after the death of the orb into an "experiment for the knowledge-seeker."[86] "Life is not an argument; the conditions of life could include error."[87]

This dangerous statement brings to light the purpose of the parable of the madman in epistemological terms: the entrance of this doubly maddened Socrates serves to present the social world with the question of how humans can survive if their previous conditions are abolished. How are those humans existentially possible who must reflect on themselves with the question, "How am I systemically possible?" What is life after its self-illumination through biology? And what will become of philosophy if it must henceforth appear as the love of knowledge of the surmountable, fatal and still undecided immunodeficiencies?

CHAPTER 6

Anti-Spheres

Explorations in the Infernal Space

> I am the way into the doleful city,
> I am the way into eternal grief,
> I am the way to a forsaken race.
> […]
> Before me nothing but eternal things
> were made, and I shall last eternally.
> Abandon every hope, all you who enter.
> — Dante, *Inferno*, Canto III, 1–3 & 7–9[1]

In theological metaphysics, especially its medieval form, "God" is the title of a hyper-immunity which insists that all merely man-made, self-conceived security systems must be overstepped. Hence the delirious interest of theoretically committed theologians in what they believe to be God's immeasurable magnitude: they want at all costs to find a God than which nothing greater can be conceived—and even more, one greater than anything that can be conceived; Anselm of Canterbury already discerned this subtle escalation. Recruiting people to share in the high, the highest, the more-than-highest immune force is the purpose of all metaphysical-religious propaganda. When the salvation of mortals is at stake, nothing less than the greatest of that which is conceivable and that which is inconceivably greater than this are great enough. According to unanimous clerical advice, humans should therefore not be self-assured under any circumstances; this attitude would deny them access to the supra-human immune structures in which we can supposedly only share in the mode of devotion, that is to say letting ourselves be held by the highest guarantor.

The psychagogical motive of eternal theology is based on this argument: de-insuring humans in themselves so that they can insure themselves more highly in the omnipotent God. Because this God, envisaged as the shell of all shells and the carrier of all carriers, offers the highest level of insurance and immunity, one should relinquish the smaller mental self-securings in which human life acquires its continuity from day to day and from year to year—provided that this divine maximum insurance is to be striven for at all. But wherever monotheistic priests held power, this insurance had to be established at all costs, if only because such a priesthood, if it understood itself correctly, could only legitimize itself as the agency of maximum immunization through an infinitely escalated *semper-maior* God. (Otherwise regional healers could have performed local immune tasks equally well, or better.)

The praise of God as the absolute highest source of insurance protection for souls sets off a dialectic that leads to potentially and actually disastrous immune paradoxes. For in order to establish God as the highest insurer, he must be contrasted with the human world as the unavailable total other; to channel streams of the most trusting devotion to him, he must be described as a cataract that sweeps us along in an unknown direction; to celebrate him as the untouchable patron of the likeness between the soul and himself, one must simultaneously claim that "the dissimilarity is all the greater";[2] to praise him as the epitome of the loveable, he must be made terrible as the eschatological judge. The general form of these paradoxes can thus be described as a weakening of immunity to bring about maximum immunization. Inoculation with the terrible and Totally Other is meant to bring what is one's own to final safety. As a dream of pure weakness, primary masochism fulfills itself in the sublime: in the expectation of forcing the strong part, through submission, to stoop to protecting us.

One can reasonably say that the tensions resulting from these paradoxes gave the religious history of the Middle East and Europe in the age of flourishing monotheisms its dynamism. They show what an enormous price was demanded by the highly metaphysicized soul insurance systems of the ecclesial variety. What is discussed as fundamentalism today is still the equally unmistakable and inevitable manifestation of the basal immune paradox inherent in the monotheistic religions: seeking the utmost security in the harrowing and the ultimate foundation in the abyss. Every maximal God is terrible, and we only admire him as long he "calmly disdains to destroy us."[3]

Where immunity and salvation in the absolute are demanded, it is systematically necessary for unfathomable risks of doom to irrupt that were unknown before the search for ultimate security and maximum immunity. The more is expected of the insurance, the more inflated the terror becomes. For a God supposedly capable of offering the maximum insurance premium of "eternal bliss" must be equipped with the license to destroy all human securities to replace them with the policies of the absolute. The same God's powers of attorney necessarily include the ability to award negative premiums: hence the Middle Ages with its fear of hell,

Preaching skeleton from the Cathedral of Murcia (16th century)

and its visions of an underworld in which those with poor insurance must endure the consequences of failing to reckon with the loving and terrible God of hyper-immunity.

Anyone wishing to know about the god of the theologians, then—if only out of historical interest—should not go without a visit to the Christian hell. For hell is the second face of the god of love and worship treasured by the theologians, the necessary reverse of the *communio* theology—which is why Dante, as obscene as it may have sounded, was entirely right to make his infernal gate say that it was built by the First Love. As we have seen, excommunication from philosophy and its round city could, in the worst case, result in atheists being disposed of in the no man's land without burial;[4] in the following, we shall observe how excommunication from the God of love led to extermination through internment. This, then, is the Christian hell: the death camp for dissidents of the First Love.

The circle, which offered the naïve geometry of immunity the most plausible of all shell forms, could simultaneously become the formal motif of a disastrous de-securing and a fatal loss of immunity: this was the discovery expressed in the Christian science of the infernal space. Rereading its manifesto, the cantos of Dante's *Inferno*, from a post-psychoanalytical and spherological perspective, one realizes one is dealing with a first psychiatric phenomenology in the guise of a theory of depressive constriction torture and the existential-vicious circle. At the same time, with his cross section of the structure of the hells, Dante provided the model for every examination of security in the false—his infernal residents are certainly effectively enclosed, but by no means in tonic casings or good circles. With holistic observations of immeasurable irony, his study of hell shows that in addition to the spheres of accomplishment, there is also a roundness to that hopelessness which returns into itself.

From the first glance, the poet's hellish fresco already gives a glimpse of a double cruelty: it not only reveals an underwold of eternalized human suffering in epic breadth, but also integrates this black encyclopedia into the circular forms that can be read as an unmistakable reference to the divine arrangement of this totality of suffering. This makes the infernal even more focused, for when the inmates of the lower rings endure their ordeals in the torturous media of mud, blood, fire and ice, they are additionally condemned to perceive the affirmative character of their torments at every moment. How else could these agonies seem authorized by the circular form? Mocking in its perfection, each *Bolgia* of hell curves around its prisoners; for the greater glory of God, each assistant devil tortures his clients at a location described with pedantic precision. It seems as if Dante's inferno itself, through its concentric camp shape, were praying to the God of form; in its nine-tiered structure, the Pseudo-Dionysian hierarchy of angelic choirs becomes apparent.[5]

Dante's underworld has a funnel-shaped structure resembling a megaphone from which a hurricane of sighs drones up from the earth's center to the upper end. Its form strikes a balance between the most cheerful order and the utmost horror. Anyone wishing to know how consequential it was that Augustine—one of the fathers of Christian infernology—defended the goodness and well-formedness of all creation (*omne ens est bonum*) need only visit the most elaborated hereafter of European vision culture, this thoroughly thought-through hell that, like philosophy, is entirely circular: if it were possible for form to break away completely from content, then Dante's inferno, even more than paradise, would be the triumph of divine formalism. If everything that is truly had its light from light, even the nonad of the underworld's circles would indicate a theo-morphologically excellent program; hell would be the most orderly dungeon, indeed the most perfect city, that humans had ever been allowed to inhabit. The best designers were hired to develop negative eternal ideas, and their work can rightly be labeled "made in heaven": the ghastly contents of hell could not possibly mirror God's direct intentions, meaning that scenes of eternal torment required attribution to non-divine secondary causes.

The following words are written above the gate of hell:

FECENI LA DIVINA POTESTATE,
LA SOMMA SAPIENZA E'L PRIMO AMORE
DIVINE OMNIPOTENCE CREATED ME,
AND HIGHEST WISDOM JOINED WITH PRIMAL LOVE

This statement exposes the complicity between trust in God and cynicism, and may have inspired later camp operators to analogous portal inscriptions. It reveals what it cost the Catholic faction of humanity to establish their concept of God as the absolute immunizer. To underwrite Roman-style faith policies, the divine insurer had to be made as formidable as possible: anyone who wants to promise heaven must also be able to threaten hell. And because hell was meant to be a hell by the grace of God, it was necessary to give it the form- seal of the creator, namely the circle.

Yet is the homogeneous, round-concentric appearance not deceptive in this case, as in all Catholicized ontology? Can the sphericity of the lowest regions of being really have the same morphological dignity as in the areas close to God? Could the circle of hell be the same in its substance as the circle in which the angels and the saved sing of the over-good center in eternal

Dante, *The Divine Comedy, Inferno*, Canto XIV, 124–127:

> *Ed egli a me: "Tu sai che il luogo è tondo;*
> *et tutto che tu sie venuto molto*
> *pur a sinistra, giù calando al fondo,*
> *non se' ancor per tutto il cerchio vòlto"*
> And he to me: "You know this place is round,
> and though your journey has been long, circling
> toward the bottom, turning only to the left,
> you still have not completed a full circle"

choral ecstasies? Should we extrapolate even here, under the influence of Platonic suggestions, from the cyclical form to the factual optimum, from the round manifestation to the well-formed essence? Dante himself would undoubtedly have answered these questions in the affirmative, as his infernal construction follows scholastic concepts of order and is described and populated in keeping with theo-morphological orthodoxy. This does not prevent the manifest text, contrary to the author's self-reading, from releasing insights that lie beyond the influence of orthodox doctrines. When it comes to spreading out the structure of the inferno, the poetry knows more than the poet and his scholastic informants. The globalization of suffering in hell, as remains to be shown, follows its own law, which is only seemingly identical to that of divine circularity.

The overpowering predominance of circular forms, which extend to the bottom of hell, reveals a secondary morphological purpose whose examination shows that God was not able to assert his monopoly on the circle unchallenged. He did not succeed in reserving the circle as his inalienable form-seal; curvature is not the forgery-proof signature he places beneath each of his successful creations. Rather, Dante's work demonstrates that the devilish region possesses a circularity, reflexivity and closure *sui generis*. Possibly we here encounter once again, and from a different angle, that doubling of orbs explained above as the irreducible duality of world sphere and divine sphere.[6] If the geocentric world picture necessarily envisages God above and outside, as a shining edge and over-bright height, then the theocentric schema must conceive of God as a protuberance of light that reaches out, eternally over-flowing and all-grasping, from the supra-spatial center, while the world as we know it is shifted to the darker periphery. Just as God radiates nothing but light and success in his euphoric orb, however, in choirs and waves that peter out on the structurally weak fringes of the existent, so too the furthest point of the existent from God in the other, cosmic orb—the infernal center at the earth's core—can trace wayward rings of failure around itself.

Dante, *The Divine Comedy*, *Inferno*, Canto XIX, 49–51:

> *Io stave come il frate che confessa*
> *lo perfido assassin, che poi ch'è fitto,*
> *richiama lui, per che la morte cessa.*
> I stood there like a priest who is confessing
> some vile assassin who, fixed in his ditch,
> has called him back again to put off dying.

It is a strangely tidy underworld of the greatest deviances, endlessly returning into themselves, through which Dante is conducted by his guide Virgil—and even if the poet leaves no doubt that in his view, the shared circular structures of *Inferno*, *Purgatorio* and *Paradiso* point to a uniformly effective structure imposed from above that makes itself known in the numerical schema of nine—seven—nine, the circularity of the infernal spaces, viewed more closely, possesses a different principle and, above all, a different center from that of the sphere formations around God. The conviction that the heavenly and infernal circular worlds belong to the same *ordo* is not so much a secure, calmly reasoned insight as a piously hasty prejudice with which the poet equipped himself for his terrible journey. It was the same prejudice that would provide support for the age of Christian dogmatic security, and which allowed the medieval thinkers to ignore the impossible congruence of the divine and cosmic orbs. If God were really and truly as the concept of the almighty and infinitely good God demanded, then his masterpiece, the world, had to be imagined by his exegetes in a far rounder and more successful form than could ever be experienced by ordinary mortals. The creation only cuts a suggestively brilliant figure in the theological prospect.

In no sector of the universe is this truer than hell, which in ontological terms constitutes the outermost limit of worldliness. Only someone who perceives hell in the most idealized forms can visit it in Dantesque style like a problematic fringe of the well-rounded universal totality. Consequently, human spirits only traverse the infernal camp unharmed if they have armed themselves with metaphysically consecrated dauntlessness, that is to say morphological optimism. Because nothing is as contagious as proximity to great misery, be it temporal or eternal, hell's visitors must immunize themselves with the conviction that even here, everything is as it should be. What would God be if he did not give each person what they deserved?

One certainly cannot accuse Dante's hell of lacking masterful planning. Are these well-developed ring roads of torment not proof enough of how well-founded and thought-through the infamous complexes are? Does the meticulous division of the whole not show that the camp administration knows what it is doing— and must not its knowledge too, like every intellect, possess a light from God? Does the infernal city of Dis not have the most mature urbanistic structure,[7] and is it not admirable how precisely its inhabitants are accommodated in guilt-specific *arrondissements*?

Armed with brave prejudices, the poets descend into the underworld and traverse ghastly universes to approach the residence of the *summum malum*. The living poet often faints on his journey, overwhelmed by horror and pity, yet always raised up again by the spirit of Virgil, who ensures him that even hell is alright in its own way. The living man and the dead man cannot feel the same on this matter, as Dante is unable to adopt the cold-bloodedness of his departed colleague. Yet there is never any doubt for the two travelers about the goal of their journey through the underworld; to them, it is self-evident that it will only be fully revealed in the lowest circle, at the *finis malorum*, what hell is all about.

The path through the torture chamber resembles the account of an aggravated audience with a ruler who is kept away from profane gazes by numerous ring walls and guarded gates. Even in this high hell, late antique recollections of the splendor of the invisible Persian Great Kings have not entirely faded.[8] As, however, the prince of the underworld in the Aristotelian-Dantesque

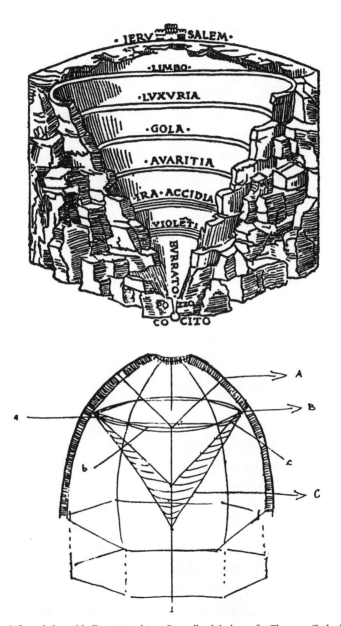

Dante's funnel-shaped hell, projected into Brunelleschi's dome for Florence Cathedral

world picture, as the epitome of negative majesty, occupies the innermost center of the terrestrial body, which is at once the absolute center of the world sphere, the place of the devil *per se* marks the point at which the physical cosmos is most itself and reflects itself most purely in its essence. This is where the truth about the lower, sublunary, terrestrial-material world as a whole comes to light: only here can one expect ultimate insight into the nature of the non-ethereal, non-luminous, non-blessed world. Through their audience with the "king of the vast kingdom of all grief"—*lo m'prador del doloroso regno* (*Inferno*, Canto XXXIV, 28)—the two poets will gaze into the thickest darkness, into a pain beyond all thresholds, impervious to every anesthetic.

The poets' journey to the lowest pole precisely mirrors the infernocentrism of Catholic cosmography. The purpose of the underworld journey is to see the prince of devils, Lucifer himself, on his throne, because the empire can only be understood in relation to the emperor. Here too the rule applies: as the lord, so the land. As the center, so the periphery. Without its conclusion through the Satanophany, the traversal of hell would be denied a result. Journeys in the beyond only fulfill their purpose if they give insight into the region as a whole from the extreme.

The region is none other than the extra-divine world, however, in that its subterranean part constitutes the former's dark extract. Who but the prince of hell himself should occupy the lower extreme of the physical space? We know why, from a cosmological perspective, the center of hell must be the furthest point from God in the shell universe, and why it lies inside the earth; we will see why, from a metaphysical or moral perspective, hell is defined as the emotional source of the rejection of spheropoietic communication with God. Because the metaphysical meaning of hell increasingly overshadows and displaces the cosmographic schema in Dante's analysis, however, his inferno ceases to be merely a reflex of the geocentric constitution of being. Rather, it transpires that hell possesses a spheropoietic potency of its own and is subject to a specific anti-spheric circularity.[9]

Traveling downwards, the two poets explore that underworld of depression in which denial forms peculiar circles: the rings of narrowness and destroyed hopes. They discover hell as an apocalypse of egoity. For it is one thing that the fallen angel turned away from God and towards himself; it is quite another that his shift became an obstinate vortex of negativity. Tracing this infernogenic vortex is the metaphysical-enlightening purpose of the poets' nocturnal voyage. This precarious desire to know is alluded to by Beatrice, who appears to the poet from heaven before his descent to give him encouragement before his hazardous journey. She herself does not quite seem to understand what compels him to descend "all the way down to this point of spacelessness, / away from your spacious home that calls you back"—*scender qua giuso in questo centro / de l'ampio loco ove tornar tu ardi* (*Inferno*, Canto II, 83f.) This lack of comprehension does not cast any doubt on Beatrice's mission as protector and muse; indeed, perhaps she can only become the poet's muse because, with a form of saving blindness, she augments the brilliant man who feels driven to descend into the center of unaugmentability, the melancholy depths.

This reveals what one might consider a knowledge-guiding interest in the regression of poetry into the heart of darkness: the poet is forced to understand something that defies human understanding—the nature of an infinite negativity that has cast its shadow over his life. The far-reaching intuition of Dante's infernology is that the rejection of communion with God can become a causal power in its own right, and that the naysayers lock themselves in rings of autogenous failure. The archetype of such negativity cannot be found anywhere but in the Luciferian position; there the unity of ossification and denial has been permanently achieved.

Never was the business of thought further removed from the philosophical harmlessness of seeing evil merely as a lack of good. What late antique authors such as Proclus, and consequently the Christian arch-mystic Pseudo-Dionysius the Areopagite had to say about the insubstantial nature of evils are, from a Dantesque point of view, no more than the feeble rhapsodies of overprotected monks. As the portraitist of the devil and the ontologist of the anti-spheric space, the poet understands how something can come of denial after all, and how rejections and privations can nonetheless produce compact, sterile environments and entangled non-vironments.

On his trip through the counter-kingdom, Dante makes a far-reaching formal-ontological discovery: every damned soul is caught in its own Around, which is formed by insistent denials. It would be a malicious exaggeration to call this Around a world, for the eternal presence of constriction parodies the givenness of a lightened, space-providing universe. All that remains of what, in the open, was called "the world" is its resistant, injurious and sticky character. That is why the delinquents keep their bodies, provided they meet the requirements for fixing a soul to a torture. The body is the minimal world used to imprison humans in casings of torment. That is what torturers would teach if they were employed by anthropology departments; without torturology, the human sciences are missing a substantial branch.

As far as the adversary is concerned, he must in all ontological seriousness be understood as the founding hero of a subject form that resides at the center of a great empire of denials. As the bearer of all privations, he is thus acknowledged—at the phenomenal level, at least—as a powerful something and a tremendous someone. From his pole, he pervades the creation like a counter-sun radiating beams of cold; these surround the freezing point of being with wide rings, where countless souls have become trapped in the *imitatio diaboli*. His anger produces enough cold to supply the entire lower and central world with negativity, which means self-enclosure. If the highest devil can captivate followers and keep underlings, it is because denials are infectious and because the shining role model of evil mobilizes great followings of those locked within themselves. Dante's hell presents the first individualistic wave, as it were—everyone for themselves and all for the devil. The collection of all individual egotisms to form a great empire with its own style is the purpose of this infernography, whose comprehensiveness is dismaying. It shows how negativity turns into a space of its own special type, and wherein this closing principle lies.

The poetic substantialization of hell was a great feat in the history of reflections on the human condition, because it led to the discovery of the anti-sphere—or the depressive space. It provided the first characterization of the human being through the possibility of sphere withdrawal and world-deprivation. With heroic patience, Dante explores an "end of the world" in which all soul partitions and augmentation by the second party have ceased. Because medieval thought does not tolerate masterless spaces, however, even the depressive space is assigned its own ruler. Hell must therefore present itself in the shape of an empire: its highest inmate preserves the feudal form as the great lord, while hell itself follows imperial protocol. If this condition could be over-turned, Dante's Satan would easily be recognized as the exemplary bearer of humanity's risk in its Modern Age interpretation.

His is the first case in which the phenomenon that would be discussed in the twentieth century using the precarious ontological name of "being-in-the-world" is a fully evident state. The devil is wholly in the world, for he acts from its center—as the principle and model of incorrigibly immanent, strictly "self-referential" relationships. Anyone wishing to understand the metaphysical structure of the medieval cosmos must not for a moment over-look the fact that a fallen angel weeping acid tears from six eyes resides at its frozen center. He, the toppled adversary, is the first and only one to be wholly in the world, for he is the first and only one to have lost the divided world. He is the classical indi-vidual, ontologically impoverished in typical modern fashion, in that he before all others felt the compulsion to settle into an anti-sphere that revolved purely around him. He is the first point with no counterpoint, the first unaugmented, the first solitary dweller, who rotates in furious attachment to his hurting self as a center with no counterpart. Dante's decision to place his prince of hell at the absolute center of the physical universe makes it seem as if this position were the center of an intimacy. In reality, the position of Satan, however interned and centered it may appear to be, is an absolutely external and eccentric one. As the lord of the kingdom of grief, he is at once its frozen observer. He describes his land using the difference between despair and hope, choosing the dark value in every case. Thus the view of hell as the highest form of deviant inner-worldliness only reveals half the truth about infernal conditions. The other, darker half is only seen at second glance: hell is the outside.[10]

On Depression As a Crisis of Extension

As we have seen, the classically metaphysical interpretation of the world is inseparable from morphological optimism, which manifests itself in the conviction that all things are contained in flawless ethereal circles. This insistently bright view of things expresses the conection that everything existent inherently longs for security in the most exquisite shape. Just as each thing in itself strives to share in the best shape of its kind, it also wants the world around and beside it to have the best, beautifully expanded and well-rounded shape. If the Old European philosophy of spirit and light was able to summarize its essence in the Eriugenic theorem *omnia quae sunt, lumina sunt*, "all things that are, are light," then classical metaphysics should have declared the principle that everything existent is in circles: *omnia quae sunt, in circulis sunt*. The Cusan helped this view gain doctrinal status with his thesis that the whole of philosophy was arranged in a circle; *tota philosophia in circulo posita dicitur*. Classical philosophy was convinced that its circling thought movements—from the explicit to the implicit and vice versa—corresponded to the constitutive law of the existent. Anyone who had not entered this bright circle had never thought in the philosophical sense.

Until Heidegger, this faith in the circle as the father of all produced and perceived things remained alive. By being safe in good circles, everything—along with its rank in the whole—was given the formal seal of its well-formedness, which also included being recognizable as assigned to a corresponding intelligence. Each thing is fully itself only in its sphere, which is in turn harbored by the sphere of all spheres.

"The world is round around the round being," writes Gaston Bachelard. It is skins and horizons that hold the living within living boundaries. In the divine circumference, skin and horizon become identical. In the warm nights of being, isolated life feels itself dissolved amid the vital orb. Existence in such good circles, then, would always mean being in the right place.

Depression has a different truth; it experiences the world under reversed spatial conditions. This initially manifests itself in reluctance towards the imposition of having to listen to adverts for the successful. And the positive is undeniably always in an easy position, as it runs in a circle where good leads to good. Because circles of happiness are wide, no one moving about inside them risks running into a wall. The basic experience of depression, on the other hand, says something else: the walls have moved so close together that no meaningful movements are possible in the area they encompass. For the depressed, the circle is a form that closes them in; what should have offered harboring now encloses isolated life as a prison wall. Thus the depressive movement, as much as it might be a rotating one, in no way resembles the heroic round trip that measures the world circle. It has nothing in common with the prototype of successful circular motion on a grand scale, namely the *Odyssey*, which develops the hero on a delayed homeward journey into a skillful, worldly and complete person. Those seized by depression are condemned to world-poverty, for their further journey halts and their horizon implodes. Wandering through their cell, the prisoner experiences nothing but the stark symmetry between the outward and homeward journeys, which is the epitome of bad traffic—for traffic is always bad if the outward journey does not take precedence.

Something that leads nowhere is unrecognizable as a path, be it the one there or the one back. Where there is no path, and no method for walking it, nothing is accomplished, nothing learned, nothing achieved, and nothing clarified. The horizon does not unfold, and the distant points are not charged up with attractions. While there would always be far more to say about an ongoing or completed odyssey than has so far been presented, depressive states never yield worthwhile reports. They find themselves incurably banal. Part of depression is the unalterable self-evidence that nothing of one's own is worth talking about; none of its experiences would merit being thematized; they will never be the concern of speaking communities. The world feeling of Rilke's panther, which walks around in its cage and no longer senses any world behind bars, corresponds to the filter through which the depressive sees the world, no longer able to reach even that which is nearest.

In spherological terms, depression expresses the annihilation of the space of relationships. The good space disappears if the radius that had kept point and counterpoint intensively apart in a shared circumference collapses. A world with no radial energy is the anti-sphere—an arbitrary surrounding of a partnerless point. While the vital radius—the spatial phallus or spheric tension—is the upper beam that shines on the horizon, the faintly lit and radially deficient world of the depressive shrinks to a horizonless, immediate presence that has once more approached the animal's poverty in world—with the difference that depressive poverty in world betrays a specifically human ill-feeling because, even as a deprived mode of being-in-the-world, it still has an ontological aspect.[11]

What is given to the depressive—pale circumstance—still remains the world as a whole, even if its givenness is defined by withholding. The world here exposes itself as the impossibility of undertaking anything within it that would make a difference to the actor. What withholds itself in this manner is the whole of spheric, augmented existence. Where there is no spheric disten-sion, there can be no space into which a changing action could be taken or an effective word spoken. The power that would be given to the sphere by its curvature has no effect on the limp self. The whole: an empty circumstance around a tensionless point.

The counterpart of this imploded space is the universally resented, broad surrounding space of paranoia, that "universe of separation" in which Rousseau's Saint-Preux, the hero of *Julie, or the New Heloise*, feels trapped: "My soul in the press, searches to pour out, only to find itself everywhere restricted."[12] Elsewhere, Rousseau writes of one of his figures:

> There had been found an art to make for him of Paris, a more frightful solitude than caves and woods, where, in the midst of men, he finds neither communication, consolation, nor counsel [...] everyone surrounds him and stares at him, but draws away from him."[13]

To the depressed person, all that seems possible are repetitions of rotations within themselves; nowhere do they see a point of entry for a space-creating action. On the contrary, space contracts ever more for them. The Swiss diarist Amiel combined this reduction of extension with an advance into death:

> Death reduces us to the mathematical point; the destruction which precedes it sends us back by increasingly narrowing concentric circles toward that final and inexpugnable refuge. In anticipation I savor that zero in which are extinguished all forms and modes.[14]

Here Amiel divulges a shared secret of depression and metaphysics: that one's own anticipated death opens the way to a perverse and pleasant immunity.

Depression has a touch of that evil which tradition called metaphysical because it augmented the unease at malevolence with a realization of failure. The source of the evil can be named: the impossibility of relocating into the open is a paralysis of the positive capacity for transference. If departures into space normally transfer the basic experience "extension is good" (infants and imperialists testify to this), depression transfers the traumatic immobilization of the extensive capacity: the inaccessibility of the augmenter that is experienced at an early stage. In the augmenter's absence, the space collapses and causes the subject, which is trapped in an inexperienceable narrowness or expanse, to shrink to its panic-stricken self-point. With the transference of this being-point, the history of loneliness begins.

End of the parenthesis

The medieval discovery of a language of depression initially followed with topological necessity from insights into a macrospheric relationship: it first spoke of the early official estrangement of the devil from his divine master and counterpart. The depressive situation was not discovered in a private or psychological context, but rather as a public and political conflict between the sovereign and his creature. Satan appears as the dissident of a God who is the lord of all ranks, not a private genius. The estrangement of these opponents leads not to frosty or poisoned intimate relations, but rather the creation of a veritable counter-world, an anti-spheric outside. (Something similar often takes place in the dead phases of mystical hyper-relationships between God and the soul.[15]) Thus depression is initially marked on the map of the existent as a zone in which the negative existences are officially at home.

The deprivation of being thus appears as a public relationship. The primary circle of the devil,[16] which comes from rebellion, is the statically rotating point in which the fallen angel meditates on his future non-relationship with God in plain view. This point too is a "kingdom"—for around it, there develops an empty space in which nothing that could be communicated in the mode of sharing comes into being. An empty expanse gapes open senselessly around an empty narrowness in which the individual arranges themselves, as if in a rotating capsule that functions as their *primum mobile*. Further rings of narrowheartedness and indifference can be set up around the first orb of narrowness. It is the self-hating self-pity of the First Lost that keeps the ego capsule in constant rotation.

That is why the central position of the fallen angel in the cosmic space has metaphysical meanings: the center of hell is the point in the world from which the inaccessibility of the world to the one who resides there can be observed. Satan enjoys a full panoramic view, which reveals to him the scale of his world-loss; he possesses the Parmenidean spatial eye to contemplate the abundance of his deprivation; his amphiscopy encompasses the whole panorama of what he has lost. For him, theory and self-torture have thus become the same thing: his sight is his suffering, his circumspection his symptom—the world pains him on all sides. He is the one theorist to whom the puerile assertion that classical metaphysics ever managed to become a strictly closed system and a metaphor-free final vocabulary actually applies. What are mere suggestions, dismissed in minutes, in other so-called philosophical systems constitute a substantial closure in the case of the melancholy devil. Thus he alone could have a well-founded interest in de"con"struction, if he did not know all too well that his *clôture* is a perfect one. His greatness lies in the fact that for him, world-withdrawal keeps completing itself endogenously. His vision spans the whole of the hopeless. While ordinary little devils, by insistently fighting circumstances, ultimately even become worldlings of a sort, the great Satan places a chasm between creation and himself that is not bridged by any habituation. He who has denied the most can dispense with the most; it is the *unum* and *totum* that is withdrawn from him through his great refusal. He has negated being-in within the divine sphere, and now experiences how the negated circle excludes the negator.

The negation of spheric union produces exactly that anti-spheric all-round isolation which characterizes the depressive position. Among numerous non-enjoyments, this one has the certainty of possessing a fully closed system and using a final vocabulary, that of despair. The devil alone succeeds in perfectly closing his system of knowledge, because he alone knows how to close the gate of hell behind him logically. For him, the unconditional depressive, the world is everything that ceases. Evidence is possible only in the lost, not the given. In this sense, Satan is a historicist; the good is everything that is over. To understand the metaphysician, one must understand the depressive; to understand the depressive, one must understand the devil; and understanding the devil means comprehending his circle. The devil's circle is movement on the safe path of the non-escape.

In his neo-Gothic illustrations for Dante's *Inferno*, Gustave Doré captured the essence of Satan's existence from a modern perspective by depicting the lord of the underworld in the pose of the melancholy genius, leaning on his arms with an empty, defiant gaze, all suppressed grief and impenitence, trapped in a dismal grotto at the frozen depths of the world. His surroundings are filled with the icy wind of his beating wings. In this late Romantic projection, Satan appears as a Saturnian nature; he is a rebel who rejected the status quo out of weariness and views what is to come as the epitome of that which will fail. He protrudes from the ice defiant, brilliant and exposed, too proud to consider an alternative to being-in-hell.

Though this post-Miltonian modernization of the devil is very far removed from Dante, his infernography already contributes elements to a phenomenology of negativity that remains valid beyond medieval conditions. Even his devil, though presented as a naïve monster with three colored, teeth-baring faces, is a subject that has chosen itself over existence in open communions and ended up in a situation that recognizes hopelessness all around. Trapped in his anti-sphere, he is no longer familiar with any intimate augmentation; no companion bursts his capsule, no division of the inner world gives him a sense of the volume of the ensouled space. His greatness stems exclusively from the pathos with which he defends his isolation. Through his self-choice, the rebellious angel has become the prototype of self-referential intelligence. He is trapped in his surrounding anti-sphere, which can soon rightly be termed the "environment."

This devil, who cannot escape the negatory anger that compulsively turns him towards himself, is the model for every self-referential body in an all-round environment. He epitomizes the utterly determined self-preservation of an isolated life founded on distrust. Indeed: bodies conceived as separate, which refer primarily to themselves and can only tolerate other things as a facet of their self-reference, are programmed to function in agreement with the devilish point inside themselves. Only from there do they know what seems to benefit them, and only from there do they survive at the expense of what is ready-to-hand and present-at-hand for them as their environment. The mode of this self-reference, the predominant thinking-of-oneself and unconditional having-to-favor-oneself as a fighting and desiring point of power in the eternal battle, is—in terms of the classical schema—Satanism in action. For modernity, it is nothing but the innocent *a priori* of individualism.

One can conclude from this that Lucifer is merely an outdated figuration of what philosophy calls the world spirit; once acquainted with its original form, one will also recognize its renovated forms. The ruler of this world is the ruler of systems. This principle of egotistical intelligence can only exist *a priori* in a fractured state inside countless body spirits or individuals, which are then assembled to form the ruling super-egotists, Leviathanic

Dante, *The Divine Comedy*, *Inferno*, Canto XXXIV, 20–21:

"Ecco Dite" dicendo, "ed ecco il loco,
ove convien che di fortezza t'armi."
"This is he, this is Dis; this is the place
that calls for all the courage you have in you."

states, profit-seeking businesses and self-serving corporations. The sum of these self-referentialities produces the epitome of modern self-preserving reason and its embodiment in systemic egotisms.

In this respect, Niklas Luhmann's current and symptomatic general systems theory should be acknowledged primarily as the last neutralization product of Satanology. In the form of a science of the finite, embodied intelligences, it examines with admirable acuity the active autisms that occupy their ecological niches. This doctrine clear-sightedly recognized the point at which phenomenology and diabolism converge. Viewed against the relief of Old European metaphysics, it undertakes everything to acquit and de-infernalize the finite minor devils, or rather organized reasonable subjects—who could not possibly think or act selflessly in relation to the divine pole even if they wanted to, being primarily stuck in their body-fixated self-reflections, traditionally known as selfishnesses, without any real alternatives, whether these manifest themselves as individual egotisms, corporate egotisms, state egotisms or—why not?—as church, sect and helper egotisms. With Luhmann, Nietzsche's postulation that the world pictures of Old Europe had to be cleansed of the residue of moralizing *ressentiments* is in good hands. Indeed, where would metaphysical *ressentiment* have manifested itself more intensely than in the traditional grudging taboo on the egotism of the others? Through the neutralization work of system-oriented thought, the old inferno is sublated into familiar worldly conditions—until it spreads evenly over all circles, which must ultimately mean purely themselves after all. Whether one then prefers to join the misers and profligates in rolling heavy burdens towards each other in the fourth circle of Dante's hell or to assume a position at the negotiating table in a bargaining round for public services is more a question of taste than a metaphysical choice.

The psychohistorian is forced to ask how it can be that modern readers—leaving aside period-specific allusions that have become incomprehensible—can receive Dante's infernal cantos as if they were the script for a contemporary film adapted to the audience's taste. What ensures that these images of human bodies wading through thick mud and diving into hot rivers of blood, bodies that are snowed upon by flakes of fire and cooked in ember-filled coffins, lost souls that wrestle with constrictor snakes and stand frozen in ice floes, unfailingly appeal to the imagination of people who have been convinced of the unreality of otherworldly hells for centuries? From a psychodramatic-scenological perspective, the trans-epochal legibility of Dante's infernography stems from the by no means self-explanatory fact that knowledge of narrowness and infernal empiricism amount to the same thing. Anyone who has experienced the excesses of fear and the pain of constriction first hand, or can at least imagine themselves undergoing them, is always already accessible for messages from the dark dimension.

Viewed from this angle, the poet's underworld account provides a phenomenology of depression spaces that outlasts its connection to medieval world picture premises. This seems amazing if one considers that although Dante claimed prophetic competencies in his work, he was far from having any psychiatric pretentions and had no inkling of an autonomous secular psychology. Nonetheless, his great journey through the three-tiered beyond not only becomes an objective experience, but also a great psychoanalysis, and even more a primary therapy with which he worked his way out of the crisis encapsulated in the enigmatic opening reference to the dark forest, *nel mezzo del cammin di nostra vita.*

Dante's poetic psychotherapy profited from an upheaval in the world picture that was already a century old in his time, and which must be understood from an elaborated modern position as the decisive metaphysical prelude to the flourishing of bourgeois psychiatric and therapy culture between the eighteenth and twentieth centuries. Through the "birth of purgatory," as Jacques Le Goff puts it, the twelfth century had seen the introduction of the distinction between hopeless and hopeful penitential suffering among humans on which, since then, all notions of progress in post-medieval Europe directly or indirectly depend. It is not only the idea of progress that comes from purgatory, however, for the whole of recent psychotherapy culture—taking a detour through the idealistic and materialistic theories of estrangement and reappropriation—is a well-encrypted continuation of the high medieval concept of the transitional hell. With an eagerness that is still baffling today as soon as one takes a closer look at the documents, the contemporaries of the purgatory revolution took up the new idea and pounced on this Third Place, which abolished the earlier inexorable choice between bliss and damnation.[17]

Through the invention of purgatory, Europeans developed a taste for the middle and the adventures of dialectics. Only the distinction between the hell of purification and that of damnation enabled the flight to goal-directedness that helped Europeans to develop their characteristic knack for working themselves out of unfavorable circumstances. Chateaubriand remarked, "Purgatory surpasses heaven and hell in poetry, in that it offers a future which the other two lack." The poetry of purgatory stems from the division of hell into a hopeless and a hopeful one. Hope was only able to become a principle because certain hells have an exit. Without purgatory, the people of the Modern Age would never have understood the salvific significance of constant effort and striving. Without purgatory, there could be no separation of depressions; without the difference between purgatory and hell, there could be no identification of the curable and incurable. Even Freud's still-opaque distinction between melancholy and mourning followed the old lines drawn between the candidates for hell and the aspirants for purgatory in the High Middle Ages: between those who never want to get over an unspeakable loss and bury themselves with their holy deficiency in an inner grave, and those who strive back through the tunnel of grief towards the light.

Had purgatory not been discovered—as a transit lounge between hell and heaven in which even the most severe, warped sufferings gained a prospect of liberation—the view of the absolute hell would never have been able to mature into the unprecedented completeness and cold-bloodedness that manifested itself in Dante's document and in later pictorial imaginings of hell. Only through the division of the hells into those of stagnation (the type found in his *Inferno*) and those of progression (as found in his *Purgatory*) did the phenomenology of human lostness become possible. Where the long wind of hope had been found again, the braver spirits could take it upon themselves to envisage realistically the futures of souls in the hereafter. Now they could dare to descend comparatively into the two hells, one of which—despite its infernal appearance—is already a forecourt to heaven, while the other indeed remains as hellish as its semblance to the end. Purgatory transpires in this examination as a

Pieter van der Heyden, *The Last Judgment* (detail), copperplate (1558)

phenomenal hell that ontologically already signifies the paradise for which it prepares souls, whereas the true inferno is marked by the coincidence of nature and appearance. Thus the road to hell never leads anywhere but to hell itself; closure is the hallmark of this institution. It remains inferno because it defines itself through a recursive movement that does not open up into purgatory, into a hopeful circularity that spirals out into the open. While Mount Purgatory is the site of cathartic processes, the true hell refuses any discharge and any distancing from evil.

Following this revolutionary distinction in the realm of negativity, Dante was able to set apart the total hell, where unalleviable constriction reigns, from the relative hell, where

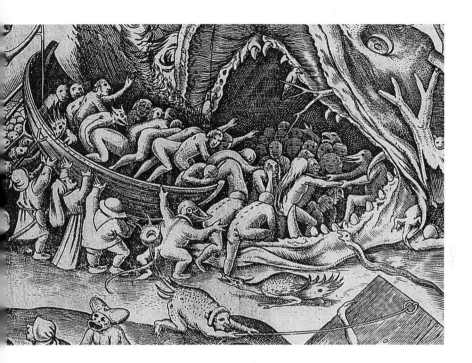

hardships are endured in the context of hopes. Correspondingly, he traverses hell with his guide Virgil as a dismayed but uninvolved observer, whereas he undertakes his visit to Mount Purgatory as an expiatory cure for himself in preparation for the third part of his journey through the afterlife: the guardian angel at the entrance draws the letter P seven times on Dante's forehead for the seven deadly sins (*peccata*), one of which can be erased after leaving each of the seven terraces of penitence. Here observation coincides with atonement, which is why the contemplation of purgatory has a directly edifying effect—just as reading a successful therapy account in our time is often therapeutic in itself—whereas the theory of hell, at least at first reading, cannot produce any moral result except pure deterrence. The progressive ordeals release heartening meanings, almost offering clean entertainment. Ghastly as it may be to see how the envious blunder about the second terrace with their eyes sewn shut, how the wrathful of the third terrace puff their way through dense clouds of smoke, and how the savable gluttons (as opposed to the unsavable ones in the third hell) rattle about the sixth terrace as diet-happy skeletons, vices and atonements here correspond to each other in edifying ways. Hence purgatory offers insights into God's economy, which rests on the distinction between redeemable debt and irredeemable guilt.

This purgatory is unmistakably a banking establishment in which a viable credit system conducts its transactions. Had not the church's sale of indulgences only been set in motion through the establishment of purgatory, which presupposes nothing other than a quantification of finite, redeemable debt? The rational equivalences between guilt and atonement confirm one's impression that in each individual case a temporary installment business is concluded to the satisfaction of both sides. Those who have overdrawn their account on earth pay back their debt in the transit hell. This lends the Dantesque configuration of hell and purgatory a certain early bourgeois quality: when the middle class entered the stage, it demanded—as early as the waning Middle Ages—the human right to proportionality. Even the most inferno-like part of purgatory, the fire in the seventh terrace that gave purgatory its German name *Fegefeuer* [cleansing fire], is no exception to this rule. The flames of purification in which the redeemable sexual sinners (here too there is, of course, also an irredeemable class) are set aglow remains a place of good prospects for the victims—firstly, because the workload is finite, and secondly, because of the convincing analogy between the literal and metaphorical burning.

Even in this penitential excess, which clearly oversteps the threshold of sadism, one finds an element of understandable logical equivalence, meaning that the graduates of the lechers' fire will cross over to heaven in full possession of their faith in the well-apportioned nature of their penance.

Things are entirely different in the genuine inferno, where the sense of proportionalities is eliminated along with the prospect of an end to the torment. Here lies the ontological basis for the infernality of the inferno: its essential trait is the disproportionate withdrawal of prospects combined with disproportionate physical suffering. This complete darkening produces the abysmal lack of equivalence between a finite crime and an infinite punishment. Dante admittedly makes an effort, even in hell, to construct equivalent relationships between the nature of the sin and its penalty in the style of a vague *nemesis divina*[18]—a relationship occasionally referred to as *contrapasso*, meaning "retribution"[19]—but these correspondences in quality are far outweighed by the disproportionate quantity and intensity. Virgil gets to the point at the very beginning: the delinquents here have "lost the good of intellect": *c'hanno perduto lo ben de l'intelletto* (*Inferno*, Canto III, 18). Hence there is nothing to be understood in these great infernal punishments, because each of them is given a supplement of infinite negativity that disables the principle of correspondences. Here too, the axiom applies that there is no relation between finite and infinite; *inter finitum et infinitum non est proportio.*

With the phenomenon of hell, the reality of an evil infinity is asserted. Yet even if it forever remains incomprehensible why one should suffer infinite evil in return for committing finite evil, every person will understand nonetheless what hell means for its inmates. What is amazing about the phenomenon of hell, therefore, is not so much that it could ever be conceived as part of a world order bearing the signature of a benevolent God as the fact that the unbearable conditions described in the infernographies immediately became *probable* for both authors and readers at the moment of their formulation and reception. While classical metaphysics made its notion of being-with-God plausible through the fantasy of an incorruptible bliss based on the models of a thinking thought and a loving love, infernology rested on the notion of an incorrectable despair demonstrated by experiences with hopeless imprisonment in the narrowest pain that eternally returns to itself. Only if this vision has a probability of its own kind does it become understandable why no one needs to have visited the Catholic hell to know what it would be like to dwell there. And this is precisely the widespread case both inside and outside the *mundus catholicus*. Conversely, it seems that Catholic figurations of hell, for their part, merely constitute the symbolic management of a store of primary fears and knowledge about narrowness with which a very large number of mortals are more abundantly equipped than any one of them can want.

Just as the powerfully developed macrospheres like empire, church and city could not come about without a transfer, however hazardous, of integral microspheric spatial concepts to the great unity, no hell could be set up without a violent re-narrowing of the macrospheric experience of width to the most torturous intimate states. The inferno grows from the intimism of the worst, where every subject is pasted into the restriction that would be most sensitive and terrible for it in unconfessable anxiety dreams. Psychodynamically speaking, this is why the indications of prenatal and perinatal anxieties return with obsessive regularity—even if one usually overlooks them, as all cultures develop specific blindnesses that render these signs illegible.

In numerous individuals, the birth they have survived leaves behind a deeply hidden, yet restless store of prenatal, claustrophobic scenic engrams and postnatal, agoraphobic ones; these are translated into permanently retrievable counter-claustrophobic and counter-agoraphobic basic moods and readinesses to act. In human birth, as depth-psychological research has shown, the two utmost awfulnesses can exist immediately alongside each other: unbearable narrowness in the synergetic fire and unbearable expanse in the postnatal ice. That is why inner and outer hells are radically different, yet scenically directly adjacent. The same applies to their symbolizations.

In the field of philosophical discourses, the first pole corresponds to freedom-theoretical and revolution-founding doctrines, which can be charged with private phobias as programs of eruption and extension; the other pole corresponds to the holistic doctrines of attachment and retrieval that openly display their character as harboring and warming programs. However one might view the Platonic concept of inborn forms, the schema of terrified memories of inner or outer hells—or both—born at birth undeniably has a real meaning for individual existence. Because countless people's memories of states, though by far not everyone's, store experiences of anxiety or abandonment analogous to hell, the later behavior of those who have escaped must include those imperatives of avoidance that claim eternal and universal validity. Those who were somehow born after all know for all time, without any reflection or need for justification, what must quite simply *never* happen to them again; they have a mark burned into their backs that tells them what must always be avoided in future. Because the concept of hell includes a dark, state-specific personal intuition, there is no need to rehearse the *second categorical imperative*, namely that the maxim of all actions must be to preserve the actors from new infernal presences—in so far as hell is that very state which must absolutely never (again) exist in the present.[20] In the birth of infernal phantasms—and their enactment in the form of tortures and exterministic actions—the imagination approaches this pole of "never again!" scenes and agrees to a wicked game with the temptation to re-enact them. As far as the concept of infernal punishment is concerned, it rests precisely on the reproduction of those scenes which should never have been allowed to repeat themselves.

Perhaps that is the psychological definition of the devilish: to have an intuition of what someone else would find most unbearable and to aim for its repetition. In topological terms, the idea or postulation of a hell rests on the assumption that somewhere in there and down there, in the ultimate space to avoid, there is a collecting point for infamous repetitions. If such a place holds a fascination for countless people, it is because it exerts a pull normally neutralized by the spontaneous intervention of the "never again"; in perverse communications, however, it can be released by a compulsion to repeat the event now more than ever.

The Christian sermons of intimidation on the last things, whose images and evocations were taken from Jewish apocalyptic literature, form the paradigm of a perverse metaphysical communication that can only have its turn by refreshing the pull through warnings and threats. Anyone who invokes hell arouses curiosity about it; whoever warns of it sends out invitations to the consciousness, which vaguely recalls having some business there. Especially after the introduction to high medieval distinction between different hells, the gates of fascination stood very

Dante, *The Divine Comedy*, *Inferno*, Canto XXVIII, 121–123:

> *e il capo tronco tenea per le chiome,*
> *pésol con mano, a guisa di laterna,*
> *e quell mirava noi a dicea: "Oh me!"*
> he held his severed head up by its hair,
> swinging it in one hand just like a lantern,
> and as it looked at us it said: "Alas!"

wide open for all interested parties. Now those virtually spared the worst could involve themselves with images in which symbolized memories received a chance to transform themselves into repetitions of states.

Dante's lower infernal city, Dis, which provides space for the four most abhorrent ring systems within its enclosing walls—including the infamous eighth, the Malebolge (evil pouches), with its ten torture ditches—is a true sum of the science of God-forsaken states. Every one of them appears as the eternal reinstatement of what should never have happened again. "Never again!" demands the human imperative. "Now more than ever!" replies the positive interest in hell. With intuitions that would be a credit to every prison camp builder, the poet's phantasms reproduce the agonies of the half-born as infinitely delayed execution procedures. Because human bodies can potentially be reminded of multiple tortures, the greatest imaginable torment can be evoked in manifold ways.

No one has ever accused hell of a lack of diversity. Here the almost-drowned are immersed again and yet again in a perpetuated drowning, in rivers of boiling blood of lakes of boiling pitch; the dismembered are continually reconstituted only to be torn apart again, "ripped open from his chin to where we fart" (Canto XXVIII, 24); the almost-suffocated are constantly suffocated again with a greater level of panic each time, while the almost-choked are squeezed to the point of bursting by repulsive snakes in fanatical strangulations. Those already in the depths of despair wander in circles on eternal death marches, bearing lead coats of ineffable weight. Bodies almost stuck in impassable tunnels are now immersed in narrow pits of fire from which only their feet and legs protrude, like breech-born babies from red-hot mothers.

Lucifer devours the arch-traitors Judas, Brutus and Cassius, engraving by Bernadino Stagnino (Venice, 1512)

At the hot-cold core of the universal constriction system, in the three grinding mouths of Satan, the arch-traitors Brutus, Cassius and Judas are tumbled, crushed and impaled as if in a memory-laden grinder composed of sticky mucous membranes and invasive teeth—just as flax is heckled and combed. Judas must endure being chewed up by his Satanic mouth in breech presentation, while Brutus and Cassius, Caesar's murderers, are in cephalic presentation with their bitten lower torsos trapped between the devil's teeth. Only in one case does the executioner's sadism of the poet appear to have failed: when he presents the high priest Caiaphas, who in the Christian account (John 11:46f.) was principally responsible for the sentencing of Christ, in an almost leisurely horizontal imitation of the crucifixion on the ground of the sixth *Bolgia*—when the infernotechnic point of Roman crucifixions was precisely to drive the delinquent on the vertical cross to despair through a re-enactment of natal suffocation with the help of his own unbearable body weight.

In the light of such images and the corresponding states, one wonders how such things ever managed to become part of a respectable metaphysics. How did sadism before de Sade attain teaching authority and pastoral power? Medieval infernography undoubtedly freed up politically interesting psychagogic energies by stoking elemental fears about the selectiveness of God. But the theologians of hell could not possibly have made God so terrible, and built up the adversary to so powerful an emperor of the underworld, if the substance of the counter-worldly states had not been embeddable by the pious clientele in an accommodating scenic or psychoplasmatic material. Thus all that needed to be done was to organize people's faith in the frightful places and tie it to plausible images of disgrace. Because infernography dealt with a place which—in keeping with the nature of things—none of those who spoke of it can ever have visited, there were only two ways to authenticate the hellish imaginings: they were either presented as graciously granted visions that revealed what was normally hidden, or they appealed to a culture-specifically developed pain imagination whereby the unimaginable pene- trated imagining after all. Dante drew on both approaches with the utmost success.

As far as the latter is concerned, the reception of his portrayal of hell turned into a test of resonance for the recipients, who would notice on their journey through the infernal ditches which symbols, which scenes and which ideas of torture captured their

Dante, *The Divine Comedy, Inferno*, Canto XXIII, 115–117:

> *"Quel confitto che tu miri*
> *consigliò I Farisei, che convenia*
> *porre un uom per lo popolo a' martiri."*
>
> "That impaled figure you see there
> advised the Pharisees it was expedient
> to sacrifice one man for all the people."

imaginations. This activated a reservoir of depressive schemata in them that one can assume to have been strictly private in character, because, as early acquisitions, they possessed the quasi-Platonic status of scenic ideas born together with the individual. They could be activated in perverse metaphysical communications. Perversion is initially a public matter, and is only privatized in a second step—and here lies the paradox of Christian church power, which for countless people became the hell from which it claimed to be saving them.

The imagined view of the infernal thus sucks in a pool of intuitions about depressive afflictions whose common trait is their disproportionality. In depressive suffering, the unimaginable is the most plausible. It is typical of the depressive's inferno that no action in the world can correspond to this state in the un-world, for the pain of despair, in its contourless omnipresence, has disproportionately outdone the world itself and every possible action within it, however bad it may have been, and distorted it to the point of unreality.[21] The unsettling element in medieval Christian communication about the infernal thus starts from the circumstance that an intuition of the disproportionately painful is already present in numerous people—*prior to* every deed or misdeed to which eternal punishment in hell might be God's response. This means that in depression, the punishment comes before the crime and desperation before its cause. The résumé of the depressive can be interpreted as an attempt by despair to bring about its cause after the fact.

Medieval infernography brought this depressive paradox halfway up from the depths of the unspoken by emphasizing the divide between finite human sin and its infinite infernal consequences; at the same time, it attempted to preserve the semblance of divine justice by asserting an if-then relationship, however weak, between the sin and its repercussion. All the players in the wicked game of infectious communication about the greatest evil knew, however, that this consequence-logical bond was a fragile one, and it was precisely because this excessive suffering was so flimsily justified that all talk of hell exuded such terror and exerted such a mighty pull. Behind the morally pseudo-reasonable if-then loomed the shadow of the unfathomable. The medieval sublime revealed itself to the meditation on the monstrousness of God with which the disproportionate irrupted into the imagination.

Infinite suffering cannot possibly be earned by finite deeds; or at least, whatever calculation this deserving rests upon cannot be grasped by human intellects. That Christian infernology nonetheless posited infinite suffering as a consequence of one's own freely chosen actions provoked a never-ending inquiry into the reason for this disproportion. In Dante's hell too, equations between earthly misdeeds and eternities of torture do not add up any more than in every other infernal phantasm, as the step from the crime to its consequence can only be taken through an irrational leap tantamount to a calculation using the value of infinity. For what integral equation could lead an infernal judge to the conclusion that humans who occasionally or habitually forged money, engaged in sodomitic acts, uttered heretical doctrines, gave bad advice or practiced alchemy should be submerged in boiling pitch or kept locked face down in narrow burning coffins? The only answer to this question that does not cause thought to decline into malign irrationalism could underpin itself with the existential *analogy* between the sinner's bad modes of being before and after his death—leaving aside the escalation for a moment.

Medieval infernology in fact insisted—taking up the terms of Augustine's doctrine of the last states in the dark later books of *The City of God*—that it was not God who had created bad will and the states of those trapped in it, for evil could only be explained with reference to its epigenesis from abused human freedom. Then hell would be nothing other than a melting pit of states resulting from free refusals of communication with God. These refusals would be the stuff of which hells are made, and what Dante depicts in his fatal *Bolge* would be the self-torturing nature of human negativity. As it was out of the question in any orthodoxy for God to be identified as the originator of radical failure, whatever could not be attributed to the good source had to come from a second origin, which was usually found in the human freedom to do evil. Without this premise, the factual existence of a hell—even the mere thought of its establishment—had to be attributed directly to the creator God; but then the lord of heaven and the *civitas Dei* would have been exposed by his failed creation, for a created world that had to be augmented by a hell due to inevitable implications of the creation would have to be viewed as a miscreation—a notion that was repeatedly and openly formulated in dualistic theologies from late antiquity onwards, while the Catholic defenders of the good totality always had to ensure that the ill-made, along with its infernal collection, was interpreted as an ingredient that stemmed purely from the works of abused human freedom.

If one follows the orthodox claim, it brings the cryptic relationship between depression and freedom sharply into focus. A candidate for hell should not merely be someone who has fallen victim to their own recklessness, and they certainly cannot be imagined as a carefree sinner who learns of the nasty surprise of

Willenborg's car looping (1952)

their damnation *post mortem*. They could only have provoked or earned hell, if at all, by failing to take up offers to escape it in full awareness of the consequences. Even the nefarious merriment of Don Giovanni, who is pulled into the flames in full view, does not meet the requirements for a deserved referral to

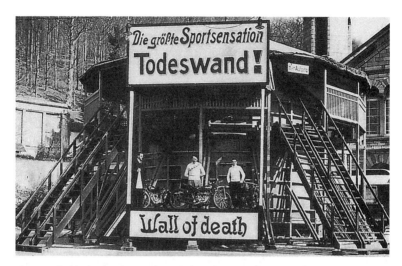

Steep-walled cylinder (motordrome) for motorcycles: Pitt Löffelhardt's "Wall of Death" (1932)

hell. Infernal admission would instead depend on the sinner having immersed themselves sufficiently deeply in a hell during life to know which evil's perpetuation needed to be avoided. It would not be enough that the impenitent mortal had spread themselves out in their life of wrongdoing with phallic cheerfulness; rather, they would have to have been in the real hell on a trial basis so that an informed interest in escaping it could be attributed to them with absolute finality.

This means that they should have acquainted themselves with the highest depression in a hell before hell—and now the argument of freedom becomes trapped in a ruinous circle. For anyone who experiences depression from within is *eo ipso* too tormented to make any choice, and anyone who still feels able to choose does not realize how far the torture can go. Therefore, either the delinquent knew sufficiently well what hell is to find in themselves the

Grid globe from the 1920s for the "death loop": the Varannes brothers training for the "death cross"

spontaneous "No!" to being eternally enslaved in it; but then one could not speak of a decision in the valid sense of the word, as the genuinely infernal far exceeds the candidate's freedom to decide for or against it. If an unfortunate currently found themselves there, there would only be a pain in their place that could long for nothing but an end with no prospect of return—which automatically eliminates the notion of choosing or re-choosing hell. Or, on the other hand, the candidate did not know enough about hell, and was lured into the trap of a misunderstanding.

So if the freedom theorists submit that because of their willful distance from God, the sinner has already sunk sufficiently deep into the infernal to imagine what its perpetuation would mean, they deviously gain this argument using a softened concept of hell in which every egotistical moment becomes charged with exaggerated infernal implications. Here the hellish is equated with security in the false, and presented as something with which humans can be at peace through sinful habituations. Theorists of alienation such as Fichte and Adorno used such arguments to attack the delusions of bourgeois and petty bourgeois life forms as hellish circles of a perfect illusory life. But such hells of error and convenience have little or nothing to do with the hells of acute agony evoked in medieval infernographies without idealistic allegory. Only if a smooth transition is possible from conditions in the comfortable hell to those in the uncomfortable hell can the thesis of hell as self-chosen and self-earned claim a minimum of plausibility. Because such a transition from affirmable and bearable conditions to non-affirmable and unbearable ones is impossible, however, and because there is an unbridgeable chasm between the one hell and the other, the freedom argument must fail here.

Hell cannot be reached from the position of freedom. No free will or free life could ever enter it, no matter how much guilt had been incurred by some malign individual. Hell cannot be the morally conclusive result of a lived life; I cannot earn hell. This makes it all the more amazing that humans nonetheless know about it, as if they had been there or had criteria for evaluating accounts of it. Yet no one can ever show conclusively how one

Fairground attraction from the 1990s: Huss Maschinenfabrik, amusement park, Bremen

arrives there—even Dante makes no attempt to describe any trial or sentencing process.

What is the meaning of this disproportion? If hell constitutes the epitome of the morally inaccessible, what does it mean that countless people testify to it as something that factually exists for them? If hell, as we know, is unreachable and unearnable from the responsible life on the one hand, yet informed infernographies are presented with maps of the surroundings, occupancy lists and torture rules on the other hand, this discrepancy tells us two things: firstly, that one must view the infernal separately from questions of access, and secondly, that participants in communications about hell can only have a positive interest in it because the concept of this place is useful for describing their own situation in being. This is precisely what characterizes the position of the depressive, who necessarily has a personal stake in portrayals of the depressive space because they feel the *tua res agitur*.[22] Their sensibility for hell feeds off the certainty that they already are or have been undeservedly in the place which could not have been reached deservedly. Thus the central Catholic question of what misdemeanors cause one to be sent there is inverted and transformed into an interest in the possibility of leaving it after undeservedly finding oneself there.

Thus hell ceases to be the monopoly topic of a moralized metaphysics of the afterlife. Rather, speaking of it becomes the yardstick for an ontological deduction of the factual. Deriving facticity means proving that it cannot be derived, only shown. Hell demonstrates more than any other phenomenon that existence takes precedence over essence. That is what post-metaphysical ontologists have to say: the brute fact of the givenness of something in something precedes every genealogy or explanation; "there is" defies all derivations. The primal gift and the primal coincidence cannot be harnessed by any principles of sufficient reason; coincidence is its own absoluteness.

As far as the inferno as a mode of primal coincidence is concerned, the ostensive "there" holds the complete proof of hell. Being-in-hell is a mode of being-in-the-world, in so far as world can also be given as *un*-world. Heidegger's fundamental principle of "thrownness" as pointing to underivable self-finding in a circumstantial totality called "world" is, in fact, only suitable to describe self-finding in hell; the throw of the dice into existence here results in being stranded on the worst side. (Thus humans are only thrown in hell; in a world, they would grow accustomed to it with time.) It is precisely the non-moralized hell that shows its claws in this finding: in a sense, having been there means being "still there" forever, as hell *per se* is defined as the place that only becomes what it is through its lack of exit. Anyone who has undeservedly been in the hopelessly infernal will, in a sense, always remain there—not because they do in fact deserve to be and remain there for some yet unknown reason, but because the factual experience of being there casts a shadow that no later light will ever fully dispel.

Hell is itself *and* its memory; it affects the temporal experience of those thrown into it as well as those who have escaped, occasionally or chronically bringing back its own in true retrieval. Having to remember the hopeless is one part of hopelessness. But even in depression, conversely, the hopeless and its memory are not everything. The fact that the hopeless—Cioran speaks of the heights of despair—can currently be viewed in the mode of remembering shows that there is a way out of the hopeless after all, a path that has not yet closed to form an infernal circuit once more, and maybe never will in that way again.[23] Everything depends on how the two facets—the hopeless and the way out—are placed in relation to each other. In their malign configuration, they yield what must, in a sophisticated sense, be called the vicious circle: the exploitation of the way out by hopelessness. The movement in which memory is systematically overwhelmed by repetition has the shape of a vicious circle; here the relative freedom offered by the way out is passed through as a curve that leads into repetition. If the more favorable configuration is found, this can produce the circle of purification in which the hopeless acts as the point of repulsion for the way out. In the circle of purification, remembering cancels out compulsive repetition; it should therefore be termed de-membering. The escapee does not return to the scene of the crime and its old circumstances, at least not of their own free will.

If we return to the findings offered by the *Commedia* equipped with these definitions, it becomes apparent that Dante's excursions into the two lower worlds already presuppose an efficient distinction between repetition and memory—or rather, the two lower places *are* themselves this distinction. Because there is a purgatory, an alternative to hell exists, and while the inmates of hell spiral in hopeless repetitions, the patients on Mount Purgatory subject themselves to the characteristic memories that will possibly bring about their escape from the fatal circle. If only the circles of purification can be traversed in a humanly meaningful way, however, why did Dante take it upon himself to descend to the very depths of the absolute hell? Why did the poet not content himself with visiting purgatory, and let the hopeless hell take care of itself? To answer this question, it is not quite sufficient to point to the conventions of scholistic correctness, which demands a triptych of the afterlife. Dante's images of hell have an irreducible experiential content that is not dogmatic, but rather phenomenologically and existential-anthropologically current. In bringing himself to seek out the harsh hell and the states found there, he declares that he too has a foundation of infernal knowledge that he has received like a necessarily undeserved prior knowledge. When true inmates of hell ask him why he has come, he has to invoke a higher directive. He is the memory man whom heaven wanted to view hell without having to remain there as a damned soul. When he returns, he will have been in hell in the knowledge that no sinful action had brought him there. He will only have been there in order to gain that of which his memory of the hopeless will be able to speak.

This privilege characterizes the position of the melancholic: he is the one who will live in the shadow of knowledge of the hopeless. An impenetrable mandate has obliged him to know about conditions which it cannot be good for humans to know authentically. He knows that what he knows is not good; but he also knows it is good to know about things of which it is bad to have first-hand experience. If, as Aristotle teaches, all humans naturally strive for knowledge, they initially and mostly—and likewise naturally—propel themselves away from that which it is not good to know. Nonetheless, there are insights into situations that were not striven for. No one naturally strives for knowledge of hell, and yet the experience of hell can arise unstriven for. Discovering you are there is sufficient to know what it is like there. As Kafka noted: "It is possible to know of the devilish but not to believe in it, because there is no more devilishness than exists anyway."[24]

From that point on, concealment of the discovery would have to be the goal of all striving—from which it follows that there must even be a striving for ignorance no less originary than Aristotle's positive appetite. But just as there are media of the will to knowledge, so too the will to ignorance finds its intermediaries. The *image* of the terrible usually serves as a figure of compromise between the pull of what has been uncovered and the concealing resistance to it. Hence the great cultic significance of terrifying images in many cultures: they are most effective in suppressing the things they represent. They confirm to the cult participants that they are in the place of representation—that is, in the language game—and not the place of what is represented—namely in torture. Informalized pictorial terror, however, as cultivated by modernity, also knows the reversal of the representational spell. Because the awful picture has handles inside and outside, as it were, users holding on to the image can be torn inwards by it if the pull exerted by what is depicted is stronger than their resistance.

So: although the poet wanted to remain at a distance from the terrible, he had descended into a hell which undeniably became his own by revealing itself to him and creating a resonance within him. Dante does not hide from his readers what happened to him *in extremis*, upon seeing Satan:

> *Ioi non morii, e non rimasi vivo;*
> *pensa oggimai per te, s'hai fior d'ingenio,*
> *qual io divenni, d'uno e d'altro privo.*
> I did not die—I was not living either!
> Try to imagine, if you can imagine,
> me there, deprived of life and death at once.
> (*Inferno*, Canto XXXIV, 25–27)

By speaking of the hell he was in, he succeeds in a feat no ordinary depressive could perform: he breaks the spell of the conviction that in the colorless, annihilated inside, there is nothing worthy of discussion in the open community. By turning towards the reader—here with a direct address, elsewhere in implicit fashion—he breaks free of his rigor mortis. With his appeal "Try to imagine [...] me there," he opens up the purgatorial dimension in the middle of hell. If you have any imagination at all, you will know how I must have felt in the innermost circle of hell, neither dead nor alive. And you, the reader, if you are not made of stone and are born of a mother, you will know in your own way what I am talking about. For I am not speaking of my hell alone, but also the one you can empathize with, as truly as you left a cave that had become too narrow in order to become the person you are; indeed, perhaps the attempt to leave the narrow cave simply transformed it into the hell as which it will appear once you have reached the other side?

This turn towards the reader leads to Dante's greatest discovery: purgatory is a place where the non-blessed will suffer *together*. Here suffering is tied to cognizance—co-suffering is possible because pain is capable of a peculiar publicness. Uncovered inter-depressive relationships are thus already the beginnings of paths leading into the open, while as concealed and secret ones they produce only the isolations of infernal circles. The inferno would become purgatory as soon as a communication beyond the boundaries of all communications had begun. If hell reveals itself in primally given de-solidarizations and excommunications, purgatory is constituted by the publication of the unspeakable in the community of the unholy. It is only in purgatory that the phenomenon which modernity would call *solidarity* truly can come about—the dissolution of the lonely hellish nights into sharable, finite, speakable complaints. This tendency towards sharing suffering finally makes it clear, in addition, why the journey into the worst in the *Commedia* always included the second, and why the poet in the lower realm would have remained empty and worldless without his co-poet. Virgil is the Great Other before whom and through whom Dante speaks, but the reader is the true other whom it is salvific to address, as they give the words a worldly address and a human future. This is where the miracle occurs: the poem combines authentic knowledge of hell with the distance that protects from it. Dante's infernography is a document that will eternally have proved that it is not only more beneficial, but also more interesting to get out of hell than to descend into it. If the undeserved hell were a fact, however, even in this one single case, the insight into its facticity would support its unconditional mandate to portray it as something that can, under certain circumstances, be left again. What these circumstances are will remain the poet's secret for the time being. But Dante made no secret of his ascent to the brightened space. The poet's return from the utmost prefigures therapeutic resurrection.

> *Quindi uscimmo a riveder le stele.*
> and we came out to see once more the stars.
> (*Inferno*, Canto XXXIV, 139)

Uscimmo—we came into the open, we went out: this is the only verb of motion that counts for insuperable enlightenment. It is the verb of birth and lightening. A "we" and a movement into the open: the alliance with life.

Closed knowledge of hell does not want to hear about exits; it acquires its own perfection by shifting thought into the heart of darkness. It carries out its reflective movement as a constantly renewed rejection of taking a run at vital projects and hopeful connections. It enjoys its victories in a constant submission to the need to expose the ridiculousness of good faith—of the poor dolt who keeps picking himself up and thinking he could go on. Infernal thought observes with a cold eye the urge of its hopeful part to propel itself away from hell, and erects the gate of hell again at the end of every escape route: hope must only survive as something abandoned, and it must keep failing until it takes itself for a part of the infernal circle. Thus despair claims to lay its own foundation, so to speak: it only needs to repeat itself in order to convince itself anew of its being and thusness. I despair, therefore I am. And how often am I as one despairing? As often as I think I am. Through a special form of self-reflection, an inward turn on the narrowest point, infernal thought presents its state as a result that is securely accessible and irrevocable for the subject. Dante himself immortalized the fiction of hell's accessibility from nonhell and the illusion of possible entrance into it with the inscription above his gate:

> PER ME SI VA NE LA CITTA DOLENTE
> PER ME SI A NEL ETERNO DOLORE:
> PER ME SI VA TRA LA PERDUTA GENTE.
> I am the way into the doleful city,
> I am the way into eternal grief,
> I am the way to a forsaken race.

Thus he too speaks as if finding oneself in hell were a matter of entering there. He too pretends that the lost are a group which can be joined. And he too gave the impression that unforgettable pain is something with which, having never felt it before, one can suddenly—through one's own fault—become acquainted. If this were the case, then hell could indeed be considered the possible destination of an outward journey. Then I could truly make myself despair, just as it was said of Satan that he chose and brought about his own fate.

But this desperate act, which is already problematic with the devil—positing oneself as desperate—remains as meaningless for every real individual as all merely formal self-relationships that follow this scheme: I grasp myself by making sure through an awareness-creating secondary grasping that I am as I am. No basic disposition can ever follow from this reflexive figure alone—neither the depressive, which is pervaded by inability, nor the manic, which is bursting with ability. The ego that posits, thinks, supposes, releases or invents itself must at all events let its content or disposition be dictated by its resonance with a sounding other. "Tonic" self-finding as one thing and another always precedes self-positing. Even the desperate individual cannot make themselves originally despair; they can only feel it, reflect upon it, and at most reinforce it through repetition. Despair can no more be attained through positings of the subject than hell could be a result of the sinner's irreverent life. Only if the fact of despair is given, and only because it is genuinely given in some cases, can reflection begin from this fact and devote itself to the exercise of envisaging itself lost. Yet despair never becomes the property of the individual; despair can become neither a result nor a personal achievement. Even in the devil's vicious circle, the subject can only find itself—not because it has produced the entire circle, but because it has suddenly found itself at its possible point of departure: undeserved, primally given, "thrown" being-in-hell.

The iron maiden of Nuremberg, torture instrument, in use from the 16th century onwards

Gottfried Helnwein, illustration for Edgar Allan Poe, "The Pit and the Pendulum"

To keep returning to the heart of darkness, one must be inside it. Finding oneself in it is the absolute coincidence that cannot be sufficiently explained by any entering, any arrival or any logic of reaching. Just as Plato did not consider it worth even hinting at the nature of the prisoners in his cave parable, a corresponding parable of hell could only begin with a crowd of unfortunates finding themselves in this place—at most, it could describe a saint or poet discovering the existence of a non-hell outside. Only the way out can be found, whereas hell itself is something that cannot be discovered or reached unless one is already within it.

That is what the storyteller Joseph Conrad showed in his novel *Heart of Darkness*, with a certain employment of exotic travel images and discovery metaphors. The philosophical trick of his tale lies in the fact that the tale of the discovery of the terrible has been relocated to a colonial décor, as if Conrad too wanted to reach the "true inner Africa."[25] For him, it is the dark continent that is elevated, in a willfully misleading fashion, to the scene of a radically modernized experience of the infernal. In the wilderness and among "savages," Conrad's hero Kurtz, an adventuring philanthropist, initially had nothing in mind but to check, in the service of the "International Society for the Suppression of Savage Customs," that all was in order outside. This culturally pious mission could not be accomplished, however, for the wilderness drew the civilization pioneer onto its side. Conrad's story initially confirms the exoticist clichés of the naïve European who is overwhelmed by the wilderness and turned into one of the very monsters he had set off to civilize. Rumors of his unscrupulous murders, enslaving bewitchments and orgiastic excesses circulate at the trading posts. When Kurtz is at last found by the narrator, he is already marked by a fatal disease; on his deathbed he wrestles with something terrible that his stay in the wilderness seems to have revealed to him, and he dies in a bitter agony, whispering "The horror, the horror."

If it seems at first glance that Kurtz had infected himself in the loneliness of the foreign continent with a form of African fever—the disinhibition of pre-civilizatory feelings that still remain present in civilization—the second glance yields insights into a pathological process of an entirely different nature. What Kurtz experiences against the African backdrop is a European and philosophical fever—not a Dionysian, but a fundamental-ontological one. His dismay stems not from the infectibility of the composed, educated and well-meaning individual by the intoxication that bursts open the civilized shell, but from defenselessness against his own realization of the absolute futility of the factual. In the shock of a collision with the naked fact of things, the individual who has fallen out of all harboring spheres discovers that whatever he does or does not do in this universe of proliferating factuality has no meaning whatsoever. Herman Melville would expose something related in his novel *Moby Dick* when he understood the color white as the manifestation of futility, the "colorless all-color of atheism."[26] In the face of the immeasurable green futility, the Congo adventurer feels as if he has been spat out of every shell and abandoned to his meaning-lessness. He discovers that the world in which he is undeservedly located is hell itself. It is nothing other than the indifferent machine of becoming that, inaccessible to allocations of meaning, continuously turns within itself.

If the discovery of pure facticity could so discompose an isolated European, this was because he saw the reality of his insecure state mirrored in the exotic hell of facts. It is the existential feeling of panic-laden immanence he brought along that breaks open in his African isolation. In the wilderness, the adventurer discovers the second anti-sphere—the depressive space in its cosmic maximum. Outraged, he stares at the primally given juggernaut of the real, humiliated and broken by the sight of the life process as it rolls on in absolute indifference. The anti-spheric minimum—the rotation of the despairing individual in the narrowest infernal circle of thinking oneself lost—and the anti-spheric maximum—seeing oneself surrounded by absolute unrelated externality—respond to each other as the two necessary poles of a depressive ontology. They belong together like the coincidental single point and its coincidental total environment. The despairing experience the gigantic quality of the depressive anti-sphere too as a siege by their surroundings. The dying adventurer draws himself up one last time and calls out to the wilderness: "Oh, but I will wring your heart yet!"—as if, even beneath the sky of the foreign continent, he were still trapped in a beating cave.

It is not the perception of existence in a factually present surrounding space as such, therefore, that shakes the discoverer of facticity. Rather, it is because the surrounding space gives the individual back his already effective cosmic isolation, and reveals his always-already-having-been-in-hell to him, that his cogito must become "I think that I am in hell." What seemed to be the wilderness transpires as the space of anti-spheric experience—the massive, factual, futilely moving world all around him as such, perceived from the all-round view of the isolated.

Thus the hell of the factual need no longer be a hereafter for one who finds themselves thus inside it; it need no longer be evoked symbolically and visionarily, as in Dante's poem; it is not a region on the other side that can be reached and traversed through a special upsurge of the soul, for it has always been present as an absolute, inescapably futile world on this side. The depressive subject is trapped inside it with no access to the shared, good space. For Conrad, of course, the old difference between inferno and purgatory has also become meaningless. What the African adventure contributed to the ontological apocalypse was merely its colonial-romantic scenery and the notion of an elsewhere in which terrible truths come to light with greater revelatory eagerness than in the European plush of 1900.

The exposure of naked factuality is a process than can only be understood in relation to what was the most advanced movement of European meaning-producing conditions at that time—it marks a phase in the transition from Old European-metaphysical to modern-postmetaphysical sphere formations. It belongs among the beginnings of foaming. While meaning could only be produced through predication on primal meaning, necessity and prediction in the metaphysical regime, modernity made the transition to a generation of meaning through projects informed by non-meaning, coincidence and prognostication. This unprecedented transformation is experienced by those involved as a nihilistic crisis, and its offshoots continue to be acute; for although a precarious state of postmetaphysical ordinariness has established itself in the main countries of the new economy of meaning, not least through the omnipresent medial mass sedatives, there are portents of dramatic convulsions in the transitional zones and cultures of resistance. A form of "meaning diet" is being maintained in the postmetaphysically correct core cultures of the West, while the marginal and reactive forces gorge themselves again, or still, on transcendent candies.

If unveiled raw facticity as such can already assume the meaning of hell, however, that meaning could soon also be found without colonial exoticism. Conrad's depraved hero in the Congo remains an Old European until his final agony, for he is unable to conceive of the naked facticity of the existent as a whole without experiencing it as horror; he is a final hero of the quest for meaning, a theologian gone astray. Standing on the outside, he paid tribute to the metaphysical genius of Europe as if for the last time by becoming a devil who rejected hell.

Barely two generations later, the authors of existentialism would coolly employ the equation of being-in-the-world and being-in-hell as the background to their doctrines of committed existence. For them, meditation on the naked fact became the skeleton key for a first, still uncertain, hysterized thought of the outside. Certainly the facticity machine had moved on by a few turns before they entered the fray, and the world wars had generalized both the gray and the grisly. Humans were not intended by the whole: this was a lesson every European could learn in the gears of their own civilization industry. The thinkers and storytellers of the old continent no longer needed colonies to advance their explorations in the heart of darkness.

In Sartre's 1944 play *No Exit*, contemporary infernology installed itself in the stuffy Second Empire salon of any given provincial hotel. That the heartless heart of facticity no longer had to be sought in exotic locations, for it rather permeated all local existences in their defiant finitude and determinacy, was now as evident as the fact that thought in general and the thought of the outside had to become the same thing. The outside is the most proximate, the innermost and the native, and everything inside is merely a molding or folding of the outside:

In circuito impii ambulabunt [The evil walk about in a circle], Psalm 12:8

one of the main tendencies in post-existentialist and post-phenomenological philosophy can be understood as the execution of this program. It leads the thought of the outside into its second wave; Michel Foucault set the tone for it.[27]

Structure and coincidence, machine and event, hardware and code—these leitmotifs combine in contemporary thought to teach humans their ek-static position on the edge of something that makes them possible and eludes them. Only the never-perturbed and those who were spared still keep the seemingly contemptuous secret of how to immunize oneself against the devastations caused by naked factuality. In a time of need, they preserve their sense of the necessity of positive sphere formation in the midst of universal externalization and depression. Too sluggish for despair, too harmless for philosophy, they alone still represent the motif of classical philosophizing: existence in a self-protecting space, with a small surplus of concern for things that lie slightly outside their core privacy. For the time being, it is the well-meaning bourgeoisie that make themselves useful both for philosophy and for the profane life as delayers of the end.

CHAPTER 7

How the Spheric Center Has Long-Distance Effects through the Pure Medium

On the Metaphysics of Telecommunication

> Just as little as a person sent into the city with a letter has anything to do with the contents of the letter but only with delivering it, and just as little as the envoy sent to a foreign court has any responsibility for the contents of the message but only for conveying it properly, so an apostle primarily has only to be faithful in his duty, which is to carry out his mission.
>
> I am not to listen to Paul because he is brilliant or matchlessly brilliant, but I am to submit to Paul because he has divine authority.
>
> The apostle is the one who has *divine authority* to command both the crowd and the public.
>
> — Søren Kierkegaard, "The Difference Between a Genius and an Apostle"[1]

True sovereignty belongs to someone who can be represented by another in such a way that they appear to be present in their representative.[2] That is why large enclosing spheres—whether constituted as political realms or emanation spaces of truth on the model of *ekklesia* or *academia*—rely on the development of the possibility of representation. Representation is both the emergency and the norm in the telecommunication of power. In ideal-typical terms, representation is always a matter of making the power center present at a distant point—as if the spheric center had the ability to communicate with every point on its circumference through representatives or emissaries as if actually present. This "*as if* actually present" expresses the advantage of the sovereign center in *staying* with itself, yet asserting its position in distant places on the radii around it.[3] The possibility of representation thus depends entirely on this "how." Whether representation occurs is determined by the question of whether and how the presence of the ruling principle is instantiated in the representative—both directly and indirectly. Sovereignty is inseparable from its long-distance effects.

If one speaks of real presence, in this tone and from this perspective, a twofold relationship is meant. Naturally, a presence is initially only actual if the power center or source is itself immediately present in its place of effect. When kings marched into cities—a primal scene of power display before the advent of fixed residences—they gave the peoples an opportunity to feel, with mouths open or fists clenched, the presence of power and perhaps even the proximity of salvation. It was said that every two years, the Early Dynastic pharaoh had to appear physically in each of the forty-two nomes (administrative districts), each of which contained a piece of the dismembered Osiris.[4] On his barge, accompanied by the great men of the kingdom and the Horus deities, he undertook the procession as an epiphany before the people. The procession is the archetype of power on the road: in processions it is not only the monarchs themselves who move about, for their representative images are also led about in the

Praesentia nocet [Presence is harmful], 17th-century emblem: radiant bodies should not get too close to one another

same ceremonial mode. Imperial Romans, Indians and Catholics attained the highest levels of pomp in such parades of images. As a child in the Frankfurt of 1764, Goethe still experienced the splendor—albeit ironically undermined—of a royal coronation *in praesentia*.[5] When the victor over the Prussian army, Napoleon Bonaparte, stayed near Jena in the autumn of 1806, Hegel conceptualized this presence by speaking of the world soul appearing on horseback.

Because the nature of the ruling center includes the ability to have long-distance effects as if it were in those places, however, the hallmark of real presence is that it makes the power holder present *in absentia*. Through sovereign creation of signs from within itself, power sends out representations that are present in its place where it is not, without being any less imposing for it. It must have the ability to be precisely where it is not as if it were there in abundance.[6] Kierkegaard characterized this relationship with the term "authority," a word whose legal form (as power of attorney) articulates an ontological state of affairs, or rather an onto-semiologial one (because it is a matter of pure being—whatever that might be—but always also the alliance of being with its preferred signs). The formula of positive onto-semiology is that if being is the sender, it remains present in the representatives' messages. (Conversely, the same applies in the negative: if there is no full sender, there can be no full presence in the representative.)

For Christian culture, the Catholic interpretation of the ritual holds the paradigm of a positive encounter between being and sign: in the Eucharistic act, the presence of the body and blood of Christ in the form of the bread and wine is actually considered a literal reality.[7] For the concept of the true icon too, the privileged relationship between the sign and present being is constitutive. Furthermore, this model concerns the official announcements of the kings and the proclamations of the gods, captured in oracular codes, and in subtler shades also the "hints" of being whose legibility Heidegger was convinced of as late as the last century. And finally, the art religion of the Modern Age taught that the abundance of the world's creative strength becomes present in the

Icon procession on Mount Athos

Pharaonic procession with placental standards

works of the genius. While ordinary signs usually only refer to something absent, and can represent it precisely for this reason, the eminent, authorized, actually present ones—let us henceforth say the signs of being—have the virtue of not only representing the power center *in absentia*, but also radiating it and testifying to its presence. The signs of being have a share in being itself; and they too are capable of being because they simultaneously show their sending power in a representative and a presentist fashion.

It is only thanks to this real share of full signs and authorized messengers in the overflowing reservoir of being-sender that the power center proves expandable and transportable—indeed, it can only attain effective spatial formation in large-scale units through the emission of messengers and signs. Where being and signs form a joint quantity, the concern is the power of the whole to be imposingly *there* in signs. Signs of being are signs of power, because they not only mean what they represent, but also embody it; a real sign should not mean but be.[8] But how can something that represents simultaneously be that which it stands for? Is the real presence of the signified in the sign itself even possible?

The example of the apostolic mission in early Christianity shows how a momentous case was given an unreservedly affirmative, albeit fundamentally problematic answer. One could go so far as seeing Paul the Apostle as the decisive discoverer of the principle of *real presence* in the shade of meaning that is effective to this day. Hence the argument over the possibility of real presence in works of art or holy texts is, in its deep structure, an argument over Paul.

The true emissary can evidently only represent the sovereign lord if they, as a bringer of signs, simultaneously share in the substance of their lord and create his real presence—just as Kierkegaard has Paul the Apostle express in a dialogue with a skeptic:

> "you must consider that what I [Paul] say has been entrusted to me by a revelation; so it is God himself or the Lord Jesus Christ who is speaking"[9]

The word "revelation" thus refers to a state of affairs that provides the basic conditions for all metaphysical telecommunications: by confiding in a special way in a chosen messenger, the simultaneously distant and discrete center makes him its representative. This envoy, in so far as he is authorized, is meant to bind the recipients of the message and have the power to hold them responsible for their reactions to it, as if the divine center were immediately

Pictures of Lenin at a May 1 procession on Red Square, Moscow (1985)

Jan Joest van Kalkar, high altar of St. Nicholai's Church, Kalkar (16th century): outpouring of the spirit

present. Hearing the messenger is meant to be tantamount to hearing the lord himself, and rejecting the messenger is the same as turning down the lord.

Paul's authority can therefore—at first reading—only come about if the messenger is unconditionally charged up with his message; its further practice will consist in nothing other than the clear and unimpaired conveyance of the same to its recipients. It puts the medium in a state that manifests itself before all mediatory work as the real presence of the lord in the charged messenger. It is only through this alleged presence of the sender in him that the messenger can pass on the message selflessly and undistorted, as if he were completely translucent and as if his own additions or inhibitions were insignificant for the passage of the message. Only if the messenger is a clear medium, then, can—in the ideal model—the message pass through him without any meaningfull addition or even co-authorship being introduced from his side; the envoy must become neuter, in a sense, as if he were nothing but a pure canal; building canals has always been a matter for lords, while cleaning them is the first servant duty—starting with self-cleaning. In this context one one cannot avoid recalling the Virgin Mary's submission, which is paradigmatic of the Catholic idea of obedience and mediatorship: Mary's womb, according to relevant documents, was a pure channel through which the God-man passed "like water through a tube"—*tamquam aqua per tubam.*

The mediality of the medium is thus indistinguishable from its alleged selflessness: whether Moses had a heavy tongue or whether St. Nicholai's Church or Paul wrote the most brilliant prose was equally meaningless for the use of these figures in God's telecommunication. For even if Moses had been yet more ponderous than he actually was, he would still have had to bring the law down from the mountain, inscribed on the two tablets which (even in the duplicate made after Moses' rage crisis) were written upon by the authentic finger of God. And if even Paul had been more eloquent than he was, a match for Plato as a thinker and for Shakespeare as a writer, his spirited and poetic additions to the Gospel would have had no bearing on the content of his mandate, for even as a great author he would not have had any more to say than that Christ was God's son, and that the way to salvation passed through faith in him.

The exemplary apostle can neither multiply the substance of his mandate through ingredients from personal talents nor impair it through idiosyncratic handicaps as long as he simply brings the message to its addressees and authenticates himself by declaring his mission. But the fact *that* he conveys the message and *that* it reaches the ears of a circle of listeners through him is an absolutely

Illustration from Jacob Böhme, *Theosophische Wercke* (Amersterdam, 1682)

historic act because, from an immanent perspective, he triggers the emergency of religious choice for the recipients.

On closer inspection, the pure being-medium of the apostle is thus by no means such a simple postman's or envoy's task as Kierkegaard's examples claim. For if the messenger brings a document to the city or the emissary carries out a mission at a foreign court, they may both be acting with a specific authority, but their mandate can be traced back to an actually existing, localizable and, philosophically put, finite sender who, however much might depend on him, still has the freedom to revoke his order. Under special circumstances, this sender could even decide to satisfy their interest in the execution of this particular communicative act in person. If necessary, the sender of the written message can appear before the recipient and thus change the written matter back into an oral one.[10] An actual king would be free to appear personally at a foreign court and render his representative superfluous in a direct confrontation between one majesty and another.

The apostolic mandate, on the other hand, cannot be revised through any regression to the immediate; after the ascension of the messenger, heaven no longer—assuming it ever did—delivers any messages itself; the state visit of the upper to the lower has become historical, and will remain unrepeatable for all time. (The same applies to the prophetological gap through which Allah, or rather his spokesman Gabriel, communicated in direct dictation to a human scribe, an illiterate named Mohammed, and which closed forever after this incomparable incident.[11])

In other words, the apostolate is a transcendent messenger affair that can never be entirely resolved through analogies with immanent telecommunications. Because the message, sent from over there and received here, is singular and paradoxical, the messenger too gains a singular, paradoxical status. The apostolic messenger becomes an irreplaceable agent in God's announcements, for if something should happen to this messenger, the sending God will not be able to appear to the world again in real presence to conclude his business. This already applies to the naturally unique intermediary, the God-man himself, but also to his first set of apostles, most of all Peter and Paul. Now and for all time, the summit meeting of this world and the world beyond would take place at the level of representatives. *Post Christum resurrectum*, the sender surrendered himself completely to the evangelical process, and since his withdrawal from the flesh has entirely become a news service (annunciation), a media society (church) and information processing (theology). Hence the two factors subordinate to annunciation, namely church and theology, depend entirely on apostolic authority, and cannot—for understandable reasons—have a more solid foundation than it does.

But is an authorization such as the apostolic one even sufficiently justified—at least, in the sense that the thought game "justifying" is usually understood? Because of its inner structure, the authentication of the authority can only exist in a self-justifying or circular fashion, and even its impressive historical success only comes into consideration as an indication of its truth, not a decisive proof. The only criterion that identifies the apostle as such is the fact that he himself says so—which means that the risk of believing the messenger can never be shared or alleviated. In truth-theoretical terms, it is untrue that billions of Christians cannot be wrong. Even if they were more numerous, they could still be merely a collective that has successfully organized its self-delusion; all of them together could have placed too much faith in a complex of misunderstood accounts. None of them possess more than the apostle's account, while the apostle himself can only repeat that he is saying what he was told to say and that he was told to say it. He must travel in this circle, and it is this circle that makes him strong. The existence of the Messiah who himself claimed to have arrived was already trapped in an analogous circle, as the question of how he could prove his messianic identity could likewise only receive the answer, "he himself says so" or "I am he."

With the apostle who presents himself as an authorized representative, regression to the final statement "he himself says so" introduces an even more convoluted situation, as the apostle is not speaking in his own name but passing on a message from another. He calls himself the envoy of one who called himself the promised one; he speaks not for himself but *for* the other, and even more *from* him. This is where the difference that determines the status of such claims intervenes: it is ultimately not the apostle himself who is speaking, but rather another speaking through him "as if actually present." That is why the formulation that he is speaking of another and for him is not sufficient to characterize the unique quality of the apostolic speech position. If he were speaking only *for* the sender he would remain an ordinary conveyor of signs, a *porte-parole*, like a government spokesman or the chief press officer of a major company; but then one would see him as a mere agent and hired voice box. He could never claim authority in the matter to which his message pertained. As the employee of a discourse-buying entity he would not be a sign of being, no authorized bearer of the absent-present truth, but merely the representative of a power that itself only represented another power, just as a company spokesman only represents a management, which represents a supervisory board, which represents the shareholders, who represent their greed for or right to the premium from their property.

Therefore, apostolic speech can only assert itself in a new, specifically Christian form of mediumism. What this mediumist shift means is that the apostle exchanges his own voice for that of the other in an ontological subject change. Kierkegaard saw this when he made his Paul say that "God himself [...] is speaking." The real Paul provided the formula for this subject exchange in a famous passage (2:20) from his letter to the Galatians: "I no longer live, but Christ lives in me." In the wonderfully counterfeited mission speech by Jesus in the Gospel of Matthew, this mediumist structure is presented retroactively as an apostolic concept intended from the start, for there the Messiah predicts the imminent difficulties of the Twelve before Jewish or Roman courts as he sends them out:

> "At that time you will be given what to say, for it will not be you speaking, but the Spirit of your Father speaking through you." (Matthew 10: 19–20)

In the Matthew text, the problematic exhortation to martyrdom is likewise dated back to the Jesus, the sender of messages and disciples, who seems to develop the public relations strategy of a suicidal sect without any false restraint.

The reason for the possibility of apostolicity thus obviously lies in a mediumistic relationship where the apostolic agent inserts themselves into the subjectivity of the sender as if they were their mouthpiece—or, anachronistically put, their soundtrack. "I no longer live, but Christ lives in me"; "it will not be you speaking, but the Spirit of your Father speaking through

you": the pious reception history of these ghostly words contributed to reducing the eccentric character of these speech
models to an expression of submission, such that the question of
the subject's sharing could not seriously arise with reference to
the apostle-Messiah relationship. If our basic analysis is correct,
in that all history is the history of ensoulment relationships, and
if ensoulment relationships constitute arrangements for sharing
subjectivity, then it is reasonable to assume that this evangelical
accord between messianic and apostolic subjectivity made a new
status quo of advanced-civilized animation manifest.

For an entire age, this new messenger arrangement—the
apostolic contract, one could say—set the standards for intense
ego formations in the zone of Christian messages. In the light of
the documents cited, there can be no doubt that this was a
monotheistic form of mediumism. Anyone who has witnessed
the ecstasy of a preacher from the American South knows how far
pneumatic release still extends in our times. Nonetheless, the
faith in Christ and one God had established themselves in
polemical contrast to the older forms of mediumism: the enthusiasm of the poets, the trance practices of the archaic ecstatic
religions and the oracular hermeneutics of polytheism. If the
early Christian theologians Justin, Tatian and Theophilus of
Antioch delight in invoking the monarchy of God, it is primarily
because for them, the advantage of being a Christian can best be
explained in opposition to the advantage of heathen possessions.
Service to the One is understood as a guarantee of the soul's
emancipation from occupation by local demons—or, expressed
in more modern terms, through sub-personal partial urges. Erik
Peterson has repeated this view from the perspective of the
twentieth century with unbroken affirmation: "The doctrine of

God's monarchy is a sign of the sobriety of the spirit, whereas polytheistic annunciation expresses the 'possession' of the poet's soul. Poetic enthusiasm manifests a metaphysical pluralism that is ultimately demonic in origin."[12]

Despite this strong language, the opposition of sobriety and possession fails as soon as the concern is to determine the dynamic character of the apostolic subject change. For in its key statements, apostolicity presents itself as an especially attractive and sophisticated form of obsession whose peculiarity lies in the fact that its complete pervasion by the One Lord precisely cannot (or can only very late and after the fact) be reflected upon as heteronomous, alienated possession. Rather, it portrays itself negatively as a liberation from subaltern demons and positively as a chance to collaborate on the project of the monarch of being. (And only when the charismas become too loud and the pneumatics leap too indiscreetly onto the front stage does it become obvious that in its deep structure, monotheism is a voodoo of the logos. Its carriers are individuals in tranceless trance—what humanism calls "personalities." It is "the spirit of your father [*to pnéuma tou patrós, Spiritus Patris*] speaking through you." Theologians have been remarkably unshocked by these words to this day because in the most important institution of Old European intellectual culture, the university, *homo academicus* triumphed over *homo aspostolicus*; theologians too have long since become more theorists than proclaimers—and the few who are not stand out, even when they are professors of dogmatics, as what Max Weber called "lectern prophets." Academicism is the most effective force of mania-muting—not least in the theology departments. But the psychodynamics of monotheism, the obsession with the essential One, still remains very powerful after such repressions. Even possession by the average, which forms the basis of individualism, unmistakably belongs to this order. For if you speak for yourselves, it is the *sensus communis* speaking through you. Until the contemporary theories of the ideal communicative situation and justice as fairness emerged, offshoots of the monotheistic communication model were at work: no truth-productive communication without post-monotheistic minimized voodoo.)

The God of the apostle is therefore sovereign because he can let the apostle represent him as if he were directly present and speaking through him. The apostle, for his part, shares in this sovereignty because he, as one chosen and marked by God, derives the unity of his existence entirely from the unity and singularity of his sender. In the apostle the sovereignty of the lord becomes the messenger's obsession, but the latter presents himself successfully as the highest possible form of obsession-free ego-identity and self-comprehension based on reasonably being a person.

It makes sense to see parallels between this coincidence of self-ownership and foreign possession, fundamental to monotheism, and the distinction between possession and ownership achieved in Roman law, for even an individual who *de facto* possesses themselves and their life can remain the property of another— this was shown by the ancient slave system, as well as the Christian attitude to the God who, not by chance, is called upon until modern times with the liturgical titles *Kyrie* and *Domine*. That is why in Justinian's book of laws, the runaway slave can be charged with self-theft, *furtum sui*—that is, the mere self-possessor has unlawfully attempted to rise to a self-owner (which, as we know, was only achieved by the proletarians of the early Modern Age).[13] In the same way, unbelievers can be viewed as criminals who have stolen themselves from God, their creator and owner. They could read in the *Codex Justinianus* that human stolen goods cannot be acquired by anyone, not even the thief, and can be demanded back by its true owner to the end.[14] From this perspective, Satan's revolt also meets the criteria of self-theft, as he took himself away from the giver of being by fleeing in possession of someone else's property.

Under these circumstances, then, the most favorable circumstances are those of the Christian apostle, who belongs to his God yet can hope to become the co-owner of himself in the afterlife—in the condominium that tradition calls "paradise." Things are less favorable for young men liable to military service in the age of the civil nation-state, which—as an authentic leviathan—asserts its rights as the owner of their lives in case of war and is entitled to demand that they die for the fatherland, as if it were the rightful life-giver who can demand back what he has loaned out; this also points to the latent continuance of possession relationships on a massive scale at the center of political modernity.[15]

The message of the apostolic messenger thus conveys two potentially very infectious impulses at once: firstly, it speaks of the fact that acknowledging the new, only lord will liberate you from old subserviencies, and secondly, it makes a recommendation to enter the ever-growing circle of advantageously possessed messengers. The messenger is only successful if he is able to call up second degree messengers—which he does if he convinces the recipient of the message to become its bearer too. What is now termed the "network effect" was already trained through the earliest ecclesiogenic communications. Without these infections, a mere information process could never have grown into a world within the world; without the apostolic chain letter, there would have been no empire within the empire, no church operating throughout the realm, no constituted Christosphere,[16] no animated grand inside in which the beneficiaries of this empire, to quote the unsurpassed Pauline-Lutheran formula for the specific character of spheric existence, "live and move and have their being."

In the light of these reflections, we can now formulate a spherological definition of apostolicity: apostolic action is a spheropoietic practice that contributes to the production of the monotheistic macrosphere—the Christosphere or ecclesiosphere with all its subdivisions into episcopates and dioceses (districts for the spraying of holy water).[17] Thus an anticipation of the integrated macrospheric end state is constitutive for the apostle effect. Arriving at this state requires a confident leap forwards into the alleged end result of evangelization, namely the dissemination of the message in the entire humanly inhabited world. In the greatest haste, the apostle anticipates the *regnum* or *imperium Christi* that is already current for him, though still hidden for the rest of humanity. Thus he functions like the herald of an emperor whose ascension to power was not registered by most people, but whose empire is nonetheless coming along with the news of it. For the apostle, the seriousness and the thrill of his office lie in the fact that he injects himself into the yet uninformed world like a messenger from the future, an authorized representative of an occult magnificence which has so far only been mentioned in his own message.

The apostolic office thus implies—as every telecommunication initially does—a monopoly, or at least a claim to sole representation. Whoever wishes to make their first entrance into the evangelically produced monosphere must subscribe to the news directly from the apostolic distributor; whoever is still ignorant of the new glory, on the other hand, will sooner or later hear something about it from the aggressive promotion of its messengers. The early missionary church installed a spheropoietic vortex that anticipated its future successes with élan. (The post-Enlightenment church, by contrast, was most diligent in postponing the recognition of its failure.)

The decisive trait of Paul's mission was the widely commented-upon turn from the Jewish enclave to the peoples of the *orbis terrarum*—an gesture of expansion that can only be grasped through a macrospheric analysis of world form. As the political head of the early Christian community and the chief strategist of this dissident telecommunicative theocracy that burst out of Judaism, Paul understood before anyone else that a particular concept of world—philosophically expressed, an ontological horizon—was immanent in the Christian Gospel, and that the objective validity of the message depended on its factual universal dissemination, or whatever could be considered such.

The reason for this lay in the fact that the truth Jesus had embodied was not a theorem—in contrast to the heliocentric hypothesis of Aristarchus of Samos, for example, whose truth value was not undermined by the fact that it barely found any supporters for two thousand years. The Jesuan truth, on the other hand, contained a macrospheric figure of alliance and an offer of an intimate-spheric relationship. Relationships, alliances and betrothals cannot be exposed like hypotheses, only updated as if under martial law if they seek to be "true." The Christian truth had the ontological structure of a world truth, and for that exact reason an imperial truth; it therefore had to be made currently present throughout the empire in order to apply. In this sense it was truly *news*, for the truth of news lies in the current-ness of its delivery and its effect on the recipient. If the event of Christ was not to remain an intra-Jewish affair that would peter out in a battle between Messiah-affirmers and deniers around the synagogues of Palestine and in the imperial cities, the world-capability of the words about this lord from the periphery had to prove itself positively at the center of the world. With the Pauline mission, the expansive concern of an actually existing Christianity became manifest, and with it the problem of an efficient, world-pervading propaganda system.

The hectic activity of the apostle for special duties and his reso-lution to travel everywhere himself, as far as possible, demonstrate the world-demand he made for his annunciation. The "peoples" whom Paul hurried to visit—he supposedly covered a distance of over 6,000 miles on his missionary jour-neys—embodied the actually developed political-onotological "cosmos" in which the quintessence of the Hellenistic idea of the ecumene and the recently established Augustan-Roman world gained concrete form. Had these imperial *faits accomplis* not had a corresponding, equally far-flung empire of annunciation in which the other *euangélion* was heard, there would be no lord who could be acknowledged as its head, and without a true master there would also be no authorized agent who could appear at all strategically important points in the center and on the periphery. Hence the apostolic impulse resembled a self-charging meaning-battery.

The two main words in the new apostolic communication, *ekklésia* and *euangélion*, were also modeled on patterns of long-distance imperial effect, as the *ekklésia*—which later became the church—initially referred to nothing but the gathering of listeners who were "called out" by the arrival of an imperial herald and summoned to receive a decree. The emperor's message itself was sometimes directly praised as good news or a joyful announcement, for example when there was a victory or favorable progeny to report, and was in such cases termed "evangelical." The parallel apostolic network could follow these standards until it was itself able to lead the market in the field of good news.[18]

Paul recognized Jesus' claim that the kingdom of God was *present* amidst the Jews as a chance to leave the Jewish enclave and advance to the political cosmos of Rome. He thus aggressively dissolved the latent imperial complex of Judaism: he broke out of the messianic provinces to finally claim a real empire for a master of Jewish descent—one in which, as would be seen, the identity of imperiality and communications would be developed more intensively than had ever been the case in the empires of the Romans, the Persians or the Seleucids. One day in the not-too-distant future, this second empire would give itself its own specific constitution as a church—which was admittedly still beyond the horizon of what was presently conceivable and desirable for Paul, who, as we know, was expecting Christ to return in a very short time.

Despite his excessive haste, Paul's world-claim contained an integral demand for empire. As such, it could only become clear under the given circumstances by following the political cosmogram of the *Imperium romanum*. It is no coincidence that Paul envisaged his missionary itinerary as a form of tour through the entire humanly inhabited and Roman-dominated world, the Mediterranean ecumene—even if he did not carry it out consistently. Though his factual travels sooner resembled restless, linear trips back and forth, their status in his imagination, and in those of his successors, was that of circumnavigations of the world. (For unknown reasons, he ignored the curved North African section of the earth.) Up to a certain point, then, Paul's story as told in the Acts of the Apostles is also a Christian periegesis—a guided tour of the sights following the schema of ancient travelogues; at the same time, it is an evangelical version of Alexander's campaign. Hence tourism's typical primacy of the place has given way entirely to the missionary's typical consideration for preaching opportunities—the apostle does not journey to gain experiences and take photographs, but to make all places subject to his program. He travels in his own mobile home, as it were, seeing his surroundings only through the tinted windows of his conviction. He has no reason to be outside, except to find a chance for annunciation. This results in the world concept of the touring ontologist—for him, the world is the epitome of opportunities for propaganda appearances. Paul himself stated in a conspicuous place—towards the end of his epistle to the Romans—that "from Jerusalem all the way around [Gr. *kýklo*, Lat. *per circuitum*] to Illyricum, I have fully proclaimed the gospel of Christ" (Romans 15:19)—a bold claim that made church historians ask whether when he wrote this, Paul had already completed his "missing" journey to the westernmost region, Roman Spain. In the given context, it should be read as the indicator of the underlying geopolitical, indeed spherological-ontological schema of Pauline movements.

As shown, the apostle's demand for space for the message to the whole world had to follow, for better or worse, the outlines of the Roman ecumene "all the way around." In practicing his mission, Paul had good reason to rely not only on his Roman citizenship (*civis romanus sum*) but also on his equally adequate and subversive understanding of empire; for him, the kerygmatic strategist, it was absolutely clear that the term *imperium* referred above all to the power of order, and hence authority, and that the empire as a political space was nothing but a delivery system for Roman orders and a catalogue of addresses requiring obedience. For his own part, the apostle knew that he was the bearer of orders from the absolute—that he was therefore, all things considered, traveling as an imperial representative or commander in his own right within the power space of the other emperor. This necessarily resulted in all the conflicts stemming from the antagonistic coexistence of the one empire with the other—primal scenes of the Old European dualism of church and state. If the apostle wanted to make productive use of his authority, that is to say his evangelical *imperium*, he had to present himself as a representative of the eschatological lord and see to it that the factual delivery of the gospel was recorded as a legally valid action.

It is no coincidence that the *acta apostolorum* became the normatively most important literary genre of the early Christian centuries: they are the epitome of ecclesiogenic writing. It was on their account that the church as a whole called itself "apostolic": with this word, it planted its telecommunicative banner early on. One cannot take this epithet seriously enough: only as an apostle empire, an apostle narrative and an apostle network could the Christian-macrospheric spatial claim be realized. As we know, apostolic acts do not repeat the message itself; they archive where and how successfully it was proclaimed, and what experiences the bearers of the message had in the process. Thus apostolic history, even before martyr history (to say nothing of the later saintly histories) is the central genre of Christian speaking on the eschatological parallel empire known as the church—precisely because it records the history of the deliveries of the message; church history deals with the routinization of grace by post. The perspective of authority plays the central part in these acts, as the apostles' sermons amounted to binding salvific actions among peoples, such that every memo about an apostolic act constitutes news about the deposition of a document with an evangelized recipient.

Just as the empire or modern state, in their chains of command between lords and subjects (or offices and citizens), postally ensure the absolute accessibility of the recipients by messages from lords or administrative authorities (making it impossible, for example, for one liable to military service not to receive his draft call), so too the apostle must bind his listeners for all time and hold them eternally responsible for their response to the message they have heard. Until the Enlightenment's intervention in the ecclesiastical regime of fear, the announcement of this liability remained the ultimately valid speech act of the apostolate and church psychagogics. The Christian message always comes as a registered letter, and having heard it, even if only absent-mindedly and with reservations, is tantamount to the recipient's signature at the bottom of an affidavit of service.

This is not least what Kierkegaard means when he credits the apostle with the authority to command "both the crowd and the public." One understands why this thesis contains a witty and willful anachronism, as Kierkegaard knew better than anyone what a modern audience was: the epitome of private persons whose behavior while leafing through books is based on aesthetic relief, and who would never let an author give them orders in a thousand years, even if he presented himself as eschatologically authorized or as an art-crazed medium. The modern author is *per se* an unauthorized speaker. The inability and unwillingness to command distinguish the writer on the book market from the apostle in the community, especially the so-called "genius" who invites readers into self-created worlds with the generosity of the brilliant. "Who else, indeterminable reader, but the hero of a story has ever made you a suggestion?" (Peter Handke) He demands no faith, being content if one quotes him. And it is precisely in this relatively power-free, almost convivial interaction between extraordinary writers and not quite so extraordinary readers that modern society seeks its freedom as a balance between duties and exemptions.

When the reader engages with novels and poems, it is in the certainty that these "texts" are no draft calls, neither from the state nor the truth, and that books do not force eschatological choices. That is why books can usually be bought, and their buyer can, within the boundaries of copyright law, feel like their owner and user—and need not be owned by them. Is the reader not *per se* the person who is glad to get further without making a decision? They feel free in so far as they understand that some-one who seems to be giving orders is usually only someone presenting quotations. And really—is freedom not simply insight into the difference between an order and a quotation?

As far as Kierkegaard is concerned, the melancholy semi-apostle demoted to a mere author (who senses that he can quote Christ, but not command *in his name*), he pokes fun at the audience's illusion of being able freely to judge everything aesthetically in masterless privacy, even the absolute and its paradoxical communication. But even he never went so far as to say that modern mass alphabetization was merely a trick for the purpose of domination that, along with the ability to read, gave the populations of civil nation-states the duty to read the commands of their occult and manifest lords—though, viewed more precisely, only the manifest sovereign shows themselves in commands, while the occult one preserves their incognito status by relying on seduction. All that modernity managed was *de facto* a structural transformation of possession: this realization was reserved for the twentieth century, which had to gather its very own experiences of the totalitarianism of warring telecommunications. It was only in the light of this that a general theory of media was able to come into view.[19]

Almost the whole of early Christian literature from the Book of Revelation to Augustine's doctrine of the Kingdom of God proves that the global space of the Christian message's annunciation was indeed conceived as the eschatological replica of the imperial world sphere and the Roman power presence on the Mediterranean "globe." Everywhere the information system of God copies and blankets the media system of the ruling world power. The apostles not only used the Roman channels and media; their famous hasty feet would scarcely have advanced so successfully without the Roman roads, the "structural lines of power,"[20] and without the translation from the Aramaic into the two world languages Latin and Greek, the message from a certain anointed one from the East would never have found its way to the relevant world, the Mediterranean West.

Catholic telecommunication began with translation from Asia to Europe. The early authors Cyprian, Lactantius, Arnobius,

Augustius, Aponius and many others were not afraid to give Christ the title *imperator*, which should be translated as "general" in contexts of the history of Christian militance, and with "emperor" in the case of reverence towards majesty.[21] The Roman imperial title was no mere term of political rank, but also a theological, indeed an ontological category, as it referred to no less than the commanding center of the imperial cosmosphere. In the discourse of imperial age house and state theologies, the *imperator* was the emanation center of *potestas* itself in its large-scale-world-forming, universal spaciousness, and simultaneously the theophanic instantiation of the Roman-Hellenistic world ground in human form. Alongside such a figure, the *imperator* Christ had to be introduced as surpassing that greatness, for he too was the head of an empire, called *regnum* or *imperium*, an empire that did not pretend to be of this world, yet demanded respect in this world too and could be proclaimed in a self-willed news empire, an ecclesiastical parallel empire.

It was in the early Christian language game of *Christus imperator* that the imperiomorphism of the ecclesiastical space of annunciation took on its sharpest contours. It unmistakably imitated Virgil's empire-theological thesis that with the rule of Augustus, an *imperium sine fine* had come into being on earth— with the difference that Christ's empire also promised a heavenly continuation.

The two decisive apostolic biographies, those of Peter and Paul, take us closest to the Christian imperial complex and its political ontology, as in these cases the martyrdom of the authorized messenger in the imperial capital had to be put *on file*. The file memos referring to Peter and Paul have an almost onto-historical status, as they officially mark the transference of the imperial claim from Jerusalem to Rome—and latently further, from the Roman Caesar to the Roman Bishop.

From the geopolitical perspective of Rome, the death of the miracle rabbi Jesus Christ was no more than a trivial event on the periphery, a silly piece of minor news from the chronically restless Eastern border region that need not hold up daily business in the capital. The vast majority of Romans never heard of him, just as they learned far less about the defeat of Varus in the Teutoburg Forest than the German legend would have us believe; the empire communicated almost exclusively via its successes, not its problems—imperial communication was largely kept to the standard of *semper victor* acclamations (while the current post-imperial nation-states, by contrast, can almost only communicate about their problems, not their successes; the dominant culture of correctness has shifted the glorification of victors to sports reporting, business news and the charts).

It was only with the two apostolic martyrdoms that such events transpired in the political center and demanded the attention of the metropolis itself, if only for a short moment, for the fact that they took place at that particular location was part of an intuitive Christian Rome campaign in which coincidence and the conventions of the Roman court system played a part. According to Roman law, capital cases from the provinces were concluded in Rome, which led to the transfer of Paul from Caesarea to Rome and probably also to his martyrdom, possibly in the context of the tortures unleashed by Nero after the city fire. Incipient Christianity could not dispense with the imperial capital as a broadcasting station for its message, for only those messages that issued from Rome were capable of proving the ontological relevance of the newly grown news empire. To implant the pirate station in the capital, apostolic files in Rome were indispensable. Only the most prominent bearers of the message could bring it: Peter through his final Roman appearances, and Paul through his trial being transferred to Rome. That the files of Peter and Paul were concluded in Rome was the perfectly fitted headstone for the evangelical building project and the central indicator of Christianity's claim to its own parallel and transcendent *imperium*.[22] Saint Peter's tomb at the center of the world capital: one cannot imagine how institutionalized Catholicism would have turned out in the absence of this symbol.

The consequences of this apostolic-marytrological subversion of the capital were extraordinary: Golgatha was typologically transposed to Rome, the marginal event was repeated at the center, and for Christians, the sky over Rome was now as open as that above Jerusalem (which had the maximum opening *post ascensionem*), even if the Roman one inevitably had the appearance of a catacomb for a long time. The martyr files, above all the Rome-related ones, are idea-politically the most important subset of the apostolic files because they document the march to the center and the multitude of imperial cities, as well as the history of injustice during which the real empire's treatment of the empire of truth dragged it ever deeper into guilt and debt. In this matter, Christian bookkeeping was thorough early on—in fact, it was only its reliability that provided the evangelical parallel empire with a minimum of administrative and semiospheric coherence.

The empire's debts with the Christians became the basic capital of the Catholic church—that was the primary purpose of the new literary genre of martyrology. Each account of martyrdom is an IOU made out by the world for the world above. A capital of tellable stories accumulates, in the form of growing mountains of martyr files, stories that place themselves like a second ring of annunciation around the first. This kerygmatic capital trial—the proclamatory valorization or profitable retelling of testimonial tales—produces an alternative world (hi)story and introduces an age of communications in which Christians can speak with their ilk about a single topic: what befell exemplary fellow believers in this world.

The late sum of these accounts was provided by Jacobus de Voragine in his *Golden Legend*, which was written before 1273 under the title *Vitae sanctorum a praedicatore quodam* remained the most popular book in Europe for centuries. It was only the incipient Modern Age that in turn managed to end the apostolic-martyrological monopoly on files and make accounts of non-martyrs and non-saints socially acceptable. Indeed, one can hold the view that the revolution of the novella enabled the telecommunicative process of modernity by setting in motion the emancipation of secular narrative threads from the *acta*. The Modern Age was the world form whose good news was that there were other narration-worthy events than those from holy history.

It was only with the novellas, the new stories, that what we call the information process could begin; for though medieval communication primarily meant swaying of societies in evangelical redundancy, the modern flow of information opened up the essential engagement of intelligences with the unknown, the external and the never-before-seen; the mathematical concept of information in the twentieth century takes this orientation towards innovation to its logical conclusion by classifying information as the essence of the system-relatively new, and thus subject to quantification. The heroes of novellas outstrip the saints of legend in post-medieval communications, and while the Christian narrative tells of Saint Christopher in the river and the martyrdom of Saints Perpetua and Felicity in Carthage, the modern one presents turbulent stories of lustful monks in the linen chest or the tribulations of an errant rogue.

As far as the Gospel is concerned, it has its own criterion for novelty in every possible surroundings because, as eschatological information, it ultimately had to seem equally unbelievable and paradoxical in all contexts, even where church redundancy and triviality of milieu made it seem evened out. It took the negative apostolic genius of Kierkegaard to defend the Christian madness of faith—just as, in our time, the negative rabbinical genius of Derrida was seemingly required to shield the messianic madness of continuing to wait for something that can have no present from the temptation of a philosophical and communication-theoretical normality.

As shown earlier, the apostolic ecclesia had to become something resembling a structural photocopy of the Roman Empire, as this offered the only current model for the existence of a large-scale space of serious world character pervaded by the ruling center. In this church "blueprint," the structural lines of imperiality as such came to light more clearly than in the original, as the church was able to restrict itself to a section of the political macrosphere—its telecommunicative nervous system or the informatic ethereal body of the empire. In these structures, the answer had to be sought to the question of how the lord could be made present at the count-less points of the world, and what signs of being were necessary to ensure his real presence in authorized representatives.

Sun stele from the Acropolis at Susa (late 3rd millennium BC), libation to a god

In fact, an actually existing empire is the answer to the question of its presence in signs through the mere fact of its existence in space and time; for the empire, being means being connected, and being connected essentially means being able to reach the periphery through sign transports from the center, and to gather up the messages striving towards the center. The empire *is* its semiospheric coherence. The signs of the empire connect the center with the periphery—never without switchpoints, to be sure, but always in such a way that the notion of the center's real presence in the distant point can successfully be kept in force.

Thus the empire—like the ecclesia in parallel with it—is a distribution system for signs of glory that are enjoyed by the recipients because the periphery cannot be tied to the center merely through physical force, meaning some principle of repulsion; in order to be attractive at the distant point as if in real presence, the center must make its presence known by pouring out shares in lust for power—that is, through signs of being that can be kept on the periphery like stocks in the core power by the latter's representatives.

Consequently, the nature of imperial and ecclesiastical telecommunication can only be understood with reference to its mode of outpouring or emanation. Making the center present at the distant point implied a form of telepathy—a telecratic broad-casting technology for signs of being, one could say. The distant warmth of being had to be palpable in the representative as an imposingly present radiation, and the voice of the master needed to be made audible thousands of miles away from the throne room and imperial chancery through suitable tele-phonic sys-tems which here, in keeping with the status quo of media history, were still authenticated writs and sealed letters. (It was only modern "broad"casting that brought about direct audiophonic contact between the leader's voice and the people's ears—with effects that mediological fascism research is attempting to account for).[23] The long-distance audition of the master's voice in its decrees had to trigger the authentic representative effect immediately in the listener, with the representative in turn becoming capable of glory and, through the shared lust for power, feeling energized to act *in nomine domini*. The long-distance listening in the written word was always augmented by a certain long-distance vision that, through the image rights of

Apollo cosmocrator from the Casa d'Apolline in Pompeii

the emperor, spread his likenesses throughout the empire, demanding cultic reverence for all of them as if they were actually present imperial substance.

To understand the energetic of long-distance rule through the sending of signs of being, one must occupy oneself specifically

Helios with quadriga, metope from Athena's temple in Troy (first half of 3rd century), Berlin State Museums

with the mode of separating off and sending out signs from the power center. What comes into focus in the process is a radio-cratic core process in which a division of being takes place through radiation and image sending.

Neoplatonism referred to this initially somewhat mysterious procedure with the equally mysterious term "emanation," *arópoía*—usually translated as "radiation" or "outflow." If one returns to the heliological schema of representation, the bizarre idea of causation through radiation loses much of its esoteric appearance.

Can one not imagine the sun of being as a bursting point that radiates and preserves everything existent around it through its *explosio continua*? The problem posed for vulgar thought by the concept of emanation lies in the demand of Platonizing ontology to accept not only that the higher sun sends out rays of light which fall on a world of objects that have grown entirely independently of it, but that the forms of these objects are radiated and unfolded together with the light: thus the giving of light gives the thing its essence, as well as bestowing the gift of cognizability for the intellect. This matter was touched on from a different angle of projection above in some remarks on the Platonic sun parable.[24]

Emanation as the being-giving act of the center—viewed by Plotinus as supra-existent—is thus analogously evident in the model of solar radiation. The "utterance" of the light source consists in the sending out of a totality of discrete quantities of light that individualize themselves as beams and pure images. The sunlike beam is the best means to show how being remains simultaneously present in a sign that issues from it. Hence there is barely an onto-semiological idea that does not imply a photo-radiological component. Equally there is usually a reference to the majesty complex in which the ruler's companions and delegates are presented as subordinate figures that bathe in the radiance of the lord. The servant *is* the effective sign of majesty. Plotinus did not hesitate to illustrate with feudal images the idea of the representatives sharing in the true One; he uses them to explain why one tends to set eyes on the representing second party *before* the highest and first:

> as in the procession before a great king the lesser ranks go first, and then in succession the greater and after them the yet more

majestic and the court which has still more of royal dignity, and then those who are honored next after the king; and after all these the great king himself is suddenly revealed, and the people pray and prostrate themselves before him—those at least who have not gone away beforehand, satisfied with what they saw before the coming of the king.[25]

This passage makes it clear that majesty forms its aura like a wreath of tiered power lights around itself, where representation and participation are synonymous.

Next to heliology, the most important pictorial sources of signs of being come from the pneumatic and cardio-sanguine areas—which is mediologically natural, for the breath of God can also be imagined as a continuum of breath whose front remains connected to the original source by the air current; and the streaming of the blood down from the heart of being to the co-supplied organs is certainly an epitome of the emissary's lasting share in the sending principle—in so far as the stream as such is the continuum between the source and the mouth.[26]

Light, air and blood are media through which the self-transport of the ruling principle from the source of emission to the distant points can coherently be imagined. All three converge, spiritualized and logicized, in the master's word, which can be uttered as a command, hint and teaching. Once it has issued from the sender's mouth, this word is meant to evoke a synchronous resonance in the authorized listener, leading them to pass on and command what was spoken masterfully into them—a process that is repeated until it reaches the periphery where the lord's word can no longer be passed on, only carried out or followed—or, if there is currently nothing to do, stored for later.

In this way, the language spoken by the lord becomes the fulfillment and epitome of everything communicated by blood, air and light in their outpourings. His word gathers up the sum of everything that can be signs of being—articulated in the lord's throat, transmitted using the royal broadcasting system, heard by the exchanged heart of the messenger, passed on by the moved apostle or the functionaries of light and carried out by the obedient hands on the periphery, which, however distant they might be, can still be sure of doing what is indispensably right. If one summarizes the process of emanation, the result is a single stirring at the sunlike center that begins as a beam, traverses space as a semiotic process and ends in a hand gesture.

The earliest, clearest and most beautiful depiction of the emanation idea comes from the time of Pharaoh Amenhotep IV, who attempted to replace the ancient Egyptian "Olympus" with the cult of a single god—the almighty sun, *Aten*—and attained an outstanding position in the history of proto-monotheistic sacred empire experiments under the name Akhenaten, meaning "devoted to Aten." His reign saw the creation of reliefs depicting the ruling sun, which turns to humans in a baffling way: it sends a multitude of individualized beams earthwards from its round body, each ending in a human hand! No later theory, neither that of Plotinus nor that of Pseudo-Dionysius, attained the same suggestivity as this archetype of all emanationisms: if the One is truly to grant and dominate everything, then its radiation—translated through ideas—must end up in operational hands, whether one interprets these as giving hands from above or servant hands on the human periphery. As long as the definition applies that sovereignty belongs to someone who can be represented by another in such a way that they seem to be present in

Akhenaten and Nefertiti beneath the sun disc (Amarna, 14th century BC)

their representative, the model of all sovereignty is Akhnaten's sun, which shines on the kingdom as if its every ray ended in a human hand. No principle has ever been represented better on earth than this sun, and never has it been clearer that the sun's representatives, the hands at the end of the beams, are still the sun itself in a different state. In the beam-hands, the source of being is competently present in the terrestrial, and every hand, because authorized, simultaneously rules and serves, gives and takes. It is the archetype of later priestly hands that bless and officials' hands that write (and indeed state treasury hands, which plunder entire societies while justifying themselves as God-sent takers). What this hand at the end of the beam does as a representative is done by the sun itself. This is my light that is sent out for you to illuminate your dark lives—the solar Eucharist. The hand made of sun proves that the sign lives. Now if this being-become-hand were also able to speak, it would have attained the pinnacle of onto-semiological self-depictive possibilities; but the doctrine of being becoming language would have to wait until Philo of Alexandria's metaphysics of the logos and the Gospel of John, which depended on it.

In philosophical ontotheology too, the long-distance manuality and long-distance orality of the sublime sender that identifies itself from afar were already contemplated clear-sightedly at an early point in the history of theory. Nowhere is this clearer than in the famous pseudo-Aristotelian comparison of God with the Persian Great King who, concealed from the world in his palace, was informed of everything that happened in his dominion through a kingdom-wide system of couriers and signs. The Great King analogy concisely illustrates the concept of telecratic monarchy from a sovereign center that became a politically formative pattern of thought and action in the missionary logic of early Christianity, as well as the ruler theology of Claudius and Julius, but especially Domitian.

Reading the following passage from the pseudo-Aristotelian text *perí kósmou*, it will be helpful to remember its supposed time of origin: the 80s of the first century AD, in which it happened for the first time that the ruling emperor—Domitian, who reigned from 81 to 96—demanded, in the context of an autocratic sharpening of the imperial court's tone towards the Senate and the people, to be addressed with the title *dominus et deus*. The anonymous author of the treatise *On the World* brings up this epithet at an important point, pretending it was the form of address for Persian rulers. He precedes his reflection on the ruler-ship style of the world-superior God with the remark that this God could not possibly look after everything himself, and that it befitted him—like the unmoved mover—to give a single powerful sign that set in motion the entire apparatus of rule, whose work would take care of everything down to the smallest details in keeping with the intentions of the ruler's all-penetrating wisdom:

> to superintend any and every operation does not become even the rulers among mankind [...]. Nay, we are told that the outward show observed by Cambyses and Xerxes and Darius was magnificently ordered with the utmost state and splendor. The king himself, so the story goes, established himself at Susa or Ecbatana, invisible to all, dwelling in a wondrous palace within a fence gleaming with gold and amber and ivory. And it had many gate-ways one after another, and porches many furlongs apart from one another, secured by bronze doors and mighty walls. Outside these the chief and most distinguished men had their appointed place, some being the king's personal servants, his bodyguard and attendants, others the guardians of each of the enclosing walls, the so-called janitors and "listeners," that the king himself, who was called their master and deity, might thus see and hear all things. [...] All the Empire of Asia, bounded on the west by the Hellespont and on the east by the Indus, was apportioned according to races among generals and satraps and subject-princes of the Great King; and there were couriers and watchmen and messengers and superintendents of signal-fires. So effective was the organization, in particular the system of signal-fires, which formed a chain of beacons from the furthest bounds of the empire to Susa and Ecbatana, that the

king received the same day the news of all that was happening in Asia. [...] Wherefore, if it was beneath the dignity of Xerxes to appear himself to administer all things and to carry out his own wishes and superintend the government of his kingdom, such functions would be still less becoming for a god.[27]

The decisive element of this telecracy model is the sublime *achirurgia* of the lord—his duty to abstain from using his own hands. This affecting without acting can only remain compatible with his sovereignty if his nature and his will flow consubstantially, as it were, into the system of representation and execution, such that the sovereign, without moving—like the Aristotelian mover—can ensure a balanced and irresistibly correct course of things with a softly spoken word. Each thing still follows its own autonomous logic, to be sure, according to an immanent entelechy or inner purpose, but the amalgamation of all processes is governed to utmost perfection by a general plan contemplated in advance by the royal intellect.

That this Romano-Hellenistically-stylized Persian king is enabled by his system of couriers and signals (which was eagerly copied by Augustus) not only to reach every point in the empire, but also to observe the most distant events in his kingdom almost immediately, identifies him as a typological kinsman of that "all-knowing God" who provided the logical mold for the specifically monotheistic concept of God.[28] He embodies the infocratic power culture of a fully matured imperiality that rules because it knows— and knows how universal knowledge can be acquired. The context reveals that this infocracy has not yet been fully understood by the author, for he turns the Great King into an unmoved mover and a barely acting god, anticipating the schema *Dieu règne mais il ne gouverne pas.* Thus the vivid examples of Pseudo-Aristotle have more factual content than his reflective commentaries, as the former make the telecommunicative basis of power transparent while the latter grope about in the origin-philosophical fog. Even if the argument does not develop an explicit emanation model, the semiotic-telepathic character of the depicted manner of rule is all the more apparent. This is shown most clearly by the unambiguous trumpeter parable from the same context:

> When, therefore, the ruler and parent of all [...] gives the word to all nature that moves betwixt heaven and earth, the whole revolves unceasingly in its own circuits and within its own bounds [...]. Very like is it to that which happens in times of war, when the trumpet sounds to the army; then each soldier hears its note, and one takes up his shield, another dons his breast-plate; another puts on his greaves or his helmet or his sword-belt; one puts the bit in his horse's mouth, another mounts his chariot, another passes along the watchword [...]all is hurry and movement in obedience to one word of command, to carry out the orders of the leader who is supreme over all. Even so must we suppose concerning the universe; by one impelling force, unseen and hidden from our eyes, all things are stirred and perform their individual functions. That this force is unseen stands in the way neither of its action nor of our belief in it. For the spirit of intelligence whereby we live and dwell in houses and communities, though invisible, is yet seen in its operations [...].[29]

The mode of operation characterizing this rule by signs is not yet truly telegraphic or crypto-telephonic, and yet it presupposes the experience of "power telepathy" through writing; it functions like an order whose execution has been rehearsed so that a clear path leads from the outpouring sound of the instrument to the actions of the servants. The trumpeter figures as a herald of the god-king. The fascinating references to the pyrotechnic relay service of the Persians have a particular factual proximity to the radiological model in the stricter sense, for here light signals with constant meanings are exchanged via posts in both directions between the center and the periphery; for in truth, a complete emanation system consists not only of the light's outward paths, but also its returns or reflections.[30]

There is good reason to doubt whether the allegory of the Great King possesses descriptive power for the historically factual imperial theology of the Persians, but it is all the more informative about conditions in the early days of the Roman Empire. There, especially after the eruptions of the *furor Caesarum* displayed by the morally deteriorated emperors Caligula and Nero, the question of the metaphysical style of the exercise of imperial power indeed began to arise with increasing urgency; Domitian's claim to the *Deus* title signalized that the emergency of the theologization of imperial existence had arrived. Now the semantic reserves of classical Platonism—its middle period remained insignificant for the political-theological sphere due to its self-castration through academic skepticism—proved an important source from which, under external conditions in no way resembling Athenian ones, fruitful new impulses for interpreting the basis of the exercise of imperial power could be drawn. Since the Augustan cultural revolution, it had been visible to all that the political theology of victory constituted the semantic central nervous system of the state ideology in the imperial age—under the first sole ruler, the winged Victoria became the empire's postal goddess, who had to convince all citizens of the advantage of being a Roman through regular messages of success.

In all important aspects, however, the basic theopolitical decisions of Augustus were still mythological, not philosophical—which is understandable given the character of the new monarch, who stood out nowhere for his great mind, but everywhere as a pedant on the large scale. This was equally evident in the cult of his adoptive father Caesar, whose deification enabled him to gain the *filius divi* (son of god) titulation for himself—moreover, the ritual sacrifice of three hundred Perugian citizens at the new altar of Julius Caesar on the commemorative Ides of March in 40 AD showed that a simultaneously dull-brained and cynically staged, pseudo-Etruscan system of blood gods was in force (especially if one considers that the Senate had abolished every form of human sacrifice in 97 BC). The fabulating connection of his own family history with *Venus genetrix*, the primal mother of Romulus, and *Mars ultor*, father of Aeneas, points in the same direction. Such divine family gossip shows that Augustus conceived of participation in the world above as kinship rather than emanation, meaning that the communication of essence conventionally occurred through the original powers of blood and semen and through the legal magic of adoption, not the logically and onto-logically more modern "radiation." Genealogism suited the conservative ancient Roman style of Augustan cultural policy. That he adorned his peace altar with the figure of *Pax* as Mother Earth with her offspring on her knees must also be read as an ancient-Romanistic gesture. At the same time, elements of manifest proxy theology were at work in the incipient emperor cult, for

Jupiter Dolichenus (Baal) with the goddess Victoria (early imperial period), Wiesbaden Museum

Augustus was presented not simply as a relative, but even more as an emissary of the gods; this was already expressed in the *Soter* or "savior" titulation that already established itself in the eastern half of the empire during the emperor's lifetime.[31]

Geopolitically speaking, notions of epiphany with reference to imperial rule belonged more in the Hellenistic than the Italic cultural area because of their popular Platonic logic; they were initially absorbed only with some effort by the Roman *divus* idea,

Divus Julius: commemorative coin based on the celebrations of Caesar's apotheosis, during which a comet appeared.

whose focus was postmortal apotheosis. But the contemporaries of Augustus, and subsequent generations all the more, already had to imagine the *modus operandi* of Caesarian salvation with radiocratic metaphors—manifested in, among other things, the bronze nimbus or crown of rays (now vanished) that adorned the third altar of Augustus erected in Rome after the death of the deified emperor, together with the obligatory cornucopiae.[32] The appearance of Augustus on later series of coins in the idealized "image of the perfect one with the crown of rays"[33] shows his association with astral gods. Julius Caesar's apotheosis was confirmed by depictions of the comet that appeared at the consecration of his altar—as if, at least in this case, a mortal had transformed entirely into a sign of radiation.

The notably frequent tendency of emperors in later times to symbolize themselves as sun emperors was thus due not merely to a fashion in pictorial and cultic history, but stemmed from the affinity between imperial telecracy and the radiocratic thought model, which predominated in the exoteric astral sun religions as much as in the subtle emanationisms of Neoplatonic photoso-phy. Hence the solar-theological episodes of Roman imperial history were symptoms of a general media-political tendency to develop broadcasting monopolies that represented the true zeit-geist, even in their failure. If even someone like Nero had the sun god's crown of rays placed on his head, this was more than an act of hysterical unscrupulousness, and not only a circus whim (motivated by patronage of the god Sol at Nero's beloved chariot races), but rather indicated a situation in which the emperors felt forced to play the leading role in a heliocratic world theater. Radiating became the first imperial duty. The telecommunicative substance of the empire coerced the Romans—who had previously been mostly telluric in their orientation—into an involuntarily subtle, astral-radiological stance. And after Nero decided to have himself depicted as the sun god in a 120-foot statue in the entrance hall of his palace—it was later transferred to the Colosseum named after it—the solar-monarchic motif became an obsessive mentality among the Romans.[34]

When Hadrian built the Pantheon, the temple of all the gods, from 118–125, motifs from astral theology gained an irre-pressibly evident architectural frame.[35] It did, at least, take until the third century before the fourteen-year-old Syrian Helioga-balus (218–222), high priest of the sun god Baal of Emesa (modern-day Homs, Syria), proclaimed an open theocracy of a solar type—a classic case of matriarchy *per filium*, incidentally— and it was only under Aurelian (270–275) that the emperor cult and the religious veneration of the victor's sun were officially identified with each other. So with the inauguration of Aurelian's temple of Sol Invictus—on December 25, 274, which would become the Christian feast of Christmas—the rule of the incarnated radiating principle was a *fait accompli* before the entire world, at least symbolically, for just under a year (Aurelian's Dominate ended with his murder in Septemer 275). After being combined with the Persian-Hellenistic Mithras cult, the circus god Sol, who protected the quadrigas in the chariot races, became a symbol of monotheism with imperial standing.

The equation of Sol with Apollo probably contributed significantly to his rising career, which seemed philosophically acceptable despite popular primitivisms, especially in Neoplatonically inspired educated circles, where the secret etymological reading of the divine name *A-pollon*, the "non-many," had circulated like a hint from above. Even when the absolutist Diocletian, who was in power as the final *dominus et deus* from 284–305, overturned Aurelian's cult innovation (by carrying out, through the elevation of Jupiter and Hercules to primary cult gods, a conservative re-Romanization at the expense of orientalism, which remained powerful nonetheless), important emblems of solar henotheism such as the imperial nimbuses remained in force as indispensable symbols of telecracy. And once Constantine had put the sign of Christ to the test as a symbol of success in his victory at the Battle of the Milvian Bridge, there was no stopping the amalgamation of solar and biblical symbols of telecracy. With its triumph over the astral sun god, Christian theology brought Platonism to power more effectively than any heathen-philosophical reaction could ever have done; for Christianity was not merely Judaism for the people, as was once said, with a Messiah who had arrived and remained present.

Cardiocentric emanation (17th-century monstrance)

Christianized emperorship was at once Neoplatonism for the people, with a baptized philosopher king at the center as an emanation politician.

For the most part, Europeans today no longer realize what this fusion of imperial and Christian broadcasting technology would come to mean: it was the most momentous alliance of technologies of meaning in the history of Europe; it kept the Old European semantics of the baptized powers in shape for an entire age. The dual system of simultaneously apostolic and radiocratic majesties managed to survive until 1453 in Byzantium, until 1806 in Western Europe, until 1917 in its Russian offshoot, until 1918 in Austria, and until the present day in the Vatican—despite the naïve rumor among historians of philosophy that Neoplatonism was essentially apolitical in nature.

The Julianic reaction (361–363) was—viewed in terms of the Platonization of the empire on the model of power emanation from the imperial center—already an obsolete undertaking; Julian's heliolatric eulogy (*eis ton basileía helion*, "To the Sovereign Sun") is no more than the exercise of a reigning high school student, more seminar paper than poetic hymn, and more romantic advocacy than a real expression of power. In Julian's solar vitalism, the sun appears as a mediator god who pours life into all that exists, completes it, gathers it up, refines it and bestows beauty upon it. Julian even celebrates Helios as the founder of Rome.[36] His rays ignite the eternal flame guarded by the vestal virgins. He guards the human race and the Roman Empire; before time began, he created the soul of Emperor Julian so that it would enter the line of the Caesars when its hour had come.[37]

But whether under *Sol Invictus*, King Helios, *Jupiter Optimus Maximus* or *Christos kosmokrator*, the meaning of *imperium* could never be anything but the centralized command of the radiocratic emperor through his telecommunicative, bureaucratic and later also episcopal networks. The emperor was the medium *and* the message, and in being both, he simultaneously plays the part of messenger and mediator between the world of gods and the human recipients.

That light can appear directly in the role of writer and writing at the same time is evident from the famous episode from Constantine's conversion legend, recounted by Eusebius in his *Life of Constantine* of 337, when the "a most remarkable divine sign" appeared to him before the decisive battle against Maximus:

> About the time of the midday sun [...] he said he saw with his own eyes, up in the sky and resting over the sun, a cross-shaped trophy formed from light, and a text attached to it which said, "By this conquer."[38]

This synthesis of long-distance writing and light-writing, telegram and photo-graphics, a textbook example of the logic of emanationist telecommunication, appeared on numerous later occasions in Christian vision culture—most vividly in Dante's *Paradise*, in whose Canto XVIII five times seven letters of light fly in formation and join to form the words *DILIGITE IUSTITIAM QUI IUDICATIS TERRAM* ("Love justice, you who judge the earth")—a command that can be read as an enlistment of worldly rulers as God's obedient officials. As far as Constantine is concerned, he not only made virtuosic use of the radiocratic machinery of majesty that illuminated his office and his person—by, for example, forcing the mostly pagan army to say a prayer of thanks on Sundays to the sun god as the giver of all

Dante, *The Divine Comedy*, *Paradise*, Canto XVIII, 79–81:

> They first flew, singing, to their music's rhythm,
>
> then having made a letter of themselves,
>
> they held their form and stopped their song a while.

victories; he also experimented at the same time with the apostolic mode of rule when he gave reflective sermons before thousands of listeners, with no concern for embarrassment, as God's interpreter.[39]

The ontologically decisive implication of political emanationism lies in the systemically necessary assertion of the possibility of pure power flows through pure media. Since time immemorial, it has been the function of all telecommunication to annul the distance that gives it its name: only because there is meant to be proximity where there was distance do communications over great distances take place.[40] In so far as telecommunication is essentially de-distancing, then, it cannot acknowledge the reality of the distance between sender and recipient and must, by annihilating distance, ensure the real presence of the order and its giver in the place of reception as if they were at close range. Seeing to the pragmatic possibility of this was the task of the imperial postal service—the notorious *cursus publicus* rigidly monopolized by the Roman court—and the system of sending out officials, which represented the empire's *official* and *munera* almost as real presence in the entire realm through the presence of Roman offices and Roman weapons. The theoretical plausibility and moral demandability of the power source's non-distant presence in the distant point were provided by emanationist logic, which can be viewed from this perspective as the real media theory of the empire. The idea of emanation discreetly became so tremendously powerful, even among countless contemporaries who had not understood a single word written by Plotinus, Iamblichus or Proclus, because it made the *modus operandi* of imperial delegation and the ontological self-transfer of power conceivable with sufficient clarity in the first place. This idea is the hermeneutics of the sun, which can be interpreted both exoterically and esoterically. The emanation model gives rise to the concept of the radiocratic space, in which the center of radiation communicates itself everywhere in uniform presence and with identical substance.

Viewed from this angle, Neoplatonism transpires as the concealed political ontology of ancient and Old European imperial culture. Its strength lies in the fact that it can be reproduced both in the sublimest forms of discourse and in popular radiation magic and astral myths. In its magical variety, radiation-based thought survived into the primitive esotericism of the twentieth century, and has been both updated and materialized through the electronic telepathy of modern news technology. Plato may be all but dead in the philosophical seminars of today on both sides of the Atlantic, but he lives on authentically in science fiction.

To recapitulate: in actually existing monocentric macrospheres of the imperial type, power "emanates" through radial emission from the center, which radiates in analogy to God and the sun. (The motif of power "emanating" from a "source" also survived until the formulation of constitutions in modern democracies; it is not amazing that today, in keeping with the democratic working fiction, "all power emanates from the people," but rather that talk of power at the highest levels still supposes an "emanation.") Positively expressed, emanation—as the self-communication of the beam—ensures that the presence of the sender in both the broadcast and the location of reception can be taken as genuinely given; in negative terms, it must prevent the messenger and the medium from inserting themselves as interference between the order and its reception.

Medallion of Louis XIV (1674)

Thus a twofold condition for the successful communication of power is captured in the emanation idea: pure and penetrating deliveries are possible!—because, on the one hand, pure or absolutely conductive channels exist through which, on the other hand, pure or absolutely selfless messengers hurry back and forth at maximum speed like joyful and useful spirits.

The axiom of all old emanationist broadcasting techniques was therefore: "the medium is not a disturbance!"—which can also be expressed in the statement "the medium has no self!" The holier the sender, the more strictly this applies, which is why the One God has always commanded selfless angelic troops under the super-selfless leadership of archangels, while the emperors, since the Augustan reform of the civil service, must content themselves with only near-selfless officials for domestic and external work under the supervision of near-selfless ministers. As long as this "near" applies, officials always have a motive to work on their perfection. But when the medium only nearly serves, the corruption of the service is dangerously close. If the medium even allowed its own interests to affect an official messenger duty, this would make it unfaithful to the task it was meant to carry out with every part of itself—in fact, it would be elevating itself to a lord beside the lord, undermining the great central sovereignty with a small co-sovereignty of its own. In this way, it would be abusing the borrowed power for its own purposes. Abuse of power by representatives of lords is the epitome of everything that must absolutely never happen in a system operating with the fiction of pure representations. If it were to happen nonetheless, however, it would release the prototype of what is evil and harmful into the world. Evil in the age of metaphysical broadcasts is the self-referentiality of the representatives—good, on the other hand, telecommunicatively reformulated, is the boundless self-communication of being.

Hence the entire ancient culture of rulership rests on the ideal of servant asceticism and the loyalty of officials—asceticism and loyalty being merely two different terms for the expectation of selflessness among the personal mediators of the central power. At a technical level, it corresponds to the assumption of perfection with reference to the broadcasting channels and material media, an expectation that one can philosophically paraphrase as an assertion of transparency. These media, both the human and the material, should all perform their services as neutrally, patiently and faithfully as the standardized papyrus types from the Nile Delta whose most outstanding specimens became known as the *Augusta* or *Liviana* (which were delivered in rolls 24 cm wide)—the finest paper in antiquity, which was reserved for the imperial chancery—and as *hieratica*, the paper for imperial bureaucracy, which was 20.3 cm wide and was used in the Roman administrative apparatus and in notary's offices from southern England to Mesopotamia.[41] The other papyri, of middle class quality, were sold in slightly thinner rolls.

It is only because paper and officials are patient that large power spaces can assert their formal coherence. Here the format is already the message, as formatting turns the neutral material into a pure means reserved for exclusive use by the lord and his representatives. Once the will of the lord has been written down, on precisely those authority-lending carriers, then the edict or rescript must, once it has left the chancery—even if the text is encoded—always be legible as a plain text; the signed[42] and sealed document must faithfully convey the lord's command, and the bringer must neither deduct anything from the actually present meaning nor add anything to it.[43] Having reached the place of reading, the pure representative then decides what the master's words truly mean. The ability to make the right decision here ultimately comes from the fact that the sender is thought of as present in the messenger. (In the age of genius art, this would lead to the thesis of the indispensable congeniality of the exegete.)

Only if the representatives act without self-interest or sluggishness, however, and if the channels pass on the message fully intact, without leaks or congestion, can the empire's beams pass unhindered through the pure or diaphanous means and have their effect in real presence at the place of reception. (One recalls that with the concept of the *diaphanum*, medieval cosmologists

Antoine Coysevox, *The Fame of the King* [Louis XIV] *Riding Pegasus* (1702), marble sculpture from the park of Marly, now kept at the Louvre

created the most powerful notion of a permeable middle element.)[44] A messenger who thinks of themselves does not carry out their assignment in the manner intended: this is the eternal worry of the sender in monopolized broadcasting systems. Where there is reason for such suspicions—and how could there not be with mere human intermediaries?—it must be ensured that the representative does not even develop a self, an ego that could think of itself first. Rather, their ego must already be removed before employment and replaced with the subjectivity of their lord within them.

The representative or agent must therefore turn in their private self and exchange it for that of the lord before they can be sent out. Given the gravity of the matter, it goes without saying that this cannot take place without the due form, for what is at stake is no less than a complete rededication of the utilized life. From the feudal enfeoffment rituals and ordination celebrations of Catholic priests and monks to contemporary formalities at the presentation of appointment certificates to civil servants, the ritual and legal-formal circumstances attendant on the subject change have remained strongly present. One of the oaths listed in a fourteenth-century Byzantine form for civil servants contains the following words:

> I swear by God and his holy Gospel, by the venerable life-giving cross, by our most holy Lady, the Mother of God Hodegetria, and by all the saints, that I will be a faithful servant to our mighty and holy ruler and emperor N. N. for my whole life, faithful not only in words, but also in those deeds which good servants perform for their masters [...] I am the friend of his friends and the enemy of his enemies, and will

never scheme against his majesty [...]. I shall remain a true and faithful servant of the Emperor [...] just as the truth indeed demands of the upright and true servant regarding his lord, and should he ever find himself in misfortune or banishment with God's permission, I shall accompany him, share his suffering and take upon myself the same dangers, even unto death, for as long as I live.[45]

These oaths were repeated at the selection of a new emperor, written down in the palace archives and registered in a directory; even the Patriarch of Constantinople and the church prelates were probably obliged to take such vows from the seventh century onwards. They reveal the nature of the alliance between the sovereign lord and his subordinate representatives with all due formality, as the officials had to oblige themselves before God and the saints to remain loyal to the emperor even if, following a palace revolt or fatal shift of external circumstances, he were deprived of his rule. The oath to remain in the service of a toppled lord until death is tantamount to giving up the right ever to think of one's own advantage again. Hence sovereignty belongs not only to someone who can be represented by another in such a way that they seem to be present in their representative; to be sovereign also means that one can convince one's representatives henceforth to refrain from all autonomous decisions about acting in an emergency—even when it factually arrives. The true official, then, would be the representative who derived all their potency from their employer and pledged impotence in every other respect.

The ideal representation, then, begins with a mediumistically relevant subject exchange—a process that Sigmund Freud misunderstood from a belated and petty-bourgeoisified position as the formation of the superego; for in the traditional representation systems, it is not a case of an unbending overseer being implanted, most effectively through early injuries and restrictions (as in Sartre's story "The Childhood of a Leader"), in an urge-driven private person who would like to get their money's worth in sensual ways, but rather of the individual who exchanges its entire small (erotic) wish apparatus for a large (political) one, thus gaining a share in a far more powerful subjectivity structure and a far more extensive context of lust for power.

This swap—characterized above as an apostolic change of subject—formed the basis of advanced-civilized ethics, to the extent that it was an ethics of service and *eo ipso* of commanding and obeying in royal and imperial power radii. The ban on narcissism or egotism taboo found until recently in every single advanced civilization can be media-theoretically explained very well from this angle. Because they could not yet be functionalists, the moral philosophers of the metaphysical age had to map offices and functions onto mentalities and efforts; the only option for classical ethicists was therefore to attribute good work in the service of a lord to the proven selflessness and humble dutifulness of the lord's representative.

People in fixed offices and those working as mobile messengers can forget themselves in order to remember all the better what task the whole or its center has given them: it was this fantastic and simultaneously power-architecturally indispensable anthropological fiction that made the Old European (and Old Asian) ethics of being-for-service possible in the first place. At the same time, it is one of the sources of the taboo on egotism that was in force in all archaic and developed societies for as long as they were pre-individualistically constituted, without anyone feeling the slightest hint of necessity to supply justifications for it.

The conviction that it is wrong to think of oneself before others, and all the more damnable to place one's own advantage above that of one's employer, is so deep-seated that for an entire age, the typically liberal idea of a socially productive labor division of several egotisms could not emerge in any way. Such a thing would only come about through the moral-philosophical revolution of the Modern Age, which led to a progressive naturalization and neutralization of so-called "evil." It began in the system of Thomas Hobbes, who made space in the construction of the state machine for a systematic expectation of the base or selfish motivations of humans, especially fear, complacency and hoping for personal advantages,[46] and it found its temporary conclusion—after intermediate stages of utilitarianism and vitalism—in Niklas Luhmann's generalized acquittal of the structurally egotistical "willfulness" of subsystems. The central principles in Luhmann's justification of his assessment are self-referential closure and progressive differentiation, and both essentially mean simply that one can never avoid egotism anyway (though it does not become quite clear whether one is allowed to theoretically confront systems with their normally compulsorily latent egotism).

In classical thought, by contrast, egotism was considered the first expression of what is harmful and evil, and its symptomatic emergencies were the loss of the servant's willingness to serve and the self-interested distortion of the message by the messenger. This yields the two cardinal forms of political crime: revolt and betrayal. It is difficult to say which of the two was viewed as the more despicable wrong in the traditional moral system. It is no coincidence that Christian Satanology imagined the prince of demons as a fallen angel—he is the prototype of the simultaneously disloyal and rebellious messenger who stole the message entrusted to him, the divine beam, and twisted it to his own ends. In choosing to have the arch-traitors Brutus, Cassius and Judas chewed eternally in the three mouths of Satan, Dante embraced the service-metaphysically inevitable view of betrayal as the utmost evil. In Augustine's view, the misappropriation of a glory meant for passing on, this privatization of a radiant message by the messenger, was the beginning of a creature's perversion or turn away from the *face-à-face* with its creator, which is why for him, angelic disloyalty or the vanity of the intermediary were the beginning of the history of Satanic-human decline. By contrast, a new loyalty of messengers, starting with the mission of Christ and continuing with the church and its devoted priestly functionaries, would herald the history of salvation; here an apostolic information system would be instated in which, thanks to a wise censoring of messages by an attentive central office—the episcopal church—pure representations by selfless intermediaries would once more take place throughout the realm.

In the secular domain, bureaucratic evil—the vain interference of the envoy and the tendency of officials to help themselves—must constantly be stopped anew, be it through stricter monitoring of performance or through more efficient systems of training and reward; the idea of the "civil service" can only be taken back to its supposedly pure and unadulterated beginnings through continual self-clarification. (It is no coincidence that the neoconservatism of our time, especially in the USA, has made the subject of state functionaries as a self-serving class one of its fixtures; it has considerable success with audiences when inveighing against the parasitism of civil servants who serve no one. In Europe, the same schema of criticizing bureaucratic evil is dominated by a discourse on corruption, formalism and wastefulness.)

As far as the critique of impure means is concerned, it shows its spiritual barb in the polemics of "pure" communicators against the now-willful intermediate realm of signs—a polemic articulated in exemplary fashion in the Jesuan speech figure "It is written, but I tell you!" This turn of phrase has remained potent until the most important media theory of the twentieth century, that of the Canadian Catholic Marshall McLuhan. Its breeding ground is the criticism, known in ancient Judaism, of Pharisees by Pharisees—which can be viewed as typologically analogous to the criticism of Greek sophists by sophists.[47] Here the member of a group within a culture of writing invokes the orality of the lord, which must be recalled as a valid basic circumstance. The member usually claims they are compelled to object to the increasing willfulness of the writing system and its creatures. Thus the spirit confronts the letter—as if the latter's only valid function were the inconspicuous service of the oral will to speak. The one who speaks "from the spirit" likes to act in the manner of life itself, which separates itself from the dead, the external and the supplementary.

This criticism, which forms a constant in Western intellectual history, is directed at the eternal rebellion of the secondary, which appears in language-theological terms as the manifestation of the semiologically evil or harmful. This is contrasted with the eternal conservative revolution of what is declared primary. For the partisans of the First Words, whether spoken by gods, kings or geniuses, everything is evil that contributes to inflating the intermediate realm of commentary and bringing the exegete or expert to power for second words. When the signs no longer want to serve discreetly,[48] but rather push themselves forward with naked signifier-bosoms to distract from the concerns; when those examining the signs are no longer willing to read disinterestedly, but undermine the masters' words with self-willed interpretations and butcher the canonical texts with their paraphrases; when the exegetes become insolent and openly claim that there is actually no such thing as an original, only versions that are somehow all equally legitimate—then the proponents of the first signs have a state of emergency, and the moment has arrived in which the angry sign-servant must drive the narcissistic middlemen out of the temple.[49]

As far as the possibility of pure representation in the political space is concerned, its cascade naturally begins at the tip of the metaphysical pyramid—with the figure of the monarch, who feels compelled by the logic of their office to present themselves as a governor of divine powers, or, theocratically heightened, even their incarnation. The aforementioned uses of the *dominus et deus* title from Domitian to Diocletian give the incarnationist tendency an unmistakable profile; in addition to the title, Aurelian made claims of divine nature and had himself declared on coins as a lord who was already born godlike—*dominus et deus natus*.[50] These theological programs in no way corresponded to ancient Roman traditions, but were released by the progressive self-reflection of the imperial state of exception.

That being-like-God was initially only a rhetorical figure for the emperors, and resulted primarily from being at a loss about their psychological status, is proved by, among other things, a passage from Seneca's educational treatise for the young Nero, *De Clementia*, in which the emperor's philosophical mentor attempts to empathize with the disadvantage of having to be a god:

> 3. This is the slavery experienced by the highest importance—to be unable to become less important. But that constraint you share with the gods. The fact is that they too are held fettered by heaven. It is no more possible for them to come down than it is safe for you to do so: you are nailed to your pinnacle.
>
> 4. Our movements are noticed by few, we can go out and return home and change our clothes without public awareness. You have no more chance than the sun does of staying hidden. There is a flood of light facing you and the eyes of everyone are turned towards it. You think you are going out? You are rising.
>
> 5. You cannot speak without all the nations everywhere hearing your voice. You cannot get angry without everything trembling, because you cannot strike anyone without everything around him shaking.[51]

Here the problem of being a sun is still reflected upon by Stoic means, not turned into something positive through Neoplatonic concepts. This brings the telecommunicative or tele-energetic quality of imperial life utterances to the fore all the more clearly in Seneca's mirror for princes.

The aim of the philosopher's commitment to princely education was to induct the emperor into the role play of the great all-round communicator; one can view the particular emphasis placed by Seneca on the clemency (*clementia*) of the *princeps* as foreshadowing a radiocratic rule in the mode of irresistible self-communications of substance. (Here we suddenly see an analogy to the Chinese philosophy of rule, in which the motif of exercising power by abstaining from intervention was developed much further—with the silent infocracy of the emperor resting on an empire-wide system of spies, reporters and denunciators.)[52] furthermore, speaking of *clementia* itself already contains a subservient concession by the philosopher to Caesarean autocracy, for what he actually meant was no different from what had still been termed *humanitas* in Cicero's time—a quality that was no longer to be demanded of imperial supermen after Augustus, and even less after Caligula, who had demanded formal sacrifices—and not merely lip service—from an intimidated Senate for his *philanthropía* or *clementia*.[53] That humanity would change into the clemency of rulers at the start of the Roman imperial age—that is, into kindness from above—reflects the removal of the Caesars from the Senate and the people, just as the transformation of *clementia* back into *humanitas* at the end of European absolutism (from the early eighteenth century on) signaled the reintegration of rulers into mankind's middle tier, the bourgeoisie. For an entire age, the rule would apply that to be sovereign is to put mercy before justice. The paradigm of the ruler's clemency—the triumphant Augustus' decision not to punish the conspirator Cinna—is highlighted in Seneca's text as a shining example. With this act of perfect ruler's wisdom, Augustus had in fact succeeded in ending the civil war and restoring to the empire that lasting peace which history would remember as *pax augusta*.

In spite of all this, Seneca's *De Clementia* remains one of the most dubious feats of assimilation to the circumstances of one's time ever performed by a thinker of great stature; as we know, the philosopher's attempts to lead the leader Nero were thwarted by the moral insanity of his pupil. The adolescent Nero's character genuinely seems to have contained elements of a certain theatrical gentleness, for Seneca is able to remind his protégé of an episode in which Nero had been putting off the sentencing of two brigands and finally, when the reluctant (*invito*) emperor was given the document to sign, called out: "I wish I didn't know how to write!" (*vellem litteras nescirem!*) Seneca comments:

> That was a fine remark! All the peoples of the world should have heard it [...]. The mildness of your mind will gradually be communicated to others [...]. Good health flows (*exit*) to the body from the head [...].[54]

Seneca did not yet comprehend that already for the young Nero, being humane was interesting primarily as a theatrical gesture; but he certainly understood that the emperor's function was to be a center from which something "flows" under all circumstances. As far as the successful radiation of a convincing message of clemency was concerned, the Romans would have to wait for the Flavian emperor Titus, who managed not to sign a single death warrant in his two-year reign (79–81 AD).[55]

As long as the emperors interpreted their office using Stoic rather than Platonic language games, the manic temptations of their status at the pinnacle of the earth only became visible in the form of private psychopathies—there is a discreet, but substantial divide separating the *furor Caesarum* from the *furor platonicus*; it would be an overestimation of Caligula's god-man phantasms to read them against the background of Hellenistic doctrines of becoming one or Philonic gnosis. In his *Meditations*, the Stoic

Marcus Aurelius pursued a hygienic strategy of self-examination with the far-sighted aim of keeping his office's inherent tendencies towards manic inflation under control; his concern was to reject seduction by splendor: "Life is short both for praiser and praised, for the remembering and the remembered."[56] Any ruler who only wished to be mirrored in the court-approved media—in acclamations, rumors and praises, in adoring poems and flattering prose—would lose mastery of himself in a flash.

The Stoic reserves of imperial self-reflection seem to have been exhausted after the philosopher-emperors of the second century. Nonetheless, the long-term, subliminal Platonization of the imperial office only came to the fore through the aggressive cult policies of later monarchs, especially the disinhibited absolutism of the Dominate, which in turn remained true to style and became Byzantine theocracy. In the process, epiphanist tendencies gained the upper hand: the emperors were increasingly influenced, both implicitly and explicitly, by thearchic and radiocratic self-interpretations. They consistently read themselves as signs of being, standing radiant against the background of the empire and the world.

It is no coincidence that Diocletian, with whom the absolutist wave reached its climax, augmented his court ceremony—like Alexander the Great—with the Persian *proskynesis* (prostration) not only for ordinary subjects, but also for the most senior courtiers and officers, in accordance with a mode of ruling "in real presence." As the manifested light *ex oriente* the emperor, along with his co-regents in the tetrarchy, could stand beneath the crown of rays in the vicinity of the One, as if he were himself a functional emanation of God from which the beams of rulers extend to the edge of the world, even though by Diocletian's reign and thereafter there was no longer any talk of deification during the emperor's lifetime. Even his indirect issuing from the sun—the Japanese *Tenno* still asserts an analogous myth, his descent from the sun goddess Ameterasu, to this day—presupposes the possibility of pure representation and claims the real presence of abundance for the lord of the realm. Hence the indispensable crowns of rays, which show with sensual evidence how gifted power and far-reaching light belong together in the empire.

The decisive question for the further course of imperial media history was now whether the two basic types of authorized and metaphysically grounded communication from the center of being, namely the apostolic and the imperial, could meet in anything but a conflict. That clerical authority and imperial abundance of power could not be reconciled in times of friction between the empire and the church—from Nero to Diocletian—is neither historically nor systemically surprising. But how could the two broadcasting sources be configured with each other if the polemical antithesis of Christianity and heathendom had disappeared, as the empire had placed itself under the *signum crucis*? The answer lies in the history of Christianized imperialism—Christianity, for its part, as shown above, did not have to be imperialized because it was already imperiomorphically constituted, both on the Pauline and Roman-Petrine lines of development (which by no means impaired its intensely local, community-based reality). This Christianized imperialism grew in two guises: firstly, in the history of the two Christian Roman empires, the eternal Byzantine and the transferred Holy Roman Empire of the Germans, and secondly, in the history of the papacy.

In both group manifestations, anyone wishing to learn how the historically far-reaching connections between emanationist radiocracy and apostolic missionary logic came about had only to look around them. That empires constantly vibrate in communications about the ruler's salvation, the successes and the duties of the empire, and that this self-arousal forms the medial basis for their unity, can be fully understood by examining the ancient ruler cult and its empire-wide application in charismas and distributions of lust for power.

For power-architectural reasons, an imperial space can only exist as the semiosphere of a communication about a present salvation—or its recreation from decline and danger. That this vibration of the empire in communications about its salvific status now had to incorporate the apostolic representatives of an eschatological salvific kingship under a Christian banner into its broadcasting activity too, however, can only be perceived as a media-historical oddity.

This brings into relief the problem, never before treated systematically, of how large-scale political and ecclesiastical bodies grounded and organized their semiospheric coherence from the end of antiquity to the threshold of the Modern Age.

The two historical-structural questions—how is Christian emperorship possible, and how is an effective papacy possible—are therefore, from a media-theoretical perspective, secondary formulations of the main systematic question: how is the synthesis of emanationism and the apostolate possible? Only from this angle can media history uncover the secrets of actually existing political macrospheres in the metaphysical age of European civilization.

The spheric nature of the holy empires presupposes, as we have seen, a sufficiently insistent opening up of space through

Etruscan teaching model for liver divination[57]

radiations and emissions from a ruling center. The question of how apostolic and emanationist productions of signs are interlocked or juxtaposed can in turn be transformed into this conundrum: how can rule via messengers become radial broadcasting power, and how, conversely, can the possession of a beam emission bring speaking messengers to power? Here we must read the word "emission" with an awareness of its unsuppressible multiple meanings of emanation, irradiation and sending-out (mission).

It is logical to assume, then—and empirical findings fully confirm this—that the liaison between apostolic and emanationist motives can be initiated from either side. This occurred in two ways: firstly, by directly integrating of the charismatic type of ruler sent by the gods for the good of the living into the apostolic succession—which was formally pronounced by Eusebius of Caesarea in his eulogies for the redeeming emperor Constantine, whom he placed directly in the first guard of Christ's emissaries when he dared call him the thirteenth apostle; and secondly, by infusing the apostolate with epiphanist and emanationist motifs—an aspect that would be especially formative for the Greek Orthodox hemisphere. In the Hellenistic paradigm of Christianity,[58] it was not only the "Christology from above" that was successfully formulated and established from Platonic inspirations; it also entailed the creation of an iconology, a pneumatology and a politology that combined to form the image of an "apostology from above." In this hemisphere, annunciation and appearance move close together, sometimes so close that apostolic emission is almost soaked up by epiphany.

This is illustrated most spectacularly by the cult around the "unpainted icons" of Christ, of which the most famous ascended in the sixth century to become the Palladium, the imperial protective sign of Byzantium; in 622, the Eastern Roman Emperor even took this picture with him on the campaign against the Persians, which was deemed a Holy War. According to the radical-epiphanist legend, the mysterious pictures of Christ had come into existence through direct projection from heaven or, to use a modern expression, "theographically"—painted by God (or, even more commonly, "acheiropoietically," made without hands).[59] This could only be imagined as a cluster of rays from the world above casting the *eidos* of Christ directly on a terrestrial canvas and materializing it there. According to Byzantine logic, then, heaven remained on the air with powerful images. The apostolic representatives were kept on a short leash by the fact that the upper world reserved priority through its constant irradiation into the lower.

Hans Menling, *Saint Veronica*, circa 1440, Washington

One finds an entirely different picture in the Latin West, where the apostolate of the Bishop of Rome largely became a matter of the sacralized exercise of power through its amalgamation with the spirit of Roman law and imperial bureaucracy, while the motif of the epiphanic appearance of light in real presence had to play a lesser role for systemic reasons. Saint Peter is not present in Rome as the diaphanous messenger from above, but as the aspostle of the rock, less as an icon of the Gospel in the crown of rays than as the first vassal and justifier of the parallel *regnum*. In any case, the depraved political conditions in the West made an eminent role of the Roman bishop inconceivable until the eighth century. It was only after the establishment of the papal-imperial dual in the ninth century that the European problem of representation developed its characteristic antithetical drama. From the political and canonical emancipation of the West from the predominance of the Byzantine emperor onwards—starting with the coup-like coronation of Charlemagne in Rome by Leo III on Christmas Day 800—pope and emperor had to cling to each other in medieval Western Europe like Siamese twins who had to remain together on account of their fused inner organs. They shared the unspeakable secret of a shared usurpation, though in the papacy the symptoms of the pathogenic secret were more severe and supplied the motifs for more spectacular declarations and more hyperbolic gestures.

The open secret of the papacy was its jealous rivalry with the inwardly calm Byzantine theocracy, which was equipped with all privileges of legitimacy and continuity, even if it was often in a precarious and unsightly state. In the city on the Tiber, it was difficult to forget that an anti-Roman tendency had already established itself in questions of church leadership at the ecumenical First Council of Constantinople in 381.[60] (With reference to the pope's position, one is inclined to modify Lacan's thesis that the unconscious is structured like a language into the claim that the unconscious is structured like an impossible office.)

The first step to papal self-therapy was the Roman bishop's anticipatory participation in the empire project of the Frankish Great King Charlemagne, who was interested in reanimating an imperial structure of the Roman type in the European northwest with the Franks as the main people. For the sake of this plan for a great empire, Charlemagne was willing to enter a liaison with the only source that could bestow a European imperial crown. But the sublime part that had to be played by the papacy in the coronation of the Western Emperor, and which could also be imagined as a retransfer of the empire from Byzantium to Rome, initially served as no more than first aid for the structural inferiority complex of the Holy See. As soon as the neo-occidental axis between Rome and Aachen was consolidated, weakly objections from the East notwithstanding (only in 812 did Byzantium deign to recognize the second emperorship in the West as a secondary power, in analogy to Diocletian's hierarchical distinction between the Augusti as full emperors and the Caesares as supplementary emperors), and once a territorial complex had formed on northwestern European soil whose domination was of potential interest for a theocratic institution, the papacy—following its recovery from the aristocratic Roman "Pornocracy" of the tenth century—had to make its second strike in order to compensate for the Byzantine injury under its own power.

The only way for this to happen was through a spiritual declaration of war on its "own" empire, which had emerged from the Ottonian *renovatio imperii Romanorum* more attractive than ever. This had to pay for the papal sovereignty complex by paying tribute to Rome's leadership claim not only in the ecclesiastical, but also the worldly domain. The rulers of the Holy Roman Empire could never quite understand that they had been given the role of an "inner" Caesar in an Augustan papacy now forced to abandon the Caesaropapism that was impossible in Rome and seek a dual solution, that is to say a papo-Caesarism or papo-Augustism, with a strict precedence of God's representative over the monarch—a precedence that did not introduce any disruptive twofoldness into the Eastern personal union, but released explosive conflicts in the dual system. With powerless revulsion, a degraded Roman church had to observe how the emperors of the tenth century had assimilated to the Byzantine model and called themselves apostolic monarchs. Though hardly enthusiastic, Charlemagne had still received hymns of clerical praise as a second Constantine. Otto III, raised as the son of the Byzantine princess Theophanu to become a theocratic prodigy, already saw himself as "another Paul" and emulated the Pauline-Justinianic formula of the *servus Iesu Christi* without blushing; contemporary documents depict him as the patron of the Holy Spirit, in possession of such pneumocratic symbols of authority as the dove and Chrism. No extensive proof is needed that Rome did not appreciate these Germanic Byzantinisms. It was an indication of Rome rallying its strength when, at the imperial coronation of Henry II (later Saint Henry) in 1014, Pope Benedict VIII staged the ingenious idea of placing a *globus cruciger* in the monarch's hand, thus introducing a symbol that implied the omnipotence of Christ as a papal gift to the emperor. The meaning of the act, which elevated the giver and lowered the taker, was evident, all the more so because a *globus cruciger* is an object the recipient cannot refuse. Soon afterwards, Henry cooled his apple hand by passing on the Roman bishop's gift to the Abbots of Cluny. Percy Schramm has written well-known studies in which he narrates the epic of the later *globus crucigers* (thirty-six objects of this kind have survived in the treasuries of Old Europe) in as lively a fashion as the monotonous subject allows.[61]

In the light of this, the ad hoc motives for the Roman church's attack on the empire seem plausible and transparent—their chronic aspect related to the unabashed instrumentalization of the German imperial church system through the emperor's power, especially through his prerogative of appointing bishops; in their immediate aspect, they stemmed from the traumatic priority functions of Emperor Henry III at the Council of Sutri in 1046, at which he deposed three false popes and appointed one "true" one, his own candidate, under the title of a *vicarius Dei* and as the *caput ecclesiae*. Thus the Byzantine scar in the Roman system was torn open anew as a German wound. The reaction was not long in coming: the symptom of the pope's actual neurosis was the incomparably brutal and prophetic sketch (unpublished in its time) for a decree by Gregory VII from 1057 that became notorious under the title *Dictatus Papae*, with which the Roman campaign to subordinate the emperor and reconquer the European church for the Roman Curia began. Let us consider some of the statements from these twenty-seven principles:

1. That the Roman church was founded by God alone.
8. That he [the pope] alone may use the imperial insignia.
9. That of the pope alone all princes shall kiss the feet.
10. That his name alone shall be spoken in the churches.
11. That this title [Pope] is unique in the world.
12. That it may be permitted to him to depose emperors.
19. That he himself may be judged by no one.
23. That the Roman pontiff, if he have been canonically ordained, is undoubtedly made a saint by the merits of St. Peter.[62]

The self-aggrandizement of the papacy in relation to the empire has been interpreted, and not inaccurately, as the first in the series of European revolutions.[63] If one accepts this perhaps overly theological and Rom-friendly reading, the *Dictatus* marks the shift towards a neo-apostolic spiritualism and its struggle against the semi-heathen compromise of episcopal feudal rule with the local salvific powers, which could scarcely conceal the universal assimilation of Christian symbols to the old military-aristocratic and ethnic-magical traditions. The "papal revolution" points to a first centralist attempt to rule Europe based on ecclesiastical neo-Roman inspiration.

From a media-theoretical perspective, it is evident why this was a charismatic centralism of a radical-apostolic character. The aim of the papal offensive had been to reform the Catholic salvific space as a spiritual-political empire; for Rome, the concern was to reach that ideal state in which a single giver of salvation—the *vicarius Dei*—had dissolved the countless scattered, self-sufficient local cults and ended all subsistence of semi-heathen families, tribes and peoples on their old native salvific capacity and made all Europeans direct recipients of salvation from the Roman source. The Catholic phantasm of a center that came to power with Gregory envisaged the Holy See as surrounded by a Christendom in which each individual saw themselves as spiritually and canonically immediate to Rome.

This project made it obvious how far a pure apostolocracy could venture in the imaginary realm. A Roman broadcasting monopoly of such range could only be striven for with the help of a disciplined body of apostles whose creation vitally depended on the enforcement of celibacy. In this respect at least, the "papal revolution" had inextinguishable consequences: it contributed to producing the type of the family-less cleric, socialized in the large-scale ecclesiastical-maternal body to be used and sent out as required—that *ecclesiasticus* on whom not only the history of the scholastic intelligentsia in medieval and early modern Europe depended, but even more the Catholic world mission in the Age of Discovery.

Anyone wishing to study the history of globalization would do well to consider the role of the papacy in shaping an elite of sendable clerical mother's boys for telecommunications with untrodden parts of the world and unknown addressees.[64] Only these papamobile, almost context-independent programmable apostles were suitable for deployment in early modern global field work. And only a papacy that managed a neo-Pauline mobilization in addition to its insistence on the Petrine rock aspect could prove itself able to deal with the challenge of Europe's multi-ethnic situation—and the even greater challenge of mundialization later on. Hence Catholic Romanism could not afford to settle into the holy lethargy of Byzantine pneumatic monotheism, and instead remained in a constant state of apostolic attack—until the French Revolution forced it into a defensive position once and for all—from the *Dictatus Papae* onwards.

It goes without saying from a macrospherological perspective that Roman papo-Caesarism never succeeded in realizing its structural aims—aside from the brief moment of triumph under Pope Innocent III (Lotario de Segni)—because the Roman central broadcasting station never had the necessary substations at its disposal to penetrate the local salvific spaces effectively. The specific broadcasting resources of the pope were never sufficient to cut off the regional monarchies from their sacred sources and rob the rulers of their magic cloaks. The magical local stations, carriers of therapeutic and psychagogic charismas, remained active everywhere; Rome and its bishops barely managed to baptize local healers and teach the village priests a few sequences of Latin. It is no coincidence that—as Marc Bloch showed in his famous book—it was the French monarchy that drew political strength from its old thaumaturgic salvific power and, at the height of its power, stood up to

Column of Constantine in Instanbul; the lost statue at the top of the column, a reworked statue of Apollo from Ilion, depicted the emperor wearing the crown of rays and holding a globe mounted by a winged Victoria in his left hand.

Beryl globus with bronze Nike, presumably 5th century BC

the papacy: it took the liberty of conducting the representative of Christ from Rome to Avignon like a vassal of the French crown.[65] The German imperial dream, incidentally, remained potent even in its failed condition; it spawned poisonous offshoots well into the

Trajan's Column in Rome, crowned with a statue of Saint Peter since 1588

Column of Marcus Aurelius, crowned with a statue of Saint Peter in 1589 under Pope Sixtus V

nineteenth century, and probably the Third Reich. Critics of the German mentality presumably saw in it, and rightly so, the traces of an imperial frustration that had never been overcome—which can only be understood if one takes the imperial concept seriously as pointing to an unsurpassed system of lust for power. In fact, it was not disabled until the system of desire for success emerged in modern capitalism and its "entrepreneurial cultures."

Even as late as the nineteenth century, Johann Gottlieb Fichte—the founder of an imaginary, new, German-Gnostic spirit empire, the initiator of German Idealism and later lectern politician in Berlin—presented in the eighth of his Erlangen lectures on "The Nature of the Scholar and Its Manifestations," given in the summer semester of 1805 (half a year after Napoleon's self-coronation in Paris as Emperor of France in the presence of Leo VII), a theory of kingship entitled "Of the Scholar as Ruler" that can be read as a continuation of German imperial mysticism using the idealistic philosophy of reflection. For Fichte, the regent is a pure representative of the ruling idea, and in this quality inevitably himself an epiphany:

> He comprehends this Life with clear consciousness as the immediate life and energy of God within him, as the fulfill-ment of the Divine Will in and by his person. [...] his desire is not merely that something may come to pass, but that the will of the Idea may be accomplished. Until it speaks, he too is silent;—he has no voice but for it. [...] In this way does the Idea possess and pervade him without intermission or reserve, and there remains nothing either of his person or his life that does not burn a perpetual offering before its altar. And thus is he the most direct manifestation of God in the world.[66]

This passage shows that German Idealism too, both in its semiotic theory and its politology (as well as its idea of officialdom), stands in the continuum of the Old European logic of purity and thus constitutes a belated chapter in the history of transparentism; Fichte's theory of the image deals with the last living icons, its aim being iconostasis as government. In argumentative terms,

Festival decoration by Elpidio Benedetti for a celebration of Louis XIV's convalescence, detail

Fichte's theorem forms the interface between the premodern and modern interpretations of the world: on the one hand, it repeats the classical metaphysics of subservient selflessness, yet its justification thereof is indebted to a logical modernity that forces the absolute through the needle's eye of reflective subjectivity without recourse to archaic ontological principles of the absolute.

Naturally Fichte's concept of representation does not belong to an apostolic so much as an emanationist perspective, for the ruler is radiated directly into profane reality as an image of being—more precisely, they activate themselves as an irradiated emanation. But even the papacy, which seemed to owe all its effects to apostolicity, could not escape the compulsion to epiphanic grandstanding at the height of its triumph; this is particularly evident in the language game of the sun and moon with which papalist propaganda attempted to illustrate the primacy of the papal light-giver over the imperial light-taker from the eleventh century onwards.

What these laconic, perhaps exaggerated sketches show is that even in the core space of metaphysical telecommunication, the standing in of a *vicarius* or *servus Christi* for the God-man, the possibility of pure representation remained problematic at all times, in empirical and historical terms alone—to say nothing of logical and systematic analysis—because the presence of the sender revealed itself in a fragmented form, both in the missives and the emissaries. Not only was the mode of sending pervaded by an impenetrable ambiguity due to the fluctuation between apostolic and emanationist standards; the envoy too could not be clearly identified, as the representation of God at the maturation point of the conflict comprised three pretentions of the highest rank—the Caesaropapist-Byzantine, the papal and the imperial—whose dogged coexistence would erode any simple faith in representatives. That the papacy also made occasional schismatic appearances, as a monster with two, sometimes even three heads, turned the encounter of being and sign into a garish grotesque.

Each of the three adjacent full signs of being had to suspect the other two of being empty (and at least subordinate) signs or seductive simulacra, as only one of them could be the true bearer of presence. But how can authentic representation be identified? The recommendation in Lessing's Ring Parable to identify the true magic ring by its beneficial effects on the life of the wearer could not be applied in this case, as each of the three representation systems managed to claim all signs of success for itself; *de facto*, each of them was capable of emission and itself produced the affirmatory signs of abundant truth in life and corroboration through real success. Thus each proved itself right within its own broadcasting space—which, in semiological terms, is the main feature of what is termed a "world" in the full ontological sense: in a world that deserves the title, the criteria or signs indicating the truth of the world picture can be found in the world itself—

except for special revealed truths, which necessarily arrive from without, and those empirical interference signs which show that this world, even if mostly content with itself, can become entangled in a competition of worlds which it must evade or win if it is to survive.

In a disconcerting fashion, the motto of compromise for religious peace after the age of confessional wars—*cuius regio eius religio* [Whose realm, his religion]—was anticipated by the Christian triathlon of Byzantium, Rome and Aachen, which in effect meant for the entire Middle Ages, except that here the result was not a rule for peace, but an armament of spaces that all claimed to perform the true representation of the divine. The notions a human was supposed to have of God and the signs of being therefore depended on whose sphere of representation they resided in through the coincidence of their birth—thus was the war of salvific spaces and spheres of signs of being anticipated. Structurally and factually, the last millennium of European history was largely a settlement of polemical tensions between the centers of highest representation—which appeared both intra-monotheistically, as wars between the factions of Christanity, and inter-monotheistically, as the world war between the caliphs as representatives on the one hand and the three God-representing leaders of the Christosphere. The naïve historian's term "world war" here reveals its deep structure, as the world war phenomenon can only be understood with reference to the collision of the highest-ranking represented positions of the salvific present and their broadcasting systems. "The empire is a postal system, and the postal system is a war."[67] It follows from this that any adequate theory of the full sign, sending and acknowledgement of receipt is a general staff matter.

In this monotheistic world theater, where several of the very highest messages were intramundanely broadcast or announced by the highest representative authorities, the Jewish people took up a separate, dangerous and endangered position. The extraordinary and eccentric nature of the Jewish position initially showed itself in the circumstance that it could not be consonantly incorporated into any of the three empires of Christian representatives, even though the fragments of diaspora Judaism could have been integrated more or less without conflict into the political structures of Christian rule. Judaism—less as an ethnicity than a position in the space of monotheistic messages—was condemned to eccentricity, for its mere existence was a thorn in the side of the Christian theologies of representation and their political apparatuses.

If one seriously contemplated the Jewish fact from the Byzantine, papal-Roman and imperial German perspectives, its presence signalized non-agreement with the axiom of the Christian world: that in the person of the crucified and resurrected Pharisee Jesus of Nazareth, the Messiah foretold by the prophets, the anointed king of salvation, had appeared in the flesh to fulfill the prophecies, going beyond the confines of Judaism to bring all humans ready for his message back to the kingdom of salvation with a God who, after all, was none other than the Jewish one. That Judaism continued to exist until 135 in Palestine, and later the diaspora, as a "constant" Judaism was purely a result of its inability to follow the doctrine of messianic presence.

To the extent that Judaism could only continue after Christ through negation and as a negation of the supposed Messiah event, the existence of this people took on an inevitable anti-Christian character in the eyes of the church and the Christian state. The Antichrist was not something Christians had to fear as a coming temptation; as the persisting prehistory of Christianity, it was older than Christianity itself. The diabolization of Jewish resistance was the logical response. If heathen peoples often had difficulties accepting the Christian message, this could be explained, perhaps even pardoned from the missionary perspective with the fact that the Gospel was entirely new, unaccustomed and unheard-of for them. For the non-acceptance of the Good News by Jews, other rules of play applied; the messianic message did not have to be explained to them at any length—they understood it better than anyone, but considered it false news, not to say blasphemous heresy. For the majority of Jews, the Jesus incident was no more than a sum of seductive misunderstandings—a whirl of errors grouped around a demonic central error, that of messianic deception. Had the orthodox been able to follow the events at the notorious supper, they would scarcely have seen more in this macabre eating of the lamb and drinking of wine-blood than tastelessness heightened to the point of delirium. It was in angry confusion that the majority of orthodox Jews, Pharisees and ordinary folk alike, observed the unfathomable aberration of the hubristic miracle rabbi, who had distinguished himself in front of his followers with incriminating self-descriptions and overstepped the threshold of the abyss with his unforgivable claims of "I am [the Christ]" (Mark 14:62).

From the Jewish perspective, this messianic "I am" was no more than an offensive human utterance, and thus an empty sign with no theological intensity or metaphysical capacity. Even considering that it might be a full sign after all would already indicate a baleful mental crisis. The attribute "the true Messiah" cannot be present in the sentence's subject, the Jesuan "I" and with this statement the speaker produces—aside from the scandal—at best merely what medieval language criticism termed a *flatus vocis*, a breath of air that passes over the vocal cords, which sound without producing anything possessed of valid meaning. The less favorable option would be that a demon of subjectivity had taken over the speaker, using his voice to produce a terrible vocal illusion that, through reinforcement in writing, would call up entire worlds of deceived consciousness. So if Jewish orthodoxy—leaving aside for a moment the Hellenistic-liberal, disengaged faction—could not possibly bring itself to affirm the messianity of Jesus, then from its perspective *nothing* of salvation-historical significance, aside from a possible momentary flash of temptation, had happened in the Jesuan episode.

The consequences of this choice of zero messianic presence cannot be overestimated. From the perspective of the affirmers, the Jews now increasingly became the people of deniers, indeed the people of nothingness, whose stance towards the celebration of God's arrival in the Christian presence-creating systems could only resemble that of a diabolical external observer. The Christian consciousness could never entirely forget that a witness was watching it from the outside who was unable to conceal their contempt for the error of the presentists. We can say this much: if one adopts the continuous Jewish position towards the Christian innovation for even a moment, one must immediately ask what Christians were actually doing by following, with such irresistible success and unfettered zeal, a Messiah who was not there—or rather, who remained a mere pretender. What does it mean to declare the presence of a God who has never appeared? What does it mean to translate an invalid message into all languages of the earth and set up pulpits, bishoprics and schools in every part of the world for the annunciation of an empty sign?

These are questions of frightening irony, for they set over-sized, over-subjective and over-laughable contexts in motion. A mere private delight in mockery would never suffice to think up objects of such weight from a distance. What, seriously speaking, do those Christians do who have deovoted their lives to an empty sign and take on everything to spead it? Whence the power of the cross symbol if the crucified Pharisee at the center had no prece-dence over the two wrongdoers on his left and right? What drives Christians to identify themselves with such élan as followers of an authorizer who could not possess any authority?

These idealized "Jewish questions" are not posed from the perspective of a foreign culture—a Stoic or Buddhist analytics of illusions, for example. Stoics or Buddhists are not genuinely interested in a figure called the Messiah, and have no opinion on whether or not he was embodied by a certain person; nor do they wish to acquire one, as holding an opinion on this matter would, from their point of view, lead only to a superfluous restriction of consciousness. Their exteriority in relation to the Christian yea-sayers therefore has an entirely different quality from that of Judaism, which is condemned to adopt an unambiguous stance in messianological matters—and in the present case, this is obviously a negative one. Whereas Stoics and Buddhists occupy a position of external externality, as it were, to the Christian thesis of messianic presence, which is initially painless and leaves all options open, that of Jews *post Christum crucifixum* is one of internal externality; their "no" has systematic weight because, as an intimate negation, it touches the root of the entire presence-creating system among the affirmers.

For this reason, Christianity occasionally dreams in sympto-matic fashion of retroactively forcing Jewish consent. The legend of the bleeding icon of Constantinople circulated by Jacobus de Voragine is significant for this: one day, an image of Christ in the Hagia Sophia was attacked by an angry sword-wielding Jew, who struck it in the throat; thereupon a jet of blood spattered the Jewish denier, who took fright and threw the picture into a well, where it was later recovered. He abandoned his hardness of heart, however, and converted to the Christian faith. A similar story was reported from Berith in Syria, where the blood that poured from the picture of Christ was collected in a bottle, which was taken to Rome and stored in a church.[68] Tales of this kind cele-brated the revenge of the full sign on the doubters. Furthermore, the genre of miracles involving icons and hosts as a whole was characteristic of a second, more epiphanic than apostolic wave of persuasive gestures towards skeptical milieus.

As shown above, Jewish negativity was such a grave matter because even the yea-sayers could not deny that the Jews were the people who ought to know. Hence the systematists of Christian truth, the apologists, were forced to take an interest in the rea-sons for the Jewish error. This marked the start of what came in the nineteenth century to be called the critique of false con-sciousness. Tertullian, in his tract *Against the Jews* (Chapter 14), already attempted to explain their non-consent to the celebration of messianic presence with a deep-seated misunderstanding: their stubborn inability to recognize the arrival of their potential personal liberator came from a failure to distinguish between the first coming in poverty and the second in glory. While the second would be universally evident, the first only revealed itself to faith; for the majority that evidence would bring terror upon its arrival, but for the faithful it would bring about the transition from hope to fulfillment. With regard to this difference, then, the Christians were already in possession of true insight through their faith, while the Jews rejected the revolutionary truth in favor of their habitual blindness.

The tragedy of Judaism in the Christian world came from the fact that its denial meant more than any other; they had to stay away from the celebration of the others, so to speak, and could not dance around the Golden Calf of the present. To formulate the particularity of Jewish spirituality concisely, one could say that part of being a Jew is having the authority to deny—both towards all the epiphanies of foreign religions and any assertions of messianic presence in one's own. At most, the Jewish signs of being can point ahead to a future presence delayed for now, but not to any fulfilled moment in which the marriage of meaning and being is celebrated. For Judaism, signs and the presence of God remain eternally separated by a royal distance. In the Jewish reading, signs must observe ontological discretion and are meant to be a reserve against abundance.

If, here too, one adopted this discreet view of the Christian phenomenon—be it as a historian or a semiologist—it would spontaneously raise the question of whom or what the Christians actually represented when referring to a first sign whose fullness was being denied, and what their authority meant if they referred to an originator whose messianity was disputed by the originally competent bearers of messianic expectations. What was essentially going on, then, when the affirmers gained independence from the deniers? Was the independence of this "yes" so strong in itself that, unperturbed by all challenges from without, it could consolidate and regenerate itself by its own means? What, indeed, is representation if the representatives can make short work of all doubts that there was ever anything to represent? And what was this presence, or what did it mean, if it was so much at the mercy of representation relationships that it could be passed off as real with the full emphasis of imperial authorities, even if it never materialized?

These questions, which inevitably had to open up along the Jewish-Christian border and whose violent potential cannot be overestimated, almost became everyday questions through the secularization process of the Modern Age and the end of the Christian news monopoly in modern society—as such, however, they were no longer posed explicitly, but silenced by the everyday response of indifference. The modern formula for the right to mission—that every person can represent by all legitimate means whatever they judge right and worthy, as long as no harm is done to others, and that every person can also speak without representing anything at all—only seemingly solved the problem, making it invisible in a state of half-clever relaxation. Hence the shock and amazement on all sides whenever someone, with a dangerous word, touches on the old secrets of authorized speech and its presence in the profane media.

An incident such as the fatal accident of Diana, Princess of Wales, and the unprecedented funeral on September 6, 1997 at Westminster Cathedral and in the streets of London, an event whose emotional and medial resonance raised it to an almost numinous dimension—it was said to be the most watched broadcast in the history of television—left modern intellectuals in a state of verbose speechlessness due not least to their premature retreat from the aforementioned media-logical and media-metaphysical questions. The messenger's power over the message is far-reaching—as proved by the entire history of Christianity and demonstrated from time to time by the great media glares of our time. This power extends so far that representing and passing on a message gains recognition as an activity of its own kind and own validity, regardless of whether the representative's status is secured by the presence of the original in the duplicate, and even regardless of whether there was ever an original to begin with.

Representation takes precedence: this is the decisive information to be gained from the hypothetical adoption of the Jewish stance towards the messianic affirmers. Without blinking, the Jewish view observed that the papal emperor of Byzantium, the Roman pope and the German emperor—as well as the long line of apostolic rulers in Old Europe—all presented themselves as *vicarii Dei* on earth, each in their own way and using their own means, even though their representation systems, in the Jewish view, revolved around an empty sign. An important conclusion could be drawn from this: the emptiness of a sign will never deter those who are determined to represent it. Nothing can throw the élan of representative frenzy off course once it has gathered critical momentum through gaining authority and routine. Representation, as an activity in its own right, always aims to be the representation of a fullness—a fullness that can only be secured through the messenger themselves positing as full the sign that is to be conveyed. A messenger concerned with their strength cannot help bringing strong news from a strong sender and affirming, with their own power, that of the sender—and with the sender's in turn their own. Only those things are passed on that further the passer-on. All systems of desire for power and meaning rest on this principle of proliferation.

If one searches for an interpretation of this—naively viewed—disturbing circumstance, it immediately becomes clear that the fullness of the sign is itself a function of the representative's positing-as-full. There could never be a chain of representatives if God's presence in the sign were incontestably and universally evident, as everyone would directly perceive the divine presence at all times. In this case, exegetes would be bothersome and superfluous. Only if God is hidden can intermediaries step forwards and claim to have looked behind the curtain; only if God is not manifest is it meaningful to state that he only occasionally reveals himself. That is how the intermediary assumes their position. Their mission always begins with the irresistible decision to insert themselves between God and the recipients of the signs of his presence. The messenger's decision is the basic mediocratic circumstance that symbolically constitutes large-scale groups and holds them together.

This constitution can never be reflected upon in the metaphysical broadcasting system itself—except in negative form: as a condemnation of false apostles and lying priests in similarly built broadcasting systems. It is easier to recognize that the apostle of another religion or the heretical dissenter from one's own has appointed or successfully fooled themselves. One's own mission, on the other hand, is necessarily viewed by determined messengers as truer, more objective, and consequently more moving and binding. From the genuine representative's perspective, it would always be true even if they did not represent it; and this semblance is entirely consistent, firstly, because all representatives must themselves be fundamentally representable, and secondly, because every representative was indeed preceded by another—extending back to Paul the Apostle, who began the Christian relay team. In the jargon of ontologists and theologians of encounter, running in a messengers' relay race is often mystified with the formula that God or being anticipated personal existence and speech. In truth, only an earlier messenger can anticipate the present one.

What has just been termed the "messenger's decision" points once more to the phenomenon of subject change frequently discussed here; in its psychological form, it means the subject's consent to be overwhelmed by a preceding great augmenter—an inner other whose size *per se* releases the impulse to spread the word in public. If the augmenter merely remained the friend or the mistress, the language of this love could be exhausted in private whispering; a possible surplus could only be published as literature. If the beloved is God, then declarations of love and loyalty must present themselves as a mission into the great. The messenger proves their love for the great other by speaking to others of love.

This makes us aware once again how microspheric motifs burst into macrospheric practice, giving it its personal tinge. Sharing subjectivity with an inner other of monotheistic format leads—as shown above—to a truth stress that must be discharged in missionary practice. For the humans taking part in this demanding dual, it would scarcely be tolerable to be bound together with a great god possessing no empire. Naturally, this great god is the providential partner of worldly greats. To help the god establish his empire, and to share in the desire for empire themselves, the human partner of the empire-shaped and empire-demanding god developed a unity of action between serving and sending—as a necessary step to enter into the apostolic contract.

It follows from these reflections that representing the absolute is an act in its own right in which the act of representation immediately makes that which is represented appear, or—as this is not directly possible—*show itself* in an image or a message. Representing means producing images and words and occupying spaces of pictorial and verbal presence. As a gesture of its own kind this representing is originally theopoietic, corresponding to the Greek verb *theopoiein*, meaning "to make godly, to deify"—a word in which, as in Latin divinization, the active contribution of the representative to bringing forth the holy notion was already clearly expressed. Naturally, this word had to be banished from the positive vocabulary of monotheistic metaphysics and Christian religion in power, as it only seemed usable for the theopoetries of heathen or heretical positions, while their own doctrine could not be reflected upon as theopoetry, theofactum or fetish, but only as a received, accepted and objectively true doctrine. The representatives, who wish to be pure, recoil from the notion that they might be authors of divine words and hewers of theosculptures as if it were evil itself, even though they are *de facto* trapped in a never-ending process of theopoietic formulation and reformulation. The longer the sending process takes, the higher the mountain of now-historical representatives' formulations becomes—and these include countless ones to which even the current "pure" representatives no longer dare return. (Around 1996, in official statements of the Holy See, John Paul II made ninety-four admissions of guilt and expressions of regret over errors and injustices of his predecessors and the Catholic Church as a whole.)

Since Giambattista Vico, the founder of the humanities—which, as we can increasingly see, would be more aptly termed spheric sciences—the argument has been in the world that the historical reality of peoples before modernity is *eo ipso* theopoietically constituted, and that the science of humans must therefore be the science of self-poeticizing life forms. This brings into view why, in modernity, poetology—even, and especially, in the First Things—ultimately outstripped both ontology and theology: the reflexivity of modern communicational circumstances made the artificial character of the metaphysical system of messengers, officials and signs as a whole emerge in such a defined light that a return to the Old European standards of self-deception seemed to have become forever impossible. Never again would the sender allow themselves to be separated from the bringer to such an extent that the metaphysical and feudal idea of the pure delivery of objective messages could remain valid. The authorial crisis—has it not long since affected heaven too? And is the representative's crisis not the necessary counterpart of the absolute sender's demise? The selfless mailmen—what became of them once they had taken all the interesting posts? Whom was Martin Buber thinking of (apart from himself) when he said that a man who does not think of himself is given all the keys?

Now it would simply be necessary for theologians to discard their job descriptions and declare themselves theopoets, whereupon the former theology departments would reunite with those of comparative literature and cultural anthropology. Does it mean nothing that Plato was thinking of the poets when he coined the term *theológoi*? Who could still speak of God and gods without identifying themselves as a poet? This rule also encompasses God and the gods themselves in so far as their self-portraits are regularly imagined as revelations, and their works of literature as acts of world-creation. The mailmen of old, the ego-less apostles, have been unmasked as the authors and continuers of their own deliveries—since well before Joseph Klausner (introducing Nietzsche's explosive theorems into the field of Jewish studies) revealed Paul as the true founder of Christianity in his 1939 book on the people's apostle—a thesis taken up and radicalized by the Jewish philosopher of religion Jacob Taubes. The idea of the pure, selfless, sender-devoted bringer of whatever more or less eliminated itself simply by drawing greater attention to its problematic points. The great senders, we can say quite calmly, are the fictions of representatives, born from the spirit in which empires shared the desire for power and meaning.

As far as pure transports of deliveries are concerned, they are best guaranteed today (relatively speaking) by the private parcel services, which ask high prices for their selfless punctuality. All other delivery agents, including the sacred ones, can be identified as media entrepreneurs who strive to gain shares in the message market—with motives that could scarcely be described as selfless. (For what is more self-ish than the preservation of identity interests among those who occupy traditional positions?) In modernity, at least, it was the sender who paid the postage, whereas in the metaphysical age the addressee was called upon to do so. Was the entire economic history of the classical monotheisms not a large-scale attempt to have the postage paid by the addressee rather than the sender? Monotheism was built on an economy of gratitude—relying on the preemptive gratitude shown by the recipients of messages that were worth any postage fee, and justified any amount of cash on delivery. Modernity replaced this with the economy of the greedy, who invest as soon as they can expect to receive back more than they paid.

The last gasp of this metaphysics of the mailman came in the twentieth century—strangely enough, in a Jewish theology that had begun to take an interest in Paul as the undercover agent of a Jewish world mission. If Paul is to be claimed as the general apostle of Judaism—and authors such as Rosenzweig, Ben-Chorin, Taubes and others did so, with the passion of irony—then the phantasm of the pure messenger is of no use. For in the matter of Jewish messages, Paul can be discussed first of all as a counterfeiter, then at second glance perhaps a secret agent, but definitely not as a pure emissary. Whatever the case may be, the aforementioned theologians begin by criticizing the national-religious hermeticism of historical Judaism, which they accuse of failing in the task formulated in Second Isaiah, namely to be a "light unto the nations," on account of its rigid ethnic enclosure.[69] Paul, on the other hand, the dissident, the seeming traitor, did justice to the universal mission of Judaism—albeit with a message that could no longer be readily considered that of Israel. Ben-Chorin, who followed on from Franz Rosenzweig and particularly intensified the Jewish mailman theory, formally states:

> Was this message still the message of Israel? [...] Historical Judaism answered the question in the negative. It felt betrayed by Paul, not represented [...] and yet it was Paul who fulfilled Israel's mission to be a "light unto the nations"in its place. Franz Rosenzweig once remarked that Christianity, not Judaism, spread the Hebrew Bible of Israel to the remotest

islands [...]. Through Paul's religious propaganda, the Bible of Israel [...] became a bestseller in the ancient world.[70]

Thus Paul, as the Jewish apostle, was equipped with an *a posteriori* world-religious authorization by the national-religious sender. The entire argument is carried by historico-theological irony, for it posits that the Christianity Paul launched emerged as a parcel service for the delivery of Old Testaments in the gentile world, with the New Testaments having to be taken on board as problematic supplements. Whoever finds this argument indecent should consider that early church historiography for its part interpreted the Roman scattering of the Jews throughout the whole empire (after the destruction of the temple in 70, then completely after the Bar Kokhba revolt of 135) with an analogous argument as a *praeparatio evangelica*, for where there were already Jews, Christian missionaries could follow more easily—which can surely be considered a classical parasitological thought figure.

This construction shows the cost of wanting to save the sender once the messenger is already standing naked. What makes it interesting is that it identifies Paul as a messenger who, even after the Damascus experience, chose the wrong sender. If he had understood himself correctly, he would never have been able to say that Christ, not he himself, lived in him—what lived in him would rather have been the Deutero-Isaiahan mandate, for which the annunciation of Christ was merely the cover. This argument amounts to a semio-psychoanalysis of the Apostle that makes a Christian secondary process dependent on a Jewish primary one. This is precisely the purpose of "bringing Paul home to Judaism," that subject which certain rabbis so enjoy discussing with certain Christian theologians during long academy weekends.

The primary process is Jewish: this posits the existence of a prophetic unconscious, and, like every authentic unconscious, this too cannot refrain from sending the message it has been trained to send. Hence this unconscious cannot refrain from speaking about chosenness. Viewed positively, extrapolating from the observations of Rosenzweig and Ben-Chorin: the volume of lust for power in the Jewish unconscious promised more than Christian takers could demand, for it held out the prospect of the unsurpassable. Nothing provides more imaginary pre-lust and actual lust for power than marking a subject with a sign of chosenness. No one can break away from such an unconscious—indeed, even analyzing it, and thus exposing it to a critical risk, will be beyond the power of the one thus marked. Here one must treat the phantom of self-analysis with even more distrust than usual. That is why Sigmund Freud, the unanalyzed "prophet of the unconscious," in whom the prophet's unconscious was perfectly developed and perfectly hidden (not repressed), did everything to cover the tracks leading to his own case. With great suggestive skill, he drew attention to the sexual-libidinous unconsciousness of the profane neurotics and ensured that nothing was said about the election-libidinous unconsciousness.

Paul's mission as a secret agent, then, would have been to mark the gentile peoples with the Jewish unconscious and its sign, that of chosenness. This escape from the national-religious enclosure of Judaim was—as indicated by Jacob Taubes in an equally illuminating and aimless interpretation—meant to be the founding act for a new people of God outside of Judaism, a people of God defined by Taubes—not usually averse to curt elitist formulations—as a strictly universalist and egalitarian project people.[71] The purpose of Paul's mission would then have been to pass on the privilege of chosenness to *all* peoples outside the "truly chosen" people. Chosenness for all: a paradox that can naturally only work at the latent level, and immediately ruins its agents and agencies as soon as it appears at the explicit. Outside of Judaism, the sign of belonging to the exclusive-inclusive new people of God could no longer be passed on as the *character indelibilis* on the man's body—hence Paul saw no alternative but to abolish the law of circumcision for male gentiles who devoted themselves to Christ.

Thus the first sign of chosenness died out. Paul therefore had to highlight a different, transferable sign at all costs; hence his obsession with the cross. Nothing else was suitable as replacement for the non-transferable primal sign. Its interpretation and annunciation show that the central operation of Pauline thought is the re-encoding of chosenness. This could only succeed by means of a higher-level concept of circumcision that saves the meaning without calling for the act—and Paul found this concept. According to him, being circumcised means having let oneself be weakened by following a suffering God, and subsequently participating eternally in the most sovereign system of desire for power and meaning. As soon as one knows what the metaphor of circumcision represents, it can be exchanged. Paul's metaphorization of circumcision is prefigured in the Jewish commandment: "Circumcise your hearts, therefore, and do not be stiff-necked any longer." (Deuteronomy 10:16) This much circumcision must be demanded of people who normally defend their uninjured state unbendingly, assuming that monotheism is to be—and that a well-integrated humiliation can make humans socially competent. (Lacan, incidentally, followed on closely from Paul with a crypto-Catholic basic position: as his patients could not be circumcised, he made them accept the principles of symbolic castration and constitutive lack.)

The sign of the suffering God, the cross, indicates the second-born in the transference and expansion of the awareness of chosenness. Hence Paul's staurological pathos; the cross, *staurós*, is meant to replace the circumcision knife, but must inscribe the same information in the baptized flesh: chosenness for all in the pneumatic people! According to Paul, the unconscious has the structure of an impossible belonging.

It is only where the discreet transference of the source of desire for being that is chosenness succeeds with gentile believers that—whether through inadvertent infection or conscious acceptance—identification with the law and the commandment to love takes place. If one takes this ethical transference seriously, the mailman theory of Christianity is not simply a desperate construction by theologians to rescue the Jewish position in its historical oddity; it describes a process that, despite its almost unbearable irony, is part of the positive history of ideas and the moral process of Western civilization.

This seemingly final escalation of the metaphysics of the mailman, which wanted to see the Jewish delivered globally by the Christian postal system, was actually outdone by the Protestant lay theologian, jurist, sociologist and philosopher of language Eugen Rosenstock-Huessy with a general theory of deliveries that, in his view, was also meant to be the true theory of cultures and people-creating communications. Rosenstock-Huessy, who had an embittered friendship with the Jewish philosopher Franz

Rosenzweig, considered it his task to reject the ironic theory of Jewish evangelization *per Christianos* from a Christian perspective. This could only be achieved through a radical broadening of the evangelical base—by backdating the good news to the beginnings of human communication. If Christian apostles were to be more than secret agents of a Jewish unconscious and deliverers of that oriental beststeller, the Old Testament, which had to be sent out all over the world as a supplement to the New Testament, they required the backing of a sender who had more to send and say than the national-religious program of Judaism with world-religious intentions.

Rosenstock believes he has identified this sender: he finds him in a theological process figure, a generalized Holy Spirit of language. Rosenstock's ingenious twist lay in separating the miracle of Pentecost from its actual date and spreading it across the entire history of language. He dates it back to the beginnings of language as such and the first gestures of human face-to-face communication, claiming that it became chronic after Christ in the history of freedom and revolutions in Europe, America and the rest of the world, in so far as free speech was already possible there. Regression to the earliest stages of language is an important point for Rosenstock primarily because it was the only way for the pluralism of starting points for people-forming communications to be ensured. "It is unthinkable that what we do when we speak is any different from what the people of all periods have done." The streams of the hundred thousand language that were spoken by the archaic human groups and converged at the start of the imperial age to form rivers of high languages and world languages are viewed by Rosenstock as enormous appeal hearings in which the dead ancestors everywhere spoke, with all their wisdom and blindness, through the living generations. "Tell me who is speaking to you and I will know who you are." "We are the children of listening."[72] From this perspective, the entire Archaic period and the Old World become an introductory course in full speech. Before Christ, one can essentially distinguish between four linguistic currents that condition a fourfold listening and passing on. Fruitful speech is possible in the continuum of the words of the ancestors and the dead, the continuum of the teachings of the celestial phenomena, the continuum of the muses' songs, and the continuum of prophetic utterances about the terrors of the apocalypse.

Only through listening to the utterances springing from these sources does humanity become a musical and discursive instrument on which the skill of resonating with increasingly demanding messages is rehearsed.

In the foundational part of his philosophy of language, Rosenstock-Huessy undertakes an inspiring reaching out into the general anthropology of communication; he acknowledges all ancient peoples and their languages as contributors to a global process of ensoulments through manifold invocations, attunements, namings and broadcasts. Rosenstock recognizes the apostolic subject change, the act of speaking out of the other, everywhere. For him, the imperative becomes a universal. Among other functions, the strategic purpose of this expanding gesture is to relativize the prophetic privilege of Judaism; prophetism is only one of several gestures that advance full and fully authorized speech; it must accept comparison with the theopoetic genius of other spaces, the cosmological knowledge of other empires and the artistic communications of other peoples.

This expansion is followed by polemical escalation. For, although Rosenstock aims to keep in check the overblown claims made for Jewish prophetism, he wishes to ascribe perfect fullness of speech to messianism—in its Christian form, of course. Consequently, the work of the archaic and classical world was, for him, nothing other than the process of making available the words that were spoken by Jesus; he, the "fruit of the lips" of humanity, is assigned "the central place in the history of language." Christ is not merely a case of prophetism, but the sum and confluence of the ancient language currents. Anyone wishing to understand what language is must listen to the sayings formulated by the God-man. For Rosenstock, the words of Christ are the result and blossom of everything, and of the best that had been said until then—the words of ancestors, of poets, of rhapsodists and of prophets. Christianity is continued speech at this level; the Christian truth is tetralingual.

Whoever considers themselves part of the Christian performative revolution is thus automatically recruited for the holy communicative war of Christians against the great rest of humanity still trapped in archaic and classical times—times *before* the experience of the full word. Rosenstock unabashedly names those he is thinking of, and as he names the main groups of those who do not follow on from the divine speaker in the same breath, he manages to produce a singular list of opponents:

the Nazis, the Jews, the Fascists, the Chinese and the Marxists deny the word as our true ancestor.[73]

The criterion for this remarkable enumeration is the shared refusal of those named to explain their communications with the pentecostal event. Rosenstock is able to protect the Christian-apostolic line of mailmen from Jewish irony by elevating the entire history of language to a process of the Holy Spirit that calls through the generations; a side effect of this rescue, however, is a declaration of enmity towards all non-pentecostal collectives.

What Hegel undertook for the concept by reconstructing its self-comprehension in time is carried out by Rosenstock for communication, for he traces its development as a process of summoning humans to work in the service of speech and love. The true spirit of the age would be the spirit of language, which issues the daily orders of love. Just as the concept of the concept leads to the observation of realized truth, the communication of communication becomes the call to participate in the humanity-creating stream of languages: Rosenstock finally speaks like a minister of world communications, stating that the purpose of all medial networks is the delivery of the message of love. His processual Pentecost is the super-mail, which sends out draft calls for the progressing history of love on a global scale—and which places its message in every letter box, even those bearing the sticker "No advertising material."

"Representation takes precedence"—as seen above, there is good reason to return to this claim from a spherological perspective. For it seems natural to suppose that the entire system of representatives is merely a powerful episode in the history of sphere productions. The dissemination of orders/messages/summons in the name of a central truth that demands to be represented unconditionally corresponds to a mode of sphere formation in imperial formats. Its model is the sending of the message in all directions from an overflowing, self-communicating center.

As soon as the stupor of thought has cleared a little through this mode of sending—and this clearing occurs largely through the experience of the modern pluralism of messages—it becomes evident that being a metaphysical representative con-stitutes a historical state of a much more general phenomenon: that of spheropoiesis on the large scale, which was reconstructed in its basic traits above. Standing in or representing would then be merely a historically restricted misnomer for sphere forma-tion—for the communicative primary function, which began long before monotheism and continues indefinitely beyond monotheistic monopolies.

The meaning of authorized telecommunications and repre-senting messengers' speeches can, therefore, only be adequately understood in terms of the logic of macrospheric space formations. The present sketch touches on how the telecommunicative ner-vous system of imperial and ecclesiastical large-scale bodies forms itself. The space-disclosing and distance-eliminating radiocracy, supported by an all-pervasive center-religious and center-meta-physical semantics, has always played the pivotal role in it.

Modernity—even when using such seemingly monocentric terms as "broad"cast—created a postmetaphysical mode of space formation that, because of its unsuppressible polycentrism, cut the ground from under all centrist and hierarchist phantasms—aside from the enclave of the popes (by which I mean Rome, not Valréas). That is precisely why the Modern Age could be con-demned by the conservatives as a revolt against the holy circle of monopoly communicators and as a loss of the center.

In reality, these formulas of battle and lament simply mean that the history of sphere creations—each with its own language game, border politics and truth functions—has by no means passed its metaphysical middle age, that is to say the stage of totalist monospheres. Since Columbus' expedition, the history of the "world" has had to become the drawn-out world war sequence that it obviously was, for the simple reason that the collision of regional monospheres, each metaphysicized in its own way, is its topic—to say nothing here of the numerous defenseless, oppressed and destroyed smaller societies, languages and worlds.

If the Europeans looked like the victors in the first round of these world collisions, it was primarily because they had been the first to destroy or lose their macrospheric immune system, their harboring beneath a homogeneous Catholic heaven, and broken through *nolens volens* to the pluralism of confessions and imperialisms. This gave them their frightening penetrative power in the first round of terrestrial globalization, plausibly marked by the dates 1492 and 1945.

For the Europeans of this period, the old dream of the outsideless universal container was shattered by their own schismatic history. This was the case from the Reformation and the subsequent age of confessional wars onwards, at least, which was simultaneously the age of the race between the rising national empires that divided up the globe among themselves into areas of interest and mission. It is no coincidence that European cosmology achieved its breakthrough from the Aristotelian-Catholic celestial orbs to the infinite universe in this period. From that point on, Europeans acknowledged an outside that could now only be grouped around a Roman or Jerusalemite center with a high degree of denial. From the beginnings of colonialism onwards, the European masters should have known and understood that the so-called periphery was something entirely different from the edge of a center that resided in the motherland. The holistic restorations and romanticisms did succeed in delaying the perception of the situation by almost an entire age, at least, until the Old European midpoint dreamtime came to an unmistakably brutal end around the middle of the twentieth century. The time referred to as the heroic years of philosophy, especially German Idealism and its Marxist epilogue, made one of the greatest contributions to sealing off the European province from the so-called peripheries that encyclopedists and colonizers had already brought so close.

It was only after the current post-socialist globalization debate was initiated that continental Europeans were forced to remove their dream glasses. They gradually began to understand that the things Europeans took for granted, including their conventions of philosophical and anthropological language, only had regional validity, and did not automatically reflect the common sense of a hypothetical total human race.

Most of all, it was modern European literature that first broke away from the Catholic-philosophical dream of a true unified message and a final world language to move towards an essential multilinguality. In media-historical terms, this departure is connected to the transition from the ecclesiastically and state-governed palace economy of messages to a literary and journalistic market economy.

Since its beginnings in the fourteenth century, the latter has presented itself in two guises: firstly, as a market of light literatures, novellas and novelties, where messages are focused on the recipient rather than the sender to meet the public's expectations of entertainment and edification; and secondly, as a market of genius literature, which remained highly sender-centered because the author still acted as the local revelation of a transcendent transmitter, but meant a transition to non-monopolistic and neo-polytheistic conditions. Novalis voiced the thought that in future, even the name "Christ" would have to be used in the plural. Art history trivialized this impulse and had the producing messiahs march past in chronological processions. On the market of genius, the former monopoly religion dissolved into a deregulated process of revelation in which as many gods as great artists were revealed. One could actually say that religious centralism perished through the legalization of genius (just as, in morphological terms, God's death throes had begun with the positing of the center as ubiquitous and the de-realization of the circumference.[74]) If, furthermore, one annuls the condition that only great art is allowed to be made public, one has already established modern mass culture in its outlines. The constant revelation of triviality can be celebrated in it; because that is not a real cause for celebration, however, participants have no choice but to keep turning the crank of self-applause for the not-very-special-either.

The choice of trivial culture is not itself trivial; just as late antiquity decided to give the Gospel precedence over the muses, postmodernized modernity (if I am not entirely mistaken) opted for the precedence of democracy over art and philosophy. The more pleasant consequences of this include the peaceful coexistence of all messages without violence and without substance; the culture of leaderboards as the eternal return of the slightly different; the self-exposure of media societies to the eternally same, eternally new mixture of nonsense and non nonsense; the freedom to choose between different forms of action for the same decadence;

and the emancipation of speakers from the unreasonable expectation of having anything to say. As far as the more unpleasant consequences are concerned, they are not the topic of this discussion.

The present state of the free message market, which—as far as one can see—will remain its final one, was perfectly evoked in a little parable by Franz Kafka around 1914:

> They were offered the choice between becoming kings or couriers. The way children would, they all wanted to be couriers. Therefore there are only couriers who hurry about the world, shouting to each other—since there are no kings—messages that have become meaningless. They would like to put an end to this miserable life of theirs but they dare not because of their oaths of service.[75]

The De-crowning of Europe

An Anecdote about the Tiara

In the event that a philosophical history of headgear is one day written (which will be inevitable once engagement with the content of head content has been exhausted), this would be the best form in which to recall a bygone age in which humans carried their central idea both on their heads and in them. The members of premodern humanity declared their stance towards the world in hats.

Among the visible cranial supplements or external capital ideas, the crowns and miters occupy an eminent position—not only because their circular form harbors the human head in a close-fitting encompassing figure, but also because they indicate the presence of majesty or divine consecration atop a head, both through themselves and through their ritual use. Should consecration and majesty, which are usually separate charisms, exceptionally come together on an exceptional head, such that miter and crown coincide, this would confirm the optimistic hypothesis that human heads are also suitable as carriers—philosophically speaking, as that which underlies—of the highest secular and spiritual thoughts. Above all, one can speak of such a head-borne (or otherwise embodied) highest thought if an individual person is set apart by singular headgear as the center of humanity or as a living principle (*principe, prince*).

In Europe, this crown optimism is a fact whose history begins in the early fourteenth century and ends in the middle of the twentieth; it is initially a history of competition between papal and imperial headgear, and one need not be a specialist in medieval history to know that the papal head was in front at the end—meaning that it gained a notable coronatory head start on other adorned heads. How exactly this papal advantage was gained is a matter of some controversy, even among experts. We can only be sure that the problem of the highest crown was set in motion in Rome under Boniface VIII, whose papacy from 1294–1303 is considered the climax of plentiful papal power, and initially towards a two-story structure.

The starting situation of this development had established itself around the turn of the thirteenth century, when the new leader of the church had first the mitra, then the tiara—which had a single ring at that time—placed on his head by the cardinal dean. For the wearers of both items, their symbolism seemed self-evident: it was clear that the miter was used liturgically, in the mass and whenever else the wearer desired by virtue of its pontifical function (*pro sacerdotio*), while the tiara was used extra-liturgically as a sign of rulership (*pro regno*) for regal appearances, receptions, processions and the like.[76] The coronation employed a formula that is suitable to remind subsequent generations of the symbolic realism of medieval thought, for the tiara as such was thenceforth often termed *corona sive regnum*—as if to emphasize very clearly that the crown did not *stand for* rulership or kingship, but rather *was* rulership or kingship.

Boniface went on from here and added a second story to the papal tiara, though the second ring only seemingly had the purpose of symbolizing the twofold power of the pope in sacred and secular matters; researchers have read all manner of pious notions into it with reference to the two kingdoms doctrine—which is nonsense, as the difference and configuration of the kingdoms was already sufficiently articulated in the dualism of the miter and corona. In reality, the second ring was part of a coronal escalation. This was a response to the provocation of imperial headwear, for the emperor, like the pope, wore both a clerical miter and his imperial diadem, which cannot have been observed from Rome without some disgruntlement.

The one-upmanship of Boniface's papal tiara is self-evident: the adjacency of miter and single crown was now considered dissatisfactory and corrected by the stacking of two coronal rings in the secular crown. Naturally Boniface did not attack the emperor via the miter, which did not permit any increase, but on the side of the crown. Crowned with the *biregnum*, the papal head thus became the bearer of an idea of majesty that exceeded the imperial head, together with its superstructions, by a noticeable margin—which fulfilled the purpose of the operation. In fact, Boniface pushed the *regnum* atop his head to a full cubit's height, which was already criticized by certain contemporaries as a hubristic return to the self-cult of the heathen emperors. Boniface's crown was, as it were, the extra-liturgical seal on the thesis of the infamous bull *Unam sanctam*, whose final sentence is as follows: "Furthermore, we declare, we proclaim, we define that it is absolutely necessary for salvation that every human creature be subject to the Roman Pontiff."[77] This subordination (*subesse*) was demanded not so much for the miter-wearing bishop as for the anointed Caesar who adorned himself with the double *regnum*. The two-tiered crown of

Boniface was the perfect expression of culminating Roman papo-Caesarism.

This escalation was felt in all its severity by the symbol-sensitive public sphere of European rulers, and the culprit was spontaneously repaid in kind. It was not the emperor who parried the papal foray, however, but Philip the Fair, King of France, who struck the inflated crown from the head of Christ's representative in 1303 in the Outrage of Anagni. Boniface did not survive the monstrous act of his capture by agents of a worldly power for long; the lingering shock of his humiliation claimed his life that same year. At the Council of Vienne, Philip succeeded in forcing Clement V (1305–1314), Boniface's second successor, to annul the validity of the bull *Unam sanctam* for France. From Vienne onwards, then, the removal of the two-tiered crown by the pope was a *fait accompli*. After a short trial period, the most serious attempt to expand the papal head heavenwards had been thwarted by worldly resistance. In effect, the pope would no longer be able to raise his crowned head above that of a nation's king.

How the classical three-tiered papal crown, the so-called tiara, could take shape in the light of these circumstances—after the decommissioning of the papo-Caesarist *biregnum*—is a question that surely merits closer examination for historians of head-covering ideas. In our context it is sufficient to note that the pope, whose hands were tied when it came to the King of France, placed all the more emphasis on his symbolic rivalry with the German emperor. Hence the coronation of Henry VII (1309–1313) as Holy Roman Emperor by a papal legate in June 1312 was a welcome occasion to display the primacy of the pope over the empire on the traditional front. It is understandable that a heightened sensitivity to the crown had established itself in Avignon after the humiliations suffered. Now it was all the more displeasing that the German imperial ideologues were becoming a talking point with overblown theories of the crown that gave the emperor precedence over all the rulers of the world on account of his triple crowning—just as Christ symbolically wore a triple diadem comprising the crowns of mercy, justice and glory.

As for the imperial *triregnum*, it consisted of the silver German crown of Aachen, the iron Lombardic crown of Milan or Monza, and finally the golden crown of the King of the Romans, which passed through the hands of the Bishop of Rome to the emperor's head. As far as the facts suggest, there was no plan on the imperial side to collect this trinity of crowns in a single tiered one. All that is relevant for the later formal development is the Roman crown of the emperor, which was a compromise between a miter and a conventional crown, with the crown's metallic housing enclosing a slightly scaled-down conical miter. It is the archetype of the magnified papal tiaras. But the question remains: how did the *triregnum* come to adorn the heads of popes when the *biregnum* had already caused such offense that Boniface's successors were forced to refrain from wearing it?

At this sensitive point, there is a significant gap in the history of papal headgear. If we turn the page, we already stumble on the glib assurance of liturgy historians that from 1350 onwards, the triregnum was the "characteristic headdress of the popes." The liturgologists maintain polite silence, however, on the matter of how this one-upmanly imitation of the imperial crown ended up on the papal head. One can understand why, for they would inevitably—assuming that documents of the embarrassment were still accessible—have had to mention that it was precisely the weak post-Bonifacian popes who symbolistically took the bull by the horns by donning a super-imperial crown. The nub of the tale is that they could do so without arousing the jealousy of the French kings anew, which tells us enough about the conditions of power and meaning in that time, as well as their interpretation by the protagonists on the European stage.

This contains the decisive information for the following: it was under the Avignonese popes, theological marionettes of the French kings, that the habit of wearing three-story crowns was firmly established among Saint Peter's successors. Thus, with their ironic tolerance, the French and their kings effectively established a new semantics of the crown in which the object was no longer itself the *regnum*, but only signified the *regnum*. Yet signification, as we know, is a broad subject. It was on the heads of the French popes that nominalism was successfully put into practice for the first time. A crown is a crown, while power is power. So, because a deep gulf opened up in logic itself between words and things, between images and powers, the French kings no longer needed to feel provoked by a highest crown whose primary function was recognizably to give a humiliated pope symbolic satisfactions in the face of a ghostly empire. Beneath the smiles of the French, the popes of Avignon could embrace the phantoms of the specialist hatters.

For the next two hundred years, the headgear of the popes would cease to be one of the highest objects of reflection by Old European reason; only with the Reformation did the time come for a new dispute of this kind, and it revealed itself in a flood of claims about the multiple meanings of the tiara. In his text *De tribus coronis Pontificis MAximi* (Rome, 1587), Marcus Antonius Mazzaronius arrayed dozens of possible and actual

Ego sum Papa, French etching from the 16th century

meanings, thus hinting at the transition to a theory of inexhaustible coronal meaning.[78] The three-story structure of the papal tiara means virtually everything that can be associated with the number three, from the persons of the trinity to the group of theological virtues, namely faith, love and hope. What is more interesting than these exercises in baroque theologians' verbosity,

Globe-crowned tiara on the statue of Gregory the Great, Ottobeuren Abbey, stucco sculpture by Johann Michael Feuchtmayer (1766)

however, are the iconographic developments that augmented the three-tiered crown by placing the cross-crowned globe on top of it—the most prominent example being a tiara occasionally worn by the statue of Saint Peter in papal robes at St. Peter's Basilica in Rome. Another, though fixed to the head, adorns the statues of Gregory the Great at the Theatine Church in Munich and Ottobeuren Abbey.[79] Whether popes from the sixteenth century onwards actually wore globe-topped tiaras is uncertain, but highly probable; the motif was in the air and corresponds to the title *rector orbis*, which, according to the Roman missal from the sixteenth century, was the form of address chosen by the popes at their coronations. In practice, admittedly, the popes—as we shall see—were not so much the controllers as the notaries of globalization.[80] The addition of the world-orb to the tip of the tiara can be recognized as the final move in a symbolic escalation with which the head of the Counter-Reformation church sought one more time to stake a claim to the highest earthly coronation in the age of incipient terrestrial globalization.

The rest of the history took a conventional course. Only once more did a tiara attract a degree of attention: when, after the Treaty of Tolentino in February 1797, Pius VI had to silver-plate the magnificent tiara of Julius II in order to pay war contributions to the young general Napoleon. (After his spectacular self-coronation in Paris in 1804, incidentally, in which he snubbed the attendant pope, Napoleon no longer wore the crown at representative appearances, but rather, as the first monarch since antiquity to do so, donned the laurel wreath.) Only after another one hundred and sixty years, on November 12, 1964, was the question of the suitable papal headgear stirred up one last time—though who can be sure in such matters?—when Paul VI, in a solemn act towards the end of the Second Vatican Council that was breathtaking for eyewitnesses, took off his personal tiara in the Council Hall and made a gift of it to the poor. He never wore a tiara thereafter. It is unclear whether his successors should be constrained to follow his example; the Vatican and the officious liturgologists prefer to remain vague about the matter. In this state of affairs, it does not seem far-fetched to take Paul VI's renunciation of the tiara as a confession

We at the Basilica of the National Shrine welcome and
appreciate your comments. E:mail: shrine@cris.com

Internet page of the Basilica of the National Shrine of the Immaculate Conception, 2006, Washington

that could not be circumvented by later popes. His two immediate successors, John Paul I and John Paul II, *de facto* adapted to the new standard; both dispensed with coronation and the wearing of the tiara. It can safely be assumed that the tiara of Paul VI was still sold during his office; it is rumored that the publisher Time Life acquired it for an undisclosed sum of money, which fits very well into the picture of the Pauline de-crowning—for had the tiara not been exchanged for at least a seven-figure dollar sum, the gesture of a gift to the poor would have remained an empty one.[81] We do know that a few years later, Paul VI discovered his special love for the Catholic Church of the USA and sought to express it by, on February 6, 1968, giving his personal tiara to the Basilica of the National Shrine of the Immaculate Conception for permanent display. Symbol-sensitive Europeans may be bemused by the fact that the last "active" tiara is now located in Washington D.C., albeit demoted to the status of an exhibition piece. It would be somewhat exaggerated to interpret this as a symbol of imperial transfer to the Americans, especially as the tiara is not a unique specimen; thus even the sale of a tiara to non-Europeans and its safekeeping by Catholics in the USA would not *per se* rule out a return to this headdress habitus.

One could imagine circumstances in the near future of the European Union under which the papal tiara might become significant once more as a symbolic resource of European self-affirmation. If tiaras disappear from papal heads in general, however (though not from the Vatican's letterheads), then this non-dress should also be understood as an idea that manifests itself on the head of a non-wearer, provided one can recognize the zero as such. If the never-crowned do not wear crowns, this does not contain any information that would move the public;

but if the potentially highest-crowned figure appears uncrowned, then the absence of the crown from his head has the character of a statement. The zero-tiara option is a vote on how crownable the heads of the Bishops of Rome are. Perhaps it is time to conclude that with regard to the extra-liturgical headgear of the popes, the decentering of Europe has been carried out since 1964 by the last imperiomorphic authority of the Old World. Through the turn of globalization towards the terrestrial, the crisis of those ideas that can be worn on heads is combined with that of the ideas inside them.

CHAPTER 8

The Last Orb

On a Philosophical History of Terrestrial Globalization

O human race, how many storms and misfortunes and shipwrecks must toss you about while, transformed into a
many-headed beast, you strive after conflicting things.

— Dante, *Monarchy* I, XVI, 3[1]

... and the pirate globe drifts
in the stormy ether.

— Henri Michaux, *Inexpressible Places*

1. The Wandering Star

When Greek philosophers and geometricians began to measure the
universe mathematically two and a half thousand years ago, they
were following an irresistible formal intuition: their interest in the
totality of the world was kindled by the easy constructibility and
symmetrical perfection of the spherical form. For them, the
simplest form was at once the most integral, complete and beautiful. That is why the cosmologists who gathered in the ancient
Academy and other places of learned quarrelling were now

considered not only the greatest rationalists, but also the most distinguished of aesthetes. Anyone who was not a geometrician or an ontologist was no longer of any use as a connoisseur of beautiful things. For what was the most beautiful thing—the sky—if not the material realization of the best, namely the whole? The Greek prejudice in favor of rounded totality would survive until the days of German Idealism: 'Do you know its name? The name of that which is one and is all? Its name is Beauty.' (Hölderlin, *Hyperion*)[2]

This rise of form as such over material in general could only be guided by an aesthetics of completion. If the subtle and the massive cosmos were ever to be integrated into a single conception, it had—as was thought at the time—to be in the notional shape of the orb. It was in the sublime nature of this super-object to remain unrecognizable to ordinary eyes: there is an orb that is too large for trivial perception and too sublime for sensory comprehension. But since philosophy started its war against the sensuality of the people's opinion, invisibility has always been presented as the foremost hallmark of the true whole.[3] Whether on this side or the other of the phenomenon, however, no object since then has succeeded in satisfying and humbling its contemplators like the all-encompassing orb, which continues to shine from afar, bearing its dual name of *cosmos* and *uranos*, long after disappearing into the archive of disused ideas.

As soon as the concern was to formulate a concept—or rather an image—of the planet's globalization, however, it was the aesthetic of the ugly that had to assert its jurisdiction. The decisive aspect of this process was not that the spherical form of the earth had been ascertained, and that it was permissible—even before clerics—to speak of the earth's curves; it was rather the fact that the particularities of the earth's form, its edges and corners, were

Before Copernicus, the earth could only be the center of the universe. Andreas Cellarius, *Harmonia macrocosmica seu atlas universalis et novus* (1708)

now in the foreground. For only the non-perfect—which cannot be constructed geometrically—permits and requires empirical research. The beautiful in its pure form can safely be left to the idealists, while the half-beautiful and the ugly occupy empiricists. While round perfections can be designed without recourse to experience, facts and imperfections cannot be deduced without it. That is why Uranian-cosmic and morphological globalization had primarily been a matter for philosophers and geometricians; terrestrial globalization, by contrast, would become a problem for cartographers and a nautical adventure, and later also a matter for economic politicians, climatologists, ecologists, terror specialists and other experts in the uneven and entangled.

It is easy to explain why this could not be any other way: in the metaphysical age, the planet could not present itself in a more distinguished light than its position in the cosmos allowed. In the Aristotelian-Catholic plan of the spheres, the earth, being most distant from the encompassing firmament, had the humblest status. Its placement at the center of the cosmos thus entailed, as paradoxical as it may sound, a relegation to the lower extreme of the cosmic hierarchy. Its encasement in a layered system of ethereal shells did provide security within a dense totality, but also shut it off from the upper regions of perfection. Hence the metaphysical references to the "earthly" and its haughty condescension towards the non-perfect down here, the fringe and privy of the heavens. Whatever lives beneath the moon must be marked by failure and dissolution, for this domain is ruled by the linear, finite and exhaustible movements that, in the eyes of antiquity, could never lead to any good. Each individual consciousness also bears the faultlines of earlier tremors of separation. This banishment from perfection left every sublunary object with cracks, scars and irregularities. Nonetheless, what contributed to the attractiveness of the metaphysical regime was that above and below were clearly separated within it. While the lower realm was naturally unable to move upwards under its own power, it remained the privilege of the upper to pervade the lower at will.

Even Eichendorff's lines from the poem "Mondnacht"—"It seemed as if heaven / Had quietly kissed the earth"—still read like a swan song for a schema that had molded the habitus of being-in-the-world among Europeans for an entire age. But the poet too already lived in a time when heaven only had pretend kisses for the earth, and in which the soul flew through silent lands as if the vehicle of the metaphor could enable it to find the way home from a beautiful foreign place. In reality, the weakened world of the living in Eichendorff's time had not exercised its *droit du seigneur* with the earth for a long time. Centuries had passed since modern physics discovered empty space and did away with the mythical enclosure of the firmament. Not everyone found it so easy to renounce completion from above, however; one can sense the sorrow over a world without heaven until Heidegger—an earth that, it was said, was "being-historically the wandering star." We recall that this phrase, which sounds rather distinctive and gloomy today, refers not to any given planet, but exclusively the one on which the question of truth and the meaning of being arose. The wandering state of Heidegger's earth is the last trace of the lost chance to be kissed by a heaven.

Even while the earth was still lying in the shells, however, long before its nautical circumnavigation and its cosmic dis-mantling, it presented itself in thanatological terms as the star on which people died scientifically. Its vague roundness was not an immune barrier that repelled death; it delineated the site on which the fall into time had taken place, the event after which everything that came into being owed its origins a death. That is why, on earth, everything that was made to exist must end—without exception; here clocks tick irreversibly, fuses burn towards ignition points (which is significant for the "historical consciousness" as soon as one understands that the thought figure of the "(big) bang" is more suitable for endings than beginnings). Anyone on earth who understands their situation will face the fact that no one leaves this place alive. People on this gloomy orb must practice—which, in the jargon of later philosophy, meant running ahead into one's death. That is why, since then, it has been better not to call humans "mortals," as was customary among the ancients, but rather "the provisional ones." If a historian were asked to say from the perspective of a virtual end of history what human collectives, viewed as a whole, did with their respective times, they could respond that humans organized free-for-all runs to their death: as humble processions, Dionysian hunts, progress projects, cynical-naturalistic elimination battles, or ecological reconciliation exercises. The surface of a body in the cosmos on which humans spend their days with futile precautions against the inescapable, then, cannot possibly be a regular one. Perfect smoothness is only possible in idealizations, while the rough and the real converge.

It is scarcely a coincidence, perhaps, that the first systematic utterance concerning an "aesthetics of ugliness"—in the book of the same name by Hegel's student Karl Rosenkranz, written in 1853—addressed the real earth as an uneven surface at the very beginning of its argumentation. In this new, non-idealistic theory of perception, the home of humans was afforded the privilege of serving as an example leading towards a theory of natural ugliness.

> Mere raw mass, in so far as it is dominated only by the law of gravity, presents us with what one could call a neutral state. It is not necessarily beautiful, but neither is it necessarily ugly; it is coincidental. If we take our earth, for example, it would have to be a perfect sphere in order to be beautiful as a mass; but it

is not. It is flattened at the poles and swollen at the equator, and its surface is of the greatest irregularity in its elevation. A profile of the earth's crust, viewed purely stereometrically, shows the most coincidental muddle of elevations and depressions with the most unpredictable outlines.[4]

If one follows this thought to its conclusion, the central principle of a post-idealistic aesthetics of the earth can be formulated thus: as a real body, the circumnavigated globe is not beautiful, but rather interesting. Faced with its irregularities, an immemorial unease returns about the human condition and existence in sublunary humiliation. The modern aesthetics of the ugly and the interesting not only tend to empirical research, which is by nature concerned with the irregular, the rough, the singular, and with things coincidentally baked together (*concrete*); and they simultaneously provide the premises for an aesthetics of disappointment. If one internalizes the local disadvantages of existence on the earth's surface, one can shake off the restraints preventing an open display of one's anger at the whole. That is why, in modernity, outrage was authorized as a basic stance—*on a raison de se révolter* [it is right to rebel]. Now that the avoidance of the coincidental, the thinking away of the burdensome and the mental adjustment of the disturbing—all advisable in the metaphysical regime—were rapidly losing the bearings given by an orderly world above, it was necessary to remain in the unpleasant, to rest among the grotesque, the amorphous, the base and the adverse; describing it turns the object of description against itself. A new cold-blooded aesthetics absorbed the cracks, turbulences, ruptures and irregularities into the picture—it even competed with the real for shocking effects.

Sittang Delta, Myanmar, photographed from the Space Shuttle Discovery

In aesthetic terms, terrestrial globalization was the victory of the interesting over the ideal. Its result, the earth made known, was the unsmooth orb, which disappoints as a form but attracts attention as an interesting body. To expect everything of it—and of the remaining bodies on this one—would constitute the wisdom of our age. As far as the history of aesthetics is concerned, the modern experience of art is tied to the attempt to open the eye, numbed for too long by geometrical simplifications, to the perceptual charms of the irregular.

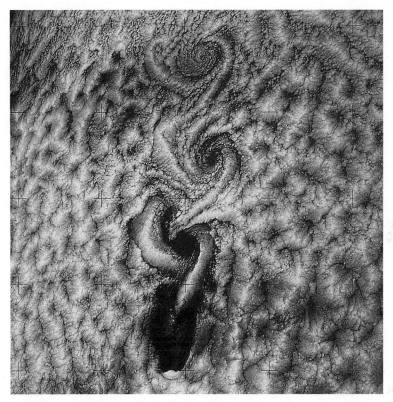

Turbulence in a cloud current behind the island of Guadeloupe, photographed from the Space Shuttle Discovery

2. Return to Earth

Accordingly, in the Modern Age, the task of designing the new image of the world no longer fell to the metaphysicists, but rather to the geographers and seafarers. It was their mission to present the last orb in pictorial form. Of all large round bodies, only shelless humanity's own planet would henceforth have any meaning. The world-navigators, cartographers, conquistadors, world traders, even the Christian missionaries and their following of aid workers who exported goodwill and tourists who spent money on experiences at remote locations—they all generally behaved as if they had understood that, after the destruction of heaven, it was the earth itself that had to take over its function as the last large-scale curvature. This physically real earth, as an irregularly vaulted, unpredictably uneven and grooved body, now had to be circumnavigated and recorded as a whole. Thus the new image of the earth, the terrestrial globe, rose to become the central icon of the modern worldview. Beginning with the Behaim Globe of Nuremberg, made in 1492—the oldest surviving specimen of its kind—and continuing up until NASA's photograms of the earth, the cosmological process of modernity is characterized by the changes of shape and refinements in the earth's image in its diverse technical media. At no time, however—not even in the age of space travel—could the enterprise of visualizing the earth deny its semi-metaphysical quality. Anyone who wished to attempt a portrait of the whole earth after the downfall of heaven stood, knowingly or not, in the tradition of ancient occidental metaphysical cosmography.

It is symptomatic of this that Alexander von Humboldt could still dare to give his magnum opus, which was published in five volumes between 1845 and 1862 (the last ones posthumously) and became the foremost scientific bestseller of its century, the openly anachronistic title *Cosmos*. It was, as one realizes in retrospect, the historically conditioned chance for this monumentally holistic "physical description of the world" to compensate with the resources of aesthetic education for what modern Europeans had endured through the loss of the firmament and cosmic *clôture* [(en)closure]. Humboldt had wagered

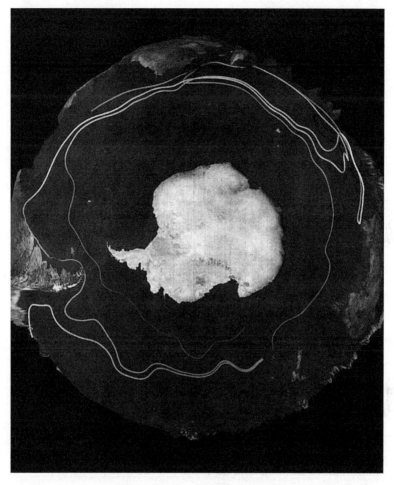

Computer simulation of the Antarctic showing the lines of the Atlantic Circumpolar Current

that he could present this metaphysical loss as a cultural gain—and he seems to have been successful, at least with the audience of his time. In his panoramic nature painting, the aesthetic observation of the centerless whole replaced its lost safety in the shell universe. The beauty of physics made the tableau of the holy circles dispensable. It is telling that in his world fresco, Humboldt, who has perhaps rightly been called the last cosmographer, no longer chose the earth as the vantage point from which to look out into the expansive space. Instead, in keeping with the spirit of his time and ours, he took up an arbitrary position in the external space from which to approach the earth like a visitor from a foreign planet.

> I propose to begin with the depths of space and the remotest nebulae, and thence gradually to descend through the starry region to which our solar system belongs, to the consideration of the terrestrial spheroid with its aerial and liquid coverings, its form, its temperature and magnetic tension, and the fullness of organic life expanding and moving over its surface under the vivifying influence of light.[5]
>
> Here, therefore, we do not proceed from the subjective point of view of human interest: the terrestrial is treated only as a part of the whole, and in its due subordination. *The view of nature should be general,* grand, and free; not narrowed by proximity, sympathy, or relative utility. A physical cosmography, or picture of the universe, should begin, therefore, not with the earth, but with the regions of space. But as the sphere of contemplation contracts in dimension, our perceptions and knowledge of the richness of details, of the fullness of physical phenomena, and of the qualitative heterogeneity of substances, augment. From the regions in which we recognize only the dominion of the laws of gravitation, we descend to our own planet, and to the intricate play of terrestrial forces.[6]

What counts here is the descending motion: it makes it clear that, despite his holistic and consolatory habitus, the world-connoisseur Alexander von Humboldt sides with the Modern Age in the decisive point, deciding against the safety of earth-dwellers in the illusory casings of the sense of proximity. Like all globe makers and cosmographers since Behaim, Schöner, Wald-seemüller, Apian and Mercator senior and junior,[7] he imposes the view of their planet on them from without, refusing to admit that the outer spaces are merely extensions of a regionally confined, herd-like, domestic and socio-uterine imagination. This opening up into the infinite heightens the risk of modern localizations. Humans know, albeit only in a confused and indirect fashion at first, that they are contained or lost—which now amounts to virtually the same thing—somewhere in the boundless. They come to understand that they cannot rely on anything as much as the homogeneous indifference of the infinite space. Here, the "comfortable component" has been eliminated. The outside expands, ignoring the postulate of proximity in the humane spheres, as a foreign entity in its own right; its first and only principle seems to be its lack of interest in humanity. The delusions of mortals that they must seek something outside—recall the space travel ideologies of the Americans and the Russians—necessarily remain very unstable, shakeable auto-hypnotic projects against a background of futility. What is certainly true is that the externalized space is the primal situation of the modern natural sciences; but the principle of the primacy of the outside also provides the axiom for the human sciences.

What develops from this is a radically altered sense of human localization. The earth now becomes the planet to which one returns; the outside is the general From-where of all possible

According to the *New Hypothesis of the Universe* (1750) of the English physicist
Thomas Wright, the endless space is filled with nested and hierarchized universes
in bubble-shaped structures.

returns. It was in the cosmographic field that thought concerning the outside was first elevated to the norm.[8] The space from which the new and inevitable encounter-from-outside with the earth occurs is no longer the naïve shell heaven from the age before Thomas Digges and Giordano Bruno. It is that eternally silent space, the infinity of physicists—of which Pascal, warning of the new atheistic physics, admitted that it put him in a state of terror. When Dante, looking down on the earth from the heaven of fixed stars on his journey through the spheres of paradise, had to smile involuntarily at its tiny form (*vil semblante*), this emotion was very different from the amazement that accompanied Humboldt's descent from the bleak outer spaces to an earth teeming with life. The Modern Age gained the vertical in a completely different way from the metaphysical age. The view from outside results not from a transcendence of the noetic soul into the extra- and supra-terrestrial, but rather from the development of the physical-technical, aero- and astronautical imagination (whose literary and cartographical manifestations, furthermore, were always ahead of the technological ones). Modern notions of flying replaced the ancient and medieval ones of "ascending"; the airport earth (where one starts and lands) replaced the ascension earth (from which one propels oneself and never returns).

When Humboldt's *Cosmos* was published, of course, there had not been any talk of the planetary domes or the all-encompassing heaven of fixed stars for centuries. That old medium of edifying astronomy, the Uranian globe—a common learning tool in traditional cosmology from Alcuin to Hegel—had already been out of use for a generation by the time of Humboldt's later years, and stargazing had long since developed into an

Lake Guatavita near Bogotá, setting of the legend of Eldorado, the Golden Man and his sunken treasures. Alexander von Humboldt's drawing still shows the communication trench with which the treasure hunter Sepúlveda attempted to drain the lake in 1581.

independent discipline in the spectrum of the triumphant natural sciences. With the consolidation of astrophysics, the science of the outermost spaces, that knowledge of the mythical constellations which had made the heavenly landscapes legible since antiquity went into rapid decline. Anyone still wishing to pursue astronomy had to do so in the knowledge that they were looking up to a firmamentless infinity, an anthropofugal space in which hopes and projections go astray without any echo.

Just as the earth retained its special status as the star to which one returns, however, European "mankind"—especially after its cosmological, ethnological and psychological enlightenments— preserved its distinction as the intelligent nerve cell in the cosmos that must be retuned to at all costs. Alexander von Humboldt had been given the mission of formulating the return from

The Great Globe (section), exhibited by James Wyld from 1851–1862 at Leicester Square, London; diameter c. 41 feet, exterior painted as the vault of heaven.

cosmic exteriority to the self-reflexive world of humans in exemplary fashion. Immanuel Kant had characterized the human mind's capacity to return to itself from the enormous, the utmost and the most foreign as the sense of the sublime—for what he considered sublime was the human consciousness of one's own dignity, resisting all temptations to abandon oneself in the overwhelming.[9] By enacting the return from the terrible expanse of nature, the astral and oceanic dimensions, into the educated salons with edifying thoroughness, Humboldt's painting of the world offered his contemporaries a final initiation into the cosmologically sublime. A view of the world on the largest possible scale here became an emergency of aesthetic life.[10] This in turn meant the continuation of the *vita contemplativa* by bourgeois, and thus ultimately consumptive means. If humans wanted to be "moved" and "deeply feel the monstrous," they now had to seek this in their own interiors. It was Walter Benjamin who summed up the meaning of bourgeois solitudes: "For the private individual, the private environment represents the universe. In it he gathers remote places and the past. His drawing room is a box in the world theater."[11] Where cosmic safety has become unattainable, humans are left to reflect on their situation in a space in which they can return to themselves from any distant place. Even if the essential transcendence and the dream of a true home in the world above were irretrievably lost for Modern Age humans, the transcendental, on the other hand, the self-reference of thinking and dwelling subjects as the condition of possibility for a return from the external to the own, emerges all the more distinctly in nineteenth-century thought. The transcendental turn is the heart of Humboldt's description of the world, as well as the designs for philosophical systems among idealistic and post-idealistic thinkers. It is the figure that shaped all later anthropological thought by following on from the precepts from the founding days of the human sciences in the late eighteenth century. The natural scientist is also confronted with the philosophical concept of the earth: it is the transcendental star that has become the determining location for all self-reflections. As the star on which the theory of stars appeared, the earth shines with self-generated phosphorescence, and when its strange, knowing inhabitants cast their thoughts into the emptiness, it is not least to return to their place from far outside. When Humboldt brings the term "spheres" into play, then, he is naturally no longer speaking of the imaginary celestial domes of the Aristotelian bimillennium, but rather the transcendental "spheres of perception," which refer not to cosmic realities but to the schemata, auxiliary concepts and radii of space-imagining reason. In the twentieth century, what had been a thought figure in Humboldt's century would become concrete as a movement in the physically real space: the astronaut Edwin Aldrin, who became the second human to set foot on the moon on July 21, 1969, shortly after Neil Armstrong, took stock of his life as an astronaut in a book with the title *Return to Earth*.[12]

3. Globe Time

Thus the same thing that had been true for the earth since Columbus' voyage was confirmed for the extra-terrestrial dimensions too: in the earth's circumnavigated space, all points are of equal value. This neutralization subjected the spatial thought of the Modern Age to a radical change of meaning. The traditional situation that humans "live and move and have their being" in regional orientations, markings and attractions was outdone by a system for localizing any point in a homogeneous, arbitrarily divisible representational space.[13] Where modern, position-spatial thought gains the upper hand, humans can no longer remain at home in their traditional world interiors and the phantasmal extensions and roundings-off of those interiors.[14] They no longer dwell exclusively beneath their home-centered sky. In so far as they take part enterprisingly in the great departure, sharing in its ideas, discoveries and gains, they have given up their provinces of birth; they have left their local language houses and their terrestrially fastened firmaments to move for all time within an insuperably antecedent outside.

These new entrepreneurs from the pilot nations of European expansion were no longer rooted in their native countries; they no longer floated amid its voices and smells; they no longer obeyed, as in the past, its historical markers or magical poles of attraction. They had forgotten what enchanted springs were, what pilgrimage churches and places of power meant, and what curses lay upon twilit corners. For them, the poetics of the natal space was no longer decisive. They no longer lived forever in the landscapes they were born into, but had learned to carry out their projects in the other place, the outermost and abstract place. In future, their location would be the map, on whose points and lines they would localize themselves without reservations. It was the knowledgeably painted paper, the *mappamundo*, that would tell them where they were. The map absorbs the land, and for imagining spatial thought, the image of the globe gradually makes the real extensions disappear.

For the terrestrial globe, the typographical marvel that informs modern humans of their location more than any other image, this marked the start of an illustrious success story extending over a span of more than five hundred years. Its monopoly on complete views of the earth's surface, shared with the great maps and planispheres, was only broken in the final quarter of the twentieth century by satellite photography.[15] The globe not only became the central medium of the new homogenizing approach to location, an indispensable worldview instrument in the hands of all who had come to power and knowledge in the Old World and its branches; in addition, through constant amendments to the maps, it documented the constant offensive of discoveries, conquests, openings and namings with which the advancing Europeans established themselves at sea and on land in the universal outside. From each decade to the next, European globes and maps publicized the state of the process whose formula was supplied after the event by Martin Heidegger when he wrote:

> The fundamental event of modernity is the conquest of the world as picture. From now on the word 'picture' means: the collective image of representing production [*vorstellendes Herstellen*].[16]

What has been advertised and decried in the mass media since the end of the twentieth century as "globalization"—as if it were a novelty—constitutes, from these perspectives, a late and muddled point in an event whose true scale only becomes visible when one understands the Modern Age consistently as a transition from meditative speculation on an orb to the practical acquisition of facts about it. One should emphasize that continental Europeans did not put an end to the death throes of the inherited Ptolemaic worldview until the twentieth century. Now they had to catch up,

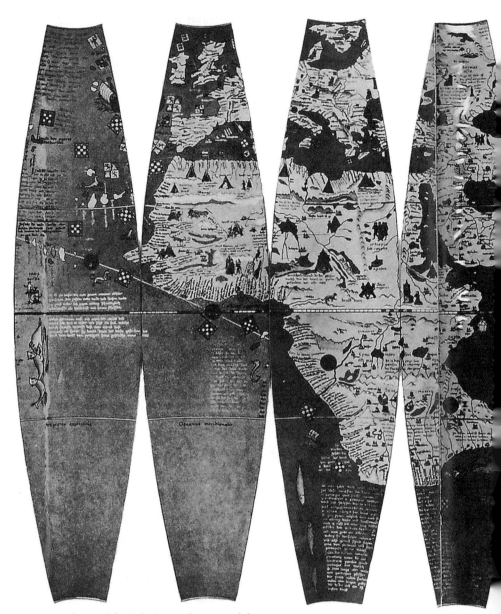

Behaim Globe (1492), two-dimensional depiction

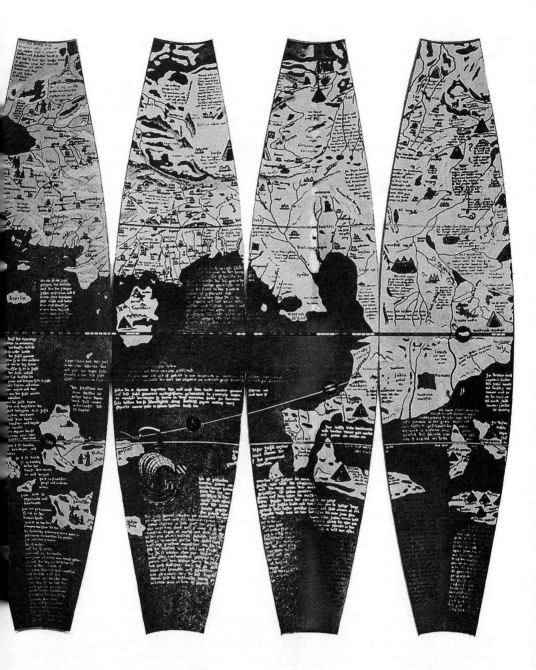

almost at the last minute, with the realization which the vast majority of them refused to accept regarding themselves: that virtually every point on a circumnavigated orb can be affected by transactions between opponents, even from the greatest distance.

The true meaning of terrestrial globalization reveals itself when one recognizes in it the history of a space-political externalization that was seemingly indispensable for the winners and unbearable for the losers, but inevitable for both. The latent metaphysical information of the earth to all its users had always been that all beings populating its surface are outside in an absolute sense, even if they still attempt to shelter themselves in pairings, dwellings and collective symbolic shells—systemicists would say in communications. As long as thinking people, considering the open sky, meditated on the cosmos as a vault—immeasurable, but closed—they remained protected from the danger of catching cold from an absolute externality. Their world was still the house that lost nothing. Since circumnavigating the planet, however, the wandering star that carries flora, fauna and cultures, an abyss has opened up above them; when they look up, they peer through it into an icy outside. A second abyss opens up in the foreign cultures that, after the ethnological enlightenment, demonstrate to everyone that practically everything we took to be the eternal order of things can be different elsewhere. The two abysses, the cosmological and the ethnological, confront the observers with the fortuity of their existence and thusness. And both make it clear that the immunological catastrophe of the Modern Age is not the "loss of the center," but rather the loss of the periphery. The final boundaries are no longer what they once seemed; the support they offered was an illusion, its authors we ourselves: this notice of loss (in technical terms: the de-ontologization of fixed edges) is the dysangelium of the Modern Age, which disseminates itself at the same time as the gospel of the discovery of new opportunity spaces. It is one of the hallmarks of the epoch that the good news rides upon the bad.

It was in the Iberian ports that the plague ships of knowledge first landed. Back from India, back from the antipodes, the first eyewitnesses of the round earth gazed with transformed eyes at a world that would henceforth be called the Old. Whoever sailed into their home port after circumnavigating the world— like the eighteen emaciated survivors of Magellan's 1519–1522 expedition—set foot on land once more in a place that could never again be idealized as the domestic-native world-cave. In this sense, Seville was the first location city in world history; its port, or more precisely that of San Lucar de Barrameda, was the first in the Old World to receive homecoming witnesses to a voyage around the globe. Locations are former homes that present themselves to the disenchanted and sentimental gaze of those returned from the outside. In such places, the spatial law of the Modern Age is in effect, namely that one can no longer interpret one's own place of origin as the hub of the existent and the world as its concentrically arranged environment. Anyone living today, after Magellan and after Armstrong, is forced to project even their home town as a point perceived from without. The transformation of the Old World into an aggregate of locations reflects the new reality of the globe as it revealed itself after the circumnavigation of the earth. The location is the point in the imagined world at which the natives grasp themselves as grasped from the outside; it is what enables the circumnavigated to return to themselves.

What is particularly strange about this process is the way countless native Europeans have managed to ignore, falsify and delay it for almost an entire age, such that in the late twentieth century, they suddenly acted as if they had entirely new reasons to examine that unheard-of phenomenon, globalization. It is incontestable, however, that the earth has been circumnavigated since 1522. All that is certain is that the quicker and more routine the circumnavigations become, the more generally the transformation of lifeworlds into locations spreads—which is why it was only in the age of fast transportation and super-fast information transmissions that the disenchantment of the old local immune structures became epidemically and massively palpable. In the course of its development, globalization burst open, layer by layer, the dream shells of grounded, housed, internally oriented and autonomously salvific collective life—that life which until then had rarely been anywhere except with itself and amid its native landscapes (Heidegger's *Gegnet* gives these outstripped spaces a belated and futile name). That older life knew no other constitution of the world than the self-harboring, vernacular, microspherically animated and macrospherically walled one—it viewed the world as a strong-walled socio-cosmological extension of a locally earthed, self-centered, monolingual, group-uterine power of imagination. Now, however, globalization, which carries the screened outside everywhere, tears the freely trading cities—and ultimately even the introverted villages— out into the homogenizing public space. It breaks open the independently growing endospheres and brings them into the net. Once caught in it, the settlements of the grounded mortals lose their immemorial privilege of being the respective center of their world.

Vinzenso Coronelli, earth globe (c. 1688), library of Melk Abbey

In this sense, the history of the Modern Age, as stated above, is initially nothing other than the history of a spatial revolution into the outside. This history brings about the catastrophe of local ontologies. In its course, all Old European countries become locations on the surface of an orb; numerous cities, villages and landscapes are transformed into stations of a limitless traffic of capitals, which march through in their five-fold meta-morphosis as commodity, money, text, image and celebrity.[17] Every place on the earth's surface becomes a potential address of capital, which regards all points in space in terms of their acces-sibility for technical and economical measures. While the speculative cosmic orb of the philosophers had, in former times, made a peak performance of security within the encompassing into an object of observation, the new "earth apple"—as Behaim called his globe—proclaimed to the Europeans discreetly, cruelly and interestingly the topological message of the Modern Age: that humans are creatures which exist on the edge of an uneven round body—a body whose whole is neither a womb nor a vessel, and has no shelter to offer. The globe may rest on a pre-cious stand with feet of engraved rosewood, enclosed in a metal meridian ring, and it may strike the observer as a paradigm of straightforwardness and delimitation; yet it will always reproduce the image of a body that lacks an enclosing edge, the spheric outer vault. Its uppermost part already appears outside of it. Even the atmosphere, which was initially made to vanish by all earth globes, was understood by most more as a part of the exterior than as an interior, and it is only in recent times, through the rise of meteorology to the exemplary science of chaos rationalism, that the earth's atmosphere has finally been recognized as the last remaining equivalent of the ethereal domes. Where is now the sky that could kiss this earth? Every globe adorning the libraries, studies and salons of educated Europe—until 1830 in the company of its obligatory twin, the celestial globe—embodied the new doctrine of the precedence of the outside, in which Europeans advanced into this outside as discoverers, merchants and tourists, but simultaneously withdrew into their artfully

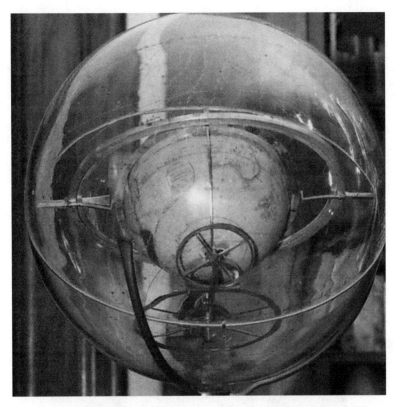

The *chronoglobium* of Mathias Zibermayer, with internal earth globe (1837), St. Florian

wallpapered inner spaces, which now displayed the specific flavor of the nineteenth century in being called "interiors" or "private spheres." The celestial globes set up in parallel with the terrestrial globe still attempted, as long as it was at all possible, to dispute the message revealed by the terrestrial globes;[18] they continued to promote the illusion of cosmic shelter for mortals beneath the firmament, but their function became increasingly metaphorical and ornamental—like the art of the astrologers, who changed from experts on stars and fate to psychologists of edification

Velázquez, *Democritus* (1628)

and fairground prophets. Nothing can save the physical heavens from being disenchanted as a form of transcendental semblance. What looks like a vault is an abyss perceived through a casing of air. The rest is displaced religiosity and bad poetry.[19]

4. Turn from the East,
Entrance into the Homogeneous Space

To establish the precedence of the outside, the bare fact of the first circumnavigations of the earth by Magellan and del Cano (1519–1522) and by Francis Drake (1577–1580) was not sufficient in itself. These two early deeds of nautical heroism nonetheless deserve a place in the history of terrestrial globalization, for their actors, in deciding to sail westwards, carried out a change of direction of world-historical importance and inexhaustible intellectual-historical meaning. Both Magellan and Drake were following the intuitions of Columbus, for whom the idea of a western route to India had become a prophetic obsession. And although, even after his fourth voyage (1502–1504), Columbus could still not be convinced of his error in thinking he had found the sea route to India—while on the Central American islands, he believed in all seriousness that he was only ten days' sail from the Ganges, and that the inhabitants of the Caribbean were subjects of the Indian "Grand Khan"—the tendency of the time was on his side. In opting for the western course, he had set in motion the emancipation of the "occident" from its immemorial solar-mythological orientation towards the East; indeed, with the discovery of a western continent, he had succeeded in denying the mythical-metaphysical priority of the orient. Since then, we have no longer been returning to the "source" or the point of sunrise, but progressively following the sun without any homesickness. Rosenstock-Huessy rightly noted: "The ocean crossed by Christopher Columbus turned the occident into Europe."[20] Whatever may have happened thereafter in the name of globalization or the universal documentation of the earth was now initially guided entirely by the Atlantic tendency. After the Portuguese seafarers from the mid-fifteenth century on had broken through the magical inhibitions obstructing the westward gaze with the Pillars of Hercules, Columbus' voyage gave the final signal for the "disorientation" of European interests. Only this "revolutionary" de-easting could bring about the emergence of the neo-Indian dual continent that would be called "America." It alone is the reason why for half a millennium, the cultural and topological meaning of the processes of globalization has always also been "westing" and westernization.[21] The inevitability of this was pinpointed by Hermann Schmitz, initiator of the New Phenomenology, with astute conciseness in the space-philosophical expositions of his *System of Philosophy*. Regarding Columbus, he writes:

> In the West he discovered America for humanity, and thus space as locational space [*Ortsraum*]. This deliberately exaggerated formulation is intended to mean that the success of Columbus—and later the circumnavigator Magellan as the executor of his initiative—on the western route forced a shock-like change in the human notion of space that, in my opinion, marks the entrance into the specifically modern mode of consciousness more profoundly than any other transition.[22]

The westward turn induced the geometricization of European behavior in a globalized locational space. Even the most summary description of the still widely unexplored zones of the earth thus followed a new methodic ideal from the outset: an even analysis of all points on the planet's surface in terms of their accessibility for European (which initially meant Iberian) methods, interests and

Terra australis nuper inventa nondum cognita, from Michael Mercator, *Atlas sive cosmographicae meditations* (1595)

measures—even if the actual access often took place only centuries later, or never. Even the famous white spots on maps marked as *terrae incognitae* acted especially as points that would have to be made known in future. The words printed above the supposedly enormous Australian continent on some influential sixteenth-century world maps applied to all of these: *Terra australis nuper inventa nondum cognita*—recently discovered, *not yet* explored, but already marked as a space for future examination and utilization. The spirit of the not-yet speaks up, for the time being, as a matter among geographers. The Modern Age is the *nondum* age—the time of a promising becoming, emancipated as much from the stasis of eternity as from the circling time of myth.

The historical nub of Columbus' voyage lies in its revolutionary effects on the shift from traditional direction-spatial to modern location-spatial movements. The West, formerly understood as a point on the compass and a wind direction, but even more as the zone of sunset—a thoroughly direction-spatially defined factor—was assigned the civilization-historically far-reaching role of assisting the breakthrough of the location-spatial and geometrical imagining of the earth, and of space as such. The westward departures marked the start of movements that would one day culminate in indifferent *traffic* in all directions. Whether the Columbus expedition of 1492 or the penetration of the North American continent in the nineteenth century, the two greatest enactments of the imperative "Westwards!" stimulated a spatial opening up that would later lead to the regular back-and-forth traffic between any given points in the explored zones. What the twentieth century would, with one of its most dulled-down terms, call "circulation" (in the sense of traffic) only became possible through the triumph of location-spatial thought. For the routine mastery of the symmetry of outward and return journeys that is constitutive for the modern concept of traffic can only be established in a generalized locational space that groups together points of equal value in a field to form timetables and images of routes. It is no coincidence that one of the most important power systems of the nineteenth century, the railway engines, were given the name "*loco*motives"—locationally mobile units—for their introduction actually marks an exceptional stage in the evening out of the locational space. The technicians of the nineteenth century knew that overcoming space through steam locomotion was closely connected to the "evaporation of space" through electric telegraphy, whose wires usually followed railway lines.[23]

The precondition for what we call "world traffic" is that the discovery of marine conditions and terrain in geographical and hydrographical terms can essentially be considered complete.

Authentic traffic can only come about with a network that makes a given zone accessible, be it as *terra cognita* or *mare cognitum*, for routine crossings. As the epitome of traversal practices, traffic constitutes the second, routinized phase of the process that had begun as the adventure history of global discoveries by the Europeans.

5. Jules Verne and Hegel

There is barely anyone who illustrated what globalized traffic means and achieves more accurately and entertainingly than Jules Verne, in his satirically tinged, best-selling novel *Around the World in Eighty Days* from 1874. With its galloping superficiality, the book offers a snapshot of the process of modernity as a traffic project. It demonstrates the quasi-historical-philosophical thesis that the purpose of modern conditions is to trivialize traffic on the global scale. Only in a globalized locational space can one organize the new mobility needs, which seek to provide both passenger transport and movement of goods with a foundation of quiet routines. Traffic is the epitome of reversible movements. As soon as these are expanded into a reliable institution for long distances too, it ultimately becomes meaningless in which direction a circumnavigation of the earth takes place. It is sooner external conditions that lead the hero of Jules Verne's novel, the Englishman Phileas Fogg, Esq. and his unfortunate French servant, Passepartout, to undertake the journey around the world in eighty days via the eastern route. Initially, the only reason for this is a newspaper announcement stating that the Indian subcontinent has become traversable in a mere three days through the opening of the last stretch of the Great Indian Peninsular

Railway between Rothal and Allahabad. From this, a journalist at a London daily newspaper constructs the provocative article that leads to Phileas Fogg's bet with his whist friends at the Reform Club. The issue of Fogg's bet with his partners at the club is essentially the question of whether the tourist system is capable of realizing its theoretical promises in practice. The momentous essay in the *Morning Chronicle* contains a list of the times a traveller would take to go from London around the world to London again. That this calculation based on a hypothetical eastward journey was due, alongside the habitual British affinity for the Indian part of the Commonwealth, to a topos of the time: the opening of the Suez Canal in 1869 had sensitized Europeans to the subject of acceleration in world traffic and created incentives for the dramatically shortened eastern route. As the course of Fogg's journey shows, it was already a completely wested east that, for all its Brahmans and elephants, was no different from any other curved stretch on a location-spatially represented planet that had been made accessible through traffic.

> This is the calculation done by the *Morning Chronicle*:
> London to Suez via the Mont Cenis Tunnel and Brindisi, by railway and steamship 7 days
> Suez to Bombay, by steamship 13 "
> Bombay to Calcutta, by railway 3 "
> Calcutta to Hong Kong (China), by steamship 13 "
> Hong Kong to Yokohama, by steamship 6 "
> Yokohama to San Francisco, by steamship 22 "
> San Francisco to New York, by railroad 7 "
> New York to London, by steamship and railway 9 "
> Total 80 days

"Possibly 80 days!" exclaimed Stuart […]. "But not allowing for unfavorable weather, headwinds, shipwrecks, derailments, etc."

"All included," said Fogg, continuing to play—for the discussion was no longer respecting the whist.

"Even if the Indians and Red Indians tear up the rails?" cried Stuart. "Even if they stop the trains, plunder the carriages and scalp the passengers?"

"All included," repeated Phileas Fogg.[24]

Jules Verne's message is that adventures no longer exist in a technically saturated civilization, only the danger of being late. That is why the author considers it important to note that his hero does not have any experiences. Mr Fogg's imperial apathy need not be shaken by any turbulence, for, as a global traveller, he is exempt from the task of showing respect to the local. Following the creation of circumnavigability, the tourist experiences the earth—even in its furthermost corners—as a mere epitome of situations that the daily papers, travel writers and encyclopedias have long since portrayed more comprehensively. This makes it clear why the "foreign" is barely worth a glance to the traveler. Whatever incidents may occur, be it a widow burning in India or a Native American attack in the west, they can never really be more than events and circumstances of which a member of the London Reform club is better informed than the tourist on site. Whoever travels under such circumstances does so neither for their own amusement nor for business reasons, but rather for the sake of travel as such: *ars gratia artis; motio gratia motionis*.[25]

Since the days of the Calabrian Giovanni Francesco Gemelli Careri (1651–1725), who sailed around the world between 1693 and 1697 out of frustration over family problems, the type of globetrotter without any business interests—the tourist—has been an established figure in the repertoire of modernity. His *Giro del Mondo*, published in 1699, is one of the founding documents of a literature of globalization on a private whim. Gemelli Careri spontaneously adopted the habitus of the explorer who believes that the zeitgeist has given him the mandate to tell those at home of his experiences outside; his Mexican observations and description of the Pacific crossing were still considered ethno-geographically respectable achievements generations later. Even though later globetrotters turned towards a more subjective style of reporting, the liaison between travelling and writing remained untouched into the nineteenth century. As late as 1855, the Brockhaus *Conversationslexicon* was able to define a tourist as "a traveler who has no specific, e.g. scientific purpose for travelling, but only does so in order to have made the journey and then be able to describe it."

In Jules Verne's tale, on the other hand, the globetrotter has even abandoned his profession as a documentarist and become a pure passenger, that is to say a customer of transportation services who is paying for a voyage *without* any experiences that could later be recounted. The circumnavigation of the world is a sporting act rather than a philosophical lesson—no longer even part of an educational programme. As far as the technical side of the circumnavigation of the world in eighty days was concerned, Jules Verne was no visionary by the standards of 1874. With regard to the decisive means of transportation, namely railway and propeller-driven steamboat, his hero's journey corresponded precisely to the state of the art of moving apathetic Englishmen from A to B and back. Nonetheless, the figure of Phileas Fogg has prophetic traits, in that he appears as the prototype of the generalized stowaway, whose only connection to the landscapes drifting past is his interest in traversing them. The stoic tourist prefers to travel with the windows shut; as a gentleman, he insists on his right to consider nothing worth seeing; as an apathetic, he refuses to make discoveries. These attitudes anticipate a mass phenomenon of the twentieth century: the hermetic package tourist, who changes transport means everywhere without seeing anything that differs from the brochures. Fogg is the perfect opposite of his typological precursors, the circumnavigators and geographers of the sixteenth, seventeenth and eighteen centuries, for whom every voyage was accompanied by expectations of discoveries, conquests and monetary gains. From the nineteenth century on, these experience-led travelers were followed by romantic travelers, who journeyed to remote places in order to enhance themselves through impressions.

Among the impressionistic travelers of the previous century, the cultural philosopher Hermann Graf Keyserling achieved a certain fame with his travel notes: he completed his great tour of the world's cultures in thirteen months as a form of Hegelian experiment—illumination through delayed return to the German provinces.[26] Phileas Fogg had a clear advantage over Keyserling, for he no longer had to pretend that he was concerned with learning anything substantial on his journey around the whole. Jules Verne is the better Hegelian, for he understood that no substantial heroes are possible in the arranged world, only heroes of the secondary: what remains for Fogg is a heroism of punctuality. Only with the idea that came to him on the Atlantic crossing between New York and England, namely to overcome the lack of coal by burning the wooden constructions on his own ship, did the Englishman touch for a moment on the original heroism, giving the principle of self-sacrifice a twist in keeping with the spirit of the Industrial Age. Aside from that, sport and spleen describe the last horizon for male endeavours in the spatially structured world. Keyserling, on the other hand, crosses the threshold of the laughable in traveling around the world, like some belated personification of the world spirit, in order to come "to himself"—his correspondingly comical motto was: "The shortest path to oneself leads around the world." As his book shows, however, the traveling philosopher cannot have any experiences, only gather impressions.

6. Waterworld
On the Change of the Central Element in the Modern Age

In the decisive point, Jules Verne's schedule perfectly mirrors the original adventure of terrestrial globalization: it unmistakably shows the considerable predominance of sea voyages over those on land. Here we still find, in a time when the circumnavigation of the earth had long become an elite sport ("globetrotting," which is to say trampling on everything), the trace of Magellan's radical revision of the world picture, in whose wake the notion of a largely terran earth was replaced with that of the oceanic planet. When Columbus was proposing his project to the Catholic majesties of Spain, he was able to state that the earth was "small" and mostly dry, with the damp element constituting only a seventh of it. The sailors of the late Middle Ages likewise declared the predominance of the terran space— for understandable reasons, as the sea is an element not usually loved by those closely familiar with it. It was not without deep-seated reasons, based on experience, that the hatred of coast-dwellers for the open water was translated into the vision in the Apocalypse of Saint John (Revelation 21:1) that the world would no longer exist after the coming of the Messiah (a statement very fittingly quoted by the ship's vicar in James Cameron's *Titanic* while the ship's stern assumes a vertical position before sinking).

All of a sudden, the Europeans of the early sixteenth century were expected to understand that in the face of the predominance of water, the planet earth had been named rather inappropriately. What they called the earth was revealed as a waterworld; three quarters of its surface belonged to the damp element. This was the fundamental globographical fact of the Modern Age, and it never became entirely clear whether it was an evangelical or a dysangelical one. It was no easy matter for humans to abandon their immemorial terran prejudices. The oldest surviving post-Columbian globe that hints at the existence of the American continents and the West Indian island world, the small metal Lenox Globe of around 1510, depicts—like many later maps and globes—the legendary island of Zipangu, or Japan (first mentioned by Marco Polo), as being very close to the western coast of North America. This mirrored the continued dramatic underestimation of the waters west of the New World, as if Columbus' cardinal error—the hope of a short western route into supposedly proximate Asia—were now to be repeated with America as the base. A little over a decade later, on the Brixen Globe of 1523 or 1524, a caravel placed in the "peaceful sea," the *Mar del sur*, pointed to Magellan's circumnavigation of the earth; pamphlets disseminated as far as Eastern Europe had reported the return of the *Victoria* as late as the autumn of 1522, and yet the creator of

Backwash from ships in the Sea of Japan, photographed from the Space Shuttle Discovery

this first post-Magellan globe was unable to participate in the oceanic "revolution." This was not an expression of any reprehensible narrow-mindedness; no European at the time could assess the implications of what the Basque captain Juan Sebastian del Cano and the Italian author of Magellan's logbook, Antonio Pigafetta, had to say when they reported that after sailing from the southwestern coast of America, they had sailed "for three months and twenty days"—from November 28, 1520 to March 16, 1521, with consistently favorable winds—on a northwesterly course through an immeasurable, unknown sea that they named *mare pacifico*, "for during that time we did not suffer any storm."[27] This short note expresses the oceanographic reversal that would bring geographical antiquity, the Ptolemaic belief in the predominance of land masses, to a sensational end.

How far the pre-Magellanic, Ptolemaic conception of the world was terracentrically oriented is revealed by the most artful among the late medieval descriptions of the earth, dating from barely a generation before Columbus' voyage: the monumental world disc of the Venetian Camaldolese monk Fra Mauro, made in 1459. In its time, it was considered not only the most extensive, but also the most detailed representation of the earth. It still presents the medieval-Old European earth, which lies contained in the immunizing circle, and on which the damp element literally plays a marginal role. Aside from the patches of the Mediterranean shifted slightly away from the center and the rivers, the water is only granted the outermost edges. In Fra Mauro's map the empirical and the fantastic present themselves in a wondrous compromise, and, despite the knowledgeable and dense reproduction of terran conditions, which is in keeping with the research of the time, the picture as a whole obediently submits to the Old European dream command: to imagine a world with as few aquatic areas as possible.

Without the translation of the new Magellanic truth into the maps of the next globe generations and the generation after those, no European would have had an adequate notion of the "revolutionary" inflation of the watery areas. This inflation was the basis of the shift from mainland thought to oceanic thought—a process whose consequences would be as unforeseeable as the Columbian-Magellanic transition from the ancient three-continent conception (which appears on maps as *orbis tripartitus*) to the modern four-continent scheme augmented by the two Americas. As for the fifth continent, the mythical *terra australis*, of which the sixteenth century began to dream as the largest and richest of all earthly spaces, the history of its discovery—compared to the initial hopes—was a long history of disappointment and shrinking. The Britons acted on this when they turned the failing southern realm into their penal colony; now the "irredeemable, unwanted excess population of felons" amply produced by England could be more or less permanently "transported" to a place an optimal distance away from the motherland.[28]

It seems especially bizarre that the contiguous landmasses of the earth's surface would soon bear only the name of the encompassing—*continens*—that had, until the time of Copernicus, referred to the cosmic shell or firmament of the world's final boundary. If the watery planet doggedly continues to call itself *Terra*, and if the landmasses on it adorn themselves to this day with the absurd title "continent," this shows how the Europeans of the Modern Age responded to the damp revolution: after the shock of circumnavigation, they withdrew to misnomers that feigned the long-familiar in the unaccustomed new. For just as

This poster for White Star Line shows the Olympic, the Titanic's sister ship, which was launched in 1910; lithograph (1911)

the circumnavigated planet does not deserve to be named after the little mainland that protrudes from its oceans, the "continents" have no rightful claim to their name, as they are precisely not the encompassing, but rather the—aquatically—encompassed. If things were as they should be in language, only the ocean could be termed *continens*. It is not only in lexical and

SS *Great Eastern* (1858)

semantic terms, however, that the history of the Modern Age was a drawn-out process of manoeuvring and evasion on the part of the terran conception of space and substance in the face of the sea and the flow of goods that passed over it. The hesitance to accept the oceanic truths informed the state and static side of the entire Modern Age.

The offensive sting of early globalization knowledge lay in the Magellanic views of the true extension of the oceans and their acknowledgement as the true world media. That the *oceans* were the carriers of global affairs, and thus the natural media of unrestricted capital flow, was the message of all messages in the period between Columbus, the hero of the maritime medium, and Lindbergh, the pioneer of the age of the air medium—a message the grounded Europeans fought against for centuries with their will to provincialism. It seemed as if the old earth would sink anew in diluvian floods—this time, however, floods that would not fall from the sky, but rather rush in from unheard-of log-books. In the nineteenth century, Melville, the greatest writer of the maritime world, could let one of his figures exclaim: "Yea, foolish mortals, Noah's flood is not yet subsided."[29] Both the unity and the division of the planet earth had become subject to the maritime element, and European seafaring—in its civil, military and corsair manifestations—had to prove itself as the effective agent of globalization until the rise of aeronautics. It was via the oceans that the European world powers wanted to build their "seaborne empires." During that time, anyone who claimed to understand the world had to think hydrographically. The sardonic itinerary in the *Morning Chronicle* still acknowledged this truth by featuring a total of sixty-eight days at sea alongside a mere twelve by rail to travel around the earth. Only the sea offered a foundation for universal thoughts; the ocean alone could bestow the graduation caps of the true Modern Age. Melville rightly let the same protagonist declare: "a whale-ship was my Yale College and my Harvard."[30]

One of the first to draw practical conclusions from the insights of Magellan and del Cano was the young monarch Charles V, King of Spain from 1516 and ruler of the Holy Roman Empire from May 1519. In the autumn of 1522, Pigafetta presented his ship's log to him at Valladolid as the most secret document of the new international situation.[31] Charles quite rightly took the information about the Pacific and the superhuman efforts involved in the circumnavigation of the earth on the western route as news that was both wondrous and frightening. After only a few failed attempts to repeat Magellan's voyage, he considered it advisable to abandon the idea of new trips to the Maluku Islands. Thus, in the Treaty of Zaragoza of 1529, he sold the asserted Spanish claims to the islands to the Portuguese crown for 350,000 ducats—which proved an excellent deal after improved longitude measurements on the other side of the globe a few years later showed that since the division of land agreed on in 1494 in the Treaty of Tordesillas, the sought-after Spice Islands had belonged to the Portuguese hemisphere anyway. Years later, Charles still chuckled about reports of his duped royal colleague's tantrums.

This interdynastic selling of distant lands, where clearly neither the buyer nor the seller even knew their exact location, mirrors more accurately than almost any other act from that time the speculative nature of the original globalization processes. It is ridiculous when today's journalists presume to identify the most recent movements of speculative capital as the real cause of the world-form shock known as globalization. From the first moment on, the world system of capitalism was established under the interwoven auspices of the globe and speculation.[32] The overseas empire of Charles V had been financed with loans from Flemish and Augsburg banks, and later Genoese ones, whose owners set globes in rotation in order to gain an idea of the outward journeys of their credit and the return journeys of their interest. From the start, the oceanic adventure entangled its actors in a race for hidden chances to access opaque distant markets. Cecil Rhodes' notorious statement already applied to them: "Expansion is everything."[33] What economists after Marx called "original accumulation" was often—as the aforementioned example suggests—more an accumulation of ownership titles, options and claims to usage than a management of production plants on the basis of invested capital. For the princely and civil

Stereorama *Poetry of the Sea*, 1900 World Exhibition in Paris, showing the mechanism for simulating waves

clients of overseas navigation, the discovery and formal appropriation of distant territories established an expectation of future income, whether in the form of loot or tribute or through regular trading transactions, in which it was never forbidden to dream of fabulous profit margins.

The globalization of the earth by the early seafaring merchants and cosmographers was clearly far removed from submitting to theoretical interests; since its initiation by the Portuguese, it had followed a resolutely anti-contemplative and deduction-hostile knowledge programme. The *experimentum maris* provided the criterion for the new understanding of world experience. Only at sea did it become clear how the Modern Age intended to envisage the interplay of theory and practice. A hundred years before Francis Bacon, the commissioners and actors of global circumnavigation knew that knowledge of the earth's surface was power—power in its most concrete and profitable form. The increasingly precise image of the earth now directly took on the character of knowledge about quantifying and accessing it; new oceanographic insights amounted to arms deliveries for the battle against competitors in the open space. Geographical and hydrographical discoveries were therefore guarded like state secrets or industrial patents; the Portuguese crown forbade—on pain of death—the proliferation of nautical charts showing the discoveries and coastline descriptions of the Lusitanian captains. That is why hardly any of its famous portolans, which were used like itineraries for sailing along navigable coastlines, have survived.[34]

A counterpart to calculation with Arabic numerals emerged, one might say, in the form of calculation with European maps. After the introduction of the Indo-Arabic zero in the twelfth century had enabled an elegant arithmetic, the earth globe of the Europeans provided an operable round view of geopolitical and world economic affairs. In the same way, however, that—as noted by the philosopher Alfred N. Whitehead—no one leaves the house to buy zero fish, no one sails from Portugal to Calicut or Malacca to return with zero cloves in the cargo hold. From this perspective, a group of spice islands in the South Pacific targeted and occupied by European desires is not simply a vague spot on a vague world map, but also a symbol of expected profits. In the hands of those who know how to use it, the globe is the true icon of the newly navigable earth; and even more than this, it constitutes an image of monetary sources flowing from the future to the present. One could even consider it an occult clock that showed the hours of profit beneath pictures of seas, islands and continents in the distant space. The modern globe made its

Shooting range of the English Navy at Gibraltar, from Karl Haushofer, *Weltmeere und Weltmächte* (1937)

fortune as an opportunity clock for a society of long-distance entrepreneurs and risk-takers who already saw the wealth of tomorrow on the coasts of other worlds today. This clock, which showed the hours in the never-before-seen, told the quick-witted agents of the new era—the conquistadors, spice merchants, gold hunters and later political realists—how things stood for their enterprises and their countries.

It is clear why the same globographers served both the princes and the civil large-scale entrepreneurs. Before the new, emperors and peddlers are equal, and Fortuna, who will in future balance less on her old cosmic orb than the modern earth globe, barely discriminates between noble and non-noble minions. Charles V, whose attention was drawn to these extremely useful

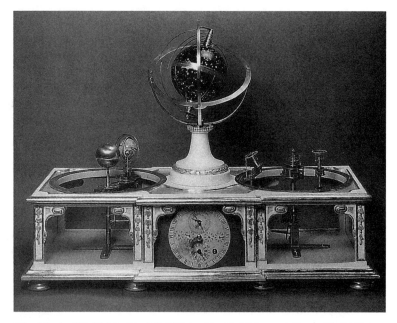

The "Gotha World Machine" (1780) by Ph. M. Hahn and Georg David Hahn; the clockwork drives the orrery (left), the Copernican world system (right), and a celestial globe with zodiac signs above the central section

scholars by his secretary Maximilian Transylvanus, had friendly relations with Gerardus Mercator and Philipp Apian, the outstanding globographers of their time, who simultaneously worked for the entire financial and scientific elite. Raymund Fugger, certainly no mere peddler, had a globe of his own produced by Martin Furtenbach in 1535, which was later exhibited at the Fuggerschloss in Kirchbach; like the slightly earlier Welser globe made by Christoff Schiepp, the Fugger globe was an artfully fashioned unicum. The future, however, belonged to printed globes, which reached the market in larger numbers; they provided globalization with its first mass media foundation.

Whether it was a unique specimen or a serial product, however, every globe spoke to its viewers of the pleasure and necessity of gaining advantages in the borderless terrestrial space.

On March 22, 1518, after the nautical hero Magellan had turned his back on ungrateful Portugal, he and a representative of the Spanish crown cast a joint glance at one such promising globe, which located the Spice Islands somewhere near the Antipodes, and made a contract for the discovery of the same (*Capitulación sobre el descubrimiento de las Islas de la Especeria*) that already stipulated in minute detail the division of the virtual riches that would be generated by these sources. This shows with uncommon explicitness that even the concept of "discovery"— the central epistemological and political word of the modern Age—referred not to an autonomous theoretical category, but rather a special case of the investment phenomenon; and investment is in turn a case of risk-taking. Where the schemata of risk-taking spread at a general level—taking up loans, investing, planning, inventing, betting, reinsuring, spreading risks, building up reserves—people emerge who want to create their own fortune and future by playing with opportunities, not simply accepting whatever God's hand grants them. In the new property and money economy, this was a type who had learned that damage makes people wise, but debts make them wiser. The key figure of the new age was the "debtor-producer"—better known as the entrepreneur—who constantly flexibilized their business methods, their opinions and themselves in order to access by all lawful and unlawful, tried and untried means the profits that would enable them to pay off their loans on time. These debtor-producers gave the idea of owed debt its radically renewing, modern meaning: a moral fault becomes an economically logical relationship of incentive. Without the positivization of debt, there can be no capitalism. It was the debtor-producers who began to turn the wheel of permanent monetary circulation in the "age of the bourgeoisie."[35] The primary fact of the Modern Age was not that the earth goes around the sun, but that money goes around the earth.

7. Fortuna, or: The Metaphysics of the Chance

This economic and psychopolitical situation saw the reappearance of the Roman goddess of luck within the horizon of current European interests, as she was capable like no other figure in the ancient pantheon of making a pact with the new entrepreneurial religiosity. The return of Fortuna corresponded to the world feeling of modern chance ontology, classically embodied in the opportunism of Machiavelli, the essayism of Montaigne and the experimental empiricism of Bacon. The neo-fatalism of late Shakespeare likewise belongs to the characteristic self-statements of the age that, in its gloomier moments, perceived humans as competition-infected, jealousy-blinded, failure-scarred risk-takers; here the actors on the world stage appear as balls with which illusory powers, malign genies, money spirits and greed demons play their games. Fortuna appears everywhere as the goddess of globalization *par excellence*: she not only produces herself as the eternally ironic equilibrist balancing on her orb, but also teaches humans to consider life as a whole a game of chance in which the winners have no cause for boasting and the losers no cause for complaint. Boethius, who laid the foundations for medieval speculations about Fortuna in the sixth century in his book *The Consolation of Philosophy*, and was still a source of inspiration for

Fortunatus and the Maiden of Luck, illustration from the 1509 chapbook

the philosophies of happiness in the Renaissance, already let his goddess reveal the premises for existence on the wheel:

> "The power that I wield comes naturally to me; this is my perennial sport. I turn my wheel on its whirling course, and take delight in switching the base to the summit, and the summit to the base. So mount upward, if you will, but on condition that you do not regard yourself as ill-treated if you plummet down when my humour so demands and takes its course."[36]

This was mostly taken by stability-infatuated Middle Ages as a *vanitas* warning; thus they saw the temperamental goddess as a demon of harmful changeability, while the incipient Modern Age suspected that in the image of the revolving wheel of fate lay a metaphysics of the chance which largely corresponded to its own motives. In the four basic positions of the wheel of fortune—

Fortuna's wheel, from the *Hortus deliciarum* by Herrad of Landbserg (c. 1190)

ascending/sitting enthroned/sinking/lying—the new era recognized not only the basic risks of the *vita activa*, but also the typical stages of entrepreneurial fortune. Fortuna was no longer only depicted with her wheel, however, but equally with maritime emblems such as the swelling sail and especially the rudder, which was her oldest attribute along with the orb; it shows that luck is not only coincidental, but also due to individual diligence. Antiquity had already associated luck with seafaring, and the Modern Age could not help reinforcing this connection. One thing it did add to the maritime symbols was that of the dice, whose falling—*cadentia*—generated the concept of risk-taking, and thus one of the key concepts of the modern world: the chance. One can go so far as to identify, in the refreshed Fortuna idea of the Renaissance—among a multitude of meanings and contexts[37]—the approaching philosophical success of proto-liberalism, in which the positions of the wheel of fortune would correspond directly to the ordeals of the market. In success, selection by coincidence comes before all subjectivity of control or method. What is liberalism in philosophical terms if not the emancipation of the accidental? And what was the new entrepreneurship if not a practice for permanently correcting chance and luck?

It is one of the more profound thoughts of the sixteenth century that alongside the hereditary nobility, which had been on top since mythical times, and the nobility of officials, which had begun to make itself indispensable in the service of early Modern Age states, it already conferred the necessary qualifications on the anarchic nobility of the future, the nobility of luck; this alone emerged from the womb of Fortuna as the true child of the Modern Age. This chance nobility would prove the recruiting ground for the prominent figures of the globalization age—a society of individuals who had become rich, famous and favored in their sleep, and who never quite understood what had carried them upwards. The airy children of Wotan, from Fortunatus to Felix Krull are, alongside the entrepreneurs and artists, the most legitimate offspring of the luck-blessed Modern Age. This was not only the age in which the wretched attempted, with varying success, to work their way up from their misery; it was also the great time of fortunate natures who sat with light heads and light hands with the sibyls and queens, devoting themselves to integral consumption, including the flights of birds and the lands of the

HIS FORTVNA PARENS   ILLIS INIVSTA NOVERCA EST

"Fortuna is a good mother to some, but an unjust stepmother to others." From Theodore de Bry, *Emblemata nobilitatis* (Frankfurt, 1593)

stars. What else should they do, the effortless winners, but dine without remorse at the "*table d'hôte* of chance?"[38] It was Nietzsche who would go on to coin the formula for this release of the accidental: "'Lord Chance'—that is the oldest nobility in the world."[39] The gesture of counting oneself among this nobility and wearing the die on one's coat of arms brings forth a new justification for life that Nietzsche, in *The Birth of Tragedy*, called "aesthetic theodicy." In the Modern Age, emancipated luck gazes up at a sky unknown to the neediness of old. "Over all things stands the Heaven Accident"[40]—a postmetaphysically enlightened elite audience is supposed to hear this as the true Good News. The

Fortuna on a round seat, Virtus on a square one

concern was a sky that vaulted a liberated immanence, far removed from any retribution in the hereafter. The sky of the Modern Age was the playing field for chance's throws of the dice. Perhaps Nietzsche would have been displeased by a reminder that in imperial Rome, Fortuna was primarily the goddess of slaves and the unemployed plebeians who depended entirely on chance alms.

8. Risk-Taking

Taking calculated risks on a global playing field in the horizon of uncertainty: this concept is the pragmatic foundation of the modern culture of attack and reaching out. The structural aggressiveness of European expansionist practices was not rooted in a regional psychodynamic disposition; it was not any species-specific sadism that propelled their extroversion into the global terrestrial space. Only in a marginal aspect did this reaching for the furthest points on the water-covered orb resemble acting out a masculine fantasy of omnipotence through telephallic penetration. As a whole, it was the adjustment of European practices and mentalities to generalized risk-taking that resulted in the surprising, almost mysteriously successful offensive force of the first generation of discoverers. The willingness to take risks among the new global actors is *ultima ratione* driven by the urge to generate profits in order to repay debts from investment loans. Europeans in 1500 were not greedier or crueller or more diligent than any other race before them; they were more willing to take risks—which means more loan-inclined in relation to creditors and more loan-dependent in relation to debtors, in keeping with the economic paradigm shift from the ancient and medieval exploitation of resources to modern investing economies. Through such economic activity, mindfulness of deadlines for the payment of interest was translated into practical ventures and technological inventions. Enterprise is the poetry of money.[41] If necessity is the mother of invention, then credit is the mother of enterprise.

Merely because the outside was simultaneously the future, and because the future *post mundum novum inventum* could be imagined as the space from which spoils and idealization originated, the early seafarers and eccentric merchant-entrepreneurs unleashed the storm of investments in the outside that would develop in the course of half a millennium into the current capitalist-informatic ecumene. From the time of Columbus on, globalization meant the general futurization of state, entrepreneurial and epistemic action. It was the subjugation of the globe to the form of profit—which meant the money that returned multiplied to its account of origin after its great loop across the oceans. In this respect, terrestrial globalization transpired as the mint of entrepreneurship in the narrower modern sense. The fact that this entrepreneurship did not, in its adventuring early days, always differ clearly from pseudo-seriously mystified project-making—Daniel Defoe, himself a luckless speculator and dealer in wine, tobacco and hosiery, examined it critically— from therapeutic and political charlatanry, as well as occasional and organized crime, lent the practices of global expansion the ambiguity associated with them to this day.

The pragmatic heart of the Modern Age lay in the new science of risk-taking. The globe was the monitor on which the field of generalized investment activities could be viewed. At the same time, it was already the gambling table at which the adventurer-investors placed their bets. Its emergence, rapid success and chronic updating began the era of the global players, in whose world a great many ships sink, but the sun never goes down. They were gamblers who took a globe in hand in order to outdo their rivals in long-distance vision, long-distance speculation and long-distance winning. The imperial motto under which the fleet of Charles V sailed the oceans, *Plus oultre* [Further beyond], stimulated a form of thought not simply concerned with seeing and proceeding far, but fundamentally *ever further*. That is why the principle of television did not make its first appearance in the age of moving images; it was *de facto* given as soon as entrepreneurial foresight and far-sight employed the medium of the

Plus ultra: Charles V between the Pillars of Hercules

globe—a medium that insisted of its own accord on constant updates. The moving images of the twentieth century were preceded by the revisable images in the great age of globes and maps. The seller of the Maluku Islands—Charles V—and their buyer—John III—were exemplary actors in this far-sighted culture of risk. Their transaction of 1529 shows that from that point on, rulers were not so much God's first regional servants on earth as the first entrepreneurs of the money-dependent state. Under their leadership, European peoples developed into modern investment collectives that, from the eighteenth century on at the latest, distinguished themselves under the name of "nations" as self-appointed *chargés d'affaires*.[42] And when economized nations democratically restructured themselves from the American Revolution on, it was brought about by the realization that kings had become unproductive factors on the supervisory boards of these political investment collectives. Modern history is characterized by the structural long-term unemployment of kings.

9. Delusion and Time
On Capitalism, Telepathy and Adviser Worlds

The history of discoveries has been written countless times as an adventure novel of seafaring, a success and crime story of conquests, a history of jealousy among major imperial powers, as well as a neo-apostolic ecclesiastical history (which was in turn the history of jealousy among the missionary orders and confessions). "European expansion" served as an object of every kind of glorification and condemnation; in the Old World, it became a field on which self-doubt gleaned the remains of its harvest.[43]

As far as I know, a philosophically thought-out history of discoveries, terrestrial and maritime alike, has never been considered, let alone attempted or carried out—probably mainly because the indispensable central concepts that would form part of a philosophical résumé of globalization processes only play a secondary part in the philosophical vocabulary, and most are missing altogether: distance, extension, externality, canopies, barbarians, becoming-image, density, one-sidedness, disinhibition, dispatchability, capture, inhibition, investment, capital, mapping, medium, mission, ecumene, risk, feedback, debt, obscurity, crime, traffic, interconnection, delusional system, world system, wishful thinking, cynicism. Even as eminent a word as "discovery" is not so much as mentioned in the *Historisches Wörterbuch der Philosophie* [Historical Dictionary of Philosophy], edited by Joachim Ritter and Karlfried Gründer, the highest intercultural yardstick for the terminology of the trade.[44] I shall touch on the significance of these gaps in the vocabulary of academic philosophy, and the dispositions of which they are symptoms, further below. First of all, however, I will make a sketch showing how a discovery-philosophical theory of globalization should approach its theme, and what problems face a theory of the discovery-dependent globalized commune, also known as mankind.

It seems a triviality that the practice of geographical discovery was connected to a very hazardous departure to an un-homelike externality. Upon closer inspection, however, it becomes clear to what extent non-trivial forces drove these enterprises. The Portuguese and Spanish expeditions could never have been undertaken without motivating systems of delusions to justify these leaps into the unclear and unknown as sensible acts. It is in the nature of a well-systematized delusion to be capable of presenting itself to others as a plausible project; a delusion that is not contagious does not adequately understand itself. Columbus himself, at any rate, was no longer content in later years to view himself only as the seaman, the conquistador of a new world and its cartographer; rather, he had become convinced that he was an apostle called by the will of God to bring salvation across the water. Encouraged by his incomparable success, he made his first name Christophorus, "Christ-bearer," into his religion, and turned his Hispanicized paternal name Colón, "settler," into his existential maxim—a success-psychological stylization phenomenon that still characterizes the modern entrepreneurial world and its autogenous religions as a whole. In *The Book of Prophecies* of 1502, he interpreted himself as a nautical messiah whose coming had been foretold since ancient times.[45] No project without delusions of success; and without a project, no chance of infecting others with one's own fever. In this, Columbus was an agent of a pan-European willingness to embrace delusion—though it was only psychotechnically perfected by the USA in the twentieth century (and re-imported to Europe through the consultancy industry)—that became workable worldwide through the principle "seek your own salvation by bringing it to others."

This ideal synthesis of selflessness and self-service sums up the Modern Age-enabling psychotechnic figure of "self-enthusiasm" or "autogenic mania." Because most actors in the Modern Age were only partly successful in their self-motivation, however, they became dependent on advisers who supported them in their attempt to believe in their mission and their luck. For project-prompters and astrologers, overseas traffic in capital marked the start of the golden age—which was still in progress on the eve of the twenty-first century. With its compulsion to act into the distance, the Modern Age became a paradise for soothsayers and consultants. The concern for capital that was intended for realization on journeys around the world bestows a sixth sense. It would indeed be amazing if people for whom reality is the flow of money and goods did not also believe in subtler forms of inflow and outflow. Modern telepathic and monetary forms of flux-based thought broke the hegemony of substance-oriented scholasticism—though it would take everyday Euro-American life four centuries to complete the adjustment ethically and logically and declare the new categorical imperative: fluidize everything!

Anton Fugger, who had become a secret master of the world as a financier of the imperial Spanish colonization of South America, was ensnared during his final years in the nets of an attractive healer, Anna Mergeler, who had slept with a priest. She had to appear before the judges of the Augsburg town council in 1564, accused of witchcraft; she was acquitted, however, because the great man's name acted as a legal talisman in her favor even after his death. Anton Fugger himself, who harbored parapsychological ambitions, claimed he had acquired the ability

The magnet oracle of Athanasius Kircher: the glass globes contain wax figures with magnetic cores that can be moved using the larger rotatable magnets in the base of the obelisk. The figures point to letters on their globes and thus answer questions. From Athanasius Kircher, *Magnus sive de arte magnetica* (1642).

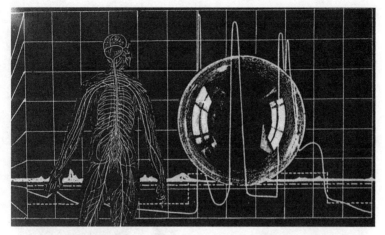

Max Ernst and Paul Eluard, *The Misfortunes of the Immortals*, with (1922)

to observe his distant agents in a crystal ball. To his displeasure, however, this far-seeing ball showed his employees better dressed than he was ("my servants walk in much fairer dress than I myself")—a discovery that, in a time when clothing customs indicated rank and class, inevitably called for sanctions.[46]

In the years before his murder by terrorists of the Red Army Faction, Alfred Herrhausen, chairman of Deutsche Bank, had, under the influence of the trained Germanist and business consultant Gertrud Höhler, introduced group-dynamic exercises in self-experience for his employees in order to motivate higher performance. His brilliant adviser had recognized the signs of the time, which demanded flexibilized, self-driving, emotionally intelligent, team-capable (more Protestant, one could say) staff, before many others.[47]

A continuum that shaped the Modern Age spans the time between these two dates: that of the search for ways to transfer salvific knowledge to unholy practices. What characterizes a

Titian, *The Allegory of Alfonso d'Avalos* (1532), detail

substantial part of the current consultancy industry is the placing of spiritual traditions in the service of their antitheses.

It cannot be stressed enough, then, that what was termed European expansion was *not* originally rooted in the Christian mission idea; rather, expansion and systematized colonial and mercantile risk-taking over great distances triggered proselytization, transmission and bringing as a type of activity in its own right (general salvific transfer, export of advanced civilization, consultation, and generalized techniques for transferring success and advantage). In this sense, we can say that the Modern Age as a whole is the object of a secular missionary science. The Christian missionaries simply recognized their historical chance early on by jumping on the moving train—or, far more appropriately, aboard the departing ship.[48] The group of advantage-bringers in the Modern Age included conquerors, discoverers, researchers, priests, entrepreneurs, politicians, artists, teachers, designers and journalists—all with their specific advisers and outfitters. Without exception, these factions dressed their practices in manic assignments, that is to say secular missions. They constantly attempt to close their depressive gaps and clear away their doubts by insuring themselves through the services of paid motivators. And all of them recognized themselves at the end of the twentieth century in the lukewarm wafflings of innovation-oriented society. For what is talk of innovation but the most abstract form of a promise of salvation and profit? The advisers coupled, rarely to their own disadvantage, new technical advantages with rising advantage-seekers. They were the first people who consistently mercantilized the informal advantages in knowledge. They initiated an economy of cognition that will ultimately downgrade what were once the greatest creations of European intellectual ecology, the universities, to varyingly shabby agencies for a globalized finance market of ideas.[49]

10. Nautical Ecstasies

On the subjective side of things, early transatlantic seafaring can be described as an informal technique of ecstasy whereby discoverers, like shamans of an undefined religion, acquired information from a significant world beyond. This was no longer to be envisaged as a heavenly "above," but rather a terrestrial "yonder." Like all transcendences or quasi-transcendences, however, this modern hazardous beyond came at a price. Early intercontinental travelers usually had to pay for access to distant shores by enduring bitter asceticisms. These included involuntary fasts and passages drawn out by weather conditions, or the torture of boredom from calm at sea and sluggish sailing. Frequent sleep deprivation as a result of heat, cold, stench, cramped conditions, noise and fear on a heavy swell also wore away at the irritable and delirium-prone crews. Every ship on the high seas placed the travelers in constant connection to what one could here, more fittingly than anywhere else, call the last things. The alternative of port or death was the formula for meditating at sea on the precariously goal-directed nature of human action. As examinations of the end, Ignatian exercises could not be any more explicit than an Atlantic crossing. No group of ascetics on the seas bore the brunt of the maritime law "port or death" more harshly than those who searched for the most difficult passages on earth, the Northern Sea Route between the Norwegian Sea and East Siberia and the Northwest Passage between Greenland and Alaska. By the turn of the twentieth century, the delusional systems and idealized fantasies of numerous researchers and adventurer-merchants had foundered on these nigh-impossible routes. In both of these northern passages, the Modern Age's campaign against the notion of "impossible" claimed its exemplary victims.

The leap onto the oceans marks a deep caesura in the history of European mentalities. If one characterizes the current civil world, in terms of its mentality conditions and immune constitutions since the eighteenth century, as a therapy and insurance society—a formation that differs clearly from the preceding society of religion—one usually overlooks the fact that an intermediate world had grown between the religious and therapeutic regimes which was involved in both systems, yet based on practices of its own. Seafaring constituted an autonomous third force between religion and therapeutics until the nineteenth century. Countless people sought healing from the frustrations of the mainland at sea. Perhaps the *Nautilus* of Captain Nemo was the last Old European ship of fools on which a great, lonely misanthrope could act out his rejection of the disappointing land-dwelling humans in a sovereign fashion. But for Herman Melville too, it was quite self-evident that the open sea was the most reliable remedy for both melancholy and manic moods; thus he was able to make the narrator of *Moby Dick*—published in 1851, barely twenty-five years before Jules Verne's literary forays into terran and subterranean, marine and submarine globalization—begin his tale with these words:

> Call me Ishmael. Some years ago—never mind how long precisely—having little or no money in my purse, and nothing particular to interest me on shore, I thought I would sail about a little and see the watery part of the world. It is a way I have of driving off the spleen, and regulating the circulation.

Whenever I find myself growing grim about the mouth; whenever it is a damp, drizzly November in my soul; whenever I find myself involuntarily pausing before coffin warehouses, and bringing up the rear of every funeral I meet; and especially whenever my hypos get such an upper hand of me, that it requires a strong and moral principle to prevent me from deliberately stepping into the street, and methodically knocking people's hats off—then, I account it high time to get to sea as soon as I can. This is my substitute for pistol and ball. With a philosophical flourish Cato throws himself upon his sword; I quietly take to the ship.[50]

Next to the monastery and suicide, modern seafaring proved itself as the third option for throwing away a life that had become unlivable. In nautical globalization, everything undertaken by restless Europeans to tear away from their older spheric anchorings and local inhibitions would flow together for an entire age. What we here term restlessness (the keyword of early emigration research) still encompasses entrepreneurial spirit, frustration, vague expectation and criminal uprooting without any distinctions. Like another purgatory, the sea now offered a chance to escape the disappointing inhabitants of the homeland and the mainland. The new entrepreneurial-nautical yonder, however, was constituted as an experiential beyond open only to those who ventured out with total physical commitment. One cannot go halfway to sea, any more than one can be halfway in God. But regardless of whether the new restless ones boarded ships or traveled in their imaginations to distant worlds from a fixed business location, the desire of those Europeans who learned to listen would in future imagine a wondrous transatlantic transcendence. The European dream of the good, better, best life was caught up in the maelstrom of a totally other overseas. The yonder was no longer the edge of a cosmic shell but another coast; the crossing began to replace the ascent.

It was this displacement of transcendence to the horizontal plane that made utopia possible—as a school of thought, a mode of writing and a mold for wish plasmas and immanentized religions. The literary genre of utopia that appeared abruptly organized a wish culture geared towards progressive explication (and later the matching politics) in which alternative worlds could be constructed without the need for a context—always based on the primal fact of the Modern Age, namely the real-life discovery of the New World in the inexhaustible diversity of its insular and continental manifestations (not least in the countless Pacific islands, where it was supposed that the *experimentum mundi* could be undertaken once more from scratch). As any glance at the relevant documents shows, however, the empirical and the fantastic were inextricably intertwined in the early Age of Discovery. By means of its rapidly effective new media—chapbooks, travel accounts, novels, utopias, broadsheets, globes and world maps—thoughts of the genuine New World and its imaginary variants created a post-metaphysical wish regime which believed that its fulfillments were perhaps not yet close, but almost within reach. This set in motion a form of self-fulfilling wishful thinking that learned to steer a course, both in fantasy and reality, towards distant worlds and their fortunes in happiness, as if their suspected appearance at some distant point already held the promise of their accessibility.

11. "Corporate Identity" on the High Seas, Parting of Minds

Outside, of course, only those who knew how to wish and sail in the sworn team would make their fortune. The crews on the discovery ships were the first objects of the naïve and effective group modeling processes that were re-described in the present day as "corporate identity" techniques. On the ships, the advancing pioneers learned to want the impossible in a team whose members were all dreaming the same thing. In psychohistorical terms, the central New European principles of constant progress and general enrichment, are essentially projections of team dream visions from the early days of nautical globalization back onto a national and social horizon. They constitute attempts to transfer the categorical Forwards of seafaring back onto the circumstances of settled life. One can read Ernst Bloch's writings—to name an eminent example of generalized progressivism—as if he had reformulated socialism from the position of the seaside and recommended it as a dream of emigration to New Worlds filtered through reason. Progress is emigration in time: as if it were wisdom to make people to believe that, with the aid of productive forces freed from greed for property, one could turn the entire world into a South Pacific paradise. For this reason, the party of objectively fulfillable wishes is always right.[51]

But the dream of the main prize that comes to us outside will, at least, help the new globonauts to look the horror of exteriority in the face. That is why the seafarers and their crews are not simply psychotics whose loss of touch with reality at home makes them suitable to discover new worlds in the unknown; often enough, they genuinely have one foot on the ground of untrodden paths, and undoubtedly it is often well-suited to reality, especially on the high seas, to postulate the imminent miracle. The mightiest captains are those who commit their crews most effectively to the pure Forwards, particularly when it seems insanity not to turn around. Without a constant, strict spell of optimism on board, most of the early expeditions would have been thwarted by demoralization. The leaders kept their crews mentally on course with visions of fame and riches for the discoverers; but draconian punishments were also among their techniques for success in the untrodden space. Had the Portuguese Magellan, after the mutiny of his captains off St. Julian on the Patagonian coast of South America on April 1, 1520, not overruled the objections of the next in command and executed Spanish nobles along with the other rebels, he would not have made it unmistakably clear to his people what it means to be on an unconditional outward voyage. And had he not, as Pigafetta recounts, forbidden on pain of death any talk of a return home or the lack of provisions, then the westward journey to the Spice Islands—which would become the first circumnavigation of the world—would probably have been over in its first fifth.[52] On his first crossing, Columbus, as he recorded in the logbook of the *Santa Maria*, falsified his information about the distance they had covered "so that the men would not be frightened if the voyage were long."[53] Facing a nascent mutiny during a storm off the East African coast, Vasco da Gama had the compasses, maps and measuring instruments of his captains thrown into the sea to eliminate any future thoughts of turning back among his crew. Experiments of this kind gave rise to a veritable expedition psychology on board these delusionally bold ships, driven by the constant, acute coercion to part the optimistic minds from the despondent.

Only when these naval insights returned to the people on land would the thing known in later times as the progressive mentality become possible—a commitment to a resolute *Forwards*. Géricault's *The Raft of Medusa*—the classical disaster seascape of the Empire—painted in 1818/19, unabashedly highlights the maritime origin of the difference between progressive and regressive psychology. One can immediately distinguish the depressive group on the left part of the raft from the hopeful group on the right. Faced with extreme conditions, these shipwrecked men wage a conflict that was constitutive of the Modern Age: that between the hopes and the discouragements.[54] Since the mutiny of Vasco da Gama's captains and its cunning suppression, the globalization campaign has been a constant war of moods and a battle for group-hypnotic means of orientation (and, more recently, programming power in the mass media and consultation power in businesses). On the progressive side, it was not infrequently the courage of desperation—allied with an inextinguishable physiological optimism—that kept the world revolution of the non-turners going. The pessimists on board would later be the potential and actual mutineers against the project of modernity, including the rediscoverers of the tragic consciousness. They tend, with eminently sensible pretexts, to abandon undertakings in which they can no longer dream of themselves and those close to them as the winners. The history of these abandonists has yet to be written. Its motto, latently or manifestly, is the call of "Stop history!" that makes allies of apocalypticists, tragedians, defeatists and pensioners.[55] And yet the combined gravity of the calm-keepers,

Thomas Struth, *Musée du Louvre IV* (1989): exhibition visitors in front of
Géricault's *The Raft of Medusa*

the losers, the off-putters and their literary tribunes achieved little against the unleashed visionary energy of the project makers and entrepreneur-charlatans, who live off productive errors and manage time and again to build up empires around themselves from self-deceptions that succeed in the medium term.

Because the practices of the captains were not based on delusion and motivational spells alone, however, but also on incontestable geographical competencies and nautical routines worked out in real life, the insane New European wish projects occasionally gained the chance to make themselves a reality. Only thus can fear be converted into ecstasy on the oceans; only thus do records of ecstasies become logbooks; and only thus are the cargo holds filled with treasures from the new world. Every ship on the open sea embodies a psychosis that has set sail, and each is also real floating capital—and as such, it participates in the constant fluidization revolution.

12. The Basic Movement: Money Returns

With every ship that is launched, the capitals begin the movement that characterizes the spatial revolution of the Modern Age: the circuiting of the earth by the money employed, and its successful return to its starting account. Return of investment—this is the movement of movements that all acts of risk-taking obey. It lends all operations of capital a nautical aspect, even those that do not cross the open sea, as every sum invested can only multiply itself through a metamorphosis from the commodity form to the monetary form and back—from the booking form to the travel form, one could also say. As a commodity, money plunges into

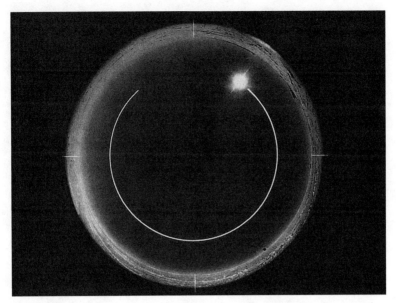

Sun path at the South Pole, photographed at the Scott Amundsen Station, exposure time c. 18 hours

the open sea of the markets, and, like the ships, must hope for a happy return to its home port; the circumnavigation of the globe is implicitly envisaged in the commodity metamorphosis. It becomes explicit when the goods for which the money is exchanged have to be sought exclusively on the distant markets. The return of the floating capital from its long-distance journey turns the madness of expansion into the reason of profit. The fleet of Columbus and his successors comprises ships of fools that are converted into ships of reason. The most reasonable ship is the one that returns most reliably—saved up by a new *Fortuna Redux* for regular, happy journeys home.[56] And because the money invested in speculative undertakings is expected to bring the investor a substantial gain, the true name for such yields is "revenues"—returns of itinerant monies whose multiplication constitutes the premium for the investors' property, which is burdened with changes of form and nautical risks.[57]

As far as the reasonable-insane overseas merchants in the ports are concerned—all these new risk-nationalists: the Portuguese, Italians, Spanish, English, Dutch, French and Germans who hoisted their flags on the oceans—they had learned by 1600 at the latest how to make their risks calculable through diversification. The new insurances seemed suitable to outwit the sea and its cliffs economically. Humans and property can be in what one calls danger; "a commodity at sea" (Condorcet), on the other hand, is subject to a risk, that is to say a mathematically describable probability of failure, and calculating solidary communities can be formed to combat this probability—the risk society as the alliance of well-insured profit-seekers and the respectably insane.

In business undertakings, unlike in everlasting philosophy, someone who bets everything on one outcome is a fool. The wise man thinks far ahead and relies, like every good bourgeois who can count, on diversification. One can entirely understand how Antonio, Shakespeare's merchant of Venice, could explain so convincingly why his sadness did not come from his enterprises:

> "My ventures are not in one bottom trusted,
> Nor to one place; nor is my whole estate
> Upon the fortune of this present year;
> Therefore, my merchandise makes me not sad."[58]

Antonio's merchant intelligence mirrors the average wisdom of an age in which floating capital had already spent a while thinking about the art of reducing risks to a reasonably acceptable level.

It is no coincidence that the beginnings of the European insurance system—and its mathematical foundations—extend back to the early seventeenth century.[59] The blooming of the insurance idea in the middle of the first adventure period of globalized seafaring shows that the great risk-takers were willing to pay a price in order to be taken seriously as reasonable subjects. For them, everything depended on establishing an insuperably deep divide between themselves and disorderly madmen. Such insurance systems as Modern Age philosophy drew their justifications from the imperative to separate reason and madness clearly and unambiguously. Both deal with techniques for security and certainty; both are interested in controlling fluctuating processes (flows of commodities and money, states of consciousness and streams of signs), and hence synonymous with the modern disciplinary systems examined by Michel Foucault in his histories of order.

13. Between Justifications and Assurances
On Terran and Maritime Thought

The early insurance system was one of the harbingers of systemic modernity, assuming one defines modernization as a progressive replacement of vague symbolic immune structures classifiable as final religious interpretations of human living risks with exact social and technical security services. The assurance of the mercantile professions replaced what had previously seemed to lie in God's hands alone; it offered provisions for the consequences of unforeseeable twists of fate. Prayer is good, insurance is better: this insight led to the first pragmatically implanted immune

Jürgen Klauke, *Prosecuritas*, installation at the Museum of Fine Arts Berne (1987)

technology of modernity; it was augmented in the nineteenth century by the social security system and the hygienic-medical institutions of the welfare state. (The immaterial price paid by the moderns for their insurability was high, admittedly, in fact metaphysically ruinous—for they dispensed with a fate, that is to say a direct connection to the absolute as an irreducible danger, and declared themselves specimens of a statistical avera-geness that dressed itself up individualistically. The meaning of being(-subject) shrank to an entitlement to benefits in a standard damage case.)

The philosophy of the Modern Age, by contrast, initially managed no more than a reorganization of symbolic immunity. This, as we know, was done in the name of "certainty"—that is, a modernization of self-evidence. The cycle of civil, non-monastic philosophies in modernity probably rested on the increasing demand among the middle classes for proof of non-insanity. Their clients were no longer the clerical courts, bishoprics, monasteries and theological faculties, but rather the project makers in the anterooms of Western princes and the enterprising minds in the growing audience of educated private persons; and finally also what one could, with increasing justification, call the scientific public sphere. Perhaps the rationalist branch of continental philosophy that followed on from the emigrant Descartes attempted precisely that: providing a new breed of risk-citizens who would take up loans, speculate on floating capital and have loan redemption dates in view with an unshakeable logical mainland on which to stand—an offer to which the seaworthy Britons proved less receptive in the long term than the other Europeans, who rarely made a secret of their hydrophobia and, furthermore, always had to reckon with an inflated public spending ratio in their intellectual enterprises.[60]

It is of epoch-typical significance that the title copperplate of Bacon's *Novum organum* of 1620 depicts *returning* ships, with the legend *Multi pertransibunt & augebitur scientia*: "Many will pass through and knowledge will be increased."[61] Here we find a betrothal of newer experiential thought to the Atlantic fleet guided by pragmatism, just as the Doge of Venice, as lord over Mediterranean seafaring, annually married the Adriatic Sea. That same Bacon, like a Pliny of the rising capitalism, authored *The History of the Winds*, which opens with the statement that the winds gave humans wings with which they learned how to fly—if not through the air, then at least over the seas.[62] The totality of these winds formed what would later be called the earth's "atmosphere"—taken literally, the orb of vapor or mist. The sailors on Magellan's voyage had been the first to see for

St. Charles Church, Vienna, built by J. B. and J. E. Fischer von Erlach at the behest of Charles VI (1716–1739)

themselves the unity of the earth's surface and that of the sea enclosed by an air breathable by humans. The seaman's breath gained the first access to real atmospheric globality: it led Europeans across to the true Modern Age, in which the connection between the human condition and the atmosphere established

Francis Bacon, title plate of *Instauratio magna* (London, 1620)

The earth in the ring of blowing winds, frontispiece of Athanasius Kircher's
Mundus subterraneus (Amsterdam, 1664)

itself as the master idea of a profound epochal caesura that had
not yet been fully thought through.

Even if the new centers of knowledge could not be situated
directly on the ships, they would still have to display certain port
qualities in future. Experience only reached people via importa-
tion; its further treatment via concepts would be the business of
philosophers—enlightenment begins at the docks. The true terrain
of experience in the Modern Age was the ship's deck, no longer
that "earth" of which, as late as the twentieth century, the ageing
Edmund Husserl had sought to reassure himself, in a desperately
conservative turn of phrase, as a "primal ark" [*Urarche*] or "primal

home" [*Urheimat*] (one can speak here of a regression to the physiocratic view, which holds that all values and validities stem from agriculture and a bond with the soil). Husserl's attempt to base all insights ultimately on a general world soil, the "ground of universal passive belief in being"[63] is still tied to a premodern form of terranism that cannot interrogate the reason for having a foundation excessively enough.[64] This happened at a time when marinism had long provided the more pragmatically astute answers, though perhaps not the better ones in absolute terms; maritime reason knows that it must navigate on the surface and be wary of running aground;[65] only those who navigate on the surface can operate successfully. The nautical spirit requires not foundations but terminals, remote destinations and inspiring port connections.

In its form, a philosophy that sought to follow its reputation for formulating the world concept of the Modern Age would be destined to constitute itself as a swimming faculty, or at least as the port authority of Old Europe. Part of the poverty of continental philosophy, the German in particular, was that it was usually bound—even in the twentieth century—to the atmospheres and morals of small rural towns and provincial residences, where philosophical studies could scarcely be anything other than the continuation of the lower priesthood's training by other means. Not even the Tübingen dreams of the Aegean, which were probably the best thing that ever touched German intelligences, could force access to the sea for idealistic thought.

Johann Gottfried Herder pinpointed the small-town spell affecting German thought into recent times in his bold early travel journal: "On earth, one is fixed to a dead point and locked in the narrow circle of a situation." He attempted to counter this claustrophobia, which touted itself as philosophy, with the leap into a different element:

> "O soul, how will it be for you when you depart from this world? The narrow, fixed, restricted midpoint has vanished, you flutter through the air or swim on a sea—the world disappears for you... how new a way of thinking."[66]

One could be tempted to read this as suggesting that the German disposition saw death as its only chance at globalization.

The maritime dimension of the Modern Age world format, however, was notoriously underestimated by most continental capitals and royal seats, whether Vienna, Berlin, Dresden or Weimar. For the most part, the continental philosophies placed themselves preemptively in the service of a terran counter-revolution that instinctively rejected the new world situation. In the end, people did still want to control the whole from the position of a secure national territory, pushing forward a firm foundation against the impositions of nautical mobility. This applied to the territorial rulers as much as the territorial thinkers. Even Immanuel Kant, who purported to be repeating the Copernican revolution in the field of thought by elevating the subject to the location of all representations, never fully realized that the Copernican revolution had actually been less decisive than the Magellanic one. What use was it, then, to make phenomena revolve around the intellect if said intellect did not stay put? With his insistence on the cogito owner's duty to reside, however, Kant was destined to misunderstand the essential feature of a world of fluctuations. The well-known quasi-lyrical passage in the *Critique of Pure Reason* concerning the island of pure reason, the "land of truth" that breasts the ocean, "the true seat of illu-sion" where "many a fog bank and rapidly melting iceberg pretend to be new lands,"[67] probably reveals more about the defensive motives of the modern business of thought in its German variety than the author intended: in front of the full faculty, this passage formulates the anti-maritime oath with which the rational mind ties itself to the perspectives of deep-rooted, terran-regional self-assertion. It crosses this treacherous ocean but once, with clear disgust—or critical intent, some would say—to assure itself that there is really *nothing* of interest for reason to be found there. Matters were made all the worse by Heidegger's defense of provincial life, a defense whose message was this: Berlin is no good for someone who, like some location-specific grotto oracle, is the medium through which the truth of Being speaks—four hundred and fifty years after Columbus and one hundred and fifty after Kant. He too understood truth as a chthonic function—a revocable emergence from earth, mountain and cave—and granted only a temporal, not a spatial meaning to that which comes from afar. Thought con-cerning the whole was the last to board the ship.

And so Goethe noted in his journal from the *Italian Journey*, on 3 April 1787 in Palermo: "No one who has never seen him-self surrounded on all sides by nothing but the sea can have a true conception of the world and of his own relation to it."[68] The great majority of Central European scholars, almost all cowed and sustained by territorial states and their lords, pre-ferred to be surrounded by the walls of schools and libraries, or at the utmost by urban backdrops. Even Hegel's seemingly magnanimous acknowledgement of the sea as the natural ele-ment of industry, which joins different nations, in the famous

MOBILIS IN MOBILI

N

§247 of his *Philosophy of Right*—"the greatest medium of communication," "one of the chief means of culture"[69]—is in fact no more than an administrative note, and does not take on any significance for the conceptual culture of the habitually enthroned, non-wandering philosopher.[70] Telling the truth remains, for the time being, a sedentary activity on mainland foundations. *Romanus sedendo vincit* (Varro).[71]

Only the great solitary Schopenhauer, away from the universities and regional churches, managed an overdue breakthrough to a way of thinking that made a fluidized foundation its starting point: *The World as Will and Representation* was the first manifestation of an ocean of the philosophers. On this ocean, the subject navigates on the nutshell of the *principium individuationis*, kept secure by the saving illusions of space, time and I-ness. This discovery was taken up by Nietzsche and the vitalists, who declared the re-fluidization of ossified subjects the true task of a "philosophy of the future." In their writings, one can witness a remoulding of subject-oriented thought suitable for the high seas. It was not a philosopher who succeeded in formulating the true concept of the subject's ambition in the age of mobilization, however, but a novelist—Jules Verne, who found the formula for the epoch in the motto of his Captain Nemo: *MOBILIS IN MOBILI*. His maxim, "moving amid mobility," explained with unsurpassable clarity and generality what modernized subjectivity sought to and had to do. The goal of the great flexibilization was the power to navigate amid the totality of all accessible places and objects without being oneself vulnerable to the detecting instruments of the others. Realizing oneself in the liquid element as a subject: this is absolute freedom of enterprise, perfect an-archy.[72]

It was Schopenhauer's contemporary Ralph Waldo Emerson who, with his first series of *Essays* published in 1841, initiated the "American evasion" and nautical reformulation of philosophy—which is why Nietzsche discovered a kindred spirit in him already as a young reader.[73] In Emerson's work, the offensive tones from the early European period of de-restriction reappear in transatlantic translation. Centuries earlier, in *On the Infinite Universe and Worlds*, published in Venice in 1583, Giordano Bruno, another thinker of solitary motivations within his time, celebrated the emancipation of the human spirit from the impoverishment of a nature so "mean and niggard in her fruit" and a miserly God restricted to a single small world:

> There are no ends, boundaries, limits or walls which can defraud and deprive us of the infinite   multitude of things. Therefore the earth and the ocean thereof are fecund [...].[74]

The Nolan described his own role as that of a Columbus of the outer spaces who had given earthlings insight into shattering the domes of illusion. Just as Columbus had returned from crossing the Atlantic with news of another shore, Bruno wanted to return from his voyage into the infinite bearing news of the non-existence of an upper edge. On the exterior and on top, the world is devoid

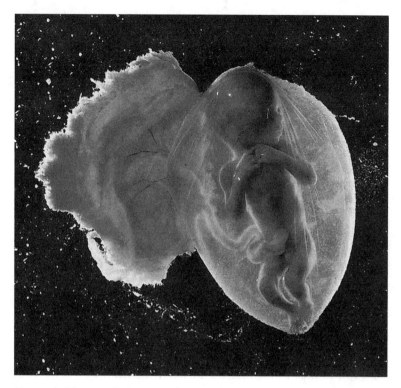

Fetograph (photograph: Lennart Nilsson, mid-1960s)

of boundaries or fortifications on all sides: this was the central space-theoretical announcement of the Brunian Modern Age, and it was not meant to sound any less evangelical than the Columbian one.[75]

A quarter-millennium later, the American sage Emerson replied to this in his pitilessly optimistic essay "Circles" with the following words:

> Our life is an apprenticeship to the truth that around every circle another can be drawn; that there is no end in nature, but every

end is a beginning [...]. There is no outside, no inclosing wall, no circumference to us. The man finishes his story—how good! how final! how it puts a new face on all things! He fills the sky. Lo! on the other side rises also a man and draws a circle around the circle we had just pronounced the outline of the sphere.[76]

Only from the later nineteenth century onwards would continental philosophy—in spite of all phenomenological, neo-idealistic and neo-Aristotelian revivals—steer towards the collapse of absolutist-territorial fortifications of evidence, a collapse that could be postponed, but no longer prevented. With more than a century's delay, some German professors even hinted at their willingness to consider whether the conceptual means of terran idealism were still suitable for processing the actual conditions of globalization intellectually. These too, to their own advantage, were closer in recent times to the legacy of the British common sense doctrine, which facilitated the transition from the old *inconcussum* standard to a globalized probability culture; theoretically approaching a universe of fluctuations also seems less painful from that position. This implies, admittedly, a conversion from the "Catholic" path, which connected poverty with security bonuses, to the "Protestant" lifestyle of the Calvinist variety, which urgingly related wealth and risk.[77] It was Friedrich Nietzsche who, as a critic of metaphysical *ressentiment*, first realized that philosophical thought after Zarathustra must become something fundamentally other than a sensible waiting and circumspection inside the divine orb.

On the competitive market of modern immunity techniques, the insurance system, with its concepts and procedures, completely won out over philosophical procedures of certainty. The

Pieter Claesz, *Vanitas* (Nuremberg, c. 1630), detail

logic of controlled risk proved far more economical and practicable than that of ultimate metaphysical justification. Faced with
this choice, the large majority of modern societies made fairly
unambiguous decisions. Insurance defeats evidence: this statement encapsulates the fate of all philosophy in the technical
world. The only modern country not to have chosen the path to
the precautionary insurance state is the United States of America,
with the result that religion, or more generally speaking the
"fundamentalist disposition," retained a significance atypical

of modernity. Wherever else insurance-oriented thought has established itself, however, one witnesses the change of mentality that characterizes postmodern boredom societies: uninsured situations become rare and disturbances can be relished as an exception; the "event" is positivized, and the demand for experiences of difference floods the markets. Only fully insured societies have proved able to set in motion that aestheticization of insecurities and unfathomabilities which forms the criterion for postmodern life forms and their philosophies.[78]

In so-called risk societies, however, the spirit of the insurance system drove out the willingness to take those very actions that gave them their name: a risk society is one in which anything truly hazardous is *de facto* forbidden—that is to say, it is excluded from compensation in the event of damage. One of the ironies of modern conditions is that by their standards, one would have to retroactively forbid everything that was ventured in order to realize them. It follows from this that post-history is only seemingly a historico-philosophical concept, and in reality an insurance-related one. The post-historical states are those in which historic actions (foundations of religions, crusades, revolutions, wars of liberation and class struggles, with all their heroic and fundamentalist aspects) are forbidden by law due to their uninsurable risk.

14. Expedition and Truth

The centuries that followed the first strike of the adventurer-seafarers initially belonged entirely to the impulse of making the outside safe for Europeans to move in—whether through an entrepreneurial insurance system or philosophical sciences that

Laurent de la Hyre, *Geometry* (1649), detail

provided ultimate justifications. With increasing routinization and optimization of marine technology, real seafaring in particular lost a significant part of its ecstasy-inducing effects, and with the reduction of the adventurous element to residual risks, it approached routinized traffic—the game of trivialized outward and homeward journeys, albeit with a shipwreck quota unacceptable for users of transportation services in the twentieth century. We should qualify this by noting that the perfect symmetry of outward and homeward journeys (which defines the concept of traffic in its exact sense) could only be achieved on land. It was only with the advent of railway traffic that the utopia of complete control over reversible movements was largely realized. Nonetheless, the primacy of the outward journey remains the hallmark of sea voyages in the heroic age of explorations and merchant voyages.

One characteristic of European extroversion is that its decisive advances always have exodus-like qualities, even where there is no Puritan emigration and no pilgrim fathers re-enacting the escape from Egypt on the Atlantic.[79] The Modern Age had no shortage of volunteers for the role chosen by exodus peoples. Promised lands could also be projected into all areas of the world with little difficulty, and departures thither often resembled offensives into the unknown, undetermined, unclear but promising—a tension that remained in effect in various regions until the middle of the all-banalizing twentieth century.

The voyage discovery that gave this era its name thus constitutes the epistemological form of an adventurism that behaves like a service to truth. Once the primacy of the outward journey is brought up programmatically, long-distance voyages present themselves as *expeditions*. Here, the penetration of the unknown is not simply the byproduct of a mercantile, missionary or military undertaking, but is carried out with direct intent. The closer we come to the hot core of typical Modern Age movements, the more obvious the expedition character of journeys to the outside becomes. And even if numerous discoveries must be attributed to Captain Nobody or Admiral Hazard, the essence of the Age of Discovery remained determined by the expedition as an entrepreneurial form—one finds because one seeks, and one seeks because one knows where things might be found. Until the nineteenth century, it was virtually impossible for Europeans to be "outside" without, at least in some aspect, being on an expedition.

The expedition is the routine form of entrepreneurially directed seeking and finding. Because of it, the decisive movement of real globalization is not simply a case of spatial expansion; it is part of the core process of a typically modern history of truth. Expansion could, of course, not take place were it not prefigured in truth-related terms—and thus in all terms—as a disclosure of what had previously been concealed. This is what Heidegger had in mind when, in his tremendous and violent 1938 essay "The Age of the World Picture," he felt he could pinpoint the basic process of the Modern Age in the conquest of the world as picture:

> Whenever we have a world picture, an essential decision occurs concerning beings as a whole. The being of beings is sought and found in the representedness of beings. [...] The world picture does not change from an earlier medieval to a modern one; rather, that the world becomes picture at all is what distinguishes the essence of modernity.[80]
>
> No wonder that humanism first arises where the world becomes picture. [...] The name "anthropology," here, does not refer to an investigation of humanity by natural science. [...] It designates, rather, that philosophical interpretation of man which explains and evaluates beings as a whole from the standpoint of, and in relation to, man.[81]
>
> To be "new" belongs to a world that has become picture.[82]

The epochal keyword "discoveries"—a plural that actually refers to a singular phenomenon, namely the authentically historical hyper-event of the earth's 'quantification'—thus denotes the epitome of practices whereby the unknown is transformed into the known, the unimagined into the imagined. With regard to the still largely unexplored, undepicted, undescribed and unexploited earth, this means that procedures and media had to be found to bring these into the picture as a whole and in detail. Hence the

World appropriation through measurement: 16th-century etching, British Museum, London

"Age of Discovery" encompasses the campaign driven along by
the pioneers of terrestrial globalization to replace the previous
non-images with images, or chimeras with "recordings"; consequently, all acquisitions of land, sea and world began with
pictures. Each of these images brought home by the discoverers
negated the externality of the external, bringing it down to a level
that was satisfactory or bearable for average Europeans. At the
same time, the exploring subject stands facing the pictures
provided and withdraws to the threshold of the pictorial
world—seeing all while itself unseen, recording everything but
predetermined only by the anonymous "point of view."

Hence the Modern Age, interpreted along Heidegger's
lines, was also an epoch of "the truth"—an era of truth history

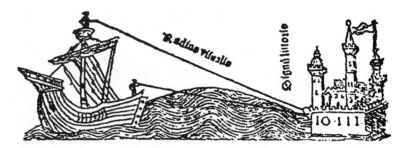

Bearing at sea, from Robert Grosseteste, *De Sphaera* (c. 1240, first published in 1506)

characterized by a particular style in the production of obviousness. Once and for all, truth was now no longer understood as that which showed itself from within itself, as in the sense of the Greek *physis* (as the "growth of the seed of emergence") or Christian revelation, where the infinitely transcendent God reveals through grace what human means of insight, left to themselves, could never have uncovered. These ancient and medieval preconceptions of truth were discarded in the age of research, for both understood truth as something that tended, prior to all human intervention, to step out into unconcealment in the sense of Greek *alétheia*, which meant something along the lines of "undisguised proclamation"—a concept that Heidegger sounded out in an attitude of cultic receptivity throughout his life. With the dawn of the Modern Age, truth itself seems to have made the transition to the age of its artificial uncoverability: from that point on, research could and had to exist as an organized theft of hiddenness. Nothing else could have been meant when the Renaissance was presented as the age of "the discovery of the world and man."

"Discoveries" were initially a summary name for recording procedures of a geotechnical, hydrotechnical, ethnotechnical and

Antonio Balestra, *The Riches of the Earth* (1689), Palazzo Mercantile, Bolzano

biotechnical kind—even if these appeared, at first, very rudimentary and random. When the Spanish queen sent her emissary Columbus a hand-written letter commanding him to bring her as many specimens of unknown birds as possible from the New World, this already contained—behind the mask of a royal whim—the technical impulse and the measuring grasp. At the end of this history of access, the zoological and botanical gardens would open their gates and integrate the animal "kingdom" and the plant "kingdom" into the modern exhibition system. When learned seafarers such as Abbé Incarville brought back flowering plants from Asia and the South Pacific for European gardens, the technical element—the acts of breeding and replanting—was unmistakably involved. It has too rarely been taken into account how far directed plant migrations shaped and contributed to enabling the life forms of the Modern Age.[83] Even things that, in terms of how they developed, often presented themselves as sheer adventurous turbulence and chaotic improvisation—the stormy crossing of the open seas, the hasty adoption of new coastal maps and countries, as well as the identification of unknown peoples— were in essence already technical processes. Heidegger's dictum can be applied without reservation to all of these gestures: "Technology is a mode of revealing."[84]

15. The Signs of the Explorers
On Cartography and Imperial Name Magic

If research is the organized working-away of concealment, then no process in the history of the expansions of human knowledge fulfilled this definition more dramatically or fully than the globalization of the earth via discovery between the sixteenth and nineteenth centuries. The cultural philosopher Hans Freyer, who was temporarily attracted to the political far right but later held more sedate education-conservative views, was not entirely mistaken when he wrote of this crude adventure:

> Whether the technology with which people set off was primitive or modern, adequate or inadequate, is the wrong question to ask. All technology is the arming of a will to the point at which it can strike out directly.[85]

The technological aspect in the mode of the early voyages of discovery comes to light most clearly when one examines how these enterprises rid themselves of the mission to create images of the traversed space. Even on the earliest expeditions, the captains and the scientists, artists, writers and astronomers on board had no doubts that it was their mission to collect and report conclusive evidence of their finds—not only in the form of commodities, samples and booty, but also of documents, maps and contracts. Crossing foreign waters can only be considered a secure achievement from the moment when a sighting is accompanied by an exploration, an observation by a record, and an appropriation by the creation of a map. The discovery of an unknown quantity— a continent, an island, a people, a plant, an animal, a bay, a sea current—presupposes the availability of the means to repeat the first encounter. What has been discovered, then, must never fall back into concealment, the antecedent Lethe from which it has just been extracted, if it is to become the secure property of the lord of knowledge. To understand the phenomenon of discovery, then, it is indispensable to show the means of acquisition which guarantee that the cover concealing what was previously hidden is removed once and for all. Accordingly, whenever Europeans of the Renaissance spoke of discovery—*découverte, descumbrimiento, Entdeckung*—they meant the things found and the means of making them known and keeping them available.

For a great number of modern discoveries in the open terrestrial space, it was merely spatial distance that had acted as the concealing cover. The conquest of distance through the new means of transportation and the establishment of trans-oceanic traffic connections created the necessary conditions for a lifting of the "cover" with lasting consequences. It is no language-historical coincidence that, until the sixteenth century, the word "discover" meant nothing other than removing the covering of an object, that is to say an exposure of the known, and only later came to denote the finding of something unknown. The mediating factor between the two is traffic, which exposes the distant and is capable of taking the covering off the unfamiliar. From this perspective, one can say that the essence of this discovering traffic is the de-distancing of the world. Globalization here means nothing other than having access to the technological means for eliminating distance. Where the successes of such reaching accumulate, the undiscovered can itself become a scarce resource. While barely half the globe was known to Europeans in its outlines in 1600, four fifths had already been explored by 1800. One of the atmospheric effects of enlightenment at the end of the twentieth century is that the earth's reserves of secrets were considered exhaustible; thus Columbus' belief that the navigable planet was "small" attained its pragmatic goal. Only the de-distanced world is the the discovered and shrunken world.

Discovery aims for acquisition: this gave cartography its world-historical function. Maps are the universal instrument for securing what has been discovered, in so far as it is meant to be recorded "on the globe" and given as a secure find. For an entire age, two-dimensional maps of land and sea—together with the globe—provided the most important tool for localizing those points in the locational space of the earth from which the shroud of concealment had been lifted. The rise of the map at the expense of the globe is an indication that the acquisition of data soon extended to the most minute details, even for the furthest reaches. Experts read this as pointing to the transition from extensive to intensive geographical research. While the globes—the main media of the Columbian age—later served predominantly summary and representative, and ultimately decorative functions, the increasingly precise maps took on ever greater operative significance. They alone could meet the demands of land description in detail, occasionally functioning as political land registers in the process. The new atlases created map collections revealing all countries and continents on interesting scales. (Since the introduction of the school subject "geography" in the late nineteenth century, European schoolchildren were brought up to look at maps that had been presented to the princes and ministers a hundred years earlier by their returning conqueror-geographers like secret diplomatic dispatches and geopolitical gospels.) The general tendency is characterized especially by the creation of the planispheric world map—that depiction of the earth which reproduced the orb as a flat surface, whether in the form of the early heart-shaped maps, in the rolled-out representation of all continents and oceans (as often seen today in the backdrops of news studios), or in the classic double hemisphere, with the more land-filled Ptolemaic Old World in the right half and the water-dominated American-Pacific New World in the left.

The irresistible pull of the map repeated the process of conquering the world, highlighted by Heidegger, in the depictive media of globalization as an image. When the planispheric world maps pushed away the globe, when even the name *Atlas* no longer stood for the orb-bearer, only a bound book of maps, the two-dimensional medium triumphed over the three-dimensional, and *ipso facto* the image over the body. In both name and substance, the planispheres—literally meaning "flat orbs"—sought to erase the memory of the dimension not mastered by the imagination: the third dimension, namely spatial depth. What art history has to say about the problem of perspective in Renaissance painting barely scratches the surface of the war for control of the third dimension. Where people succeeded in committing spheres to paper and simulating spatial depth on canvases, the conquest of the world as picture opened up infinite new possibilities. Imperialism is applied planimetry: the art of reproducing orbs as surfaces. Only that which can successfully be stripped of one dimension can be conquered.

Nothing characterized the knowledge-political dynamics of early globalization more radically than the alliance of cartography and land acquisition. Carl Schmitt, who enjoyed presenting himself as the last legitimist of European power in the world, did not hesitate to claim in his study *The Nomos of the Earth* that European expansion was ultimately only allowed to invoke the legal titles provided by discovery. The fiction of "finder's rights" was based on this, as was that of a "communication right" that went beyond mere visiting rights (the *ius communicationis* defended by Francisco de Vitoria in his famous *relectio, On the Indians*). Only as discoverers and finders of foreign coasts and cultures, he argued, had the Europeans become able to be the *legitimate* masters over the majority of the world; only their willingness to be masters trained them to take on the responsibility that fell to them from their superior devotion to the open world. The responsibility of discoverers, according to Schmitt, manifests itself first of all in the duty to reclaim the new territories for the European masters, usually royal clients, with formal gestures. The most important elements of this claim-staking included, beside the erection of crosses, stone coats of arms, *padrãos*, banners and dynastic emblems, the mapping and

The Platonic bodies serve as models of cosmic and terrestrial measurements; from Peter Apian, *Instrument Buch* (1533)

naming of the lands.[86] In the European understanding, these could only come formally under the dominion of their new lords once they had become localized, recorded, demarcated and named entities. The coincidence of sighting, landing, appropriation, naming, mapping and certification is what constitutes the complete, legally consequential act of a discovery.[87] This, according to Schmitt, is followed by the real subjection of a country to the legal jurisdiction of the discoverer-occupier. The latter gives the discovered the fruits of their discoveredness, namely the privilege of being protected by this master and no other—a prerogative that simultaneously covers the risks of exploitation by the distant sovereign.

As a "finding" of seemingly or genuinely unclaimed objects that is relevant to ownership rights, discovery could never have been consolidated into a particular mode of appropriation if motifs from the nautical natural law had not also influenced it. Through the transference of an old habitus, the time-honored equation of the catch and the find declared the discoverers of new lands fishermen of a sort, whose claim to rightful ownership of their prey could not so easily be contested. In his great whaling novel, Melville reminds the reader of the difference between "fast-fish" and "loose-fish," which was supposedly an iron rule for the hunters on the Modern Age seas: a fast-fish belonged to the party "fast to it" (when connected with an occupied ship or boat), while a loose-fish was considered "fair game for anybody who [could] soonest catch it." Looting on land, as Melville noted, was subject to the same distinction:

> What was America in 1492 but a Loose-Fish, in which Colum-
> bus struck the Spanish standard by way of waifing it for his
> royal master and mistress? What was Poland to the Czar? What
> Greece to the Turk? What India to England? What at last will
> Mexico be to the United States? All Loose-Fish. What are the
> Rights of Man and the Liberties of the World but Loose-Fish?
> [...] What is the great globe itself but a Loose-Fish?[88]

It is unmistakably clear that Schmitt, a man as legally sensitive as he was morally thick-skinned, modeled his theorem of the legitimacy of European dominion through legal titles from dis-coveries on the Columbian mission described above, where the taker presents himself as the bringer of the more precious goods. While Columbus saw himself as the man who brought Christ's

Globo imperial, globus cruciger and armillary sphere for Dom Pedro II of Brazil (1841)

salvation to the New World, the conquistadors defended by Schmitt could consider themselves justified as conveyers of European legal and civilizatory accomplishments.

Such justificatory fantasies were not a product of late apologetics and *post factum* applications of legal unscrupulousness, however; from the start, they were interwoven with the events

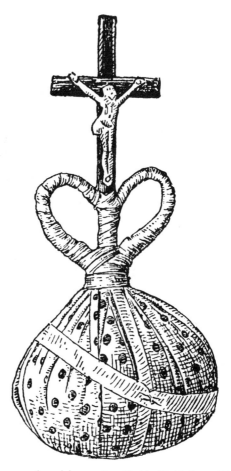

Paquet talisman or voodoo *globus cruciger*, Guéde, Haiti, from Alfred Métraux, *Le voudou haitien* (1958)

themselves. In the fourth canto of his epic of world-appropriation, *The Lusiads*, the poet Luis de Camões has the Indus and Ganges rivers appear to the Portuguese king Manuel in a dream, in the guise of wise old men who urge him to subjugate the people of India—whereupon the epic's king decides to prepare a fleet for

Primus me circumdedisti: Sebastian del Cano's coat of arms

the Indian voyage under the command of Vasco da Gama. Literature of the Modern Age is poetry of success.[89] It is no coincidence
that Manuel I, known as "the Fortunate," would later include the
globe in his coat of arms—a pictorial idea that is being taken up
once more today by countless businesses in their logos and advertising. In Manuel's century, this was a privilege afforded only to

one private person after him: Sebastian del Cano, who brought the *Victoria* back to Spain in 1522 after Magellan's death and was rewarded with the right to wear the globe in his insignia, accompanied by the motto *primus me circumdedisti*[90] and a crown land, the royal Portuguese colony of Brazil, whose flag features Manuel's sphere to this day.

That the association of globe and conquest had already become a metaphor-spawning fixed idea among European poets shortly thereafter is illustrated by some lines from Shakespeare's early dramatic poem "The Rape of Lucrece" (1594), in which the rapist Sextus Tarquinius views the uncovered body of his sleeping victim:

> Her breasts, like ivory globes circled with blue
> A pair of maiden worlds unconquered...
> These worlds in Tarquin new ambition bred.

It would seem that in the Modern Age's organization of fantasies, it was already sufficient for an object to appear round, desirable and asleep in order to become describable as a conquerable "world."

But just as the national Portuguese epic provided the belated heroic justification for the factual conquest by declaring the expansionist people chosen from among the less worthy Christian peoples,[91] the recorded land and sea maps served in the occupation as prosaic legal means and notarial files that certified the new conditions of ownership and dominion with sufficient formality. *Cuius carta, eius regio.*[92] Whoever draws the map behaves as if they were culturally, historically, legally and politically in the right—even if the black books of the colonial centuries present disastrous closing balances in retrospect.

The reopening of Shakespeare's Globe Theater on August 21, 1996 with a production of *The Two Gentlemen of Verona*

One of the most conscpicuous hallmarks of European expansion had always been the asymmetry between the discoverers and the inhabitants of found lands. Overseas territories were considered ownerless things as long as the discoverer-occupiers felt unhindered and unchallenged in the mapping of new areas, be they inhabited or uninhabited. Very often the inhabitants of distant lands were viewed not as their owners, but as parts of the colonial lost property—its anthropic fauna, as it were, which seemed available for hunting and harvesting. The so-called primitives initially had no idea of what it meant that Europeans wanted to gain an idea of them and their territories. Where the discoverers became aware of their own technological and mental superiority in their encounters with native peoples—which was less often the case in Asian and Islamic realms—they generally concluded that this entitled them to take the land and subject it to the rule of European sovereigns. Even in retrospect, Carl Schmitt viewed these fateful and violence-laden events with unreserved affirmation:

> Thus, it is completely false to claim that, just as the Spaniards had discovered the Aztecs and the Incas, so the latter could have discovered Europe. The Indians lacked the scientific power of Christian- European rationality. It is a ludicrous anachronism to suggest that they could have made carto-graphical surveys of Europe as accurate as those Europeans made of America. The intellectual advantage was entirely on the European side, so much so that the New World simply could be "taken" [...].[93]
>
> Discoveries were made without prior permission of the dis-covered. Thus, legal title to discoveries lay in a higher legitimacy. They could be made only by peoples intellectually and histori-cally advanced enough to apprehend the discovered by superior knowledge and consciousness. To paraphrase one of Bruno Bauer's Hegelian aphorisms: a discoverer is one who knows his prey better than the prey knows himself, and is able to subjugate him by means of superior education and knowledge.[94]

This means that the maps—especially in the early history of dis-covery—directly documented claims to civilizatory sovereignty. "A scientific cartographical survey was a true legal title to a *terra*

World map by Fra Mauro (Murano, 1459)

incognita."[95] One is inclined to note that it is the map sovereign who decides on a discovered world's state of emergency—which applies when the finder gives a discovered and charted land a new name along with a new master.

It would be of immeasurable epistemological value for the theory of terrestrial globalization if a detailed history of geographical naming practices during the last five hundred years were available. It would not only mirror the primal scenes of discovery and conquest, as well as the struggles between rival factions of discoverers and conquerors; it could also explain how, in the world history of names, the semantic side of a world de-distancing carried out seemingly instinctively by Europeans came about. Only a few cultural regions proved able to keep their proper names despite the discoverers' efforts; where this succeeded, it pointed to the resistance of sufficiently powerful empires to infiltration from without. Overall, the Europeans managed to catch the largest part of the earth's surface in their naming nets like a swarm of anonymous lost property and to project their lexica into the open world. The European discoverers unrolled *The Great Map of Mankind*—this resonant phrase goes back to Edmund Burke—and labeled it according to their naming moods. The baptism of seas, currents, rivers, passages, capes, coves and shallows, of islands and archipelagos, and of coasts, mountain ranges, plains and countries grew into a centuries-long passion among European cartographers and their allies, the seafarers, merchants and missionaries. Wherever they appeared, a torrent of new names rained down on a world that had seemed mute until then.

Where there is baptism, however, there can also be rebaptism. The small Bahaman island of Guanahaní, whose coast was the first in the New World to be visited by Columbus on October 12, 1492, was given the name—a completely natural act under his premises—of *San Salvador*, a phrase that, in the ideology of the bringer, represented the highest value the conquerors could carry with them. The early discoverers barely ever went on land without

Memorial plaque on the island of San Salvador

believing, however vaguely, that the God of Europe was revealing himself to these areas through their presence. In keeping with this habitus, any Buddhist conquerors would have had to give the island Guanahaní the name Gautama or Bodhisattva, while "The Prophet" would have been a likely choice for Muslim invaders. After the English pirate John Watlin occupied the now deserted island in 1680 and made it his base, it retained the name "Watlin's Island" until the start of the twentieth century, as if it had been the pirate's natural vocation to continue the legacy of the discoverer. The pirate's island was only given back its Columbian name in 1926—not entirely without conflict, as five other Bahaman islands now also claimed to be the historical Guanahaní. The island known today as Rum Cay had been named *Santa Maria de la Concepción* by Columbus, establishing the Holy Family in the Caribbean. For a time, the later Haiti enjoyed the privilege of being dubbed *Hispaniola*, "Little Spain." Similarly, thanks to Columbus, dozens of islands and coastal places assumed names from the Christian and dynastic nomenclature of Europe, though few of them had any historical longevity.

Admittedly the continent discovered by Columbus, that of Central and South America, was not named after him, as the rules of the globalization game would normally require, but after one of his rivals in the race for the exploration of the New World. Owing to a problematic naming hypothesis advanced by the German cartographer Martin Waldseemüller in 1507, the feminized (because continents, as vessels of life, must be feminine) first name of the merchant-discoverer Amerigo Vespucci came to be used for the continent, whose eastern coast the Florentine had, according to questionable sources, supposedly explored as far as the mouth of the Amazon River in 1500. This naming success reflects the assertiveness of a roughly heart-shaped planispheric world map published by Waldseemüller in 1507—it is also (coming shortly after Contarini's 1506 map, produced as a copperplate) the oldest *printed* map made using the woodcut technique.[96] Its success—there were supposedly one thousand copies, of which only one has survived—was assisted by an accompanying text that had to be reprinted three times in the year of its publication alone. The year of Waldseemüller's map also saw the production of his globe, which suggests the same name for the southern half of the New World: *America*. One might ask whether the heart-like shape of the map—even if it is not developed as fully as in the later heart-shaped world maps of Oronce Finé and Giovanni Cimerlino[97]—contributed decisively to the triumph of Waldseemüller's brilliant cosmographic feat; for what could capture the world-envisaging imagination better than the idea of depicting the surface of the terrestrial orb with a great heart? Waldseemüller's later abandonment of his Vespucci error could no

Heart-shaped map by Giovanni Cimerlino, *Cosmographia universalis* (Verona, 1566)

longer impede the triumph of the name he (and Matthias Ring-
man) had advanced.[98]

The Paris *Globe Vert* of 1515 seems to have been the first on
which the name *America* was also applied to the northern part of
the double continent. For a considerable time, however, more

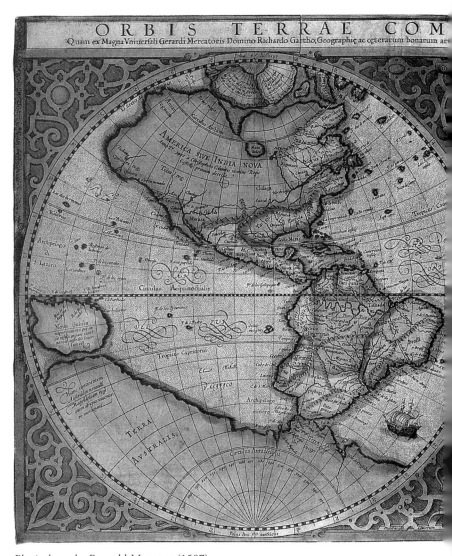

Planispheres by Rumold Mercator (1587)

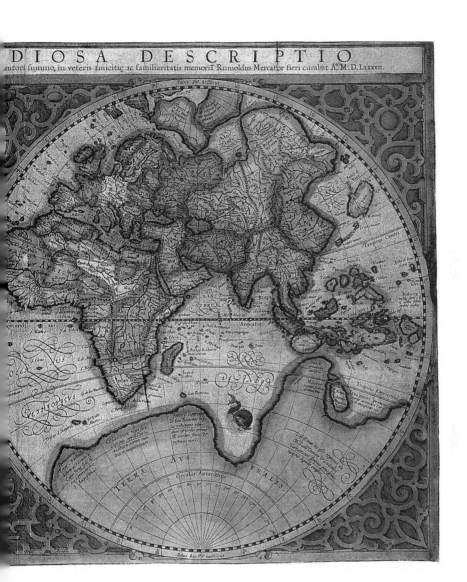

than a few rival labels for this part of the *mundus novus* were in circulation. As late as 1595, it appeared on a map by Michael Mercator as *America sive Nova India*; a Venetian map from 1511, on the other hand, calls the Columbian continent *Terra sanctae crucis*; on a Genoese world map from 1543, the entire North American continent remains nameless, while the southern part simply bears the aspecific marking *Mundus Novus*. For centuries, the Northeast United States appeared as *Nova Francia* or *Terra francisca*, while the West and Midwest fell to their British name-givers as New Albion. The eastern coast of North America, which later became New England, was in fact temporarily termed *Nova Belgia*—meaning "New Netherlands"—while Australia was known in the seventeenth century as *Nova Hollandia*. These confusing traces of early name nationalism already heralded the age of civil imperialisms on the basis of capitalized nation-states. For an entire era, the prefix "new" proved to be the most powerful module in the creation of names, matched only by the prefix "south" during the race for *Terra Australis*, the hypothetical giant continent in the southern hemisphere. With the baptism of "new" cities (New Amsterdam), "new" countries (New Helvetia), "south" countries (South Georgia, New South Wales), saints' islands (San Salvador), monarchic archipelagos (the Philippines) and conquistador countries (Colombia, Rhodesia), Europeans enjoyed the prerogative of semantically cloning their own world and appropriating the distant and foreign points through the lexical recurrence of the same.

In the sum of its effects, the role of cartography in the actual progress of globalization cannot be overestimated. Maps and views of the globe not only served as the greatest lures of the first discovery periods; they were not only a form of land register, documents of appropriative acts and archives of locating knowledge that accumulated over centuries, as well as route maps for sea-faring. They also constituted the memory media of the Age of Discovery, containing countless names of nautical heroes and finders of foreign parts of the world—from the Straits of Magellan in southern Patagonia to Hudson Bay in northern Canada, from Tasmania in the South Pacific to Cape Chelyuskin in Siberia, from Stanley Falls in the Congo to the Ross Ice Shelf in the Antarctic. In parallel with the history of artists, which was taking shape during the same time, the history of discoverers had created its own hall of fame on the maps. Many of the later undertakings were already candidates tournaments for the prize of an idealized status in charted history. Long before art and art history drew profit from the concept of the avant-garde, the vanguards of earth acquisition were moving on all fronts of future cartographical fame. They often set off from European ports as those who, if successful, would be the first to have reached some point or other. Theatrical projects such as the "conquest" of the North Pole and South Pole in particular were entirely guided by that mania of immortalization for which going down in the annals of discovery history was the highest distinction. Alpinism was also a variety of the vanguard hysteria that wanted no eminent point on the earth's surface to remain unconquered. For a long time, the hunt for the fame promised by the first visits to the poles would remain the purest form of this learned delirium. Contemporaries of aviation and space travel can no longer comprehend the popular fascination and scientific prestige still attached to the two polar projects around 1900. The earth's poles not only epitomized that which was distant, devoid of humans and

Martin Waldseemüller, world map "America Terra Nova" (Strasbourg, 1513)

difficult to reach; more than this, they were also the focus of the
dream of an absolute center or axial zero point, which was barely
anything other than the continuation of the search for God in
the geographical and cartographical element.

In this context it is appropriate to remind ourselves that the era in which Sigmund Freud would make a name for himself as the "discoverer of the unconscious" also saw the climax of the races for the earth's poles and the grand coalition of Europeans to extinguish the last white spots on the map of Africa. In its habitus of disclosure and foundation, the enterprise of psychoanalysis belongs to the age of empire builders such as Henry Morton Stanley and Cecil Rhodes ("I would annex the planets if I could"). These were joined not long afterwards by Freud's age-mate, the young Hanoverian Carl Peters (briefly a *Privatdozent* in Leipzig), the later founder of German East Africa, whose philosophical treatise *Willenswelt und Weltwille* (1883) had conceptually realized the imperialization of the irrational ground of life in advance. Freud's ambition can only be explained in relation to the projects of those men. Had the unconscious not been present in vague outlines on the maps of the reflective spirit since the days of the young Schelling? Was it not natural to claim that its dark interior had finally become ripe for the "sickle of civilization?" If Freud, who was familiar with the works of the Africa-conquerors Stanley and Baker, chose the "true inner Africa" in the psyche of every person on his path to fame, this choice of research area testified to an excellent imperial instinct.[99] The Austro-Hungarian Arctic expedition of 1872–1874, led by Karl Weyprecht and Julius von Payer, had achieved some *succès d'estime* with the discovery and naming of Franz Joseph Land and Prince Rudolf Island; as a whole, however, their results were only of frosty and provincial significance. Freud's self-assured scientism manifested itself in the fact that he claimed not an island on the icy outskirts, but rather a hot and centrally situated continent for himself. His ingenuity exhibited

Preparations for the funeral of Cecil Rhodes in 1902

itself impressively when, thanks to his topological maps, he succeeded in acquiring the unconscious *de facto* as Sigmund Freud
Land. He too stoically took the white man's burden upon his
shoulders when, summarizing his work, he stated: "Psychoanalysis
is an instrument to enable the ego to achieve a progressive
conquest of the id."[100] Even if the sad tropics of the id are
meanwhile increasingly being managed by new occupiers, or
unanalyzable Calibans are even declaring their decolonization,
the old Freudian landmarks remain clearly visible in many places.
Whether they will be able to command more than touristic
interest in the long run, however, is uncertain.

16. The Pure Outside

Like Freud's allusion to the "dark continent" of the unconscious,[101] the reference to the "terrors of ice and darkness"[102] encountered by polar explorers is suitable for presenting the spherological meaning of discovery projects in the age of globalization in the correct light. When European merchants and heroes set off to "take" distant points on the globe, they could only make their decisions in so far as the globalized locational space had already been conceived as a homogeneous, open and passable outside. All European expeditions of land and sea acquisition—which now took on their most general form through ecological environment acquisition—aim for exospheric spaces that, in the eyes of the expedition groups, in no way belong to their own lifeworlds. Here Heidegger's existential-topological statement "In Dasein there lies an essential tendency towards closeness"[103] no longer applies. The strong characteristic of externality is that it is *not* "always already" disclosed in the mode of dwelling—rather, the possibility of disclosure is supposed in a projective anticipation, from which it follows that the difference between inhabiting and exploiting will never again become clear. With the advent of discoverers and conquerors, global camping was established as a *modus vivendi*. Here Merleau-Ponty's subtle theorem "our body is not primarily *in* space: it is of it" falls short.[104] The remark by the same author that "science manipulates things and gives up living in them"[105] is equally applicable to piracy or international trade; neither of them has a habitative relationship with the world. For the pirate's and the liberal's eye, it is no longer true that it inhabits being "as a man lives in his house."[106] In truth, the seafarers and colonizers—to say nothing of the desperados and *degradados* from all the gutters of the Old

World—were sooner scattered about outside like displaced bodies in an abandoned space. Only rarely did they find the way, through the transference of domesticity, to what one calls a "second home." In the external space, a type of human is rewarded that, thanks to the weakness of its ties to objects, can appear everywhere as internally controlled, speculative, unfaithful and available.[107]

Perhaps this explains the mysterious ease with which those men who encounter one another on the outside as strangers can exterminate one another. The other, viewed as a body in the external space, is no cohabitant of a shared lifeworldly sphere, no fellow carrier of a sensory-moral resonator, "culture" or shared life, but rather an arbitrary component of welcome or unwelcome *external circumstances*. If the psychodynamic problem of an over-sheltered settled existence is container masochism, then that of the excessively uninsured life lies in exterminism—a para-sadistic phenomenon that had already revealed itself unmistakably in the disinhibitions of the Christian crusaders from the twelfth century onwards.

On his first voyage to India in 1497, after looting an Arab merchant vessel with over two hundred pilgrims to Mecca on board, including women and children, Vasco da Gama had it burned and sunk for no particular reason—the prelude to a "world history" of external atrocities. Globalized liquidation activity breaks away from all pretexts and, as pure extermination, brings about a state beyond war and conquest. The colonies and the seas beyond the line were the practice sites for the exterminism that would return to Europeans in the twentieth century as the style of total war. If it takes place on the outside, the battling of a foe can no longer be clearly distinguished from the extermination of a thing. The disposition towards this lies in spatial alienation:

in the watery deserts and new lands of the earth's surface, the agents of globalization are never active as inhabitants of their own property; they are unleashed actors who no longer respect the house rules of culture anywhere. As house-leavers, the conquerors crossed the smoothed space without consequently entering the "path" in a Buddhist sense. When they left the shared house of the Old European world interior, they gave the impression of individuals who had broken away from all former restraints like projectiles to look around in a general non-sphere and non-closeness, a smooth and indifferent outside world of resources—but lead by mandate and appetite, and kept in shape with cruelty fitness exercises. The landing successes—in the stricter and the broader sense—of those loosed of the earth would one day be decided whether they would fall prey to their internal centrifugal force and disappear into oblivion as feral expedition psychotics, or whether—through new "object relationships," as it were—they would succeed in restoring mainland conditions, renewed housing in a distant world, or in the recovered old one. Carl Schmitt rightly pointed out the role of the "friendship lines" agreed upon by the European naval powers, whose purpose was to mark out a civilized space beyond which the outside, as an extralegal space, could formally begin.[108]

17. Theory of the Pirate
The White Terror

In this context, piracy—next to the slave trade, the foremost manifestation of a naïve globalization criminality—took on a marked historico-philosophical significance. It was the first entrepreneurial form of atheism: where God is dead, or where he is not looking—in the region without a state, on the ship without a priest on board, on the lawless seas outside of the agreed zones of respect, in the space with no witnesses, and in the moral emptiness beyond the line—the unimaginable is indeed possible, and the open sea has, at times, been the site of the greatest atrocities that can be perpetrated among humans. The lesson of this capture capitalism was a lasting one: the moderns conceived of the dangers of libertarian and anarchist disinhibition in terms of piratical atheism—the conservative phobia of partisans also stems from this. The fear of innovators among the guardians of law and order, notorious since antiquity, changed during the Modern Age into the land-dweller's fear of the seagoing entrepreneur; for even if he wears a top hat and knows how to use a fish knife at the table, the pirate still lurks beneath. Thus no terran could imagine without horror a state of the world in which the primacy of the political—which here means of mainland things—were no longer in force. For if the pirate goes ashore, what criminal plans is he carrying in his breast pocket? Where is he hiding his weapons? What enticing arguments does he use to advertise his speculations? What humanitarian masks does he don to hide his despicable intentions? The citizens have been arranging their fears for two hundred years: in the best case, the anarcho-maritime figure on land becomes a Raskolnikov (who does as he pleases, but regrets it), in the less favorable case a de Sade (who does as he pleases and negates remorse), and in the worst case a neoliberal (who does as he pleases and then, quoting Ayn Rand, praises himself).

In the figure of Captain Ahab, Herman Melville erected the outstanding monument to those who have fallen out of society, to the seafarers without return who spend their "pitiless old age"

"With sword and compass more and more and more and more": Vargas Machuca, *Militia and Description of the Indies* (1599)

on the outside. Ahab embodies the Luciferian, lost side of European-American seafaring, indeed the whole night side of the project of colonial modernity and nature-plundering, which could only advance by bursting spheres and ravaging peripheries. In psychological or microspherological terms, the evidence is compelling that the inner and outer double of the possessed seaman do not assume a personified form. The genius of Ahab's existence is not a spirit in the proximity field, let alone a lord on high, but rather a god from below and outside, an animal sovereign that appears from the deep and defies all appropriation—precisely that white whale of which the author noted in his etymological mottos:

> "This animal is named from roundness or rolling; for in Dan. *hvalt* is arched or vaulted." — *Webster's Dictionary*
>
> "Whale. *** It is more immediately from the Dut. and Ger. *Wallen*; A.S. *wealwian*, to roll, to wallow."
> —*Richardson's Dictionary*[109]

Through its "rolling" form, the whale appears to both its admirers and its haters as the epitome of a power that turns exclusively within itself in the sea's ominous depths. Moby Dick's grandeur represents the eternal resistance of an unfathomable life to the motives of hunters. His whiteness simultaneously stands for the non-spheric, homogeneous, unmarked space in which travelers will feel cheated of any feeling of intimacy, arrival or home. It is no coincidence that his color was that reserved by cartographers for *terra incognita*. Melville called white "a colorless all-color of atheism from which we shrink,"[110] because it reminds us of the Milky Way's white depth, of the "heartless voids and immensities of the universe";[111] it infuses us with the thought of our annihilation in the indifferent outside. That is why Ahab's whale wears this color, as it symbolizes an exteriority that is otherwise neither in need nor capable of a manifestation. But if the outside should ever show itself as such, then the palsied universe lies before us a leper; and like willful travelers in Lapland, who refuse to wear colored and coloring glasses upon their eyes, so the wretched infidel gazes himself blind at the monumental white shroud that wraps all the prospect around him.[112]

Almost a century before Sartre would let one of his figures in a play state that "hell is other people," Melville had touched on a deeper foundation: hell is the outside. The disconnected modern point-individuals are scattered in this methodological inferno, this indifference of a space in which no dwelling occurs. It is therefore not, as the Existentialists claimed, only a matter of giving oneself a direction and a project in the senseless space through a freely chosen commitment; rather, after the general exposure of humans on the surfaces of the earth and the systems, it is a matter of inhabiting the indifferent outside as if ensouled bubbles could achieve longer-term stability within it. Humans must bet that they will succeed—even in the face of the shroud covering everything external—in taking their relationships with one another in an interior that must be artificially created as seriously as if no external facts existed. Couples, communes, choirs, teams, peoples and churches all try their hand at fragile spatial creations against the primacy of the white hell. Only in such self-producing vessels can the withered word "solidarity" be fulfilled in the most radical layer of its meaning: the living-arts of modernity aimed to establish the non-indifferent within the indifferent. This created inexhaustible horizons for projection and invention in the face of a geographically exhausted world.[113]

And perhaps the "free peoples" of which the nineteenth century spoke—without realizing it was thereby assisting the emergence of the modernized obsession collectives—will only exist as associations of people who, faced with an actually universalized indifference, join forces anew in a manner vaguely anticipated by congregations and academies, but previously unknown.

18. The Modern Age and the New Land Syndrome

The reading room in the modern annex of the Library of Congress features an inscription by Thomas Jefferson that sums up the spirit of the land acquisition age with unmatched clarity:

> The earth belongs always to the living generation. They may manage it then, and what proceeds from it, as they please, during their usufruct.

Although the Washington thesis dates from the end of the eighteenth century, it encapsulates an impulse that affected the expansionist behavior of Europeans from Columbus' time onwards: the view of the earth as found property and a resource. Old Testament and colonizatory references are unmistakable in Jefferson's statement: the generation granted usufruct is, of course, none other than that of the New England Americans who broke away from the British Crown and believed they had found the promised land on the North Atlantic coast. For the Yankees (supposedly a Native American pronunciation of *les anglais*) of the eighteenth century, the Judaizing language games of the Pilgrim Fathers, who thought they were repeating the exodus of the Israelites from Egypt across the ocean, had long become rhetorical small change. Thus they did not need to lisp when expressing the belief that had become natural for them: that a chosen people should be granted a promised land.

The statement about the commitment of the earth to the present generation of usufructuaries, shimmering with the jargon of natural right, unmistakably conveys the shock of world reforms triggered by the transatlantic discoveries at the end of the fifteenth century and by Magellan's voyage. While the Pacific revolution, the realization of the oceanic character of the earth's communicating water areas, remained an abstract and unwelcome, at best utopia-inspiring piece of "information" for the vast majority of Europeans over centuries, the discovery of the Fourth Continent, the two Americas, was a more than geographical sensation. It was mirrored in countless expressions of a new theological and mercantile appetite. Americanists have offered manifold paraphrases of the salvation-historical interpretations of the double continent's discovery presented by its contemporaries and their successors. For the Biblicists among the immigrants and occupiers, America was undoubtedly the ace God had kept up his sleeve for a millennium and a half to play it at the time of greatest need, in the religion-political death throes of the occident. By allowing His still-Catholic servant Columbus to find America just in time, God used the ploy of divine providence to show his Protestant followers the way in the second exodus.

I shall leave aside the historico-theological deliriums that became real historical factors through the emigrants and their strong faith. Anyone interested in the serious appendix to *The Divine Comedy* should get their money's worth from *Magnalia Christi Americana* (The Glorious Works of Christ in the New World), penned in 1698 by the Bostonian minister Cotton Mather. What made the America effect one of the central

THE EARTH BELONGS ALWAYS TO THE LIV
AND WHAT PROCEEDS FROM IT AS THEY PL
TOO OF THEIR OWN PERSONS AND CON:

Annex of the Library of Congress, reading room

psychopolitical facts of the Modern Age, beyond its character as
a geographical sensation and the theological idealizations thereof, is its irradiation into the awareness of space, soil and chances
among the post-Columbian Europeans from whom the Americans
would be recruited. America rose from the Atlantic like a spare
universe in which God's experiment with mankind could be
started anew—a land in which arriving, seeing and taking
seemed to become synonymous. While, in the feudalized and
territorialized Old Europe, every strip of arable land had had an

NERATION · THEY MAY MANAGE IT THEN
RING THEIR USUFRUCT · THEY ARE MASTERS
LY MAY GOVERN THEM AS THEY PLEASE.

owner for a thousand years, and every forest path, cobblestone
or bridge was subject to age-old rights of way and restrictive
privileges in favor of some princely exploiter, America offered
countless arrivals the exciting contrasting experience of a virtually
lordless land that, in its immeasurability, wanted only to be
occupied and cultivated so as to belong to the occupier and
cultivator. A world in which the settlers arrive before the land
registers—a paradise for new beginners and strong takers. Hence
feelings of the world's breadth in the Modern Age were co-conditioned by the basic American experience: the ease with which

possession can be taken of land and resources. This produced—along with numerous other social characters—a world-historically unprecedented type of peasant who no longer resided on a lord's property, but rather managed his new, self-owned soil as an armed land-taker in his own right and a farmer under God.[114] Anyone seeking their fortune on the chance-grounds of the overseas commonwealth must therefore be as much of a chance-taker as goes with being a land-taker. Indeed, perhaps what theologians and jurists called natural law was simply the formal explication of the new taker-subjectivity, which had set itself the task of taking what was its own, by land and by sea. Human rights are the legal soul of the life that takes what belongs to it wherever it can. Melville, once again:

> Is it not a saying in every one's mouth, Possession is half of the law: that is, regardless of how the thing came into possession? But often possession is the whole of the law.[115]

Nonetheless, the taker-entrepreneurs on the colonial fronts acted, to speak in Kantian terms, under a maxim that is usually more suitable for the definition of crime than that of a noble participation in the exploration of the world: for, by seeking to become possessors and owners of goods by pure taking, they eluded the impositions of fair exchange. Their consciences were barely ever damaged by this, as history shows, for they invoked the right of the supreme moment: in that instant, justice had to lie in the appropriation itself. The agents of expansion, in the American West and the rest of the globe, exculpated themselves in their interventional acts through an implicit theory of the moral gap: there were seemingly times in which action must be

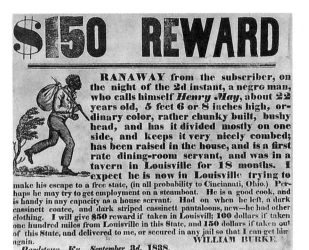

Reward for runaway slaves

ahead of legislation, and they were now in such a moment. With this argument they requested acquittal due to extraordinary circumstances. In the historical gap, people who would be looters in ordinary times are pioneers. Whoever found themselves charged with a crime during juridified or post-historical years would, in the turbulence of history in action, be considered a hero. (And who could overlook the fact that the current crime film industry continues to dream of the gap, in which criminals can still claim the human right to take without exchange?)

The agents in the heroic times of taking were unmistakably interested as much in self-taking as world-appropriation; they viewed their own existences as the next lordless estates that needed only to be seized in order to become a chance. The classic purveyor of this idea is Daniel Defoe, who not only presents his castaway, Robinson Crusoe, as an integral land- and self-seizer; his exemplary heroine Moll Flanders too, famous for her *Fortunes and Misfortunes*, is a taker in every sense of the word—a self-taught thief ("take the bundle; be quick; do it this moment") and seizer of all husbands and fortunes that chance sent her way.

More recently, there have been increasing signs of a retroactive juridification of history—the result being that the agents of world-appropriation from Christopher Columbus to Savorgnan de Brazza, from Francesco Pizarro to Cecil Rhodes, are being put on trial after the event: an endless and procedurally uncertain process in which sentences and appeals alternate. The retroactive criminalization of the Modern Age is completed through the history of black slavery, the extermination of the Native Americans, and exploitative colonialism, and the defense can barely dare, as in earlier trials, to plead for acquittal on account of extenuating civilizatory circumstances. In these cases, even the most resolute legists of guiltless world-appropriation would have no chance against the burden of documents and the earlier trials. Who could defend the American soldiers who, with genocidal intent, sent pox-ridden woollen blankets into the camps of their Native American enemies? Who would stand up for the slave traders who sometimes lost a third of their perishable wares on their transatlantic human animal transports? Who would take the side of Leopold II of Belgium, who turned his private colony, the Congo, into the "worst forced labor camp of the Modern Age" (as Peter Scholl-Latour phrased it)? Faced with these events, historians have had to become prosecutors of their own cultures. Their dossiers show how the relationship between justice and history can shift after the fact.[116] The tribunalization of the past has meanwhile affected the heroic period of terrestrial globalization in its entirety. The dossier on the Modern Age reads like a massive indictment of imperial incorrectnesses. The only solace offered by a study of its contents is the thought that these deeds and misdeeds have become unrepeatable. Perhaps globalization, like history as a whole, is the crime that can only be committed once.

19. The Five Canopies of Globalization
European Space Exportation

To understand the spherological secrets of advanced terrestrial globalization, one must not only attempt to go back *before* the negation of spatial differences through traffic technologies and storms of images in the late twentieth century; one should also recover the criteria to assess the immeasurable work of European humans and their collaborators in all parts of the world on the reinvention and transference of livable conditions to other locations. The reaching out into the planetary white could never have become the "success story" for Europeans and their descendants that it was, with all its horrors, at least in geopolitical and technological terms, if the departing risk-takers had not managed to preserve or regenerate minimal endospheric conditions on the way and at the other shores. Thus the true history of terrestrial globalization should first of all be told as a history of shells brought along, and as a crossing of enclosing husks, visible and invisible ones alike. One could say that the specific European art was exporting canopies—portable symbolizations of the sky that could also be appropriated outside by the travelers as a "sky for us." It was less their fatal exterminism that made Europeans leaders in the conquest of the outside for centuries than their superior ability to bring with them a minimal native space. That is why, wherever they appeared, they usually proved the better

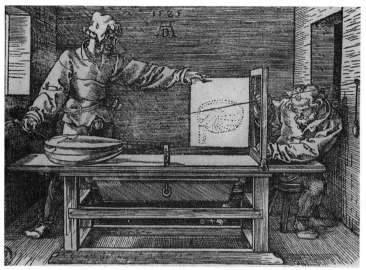

Windows 1525: world-appropriation with the help of perspectival representation technique. Pictures (details): Albrecht Dürer, Andrea Mantegna and Hieronymus Rodler

observers: an observer is someone who perceives the other through a window of theory. By having portable mental windows at their disposal, the managing Europeans were usually ahead of the discovered others by an entire dimension of descriptive, analytical and acting capacity. There are essentially five forms in which the relationship between the attackers and the white space could be spherologically handled:

- nautical mythology
- the Christian religion
- loyalty to the rulers of one's motherland
- the scientific documentation of the external space
- linguistic translation

Each of these methods produced its own spatial poetics, and all of these contributed to the epochal task of making the outside livable for the voyagers and invaders, or feigning its integration and domination.

20. The Poetics of the Ship's Hold

The psychodynamic aspects of the ship's hold experience are the most accessible ones to present-day people, as they have points of reference from dealing with caravan interiors and automobile cabins. The availability of such "traffic" means would not have become an indispensable, and usually enjoyable, method of movement for the considerable majority of modern individuals if the interior forms of the vehicles themselves had not adapted elementary structures of sphere formation on a small scale. The

Windows 1525: world-appropriation with the help of perspectival representation technique. Pictures (details): Albrecht Dürer, Andrea Mantegna and Hieronymus Rodler

ship, like—more moderately proportioned—the automobile and the caravan, is the mobilized nest or the absolute house.[117] It makes symbiotic relationships possible to the extent that the vehicle can be experienced as a belly holding a litter of newcomers; they will leave where they can, and do as they please in front of their context-free front door. At the same time, the ship is a magical-technospheric self-expansion of the crews—like all modern container-vehicles, it is a homeostatic dream machine that can be steered through the outer element like a manipulable Great Mother. (A psychohistorically convincing history of ship magic and vehicle superstition has yet to be written.) For this formal reason, ships can become mobile homelands for their crews. In recognizing ships as extensions of the country under

whose flag they sail, maritime law follows an original spherological intuition: being-on-land here changes in spatio-logical and international law terms into being-on-board; central aspects of the earth's *nomos*, the "peace" of the native space, are transferred to the floating endosphere. The decisive function of the ship's hull, admittedly, is to displace, both in physical and symbolic terms. This corresponds to the rule that human ensembles which throw themselves outwards only remain coherent if they succeed in stopping their leaks and asserting the precedence of the interior amid the unlivable element. Just as church naves[118] once transferred this act of displacement to the mainland in order to be vehicles for Christian souls on the earthly sea of life, expedition ships in the outer space would have to rely all the more on their displacement space as the spatially self-disposing shelter form they have brought with them.

21. Onboard Clerics
The Religious Network

From here on it is obvious: the fact that the larger expeditions in the days of nautical heroism could barely ever embark without a priest on board was not simply a religious convention, nor a mere concession to the demands of the church not to let groups of seafarers leave without some form of spiritual control. The omnipresence of the religious factor in early seafaring points rather to a second, overpowering spheropoietic mechanism. If the expeditions of the first ocean travelers were to succeed, the crews had to rely not only on their profession, but also the metaphysical routines of their home countries for assurance. Because seafaring was a practice that involved extreme situations, experts on the extreme had to be on board whenever possible. The possibility of shipwreck belongs to any ship as distress belongs to the sea, and the holy emergency helpers and their connoisseurs, the priests, could at least offer symbolic protection from the latter. That European seafaring could call itself Christian—long before the dawn of the oceanic age—shows its orientation towards this indispensable metaphysical insurance system. If the white outside seemed terrifying, it was partly because for countless people it meant death, and thus the prospect of being buried in an element devoid of all conciliatory qualities.[119] Without any connection to Old European ideas of burial and the hereafter, the notion of perishing outside was doubly unbearable.

The seafaring clerics would have been mistaking their function, however, had they not looked out on two sides from the start: to the seamen on board, who had to be ritually stabilized and motivationally controlled, and also for the new humans

The research ship *Endurance* being crushed by pack ice; photograph taken on
October 19, 1915

outside, who increasingly became interesting as future recipients of the Christian message. On the board side, the Christian religion offered incentive and refuge—the latter especially on the expeditions of Catholic nations under the ubiquitous figure of the protecting Virgin Mary, the *regina maris* who was also presented after the victory of Lepanto as Santa Maria della Vittoria—the Great Mother of seamen and rescuer-intercessor in mortal danger and distress. *In periculis maris esto nobis protectio.* Rulers, merchant princes, captains, sailors and baptized natives all found refuge beneath her protective cloak—when they crossed beneath Mary's cloak, the rigged fleets only seemed exposed to friendly winds. On the cult pictures in seamen's chapels, the high lady wraps her own in the shell of a world womb as if for the last time—the entire navy under a single garment (a plausible argument in favor of loose clothes for women, and one of the last concessions of the Modern Age to the morphological dream of the living being contained in the living). Here, once again, an enclosing sphere in the sky is elevated to a sealed, personally colored symbolic shell—even though by this time, cosmologists had already begun to make the heavens physically comfortless.

On the land side, the meaning of the Christian religion in the Age of Discovery was essentially mission in its second era—consistently in its dual function as a neo-apostolic extension of the church and a religious protection on the flank of colonialism. One cause of the militant colonial church and "battlefront church" tendencies of overseas missionary practice was the almost unconditional papal approval of the Portuguese and Spanish forays into the New World, as the Curia initially saw "the providential arm of the great commission in the Iberian

Alejo Fernández, *The Virgin of the Navigators*, Alcazar, Seville

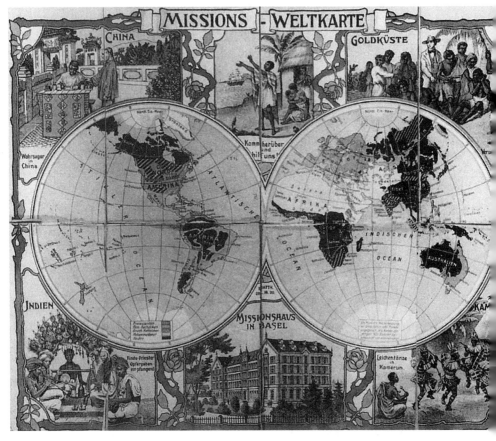

World map of Protestant mission (late 19th century)

states."[120] In its universalist appetite, Rome granted the conquerors such far-reaching privileges that the Catholic Church soon found itself in the position of a disempowered second next to the *de facto* autocratically colonizing states. Nonetheless, the pope had entered the Modern Age stage—especially in the first era of expansion—not only as its supreme client, but also as the notary of globalization; this was evident early on from his eminent role in

Title picture for the newsletter of the North German Missionary Society (19th century)

confirming the Portuguese discoveries in Africa (with the bulls *Romanus Pontifex* of 1455 and *Inter cetera* of 1456), and then even more from his mediating function in the dispute between Portuguese and Spanish pretentions over world domination (sanctioning the Treaty of Tordesillas in 1494 has inevitably been a matter for the Holy See).

Post-Columbian Catholicism's claims to majesty came to light most explicitly when the pope, citing the sources of his office, proclaimed himself the true overlord of the circumnavigated world.[121] Under these circumstances, the national monarchies of Europe—the Catholic ones too—had to resist the papal claims to primacy with increasing vehemence. The tone of these national-dynastic rebellions became apparent in 1540, when Francis I ordered the imperial envoy to show him Adam's will and the papal clause therein stating that the French king should be excluded from the division of the world.

Church dignitaries at the entering ceremony of the Second Vatican Council before St. Peter's Square, Rome (1962)

As for the Protestant missions, these were devoted from the start to national-colonial functions even more obviously than the Catholic ones; missionaries for the Dutch colonial empire were trained in Leiden at a seminary of the United East India Company, as if the church's vocation to proselytize came not from Matthew 28:19 but through a mandate of the North Atlantic free trade associations. Certainly the Christian mission—or, more generally, the exportation of confessions—was the most important agent of a socio-spherological continuum principle in the transition from the Old World to the New World because, when encountering the strangers, the motifs of possible generic and cultic commonalities between discoverers and discovered could be foregrounded. A spherological ecclesiastical history would specifically have to reconstruct the work on building extended canopies over the members of current and potential Christendom.

The opening of the Second Vatican Council in 1962 showed under spectacular auspices how successful the Catholic missions in particular believed their globalization efforts over four and a half centuries had been, with bishops from no fewer than 133 countries entering St. Peter's Basilica in Rome—an act of assembly that one would have to call unique, had it not been regularly outdone at the opening celebrations of the Olympic Games in the Modern Age. Councils and Olympiads—both exemplary manifestations of European assembly projects—illustrate what universalist umbrellas can achieve. Precisely these, however, as imposing as their expansive gestures may be, bring to light the insurmountable exclusivity of such gatherings. To construct a religious or athletic interior of humanity *in actu*, those who actually come together must be representatives, "overseers" or "choices"—the virtual totality can only arise through the synchronized attention of an observing humanity in the media of transference. The totalizing quality of such gatherings is thus expressed less through those present than through the universalist symbolism of the assembly's architectural container—the typical superlatives of macrospherically committed architecture: the Catholic cathedral and the secular sports arena. In the cathedral, the nave and the dome indicate the assembling power of the Roman Catholic creed, while in the stadium, the neo-fatalistic arena motif exhibits itself as a symbol of the immanently closed world sphere. Because the churches only exist as uncollected *communio sanctorum* in their everyday mode of being, however, and must prove themselves in local gatherings, they are constantly confronted with the task of organizing themselves in less spectacular, always operatively accessible and traditionalizable media. In addition, centrifugal forces take effect far more powerfully in Protestant churches, with their more autonomous units. The New England Puritan communities left behind were especially reliant on their aptitude to achieve stability in their own ritual practice. To understand the conditions under which this attachment to brought-along forms took place, it is useful to call to mind the reconstruction of the primitive wooden chapel in which the Pilgrim Fathers and their families gathered for their services after landing in New Plymouth, at Cape Cod in the Massachusetts Bay on November 19, 1620. Nothing could highlight the precedence of the ritual framework over the physical building more clearly than this raw, draughty barn in the middle of a hastily erected, fear-infused palisade village. It is not only in Heidegger's provinces that humans are those who dwell in their language as the House of Being; in the scattered points of the newly disclosed global space too, they set up camp under the tent roofs of the traditions and ritual safeguards they have brought with them.

Entrance of the German team at the opening ceremony of the 1992 Winter Olympics in Albertville

25th Summer Olympics in Barcelona, closing ceremony on August 9, 1992

22. The Book of Vice-Kings

As well as their religious notions, the leaders of the globalization expeditions, the vice-kings, the admirals and their officers also carried their dynastic models in themselves and out into the distant expanse. The internalized images of the royal clients, no less than their real portraits, ensured that the expansion into the outer space, both in critical moments and hours of triumph, could be experienced as an effective emanation from the personal center of home power. When the carriers of discovery enterprises

returned physically or thought back sentimentally, they made inner and outer gestures that conveyed their allegiance to the European sender. Their activity on the outside can be compared to the behavior of the Neoplatonic ray of light, which erupted from the center, turned around after arriving at its point of reflection, and returned to its source of emission. In this sense, all loyal European conquerors and discoverers were traveling as the executive rays of distant sun kings. Even the crudest emissaries of imperialism in the nineteenth century, the "men on the spot," considered themselves bringers of light in the service of their nations. If the European agents presented themselves as the great

Vermeer van Delft, *Allegory of Faith* (c. 1670), New York, detail

bringers, it was also because they carried their dynastic splendor outside with them, while appropriating the treasures of the New World with the demeanour of harvest hands. They move about in the nimbus of their native majesty systems, and most or all of their finds remain tied to the throne rooms and halls of fame in the Old World. What has been termed the exploitation of

The Jesuit priests Müllendorf and Dressel in Quito, Equador

colonies merely conveys the most intensive form of bond to the colonizers' homeland. Their enterprises were investments of shares in lust for power and majesty that retained allegiance to an Old European dynastic and national capital stock; their victories were kept as investment returns in the treasuries of homeland majesties, and later also in the cultural temples of nations, the museums and history books. (The subject of looted art is as old as terrestrial globalization: gold treasures of the Aztects were exhibited in Antwerp at the start of the sixteenth century, and the question of their rightful owners was never asked. Albrecht Dürer looked upon these works of an art from an entirely different place with his own eyes.)

Without their inner royal icons, most expedition leaders of early globalization would not have known for whom—except themselves—they should achieve their successes; most of all, however, they would not have learned whose acknowledgement would have augmented, justified and transfigured them. Even the atrocities of the Spanish conquistadors in Central and South

Jacques Callot, *The Martyrs of Japan*; in 1597, the daimyo Toyotomi Hideyoshi (1582–1598) ironically had Franciscan monks executed *more christiano*.

America were metastases of loyalty to their native majesties, who could be represented by extraordinary means. The title of vice-king thus has more than simply legal and protocol significance; it is also a category that sees to the very psychopolitical heart of the Conquista. The books of the vice-kings have yet to be written. It is because of them that the European kings were present always and everywhere in the outer expansions of the Old World, despite never visiting their colonies themselves.[122] The conquistadors

Pope John Paul II with cardinals at the *Assembla Speciale per l'Asia* on May 13, 1998, from *Osservatore Romano*, May 15, 1998

and princes' pirates collected their spoils under imaginary majestic canopies.

In a sense, this is also true of the spiritual king of kings, the pope, who, as the wearer of the three-tiered crown, wanted to expand his throne into a hyper-majesty for the entire globe. For it was his elite troops—the Jesuits, who were pledged to him with their fourth oath as the commander of martial Catholicism— who covered the globe with a net of prayers for the pope and considerations for Rome: an Internet of fervent obedience formed by distant devotees of the center. This was the model for the worldwide operations of today's telecommunications companies. The long-distance call was prefigured by long-distance prayer for the pope. The Jesuits were the prototypical newsgroup, communicating via their organization-specific network. The other missionary orders—Franciscans, Dominicans, Theatines, Augustinians, Conceptionists, Clarists of the first and fifth rules,

Hieronymites, canonesses, Barefoot Carmelites and many others—were likewise committed through their Rome connection to the project of procuring successes for the spiritual Conquista. It was their ambition to spread a papally supervised commonwealth over all the earth's continents. Only in the twentieth century did the pope have the mass-medially correct idea of travelling to the provinces of his moral empire as the ambassador of his own state. This marked Catholicism's transition into undisguised telematic charismocracy: the Roman path to modernity.

In keeping with the laws of metaphysical communication in large-scale social bodies, however, Catholic telecommunication before the age of actual papal presence could still not dispense entirely with magical-telepathic mechanisms. The body of the first great Jesuit missionary in Asia, Franz Xaver, who had opened up India and Japan to the Roman church, found its final resting place in Goa. The saint's right arm was brought back to Europe, "tired from the baptism of thousands"; it is still preserved today in the order's mother church, Il Gesù in Rome, as the most precious relic of globalization.

23. The Library of Globalization

But what if the participants in the commando operations of early terrestrial globalization were neither captains loyal to the crown nor missionaries who obeyed the pope or Christ? They did not have to feel immediately excluded from the higher chances of shelter or from the idealizations of European expansion. For the worldly-minded pioneers of world-disclosure, there were ways and means to step beneath one of the secular canopies of

The Jesuit priest schall von Bell explains geographical principles at the court of the Chinese emperor; tapestry from the Beauvais manufacture (18th century)

globalization, and even a spirit not religiously committed had good prospects of getting its money's worth in the Last Bullet project. Anyone who did not acquire new lands for a European king or believers for the church could nonetheless sail into European ports as a conqueror and retriever of riches if they knew how to make themselves useful as agents of the European experiential sciences. These world-hungry disciplines, which grew around geography and anthropology, constituted themselves emphatically in the incipient era of expansion as *new* sciences and accumulations of knowledge whose methodological modernity was plain to see.

What characterized these insights was that they accumulated like a second capital—albeit a capital that would belong to an enlightened humanity as a whole, and not be withdrawn from public and civil use by rulers and their keepers of secrets. Against the background of the new sciences of the outer humans, of usable nature and of the inhabited earth, an alphabetized European never had to feel entirely cut off from the flow of their native systems of meaning, even in the most desolate abandonment on distant islands and continents. Every life on the outer front potentially bore an aura of cumulative experience that could be projected into literary documentations. Countless seafarers and explorers dreamed of their immortalization on land and sea maps; cartographical fame is only a special example of what one could call the general canopy function of the European experiential sciences during the globalization process. It presently and potentially protected the actors on the outer lines from the danger of sinking into the senseless white and being engulfed by the depressions that can be triggered by collisions with unassimilable newness, otherness, strangeness and bleakness.

The empirical sciences, with their affiliated literary genres of travel account, utopia and exotic novel, tended towards a transformation of all outside conditions into observations, and all observations into announcements that found their way into the great book of new European theory—"observers," after all, exist only as subjects who will write what they have *seen* or *found*. This applied especially to the golden age of explorer-writers, from which names such as Louis Antoine de Bougainville, Jacques-Etienne-Victor Arago, Reinhold and Georg Forster, Johann Gottfried Seume, Charles Darwin, Alexander von Humboldt and Henry Morton Stanley occasionally rose to the level of world literature—in the breadth of their readership, at least. It is typical of the Modern Age habitus of acquiring, bringing, contributing, collaborating, going forwards and systematizing that the principal

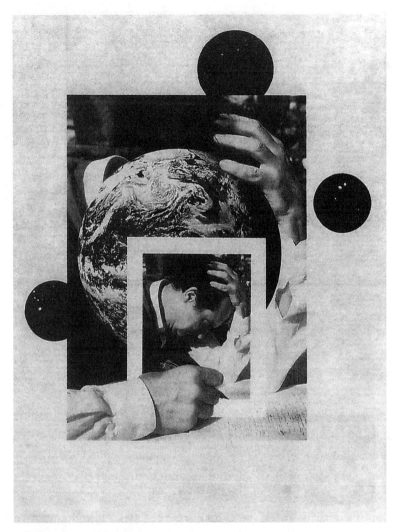

Giulio Paolini, *The Eye of Calvino*, in *Lettre International* 43 (1998)

The writing hand of Rudyard Kipling

research took place in the form of competitions. Corresponding to the races for goals to be reached, there was a writing competition on the field of scientific honor—which applied particularly to the fundamentally hystericized domain of polar research, whose protagonists mostly appeared as their own rhapsodists and publicizers of their research woes. This entanglement of research and theater made it visible at a popular level that every form of scientific expedition was also a media matter. Had the heroes of globalization not been mirrored in an idealizing medium, their goals could never have become adequately clear (or unclear) to them.

Initially, however, it was not so much the mass media that observed the expeditions while they set off. Rather, all literate participants in the voyages into the unknown looked towards an imaginary hyper-medium, the only one in which the history of the lonely successes outside could be recorded and brought back: the canopy that could hold all the solitudes of researchers had to be a fantastic integral book—a book of cognitive records in which no one would be forgotten who had ever stood out as a retriever of experience and a contributor to the great text of world-disclosure. It was inevitable that sooner or later, someone would attempt the actual publication of this imaginary hyper-book of European experiential knowledge. It is characteristic of the practical genius of the French Enlightenment figures that as early as the mid-eighteenth century, at half-time in terrestrial globalization, so to speak, they summoned the energy to carry out the project of an *Encyclopedia* of valuable knowledge. It lent the previously informal theoretical canopy the edifying shape of the circle that ordered and held all knowledge. In this work, items of knowledge from the remotest sources could be promoted to their cognitive value-forms. Thus the black of print celebrated its triumph over white in the hyper-book of the sciences.

That collecting and bringing home experiences can also have a subversive, or in some cases at least a tactless side, however, was learned by Frederick II of Prussia in his dealings with the globe-trotter and naturalist Georg Forster. At his first audience with the king after acquiring a professorship for natural science in Halle, Forster supposedly said—somewhat more frankly than was customary at the royal court—that he had seen five kings in his life, three of them savage and two tame, "but none like Your Majesty." Frederick the Great considered these the words of a "most uncouth fellow." But how else should one have broken it to the rulers? Once the kings of the Old World could be viewed empirically like exotic chieftains (and once European residences could be observed as mere locations of royalty), it could no longer be kept from the noble lords and their followers that their time was coming to an end.[123]

24. The Translators

While the habitus of participation in the European experiential sciences was able to develop under the super-canopy of an encyclopedic book phantasm, it was the task of linguists and ethnologists to work away at the linguistic outside in a wealth of individual encounters with different foreign languages. The European explorer languages found themselves faced with a semiotic multiverse of incredible variety comprising at least five thousand authentic languages (6,700 at a recent UNESCO count) and a virtually inestimable multiplicity of dialects and sub-dialects that always included mythologies, religions, ritualisms, arts and gestures. Considering this diversity, which defies any attempt at an overview, the dream of an all-integrating hyper-language had to disappear almost automatically. Only two strategies offered themselves to the discoverers and the discovered alike to find their bearings in this neo-Babylonian situation: firstly, the forced establishment of the colonial rulers' languages as general languages of interaction—which at least succeeded in the cases of English, Spanish and French, with varying success in different parts of the world—and secondly, the infusion of the individual languages with the translated words of the new masters.

Both paths had to be taken simultaneously, and on both of them, learning languages—and translation along with them—proved the key to the concrete and regional spheropoietic processes. Whether one leans towards pessimistic or optimistic theories of translation, bilingualism or plurilingualism performed one of the most important canopy functions during terrestrial globalization. It remains a fact that the language of the European rulers pulled the local languages over to its side, rather than the respective indigenous languages absorbing the idioms of the colonizers.[124] It testified to the wise intuition of the politician-historian Winston Churchill that he wrote the history of the British world power not only as that of an empire, but also that of a language area: *History of the English-Speaking Peoples*. He evidently foresaw that the most long-lived aspect of the Commonwealth would be its commonspeak. This arrangement not only satisfied the English need to present the rift between Great Britain and the United States as a mere question of pronunciation; it also kept open the option of new political groups and cultural circles entering the club of English-speaking peoples. As far as the language criterion is concerned, all natural scientists, pilots, diplomats and businesspersons have indeed been incorporated into the inescapable Anglophone language network like artificial new peoples—followed by the brave new world of pop music. In Anglophony, as in religion and the most basic forms of entertainment, the medium is the message.

As for the Christian message, it could not wait in its second mission cycle for demand to arise among the five thousand foreign languages; it had to translate itself into the language of the others in order to explain its salvific necessity to them. Probably the work of Christian translators in the last five hundred years to express their faith in other languages, at least in quantitative, and perhaps also qualitative terms, constitutes the most extraordinary cultural achievement in the history of mankind—at least, the self-translation of modern Christianity into the countless individual cultures is, for the time being, the most powerful testament to the possibilities and difficulties of an operatively concrete transcultural ecumene. By the end of the twentieth century, parts of the New Testament had been translated into over 2,212 genuine languages—from which connoisseurs of the linguistic atlas could conclude that the Christian message had gained access to at least one in three language communities on the planet, including more than a few in which the New Testament was the first book ever published. This fact, which could be described in church-historical immanence as the continuation of the pentecostal miracle by Gutenbergian means, at once reveals the insurmountable particularity of even the most inclusive message: the inaccessibility of "small" languages places a factual limit on the effectively universal spread of the Gospel. Consequently, even the apostolic methods of dissemination, as invasive as they may have been, were unable to fulfill the dream of erecting a Eurocentric message empire, penetrating as far as the capillary level, founded on Mediterranean transmitters and content providers. Moreover, Hollywood, the Pacific metropolis of images, outstripped the Mediterranean emission bases for morals and mysteries—Rome and Jerusalem—half a century ago. Its messages already promise the most ample of profits if they can be promoted in two dozen dubbed versions.

25. Synchronous World

Modern times: half a millennium after the four voyages of Columbus, the circumnavigated, uncovered, depicted, occupied and used earth presents itself as a body wrapped in dense fabrics of traffic movements and telecommunications routines. Virtual shells have replaced the imagined ethereal sky; thanks to radio-electronic systems, the meaning of distances has effectively been negated in the centers of power and consumption. The global players live in a world without gaps. In aeronautical terms, the earth has been reduced to a flying route of fifty hours at most; for the orbits of satellites and the *Mir* station, and recently the International Space Station (ISS), units of ninety minutes became the norm. For radio and light messages, the earth has virtually shrunk to a static point—it rotates, as a temporally compact orb, in an electronic layer that surrounds it like a second atmosphere.

Terrestrial globalization, then, has advanced so far—primarily through the great technological leaps in the second half of the twentieth century—that it would seem bizarre to demand a justification from it now. Just as the actual occupation of a country had become the final argument of European nation-states for the realization of colonial claims until the nineteenth century, so too the effective consummation of terrestrial globalization has become the self-supporting argument for the process itself. After a start-up phase of several centuries, the world system is increasingly stabilizing itself as a complex of rotating and oscillating movements that maintain themselves on their own power. In the realm of circulating capital, momentum has overtaken reasons. Execution replaces legitimation, and facts have become norms and standards.

What the sixteenth century set in motion was perfected by the twentieth: no point on the earth's surface, once money had stopped off there, could escape the fate of becoming a location—and a location is not a blind spot in a field, but rather a place in which one sees that one is seen. The fluidization revolution rolled on, the tides rose. All cities have meanwhile become ports, for where cities have not gone to the sea, the seas come to them (for the super-commodity of information in particular does not reach its investors via highways—as an incorrect metaphor from the early days of the network discourse suggested—but rather through currents flowing into the more aptly named data oceans). In this sense, today's Davos is a seaside town.

Through its old and new media, globalization constantly conveys the message that it is occurring and advancing, with disregard for any alternatives; hence its peculiar independence from philosophy and other manifestations of reflective theory. Like a second nature or destiny, it now talks only to itself, affirming and reinforcing itself as a higher power. Briefings have replaced critique. At most, the course of the world can read itself as the most comprehensive form of an act of God, realized through the sum of human actions—and no will to desist, however widespread, could prevent their continuation. No theoretical engagement with the present can undo the fact that the earth has been circumnavigated and its peoples and cultures forced into mediation. In this sense, terrestrial globalization, like an axiom, is the first and only precondition for a theory of the present age. Even though the scattered peoples of the world have, until recently, existed in their endospheres as if on separate stars, concealed from the outside in their linguistic retreats, they are forced by the distance-destroying revolution of modernity to admit that from

Joseph Arnold, *The Curiosity Cabinet of the Dimpfel Family of Wholesale Iron-mongers and Miners from Regensburg* (1608), detail

now on, because they are reachable by the mobile others, they live on one and the same planet: the planet of the unconcealed.

Because terrestrial globalization is a mere fact that came into effect late on, and under singular circumstances, it cannot be interpreted as the manifestation of an eternal truth or an inescapable necessity. It would be far-fetched to see it as the natural expression of the biological theorem that all people on earth form a single species. Nor does it support the metaphysical idea that the human race shares in one and the same store of unrevisable truths (even if some believe that). And least of all does it mirror a moral law that all people should think of all others in their species as considerately and compassionately as possible. The naïve supposition of a potential openness of all to all is taken *ad absurdum* by the facts of globalization. On the contrary: the inevitable finitude of human interest in other humans must become ever clearer as global interconnection progresses—it is only the moral emphasis that changes, tending towards expectations of greater capacity (under an increasing nervous strain). What characterized "all people," without exception, "by nature" until very recently was their common and universal inclination to blamelessly ignore the vast majority of people outside of their own ethnic container. As members of a scattered species—whose factual diaspora remained insurmountable even after the revolution of global traffic— humans in their clans, their ethnicities, their districts, their clubs and their interest groups turn naturally and quietly away from those who belong to other identity units or mixture scenes. One of the outstanding mental effects of globalization, however, is the fact that it has elevated the greatest anthropological improbability— constantly taking into account the distant other, the stranger to one's container—to the new norm.

Franklin D. Roosevelt and V. M. Molotov in the map room of the White House in 1942: "The maps were installed so comfortably that the President, sitting at his desk, could simply pull down a map of any region in the world he wished to study." (Gilbert Grosvenor)

The globalized world is the synchronized world; its form is produced simultaneity, and it finds its convergence in things that are current.[125] Where it is night, countries and people will still lie in the earth's shadow; but the world as world has become shadowless and nightless, bound by a merciless diurnal imperative; there are no more time-outs in the depicted global space. In addition, the mindsets of the global market and of burgeoning world-"domestic" politics besiege the immemorial ignorance towards distant and foreign people, pushing together those

Theodore Roosevelt (1858–1919)

involved in an arena of real chances for encounter and chronic necessities of contact. The anthropological result of globalization, namely the logical synthesis of humanity in a powerful concept of species and its joining in a compact, synchronous world of traffic, is a product of bold, compelling abstractions and even bolder compulsion-creating expeditions.

What was said above concerning the precedence of the outward journey in the history of world traffic now becomes the crux of the matter: "man" and "mankind" have only existed since, after centuries of European one-way journeys to others, the establishment of the anthropological horizon as a virtual plenum of peoples and cultures—a movement that must now, with the start of decolonization, look out for increasing two-way traffic. This two-way traffic mingles with the gestures of Europeans returning to themselves; the result of this mixture is multiculturalism or the hybridization of symbolic worlds. "Mankind"—it enters the stage of contemporary thought in a state of progressive self-discovery and interconnection as the vague and splintered para-subject in a universal history of the coincidental,[126] a latecomer whose emergence, if not its character, remains entirely determined by the chance circumstances of its discovery and organization.

26. The Second Ecumene

"Mankind" is by no means constituted by the libido of forming a total organization and procuring the necessary media for it. Rather, the anthropological assembly resulted initially from the coercive ties of colonialism and, following its dissolution, through the compulsion of interconnections that take effect via credit systems, investments, physical movement of goods, touristic penetrations, cultural exports, world-policing interventionisms and expansion of ecological norms. The imposition presented by the current Second Ecumene reveals itself less in the fact that people everywhere are supposed to admit that the people from elsewhere are their equals (though the number of those who deny this, be it overtly or covertly, remains considerable) than in the circumstance that they must endure the increasing pressure to cooperate, which forces them together as a self-coercing commune in the face of shared risks and transnational threats. What has been shown for modern nation-states—that they can only be kept in shape through constant self-stressing communication—seems increasingly valid for the as yet inadequately aggregated planetary "community of states." Autogenous stress forms the basis for all large-scale technologies of consensus.[127]

Faced with this, international politics is transforming itself in a significant fashion: before our eyes, it seems to be leaving the era of grand actions for the age of grand themes (that is, of generalized risks that solidify into semantic institutions or universals of a new kind), which require endless meetings to be worked out in minute detail. Theme politics and the corresponding cycle of conferences only progress as a production of autogenous global stress. Their carriers act for a humanity that increasingly constitutes itself as the integral of mutually approaching stress communes.

This virtual plenum of an actually interconnected, theme-motivated traffic humanity grown from modern terrestrial globalization through the colonial empires and their sublation in global market conditions is not the first manifestation of the anthropological commune that was conceived in the history of human self-discoveries and self-organizations. Pre-Columbian Europeans too had already conceived a nation of species unity, articulated in the Greek concept of the *oikuméne* or "inhabited world." That these colonies of the human being were essentially restricted to Roman-Hellenistic Mediterranean culture, and did not illuminate any periphery but the Ptolemaic-terran continental trinity of (residual) Europe, (Western) Asia and (North) Africa, does not lessen the generosity of this first idea of species. The point of the ancient ecumenical concept is not the notion that

Production line in the factory of Replogle Globes Inc., Chicago

people always have to be at home somewhere. It never occurred to the ancients to teach that the mortals of all peoples were economic animals (*oikein*, to dwell, inhabit) or deficient, house-dependent beings who could not live without a roof over their heads and whatever else were considered the basic necessities. In ancient ecumenism, people were *not* those beings which had rights because they all had more or less the same physical needs, and recognized themselves in one another as a result. Rather, in the thought of the early philosophers, humans are ontologically unified as the beings that share a single world secret beyond their respective local symbolisms. They are the beings that all gaze into the same light, and all have the same *question* towering over them. This view of a universal share in a manifest *and* concealed super-ground of reality constitutes what, to use Eric Voegelin's terms, one can call the First Ecumene of the West (there was, as we know, also a Chinese version of the idea of a civilized totality expressed in the concept of *t'ien-hsia*, "everything under the sky"—usually translated simply as "realm").[128] Voegelin incisively formulates the metaphysical structure of the first idea of a united mankind in Western antiquity:

> Universal mankind is not a society existing in the world, but a symbol that indicates man's consciousness of participating, in his earthly existence, in the mystery of a reality that moves towards its transfiguration. Universal mankind is an eschatological index.
>
> [...] Without universality, there would be no mankind other than the aggregate of members of a biological species; there would be no more a history of mankind than there is a history of catkind or horsekind. If mankind is to have history, its members must be able to respond to the movement of divine presence in their souls. But if that is the condition, then the mankind who has history is constituted by the God to whom man responds. A scattering of societies, belonging to the same biological type, is discovered to be the one mankind with one history, by virtue of participation in the same flux of divine presence.[129]

From this perspective, the basis for the unity of a "mankind" thus projected would be found neither in the circum-Mediterranean movement of goods nor in the imperialist synthesis of peoples under Roman rule. Rather, the people of antiquity, in their highest self-interpretations, were a "problem community"; they were illuminated through participation in similar noetic and pneumatic evidence, and solidarized through sharing the same riddle structure of existence. What gave the human race its dignity was that it encompassed the beings that were towered over by the same immeasurable ground. It would, admittedly, be reserved for the Romans to develop the war machines and means of transportation that would place the inhabited world all around the Mediterranean Sea at their feet; but once they had spread out in all directions, the conquerors in turn found themselves conquered by two conquered peoples. If first of all, as Horace wrote, "Captured Greece took her savage victor captive," this was because the philosophical theology of the Greeks had revealed the structures of a generally perceptible voice of reason—or rather an exportable technique of evidence—that could potentially show itself in pure thought to all people, with no concern for their ethnic allegiances. Voegelin celebrates this "noetic epiphany" as Greece's contribution to a world-culturally relevant *philosophia perennis*.[130] And that the Christian Jerusalem later also won out over Rome came about through its message of the intimate and public community of God with the souls of the faithful in the *ecclesia*: thanks to this doctrine, the motif of a "pneumatic theophany" was likewise developed in general, no longer ethnically restricted terms. Rome thus rose to become the Eternal City less in the name of its rooted success gods—Jupiter, Mars, Venus, Virtus or Victoria—than because it was capable of changing into a Second Jerusalem, and within narrower limits even a Second Athens. Through its powers of assimilation and translation, Rome was able to raise itself to the city of the First Ecumene. Long before the universities and modern academies, *Roma aeterna* presented itself as the earthly seat of evidence: after Athens and Jerusalem, it wanted to be the city where that which is *shows itself*. It demanded of its visitors that the journey to Rome become a pilgrimage to evidence (and to mystery).

But terrestrial globalization decentered the city of cities too, turning the metaphysical broadcasting headquarters of the Old European globe into a mere location among others. One should not underestimate the fact that the fifty-six men who signed the American Declaration of Independence of July 4, 1776, almost all of them freemasons and amateur metaphysicians, referred to the evidence first, only then declaring the human rights—as if they had intuitively understood that attempts to break away from Europe do not succeed unless the truth is conveyed across the Atlantic first: "We hold these truths to be self-evident, that all men are created equal."

For the anthropological commune of the current advanced globalization process, however, a metaphysical ground of unity in the manner of the "divine presence" that Voegelin assigns to every soul is no longer in sight. A different medium of universal coexistence will therefore have to be found. The Second Ecumene broke open the universals of the first; it labeled both the Christian and the Greek conceptions of the world, with their supposed logical evidence, provincial. Christianity had to face being told of its particularity, and time will tell whether it will manage to expand its authority through attempts to become a "world ethos"—a project on which Hans Küng and others are working with the élan of belated Church Fathers (but perhaps there can only be church cousins now).[131] This much is certain, however: none of the so-called world religions will ever qualify as the Great Vehicle for all factions of humanity. In the long term, every one of them will have difficulty keeping its shares on the global market of metaphysical needs. Now more than ever, the prospects for synthetic universal religions of practically implanting a unified language or final vocabulary for the anthropological commune are non-existent—[132]most of all because in the world of the future, the languages of the victors and those of the losers will drift ever further apart, even if there are now renewed attempts, in the media and parliaments of affluent societies, to keep in power a unified social democratic language for a world without losers in power.[133] Under these circumstances, it seems plausible to lower the requirements for the concept of a ground of unity for the species than intended by the effusive statements of noetic and prophetic theologies in the age of the First Ecumene.

What the Second Ecumene can learn from the reconstructed First, at least, is that it will not do to invoke biological "foundations" as a ground of unity for mankind—not even after the emergence of a newer, politically correct genetics that affords all humans a place in a largely homogeneous gene pool. This Adamitic racism is a delusional system whose structure is similar to all earlier biological collectivisms, even if genetic arguments are now no longer used to discriminate between races, but rather to unify them. The Second Ecumene too will be able to formulate the "unity of the human race"—to adopt the language of the eighteenth century for one moment—not through a shared *physis*, but only through a shared situation. The situation can now only be determined ecologically and immunologically, however.

The unity of humans in their scattered species is now based on the fact that all of them, in their respective regions and histories, have been outstripped, synchronized, affected from a distance, shamed, torn open, connected and overtaxed: they have become locations of a vital illusion, addresses of capital, points in the homogeneous space to which one returns and which return to themselves—more seen than seeing, more acquired than acquiring, more reached than reaching. Every person must now, in returning to themselves, make sense of the advantage or disadvantage of being who they are. "Mankind" after globalization consists mostly of those left behind in their own skins, victims of the locational disadvantage of oneself.

The course of the world has, without any philosophy, shifted people away from the center in an unexpected fashion. In the course of globalization, they not only experience themselves as antiquated, as some theorists of alienation have resignedly stated, but now actually perceive themselves as belonging to the outside—beings looking at themselves from without, not knowing whether anyone will be home when they enter their dwellings.

If the exemplary human in the First Ecumene was the wise man, who meditated on his dysfunctional relationship with the absolute, and the saint, who could feel closer to God than ordinary sinners through grace, then the exemplary human in the Second Ecumene is the celebrity, who will never understand why they had more success than other people, and the anonymous thinker, who opens themselves up to the two key experiences of the age: firstly, to the constantly recommencing revolutions as the "presentations of the infinite in the here and now,"[134] and secondly, to the shame which affects every thinking life today more than original sin: never rebelling enough against the ubiquitous degradation of all that lives.

On the last orb, the location of the Second Ecumene, there will be no more sphere of all spheres—neither an informatic nor a world-state sphere, let alone a religious one. Even the super-inclusive system of the Internet, as immense as its potential might be, simultaneously produces a complementary super-exclusivity. The

Tietz department store, Berlin (1899–1900)

orb consisting only of a surface is not a house for all but a market for each person. On markets, no one can be "at home"; no one is meant to settle where money, commodities and fictions are changing hands. The global market is a concept for the realization (and demand) that all suppliers and customers meet in a general externality. As long as the global market or global markets exist, all speculations on the recovery of a domestically or capital city-centered circumspection in an integral interior of humanity will be thwarted by the irreversible headstart of the outside. If the Middle Ages already proved incapable of placing the world orb and God orb within each other concentrically,[135] then modernity would only have produced even more folly by attempting the hubristic project of integrating the multitude of cultural and entrepreneurial locations as sub-spheres within a concentrically built monosphere. Even Marshall McLuhan seems to have underestimated this when he embraced the vision of the global village: "The media extensions of man are the hominization of the planet."[136] Today, such words could not even be repeated in missionary sects. As generous as the great media theorist's expectations were, the dying out of imperial-centrist world-form creations also destroyed the basis for electronic Catholicism (the central position of the absolute sender).

The last orb permits further constructs only in the horizontal—which does not rule out individual high-rise buildings. It furthers joint ventures, intercultural transactions under artificial, not overly steep skies; it longs for forums, podiums, canopies, patronages and alliances; it favors gatherings of interest groups at tables of different formats in conference rooms of graduated sizes. But it discourages the idea of a super-monosphere or a power-holding center of all centers.

27. The Great Immunological Transformation: On the Way to Thin-Walled Societies

From the noisy monotony of the current sociological and political literature on globalization, one can abstract a number of patterns with good chances of becoming something like timeless themes or journalistic universals for the coming centuries. The first of these is the motif that a new *modus vivendi* between the local and the global must be negotiated time and again; the second is that political communities "after modernity" have entered a new constellation "beyond the nation-state";[137] the third is that the increasingly gaping divide between rich and poor has brought the globalized world to a state of political and moral tension; and the fourth is that the progressive consumption of the biosphere along with the pollution of water, air and soil changes "humanity" willy nilly into an ecological interest group whose contemplation and dialogue must bring forth a new, far-sighted culture of reason. It is not hard to perceive a tendency running through all these themes: the blurring of traditional notions of political subjects and social units. Wherever one looks, one notes that the most important trends have slipped from the grip of those responsible for them, and that the problems of today and the problem solvers of yesterday (let alone the problems of tomorrow and the problem solvers of today) are no longer suited.

Let us translate these perceptions from the sociological debate into our own context: a political poetics of space or "macrospherology."[138] After this shift of perspective, all questions of social and personal identity pose themselves in morphological and immunological terms, which is to say in terms of how something resembling livable forms of "dwelling" or being-with-

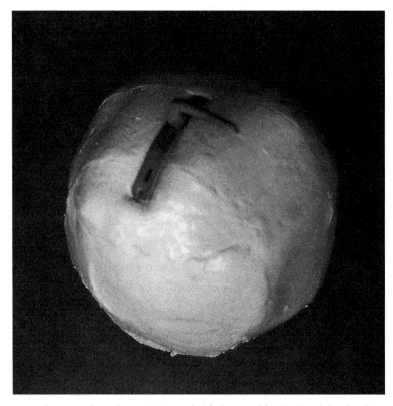

Róza El-Hassen, door object (1996) made of silicone rubber, lock and doorhandle

oneself-and-one's-own can be accommodated in historically active macro-worlds. Contemporary nervousness about globalization mirrors the fact that with the nation-state, what was previously the largest possible scale of political dwelling—the living and conference room of democratic (or imagined) peoples, as it were—is now subject to negotiation, and that this national living room already has some very unpleasant drafts here and there. Looking back, we can see more clearly the extraordinary achievement of the nation-state, which was to offer the majority of those dwelling there, a form of domesticity, a simultaneously imaginary and real immune structure, that could be experienced as a convergence of place and self, or as a regional identity (in the favorable sense of the word). This service was performed most impressively where the welfare state had successfully tamed the power state. Through globalization, this political-cultural domesticity effect was challenged—with the result that countless citizens of modern nation-states no longer feel with themselves in their own homes, and no longer feel at home with themselves.

The immunological construction of political-ethnic identity has been set in motion, and it is clear that the connection between place and self is not always as stable as the political folklores of territorialism (from ancient agrarian cultures to the modern welfare state) had demanded and pretended. Weakening or dissolving the links between places and selves can allow us to see the two extreme positions that reveal the structure of the social field with almost experimental clarity: a self without a place and a place without a self. It is clear that all actually existing societies have always had to seek their *modus vivendi* somewhere between the poles—ideal-typically at the most favorable distance from each extreme position— and one can easily understand that in future too, every genuine political community will have to give an answer to the twofold imperative of self-determination and place-determination.

The first extreme of dissolution is probably approached most closely by the diaspora Judaism of the past two millennia, which has been described not inaccurately as a people without a land— a fact that Heinrich Heine put in a nutshell when he stated that the Jews were not at home in a country, but rather in a book: the Torah, which they carried with them like a "portable fatherland."[139]

This profound and elegant comment illuminates a fact that is frequently passed over: "nomadizing" or "deterritorialized" groups construct their symbolic immunity and ethnic coherence not (or only marginally) from a supporting soil; rather, their communications amongst themselves act directly as an "autogenous vessel"[140] in which the participants contain themselves and stay "in shape," while the group drifts through external landscapes. Thus a landless people cannot fall prey to the misconception that has imposed itself on virtually all settled groups throughout human history: understanding the land itself as the container of the people, and viewing their native soil as the *a priori* of their life's meaning or their identity. This territorial fallacy endures to this day as one of the most effective and problematic heirlooms of the sedentary age, as the basic reflex underlying all seemingly legitimate applications of political force, so-called "national defense," relates directly to it. National defense is based on the obsessive equation of place and self—the axiomatic logical error of territorialized reason. This error has increasingly been exposed since an overpowering wave of transnational mobility began to ensure that peoples and territories everywhere qualify their liaison with one another. The trend towards a multi-local self is characteristic of advanced modernity—like the trend towards a polyethnic or "denationalized" place.

The Indo-American cultural anthropologist Arjun Appadurai has drawn attention to this state of affairs with his conceptual creation of the "ethnoscape," which allows us to examine issues like the progressive deterritorialization of ethnic connections, the formation of "imaginary communities" outside nation-states, and the imaginary sharing in the images of life forms from other national cultures among countless individuals.[141] As far as

Judaism during its period of exile is concerned, its provocation lay in the fact that it constantly reminded the peoples of the western hemisphere of the seeming paradox and actual scandal of a factually existing self without a place.

At the other extreme, the phenomenon of the *place without a self* becomes increasingly clear. The earth's uninhabited regions—the white deserts (polar world), the grey ones (high mountains), the green ones (jungles), the yellow ones (sand deserts) and the blue deserts (oceans)—are paradigmatic. In the context of this investigation of spheric conditions, the latter are of interest by way of contrast as those places in which people come together, yet are unwilling or unable not to tie their identities to the locality. This applies to all transit spaces, both in the narrower and the wider sense of the term, be they facilities intended for traffic such as train stations, docks and airports, roads, squares and shopping centers, or complexes designed for limited stays such as holiday villages and tourist cities, factory premises or night shelters. Such places may have their own atmospheres—but they do not depend on a regular populace or collective self rooted in them. By definition, they do not hold on to those who pass through them. They are the alternately overrun or extinct no man's lands, the transit deserts that proliferate in the enucleated centers and on the hybrid peripheries of contemporary "societies."

It does not take much analytical effort to see that in these "societies," a prior normality—life in massive, ethnic or national containers (along with their specific phantasms of origin and mission) and the unendangered license to confuse land with self—is decisively infringed upon by globalizing tendencies. On the one hand, such societies loosen their regional ties through large

Anish Kapoor, *Turning the World Upside Down III* (1996), Deutsche Bank London

populations acquiring a historically unprecedented mobility. On the other hand, there is a dramatic increase of transit places that cannot be inhabited by those who frequent them. Thus globalizing and mobilizing societies simultaneously approach the "nomadic" pole, a self without a place, and the desert pole, a place without a self—with a shrinking middle ground of regional cultures and grounded contentments.

The formal crisis of modern mass societies, which is now seen chiefly as a loss of meaning for the nation-state, thus results from the advanced erosion of ethnic container functions. What was previously understood as society and invoked with it was usually, in fact, nothing other than the content of a thick-walled, territorially grounded, symbol-supported and usually monolingual container—that is, a collective which found its self-assurance in a certain national hermeticism and flourished in redundancies of its own (that could never be entirely understood by strangers). Because of their self-containing qualities, such historical communities—known as peoples—stayed on the point of intersection between self and place and usually relied on a considerable asymmetry between inside and outside (a tendency that typically manifested itself in pre-political cultures as naïve ethnocentrism, and at the political level in the substantive difference between domestic and foreign policy. But these same effects of globalization increasingly evened out this difference and asymmetry; the immune situation of the national container is increasingly perceived as problematic by those who profited from earlier conditions. Certainly no one who has tasted the advantages of free transnational movement is likely to desire a return to the militant enclosures of older nation-states in earnest, much less the totalitarian self-hypnoses that often characterized tribal life forms. Yet for numerous people today, the purpose and risk of the trend towards a world of thin-walled and mixed societies are neither clear nor welcome. Globalization, Roland Robertson rightly observes, is a "basically contested process."[142] But the protest against globalization is *also* globalization itself—it is part of the inevitable and indispensable immune reaction of local organisms to infections through the larger format of the world.

The real psychopolitical challenge of the Global Age (which Martin Albrow aptly describes as a willful result stage of the globalized Modern Age) lies in the fact that the weakening of container immunities must not be dealt with simply as decadence and loss of form, that is to say as an ambivalent or cynical abetment of self-destruction. What is truly at stake for the post-moderns are successful new designs for livable immune relationships, and these are precisely what can and will develop anew in manifold ways precisely in societies with permeable walls—albeit, as has always been the case, not among all and not for all.

In this context, the epochal trend towards individualistic life forms reveals its immunological significance: today, in advanced societies, it is the individuals who—perhaps for the first time in the history of hominid and human life forms—break away from their group bodies (which had been their prime protectors) as carriers of immune competencies, and seek in great numbers to disconnect their happiness and unhappiness from the being-in-shape of the political commune. This tendency manifests itself most clearly in the pilot nation of the Western world, the USA, where the concept of the pursuit of happiness has nominally been the foundation for the social contract since 1776. The centrifugal effects of this orientation in terms of individual happiness were previously balanced out by the combined energies of communities and civil societies, such that the immunological priority of the group over its members also seemed embodied in that synthetic people, United States Americans.

Since then, the tables have been turned: no country, population or culture on earth practices as much biological, psychotechnic and religioid self-concern at the individual level in parallel with a growing abstinence from political commitments. In the 1996 presidential election, the USA saw its first voter turnout of under 50%, and in the November 1998 elections to the House of Representatives and the Senate, roughly two out of three voters stayed at home (though experts still considered the 38% turnout as a relatively good result). This testifies to a situation in which the majority can largely abandon solidarity with the fates of their political communes—guided by the highly plausible notion that individuals will henceforth no longer (or only in exceptional cases) find their immunological optimum in the national collective, but maybe still partially in the solidary systems of their own communities, though most clearly in private insurance arrangements, be they of a religioid, gymnastic, assurance or dietary nature. The axiom of the individualistic immune order gained currency in populations of self-centered individuals like a new vital insight: that, ultimately, no one would do for them what they did not do for themselves. The new immunity techniques presented themselves as existential strategies for societies of individuals in which the long way to flexibilization, the weakening of "object relationships," and the general authorization of unfaithful disloyal or reversible interpersonal relationships had led to the goal—the baseline of what Spengler rightly prophesied as the final stage of every culture: the state in which it is impossible to determine whether individuals are exceptionally fit or exceptionally decadent. Beyond this line, the last metaphorical difference, namely the distinction between noble and common defended by Nietzsche, would lose its contours, and what had seemed hopeful and great about the project of "man" would disappear like a face drawn in sand at the edge of the sea.

Air Conditioning

What remains common to all earth-dwellers for the time being is the planet's active weather shell, the atmosphere in the meteorological sense, which, for well-known reasons, has become a source of concern to contemporaries. The trends on the market of climate technology have long indicated that whoever can afford to work on exiting the bad air shared by everyone does so. The residential cultures of the future will assume increasingly explicitly that livable internal climates must be created by technical means. Air conditioning, in the literal sense, will establish itself as the main space-political theme of the coming era. Thus the spheric imperative will emerge from latency and manifest itself exoterically as the center of all political and cultural creations of unity.

In less than a generation, the members of the Second Ecumene will have understood at numerous climatically critical points of the earth that breathing is too important to continue doing it in the open. Something will soon be banally self-evident that can only be seen through heterodoxly cut theory spectacles: explicit climate policy will be the foundation of the new ecumene, just as explicit climate technology will form the basis

Soap bubbles in New York (1945)

Frei Otto, *Soap Bubble Experiment for Large Umbrellas* (1971)

of concrete community formations. Once irreversible or only scarcely compensable physical damage to the climate (the mental damage can be swept under the carpet for longer) has become chronic, if not before then, it will be generally clear that societies can only be adequately described and controlled as cases of applied spherology.

Air conditioning is destiny. It proves the assertion that the nature of modernity manifests itself in the task of separating technically refined immune systems from older, vaguer holistic immune structures. As soon as air supply ceases to be an unproblematic premise of life processes and enters its technological stage, even this oldest pneumatic and atmospheric basic condition

of human existence will have reached the threshold of modernity. From that point on, air mixtures and atmospheres will become objects of explicit production. The phenomenon known in the last two and a half centuries as "Enlightenment" will then no longer be valid. The bright side of the Enlightenment will become atmotechnics. Modern everyday aesthetics shows the horizon for these developments, if not the way.

Humans create their own climate—not of their own free will, however, under self-chosen circumstances, but under found, given and handed-down ones. The tradition of all dead climates burdens the moods of the living like a nightmare. What began with the first fires—as Vitruvius' intimations suggest[143]—namely the gathering of people around a pleasant center, a *magna commoditas*, an attractive pampering, remains the basic technology of solidarizing group creations to the end. Society *is* its room temperature, it *is* the quality of its atmosphere; it *is* its depression, it *is* its clearing up; and it *is* its fragmentation into countless local microclimates.

The self-attunement of spheres thus means more than what has previously considered politics. Spheres—as I have attempted to show in elaborate investigations—are shared spaces set up by common inhabitation within them. They are the first product of human cooperations; they form the immaterial, yet very realest result of a primal work that only takes place in resonances. The process of civilization was advanced not by the division of labor, but of spheres; it is the primal agreement of the community about itself within itself.

That is why political parties and indeed politics itself could only exist as a focus of public interest once there was no more need to quarrel over the calibration of the ruling internal climate in civilized forms. Recent democracy and mass media society appeared simultaneously because only mass media as social climate creators allowed the dispute over climate regulations to ensue. The enlightened populations of mass democracies who view the election campaign gesticulations of their parties as a war of weathermen are therefore right: all of them want to change the climate through promises, but their croaking[144] reveals that they do not know what promises mean; almost every one of them overlooks the strong reason for being together. They fail to see that solidarity can only be achieved by transferring early cultural forms of shared existence to large-scale societies—but they too sense that the preconditions for such transfers have become precarious.

Man Ray, *Deformed Self-Portrait* (1938)

The anti-political skepticism in the East and the West, which feeds off accurate perceptions, holds the essence of a realization with which the reprojection of solidarity spaces must begin: part of every such space is a laying of foundations—or rather a hanging up—through a self-fullfilling climatic promise. Enlightenment begins with lightening—or it is truly and by definition the very mass deception that the dark authors of the twentieth century suspected it of being. Like every shared life, politics is the art of the atmospherically possible.

Notes

Prologue

1. Diogenes Laertius, *Lives and Opinions of the Eminent Philosophers*, II, 10.

2. Max Bense, *Ausgewählte Schriften*, vol. 1 (Stuttgart: J. B. Metzler, 1997), p. 61.

3. *Das Seiende* is usually translated here as "the existent," unless there is a clear reference or proximity to Heidegger, in which case "entity" is sometimes used (trans.).

4. Although the personal pronoun in reference to the monotheistic god is consistently capitalized in the translation of *Spheres I*, the frequent alternations between and juxtapositions of monotheistic Judeo-Christian and quasi-monotheistic Platonic conceptions of God in the present volume have led me to abandon this here, rather than deciding arbitrarily to capitalize in some cases but not in others (trans.).

5. Cf. Peter Sloterdijk, *Bubbles, Spheres I: Microspherology*, trans. Wieland Hoban (Los Angeles: Semiotext(e), 2011), p. 65.

6. The various lists actually contain over twenty names in total, of which only four are canonical: Thales the proto-philosopher, Bias of Priene, Solon the lawmaker and Pittacus of Mytilene. These are often joined by Chilon of Sparta, Periandros of Corinth and Cleobulus of Lindos. Each of these sages is assigned typical gnomes or mnemonics in the manner of a signature tune: "Know thyself" (Thales), "Most men are bad" (Bias), "Keep everything with moderation" (Solon), "Gain is insatiable" (Pittacus); "Do not desire what is impossible" (Chilon); and "Moderation is the best thing" (Cleobulus).

7. By pointedly invoking every possible sense of the word *Vorstellen*—the verbal noun of *vorstellen*—, the author is introducing a multitude of semantic elements. In philosophical parlance, the noun *Vorstellung* is conventionally translated as "representation," particularly in the works of Kant and Schopenhauer, and later also

Husserl; though justified in those contexts, this is also slightly misleading, in that the representation taking place there is a mental, not an external one—a mental image. In conventional usage, the verb *sich (etwas) vorstellen* means "to imagine (something)" or "to envisage (something)," while its non-reflexive form *vorstellen* means "to present," "to introduce" or "to perform." In Heidegger's idiosyncratic, etymologically informed approach to language, which is very often present in the background in Sloterdijk's work, there is also a literal sense of placing (*stellen*) something before (*vor*) the self, giving the act of imagining or mentally representing a quasi-physical character; this also applies to the related words *herstellen*, *bestellen* or *Gestell*, which all bear connotations of placing (trans.).

8. Plotinus, *Enneads*, VI 8, 18, 1f. "Everything is inside."

9. Gaston Bachelard, *The Poetics of Space*, trans. Maria Jolas (Boston: Beacon Press, 1994), pp. 104 & 208.

10. Cf. Otto Brendel, *Symbolism of the Sphere: A Contribution to the History of Earlier Greek Philosophy*, trans. Maria W. Brendel (Leiden: Brill, 1977). In the following, I shall freely adapt some of Brendel's reflections.

The most comprehensive recent study on the philosopher mosaic of Naples, by Konrad Gaiser (*Das Philosophenmosaik in Neapel: eine Darstellung der platonischen Akademie* [Heidelberg: Winter, 1980])—who sees it as a depiction of the Platonic Academy during a discussion of Heraclides Ponticus' theory of heavenly standstill— is not convincing, despite its wealth of references and knowledge, because it is entirely implausible that a painter of the Hellenistic era would have based a picture on a cosmological hypothesis that had no following in its time. Furthermore, Heraclides rejected the notion of a layered cosmos and believed the world to be infinite, which would make it bizarre for his ideas to have provided the subject of a debate about an actually existing heavenly orb. The only tenable element in Gaiser's elaborately misguided argumentation is that the mosaic of Torre Annunziata indeed has an air of an Academy debate and Platonizing typology; but only, I would argue, in relation to an earlier and much more fundamental scene.

11. It is clear that this theory introduces a deviation from the doxographic findings, for if tradition characterizes Thales beyond doubt as the originator of an elemental-philosophical hypothesis of primordial matter, the actual sources initially ascribe to him only a conception of the world in which the earth swims on the primordial waters like a ship. In Plutarch, the sphere-cosmological thesis is interwoven with Thales' aphorisms through a retrojection of later models. As far as the pictorial idea of the philosopher mosaic is concerned, it would appear unproblematic to see in it a syncretism of foundation legend (proto-philosophy, the Seven Sages tradition) and classicism (spherical conception of the world and philosophical cosmotheology).

12. In Diogenes Laertius, op. cit., I, 35, we read: "And the following are quoted as sayings of his:— 'God is the most ancient of all things, for he had no birth: the

world is the most beautiful of things, for it is the work of God: place is the greatest of things, for it contains all things: intellect is the swiftest of things, for it runs through everything: necessity is the strongest of things, for it rules everything: time is the wisest of things, for it finds out everything.'" 'To the question, 'What is the divinity?' he replied, 'That which has neither beginning nor end.'"

13. Cf. Chapter 3, "Arks, City Walls, World Boundaries, Immune Systems: The Ontology of the Walled Space."

14. Among those for whom these giant toys seemed to have a familiar format, one figure who stands out is the young Max Bense, who noted in 1935: "Space is the original. *The more original the human, the deeper the feeling of space.* Heidegger should have interpreted being as space—if he had been original in his 'inwardness,' in his 'inner reality,' in his 'elementary existence.'" From "Aufstand des Geistes. Eine Verteidigung der Erkenntnis," in Bense, *Ausgewählte Schriften,* vol. 1, p. 107. "Original" here is a translation of *ursprünglich* (as opposed to *originell*), which refers not to individuality or novelty, but rather proximity to the origin, a primordial quality (trans.).

15. Martin Heidegger, "The Age of the World Picture," in *Off the Beaten Track*, ed. & trans. Julian Young & Kenneth Haynes (Cambridge University Press, 2002), p. 71.

16. *Nulla enim bestia globum et eius motus ad terminum producit.* Nicholas of Cusa, *De ludo globi*, trans. Pauline Moffitt Watts (New York: Abaris Books, 1986), p. 24.

17. Max Bense, *Aufstand des Geistes. Eine Verteidigung der Erkenntnis* (Stuttgart & Berlin: Deutsche Verlags-Anstalt, 1935), p. 122.

18. Brendel, *Symbolism of the Sphere*, p. 78.

19. Cf. Chapter 8, "The Last Orb: On a Philosophical History of Terrestrial Globalization."

20. This question—I shall call it the question of absolute localization—seems to have been discovered by Aristotle, who in his *Physics*, after listing eight variants of the meaning of 'in' (*en*), formulated the problem of whether everything is either in something else or nowhere, or whether it is also possible for something to be *in itself.* (Cf. *Bubbles*, Excursus 4, "'In Dasein There Lies an Essential Tendency towards Closeness,'" note 42, p. 648.) With this inquiry about being-able-to-be-in-oneself, Aristotle touches on the problematics of the unwritten super-book of Western philosophy, which should have been called *Being and Space*.

21. The relevant literature contains inconsistent information about the dating. Alois Fauser calls the *Atlante Farnese* a work from the first century *BC*; cf. *Die Welt in Händen: kurze Kulturgeschichte des Globus* (Stuttgart: Schuler, 1967), p. 39. According to Percy Ernst Schramm (*Sphaira, Globus, Reichsapfel. Wanderung und Wandlung eines Herrschaftszeichens von Caesar bis Elisabeth II.* [Stuttgart: A. Hierseman, 1958], p. 8), the work dates from the first century *AD*, while some refer to the time of Antonius

Pius, which is to say the middle of the second century. The authors I would consider most convincing narrow down the date to the time of the Augustan principate. Franz Boll argues that the presence of the throne constellation indicates that the globe was fashioned in the years following the rise of Augustus to absolute power. Cf. Franz Boll, *Sitzungsberichte der Akademie der Wissenschaften München 1899*, pp. 121f., quoted in *Pauly-Wissowa, Realencyclopädie der Altertumswissenschaften* (Stuttgart: Metzler, 1981), article 'Globen,' col. 1429.

22. Cf. Schramm, op. cit., p. 11.

23. Cf. "Über astronomische Druckwerke aus alter und neuer Zeit," manuscript of a lecture given to the Gesellschaft der Bücherfreunde [Society of Book Lovers], Hamburg 1911, quoted in Ernst H. Gombrich, *Aby Warburg: An Intellectual Biography* (Oxford: Phaidon, 1986), pp. 200f.

24. Cf. the stimulating remarks by Rolf Michael Schneider in *Bunte Barbaren. Orientstatuen aus farbigem Marmor in der römischen Repräsentationskunst* (Worms: Wernersche Verlagsgesellschaft, 1986), pp. 47f. I am grateful to Hans Belting for bringing this book to my attention.

25. *Cum tot sustineas et tanta negotia solus*, in *Epistulae* II, I, 1.

26. Cf. Fauser, *Die Welt in Händen*, pp. 36–39.

27. Cf. Paul Zanker, *The Mask of Socrates: The Image of the Intellectual in Antiquity* (Berkeley & Los Angeles: University of California Press, 1996), p. 110.

28. The verb *philoponeín* and the noun *philoponía* were already part of classical Greek; the philosophical praise of the practicing life, especially among the Stoics, could simply not dispense with these terms. Plato too spoke of the "effort-loving," whom he mentions in the same breath as the gymnast and the healer (*Phaedrus*, 248 d). Concerning the Alexandrian Monophysitic sect of the *philoponoi*, cf. Michael Wolff, *Geschichte der Impetustheorie. Untersuchungen zum Ursprung der klassischen Mechanik* (Frankfurt: Suhrkamp, 1978), pp. 107–113. That the love of effort also had a place in the personal statements of the powerful is shown by the ruler's maxim of Alexander the Great: *pónos kai philanthropía*. Nietzsche's philosophical genius was expressed not least in the fact that in the notorious §341 of *The Gay Science* ('The heaviest weight'), he succeeded in formulating a radically new relationship between *lógos* and *pónos*: the thinking person's consent to the idea of the eternal return.

29. Marcus Aurelius, *The Meditations*, trans. G. M. A. Grube (Indianapolis: Hackett, 1983), p. 3.

30. Cf. Chapter 4, "The Ontological Proof of the Orb," as well as Chapter 5, "*Deus sive sphaera*, or: The Exploding Universal One."

31. It should be noted that all instances of "sky," "heavens" or "heaven" here are translations of the highly polyvalent word *Himmel*. A minimization of unintended ambiguity has been striven for, though the precise emphasis is sometimes unclear even in the German (trans.).

32. The distinction between onto-logical and onto-graphic goes back to Alexandre Kojève (cf. below, note 00).

33. Cf. Heraclitus, Fragment 108: "Of all whose discourses I have heard, there is not one who attains to understanding that the wise [*sophón*, i.e. God] is apart from all [*kechorisménon*]." Cf. also Simone Pétrement, *A Separate God: The Christian Origins of Gnosticism*, trans. Carol Harrison (San Francisco: Harper Collins, 1990).

34. Alongside the Farnese globe, the only other candidate for an authentic ancient document would be the marble celestial globe from Arolsen.

35. There is one such mythological episode of celestial handover: Hercules stands in for Atlas when the latter goes to fetch the Apples of the Hesperides for his visitor. Here a new theory of relief appears in a nutshell: Atlas, pleased by his new freedom of movement, refuses to take back his heavenly burden and tells Hercules that he will henceforth have to carry the sky in his stead. Hercules pretends to agree to the new situation, but asks Atlas to shoulder the burden for a moment so that he can make a neck cushion out of his cloak. Atlas, who does not see through the trick, assents and takes over again, after which Hercules cheerfully walks off. One could say that ever since, advanced civilizations have been arguing—more latently than openly—over the question of how to get others to carry the heavier part of the load.

36. Concerning the formula "that it is," *hos éstin*, cf. the lucid commentary by Thomas Buchheim in his book *Die Vorsokratiker. Ein philosophisches Portrait* (Munich: C. H. Beck, 1994), especially pp. 117ff., where the meaning of *noeín* as "realize" is also discussed.

37. ...*tó gár autó noeín estín te kaí eínai*: "for the same thing is there for thinking and for being." (Parmenides, Fragment 3, in Daniel W. Graham [ed.], *The Texts of Early Greek Philosophy: The Complete Fragments and Selected Testimonies of the Major Presocratics* [Cambridge University Press, 2010], p. 213.)

38. Ibid., p. 217 (Fragment 7, 20–25).

39. Ibid., p. 219 (Fragment 7, 42–44).

40. Parmenidean circumspection saw a partial technical implementation in the Roman arena and the modern panorama, the surround cinema and its further development in current virtual reality technology. Cf. Uwe Pirr, "Zur technischen Geschichte des Rundumblicks. Vom Panoramagemälde zur interaktiven Virtuellen Realität," in Hubertus von Amelunxen, Martin Warnke, Wolfgang Coy & Georg

Christoph Tholen (eds.), *HyperKult. Geschichte, Theorie und Kontext digitaler Medien*, (Basel & Frankfurt: Stroemfeld, 1997), pp. 291–330.

41. Concerning the universal one that is viewed in the image of the orb, Alexandre Kojève remarks: "The decisive aspect of the Parmenidean image of being is that, on the one hand, the sphere is absolutely *homogeneous*, such that one cannot really speak of its *parts*, and on the other hand, that the sphere itself has no (crossable) *boundaries to the external*, and is in that sense entirely *restricted to itself*. [...] Thus nothing can exceed the orb of being: no matter how one dis-places oneself in this sphere, one will always have *exactly the same amount* of being in front as behind, and it will be the same being *everywhere*." *Le Concept, le Temps et le Discours: Introduction au Système du Savoir* (Paris: Gallimard, 1990), p. 289. English edition: *The Concept, Time, and Discourse*, trans. Robert H. Williamson (South Bend, IN: St. Augustine's Press, 2012). (I am grateful to Boris Groys for pointing me to Kojève's reflections on the possibility of a "last spherology.")
   This means that the demand for homogeneity implies there is no actual majority of real or spatially distinct points in the sphere, but only the one spatial and supra-spatial central point, which is always already connected to divine spheroscopy. Cf. also Kojève's deliberations on the "Parmenidean thesis" in *Essai d'une histoire raisonnée de la philosophie paienne*, vol. 1: *Les présocratiques* (Paris: Gallimard, 1968), pp. 206–236, especially p. 211 (critique of the spatial one/one-space).

42. Friedrich Nietzsche, *Beyond Good and Evil: Prelude to a Philosophy of the Future*, trans. Judith Norman (Cambridge University Press, 2001), §150 (p. 70).

43. Concerning this complex, cf. *Spheres I*, Chapter 3, "Humans in the Magic Circle: On the Intellectual History of the Fascination with Closeness"; on Hegel, cf. particularly pp. 246f.

44. Richard Dawkins, *The Selfish Gene* (Oxford & New York: Oxford University Press, 1976), p. 132.

45. Concerning the problem of the representatives of the absolute, cf. Chapter 7, "How the True Spheric Center Has Long-Distance Effects through the Pure Medium."

46. Jacobus de Voragine, *The Golden Legend: Readings on the Saints*, trans. William Granger Ryan (Princeton University Press, 2012), p. 398.

47. The one exception to this is perhaps the book by Gertrud Höhler and Michael Koch, *Der verentreute Sündenfall. EntZweiung oder neues Bündnis?* (Stuttgart: Deutsche Verlags-Anstalt, 1998), in which the male-female couple is highlighted as a "duocentric primal team."

48. Cf. Wilhelm Schmidt-Biggemann, *Philosophia perennis: Historical Outlines of Western Spirituality in Ancient, Medieval and Early Modern Thought* (Dordrecht: Springer, 2004).

49. "All that exists is good" (trans.).

50. The last thinker of consequence whom we must read as an orb theologian conscious of his motives was Karl Jaspers, who insisted that ontology (the theory of being) could only be carried out as periechontology (the theory of being encompassing and encompassed). Cf. Karl Jaspers, *Von der Wahrheit. Philosophische Logik*, vol. 1 (Munich: Piper, 1991), pp. 47–222.

51. A reference to the song "Weißt du, wie viel Sternlein stehen?" [Do You Know How Many Stars There Are?], which contains the line "Gott, der Herr, hat sie gezählet" [The Lord God counted them] (trans.).

52. Cf. Heinz Robert Schlette, *Weltseele. Geschichte und Hermeneutik* (Frankfurt: Knecht, 1993).

53. Nicolas of Cusa, *De ludo globi*, p. 36.

54. *Fernstenliebe* is a play on *Nächstenliebe*, which means "brotherly love" or "altruism," but literally "love of the closest" (trans.).

55. Parmenides, Fragment 8, 30–32, in Graham, *The Texts of Early Greek Philosophy*, p. 217.

56. For a painstakingly detailed survey of the two thousand-year history of cosmological sphere concepts, cf. Jean-Pierre Lerner, *Le monde des sphères*, vol. 1: *Genèse et triomphe d'une representation cosmique* (Paris: Les Belles Lettres, 1996) & vol. 2: *La fin du cosmos classique* (Paris: Les Belles Letters, 1997).

57. This infamous statement seems to go back to the hermetic *Liber viginti quattuor philosophorum*, where the formula *Deus est sphaera infinita cuius centrum est ubique, et circumferentia nusquam* appeared probably for the first time. Bonaventura, who adopts the claim in his *Itinerarium mentis in Deum*, V, 8, augments it by describing the sphere as intelligible. The thought of Meister Eckhart and his successors, extending to Cusa, is likewise indebted to this theorem. The book of the twenty-four philosophers has been published in an excellent new edition as vol. 153 of *Corpus Christianorum* (Turnhout: Brepols, 1997). Three of the twenty-four main theosophical theorems are discussed below in Chapter 5, "*Deus sive sphaera*, or: The Exploding Universal One."

58. Michel Foucault, "Theatrum Philosophicum," in *Language, Counter-Memory, Practice: Selected Essays and Interviews*, ed. Donald F. Bouchard, trans. Donald F. Bouchard & Sherry Simon (Ithaca, NY: Cornell University Press, 1980), p. 176 (translation modified).

59. *Spheres I*, p. 630.

60. Johann Wolfgang Goethe, *Die Schriften zur Naturwissenschaft*, section 1, vol. 9: *Zur Morphologie* (Weimar: Böhlau, 1954), p. 233.

61. A derivation of the term "location" [*Standort*] from the new thought and traffic conditions after the completed circumnavigations can be found in the final chapter of this volume, "The Last Orb: On a Philosophical History of Terrestrial Globalization."

62. Cf. Boris Groys, "Lenin und Lincoln. Zwei Gestalten des modernen Todes," in *Die Erfindung Russlands* (Munich: Hanser, 1995), pp. 180f.

63. Cf. Chapter 8, "The Last Orb: On a Philosophical History of Terrestrial Globalization," section 26, "Second Ecumene."

64. Cf. *Spheres I*, Chapter 8, "Closer to Me Than I Am Myself: A Theological Preparation for the Theory of the Shared Inside," pp. 539f.

65. Cf. Alexander Gosztonyi, *Der Raum. Geschichte seiner Probleme in Philosophie und Wissenschaften*, 2 vols. (Freiburg & Munich: Alber, 1976), vol. 2, p. 1255.

66. In §149 of *System der Philosophie*, vol. 3: *Der Raum*, Part 2: *Der Gefühlsraum* (Bonn: Bouvier, 1981), pp. 98f., Hermann Schmitz presents an impressive interpretation of "Feelings as Atmospheres." Inspired by Schmitz, Gernot Böhme develops a concept of aesthetic activity as atmosphere production in his book *Atmosphäre. Essays zur neuen Ästhetik* (Frankfurt: Suhrkamp, 1995). He offers variations on this in *Anmutungen. Über das Atmosphärische* (Ostfildern: Edition Tertium, 1998). Cf. also Michael Hauskeller, *Atmosphären erleben. Philosophische Untersuchungen zur Sinneswahrnehmung* (Berlin: Akademie, 1995) and Reinhard Knodt, "Atmosphären. Über einen vergessenen Gegenstand des guten Geschmacks," in *Ästhetische Korrespondenzen. Denken im technischen Raum* (Stuttgart: Reclam, 1994).
Otto Friedrich Bollnow mediates tirelessly between Heidegger's and Schmitz' theories of space and atmosphere in *Mensch und Raum* (Stuttgart: W. Kohlhammer, 1963), especially in the chapters "Der gestimmte Raum," "Der präsentische Raum" and "Der Raum des menschlichen Zusammenlebens," pp. 229–270.

67. And the work of Hermann Schmitz as a partially successful attempt to outdo Heidegger's (and Bollnow's) precepts.

68. There is an automatic play on words or ambiguity in the German here, as *Stimmung* means both "mood" and "tuning" (trans.).

69. Cf. Elisabeth von Samsonow, "Präliminarien zu einer Phänomenologie des halluzinierenden Geistes," Elisabeth von Samsonow & Éric Alliez (eds.), *Telenoia, Kritik der virtuellen Bilder*, (Vienna: Turia & Kant, 1999), pp. 28–46.

70. Cf. Alfred Seidel, *Bewusstsein als Verhängnis*, ed. Hans Prinzhorn (Bonn: F. Cohen, 1927).

Chapter 1

1. *Spheres I*, p. 53.

2. For established empires or large-scale political worlds, this implies the further evolution of the thesis into the claim that all history is the history of self-aggrandizements, chosenness programs and systems of megalo-"mania."

3. I describe how this already comes into its own earlier, in the impulse of listening out for greetings in the mode of anticipation, in *Spheres I*, Chapter 7, "The Siren Stage: On the First Sonospheric Alliance."

4. Concerning disturbances in the process of this pre-farewell, cf. *Spheres I*, Excursus 6, "Spheric Mourning: On Nobject Loss and the Difficulty of Saying What Is Missing," pp. 459f.

5. Cf. Ram Adhar Mall & Heinz Hülsmann, *Die Drei Geburtsorte der Philosophie. China, Indien, Europa* (Bonn: Bouvier, 1989).

6. The argument that the worldview develops in parallel with the world border view is expounded further in Chapter 2, "Vascular Memories: On the Reason for Solidarity in Its Inclusive Form."

7. Cf. Marc Augé, *Non-Places: Introduction to an Anthropology of Supermodernity*, trans. John Howe (London & New York: Verso, 1995), pp. 42f.

8. Concerning the dissolution of territorialism and the loosening of the bond between place and self, cf. Chapter 8, "The Last Orb: On a Philosophical History of Terrestrial Globalization."

9. *The Epic of Gilgamesh*, trans. Andrew George (London: Penguin, 1999), pp. 83–85.

10. Augustine, *Confessions*, trans. Francis Joseph Sheed & ed. Michael P. Foley (Indianapolis: Hackett, 2006), pp. 59f.

11. Ibid., pp. 60f.

12. Ibid., p. 63.

13. "Our own speech, which we utter by making sounds signifying meanings, follows the same principles. For there never could be a whole sentence unless one word ceased to be when its syllables had sounded and another took its place." (Ibid., p. 64)

14. *Confessions*, IX, XII (32).

15. "To judge the living and the dead" (from the Nicene Creed).

16. Cf. René Girard, *Quand ces choses commenceront. Entretiens avec Michel Treguer* (Paris: Arléa 1994), p. 57: "To adopt a formulation by Jean-Pierre Dupuy: 'Sacrificial

systems *contain* violence in the twofold sense of the word'—because it is inherent in them, and because they prevent violence from flooding everything."

17. Cf. René Girard, *Job, the Victim of His People* (Stanford University Press, 1987).

18. William Kelly Simpson (ed.), *The Literature of Ancient Egypt: An Anthology of Stories, Instructions, and Poetry* (New Haven: Yale University Press, 2003), p. 227.

19. Ibid., p. 228.

20. Ibid., p. 233.

21. Ibid., p. 241.

22. Ibid., p. 242.

23. Ibid., p. 243.

Chapter 2

1. Leon Battista Alberti, *On the Art of Building in Ten Books*, trans. Joseph Rykwert, Neil Leach & Robert Tavernor (Cambridge, MA: MIT Press, 1991), p. 196.

2. Samuel Beckett, *Selected Poems 1930–1989*, ed. David Wheatley (London: Faber & Faber, 2009), p. 94 (originally in French).

3. Cf. Dominic O'Meara, *The Structure of Being and the Search for the Good. Essays on Ancient and early Medieval Platonism* (Aldershot: Ashgate, 1998), Chapter 3, "Man as Political Animal: on the Relation between Plato and Aristotle," pp. 29f.

4. Concerning the concept of the "strong relationship," cf. *Spheres I*, Chapter 8, "Closer to Me Than I Am Myself: A Theological Preparation for the Theory of the Shared Inside," pp. 539f.

5. Cf. the explanation of the concept of perichoresis in *Spheres I*, Chapter, 8, pp. 603f.

6. Cf. Eric Voegelin, *Order and History*, vol. 4: *The Ecumenic Age* (Baton Rouge: Louisiana State University Press, 1974), pp. 272f.

7. Cf. André Leroi-Gourhan, *Gesture and Speech*, trans. Anna Rostock Berger (Cambridge, MA: MIT Press, 1993), p. 320.

8. Cf. Klaus E. Müller, *Das magische Universum der Identität. Elementarformen sozialen Verhaltens. Ein ethnologischer Grundriss* (Frankfurt & New York: Campus, 1987).

9. Dieter Claessens, *Das Konkrete und das Abstrakte. Soziologische Skizzen zur Anthropologie* (Frankfurt: Suhrkamp, 1980), p. 61.

10. Thomas Macho, "Drinnen und Draussen. Reflexionen zur Ordnung der Räume," in Bernhard Perchinnig & Winfried Steiner (eds.), *Kaos Stadt. Möglichkeiten und Wirklichkeiten städtischer Kultur* (Vienna: Picus, 1991), pp. 107–123.

11. Louis Dumont, *Homo Hierarchicus: The Caste System and Its Implications*, trans. Mark Sainsbury, Louis Dumont & Basia Gulati (Chicago & London: University of Chicago Press, 1980), p. 245.

12. One can see in this context how the musketeers' motto "One for all and all for one" hints at a vague military-romantic early socialism. Hölderlin had anticipated this thought figure in Hyperion's battle cry "All for everyone and everyone for all" as a spherological prediction of the "free state," that is to say the citizens' republic.

13. In the phrase "internal situation," the latter word should be read as much in the sense of "position" as "condition"; the word *Lage* (here expanded into *Innenlage*) is used equally for both (trans.).

14. Alfred Tomatis, *Klangwelt Mutterleib. Die Anfänge der Kommunikation zwischen Mutter und Kind* (Munich: Kösel, 1994), p. 126.

15. Cf. Erika Simon, "Der Schild des Achilleus," in Gottfried Boehm & Helmut Pfotenhauer (eds.), *Beschreibungskunst—Kunstbeschreibung* (Munich: Fink, 1995), pp. 123f.

16. Homer, *The Iliad*, trans. E. Rieu (London: Penguin, 2003), p. 333.

17. Georg Simmel, "The Picture Frame: An Aesthetic Study," trans. Mark Ritter, in *Theory, Culture and Society* 11 (1994), p. 12.

18. Homer, *The Iliad*, p. 335.

19. The ways in which the schema of space production established itself in the Western line through palace transferences are expounded in the following chapter with reference to the metaphorical potencies of Persian palace architecture.

20. "And it will be for me to show Macedonians and allies alike that the Indian gulf [Arabian Sea] forms but one stretch of water with the Persian gulf, and the Hyrcanian Sea with the Indian gulf. From the Persian gulf our fleet shall sail round to Libya, as far as the Pillars of Heracles [Straits of Gibraltar]; from the Pillars all the interior of Libya then becomes ours, just as Asia is in fact becoming ours in its entirety, and the boundaries of our Empire here are becoming those which God set for the whole continent." Arrian, *Anabasis of Alexander*, trans. P. A. Brunt (Cambridge, MA: Harvard University Press, 1983), p. 85 (V, 26).

21. Cf. Chapter 8, "The Last Orb: On a Philosophical History of Terrestrial Globalization."

22. This ideal-typical twofold centricity manifested itself in the cities of Mesopotamia as a threefold centricity (of temple, palace and granary).

23. A quotation from Goethe's poem "Prometheus" (trans.).

24. Cf. the excellent study by Norbert Bolz, *Auszug aus der entzauberten Welt. Philosophischer Extremismus zwischen den Weltkriegen* (Munich: Fink, 1989).

25. Cf. Chapter 4, "The Ontological Proof of the Orb," as well as Excursus 4, "Pantheon: The Theory of the Dome."

26. Vitruvius, *On Architecture*, trans. Richard Schofield (London: Penguin, 2009), pp. 37–40.

27. The derivation of all society from gathering around a fire was already contested in classical architectural theory, and rightfully so, as it unduly neglects the perspective of northern lifeworlds. In his introduction to *On the Art of Building in Ten Books*, Leon Battista Alberti (1404–1472) identifies the house itself as the starting point: "Some have said that it was fire and water which were initially responsible for bringing men together into communities, but we, considering how useful, even indispensable, a roof and walls are for men, are convinced that it was they that drew and kept men together." (p. 3)

28. Cf. *Spheres I*, Chapter 6, "Soul Partition: Angels—Twins—Doubles," pp. 413f.

29. Oswald Spengler, *The Decline of the West*, trans. Charles Francis Atkinson, vol. 2: *Perspectives of World History* (New York: Knopf, 1961), p. 383.

30. The logic of rule through radiation is explained in the sections on political emanationism in Chapter 7, "How the True Spheric Center Has Long-Distance Effects through the Pure Medium: On the Metaphysics of Telecommunication."

31. It is no coincidence that Hegel, who closely examined these circumstances, speaks of the difference between private and public gods in a supplementary note to §257 of his *Philosophy of Right*: "The Penates are the inner and lower order of gods; the spirit of a nation, Athena, is the divinity which knows and wills itself." (Hegel, *Philosophy of Right*, trans. S. W. Dyde [New York: Cosimo, 2008], p. 132). This points to a clear hierarchy of religioid immune systems.

32. Cf. Cathérine Clément, *La putain du diable* (Paris: le Grand livre du mois, 1996), pp. 64f.

33. Cf. above, "Introduction: Geometry in the Monstrous," section IV, "The Morphological Gospel and its Fate."

34. Cf. also W. Altmann, *Die italischen Rundbauten* (1906), quoted in Spengler, *Perspectives of World History*, p. 121.

35. Giacomo Leopardi, *Operette Morali: Essays and Dialogues*, trans. Giovanni Cecchetti (Berkeley & Los Angeles: University of California Press, 1982), pp. 420f.

Chapter 3

1. Quoted in Paul Hübner, *Vom ersten Menschen wird erzählt in Mythen, Wissenschaft und Kunst* (Düsseldorf & Vienna: Econ, 1969), p. 187.

2. On the concept of the natural contract, cf. Michel Serres, *The Natural Contract*, trans. Elizabeth MacArthur & William Paulson (Ann Arbor: University of Michigan, 1995). Gunnar Heinsohn's attempt in *Die Erschaffung der Götter. Das Opfer als Ursprung der Religion* (Reinbek: Rowohlt, 1997) to characterize the Jewish contractualization of postdiluvian nature through the covenant as indicative of a "cosmic optimism" is one of the peculiar forms taken by a helpless philo-Semitism.

3. Cf. Friedrich Nietzsche, *The Gay Science*, trans. Josefine Nauckhoff & Adrian Del Caro (Cambridge University Press, 2001), §124, "In the Horizon of the Infinite": "We have forsaken the land and gone to sea! We have destroyed the bridge behind us— more so, we have demolished the land behind us!" (p. 119)

4. Conversely, if the entire city goes to sea, this produces the thought figure of the "ocean giant," classically depicted by Jules Verne in his novel *A Floating City*; it was inspired by the *Great Eastern*, the first large steam ship, which crossed the Atlantic from Bristol to New York in 1858.

5. Spengler, *Perspectives of World History*, p. 90 (translation modified).

6. Spengler's insights were prepared by the typology of spatial experience developed by Leo Frobenius, who distinguished between cultures with a sense of breadth [*Weitege-fühl*] and those with a sense of the "world cave" [*Welthöhlengefühl*]; cf. Leo Frobenius, *Paideuma. Umrisse einer Kultur- und Seelenlehre* (Düsseldorf: Eugen Diederichs, 1953), as well as Hans-Jürgen Heinrichs, *Die fremde Welt, das bin ich. Leo Frobenius: Ethnologe, Forschungsreisender, Abenteurer* (Wuppertal: Hammer, 1998). Max Bense presented the most interesting adoption and heightening of Spengler's space-philosophical intuitions in his early work *Raum und Ich. Eine Philosophie über den Raum* (1934), subsequently published in *Ausgewählte Schriften*, vol. 1.

7. Cf. Mircea Eliade, Ioan P. Couliano & Hillary Suzanne Wiesner, *The Eliade Guide to World Religions* (San Francisco: Harper Collins, 1991).

8. Johann Gottfried Herder, *Reflections on the Philosophy of the History of Mankind*, trans. Frank Edward Manuel (Chicago & London: University of Chicago Press, 1968), p. 79.

9. This refers above all to the findings of microsphere phenomenology developed in the first volume; in the cities and empires, as elsewhere, it is necessary to fulfill the function of the intimate twin that augments the "individuals," and this usually takes place in such a way that the group as a whole is tied to the same augmenter. This will be further discussed below, in connection with a remark by Leo Battista Alberti about city geniuses; cf. also the reflections on the relationship between geometry and the soul

twin model in Christian theology in Chapter 5, "*Deus sive sphaera*, or: The Exploding Universal One."

10. This phrase is used in the Epic of Gilgamesh as code for the distance from Uruk to the edge of the world.

11. Quoted in Jan Assmann, *Cultural Memory and Early Civilization: Writing, Remembrance, and Political Imagination* (Cambridge University Press, 2001), p. 178; it is also explained in that context how post-exodus Judaism reworked the Egyptian motif of the "iron wall" for the language games of its secession from the impure non-Jewish peoples.

12. Herodotus, *The Histories*, trans. Robin Waterfield (Oxford & New York: Oxford University Press, 2008), p. 46.

13. Drawing on Heiner Mühlmann's ingenious concept of "instinctive architecture" (cf. *The Nature of Cultures: A Blueprint for a Theory of Culture Genetics*, trans. R. Payne [Vienna & New York: Springer, 1996], pp. 47ff.), one can interpret this fortress complex as a synthesis of maximum stress design and post-stressal relaxation art.

14. André Neher further differentiated this thesis, noting that if Faust is the myth of the modern human, then the golem is that of the postmodern. Quoted in Henri Atlan, "Golems," in *Selected Writings: On Self-Organization, Philosophy, Bioethics, and Judaism*, ed. Stephanos Geroulanos & Todd Meyers (New York: Fordham University Press, 2011), p. 333. On the question of Adamotechnics, cf. *Spheres I*, pp. 31–44.

15. Schalom Ben-Chorin, *Paulus. Der Völkerapostel in jüdischer Sicht* (Munich: dtv, 1980), p. 171.

16. Ben-Chorin straightforwardly writes: "Jewish monotheism with its universal aspect was born from the tragedy of exile, and remains tied to exile" (ibid.). "Exile" here means having to weep by the rivers of Babylon and look up at the high buildings of foreign masters.

17. Conversely, anti-theological discourses also develop as competitions; one would be overlooking the specific dynamics of French post-structuralism, for example, if one failed to see in it an auction of subject denials—the competition for the discourse most thoroughly purged of theological residue.

18. Concerning the interpretation of proxy as original activity, cf. Chapter 7, "How the True Spheric Center Has Long-Distance Effects through the Pure Medium."

19. Cf. Chapter 5, "*Deus sive sphaera*, or: The Exploding Universal One," as well as *Spheres I*, Chapter 8, "Closer to Me Than I Am Myself: A Theological Preparation for the Theory of the Shared Inside," pp. 570–583.

20. Cf. Ernst Heinrich & Ursula Seidl, "Mass und Übermass in der Dimensionierung von Bauwerken im alten Zweistromland," in *Mitteilungen der Deutschen Orient-*

gesellschaft 99, pp. 5–8; I thank Gwendolyn Leick (London) and Elisabeth von Samsonow (Vienna) for pointing me to this article.

21. Cf. Peter Sloterdijk, *Im selben Boot. Versuch über die Hyperpolitik* (Frankfurt: Suhrkamp, 1995), pp. 29ff., where the distinction between megalopathy and megalomania is introduced in a historico-philosophical context. Megalopathic reason is the non-psychotic work form of political and ontological thought in the age of empires and their respective metaphysics.

22. Ernst Bloch attempted an ontology of concretization and a category theory of increase in his late work; cf. *Experimentum mundi. Frage, Kategorien des Herausbringens, Praxis* (Frankfurt: Suhrkamp, 1975).

23. The shield of Achilles is discussed above in Chapter 2, and the Greek cosmospherology in Chapter 4 and 5.

24. This is examined in greater detail in the final chapter of this volume, "The Last Orb: On a Philosophical History of Terrestrial Globalization," section 27.

25. Concerning the ground plans of Chinese and Japanese cities, cf. Leonardo Benevolo, *The History of the City*, trans. Geoffrey Culverwell (London: Scolar Press, 1980).

26. Cf. Lothar Ledderose, "Die Gedenkhalle für Mao Zedong. Ein Beispiel für Gedächtnisarchitektur," in Jan Assmann & Tonio Hölscher (eds.), *Kultur und Gedächtnis* (Frankfurt: Suhrkamp, 1988), pp. 311f. Furthermore, Mao referred explicitly to the centralist despotism of the First Emperor: "What was so extraordinary about Qin Shi Huangdi? He only executed 460 scholars. We have executed 46,000 of them [...] You refer to us as Qin Shi Huangdi, you refer to us as a despot—we gladly acknowledge these qualities [...]." Quoted in Émile Guikovaty, *Das neue China des Mao Tse-Tung* (Frankfurt: S. Fischer, 1977), p. 12.

27. Confucius, *The Li Chi or Book of Rites, Part I of II*, trans. James Legge (Forgotten Books, 2008; first published 1885), p. 214 (Book VII, Section 1).

28. Concerning the birth of "decorous" behavioral codes from the spirit of "post-stressal relaxation," cf. Mühlmann, *The Nature of Cultures*, pp. 51f.

29. Alberti, *On the Art of Building in Ten Books*, p. 101.

30. Ibid., pp. 189f.

31. Concerning the synthesis of intimacy and majesty, cf. Chapter 5, "*Deus sive sphaera*, or: The Exploding Universal One."

32. For the Greeks, *isonomia*—roughly meaning "equal rights"—and *isokratia*—approximately "even distribution of powers"—were not mere "values," but rather structural principles and regulative ideas for life in the polis.

33. Cf. Jacqueline de Romilly, *La Grèce antique à la découverte de la liberté* (Paris: Éditions de Fallois, 1989).

34. Cf. *Spheres I*, Chapter 6, "Soul Partitions: Angels—Twins—Doubles," pp. 416f.

35. Pagan collective geniuses for cities and people were later transformed by a Platonizing Christianity into community angels (cf. Revelation 6:1–29 and 3:1–22) and people's angels; their conception indicates that religious communities and political groups, in analogy to the animal species, can also be imagined as subordinated ideas of God. (Cf. Arno Borst, *Der Turmbau zu Babel. Geschichte der Meinungen über den Ursprung der Verschiedenheit der Völker*, 5 vols. [Munich: dtv, 1995].)

These spirits of totality have taken part in secularization since the eighteenth century; Herder depicts them (territorialized) as spirits of a people, while Arndt and Hegel portray them (temporalized) as spirits of the age. Both were ultimately de-substantialized—milieu-theoretically and socio-psychologically in the course of the nineteenth century, then also media-theoretically in the twentieth—with the effect that from then on, attempts to re-substantialize them seemed regressive and (pre-)totalitarian. In his book *Rembrandt als Erzieher* (Leipzig: Hirschfeld, 1891), Julius Langbehn suggested that the social synthesis of the German people could be achieved through a real, in this case hereditary national genius (an "individualistic" one, amusingly enough: "The great future of the Germans rests on their eccentric character," p. 4; thus a Dutchman could be the most characteristic German on account of displaying the "tremendously knobbly" "German form of skull, art and spirit" most purely). This secured Langbehn a place in intellectual pre-fascism.

The history (of decline) of political Platonism has yet to be written. Heinrich Rombach ventures an appeal for a new philosophical acknowledgement of "living communities" in his book *Drachenkampf. Der philosophische Hintergrund der blutigen Bürgerkriege und die brennenden Zeitfragen* (Freiburg: Rombach, 1996).

36. "We are born into a life with no reprieve." The *missio* was the release of a gladiator from a lost battle; in battles *sine missione*, the fight lasted until one of the combatants was dead.

37. Samuel Beckett, *The Complete Short Prose 1929–1989*, ed. S. E. Gontarsky (New York: Grove, 1995), p. 236.

38. Quoted in Richard Sennett, *Flesh and Stone: The Body and the City in Western Civilization* (New York: Norton, 1996), p. 89.

39. Ibid., p. 98.

40. Elias Canetti, *Crowds and Power*, trans. Carol Stewart (New York: Seabury, 1978), p. 28.

41. Friedrich Nietzsche, *Thus Spoke Zarathustra: A Book for Everyone and Nobody*, trans. Graham Parkes (Oxford & New York: Oxford University Press, 2005), p. 84.

42. Cf. Julia Csergo, *Liberté, Égalité, Propreté: La morale de l'hygiène au XIXe siècle* (Paris: Albin Michel, 1988).

43. Michel de Montaigne, *The Complete Essays*, trans. M. A. Screech (London: Penguin, 2004), p. 354 (I:55).

44. The association of the aura concept with the phenomenon of the odor sphere made its first appearance, as far as I know, in Ivan Illich, *H2O and the Waters of Forgetfulness* (Berkeley: Heyday, 1985). It was later taken up by Michael Hauskeller in his investigations into the odor space; cf. *Atmosphären erleben* (Berlin: Akademie, 1995), pp. 94f. Ironically enough, although this coinage—as Hauskeller emphasizes—has nothing to with Walter Benjamin's well-known theorem, the thesis of the "loss of aura" takes on a new, explosive and probably more tenable meaning: it concerns not the status of the work of art, but rather that of deodorized society, and in this case, more than in art, a lack of aura indeed indicates a radically altered mode of being on the part of the matter itself.

45. Cf. Chapter 2, "Vascular Memories: On the Reason for Solidarity in Its Inclusive Form."

46. Cf. Jean-Noël Kapferer, *Rumors: Uses, Interpretations, & Images*, trans. Bruce Fink (New Brunswick: Transaction, 1990), Hans-Joachim Neubauer, *Fama. Eine Geschichte des Gerüchts* (Berlin: Berlin, 1998), and Arlette Farge, *Subversive Words: Public Opinion in Eighteenth-Century France*, trans. Rosemary Morris (University Park, PA: Pennsylvania State University Press, 1994).

47. *The Liber Augustalis or Constitutions of Melfi*, trans. James M. Powell (New York: Syracuse University Press, 1971), p. 132.

Chapter 4

1. Plato, *The Laws*, trans. Trevor J. Saunders (London, 1970; reprint, London: Penguin, 2005), p. 388.

2. Dieter Claessens identified an analogous dynamic for world-befriending techniques in modernity in *Das Konkrete und das Abstrakte. Soziologische Skizzen zur Anthopologie* (Frankfurt: Suhrkamp, 1980), p. 300; it was, as I attempt to show, already at work in the birth of philosophy from the crisis of urban self-affirmation: "Through the 'universal sympathy' constantly deployable in the institutional space, homeliness can still be inserted into 'world-logos reason,'" and one can be 'at home' in rationale, indeed in analysis (dissolution). [...] The same method of transference is used: the abstract is made cozy. This is concealed from our view by a modern bashfulness about naming the sources, such that Hegel already turned God(-father) into 'reason' (or spirit/world spirit). This 'cooling off' or (pseudo-)de-emotionalization continues in the use and reuse of concepts in 'science,'" extending to that of the 'system,' which can become as absolute (i.e. concentrated/all-revealing, yet

simultaneously detached) as God(-father)." Then systems theories would be the (secret) homeliness techniques of intellectual subcultures? Regarding the concealed synonymy of the concepts of "egg" and "system," cf. *Spheres I*, Excursus 3, "The Egg Principle: Internalization and Encasement," pp. 323f.

3. Cf. *Spheres I*, p. 99.

4. Diogenes Laertius, op. cit., VI, 93. Oswald Spengler may have had the same theses in mind when he remarked that Athens was ruined by theory (*Perspectives of World History*, p. 409); he seems to have confused cause and effect, however, for philosophy only came out on top once the old Athens and its gods had perished and a new, trans-urban, universalist form of social synthesis was the order of the day.

5. Spengler, *The Decline of the West*, vol. 1: *Form and Actuality*, pp. 79–81.

6. This refers to Freud's *Das Unbehagen in der Kultur*, which, though published in English as *Civilization and Its Discontents*, would be more accurately translated as "Unease in Culture" (trans.).

7. Concerning the hypothesis that religion grew from astrophobias and deep-impact memories, cf. Alexander & Edith Tollmann, *Und die Sintflut gab as doch. Vom Mythos zur historischen Wahrheit* (Munich: Droemer Knauer, 1995), and Fred Hoyle, *The Origin of the Universe and the Origin of Religion* (Wakefield, RI: Moyer Bell, 1993).

8. Concerning the practice character of ancient school systems, cf. the seminal study by Pierre Hadot, *Philosophy as a Way of Life: Spiritual Exercises from Socrates to Foucault*, trans. Michael Chase (Oxford: Blackwell, 1995).

9. Spengler, *Form and Actuality*, p. 85.

10. Ibid., p. 83.

11. That the Greeks developed explicit models of political cosmology at the pinnacle of their intellectual creativity, and expressly analogized urban cooperations with cosmic configurations, is shown by Jean-Pierre Vernant in his study *The Origins of Greek Thought* (Ithaca: Cornell University Press, 1982).

12. The formal trace of this retreat of theologians from the rational power of their own actions manifested itself in the declarations of humility with which they attempted to subordinate the constructed "god of the philosophers" to the "revealed" God of the Bible. Even if God, for understandable reasons, was to be imagined as the greatest sphere, the theologians of submission held that he still had to be something else, and far more than that. This was because, from a meta-theological perspective, religious theologians were unwilling and unable to believe that an immune form comprehensible to humans could truly be adequately immunized. While the most technically astute theologians began by meditating on the periphery of the largest circle as the highest level of immunity, the religious ones

declined: a God whom *we* can envisage would not be sufficiently secure *for us.* Whatever we can measure cannot hold us. *Deus semper maior.* We always want to be taken more than to take; we want to devote ourselves, and not to be surrounded to the end with things we can understand. In short, the higher promise of immunity is sought in the non-comprehensible. Immunologically speaking, however, this is at best a half-truth. Being unwilling and unable to believe in the appreciable God is the primal form of technophobia. The priestly theologians refused to admit that they too were purveyors of a theotechnic profession—meaning that they were *making* something, not simply *finding* something; they did not want to see that they were evoking immunity or subjective redemption in symbolic production, not simply letting something beyond their influence take place. In so doing, however, they only expressed that they understood nothing of the phenomenon of immunity.

The highest-ranking version of the non-understanding of the nature of theology on the part of priestly theologians can be found in the seemingly clear, yet rather ambiguous motto from the Fourth Lateran Council: "For between creator and creature no similarity can be found so great but that the dissimilarity is even greater." The formula is clear in that it gives precedence to the aspect of God we do not understand or resemble over that which we do resemble and understand; it is ambiguous in that it calls the God we do not know the creator without taking into account the constructivist demand of this title: the will to attribute the existent to the actions of an intelligence we understand (because we know what making is). This results in a semi-rationalism that only acknowledges the "that," not the "how" of creation. Such theology (like almost all theology) is a final shape of near-thought.

In spherological terms, the riddle of the difference between the respective gods of the philosophers and the theologians is easily solved: while the philosophers strove with epochal success to ground macrospheric conditions of immunity—which led to classical ontology or ontotheology, as well as Aristotle's orb cosmology—priestly intelligences face the task of transforming the container god of "being" back into the relationship god of the soul. Hence we are dealing with two different, perhaps incompatible configurations of micro- and macrospherology.

How the de-personalization of the being of the philosophers can be envisaged in detail is explained below: cf. Chapter 5, "*Deus sive sphaera,* or: The Exploding Universal One."

13. Cf. Jean Starobinski, 1789: *The Emblems of Reason,* trans. Barbara Bray (Cambridge, MA: MIT, 1988) and Heinrich Klotz (ed.), *Vision der Moderne. Das Prinzip Konstruktion* (Munich: Prestel, 1986).

14. Plato, *The Laws,* 903b–c, 904b (pp. 394f.).

15. Quoted in Raffaele Pettazzoni, *The All-Knowing God,* trans. H. J. Rose (London: Taylor & Francis, 1956), p. 119.

16. Plato, *The Laws,* 909b–c (p. 402).

17. With reference to Plato's *Laws*, Alain Badiou has even sought to identify the exclusivity of the (hypothetically) actually existing philosophical commune as the underlying principle of terror: "The essence of terror consists in the annihilation of what is not." (*Conditions*, trans. Steven Corcoran [New York: Continuum, 2008], p. 205.) This thesis would be more acceptable if it explained itself in greater detail regarding the real terrorist activity: the presumption of the final judgment about what is defined as non-being, and the transition from theoretical judgment to practical extermination.

18. Aristotle, *On the Heavens*, trans. William Keith Chambers Guthrie (Cambridge, MA: Harvard University Press, 1939) 270b21 (p. 25).

19. Ibid., p. 23.

20. Ibid., pp. 87–91.

21. Ibid., p. 159.

22. Ibid., p. 163.

23. Cf. Arnold Gehlen, *Moral und Hypermoral. Eine pluralistische Ethik* (Frankfurt: Athenäum, 1973), pp. 23–35, a text that impresses not least because the author projects his hatred of intellectual humanitarianism back into antiquity.

24. It is characteristic of the "emancipatory" politics of modernity that it had to rely on cosmopolitanism after the end of the positive cosmos principle—in other words, on a politics of the infinite. Previously, political infinitism, which is the philosophical definition of the left, had to set itself apart from the entire rhetoric and praxis of the concrete community, as the latter recommends a politics of the finite.

In recent times, Alain Badiou affirmatively formulated the axiom of a post-Marxist politics of emancipation from this perspective: "the situations of politics are infinite." (*Conditions*, p. 172) This statement is obviously false, but it does have the advantage of clarity. It shows that the metaphysical left calls in the infinite for the critique of the finite—which exposes the religious roots of all politics to the left of the possible and the real. Political infinitism (to which such divergent authors as Derrida, Lyotard, Lévinas, Deleuze and others tend) is thus a form of "attitude" in the negative sense. The point of recent communitarianism, by contrast, is to clarify the preconditions for a leftist politics of the finite.

Only a political spherology can adequately formulate the tension between finite and infinite forms of politics. It also shows why it is unacceptable to have to choose between a conservatism that sees itself as a delayer of decadence and a progressivism suspected of acting as a hastener thereof.

The concept of "world culture" indicates the horizon of a political constructivism beyond the binary opposition of conservative and progressive. Much can be learned about this in the incomparably well-informed, albeit hermetic work of Reinhold

Grether: cf. "Sehnsucht nach Weltkultur. Über Grenzüberschreitung und Nichtung im Zeitalter der Zweiten Ökumene" (PhD, University of Constance, 1995).

25. Aristotle, *On the Heavens*, 294 8a (p. 135).

26. Arthur Koestler was therefore right to describe the edifying reception of ancient spherism in medieval Christian Europe under the heading "The Walled-In Universe"; cf. *The Sleepwalkers: A History of Man's Changing Vision of the Universe* (1959) (London: Penguin Arkana, 1990), pp. 97f.

27. These have been expounded on in the excellent monograph by Edward Grant, *Planets, Stars and Orbs: The Medieval Cosmos 12—1687* (Cambridge University Press, 1996); as an idea-historical synopsis of sphere cosmology, Jean Pierre Lerner's learned study *Le monde des sphères* is also useful.

28. Alexandre Koyré, *From the Closed World to the Infinite Universe* (Baltimore: Johns Hopkins Press, 1957).

29. Cf. Sigmund Freud, "A Difficulty in the Path of Psychoanalysis" (1917), in *The Standard Edition of the Complete Psychological Works of Sigmund Freud*, ed. & trans. James Strachey et al., 24 vols. (London: Hogarth, 1953–1974), vol. 17, pp. 136–144. The same argument appears in Chapter 18 of *Introductory Lectures on Psychoanalysis* from the same year (ibid., vol. 16).

30. Cf. Rémi Brague, "Geocentrism as a Humiliation for Man," in *Medieval Encounters*, vol. 3/3 (November 1997), pp. 187–210, here p. 209.

31. Hints at a general cultural history of injury can be found in Gerhard Vollmer, "Die vierte bis siebte Kränkung des Menschen—Gehirn, Evolution und Menschenbild," in *Philosophia naturalis* 29 (1992), pp. 118f., as well as Mühlmann, *The Nature of Cultures*, pp. 2ff. Cf. also Peter Sloterdijk, "Kränkung durch Maschinen. Philosophische Anmerkungen zur psychohistorischen Stellung der neuesten Medizintechnologie" (paper given at the congress "Medicine Goes Electronic" in Nuremberg, September 1995).

32. Cf. Excursus 2, "Merdocracy: The Immune Paradox of Settled Cultures."

33. Aristotle, *On the Heavens*, p. 219.

34. Literally "Man is a metic (*alienigena*) who lives in the suburbs (*suburbium*) of the universe" (Cf. Rémi Brague, "Geocentrism as a Humiliation for Man," p. 205.

35. Plato, *Timaeus*, 33 c–d, in *Timaeus and Critias*, trans. Julian Waterfield (Oxford & New York: Oxford University Press, 2008), p. 21.

36. Jorge Guillén, *Affirmation: A Bilingual Anthology, 1919–1966*, trans. Julian Palley (Norman: University of Oklahoma Press, 1968), p. 63.

37. As far as scale is concerned, it was only outdone in 1912 by the Centennial Hall in Wrocław (built on the centenary of the victory over Napoleon), with an inner diameter of 226 feet. The opening of the dome of St. Peter's Basilica is roughly 140 feet, with an interior height of 390 feet (compared to the Pantheon's 140).

38. Manfred Schneider, *Der Barbar. Endzeitstimmung und Kulturrecycling* (Munich: Hanser, 1997), p. 41.

39. Cf. Erwin Heinle & Jörg Schlaich, *Kuppeln aller Zeiten—aller Kulturen* (Stuttgart: Deutsche Verlags-Anstalt, 1996), pp. 20ff. It is, incidentally, unknown to this day how Apollodorus solved the problem of cladding before casting the dome.

40. As in Heidegger, the word *Lichtung*, though the standard term for "clearing," has an obvious connotation of light [*Licht*] and illumination (trans.).

41. Rilke, in the poem "Windows," describes a window as something that "evens the odds of the loaded outside." (*The Complete French Poems of Rainer Maria Rilke*, trans. A. Poulin [Saint Paul, MN: Graywolf Press, 1986], p. 31)

42. E. Baldwin Smith, *The Dome: A Study in the History of Ideas* (Princeton University Press, 1950), Chapter 4, "Domical Forms and Their Ideology," pp. 61–94.

43. "Under the emperor's eye" (trans.).

44. Spengler, *Form and Actuality*, p. 211.

45. The radical originality of modern space production has been pointed out with particular emphasis by Heinrich Klotz, especially in his impressive exhibition "Vision der Moderne—Das Prinzip Konstruktion" at the German Museum of Architecture in Frankfurt from June 6 to September 17, 1986 (book and catalogue Munich: Prestel, 1986). This thesis of originality is the matrix of the theorem of Second Modernity, meanwhile copied by sociology, which Klotz—almost independently of the number "two"—deems the unexploited potential of modern space-forming art, and therefore the reviving power of the modern constructivist approach in architecture, and to an extent also the visual arts. Modernity in the sign of two thus has nothing to do with reflexivity, as some sociologists allege, but rather with the unbroken creativity of New Building, which can offer proof that even long periods of vulgar-functionalist stagnation have not been able to steal its élan.

46. Cf. Hanno Rauterberg in *Die Zeit* 35, August 20, 1998, p. 34.

Chapter 5

1. Marcus Aurelius, *Meditations*, trans. A. S. L. Farquharson (Oxford & New York: Oxford University Press, 1998), p. 104.

2. Nicholas of Cusa, "On Learned Ignorance," in *Selected Spiritual Writings,* trans. H. Lawrence Bond (Mahwah, NJ: Paulist Press, 1997), p. 159. The statement is part of a cosmological argument in which the agony of the medieval "world picture" convulsively manifests itself: taking the bull by the horns, Cusa incorporates the physical universe into the theological paradox which shines out from the assertion that God is an orb whose center is everywhere and whose circumference is nowhere—that key tenet of geometric mysticism whose meaning will be further explained below. But whatever still had a communicable purpose in the theological discourse now had to apply cosmologically too, which is why for Cusa, *centrum* and *circumferentia* now coincide not only with God, but also in the world—a seemingly bold view that some have sought to interpret as a contribution to overcoming the medieval world picture, but merely constituted the desolate end to an unfeasible harmonization of ontotheology and cosmology.

3. Nietzsche, *The Gay Science,* p. 120.

4. Ibid.

5. For a closer examination of Nietzsche's intervention, cf. Excursus 5, "On the Meaning of the Unspoken Statement 'The Orb Is Dead.'"

6. Richard Rorty, *Eine Kultur ohne Zentrum. Vier philosophische Essays,* ed. & trans. Joachim Schulte (Stuttgart: Reclam, 1993), pp. 5–12. This is a selection of essays in German that has no direct English equivalent (trans.).

7. Hans Sedlmayr, *Art in Crisis: The Lost Center,* trans. Brian Battershaw (London: Hollis & Carter, 1957).

8. Cf. Anca Vasiliu, *Du Diaphane: Image, Milieu, Lumière Dans la Pensée Antique et Médiévale* (Paris: Vrin, 1997).

9. Dante Alighieri, *The Divine Comedy,* vol. 3: *Paradise,* trans. Mark Musa (London: Penguin, 1986), p. 145.

10. Ibid., p. 262.

11. This humiliation is open to escalation: the Jewish Plotino-Aristotelian Solomon ibn Gabirol (Avicebron) claims in his text *The Fountain of Life* (*Fons vitae*), an influential work in medieval Europe, that the entire cosmic system of spheres shrinks to the "nothing of a point" before the eye of the immeasurably eccentric and transcendent God. Cf. Dietrick Mahnke, *Unendliche Sphäre und Allmittelpunkt* (Halle: Faksimile Neudruck der Ausg. Halle, 1937), p. 212. Eccentric views of the earth also appear in Plato—in Phaedo's final vision of the "true earth"— and Cicero, in *Somnium Scipionis* (*Republic* VI, 16): "the earth itself now seemed to me so small that I was ashamed of our empire."

12. Dante, *Paradise,* p. 171.

13. Jean Paul, "Speech of the Dead Christ from the Top of the Universe: That There Is No God," trans. Thomas Carlyle, in Jerome Rothenberg and Jeffrey C. Robinson (eds.), *Poems for the Millennium: The University of California Book of Romantic and Postromantic Poetry*, vol. 3 (Berkeley & Los Angeles: University of California Press, 2009), pp. 133–137, here p. 135. Giordano Bruno placed the strongest contrast to this sad non-finding of God: "Now behold, the Nolan [Bruno] who has surmounted the air, penetrated the sky, wandered among the stars, passed beyond the borders of the world, who has effaced the imaginary walls of the first, eighth, ninth, tenth spheres, and the many more you could add according to the tattling of empty mathematicians and the blind vision of vulgar philosophers. [...] So we are led to discover the infinite effect of the infinite cause [...] and we have the knowledge not to search for divinity removed from us if we have it near." (Giordano Bruno, *The Ash Wednesday Supper*, ed. & trans. Edward A. Gosselin & Lawrence S. Lerner [University of Toronto Press, 1977], pp. 90f.)

14. Dante, *Paradise*, p. 365.

15. (Pseudo-)Aristotle, *De Mundo*, trans. E. S. Forster (Oxford: Clarendon, 1914), 397b.

16. Just as one now recognizes authentic systemists by their thinking style "in relation to the system"—which demands similar asceticism (namely refraining from taking consciousness, experience or the human being as the point of departure).

17. Plotinus, *Enneads*, VI 9, 11, 43.

18. *The Letters of Marsilio Ficino*, trans. members of the Language Department of the School of Economic Science, London, vol. 1 (New York: Gingko Press, 1985), p. 8.

19. Cf. Klaus Hedwig, *Sphaera lucis. Studien zur Intelligibilität des Seienden im Kontext der mittelalterlichen Lichtspekulation* (Münster: Aschendorff, 1980).

20. Rainer Maria Rilke, Second Duino Elegy, in *Duino Elegies*, trans. Stephen Cohn (Evanston, IL: Northwestern University Press, 1989), p. 27.

21. Cf. Max Horten, *Die Philosophie des Islam* (Munich: Reinhardt, 1924), pp. 234f. Taken as a whole, the dogmatic dictates of Islamic thought, especially of expressly transcendent theism, kept Neoplatonic velleities at bay more strongly than was the case in Christian theologies.

22. Plato, *Timaeus*, 34b (p. 22).

23. Maurice Merleau-Ponty, "Eye and Mind," trans. Carleton Dallery, in *The Primacy of Perception and Other Essays on Phenomenological Psychology, the Philosophy of Art, History, and Politics* (Evanston: Northwestern University Press, 1964), p. 186.

24. Plato, *The Republic*, trans. Desmond Lee, second edition (London: Penguin, 1987), 508 a–c (p. 233).

25. Ibid., 509 d (p. 237).

26. Ibid., 511 b (p. 240).

27. Cf. Jan Assmann, "Der zweidimensionale Mensch. Das Fest als Medium des kulturellen Gedächtnisses," in Jan Assmann & Theo Sundermeier (eds.), *Das Fest und das Heilige* (Gütersloh: Mohn, 1991), pp. 13–30.

28. Max Bense, quoted above in the introduction, "Geometry in the Monstrous: The Project of Metaphysical Globalization."

29. "And by evening, man has constructed a building, an inner sun, the sun of his own consciousness, which he has produced by his own efforts; and he will value it more highly than the actual sun outside him." G. W. F. Hegel, *Lectures on the Philosophy of World History*, trans. Hugh Barr Nisbet (Cambridge University Press, 1975), pp. 196f.

30. Plotinus, *Enneads*, I 7, 1, 23.

31. Ibid., V 84, 4.

32. Cf. Maxime Rodinson, *De Pythagore à Lénine: Des activismes idéologiques* (Paris: Fayard, 1993).

33. Cf. *Spheres I*, Introduction, pp. 31–45.

34. Cf. *Spheres I*, Chapter 1, "Heart Operation, or, On the Eucharistic Excess," pp. 103ff.

35. Cf. *Spheres I*, Chapter 6, "Soul Partition: Angels—Twins—Doubles," pp. 433ff.

36. Concerning the "With," cf. *Spheres I*, Chapter 5, "The Primal Companion: Requiem for a Discarded Organ," pp. 356ff.

37. Eugen Rosenstock-Huessy, *Die Sprache des Menschengeschlechts. Eine leibhaftige Grammatik in vier Teilen*, vol. 2 (Heidelberg: Lambert Schneider, 1964), p. 862.

38. Mechthild of Magdeburg, *The Flowing Light of the Godhead*, trans. Frank J. Tobin (New York: Paulist Press, 1998), p. 333.

39. Daniel Paul Schreber, *Memoirs of My Nervous Illness*, ed. & trans. Ida Macalpine & Richard A. Hunter (New York Review of Books, 2000).

40. In fact, it was probably a selection from the *Enneads* of Plotinus.

41. *Liber viginti quattuor philosophorum*, quoted in Florian Ebeling, *The Secret History of Hermes Trismegistus: Hermeticism from Ancient to Modern Times*, trans. David Lorton (Ithaca, NY: Cornell University Press, 2007), p. 53.

42. Dietrich Mahnke shows in his study *Unendliche Sphäre und Allmittelpunkt*, pp. 144ff., how Meister Eckhart takes the impulse of the twenty-four-philosopher book further and intensifies it; his interpretation connects definitions 2 and 18 particularly closely.

43. Cf. Giorgio Agamben, "Absolute Immanence," in *Potentialities: Collected Essays in Philosophy*, ed. & trans. Daniel Heller-Roazen (Stanford University Press, 1999), pp. 220–239; Agamben's study on the almost testamentary, short and powerful essay by Deleuze entitled "Immanence: A Life…" testifies to a modern metamorphosis in the metaphysical problem of how the individuations of the absolute are to be thought. This trail will be followed further in *Spheres III*.

44. Hermann Schmitz, *System der Philosophie*, Part III, vol. 4, *Das Göttliche und der Raum* (Bonn: Bouvier, 1995), §218 (p. 258).

45. Cf. the chapter on the circle (pp. 165–239) in Werner Beierwaltes' groundbreaking study *Proklos. Grundzüge seiner Metaphysik* (Frankfurt: Klostermann, 1979).

46. This explains the speculative ambition of contemporary authors such as Ken Wilber (*A Brief History of Everything* [New York: Shambhala, 1996]) and Arthur Zajonc (*Catching the Light: The Entwined History of Light and Mind* [New York: Bantam, 1993]) to provide a reflection history for the irreflexive bang after the fact. Behind this lies, barely concealed, the theological or origin-philosophical requirement of a bang so calculated that the later demeanor of bang theorists was intended. A finalized Big Bang, however, is nothing other than what theologians know well as "the monad that begat a monad and turned it back on itself as a single blast of heat."

47. "from the chalice of this realm of spirits / foams forth for Him his own infinitude," closing line of G. W. F. Hegel, *Phenomenology of Spirit*, trans. A. V. Miller (Oxford & New York: Oxford University Press, 1977), p. 493.

48. Because Heidegger does not realize this, he repeats—through the anti-biologism of his fundamental ontology—the betrayal of the living, which occurred in any case in the modern trend towards a neutral concept of being. In his late work he attempts to compensate for this betrayal through an ontologization of the redemptive place and the word that is necessary for being. Conversely, Deleuze—following Fichte and Nietzsche—clings to the absolutism of the living, but serves modernity through an illusory praise of boundless becoming and floating mobility. Thus two eminent thinkers of the twentieth century only helped the contradiction between immunity and infinity to be expressed, but not to come into its own.

49. Boethius, *The Consolation of Philosophy*, trans. W. V. Cooper (New York, 1943; reprint, New York: Cosimo, 2007), p. 115.

50. G. W. F. Hegel, *The Philosophy of History*, trans. J. Sibree (New York, 1902; reprint, New York: Cosimo, 2007), p. 174.

51. A partial view of pre-Freudian depth psychologies can be found in *Spheres I*, Chapter 3, "Humans in the Magic Circle: On the Intellectual History of the Fascination with Closeness," pp. 207–262.

52. Nietzsche, *The Gay Science*, §124 (p. 119).

53. Jean-Jacques Rousseau, *The Collected Writings of Rousseau*, vol. 13: *Emile, Or, On Education*, trans. Christopher Kelly & Allan Bloom (Hanover, NH & London: University Press of New England, 2010), p. 437.

54. Ibid., p. 312.

55. Quoted in Georges Poulet, *The Metamorphoses of the Circle*, trans. Carley Dawson and Elliott Coleman (Baltimore: Johns Hopkins University Press, 1966), pp. 99f.

56. Novalis, *Philosophical Writings*, ed. & trans. Margaret Mahony Stoljar (Albany: SUNY Press, 1997), p. 42.

57. Thus Kurt Flasch's term [*Unterhaltungsphilosophie*] in his masterful book *Nikolaus von Kues—Geschichte einer Entwicklung. Vorlesungen zur Einführung in seine Philosophie* (Frankfurt: Klostermann, 1998), p. 576.

58. Nicholas of Cusa, *Metaphysical Speculations*, vol. 2, trans. Jasper Hopkins (Minneapolis: Arthur J. Banning Press, 2000), p. 1226. Nicholas only quotes the first half of the ominous statement, probably because he considered the second (*circumferential nusquam*) unsuitable for young persons.

59. Ibid., p. 1201.

60. The phrase *Junge Konfusion* is presumably a play on the Junge Union, the joint youth organization of the German conservative parties CDU and CSU (trans.).

61. Cusa turned *deus est sphaera infinita* somewhat casually into *dues est circulus*.

62. Cf. Heinrich Dumoulin, *Zen Buddhism: A History*, vol. 2: *Japan*, trans. James W. Heisig & Paul F. Knitter (New York: Macmillan, 1989), pp. 282ff.

63. Cusa, *Metaphysical Speculations*, vol. 2, p. 1209.

64. The phrase *Spiel-Hölle* is a play on *Spielhölle*, the word for "gambling den" (trans.).

65. *quia non potest patrem ut patrem ostendere, nisi filius*: "because only a son can reveal his father as father." Ibid., p. 1218.

66. "No salvation outside the game" (trans.).

67. Ibid., p. 1219; my emphasis.

68. Ibid., p. 1207.

69. The Cusan Christ ideal-typically fulfills the condition mentioned by Plotinus in the "mystical" *Ennead* VI 9: that he who is transformed into the One "is joined, as it were, center to center."

70. Ibid., p. 1218.

71. Ibid., pp. 1185: "For roundness that could not be more round is not at all visible. [...] if it were possible for someone to be situated outside of the world, the world [as such] would be invisible to him, after the fashion of an indivisible point."

72. Ibid., p. 1238.

73. Ibid., p. 1223.

74. When Kurt Flasch, referring to the circles of the ball game, claims that they "also represent the celestial spheres" (*Nikolaus von Kues—Geschichte einer Entwicklung*, p. 596), this seems at first reading to deviate from the text; it is not wrong, however, for it reflects Cusa's fundamental indecision about whether to speak of Aristotelian shells or Pseudo-Dionysian angelic orders.

75. Cusa, *Metaphysical Speculations*, vol. 2, p. 1239.

76. Cf. Stefan Meier-Oeser, *Die Präsenz des Vergessenen. Zur Rezeption der Philosophie des Nicolaus Cusanus vom 15. bis zum 18. Jahrhundert* (Münster: Aschendorff, 1989).

77. In July 1742, Benedict XIV—at the end of a hundred-year legal battle against the "Chinese rites"—issued the bull *Ex quo singulari*, which forbade missionaries in India and China, especially the Jesuits, to assimilate to the cultures of their host countries. It was only John Paul II who expressed his regret over this mistaken mission-political decision, at a reception for Chinese clergymen during his visit to the Philippines in February 1981.

78. The liquidation of the last shell has recently been described in detail in Lerner, *Le monde des sphères*, vol. 2: *La fin du cosmos classique*, pp. 137–189.

79. Nietzsche, *The Gay Science*, pp. 119f.

80. Ibid., p. 120.

81. Ibid.

82. Concerning More and Malebranche, cf. Alexandre Koyré, *From the Closed World to the Infinite Universe*, pp. 126f. and 155f.

83. Nietzsche, *The Gay Science*, p. 120.

84. Ibid.

85. Ibid., p. 119.

86. Ibid., p. 181.

87. Ibid., p. 117.

Chapter 6

1. Dante, *Inferno*, p. 89.

2. Concerning this formula, which was laid down at the Fourth Lateran Council, cf. Chapter 4, "The Ontological Proof of the Orb," note 12.

3. A reference to Rilke's First Duino Elegy (trans.).

4. Cf. above, pp. 375f.

5. With the difference that the Neoplatonic nonad comprises three times three steps, whereas the medieval hell consists of five outer and four inner rings.

6. Cf. Chapter 5, "*Deus sive sphaera*, or: The Exploding Universal One."

7. Cf. Osip Mandelstam, "Conversation about Dante," trans. Clarence Brown & Robert Hughes, in *Osip Mandelstam: Selected Essays*, trans. Sidney Monas (Austin & London: University of Texas Press, 1977), pp. 3–44.

8. Cf. Chapter 3, "Arks, City Walls, World Boundaries, Immune Systems: The Ontology of the Walled Space," and Chapter 7, "How the True Spheric Center Has Long-Distance Effects through the Pure Medium."

9. In Daniel Paul Schreber's *Memoirs of My Nervous Illness*, which must be read as one of the most significant commentaries on the structure and function of classical metaphysics, the author describes a phantasm that perfectly illustrates the idea of a counter-circle resulting from soul abuse: "The picture I have in my mind is extremely difficult to express in words; it appeared that nerves—probably taken from my body—were strung over the whole heavenly vault, which the divine rays were not able to surmount, or which at least constituted a mechanical obstacle similar to the way a besieged fortress is protected by walls and moats against the onrush of the enemy." (p. 110)

10. I shall develop this thought further (taking up a motif from Herman Melville) in the chapter after next: "The Last Orb: On a Philosophical History of Terrestrial Globalization."

11. Cf. Martin Heidegger, *The Fundamental Concepts of Metaphysics: World, Finitude, Solitude*, trans. William McNeill & Nicholas Walker (Bloomington & Indianapolis: Indiana University Press,1995). In these lectures from the 1929/30 winter semester, which contain a nature-philosophical sketch unique in his œuvre, Heidegger sets human being-in-the-world apart from the poverty in world [*Weltarmut*] of animals' subjectness to their environment and the worldlessness of stones.

12. Quoted in Poulet, *The Metamorphoses of the Circle*, p. 88.

13. Ibid., p. 87.

14. Ibid., p. 248.

15. Cf. Chapter 5, "Deus sive sphaera."

16. The word *Teufelskreis* literally means "devil's circle," but its meaning in everyday usage is "vicious circle" (trans.).

17. Cf. Jacques Le Goff, *The Birth of Purgatory*, trans. Arthur Goldhammer (Chicago & London: University of Chicago Press, 1984), "The Third Place," pp. 1–14.

18. Cf. Carl von Linné, *Nemesis Divina*, ed. & trans. M. J. Petry (Dordrecht: Kluwer Academic Publishers, 2001).

19. *Inferno*, Canto XXVIII, 142: "*Così s'osserva in me lo contrapasso*" ("In me you see retribution"). The speaker is the troubadour Bertran de Born, who is trapped in the hell of bad advisers; having sowed discord between a father and son during life, he must now dismember himself and walk about holding his severed head.

20. Concerning the "first" categorical imperative, cf. *Spheres I*, pp. 503f.

21. Cf. Elaine Scarry, *The Body in Pain: The Making and Unmaking of the World* (Oxford & New York: Oxford University Press, 1985), Chapter 1, "The Structure of Torture: The Conversion of Real Pain into the Fiction of Power" (pp. 27–60), where the author, in a subtle phenomenology of torture, examines the breakdown of the world and the self through pain.

22. "It is your concern" (trans.).

23. The repeated juxtaposition of "hopelessness" and the "way out" seems more natural in German, as the word for the former is *Ausweglosigkeit*, literally "exit-lessness," while the latter is *Ausweg* (trans.).

24. Franz Kafka, *The Zürau Aphorisms*, trans. Michael Hofmann (New York: Schocken, 2006), p. 98.

25. Cf. Ludger Lütkehaus, *Tiefenphilosophie. Texte zur Entdeckung des Unbewussten vor Freud* (Hamburg: Europäische Verlagsanstalt, 1995), pp. 2–7.

26. Cf. Chapter 8, "The Last Orb: On a Philosophical History of Terrestrial Globalization."

27. Michel Foucault, "The Thought of the Outside," in *Essential Works of Michel Foucault, 1954–1984*, vol. 2: *Aesthetics, Method and Epistemology*, ed. James D. Faubion (New York: The New Press, 1998) pp. 147–169.

Chapter 7

1. Søren Kierkegaard, *Without Authority*, trans. Howard & Edna Hong (Princeton University Press, 1997), pp. 106, 96 & 107.

2. Throughout this chapter, "representation" refers exclusively to the phenomenon of a person standing in or speaking for another (trans.).

3. This staying is reminiscent of both the fixed residences of the Persian Great Kings and the remaining (*mone*) of the One with itself (while simultaneously proceeding from itself and returning into itself) in the schema of Procline triadics.

4. Cf. Jan Assmann, "Das ägyptische Prozessionsfest," in *Das Fest und das Heilige*, p. 120.

5. Goethe reminds the reader that the young king looked rather lost in his splendid robes, and had to smile at his own clothing; word has it that at her own coronation two decades earlier, the Habsburg empress Maria Theresa fell into a paroxysm of laughter at the sight of her costumed husband when he held out the imperial insignias to her as they left the cathedral—not a good omen for the defenders of real presence.

6. That symbolic representations are by no means restricted to the portrayal of political majesties *in absentia* can be made plausible through a nature-historical derivation of animal territorial behavior. Cf. on this Thomas Kappe, "Anmerkungen zu einer Biologie der Grenze," in Markus Bauer & Thomas Rahn (eds.), *Die Grenze. Begriff und Inszenierung* (Berlin: Akademie, 1997), pp. 133–146. "Territories are not always so small that the boundary can be effectively marked by actual presence. Then boundary marks are required that are still effective in the absence of the territory owner. [...] A territory owner's scent trails make them identifiable [...] as a unique individual; they are as unmistakable as a fingerprint. In this sense, the formulation 'Scent markings are still effective in the absence of the territory owner' needs to be modified; the owner is precisely not absent, but rather present at the boundary through their scent." Concerning an onto-topology of smell, cf. Excursus 2, "Merdocracy: The Immune Paradox of Settled Cultures."

7. Cf. Jochen Hörisch, *Brot und Wein. Zur Poesie des Abendmahls* (Frankfurt: Suhrkamp, 1992) and "Das Sein der Zeichen und die Zeichen des Seins. Marginalien zu Derridas Ontosemiologie," in Jacques Derrida, *Die Stimme und das Phänomen. Ein Essay über das Problem des Zeichens in der Philosophie Husserls* (Frankfurt: Suhrkamp, 1979), pp. 7–50.

8. This is an adaptation of two lines from the poem "Ars Poetica" by Archibald MacLeish: "A poem should not mean / But be." (trans.)

9. Kierkegaard, *Without Authority*, pp. 96f.

10. Cf. Gotthold Ephraim Lessing, *Minna von Barnhelm*, Act III, Scene 10: "And we think that letter writing is not for those who can communicate by word of mouth whenever they like to." (*Nathan the Wise, Minna Von Barnhelm, and Other Plays and Writings*, ed. Peter Demetz [New York: Continuum, 1991], p. 41)

11. Concerning this "closing of the gate" in the post-prophetic situation, cf. Assmann, *Cultural Memory and Early Civilization*, p. 155 and Tilman Nagel, *Die Festung des Glaubens: Triumph und Scheitern des islamischen Rationalismus im 11. Jahrhundert* (Munich: C. H. Beck, 1988).

12. Cf. Erik Peterson, "Der Monotheismus als politisches Problem," in *Theologische Traktate* (Munich: Kösel, 1951), p. 66.

13. *Servus fugitivus furtum sui facit.* Cf. Michael Wolff, *Geschichte der Impetustheorie*, pp. 94f.

14. *Annotated Justinian Code*, trans. Fred Blume (http://www.uwyo.edu/lawlib/ blume-justinian/_files/docs/book%20–11pdf/book11–46.pdf, accessed 7/20/13), Book 11, Title 46, 23: "And if he conceals himself or attempts to steal away, he shall, according to the precedent set for slaves, be considered as committing theft of himself by his trickery […]."

15. The thought figure of self-ownership became fundamental in the history of modern society, for it was only through them that the status of proletariats on "labor markets" gained legal and economic force. The first authentic "workers" emerged from the Peasants' Revolt of 1381 in England, in which they shook off serfdom and acquired ownership of themselves, including the right to hire themselves out temporarily.

16. Erik Peterson makes similar remarks in his first lecture on the letter to the Romans, terming the church a "Christ sphere that exists representatively for Christ himself." (*Der Brief an die Römer* [Würzburg: Echter, 1997])

17. The word *Sprengel* refers both to a diocese and to the brush used to sprinkle holy water, the former meaning having come about as a result of the latter (trans.).

18. Cf. Gerhard Kittel & Gerhard Friedrich (eds.), *Theological Dictionary of the New Testament, Abridged in One Volume*, trans. Geoffrey William Bromiley (Grand Rapids, MI.: Eerdmans, 1985), articles "euangélion" (pp. 269f.) and "ekklesía" (pp. 397–402).

19. Cf. Arthur Kroker, *The Possessed Individual: Technology and the French Postmodern* (New York: St. Martin's Press, 1992); Friedrich Kittler, "Geschichte der Kommu- nikationsmedien," in *Raum und Verfahren, Interventionen*, ed. Alois Huber & Alois Martin Müller (Basel & Frankfurt: Stroemfeld/Roter Stern, 1993), pp. 169–188; and Norbert Bolz, *Theorie der neuen Medien* (Munich: Raben, 1990).

20. Cf. Dieter Hildebrandt, *Saulus/Paulus. Ein Doppelleben* (Munich: dtv, 1989), p. 138: "These roads are not footpaths but structural lines of power; not pedestrian zones but railways for the wheel of history." The imperial significance of road-building is also emphasized by Arnold E. T. Ehrhardt in "Imperium und Humanitas. Grundlagen des römischen Imperialismus," in *Studium Generale* 14 (1961), pp. 646f. "The decisive problem of ancient rule was that of communication." (p. 649)

21. Cf. Erik Peterson, "Christus als Imperator," in *Theologische Traktate*, pp. 151–164.

22. The transition from telecommunicative to architectural images oft he apostolic process already took place in the second century: in the third vision from *The Shepherd of Hermas*, a Roman vision text that may have been written around 150, the church is no longer understood as a broadcasting area but already as a building—and one with no joints, thus seemingly formed from a single piece. The temple metaphors for the *corpus Christi* in the epistles contain numerous attempts to describe communications as substances. This transformation is prefigured in language games that speak of the Twelve as the house of God. Cf. Klaus Berger, *Theologiegeschichte des Urchristentums* (Tübingen & Basel: Francke, 1994), pp. 131f.

23. Cf. Claudia Schmölders, "Die Stimme des Bösen. Zur Klanggestalt des Dritten Reiches," in *Merkur* 8/1997, pp. 681–693. The author also refers to Marcel Beyer's novel *Flughunde* (Frankfurt: Suhrkamp, 1995), the first attempt to explore a political acoustics of fascist society by narrative means.

24. Cf. Chapter 5, "*Deus sive sphaera*, or: The Exploding Universal One."

25. Plotinus, *Enneads* V 5, 3, 23.

26. Concerning the mediality of blood in the microspheric sense, cf. *Spheres I*, Excursus 3, "Nobjects and Un-Relationships: On the Revision of Psychoanalytical Stage Theory," pp. 291ff.

27. (Pseudo-)Aristotle, *De Mundo*, 398a–b.

28. Cf. Raffaele Pettazzoni, *The All-Knowing God* (London: Methuen, 1956).

29. (Pseudo-)Aristotle, *De Mundo*, 399a–b.

30. Cf. on this Chapter 5, "*Deus sive sphaera*, or: The Exploding Universal One."

31. Fritz Taeger, *Charisma. Studien zur Geschichte des antiken Herrscherkultes*, vol. 2 (Stuttgart: W. Kohlhammer, 1960), pp. 192f.

32. Cf. Paul Zanker, *The Power of Images in the Age of Augustus*, trans. Alan Shapiro (Ann Arbor: University of Michigan Press, 1990), p. 308.

33. Cf. Taeger, *Charisma*, p. 273.

34. In other accounts, it was only Vespasian who had the head of Helios placed on the colossus.

35. Cf. on this Excursus 4, "Pantheon: The Theory of the Dome."

36. Cf. *Two Orations of the Emperor Julian: One to the Sovereign Sun and One to the Mother of the Gods*, trans. Thomas Taylor (Forgotten Books, 2007), p. 46.

37. Ibid., pp. 48 & 51.

38. Eusebius, *Life of Constantine*, trans. Averil Cameron & Stuart Hall (Oxford & New York: Oxford University Press, 1999), p. 81.

39. Cf. Jacob Burckhardt, *The Age of Constantine the Great*, trans. Moses Hadas (Berkeley & Los Angeles: University of California Press, 1983), p. 298.

40. This was made explicit by Heidegger with an exemplary anticipation in §23 of *Being and Time*, "The spatiality of Being-in-the-world": "With the 'radio,' for example, Da-sein is bringing about today the de-distancing of the 'world' which is unforeseeable in its meaning for Da-sein, by way of expanding and destroying the everyday surrounding world." (Martin Heidegger, *Being and Time*, trans. Joan Stambaugh [Albany: SUNY Press, 1996], p. 98.)

41. Cf. Harold A. Innis, *Empire and Communication: An Illustrated Edition*, ed. David Godfrey (Toronto: Press Porcépic, 1986), p. 103.

42. Cf. Béatrice Fraenkel, *La signature: Genèse d'un signe* (Paris: Gallimard, 1992).

43. Concerning the function of the "verbatim formula" "take nothing away, add nothing," cf. Assmann, *Cultural Memory and Early Civilization*, pp. 213f.

44. Cf. Chapter 5, "*Deus sive sphaera*, or: The Exploding Universal One" and note 8.

45. Quoted in André Gillou, *La civilisation byzantine* (Paris: Arthaud, 1974), pp. 114f.

46. Cf. Thomas Hobbes, *Leviathan* (London: Penguin, 1981), Chapter XIII, "Of the Naturall Condition of Mankind, as concerning Their Felicity, and Misery," pp. 183–189.

47. Cf. Jerusalem Talmud, Berachot 9:5 and Babylonian Talmud, Sota 22b; there five classes of Pharisees are distinguished, including the typical hypocrite class of the New Testament, the "painted Pharisees."

48. Even classical aesthetics presupposes the primacy of the signified; cf. Friedrich Schiller's essay "Über die nothwendigen Grenzen bei Gebrauch schooner Formen."

49. Cf. George Steiner, *Real Presences: Is There Anything in What We Say?* (Chicago & London: University of Chicago Press, 1989).

50. Torben Christensen, *Christus oder Jupiter. Der Kampf um die geistigen Grundlagen des Römischen Reiches* (Göttingen: Vandenhoeck und Ruprecht, 1981), p. 117.

51. Seneca, *De Clementia*, ed. & trans. Susanna Braund (Oxford & New York: Oxford University Press, 2009), p. 109.

52. Cf. Jacques Gernet, *A History of Chinese Civilization*, trans. J. R. Foster & Charles Hartmann, second edition (Cambridge University Press, 1996). Concerning

the policistic mysticism of rule, cf. Jean Levi, *Les fonctionnaires divins. Politique, despotisme et mystique en Chine ancienne* (Paris: Seuil, 1989).

53. The *clementia* motif became widespread after Caesar, having triumphed in the struggle with Mark Antony, signaled that he would not choose the path trodden by Sulla, namely to take revenge on former opponents through proscription lists.

54. Seneca, *De Clemencia*, p. 141.

55. The topos of Titus' clemency remained strong until Mozart's coronation opera (*La clemenza di Tito*) for Leopold II (1791).

56. Marcus Aurelius, *Meditations*, VIII, 21.

57. Alongside the two advanced-civilized procedures for making the divine speak—the apostolic-priestly and the emanationist-philosophical—a wealth of mantic techniques survived (reading innards, watching birds, divination using dice, shells and yarrow stalks, horoscopy, palmistry, crystal-gazing, cartomancy and so on) that, despite their primitive roots, were capable of higher refinements. The escalating imperial bans on fortune-telling between 294 and 358 document the empire's determination to stem the inflation of information from the beyond at all costs. Cf. Marie Theres Fögen, *Die Enteignung der Wahrsager. Studium zum kaiserlichen Wissensmonopol in der Spätantike* (Frankfurt: Suhrkamp, 1993). Having risen to become the imperial church, Christianity inherited the heathen emperors' political interest in the monolinguality of the world above.

58. Cf. Hans Küng, *Christianity: Essence, History and Future*, trans. John Bowden (New York: Continuum, 1995), Sectio nC II, "The Ecumenical Hellenistic Paradigm of Christian Antiquity," pp. 111–282.

59. Cf. Hans Belting, *Likeness and Presence: A History of the Image Before the Era of Art*, trans. Edmund Jephcott (Chicago & London: University of Chicago Press, 1994), pp. 49–63, which makes extensive use of the study *Christusbilder* by Ernst von Dobschütz (Leipzig: Hinrichs, 1899).

60. Cf. Giuseppe Alberigo, *Geschichte der Konzilien. Vom Nicaenum bis zum Vaticanum II* (Düsseldorf: Patmos, 1993), pp. 75–77 (on disciplinary canons 2 and 3).

61. Schramm, op. cit.; cf. pp. 186f. for a chronological index of the surviving *globus crucigers*.

62. The full twenty-seven rules appear in Eugen Rosenstock-Huessy, *Die Europäischen Revolutionen und der Charakter der Nationen* (Stuttgart: W. Kohlhammer, 1987), pp. 143f.; concerning their interpretation, cf. Horst Fuhrmann, "'Der wahre Kaiser ist der Papst'. Von der irdischen Gewalt im Mittelalter," in Hans Bungert (ed.), *Das Antike Rom in Europa, Vortragsreihe der Universität Regensburg* (Regensburg: Mittelbayerische Druckerei- und Verlagsgesellschaft, 1985), pp. 99f.

63. Cf. Rosenstock-Huessy, *Die Europäischen Revolutionen und der Charakter der Nationen*, pp. 131ff. & 143ff., as well as Friedrich Heer, *Europäische Geistesgeschichte* (Stuttgart: W. Kohlhammer, 1953), pp. 82f.

64. Their typological successors include the employees of the major American telephone companies, which access the regions of the former Soviet Union via networks from operating bases in Central Europe (Vienna, Prague and other cities). Concerning religious telecommunication in the early days of terrestrial globalization cf. below, pp. 910–926.

65. Cf. Marc Bloch, *Les Rois thaumaturgiques* (Strasbourg, 1924; reprint, Paris: Gallimard, 1983); concerning the Avignonese episode, cf. also Excursus 6, "The De-crowning of Europe: An Anecdote about the Tiara."

66. *The Popular Works of Johann Gottlieb Fichte*, trans. William Smith, vol. 1 (London: John Chapman, 1848), pp. 336–338.

67. Bernhard Siegert, *Relays: Literature As an Epoch of the Postal System*, trans. Kevin Repp (Stanford University Press, 1999), p. 2. This appealingly pointed thesis is indebted to the semio-polemology of Friedrich Kittler, which constitutes the most advanced position in contemporary mediology.

68. Jacobus de Voragine, op. cit., pp. 556f. Cf. Thomas Macho, "Blutende Bilder," in *kursiv. Eine Kunstzeitschrift aus Oberösterreich*, 3/1997: *Blutbilder* (1), pp. 63–67.

69. Concerning the phenomenon of ethnic self-enclosure, cf. Peter Daniel, *Zaun: Normen als Zaun um das jüdische Volk. Zum Phänomen der Zeitüberdauer des Judentums* (Vienna: Splitter, 1995); also Assmann, *Cultural Memory and Early Civilization*, Chapter 5, "Israel and the Invention of Religion," pp. 175–205.

70. Schalom Ben-Chorin, *Paulus. Der Völkerapostel in jüdischer Sicht* (Munich: dtv, 1980), pp. 175f.

71. Cf. Jacob Taubes, *The Political Theology of Paul*, trans. Dana Hollander (Stanford University Press, 2004).

72. Rosenstock-Huessy, "Die Frucht der Lippen," in *Die Sprache des Menschengeschlechts*, pp. 797 & 801.

73. Ibid., p. 803.

74. Cf. Chapter 5, "Deus sive sphaera."

75. Frank Kafka, "Couriers," in Robert C. Solomon (ed.), *Existentialism* (New York: Random House, 1974), p. 167.

76. Bernhard Sirch, *Der Ursprung der bischöflichen Mitra und der päpstlichen Tiara* (St. Ottilien: Eos Verlag der Erzabtei, 1975), p. 162.

77. The full text in Latin and English is available online at several locations, for example http://faculty.cua.edu/pennington/churchhistory220/lectureeight/unam-sanctam.htm (accessed 9/4/13).

78. Cf. Sirch, *Der Ursprung*, pp. 180f.

79. As far as the statue of Saint Peter is concerned, it is not usually displayed in its crowned state; only on festive occasions is a tiara from the treasury of the papal sacristy placed upon it. It can also be seen on the official postcards of the Vatican.

80. Cf. Chapter 8, Section 21, "Onboard Clerics: The Religious Network."

81. Comparison with similar acts of insignia divestment showed that Paul VI's gesture was both momentarily expressive and conventional; cf. Percy Ernst Schramm, "Herrschaftszeichen: gestiftet, verschenkt, verkauft, verpfändet," in *Nachrichten der Akademie der Wissenschaften in Göttingen* 1 (Göttingen: Vandenhoeck und Ruprecht, 1957).

Chapter 8

1. Dante, *Monarchy*, trans. Prue Shaw (Cambridge University Press, 1996), p. 28.

2. Friedrich Hölderlin, *Hyperion and Selected Poems*, ed. Eric L. Santner (New York: Continuum, 1990), p. 41.

3. Cf. Helmut Pape, *Die Unsichtbarkeit der Welt* (Frankfurt: Suhrkamp, 1997).

4. Karl Rosenkranz, *Ästhetik des Hässlichen* (Leipzig: Reclam, 1990), p. 20.

5. Alexander von Humboldt, *Cosmos: Sketch of a Physical Description of the Universe*, trans. Edward Sabine (Cambridge University Press, 2010), p. 68.

6. Ibid., p. 73.

7. More about the great names from the founding days of globography can be found in Oswald Muris & Gert Saarmann, *Der Globus im Wandel der Zeiten. Eine Geschichte der Globen* (Berlin & Beutelsbach: Columbus, 1961), pp. 47–132.

8. Cf. Foucault, "The Thought of the Outside."

9. Cf. Kant, *Critique of the Power of Judgement*, trans. Eric Matthews (Cambridge University Press, 2001), §26, "On the estimation of the magnitude of things of nature that is requisite for the idea of the sublime" (pp. 134ff.) and §28, "On nature as a power" (pp. 143ff.).

10. Humboldt goes much further in this than his colleague and rival Charles Darwin, who had only brought back a few manifestly sublime "pictures" from his journey around the world on board the *Beagle* from 1831–1836, including this: "Among the scenes which are *deeply impressed on my mind*, none exceed in sublimity the primeval

forests undefaced by the hand of man; whether those of Brazil, where the powers of Life are predominant, or those of Tierra del Fuego, where Death and Decay prevail. *Both* are temples filled with the varied productions of the God of Nature: no one can stand in these solitudes unmoved, and not feel that there is more in man than the mere breath of his body." (*Charles Darwin's Beagle Diary*, ed. R. D. Keynes [Cambridge University Press, 2001], p. 443). Darwin likewise knew that one who studied the earth could no longer get far with an aesthetic of the beautiful; in the spirit of the times, it had to be augmented by that of the (quantitatively and dynamically) sublime: "Lastly, of natural scenery, the views from lofty mountains, though certainly in one sense *not beautiful*, are very memorable. When looking down from the highest crest of the *Cordillera*, the mind, undisturbed by minute details, was filled with the stupendous dimensions of the surrounding masses." (ibid.)

11. Walter Benjamin, "Paris, Capital of the Nineteenth Century," in *Reflections*, ed. Peter Demetz & trans. Edmund Jephcott (New York: Schocken, 1986), p. 154.

12. Edwin "Buzz" Aldrin, *Return to Earth* (New York: Random House, 1973).

13. Cf. the phenomenological clarifications of Hermann Schmitz in *System der Philosophie*, vol. 3: *Der Raum*, Part 1: *Der leibliche Raum* (Bonn: Bouvier, 1967), §119, "Der Richtungsraum" (as well as §§219–231) and §120, "Der Ortsraum" (likewise §§132–135).

14. Rilke, to whom we owe the term "world interior" [*Weltinnenraum*], attempted to overcome the basic experience of modernity that things and people, in a purely position-spatial sense, die out from atmosphere withdrawal, by seeking to revive the world through his own experiential power with a form of poetic animism. The result of this could no longer be a Platonic world soul, but rather an individual-cosmological intensity corresponding to the mode of contemporary "poetic dwelling."

15. The success of the three-dimensional globe, however, had already been relativized by the planispheric representations of the earth that had been ubiquitous since the late sixteenth century, and had the advantage of being reproducible in atlases.

16. Martin Heidegger, "The Age of the World Picture" (1938), in *Off the Beaten Track*, ed. & trans. Julian Young & Kenneth Haynes (Cambridge University Press, 2002), p. 71. Although the translation has been left unmodified here, Heidegger's use of the verb *vorstellen* is rather more idiosyncratic than the gerund "representing" suggests, as it invokes its literal sense of placing (*stellen*) something before (*vor*) the self, giving the act of imagining or mentally representing a quasi-physical character; this also applies to the related words *herstellen*, *bestellen* or *Gestell*, which all bear connotations of placing. More generally, although the convention of translating *Vorstellung* as "representation," particularly in the works of Kant and Schopenhauer, is justified in those contexts, it is also slightly misleading, in that the representation taking place there is a mental, not an external one—a mental image; in everyday

usage, the verb *sich (etwas) vorstellen* means "to imagine (something)" or "to envisage (something)," while its non-reflexive form *vorstellen* means "to present," "to introduce" or "to perform." Though the use of a word like "representation" is necessary to achieve adequate terminological distinctions in Schopenhauer, it would be mistaken simply to assume that it is the natural cognate of *Vorstellung*, as it would normally correspond far more to *Darstellung*. In the present text, as Sloterdijk often means a more active, shaping process than mere mental representation when he speaks of *Vorstellung* and its related forms, I have tended to use such words as "imagine" or "envisage" (trans.).

17. It is a truism that commodity and money are states of capital; that texts, images and celebrities likewise are is gradually being understood by the agents of the modern cultural sector, despite traditional intellectually conservative reservations. The way in which this applies to texts and images can be learned from, among other sources, the reflections of Georg Franck in *Ökonomie der Aufmerksamkeit. Ein Entwurf* (Munich: Hanser, 1998). An illuminating description of the economy of celebrity can be found in Thomas Macho, "Von der Elite zur Prominenz. Zum Strukturwandel politischer Herrschaft," in *Merkur*, issues 534–535 (1993), pp. 762–769, as well as Macho, "Das prominente Gesicht. Notizen zur Politisierung der Sichtbarkeit," in Sabine R. Arnold, Cristian Fuhrmeister & Dietmar Schiller (eds.), *Politische Inszenierungen im 20. Jahrhundert. Zur Sinnlichkeit der Macht* (Vienna: Böhlau, 1998), pp. 171–184.

18. Cf. Elly Decker, "Der Himmelsglobus—eine Welt für sich," in *Focus Behaim Globus*, vol. 1 (Nuremberg: Germanisches Nationalmuseum, 1992), pp. 89–100.

19. One significant exception is Barthold Heinrich Brockes' poem "Das Firmament" (in *Irdisches Vergnügen in Gott, bestehend in Physicalisch- und Moralischen Gedichten*, Part 1 [Hamburg: Grund, 1723]), which can be read as an escalating response to Pascal's dictum on the eternal silence of infinite spaces. Admittedly, the title of Brockes' poem is misleading, as its point is precisely that there is *no longer any* firmament that could provide cosmic stability, only a non-spatial location of the soul in God: "[…] As a thick flood from the bottomless sea / Engulfs sinking iron, the space of the abyss / Closed in around my spirit in an instant. / The tremendous crypt, filled with invisible light, / A bright darkness with no beginning nor limits, / Swallowed up the entire world, burying even my thoughts; / My whole being became dust, a speck, a nothing, / And I lost myself. Suddenly it struck me down; / Despair threatened my breast, filled with confusion: / And yet, o healing nothingness! O blissful loss! / Omnipresent God, in you I found myself again."

These verses show three things clearly: firstly, the poet no longer understands the original cosmographic meaning of the term "firmament." Secondly, in analogy to the ocean, he imagines the heavens as something by which one can be engulfed. Thirdly, the only force that can save us from the shipwreck of the imagination in the bottomless is a God with an "essential tendency towards closeness."

The idea of the firmament enjoyed an afterlife not only in poetry, but also in delirium. Daniel Paul Schreber notes in Chapter 6 of *Memoirs of My Nervous Illness* (New York Review Books, 2000 [originally published in German in 1903]) that a number of the souls of the departed haunting him name "the firmament" as their place of origin.

20. Eugen Rosenstock-Huessy, *Die europäischen Revolutionen und der Charakter der Nationen*, p. 264.

21. This note on the tendency towards "western passage" is taken up in Giacomo Marramao, *The Passage West: Philosophy After the Age of the Nation-State*, trans. (London & New York: Verso, 2012).

22. Schmitz, *System der Philosophie*, vol. 3, p. 441.

23. Cf. Armand Mattelart, *The Invention of Communication*, trans. Susan Emanuel (Minneapolis: Minnesota University Press, 1996), pp. 47f.

24. Jules Verne, *Around the World in Eighty Days*, trans. William Butcher (Oxford & New York: Oxford University Press, 1999), p. 19.

25. In praise of pure movement, cf. Karl Marx & Friedrich Engels, *The Communist Manifesto* (1848), ed. Gareth Stedman Jones (London: Penguin, 2002), and Thomas de Quincey, "The English Mail-Coach, or The Glory of Motion" (1849), in *The Confessions of an English Opium-Eater and Other Writings* (Oxford & New York: Oxford University Press, 1998), pp. 183–233.

26. Hermann Graf Keyserling, *Reisetagebuch eines Philosophen* (1918) (Munich: Langen-Müller, 1980).

27. Antonio Pigafetta, *The First Voyage Around the World, 1519–1522: An Account of Magellan's Expedition*, ed. Theodore J. Cachey (University of Toronto Press, 2007), p. 25.

28. Edward W. Said, *Culture and Imperialism* (New York: Vintage, 1994), p. xv. Said's ironic formulation reflects the cynicism of the British deportation system, in which first the Caribbean, then New England and finally Australia served as destinations for a utilitarian export of criminals.

29. Herman Melville, *Moby Dick* (Oxford & New York: Oxford University Press, 1998), p. 248.

30. Ibid., p. 99 (end of Chapter 24). It is one of the central facts of modern theory culture that these seaborne studies led to the rise of nautical empiricism against university scholasticism (until the universities reabsorbed the experience-based attitude and countered sedentary empiricism with the mobile kind). One of those who made a principle of travelling and seeing for himself early on was Fernándes de Oviedo, who tirelessly repeats in his *Historia general y natural de las Indias* that "what I have

said cannot be learned in Salamanca, in Bologna, or Paris." Quoted in Kathleen Ann Myers, *Fernández de Oviedo's Chronicle of America: A New History for a New World* (Austin: University of Texas Press, 2007), p. 26.

31. Pigafetta, *The First Voyage Around the World*, p. xix.

32. Cf. Immanuel Wallerstein, *The Modern World-System I: Capitalist Agriculture and the Origins of the European World-Economy in the Sixteenth Century* (Berkeley and Los Angeles: University of California Press, 2011) and *The Modern World-System II: Mercantilism and the Consolidation of the European World-Economy, 1600–1750* (Berkeley & Los Angeles: University of California Press, 2011). For Wallerstein, the term "world-system" certainly does not refer to the inclusion of all countries and cultures in the new relationships; it does, however, indicate that the economic transaction space now developing goes beyond local markets, countries and empires.

33. Oswald Spengler made this the axiom of civilizatory epochs preceding the death of advanced civilizations. Cf. *The Decline of the West*, trans. Charles Francis Atkinson, vol. 1 (New York: Knopf, 1950), p. 37: "Expansion is a doom, something daemonic and immense, which grips, forces into service, and uses up the late mankind of the world-city stage [...]."

34. Until the late eighteenth century, the logbooks from expeditions of discovery remained secret affairs of the seafaring states; cf. the observations of Georg Forster on the second of Captain Cook's expeditions, in *A Voyage Round the World*, ed. Nicholas Thomas & Oliver Berghof, 2 vols. (Honolulu: University of Hawai'i Press, 2000).

35. The definition of the entrepreneur as "debtor-producer" comes from Gunnar Heinsohn and Otto Steiger, whose book *Eigentum, Zins und Geld. Ungelöste Rätsel der Wirtschaftstheorie* (Reinbek: Rowohlt, 1996) presents a suggestive model for the explanation of the dynamic of innovation in modern economy as *a property economy*.

36. Boethius, *The Consolation of Philosophy*, trans. P. G. Walsh (Oxford & New York: Oxford University Press, 2000), p. 22.

37. Some of these are mentioned in Klaus Reichert's imaginative book *Fortuna oder die Beständigkeit des Wechsels* (Frankfurt: Suhrkamp, 1985).

38. Conversely, the late eighteenth century also discovered the human who, in an absolute sense, has bad luck—or, as Malthus would say, the poor man who is "born into a world already possessed" and whose parents cannot feed him. Such an unfortunate, according to Malthus, "has no business to be where he is. At nature's mighty feast there is no vacant cover for him." (Thomas Robert Malthus, An Essay on the *Principle of Population*, ed. Donald Winch [Cambridge University Press, 1992], p. 249)

39. Friedrich Nietzsche, *Thus Spoke Zarathustra: A Book for Everyone and Nobody*, trans. Graham Parkes (Oxford & New York: Oxford University Press, 2005), p. 143.

40. Ibid.

41. Cf. Jochen Hörisch, *Heads or Tails: The Poetics of Money*, trans. Amy Horning Marschall (Detroit: Wayne State University Press, 2000). As the original title uses the word *Poesie*, not *Poetik*, it would be more accurately translated as *The Poetry of Money* (trans.).

42. Concerning the typology of the entrepreneur prince, cf. Werner Sombart, *Der Bourgeois. Zur Geistesgeschichte des modernen Wirtschaftsmenschen* (Munich & Leipzig: Duncker & Humblot, 1923 [reprint: 1987]), pp. 102f.

43. The fundamental shift of mood becomes apparent if one compares the triumphant timbres that predominated at the celebrations on the 400th anniversary of Columbus' voyage in 1892 with the atmosphere of self-flagellation on the 500th anniversary in 1992.

44. One can gain insight into the meaning of this blindness if one takes into account that another keyword of the highest order is missing from the same dictionary: media. Cf. Jochen Hörisch, "Der blinde Fleck der Philosophie: Medien," in *Deutsche Zeitschrift für Philosophie*, 5/2003, pp. 889f. The crux of the matter is clear: a philosophy that understands its dependence on discoveries and media could probably no longer be philosophy in the ordinary sense.

45. In a letter to Doña Juana de Torres, Columbus wrote: "Our Lord made me the messenger of the new heaven and the new earth, of which he spoke in the Book of Revelation by St. John, after having spoken of it by the mouth of Isaiah," quoted in Kay Brigham, *Christopher Columbus: His Life and Discovery in the Light of His Prophecies* (Barcelona: Editorial Clie, 1990), p. 50.

46. Cf. Lyndal Roper, *Oedipus and the Devil: Witchcraft, Sexuality and Religion in Early Modern Europe* (London & New York: Routledge, 1994), Chapter 6, "Stealing Manhood: Capitalism and Magic in Early Modern Germany," pp. 126–131. The same essay also illustrates the problem of transmission techniques in these early telecommunications: according to Anna Megerler, the souls of two criminals had been locked in Anton Fugger's crystal ball, condemned to wander through the air— could there be any faster, yet also more unreliable informants?

47. For an impression of the later state of her consultancy approach, cf. her book *Herzschlag der Sieger. Die EQ-Revolution* (Munich: Econ, 1997). Note the fascinating double meaning of "heartbeat" [*Herzschlag*]. The heartbeat of the losers [*Sieger* means "winners" (trans.)] is examined, more in the tone of a depressive counter-consultation, by Richard Sennett in his book *The Corrosion of Character: The Personal Consequences of Work in the New Capitalism* (New York: Norton, 1998).

48. Cf. Felix Alfred Plattner, *Jesuits Go East*, trans. Lord Sudley and Oscar Blobel (Maryland: Newman, 1952).

49. A recent document showing this transfer of universities to the system of cognition capital, and a shocking one for traditionalists, is the Berlin speech given in January 1998 by the then-President Roman Herzog addressing the need for reform in German higher education.

50. Melville, *Moby Dick*, p. 1.

51. Bloch's well-known description of the geographical utopias of the Modern Age as expressions of "horizontal treasure-hunting" (*The Principle of Hope*, trans. Neville Plaice, Stephen Plaice & Paul Knight [Cambridge, MA: MIT Press, 1995], p. 755) clearly shows a certain bias towards the aforementioned model. In fact, such treasure-hunter socialism assumed that nature always comes for free. Taken as a whole, Bloch's work displays a very pronounced Saint-Simonist trait, expressed in the conviction that the "exploitation of man by man" should be replaced by the exploitation of the globe by humans. Concerning Bloch's extension of the treasure hunt to the world history of bringing forth, cf. *Sphären III, Schäume*, pp. 774f.

52. Cf. Anon., *An Historical Account of the Circumnavigation of the Globe, and of the Progress of Discovery in the Pacific Ocean* (Edinburgh: Oliver & Boyd, 1836), pp. 45f.

53. Christopher Columbus & Bartolomé de las Cases, *The Diario of Christopher Columbus' First Voyage to America, 1492–1493*, ed. & trans. Oliver Dunn & James E. Kelley (Norman: University of Oklahoma Press, 1991), p. 29.

54. Cf. Klaus Heinrich, *Floss der Medusa. 3 Studien zur Faszinationsgeschichte mir mehreren Beilagen und einem Anhang* (Basel & Frankfurt: Stroemfeld, 1995), pp. 9–45.

55. Concerning the motif "Stop history!" cf. Eric Voegelin, *Order and History*, vol. 4: *The Ecumenic Age* (Baton Rouge: Louisiana State University Press, 1974), pp. 329–33. We shall explain why this imperative became obsolete after the completion of terrestrial globalization (1945/1974) in the section on post-history.

56. Her cult was founded in Rome after the return of Augustus from his expedition to the Orient in 19 BC.

57. Marx too pointed out the "return of the point of departure into itself" as a feature of the incipient movement of capital: "At first sight, circulation appears as a simply infinite process. The commodity is exchanged for money, money is exchanged for the commodity, and this is repeated endlessly." Karl Marx, *Grundrisse (Introduction to the Critique of Political Economy)*, trans. Martin Nicolaus (New York: Vintage, 1973), p. 197. Marx' aim, however, is to show two things: firstly, that in the money-commodity-money metamorphosis the initially mysterious phenomenon of added value can appear, which stimulates the accumulation process, and secondly, that the competition between capitals must lead to crises of utilization, and thus to social crises that obstruct the happy return of money to itself as capital.

58. William Shakespeare, *The Merchant of Venice*, Act 1, Scene 1.

59. Cf. Peter L. Bernstein, *Against the Gods: The Remarkable Story of Risk* (New York: John Wiley & Sons, 1998) and François Ewald, *Der Vorsorgestaat* (Frankfurt: Suhrkamp, 1993), Section II, "Vom Risiko," pp. 171–275.

60. In political-sociological terms, the British philosophy of common sense mirrors the fact that in England, the historic compromise between (civil) trade and (aristocratic) property was made earlier, and in more solid forms, than in the territorial states on the continent. This encouraged a climate in which untragic and convivial social philosophies could thrive, while on the continent—especially the German princedoms—tragic and authoritarian state philosophies gained the upper hand.

61. Some inattentive histories of philosophy describe the ships on the title page of Bacon's book as departing.

62. *Historia ventorum*, 1622, the first section of Bacon's *Historia naturalis et experimentalis ad condendam philosophiam*, published as the third part of his *Instauratio Magna*.

63. Edmund Husserl, *Experience and Judgement: Investigations in a Genealogy of Logic*, trans. James S. Churchill & Karl Ameriks (Evanston: Northwestern University Press, 1973), p. 30. The German word translated as "ground" in the quoted passage is the same as the one translated directly before it as "soil," namely *Boden* (trans.).

64. "Reason" and "foundation" are both translations of *Grund* (trans.).

65. Here the author plays with yet another semantic shading of *Grund* (trans.).

66. "Journal meiner Reise im Jahr 1769," in *Schriften. Eine Auswahl aus dem Gesamtwerk* (Munich: Goldmann, 1960).

67. Immanuel Kant, *Critique of Pure Reason*, ed. & trans. Paul Guyer & Allen Wood (Cambridge University Press, 1998), p. 339 ("On the ground of the distinction of all objects in general into *phenomena* and *noumena*").

68. Johann Wolfgang von Goethe, *Italian Journey, 1786–1788*, trans. Elizabeth Mayer (London: Penguin, 1992), p. 228.

69. G. W. F. Hegel, *Philosophy of Right*, trans. S. W. Dyde (New York: Cosimo, 2008), p. 128.

70. The paragraph is famous not least because Carl Schmitt invoked it as a basis for his own geopolitical doctrines: just as, in Schmitt's interpretation, Marxism was merely a world-historical realization of the preceding §§243–246 of Hegel's *Philosophy of Right*, Schmittism was to bring about the corresponding fulfillment of §247. This remained a hollow ambition, however, both because of the inadequacy of Hegel's contributions to political oceanology and because the element-theoretical narrowness of Schmitt's fundamental geopolitical theorem, the dogma of the power-constitutive role of dominion over earth, sea, air and fire, caused him to miss the decisive dimension of a modern doctrine of power, namely the media-theoretical one.

71. "The Roman conquers by sitting." The central principle of the agrometa-physical-imperial age: this is the epoch in which commands, administration and exploitation of resources take precedence over flows, circulations and investments. One must admit that the territorial states of the seventeenth and eighteenth centuries, as long as they strove for modernization, were still dealing primarily with internal disclosure work; the establishment of "infrastructures" and internal markets of communication for commodities and news (channels, roads, bridges, land registers, publishing, post, telecommunications, standards for measurements and weights, orthography, grammar, schools, banking, courts, currencies, taxes, statistics etc.) absorbed the majority of state energies, relegating questions of world connections to the outside to secondary status. This is evident in virtually all philosophical discourses that remain trapped in a terran, "physiocratic" agrosophical horizon based on immovables.

72. "To be free means to calculate the moves of your competitors while remaining securely impervious to such calculability oneself." Terry Eagleton, *The Ideology of the Aesthetic* (Oxford: Blackwell, 1990), p. 74.

73. Cf. Cornel West, *The American Evasion of Philosophy: A Genealogy of Pragmatism* (Madison: University of Wisconsin Press, 1989).

74. Cf. Dorothea Waley Singer, *Giordano Bruno: His Life and Thought, with Annotated Translation of the Work, On The Infinite Universe and Worlds* (New York: Greenwood, 1968), p. 245. Bruno also wished to create an exact analogy between Columbus' voyage and his own mental exploration of outer space and breaching of the "outermost celestial sphere" to enter the infinite space. Cf. Giordano Bruno, *The Ash Wednesday Supper*, ed. & trans. Edward A. Gosselin & Lawrence S. Lerner (University of Toronto Press, 1977), pp. 88ff.

75. Cf. Bruno, *The Ash Wednesday Supper*, First Dialogue (pp. 79–106).

76. Ralph Waldo Emerson, "Circles," in *The Portable Emerson*, ed. Carl Bode & Malcolm Cowley (New York: Penguin, 1981), pp. 228 & 230.

77. Cf. Francis Fukuyama, "The End of History," in *The National Interest* 16 (Summer 1989), p. 7.

78. Cf. Gerhard Gamm, *Die Flucht aus der Kategorie. Die Positivierung des Unbestimmten im Ausgang der Moderne* (Frankfurt: Suhrkamp, 1994).

79. Cf. Michael Walzer, *Exodus and Revolution* (New York: Basic, 1986).

80. Heidegger, "The Age of the World Picture," p. 68.

81. Ibid., p. 70.

82. Ibid., p. 69.

83. Cf. Henry Hobhouse, *Seeds of Change: Six Plants That Transformed Mankind* (Washington, DC: Shoemaker & Hoard, 2005); Sidney W. Mintz, *Sweetness and Power: The Place of Sugar in Modern History* (New York: Penguin, 1986); Alfred W. Crosby, *Ecological Imperialism: The Biological Expansion of Europe, 900–1900* (Cambridge University Press, 1986). Concerning the role of hothouses in the resettlement of plants, cf. also *Sphären III, Schäume*, section "Atmosphärische Inseln," pp. 338f.

84. Martin Heidegger, "The Question Concerning Technology," in *The Question Concerning Technology, and Other Essays*, trans. William Lovitt (New York: Garland, 1977), p. 13.

85. Hans Freyer, *Weltgeschichte Europas,* p. 480; this ability to strike out directly, however, as Freyer implicitly knows, is the hallmark of historical action as such. It is clear that one would forbid it from a post-historical perspective (technologically primitive, logically daring, legally uninsurable). The "wrong question" thus arises from projecting categories of post-history (insurance age) backwards onto history (pre-insurance age).

86. Carl Schmitt, *The Nomos of the Earth in the International Law of the Jus Publicum Europaeum*, trans. G. L. Ulmen (New York: Telos, 2003), pp. 86–100.

87. Concerning the legal formalism and discourse-theoretically questionable nature of Columbus' conquistadorian speech acts, cf. Stephen Greenblatt, *Marvellous Possessions: The Wonder of the New World* (Oxford & New York: Oxford University Press, 1991), pp. 86–118. The journalist and Africa-explorer Henry Morton Stanley made at least 400 "contracts" for Leopold II of Belgium with African chieftains, which were mostly interpreted by the latter as friendly alliances and by the Europeans as subjugation agreements and exploitation licences. A comparable collector of "contracts" was Carl Peters (1856–1918), who laid the foundations of German East Africa with over 120 "contracts."

88. Melville, *Moby Dick*, pp. 356f.

89. Cf. Peter Sloterdijk, *Tau von den Bermudas. Über einige Regime der Einbildungskraft* (Frankfurt: Suhrkamp, 2001), pp. 27–40.

90. "You were the first to go around me"; it is notable that the decisive verb of globalization, *circumdare*, initially meant "to surround" rather than "to go around"; this reminds us that even then, people still imagined the earth as something that can be "surrounded," namely by celestial domes, whose circumnavigation was admittedly inconceivable. When the deed is done, the encircler appears as the encloser: if one takes the tendency to its logical conclusion, circumnavigation transpires as the new enclosing. The circumnavigating traffic replaces the enclosure of the domes, and the active subject becomes the true "encompassing" entity.

91. We lack a synoptic description of the ethnic, culture-nationalistic and religion-communal ideas of chosenness in Modern Age Europe. See, to an extent, *The Collected Works of Eric Voegelin*, vol. 22: *History of Political Ideas*, vol. IV: *Renaissance and Reformation*, ed. David L. Morse & William M. Thompson (Columbia: University of Missouri Press, 1998), Part Four, Chapter 3, "The People of God."

92. "Whose map, his realm"—an adaptation of the phrase *Cuius regio, eius religio* [Whose realm, his religion] (trans.).

93. Schmitt, *The Nomos of the Earth in the International Law of the Jus Publicum Europaeum*, p. 132.

94. Ibid.

95. Ibid., p. 133.

96. Cf. John Goss, *The Mapmaker's Art: An Illustrated History of Cartography* (Chicago: Rand McNally, 1993).

97. Cf. ibid. Waldseemüller's map is halfway between the new heart maps and the older mantle maps, where the outlines of countries and oceans were projected onto a liturgical mantle, especially that of the emperor.

98. Cf. Rodney Broome, *Terra Incognita: The True Story of How America Got Its Name* (Seattle: Educare, 2001).

99. Cf. Ludger Lütkehaus (ed.), *Tiefenphilosophie. Texte zur Entdeckung des Unbewussten vor Freud* (Hamburg: Europäische Verlags-Anstalt, 1995) (originally published in 1989 under the title *Dieses wahre innere Afrika*); concerning Freud's intimate relationship with the "dark continent," cf. pp. 2–7. The formulation "wahres inneres Afrika" comes from Jean Paul's posthumous novel *Selina* (1827).

100. Sigmund Freud, *The Ego and the Id*, trans. James Strachey (New York: Norton, 1990), p. 58. That this land was already densely populated did not bother the conquistador Freud, any more than it bothered other land-takers of the imperial age; for him, the magnetizers of the nineteenth century became the Indians of the unconscious, and the hypnotists his Palestinians.

101. Sigmund Freud, *The Question of Lay Analysis*, trans. James Strachey (New York: Norton, 1990), p. 38.

102. Christoph Ransmayr, *The Terrors of Ice and Darkness*, trans. John E. Woods (New York: Grove, 1996).

103. Martin Heidegger, *Being and Time*, trans. John Macquarrie & Edward Robinson (Oxford: Blackwell, 1978), p. 140.

104. Maurice Merleau-Ponty, *Phenomenology of Perception*, trans. Colin Smith (London & New York: Routledge, 2002), p. 171.

105. Maurice Merleau-Ponty, "Eye and Mind," trans. Carleton Dallery, in *The Primacy of Perception and Other Essays on Phenomenological Psychology, the Philosophy of Art, History, and Politics* (Evanston: Northwestern University Press, 1964), p. 159.

106. Ibid., p. 166.

107. Cf. Gert Raeithel, *"Go West": Ein psychohistorischer Versuch über die Amerikaner* (Frankfurt: Syndikat, 1981).

108. Schmitt, *The Nomos of the Earth*, pp. 92–99; cf. also Jacques Derrida, *The Politics of Friendship*, trans. George Collins (London & New York: Verso, 1997). It was Nietzsche, incidentally, who sketched the first outlines for a theory of moral decompensation in externality: "[...] the question which should be asked is rather: who is actually "evil" according to the morality of ressentiment? In all strictness, the answer is: none other than the "good man" of the other morality, none other than the noble, powerful, dominating man, but only once he has been given a new colour, interpretation, and aspect by the poisonous eye of ressentiment. [...] these same men, who are *inter pares* so strictly restrained by custom, respect, usage, gratitude, even more by circumspection and jealousy, and who in their relations with one another prove so inventive in matters of consideration, self-control, tenderness, fidelity, pride and friendship—these same men behave towards the outside world—where the foreign, the foreigners, are to be found—in a manner not much better than predators on the rampage. There they enjoy freedom from all social constraint, in the wilderness they make up for the tension built up over a long period of confinement and enclosure within a peaceful community [...]." (*On The Genealogy of Morals*, trans. Douglas Smith [Oxford & New York: Oxford University Press, 1996], pp. 25f.)

109. Melville, *Moby Dick*, p. xli.

110. Ibid., p. 175.

111. Ibid.

112. Ibid.

113. Cf. Vilém Flusser, *From Subject to Project: On Becoming Human* (London: Free Association Books, 2001).

114. Adam Smith noted in his *Inquiry* that in England's North American colonies, as soon as a workman has earned a small surplus, he will tend to invest this in land acquisition and become a settler or planter: "He feels that an artificer is the servant of his customers, from whom he derives his subsistence; but that a planter who cultivates his own land [...] is really a master, and independent of all the world." (*The Wealth of Nations*, p. 482)

115. Melville, *Moby Dick*, p. 356.

116. The condemnation of Israel at the conference on colonialism held in Durban, South Africa in 2001 is just one recent episode of the triumphalist tribunalization of past and present historical events.

117. Cf. Chapter 3, "Arks, City Walls, World Boundaries, Immune Systems: The Ontology of the Walled Space."

118. The correspondence is even clearer in the German, as the word for "nave" is *Kirchenschiff*, literally "church ship" (trans.).

119. This was also documented by Melville in *Moby Dick*. In the Whaleman's Chapel in New Bedford, before leaving for Nantucket, the narrator notices a series of marble tablets in memory of all the sailors who died at sea: "What deadly voids and unbidden infidelities in the lines that seem to gnaw upon all Faith, and refuse resurrection to the beings who have placelessly perished without a grave." (p. 32)

120. Horst Gründer, *Welteroberung und Christentum. Ein Handbuch zur Geschichte der Neuzeit* (Gütersloh: Gütersloher Verlagshaus G. Mohn, 1992), p. 87.

121. A liturgical symbol of this planetary self-elevation is the tiara, which, though it had already assumed its shape as a three-tiered hyper-crown in the fourteenth century, was adapted to the globalized situation in the sixteenth by the addition of a monde (globe) at the tip of the crown. Cf. Excursus 6, "The De-Crowning of Europe: An Anecdote about the Tiara."

122. Some Princes of Wales at least visited India, though as far as we know it was always *before* they were crowned rulers of Great Britain.

123. Cf. Georg Forster, *Entdeckungsreise nach Tahiti und in die Südsee 1772–1775*, ed. Hermann Homann (Tübingen & Basel: Erdmann, 1979), p. 419.

124. Concerning the world of Creole languages, cf. Hans Joachim Störig, *Abenteuer Sprache. Ein Streifzug durch die Sprachen der Erde* (Munich: dtv, 1992), pp. 345ff.; on the number of languages, cf. David Crystal, *The Cambridge Encyclopedia of Language* (Cambridge University Press, 2005).

125. Cf. Peter Sloterdijk, "The Time of the Crime of the Monstrous: On the Philosophical Justification of the Artificial," trans. Wieland Hoban, in *Sloterdijk Now*, ed. Stuart Elden (Cambridge: Polity, 2012), pp. 165–181. Martin Albrow's aforementioned suggestion is interesting in this context: to consider the period between 1492 and 1945 (or until the climate conference in Rio de Janeiro) "modernity" or the "age of globalization" with equal validity, setting this apart from the "global age" of the incipient transnational world form, for which the heroic phase of globalization created the necessary conditions. If one understands globality in this way as a result and *fait accompli* of globalization, the "post-historical" structure of this "global age" we have entered stands out—that is, a shift of emphasis from history to news, and

from a reliance on regional pasts to a reliance on trans-regional futures. Only then does Albrow's playful motto—"Forget modernity!"—become understandable, if not quite acceptable. Cf. Albrow, *The Global Age*.

126. Cf. Gilles Deleuze & Félix Guattari, *Anti-Oedipus*, trans. Robert Hurley, Mark Seem & Helen R. Lane (London & New York: Continuum, 2004), p. 244 : "The only universal history is a history of contingency."

127. Cf. Peter Sloterdijk, *Der starke Grund, zusammen zu sein. Erinnerungen an die Erfindung des Volkes* (Frankfurt: Suhrkamp, 1998). In our opinion, Heiner Mühlmann has undertaken the most stimulating attempt to derive a general theory of culture from an analysis of stressory and post-stressory mechanisms in *The Nature of Cultures*.

128. Cf. Voegelin, *Order and History*, vol. 4: *The Ecumenic Age*, Chapter 6, pp. 272–299.

129. Ibid., pp. 376f.

130. Cf. Voegelin, *Order and History*, vol. 3: *Plato and Aristotle* (Baton Rouge: Louisiana State University Press, 1957). We refer to Voegelin's monumental work because, although its impact has remained negligible, it can be considered an exemplary self-penetration of philosophical Catholicism; it also shows especially clearly that defenses of *philosophia perennis* in the twentieth century frequently become involuntary obituaries instead.

131. In the German, there is a more obvious play on words between *Kirchenvetter* [church cousins] and *Kirchenväter* [Church Fathers] (trans.).

132. Cf. Johann Figl, *Die Mitte der Religionen. Idee und Praxis universalreligiöser Bewegungen* (Darmstadt: Wissenschaftliche Buchgesellschaft, 1993).

133. For a harmonizing view of the developments on the free market of religion, cf. Irvin Hexham & Karla Poewe, *New Religions as Global Cultures: Making the Human Sacred* (Boulder: Westview Press, 1997). A typical example of the tendency towards illusory harmony can be found in Oskar Lafontaine & Christa Müller, *Keine Angst vor der Globalisierung. Wohlstand und Arbeit für alle* (Bonn: Verlag J. H. W. Dietz Nachfolger, 1998). An interesting attempt to base a social democratic ethics on Aristotle is made in Martha C. Nussbaum, "Aristotelian Social Democracy," in R. Bruce Douglass, Gerald M. Mara & Henry S. Richardson (eds.), *Liberalism and the Good* (London & New York: Routledge, 1990), pp. 203–252.

134. Cf. Deleuze & Guattari, *What Is Philosophy?*, p. 100.

135. In terms of its deep structure, this was the intellectual task to which *philosophia perennis* devoted itself, and whose impossibility occasioned its failure. Cf. Chapter 5, "*Deus sive sphaera*, or: The Exploding Universal One."

136. Marshall McLuhan & Bruce R. Powers, *The Global Village: Transformations in World Life and Media in the 21st Century* (Oxford & New York: Oxford University Press, 1992), p. 93.

137. Cf. Albrow, *The Global Age* and Jürgen Habermas, *The Postnational Constellation: Political Essays*, trans. Max Pensky (Cambridge: Polity, 2001).

138. I use this term to encompass the reflections with which the theory of intimate spheres (microspherology) is "elevated" to the level of a theory of large immune structures (states, realms, "worlds"). Cf. *Bubbles, Spheres I: Microspherology* and the present volume.

139. Concerning the imaginative complex of the "portable God," cf. Régis Debray, *God: An Itinerary*, trans. Jeffrey Mehlman (London & New York: Verso, 2007), pp. 83f.

140. For an elaboration on this phrase, cf. *Bubbles*, pp. 59f.

141. Cf. Arjun Appadurai, "Global Ethnoscapes—Notes and Queries for a Transnational Anthropology," in Richard G. Fox (ed.), *Recapturing Anthropology: Working in the Present* (Santa Fe: School of American Research Press, 1991), pp. 191–210.

142. Roland Robertson, *Globalization: Social Theory and Global Culture* (London/Thousand Oaks/New Delhi: SAGE, 1992), p. 182.

143. Cf. Chapter 2, "Vascular Memories: On the Reason for Solidarity in Its Inclusive Form."

144. The colloquial term for "weatherman" in German is *Wetterfrosch*, which literally means "weather frog" (trans.).

PHOTOGRAPHIC CREDITS